Armaments, arms control and disarmament

Armaments, arms control and disarmament

A Unesco reader
for disarmament education

Edited by Marek Thee
Director, International Peace
Research Institute, Oslo

Unesco

First published in 1981 by the United Nations
Educational, Scientific and Cultural Organization
7 place de Fontenoy, 75700 Paris
Printed by Imprimerie Darantiere, Dijon-Quetigny

Second impression 1982

ISBN 92-3-101920-1

Preface

The General Assembly of the United Nations has clearly set out the objective of disarmament education in the Final Document of its Tenth Special Session, devoted to disarmament:

With a view to contributing to a greater understanding and awareness of the problems created by the armaments race and of the need for disarmament, Governments and governmental and non-governmental international organizations are urged to take steps to develop programmes of education for disarmament and peace studies at all levels.

The same session of the General Assembly urged Unesco to 'step up this programme aimed at the development of disarmament education as a distinct field of study through the preparation, *inter alia*, of teachers' guides, textbooks, readers and audio-visual materials'.

Unesco is very pleased to present this reader as a contribution to the promotion of disarmament education at the university level. It has been conceived as background reading for an undergraduate or postgraduate course on disarmament-related issues.

Dr Marek Thee, director of the International Peace Research Institute, Oslo, and Editor-in-Chief of the *Bulletin of Peace Proposals*, has undertaken the task of general editor of this reader. While maintaining the essential ideas and arguments of the authors, he has shortened and rearranged the material (most of which has been published elsewhere) to make a coherent whole. Unesco expresses its warmest thanks to Dr Thee for his untiring efforts to co-ordinate the volume and to each of the contributors for authorizing reproduction of this material. The authors are, of course, responsible for the choice and the presentation of the facts contained in their respective contributions and the opinions contained therein, which are not necessarily those of Unesco.

Unesco hopes that this reader will encourage the creation or further development of specialized teaching and research on armaments, the arms race and disarmament in the spirit of the principles of disarmament education adopted by the World Congress on Disarmament Education (Unesco, 9–13 June 1980), reproduced in this book on pages 338–40. In presenting this reader, Unesco wishes to reiterate the importance disarmament education can have in the long run, and indeed the imperative it represents for the future. In the final words of the principles of that congress, 'the challenge is all the greater as the stakes are so high'. This reader and similar efforts will, we hope, contribute to meeting that challenge.

Contents

Foreword

The Unesco initiative to develop disarmament education as a distinct field of study and as a tool for mobilizing knowledgeable public opinion on questions of peace and war comes at a crucial moment in history after the Second World War. As we enter the 1980s, international tension is mounting and questions of peace and war trouble everyone. Threats of force and the use of force in international relations have become more frequent, the arms race has accelerated and arms-control negotiations have become bogged down in deep crisis. The spectre of a new world conflagration with the possible use of nuclear weapons is growing.

There are continuing efforts to overcome the crisis, to reduce tension and bring the arms race under control. However, one lesson brought home in the course of events is that success in these efforts depends vitally on political will and the involvement in the decision-making process of well-informed and enlightened public opinion. Questions of peace and war in the nuclear age, with highly sophisticated nuclear weapons deployed around the globe, cannot be left any longer to generals and diplomats alone. They have become a problem of survival of the human race and should become the subject of learning and debate by as many strata of concerned citizens as possible, nationally and internationally. The peoples of the world should have a decisive voice in solving problems which threaten their very life. Participatory democracy is imperative here as in no other area of human concern.

The present work is meant to further the cause of disarmament education. It should serve as an introduction to contemporary problems of armaments, arms control and disarmament. It is meant as a compendium for disarmament education in secondary schools and universities, as a handbook for concerned politicians, and as a manual for all interested in halting and reversing the arms race. The approach is pluralistic; different views are expressed. However, there is one basic message: the overriding interest of all human beings in averting war and nuclear calamity.

Three criteria guided the selection of the materials for this reader: the most objective information possible; reliable scholarly analysis; and relevance to the contemporary debate on armaments and disarmament. Thus we tried:
To supply basic data and information about the ongoing armaments buildup and

efforts at arms control and disarmament, with particular emphasis on the role of the United Nations.

To provide a historical perspective on efforts towards disarmament.

To present an analysis of the nature and dynamics of the contemporary arms race, with special regard to the race in military technology.

To visualize the intimate interrelationship between disarmament and development efforts—the allocation to purposes of destruction of human and material resources which could well be used to alleviate poverty and hunger, and to reduce the conflict-loaded gap between the developed and developing countries.

To outline some possible alternative strategies for arms control, disarmament and peaceful change.

To present a balanced view of problems of armaments and disarmament from East and West, North and South.

To appeal to reason and human rationality in order to create political will and activate public opinion for the cause of genuine disarmament and peace.

Naturally, limits of space did not allow us to include in this reader many of the very good and highly relevant materials available in the vast scholarly and political literature on the subject. The interested reader will find some of these materials indicated in the select bibliography at the end of this work. In fact, the aim of the book is to stimulate thinking and further research, provide insight and knowledge for independent judgement and engender a commitment to efforts for disarmament. Though disarmament education as an organized search for knowledge on questions of peace and war is in its initial stage only, it reflects a long-felt need for a well-informed and conscientious citizenship militating for the cause of peace. In the nuclear age we can ignore disarmament only at our own peril.

MAREK THEE
Oslo, October 1980

Part I. The armaments race and its socio-political impact

1

Arms race indicators

Stockholm International
Peace Research Institute (SIPRI)

World military expenditure

Increased military spending is one major indicator of the growing use of resources in the world for military purposes. Throughout the 1970s world military expenditure continued to increase steadily in real terms. By 1979, estimates by the Stockholm International Peace Research Institute (SIPRI) of world military expenditure had reached the figure of some $480,000 million[1] at current prices—and the 1980 figure will certainly go above $500,000 million. In real terms this represents an almost fourfold increase during the thirty years since 1948. Current budget figures indicate strongly that the rise in world military spending is accelerating. In this respect the first United Nations 'Decade for Disarmament' (the 1970s) has ended in total failure.

The waste of resources is not the only cause for concern. There are also some ominous implications in the rise in military spending. There were upswings in world military expenditure before the First World War and before the Second World War. And in the post-war period the big upswings were at the times of the Korean and the Viet Nam wars.

It is the impending figures for the two great power blocs which are especially disturbing, as experience has shown that increases by either side are often used as justification for increases by the other side. On the NATO side, we have the decision of 1978 to set a target of a 3 per cent annual rise, in real terms, in military spending. The United States has even gone beyond this figure. The United States five-year plan for military spending envisages a 4 per cent annual increase in volume from fiscal year 1980 to 1985. Over those five years, the total additional spending over and above the present level of military expenditure will be about $80,000 million (at 1980 prices). The level and trend of military spending in the Soviet Union are a matter of great argument—not helped by the incredibility of official figures released by the USSR. The United States has estimated that Soviet military spending had risen at a rate of 3–5 per cent annually in the 1970s. This estimate was given as one of the reasons for increased NATO spending.

Findings of the Stockholm International Peace Research Institute, 'World Armaments and Disarmament', *SIPRI Yearbook 1979 and 1980.*

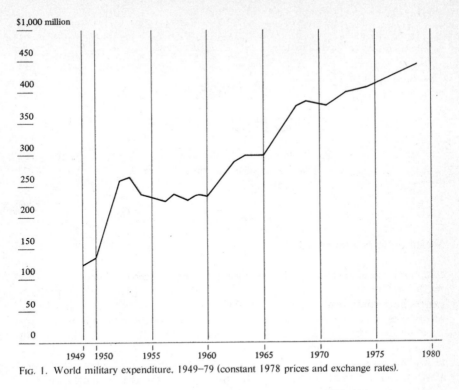

FIG. 1. World military expenditure, 1949–79 (constant 1978 prices and exchange rates).

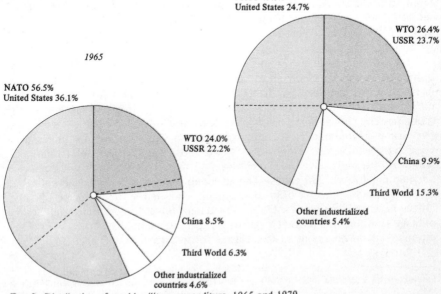

FIG. 2. Distribution of world military expenditure, 1965 and 1979.

As far as the rest of the world is concerned, the general picture is one of fairly rapid rates of growth in military expenditure over the decade. The general upward trend outside NATO, the Warsaw Treaty Organization (WTO) and China has been of the order of 7–8 per cent a year from 1970 to 1979.

There have been some groups of states where military expenditure has risen even more rapidly. For example, the members of the Organization of the Petroleum Exporting Countries (OPEC) have spent a significant part of their increased income on weapons. Their rate of increase of military expenditure, as a group, has for the past decade been 15 per cent a year in real terms. Another area where military spending has been rising rapidly is southern Africa—South Africa and the adjoining states—with an annual real growth rate in military spending of 16 per cent a year. In the Far East, Japan, although devoting less than 1 per cent of its gross domestic product to military purposes, has none the less moved up to seventh place in the world rank order of military expenditure. In South America military spending has risen to about 5 per cent a year (in real terms) on the continent as a whole.

The only area of the world where military spending (in real terms) was not much higher in 1979 than in 1970 was Oceania.

Nuclear armaments

Although the bulk of military spending goes towards the upkeep of conventional weapons and forces, nuclear weapons are by far the greatest threat to the survival of mankind.

In 1945 two nuclear bombs with a total explosive power of about 30 thousand tonnes of high explosive destroyed the cities of Hiroshima and Nagasaki, killing about 300,000 people. Since that time, the world's nuclear arsenals have grown to the equivalent of over a million Hiroshima bombs.

The nuclear arsenals of the world contain more than 60,000 nuclear weapons—an equivalent of about four tonnes of explosive per person. If even a fraction of these weapons were to be used, this would result in a catastrophe of unimaginable proportions.

Utterly catastrophic though a nuclear world war would be, many scientists believe it to be increasingly likely. The nuclear arsenals themselves have for so long been so huge as to make any further quantitative increases meaningless, at least from the military and strategic points of view. A major reason for pessimism, however, is that improvements are constantly being made in the quality, particularly as regards accuracy and reliability, of strategic weapons. New warheads for the United States Minuteman intercontinental ballistic missile, for example, are so accurate that 50 per cent should fall within 200 metres of the intended target at intercontinental ranges. The next generation of these missiles will be accurate to within a few tens of metres. All military targets would be vulnerable to such weapons.

Such precision, together with other advances, may give military decision-makers misplaced confidence that they can actually fight and win nuclear wars, rather than simply deter them. Deterrence based on mutually assured destruction will then no longer be regarded as the main role of the strategic nuclear forces, the temptation to strike first will increase dangerously, and the risk of nuclear war by miscalculation, accident or madness will increase correspondingly. This is probably not due to the deliberate decisions of political leaders, but rather to the sheer momentum of military technology. Nuclear war fighting weapons are being made available, pressures build up for their deployment and nuclear strategies are rationalized accordingly.

Planned deployments of nuclear weapons by the United States and the USSR are not significantly affected by the Strategic Arms Limitation Treaty (SALT II), which establishes equal limits for these powers on the total numbers of strategic delivery systems. Within the numerical limits set, each side is free to determine the structure of its strategic nuclear forces.

More ominous than any other weapon development is the continuing emergence of weapons with distinct nuclear warfighting capabilities.

Among such weapons being developed in the United States is the MX missile system (ICBM), with a related mobile basing scheme to reduce vulnerability. The MX will carry ten warheads, the maximum allowed by the SALT II treaty. Each warhead will have substantially greater accuracy and explosive yield than warheads on current United States Minuteman III ICBMs. Furthermore, a laser or radar system may be introduced to guide the warhead on to its target, giving it hitherto unattained accuracy. The first MX is expected to become operational in 1986, and the full force of 200 MX missiles by 1989. From then on, the MX will significantly increase the capability of the United States to threaten the Soviet fixed ICBM force.

While current submarine-launched ballistic missiles (SLBMs) do not possess the necessary combination of accuracy and explosive yield to pose a real threat to hardened targets such as missile silos, the United States is developing a new type of SLBM, the Trident II, which will probably have a definite capability against hardened targets. This new missile will eventually be deployed on new Trident submarines. A variety of sophisticated guidance mechanisms are under consideration for use on Trident II; thus Trident II may be more accurate than any strategic missile in operation today.

The United States is not alone in developing new generations of strategic nuclear weapons. The USSR has in operation, and under continued production, a series of multiple-warhead ICBMs capable of destroying a high percentage of United States fixed ICBMs. The new Soviet ICBMs—the SS-17, SS-18 and SS-19 missiles—are ostensibly a response to the United States deployment, in the early 1970s, of multiple-warhead ICBMs—the Minuteman III force. In turn, the United States MX is heralded as a response to the new Soviet ICBMs, and the USSR is likely to react to the deployment of the MX. Thus, the strategic nuclear-arms race continues.

Nuclear-weapon accidents

There are many thousands of nuclear weapons and their delivery systems in the world's arsenal, a significant portion of which are on alert. It is, therefore, hardly surprising that nuclear-weapon accidents occur. But few realize just how frequently they do occur. Data on accidents of nuclear-weapon systems given in the *SIPRI Yearbook 1977* suggest that there have been at least 125 nuclear-weapon accidents in the past thirty years—a frequency of one every three months.

Thirty-two accidents are listed, involving United States weapon systems, in which nuclear weapons were believed to have been destroyed or seriously damaged. In fifty-nine other United States accidents, nuclear weapons may have been in danger of destruction or serious damage. Also listed are twenty-two Soviet nuclear-weapon accidents, eight British and four French. And the lists, relying as they do on open sources, are certainly incomplete.

Some of the nuclear-weapon accidents are bizarre. A United States Corporal missile with a nuclear warhead is recorded as 'rolling off a truck into the Tennessee River'. On 9 April 1968 the United States strategic nuclear submarine *Robert E. Lee* 'became snagged in the nets of a French trawler' in the Irish Sea. Among the Soviet incidents is one in which 'American personnel recovered a nuclear weapon from a Russian airplane that crashed in the Sea of Japan'. And in September 1974 a Soviet guided-missile destroyer allegedly exploded and sank in the Black Sea. A number of Soviet nuclear-powered submarines have been snagged by Norwegian or Japanese fishing boats. Some have collided with United States submarines.

On at least nine occasions United States submarines, some of them armed with nuclear weapons, have collided with other, apparently Soviet, vessels within or close to Soviet territorial waters while on intelligence-gathering missions. There are probably similar incidents involving Soviet nuclear-armed submarines on intelligence missions. Such events vividly recall President Kennedy's warning of the danger of a nuclear world war being started by accident.

One incontestable fact is that nuclear-weapon accidents do occur, are quite frequent worldwide, and occur with probably all the different nuclear-weapon systems containing nuclear warheads, and in probably every kind of activity in which these weapon-delivery systems take part: in silos, in the air, in harbours, under the sea-surface, on land and so on.

It is true that in the 100 or more nuclear-weapon accidents and incidents that have occurred in the post-war years, there has been no nuclear-weapon detonation, but there has been very extensive radioactive contamination in several instances. A new aspect, the possibility of weapon capture and terrorism, is receiving increasingly serious attention in several government and international agencies. The presence of a nuclear-weapon storage site close to a civilian population centre is questionable on at least several grounds of prudence. It would seem that preventive measures of caution, care and security—such as remote locations of sites—should be of equal interest to both military and civilian administrators.

Strategic and Eurostrategic nuclear weapons

In Vienna, on 18 June 1979, after almost seven years of negotiation, President Carter and President Brezhnev signed the SALT II agreements for the limitation of strategic nuclear arms.

The treaty sets an overall limit on the number of strategic nuclear delivery vehicles and sub-limits on certain categories of these weapons. Ensuring equal numbers of strategic weapons cannot in itself create nuclear parity, because the two powers place different emphasis on various force components. However, the numerical symmetry may provide an equal basis for future reductions. Furthermore, for the first time an arms-control treaty requires the dismantling of nuclear weapons.

The aggregate ceiling, which covers intercontinental ballistic missile (ICBM) launchers, submarine-launched ballistic-missile (SLBM) launchers, heavy bombers and long-range air-to-surface ballistic missiles (ASBMs), has been set at 2,400 until the end of 1981, when the ceiling will be lowered to 2,250. Under the 2,250 limit, the United States will have to dismantle thirty-three vehicles—probably mothballed bombers and/or outdated ballistic missile launchers will be chosen for this purpose. The USSR will have to dismantle 254 operational strategic nuclear delivery vehicles, and will also probably choose obsolete weapons.

However, the sub-limits on systems able to deliver multiple independently targetable re-entry vehicles (MIRVs) are disappointingly high. Far from causing a reduction, they will in effect allow an increase in the number of missiles with multiple warheads, each warhead capable of being aimed at a separate target. A sub-limit of 1,200 on launchers of MIRVed ballistic missiles permits the United States 154 and the USSR 448 additional launchers of these sophisticated missiles. Furthermore, a sub-limit allowing 820 launchers of MIRVed ICBMs will allow this most threatening element of the strategic nuclear forces to increase in number.

With the high number of warheads permitted on ballistic missiles, plus the high number of cruise missiles permitted on current heavy bombers, the total number of deliverable warheads in the United States and Soviet strategic nuclear

Salt II limits					United States	USSR
2 250	(MIRV) 1 320	1 200	820	MIRVed ICBM launchers	550	608
				MIRVed SLBM launchers	496	144
				Heavy bombers equipped for long-range ALCMs	3	0
				Non-MIRVed ICBM launchers	504	790
				Non-MIRVed SLBM launchers	160	806
				Heavy bombers not equipped for long-range ALCMs	570	156
				Total	2 283	2 504

Total systems by deployment category	United States	USSR
ICBM launchers	1 054	1 398
SLBM launchers	656	950
Heavy bombers	573	156
Total	2 283	2 504

FIG. 3. SALT II limits and United States and Soviet strategic nuclear forces as of 18 June 1979 (Key: ALCM (air-launched cruise missile); ICBM (intercontinental ballistic missile); MIRV (multiple independently targetable re-entry vehicle); SLBM (submarine-launched ballistic missile).)

arsenals is expected to rise by 50 to 70 per cent between now and 1985. Thus, the strategic nuclear firepower of both sides will augment considerably, notwithstanding the SALT II treaty. In 1980 the United States had 10,154 strategic nuclear warheads, of which 6,610 were on MIRVed launchers, while the estimates for the USSR were 7,078 strategic nuclear warheads with 4,752 on MIRVed launchers.

Furthermore, the parties will be able to improve the accuracy and explosive yield of warheads on current ICBMs, thereby increasing their lethality. The sides will also be able to introduce one new type of ICBM, while there are no restrictions on new types of SLBMs. Certainly, the strategic nuclear forces—especially the fixed ICBMs—of both sides will be more vulnerable to a first-strike attack in 1985 than they are today. Consequently, pressures may mount to prepare for launching vulnerable missiles on very short notice—perhaps less than half an hour—to avoid their being destroyed. This compression of the time available for the evaluation of information and of options in a crisis heightens the chance of nuclear war by accident or miscalculation.

The treaty also contains some qualitative limitations, such as restrictions on the modernization of existing types of ICBMs. However, these limitations are minor and will not prevent certain important improvements to missiles on both sides. Nevertheless any limitations imposed on ICBMs must be welcomed.

Among the limits imposed by the short-term protocol is a ban on the deployment of ground- and sea-launched long-range cruise missiles as well as on the deployment of mobile ICBM launchers and on the flight testing of mobile ICBMs. The restrictions in the protocol may turn out to be pointless, however, as neither party will be ready to deploy the weapons in question by the end of 1981, when the protocol is to expire.

SALT II represents a definite step forward in that the two powers have pledged to maintain an agreed data base for weapon systems included in the various categories limited by the treaty. This regular exchange of information on the most powerful weapons possessed by the parties could serve as an important confidence-building measure.

The spotlight has recently fallen on so-called Eurostrategic weapons. Defining these weapons is extremely difficult. By and large, Eurostrategic weapons could be defined as nuclear weapons located in or targeted on Europe and having a range longer than that of the existing short-range tactical nuclear weapons, but shorter than that of the intercontinental strategic nuclear weapons. A heterogeneous array of missiles and aircraft is contained under the rubric 'Eurostrategic weapons'. Often referred to as 'grey area systems' these weapons are not covered by any of the current international arms-control negotiations.

The debate on Eurostrategic weapons is focused on the newest generation of United States and Soviet medium- and intermediate-range nuclear-weapon delivery systems. The Soviet SS-20 missile, which can carry three independently targetable nuclear warheads to ranges of up to 4,000 km, substantially increases the Soviet Union's nuclear potential in Europe. This missile has been deployed and is still under production, as is the other controversial Soviet Eurostrategic weapon, the Tu-22M Backfire bomber. It should be noted that under certain conditions the Backfire bomber is capable of carrying out intercontinental missions. This bomber was therefore a contentious issue during the SALT II negotiations, but was finally excluded from the treaty limitations. However, the USSR pledged not to produce more than thirty Backfires a year and not to upgrade the Backfire so as to carry out intercontinental missions.

Two new United States Eurostrategic systems, under development, are planned to be deployed in a number of NATO countries. These will be ground-launched cruise missiles and the Pershing II ballistic missile (replacing the Pershing I of shorter range). In December 1979, NATO decided to base 464 ground-launched United States cruise missiles and 108 United States Pershing II missiles in Western Europe. The reason given for this decision was that the Soviet SS-20 missiles and Backfire bombers posed a new threat to NATO. Both types of NATO missile will be capable of penetrating a significant distance into the Soviet Union and will possess exceptional accuracies. Furthermore, the flight-times of Pershing II missiles from their bases in the Federal Republic of Germany to targets in the Soviet Union will be extremely short—only a few minutes—affording virtually no warning of attack. The cruise missiles, although considerably slower, will be able to fly zigzag flight paths at 'tree-top' altitudes to avoid air defences. Although the protocol to the SALT II treaty prohibits the deployment of ground- and sea-launched cruise missiles with a range exceeding 600 kilometres, it does not prohibit their development. In any event, the protocol is due to expire at the end of 1981, that is, before these missiles are ready to be deployed.

These new Eurostrategic weapons, on both sides, must be seen as increasing the risk of nuclear war in Europe, which would amount, in fact, to the destruction of Europe.

Comprehensive test ban

Since August 1945, when the first bombs were dropped on Hiroshima and Nagasaki, there have been over 1,200 nuclear explosions, carried out mainly to test and improve the efficiency of nuclear weapons.

In 1963 the Partial Test-Ban Treaty (PTBT), prohibiting atmospheric tests, was signed and contained a clear commitment to seek a comprehensive ban on all nuclear testing. No such ban has been achieved. In fact, the rate of testing has gone up: an average of forty-five explosions a year after the treaty as against only twenty-seven a year before the treaty. The USSR, the United Kingdom and the United States are responsible for over 90 per cent of all nuclear explosions.

In 1979 there were fifty-three nuclear explosions, all underground, France and the USSR conducting more tests than in any year since 1963–69—nine and twenty-eight tests, respectively. The United States was responsible for fifteen explosions in 1979, the United Kingdom only one, and China none at all for the first time since it started testing in 1964. According to United States sources, a low-yield nuclear explosion may have taken place on 22 September 1979 in the southern hemisphere, somewhere in a vast area including parts of the Indian and Atlantic oceans as well as southern Africa and Antarctica.

Intensive testing in recent years has coincided with tripartite United Kingdom/United States/Soviet talks on a treaty prohibiting nuclear-weapon tests in all environments. But these talks, which started in 1977, have, as yet, produced no

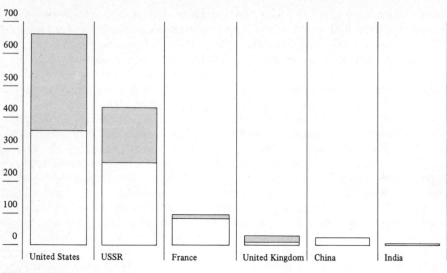

16 July 1945 to 5 August 1963 (the signing of the Partial Test Ban Treaty)
5 August 1963 to 31 December 1979

FIG. 4. Number of nuclear explosions, 1945–79 (known and presumed).

result. Multilateral talks on a test-ban treaty have not even been initiated. More intensive negotiations are needed—verification of compliance is no longer an obstacle to reaching an agreement.

A comprehensive test-ban treaty would make it difficult, if not impossible, for the nuclear-weapon powers to develop new designs of nuclear weapons or to improve the existing designs. Such a treaty would also reinforce the Non-Proliferation Treaty by demonstrating the awareness of the major nuclear powers of their obligation to halt the nuclear arms race. To be of real value, a comprehensive test-ban must be of permanent duration.

Nuclear proliferation

It is clear that the nuclear-weapon powers have a potential for massive destruction unparalleled in history, and the risk of horizontal proliferation needs to be emphasized. A by-product of the nuclear-power generation industry is plutonium-239, which can be used as an explosive in nuclear weapons. Materials that can be used for nuclear weapons are being produced in an increasing number of countries.

The technology of nuclear weapons is now widely known. To make a number of reliable, efficient and lightweight fission weapons for a national military programme is a complicated business. To construct a crude nuclear device, of unpredictable yield, however, is not beyond the capacity of small groups of people. The fear thus arises that not only governments, but also criminal and terrorist groups, could conceivably manufacture nuclear explosives.

To prevent the spread of nuclear weapons the world community relies mainly on the Treaty on the Non-Proliferation of Nuclear Weapons (NPT), which entered into force in 1970. By 1 March 1980 the number of parties to the NPT had reached 112, evidence that the non-proliferation idea had been accepted by most nations, including many highly developed states. Under the NPT, the nuclear-weapon states are committed not to transfer, while the non-nuclear-weapon states are under an obligation not to receive, manufacture or otherwise acquire, nuclear weapons or other nuclear explosive devices, nor to control them.

The non-nuclear-weapon states are obliged to conclude safeguard agreements with the International Atomic Energy Agency (IAEA) covering all their peaceful activities to ensure that there is no diversion of nuclear material to the manufacture of nuclear explosives. All parties to the treaty have the right to exploit nuclear energy for peaceful purposes, and those in a position to do so must co-operate with other countries in developing peaceful nuclear technology. All parties are committed to pursuing negotiations in good faith on effective measures contributing to the cessation of the nuclear-arms race at an early date and to nuclear disarmament, including a treaty on general and complete disarmament.

However, the NPT sets no limits as to how close a country may come to nuclear-weapon assembly. A number of countries well able to construct nuclear weapons once they decide politically to do so and which have access to fissile material are not parties to the treaty.

A treaty that denies a powerful weapon to most signatories in order to preserve a firebreak between the 'haves' and 'have-nots' has obvious limitations in its appeal. In the case of the NPT, the situation is aggravated because the 'haves' are continuing to build up their already formidable nuclear-weapon strength. To redress the glaring imbalance in NPT obligations, the United States and the USSR must now undertake specific obligations to reduce significantly their strategic and tactical armaments.

The most immediate threat to the non-proliferation regime is posed by the spread of reactor-grade plutonium, a few kilos of which are readily convertible into an explosive device. Just one reactor with an electrical energy output of 1 GW(e) can produce about 250 kg of plutonium annually—enough for about fifty Nagasaki-type bombs. So far a total of 100,000 kg of plutonium, in an unprocessed state, has been accumulated from nuclear reactors. There are at present about 230 nuclear-power reactors generating about 120,000 megawatts of electricity (MW(e)) in twenty-two countries, but another 230 or so power reactors are under construction. It has been predicted that by the year 2000, reactors generating about 600,000 MW(e) will be operational and about 250,000 kg of plutonium will be produced annually—enough to make roughly 50,000 bombs of the Nagasaki type.

With pressures towards the recycling of plutonium and a fast-breeder regime, in which large quantities of plutonium would be used, the proliferation danger could increase dramatically; in a plutonium economy, such large amounts of plutonium would need to be reprocessed that it would be almost impossible for safeguards to detect diversion. And there is certainly no feasible technical means of preventing plutonium from being diverted. The International Nuclear Fuel Cycle Evaluation (INFCE), initiated by the United States in 1977, has made it crystal clear that, if there is to be any real solution to the proliferation problem, it must be a political one.

24

TABLE 1. Power reactors as of 31 December 1979[1]

Country	Operating reactors		Reactors under construction	
	Number of units	Total MW(e)	Number of units	Total MW(e)
Argentina	1	345	1	600
Belgium	4	1 676	4	3 811
Brazil	—	—	3	3 116
Bulgaria	2	816	2	828
Canada	10	5 245	14	9 751
Cuba	—	—	1	408
Czechoslovakia	2	491	3	1 142
Finland	2	1 080	2	1 080
France	16	8 163	21	20 290
German Democratic Republic	4	1 287	5	2 040
Germany, Federal Republic of	15	8 782	10	10 638
Hungary	—	—	2	816
India	3	602	5	1 087
Italy	4	1 382	3	1 996
Japan	21	13 249	11	9 408
Mexico	—	—	2	1 308
Netherlands	2	499	—	—
Pakistan	1	125	—	—
Philippines	—	—	1	621
Republic of Korea	1	564	6	5 137
South Africa	—	—	2	1 843
Spain	3	1 073	7	6 302
Sweden	6	3 700	6	5 682
Switzerland	4	1 926	1	942
Taiwan	2	1 208	2	1 902
USSR	30	10 616	18	15 200
United Kingdom	32	6 890	6	3 714
United States	69	50 644	88	96 408
Yugoslavia	—	—	1	632
TOTAL	234	120 363	227	206 702

1. Construction in Austria and in Iran has been interrupted, so the plants are not included.
Source: Based on *Power Reactors in Member States* (IAEA, Vienna, 1979).

Internationalization of the nuclear fuel cycle would be an important element in such a solution. The sensitive parts of the cycle, that is, uranium enrichment, fuel fabrication and reprocessing, should be managed on an international scale and operated only under the authority of an international agency, with full responsibility for the security of plants. An international repository of spent fuel and a bank of fresh fuels should be established and could form a starting-point to the internationalization process. Under a scheme for internationalization, diversion risks could be reduced significantly. Also, if we do eventually enter the dangerous arena of a fast-breeder economy, it would happen under international guidance.

All efforts should be put into strengthening the non-proliferation regime, and especially the NPT—the main legal and political barrier against the spread of nuclear weapons. However, a longer-term solution must include the resolution of regional security problems, so that states do not perceive the need to develop nuclear weapons for security reasons. Also, the belief that nuclear weapons bring prestige must be disproved. So long as the nuclear-weapon powers imply, by continuously expanding and improving their nuclear arsenals, that nuclear weapons have high political and military utility, other countries may come to share this belief.

The trade in arms

The international arms trade is one of the most alarming factors contributing to the growing militarization of the world. The arms trade with Third World countries has caused the most attention and concern, both because to a large extent it represents an extension of the conflict between East and West and because the weapons supplied to these countries have been extensively used. It remains a fact that practically all wars since 1945 have been fought in the Third World and with conventional weapons supplied by the main industrialized arms-producing countries.

While the arms-manufacturing countries once supplied primarily second-hand or obsolete weapons to underdeveloped countries, they have during recent years transferred many of the most advanced conventional weapons to the Third World. Very sophisticated weapons can often be purchased on the arms market even before they enter the arsenals of the producer countries.

The trade in arms has, for many years, been increasing at an alarming rate. In 1979, for example, the value of global arms exports was five times greater than it was in 1969, and twelve times what it was in 1959. In the 1970s—the Decade for Disarmament—the total value of major arms imports[2] was about $61,000 million—three and a half times as much as that of the previous decade and seven times greater than that of the 1950s. Nor are there any signs that the average yearly rate of increase (25 per cent for the period 1975–79) will slow down. On the contrary, the early 1980s will see increased investment in conventional weaponry, which sooner or later will enter the arms market.

Not only was there a growth in the volume of the arms trade in the 1970s. There was also an increase in the number of importing countries and a demand for more sophisticated weapon systems. Furthermore, owing to the transfer of know-how, the number of countries producing weapons domestically is growing rapidly. Today some fifty-six countries produce major weapons and twenty-four of these are in the Third World. If small arms are included then the number of weapon-producing countries is much greater.

Two-thirds of the global arms trade involves transfer of weapons to the Third World, a good part of which suffers from underdevelopment, starvation and disease. In the 1970s the United States was the biggest supplier of arms to the Third World, accounting for 45 per cent of exports. The Soviet Union was the second largest arms supplier, with a share of 27 per cent. Much further behind were the next two big arms suppliers—France and the United Kingdom. After that came the new exporters of the 1970s—Italy and the Federal Republic of Germany, followed by the Third World countries as a group. The largest Third World exporters of major arms were Israel, Brazil, Iran, Jordan, South Africa, Libyan Arab Jamahiriya, Singapore and Argentina.

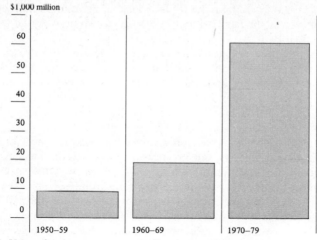

FIG. 5. Value of major weapons exports (in constant 1975 prices).

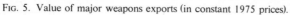

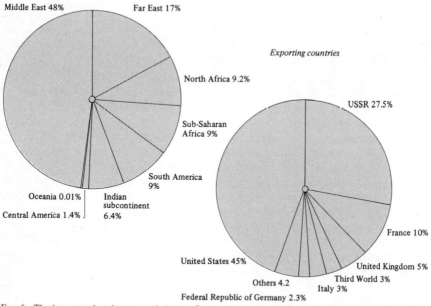

FIG. 6. The importers' and exporters' shares of major-weapon supplies to the Third World, 1970–79.

The Middle East was throughout the 1970s the largest arms-importing region in the world, followed by the Far East and by Africa, which only started its big military buildup after 1970.

The United States was the biggest arms exporter to the Middle East, the Far East and South America, while the Soviet Union was the biggest supplier to Africa, the Indian subcontinent and Central America. The international arms trade is very much a Western affair, with NATO countries responsible for 66 per cent of exports while the members of the Warsaw Treaty Organization account for 28 per cent.

Transfers of conventional arms have on several occasions been the subject of discussions in the United Nations, but no measure of control has so far been successfully negotiated. Many Third World countries view with suspicion proposals for limiting the international flow of arms, regarding such proposals as attempts to impose unilateral arms limitation on them. However, the traffic in arms is encouraged by the suppliers of these weapons. The great powers export arms to gain political or economic influence, or military bases, in Third World regions. Moreover, certain governments believe that selling weapons helps their economies, especially during economic recession. And commercial firms use their considerable political influence to obtain export licences.

There is always a danger that both the United States and the USSR could be drawn into a regional conflict, which could thus escalate into a world war. And this is more likely if these powers are the main suppliers of the weapons used in the original conflict.

Naval arms race and submarine warfare

New trends, both in the quantities of warships being procured and in the pace of their technological advancement, indicate that the naval arms race is now more intensive than ever before.

Developments in naval weapon systems provide a good example of the evolutionary character of the present qualitative arms race. New types of naval weapons do not differ much in external characteristics from their predecessors. Where they do differ is in the greater efficiency of their elementary components: more energy-rich fuel composition; greater engine efficiency; more accurate guidance systems; greater resistance to electronic, optical and other counter-measures; increased adaptability to various firing platforms; and smaller size and lower weight. In addition to these features of weapons *per se*, several technological improvements have taken place in entire weapon systems, where the weapons are only links in a whole chain—from remote surveillance, discovery and location of a target, through quick and accurate delivery of the weapon in order to execute the attack and the destruction of the target, to the assessment of the post-attack damage and to possible re-attack.

Available figures clearly show that in the past decade a steep rise has occurred in the numerical and qualitative characteristics of the world's light naval forces. The number of missile-armed fast patrol boats (FPBs) in the world grew in so short a time-span as 1975–78 from 398 to 811 (outstanding orders included), that is,

TABLE 2. Rank order of Third World major arms importers, 1975–79

Importing region	Percentage of Third World total	Largest recipient countries	Percentage of region's total	Largest supplier to each country	Largest suppliers per region
Middle East	48	Iran	31	United States	United States
		Saudi Arabia	14	United States	USSR
		Jordan	13	United States	France
		Iraq	12	USSR	United Kingdom
		Israel	10	United States	
		Syria	6	USSR	
Far East	16	Republic of Korea	38	United States	United States
		Viet Nam	16	USSR	USSR
		Taiwan	13	United States	France
		Malaysia	5	United States	China
		Philippines	5	United States	
		Indonesia	5	United States	
North Africa	11	Libya	65	USSR	USSR
		Morocco	20	France	France
		Algeria	14	USSR	United States
		Tunisia	1	Italy	United Kingdom
Sub-Saharan Africa	10	South Africa	24	France	USSR
		Ethiopia	13	USSR	France
		Angola	9	USSR	United States
		Mozambique	9	USSR	United Kingdom
		Sudan	6	France	
		Nigeria	5	United Kingdom	
South America	9	Brazil	24	United States	United States
		Peru	20	USSR	United Kingdom
		Argentina	17	United Kingdom	France
		Chile	14	France	Italy
		Venezuela	13	Italy	
		Ecuador	8	France	
Indian subcontinent	5	India	52	USSR	USSR
		Pakistan	28	France	France
		Afghanistan	13	USSR	United Kingdom
		Bangladesh	3	China	China
		Nepal	0.3	France	
		Sri Lanka	0.2	France	
Central America	1.5	Cuba	45	USSR	USSR
		Mexico	28	United Kingdom	United Kingdom
		Bahamas	6	United States	United States
		Honduras	5	United States	France
		El Salvador	5	Israel	
		Guatemala	4	Israel	
Oceania	0.02	Papua New Guinea	63	Australia	Australia
					United States
		Fiji	37	United States	

more than doubled; the number of all types of FPBs grew in the same time from 1,972 to 2,483; and the number of other patrol craft (including missile-armed corvettes) grew from 1,899 to 2,475. There is now only one region in the world where FPB forces do not exist, namely Australia and Oceania. The numbers of missile-armed FPBs, that is, vessels most suitable in a combat role, grew most rapidly in Europe, the Middle East and Far East Asia. Whereas in 1960 only one state possessed FPBs, in 1970 seventeen countries, and in 1978 more than one-third of the countries (122) having direct access to the sea—forty-five to be precise—were already operating FPB forces.

Ballistic missiles carried aboard nuclear submarines are relied upon by both the United States and the USSR to provide the most secure form of deterrent retaliatory capability. This reliance is based on the assumed invulnerability conferred by the enormous difficulty of the task of locating and destroying all the missile submarines of an opponent in the opening stages of a nuclear attack.

Because of advances in geodetic knowledge of the earth's shape, in navigation systems for submarines, and in guidance systems for the missiles, SLBMs are now acquiring the degree of accuracy that is necessary for hitting missiles buried in hardened silos. Previously each side could feel reasonably assured that SLBMs were indeed only deterrent weapons, because they were only accurate enough for such soft and extensive targets as cities.

An enormous amount of effort is being put into new command, control and communication (C3) systems for missile submarines. There is still considerable doubt as to whether C3 links to submarines can function in a nuclear-war environment. If they cannot, then the viability of the deterrent concept is endangered.

However, the biggest threat to the deterrence concept is the increasing ability of anti-submarine warfare (ASW) systems to detect and destroy missile submarines. Although there is no single breakthrough imminent which will make the oceans militarily transparent, there are a number of lines of technological progress coming to fruition which will, taken together, offer a high probability of detecting missile submarines anywhere in the ocean. If the location of the submarines is known, then their destruction becomes relatively easy.

If the invulnerability of both the submarines and their C3 systems cannot be guaranteed, then there will in turn be an increased temptation to further adapt the missile submarines to first-strike counterforce roles.

Military use of outer space

Considerable qualitative advances are being made in almost all fields of military technology. An excellent example is the military use of outer space.

Military satellites are able to navigate weapons to their targets with a high degree of accuracy; they can be used to pinpoint geographical positions with great precision so that no target can remain invulnerable; and they increase the possibility of fighting wars by remote control.

With the development of reconnaissance and early-warning satellites more emphasis seems to be placed on a strategic doctrine of flexible response and limited nuclear war. Early-warning satellites can detect almost immediately the launching of an enemy missile, while reconnaissance satellites can give precise target information and also quickly assess the damage. This allows the prompt response essential in a limited exchange of nuclear weapons.

Military satellites are used for reconnaissance, early warning of attack, communications, navigation, and for meteorological and geodetic measurement. They have also been used to observe conflict areas on earth. Over 50 per cent of all military satellites have been launched for reconnaissance purposes. They provide photographic and electronic reconnaissance, early-warning systems and a means of ocean surveillance.

The surface movements of naval forces can be closely monitored by ocean-surveillance satellites. Oceanographic satellites provide information about ocean conditions over the entire globe in real time. Such information is vital to the functioning of long-range submarine-detection systems and is also used by submarines to avoid detection.

Early-warning satellites are launched to give notice of the launching of enemy missiles. They also carry sensors to detect nuclear explosions both on the surface of the earth and in the atmosphere so as to check treaty violations.

Military communications satellites are replacing other systems for global strategic networks, for command and control of nuclear forces and for tactical battlefield and naval networks. The increasing complexity of modern means of warfare, involving a host of mobile weapon systems such as aircraft, missiles and ships, places enormous demands on new military navigation systems. Navigation satellites will play an increasing role. By means of a satellite-based system, it will be possible to guide a weapon anywhere on earth to within ten metres of its target. In addition, the detailed maps made possible by geodetic and reconnaissance satellites allow the military forces to achieve greater accuracy for some of the most advanced weapons, such as cruise missiles.

A more recent military activity in space is the development of ways of destroying hostile satellites. In addition to some conventional techniques, high-energy laser and particle-beam weapons are also envisaged for this purpose. This is a dangerous activity because early-warning satellites and reconnaissance satellites provide reassurance against nuclear attack. The threat of their destruction would cause considerable anxiety.

Another dangerous development would be systems based in space for destroying ballistic missiles in flight. Currently, high-energy lasers and heavy-particle beams are being considered for this purpose. Effective ballistic-missile defence would actively encourage thinking in terms of nuclear-war fighting.

On the positive side, military satellites play a useful role in verifying arms-control agreements. But only two nations possess the technology for such extensive data gathering. Therefore, broad international participation in verification of multilateral arms-control agreements by satellites has been demanded for many years.

Ecological warfare[3]

There is a discernible trend for modern warfare to become ever more destructive of the environment. Moreover, the weapons of mass destruction available today could be employed so as to have a catastrophic environmental impact. There is the further suggestion that man will soon attain the technological sophistication to permit the manipulation of certain forces of nature such as hurricanes, tsunamis, or earthquakes. If these abilities were to be employed for hostile purposes, their environmental impact could be truly widespread, long lasting and severe.

Hostile environmental disruption is open to *a priori* criticism since its effect, although more or less subtle, is unavoidably indiscriminate, uncontainable, and long lasting. The impact is thus felt not only by the enemy military forces, but probably as well by the civil sector, by third parties, and by future generations. Moreover, all living things on earth deserve at least some measure of respect and protection in their own right. Humans must think of themselves less as owners of the land and lords of the birds and beasts, and more as temporary residents and guardians of the land and what it supports. A concern over the ecological consequences of war does not preclude direct traditional anthropocentric concerns. It may, in fact, enhance such concerns via a civilizing influence and also perhaps by awakening a new constituency to war-related concerns. That is to say, a respect for the environment should reinforce the incentive to attain a disarmed world.

The Second Indo-China War was the first in modern history in which environmental disruption was an intentional and sustained component of the strategy of one of the belligerent powers. In an attempt to subdue a largely guerrilla opponent, the United States pioneered a variety of hostile techniques causing widespread environmental disruption which were aimed at denying its enemy concealment, freedom of movement, and local sources of food and other supplies.

The three ecologically most destructive techniques of the Second Indo-China War were: (a) the massive and sustained expenditure of high-explosive munitions (about 14 million tons of bombs, shells and the like); (b) the profligate dissemination of chemical anti-plant agents (about 55,000 tons of herbicides); and (c) the large-scale employment of heavy land-clearing tractors (about 200 so-called Rome ploughs).

Among the ecological lessons to be learned from the military tactics employed during the Second Indo-China War are: (a) that the vegetation can be severely damaged or even destroyed with relative ease over extensive areas—and, of course, with it the ecosystems for which it provides the basis; (b) that natural, agricultural and industrial-crop plant communities are all similarly vulnerable; and (c) that the ecological impact of such actions is likely to be of long duration.

Chemical weapons

Chemical weapons increasingly seem to be regarded as useful tactical weapons in specific situations. The question of eliminating chemical weapons has been on the agenda of international disarmament bodies for the past twelve years. Progress towards a ban on chemical weapons is extremely slow, mainly because of perceived problems with verification.

A major issue in discussions on chemical disarmament is how to eliminate the large existing stocks of chemical warfare (CW) agents and the facilities for their production, and how to verify that this has been done. For example, a difficult verification problem is how the existence of allegedly concealed or undeclared chemical munition stockpiles can be confirmed or refuted in situations where trust is lacking.

The maintenance of ageing stockpiles of chemical weapons in the vicinity of densely populated and heavily trafficked areas is associated with environmental hazards. Further hazards are associated with the handling and transportation of chemical weapons.

Although some highly toxic chemicals are manufactured for ordinary industrial processes, strict limitations on these chemicals as well as destruction of those suitable only for warfare purposes would diminish the capacity for waging chemical warfare, at short notice at any rate.

Complete and effective prohibition of all chemical weapons and their destruction is one of the most urgent disarmament measures.

Military research and development (R&D)

Apart from the huge increase in the volume of resources devoted to military uses the other distinguishing feature of the post-war period has been the extraordinary emphasis given to technological advances. The intensity of the drive—though not the drive itself—to develop and produce better machines is basically military in origin. A major conclusion drawn from events during the Second World War was that failure to have on hand the most technologically advanced weapons would have disastrous consequences. As a result, military research and development (R&D) was given the highest priority. In the major countries the quantity and quality of the scientific and engineering workforce were deliberately maximized (through changes in the educational system and by modifying relative wage and salary rates) to meet the enormously increased military demand.

Since these developments occurred in parallel in both East and West, the anticipated dangers of lagging technologically became a self-fulfilling prophecy. For the last thirty years new and improved weapons have emerged at an unmanageably rapid rate with no signs of any relaxation.

About 10 per cent of military spending is for military R&D. This activity—which also absorbs more than one-half of the world's most highly qualified physical and engineering scientists—is the one which makes possible the arms race. Without military R&D, the production of weapons for replacement may continue, the size of the world's arsenals may increase, and the weapons of the small and medium powers may (because of the arms trade) eventually approach in quality those of the great powers. But, in terms of the development of new, more sophisticated, more destructive and increasingly expensive weapons, the arms race would cease. In practice, however, military R&D is the hardest of all military activities to restrain. In fact, since the Second World War the only significant limits to developments in military technology have been the innovative capabilities of the Soviet and United States societies.

Notes

1. Unless otherwise indicated, throughout the work the sign $ = United States dollars.
2. The SIPRI data on transfers of major weapons include aircraft, armoured vehicles, missiles and warships. According to SIPRI statistics, major weapons account for about 40 per cent of total arms sales. The remaining 60 per cent consists mostly of related equipment, electronics, support, training, spares, guns and small arms.
3. SIPRI has dealt with the problems of war and the environment in two books, namely *The Ecological Consequences of the Second Indochina War,* Stockholm, Almqvist & Wiksell, 1976, and *Weapons of Mass Destruction and the Environment,* London, Taylor & Francis, 1977.

2

Socio-political indicators

Ruth Leger Sivard
Director, World Priorities Inc.

Creeping militarization

Worldwide, the men and women in uniform and the civilians employed by defence ministries or working in military-related jobs now add up to 100 million people, a population as large as the total labour force of Latin America. About 70 per cent of these are in the armed forces: 24 million in the regular forces, plus 22 million in paramilitary units (including people's militia) and 24 million reservists.

For both developed and developing nations, support of the armed forces represents a growing financial burden. Operating costs, i.e. outlays for personnel and maintenance, constitute the largest item in military budgets. Military pay scales have gone up in most areas, and especially rapidly in the industrialized nations. Military defence is one business in which increased productivity per man (the result in this case of society's investments in mechanization, computerization, and unprecedented advances in firepower) has not meant fewer people employed or lower prices.

Creeping militarization involves more than the piling up of weapons and the development of an arms-producing industry. With it goes a power structure dependent on arms for jobs, prestige and profits, a climate of fear and secrecy, and a single-minded concern that takes over the national purpose. These are the factors that institutionalize the arms race.

The size of today's peacetime military-industrial-labour-political complex exceeds anything known in the past. Despite mechanization and the technological miracles which have given the modern soldier mobility and firepower infinitely greater than his predecessors, the number of people under arms continues to increase. The world's armed forces, supported by an estimated 25–30 million civilians in military-related jobs, now represent a population twice as large as all the doctors, nurses and teachers in the world.

The military bureaucracy is unique not only in size but in the financial resources that it commands. In central governments its employees outnumber all

Excerpts from Ruth Leger Sivard, *World Military and Social Expenditures 1978 and 1979*, Leesburg, Va., World Priorities Inc., 1979 and 1980.

other government employees and account for a major share of public payrolls. They also administer the largest slice of government revenues. The military power structure extends into the topmost echelons of government. In over 40 per cent of developing nations, military officers now hold the key positions of power.

The military presence in political life has a growing effect on public policy. Its mission begins to govern the national purpose. National security is increasingly identified with military security. One threat, the threat of attack, becomes the dominant concern and one solution, military power, the national obsession.

Military *v.* other budgets

Of all the functions of government the most difficult for the public to assess is military power, often the single largest element in national budgets. Isolated from view by the complexities of modern technology, and often by deliberate official policy, this significant part of the public budget has been left to the control of a comparatively small band of specialists. Yet the requirements of military security cannot effectively be judged in isolation, or by specialists alone. Military adequacy is always relative, subject to factors, international and domestic, far beyond the military sphere. Specialists who judge military needs may too readily see threats and their solutions only in narrow military terms. For politicians, the final arbiters, the military budget is often the easy way out.

A review of the world's use of public funds in the 1970s does, in fact, raise troubling questions about the perspectives which governments have been bringing to the allocation process. Judged by a variety of measures of national and global welfare, budget priorities show a persistent slant towards military strength, to the neglect of other factors—economic, social and political—that are equally vital in protecting society's well-being and its security.

An essential difference between military budgets and budgets for health and education is that the latter are directly related to rising population requirements. The military budget presumably is not—i.e. the military threat to a nation does not necessarily grow as its population grows. Yet military budgets show an ability to ride out inflation, climbing faster than the price level, while social budgets find it difficult to keep up with both price and population pressures. The bare figures make striking statements about the priorities implicit in these budgets:

On a global basis, society now invests $16,000 a year per soldier, $260 a year in the education of a school-age child.

Developing nations carry three times as much insurance against military attack as against all the health problems that strike people on a day-to-day basis.

Worldwide, the support of national military forces costs $92 a year per person; support of the United Nations and all its programmes in food, health, labour, etc. $0.57 a year; international peace-keeping operations, $0.05 a year.

Military expenditures *v.* economic aid

The increasing interdependence of nations, whether developed or developing, endowed with raw materials or with technology, rich or poor, has been one of the

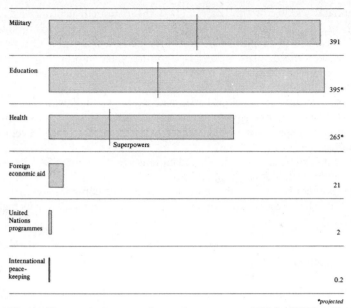

Military	391
Education	395*
Health	265*
	Superpowers
Foreign economic aid	21
United Nations programmes	2
International peace-keeping	0.2

*projected

FIG. 1. World military and other expenditures of governments, 1977 (in $1,000 million).

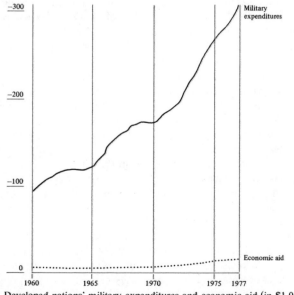

FIG. 2. Developed nations' military expenditures and economic aid (in $1,000 million).

most emphatic lessons of the latter half of the twentieth century. Economic development, growth on a broad front, is a boon to the whole community of nations. Assistance to economies in need may be returned many times over in enlarged markets, needed raw materials, a mutual stake in peaceful coexistence. Nevertheless, as Figure 2 suggests, much more of the public money has gone to the buildup of military force than to the buildup of underdeveloped economies.

Military expenditures of developed nations rose by $200,000 million between 1960 and 1977, their foreign economic assistance by $10,000 million. In 1977 their military expenditures were twenty times larger than their development assistance.

The foreign aid extended by the developed nations averaged out to $4.50 a year for each person in the developing nations.

Both superpowers have a poor record in foreign aid compared with military resources. The USSR was the lowest of all aid-givers in relation to its high rate of military spending.

Military *v.* civilian research

The search for new and more destructive weapons dwarfs all other research efforts, whether publicly or privately financed. Weapons research occupies over half a million scientists and engineers throughout the world and takes more public research money than all research on energy, health, education, food and other civilian needs combined.

Because of the enormous resources it has commanded, both in money and in skilled personnel, research for military applications has been the dominant force in the development of technology in the modern era.

One result of this effort is an explosive advance in technology unmatched in the civilian world. A constantly changing panoply of exotic weapons seems to come to life out of science fiction: a missile that with one warhead can bomb three or more separate cities 6,000-7,000 miles away; 'smart' bombs that home in on heat; high-energy lasers; hunter-killer satellites; death rays; uranium bullets.

Many of the most revolutionary modifications have occurred in the so-called conventional arms, which take the largest share of military budgets even in nuclear-weapon states. Conventional weapons have fought all wars since the Second World War, killing an estimated 25 million people.

Increasingly, the weapons themselves are capable of massive, often inhumane and indiscriminate destruction. Explosive power has been greatly enhanced. Bullets may be made to tumble and fragment within the body. Incendiary agents produce chemical fireballs. Cluster bombs carry hundreds of bomblets, each of which detonates into many steel pellets. Fuel air explosives disperse fuel into the air and then detonate the fuel cloud. For affected civilian populations, war fought with the horror of incendiaries and fragmentation weapons may be 'conventional', but for many it is as cruel and deadly as nuclear war.

Detailed data on the allocation of government R&D expenditures among programme objectives are available only for the United States and a limited number of European countries, and in some cases classifications among programmes differ.

Despite the critical importance of energy to world security almost five times as
much public money was spent on weapons research as on energy conserv-
ation and all alternative energy sources.

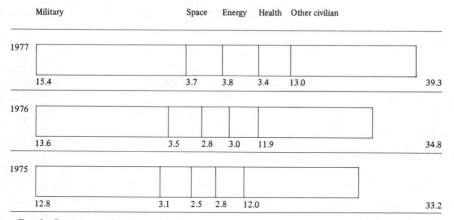

FIG. 3. Government financing of research in the United States and the European Community (in
$1,000 million).

Military and space during this three-year period took a growing share of the
research dollar, further squeezing research funds for civilian technology.
For the entire range of health needs, preventive care, environmental health,
disease control, etc., governments spent less than on space exploration.
The R&D effort is significant not only for what it has produced but also for the
continuing momentum it gives to the arms race generally. The steady improvement in technology has made the pace of national military spending essentially
independent of the existing threat to the nation. The criterion governing weapons
procurement is not necessarily need but, more commonly, availability. In the
superpower competition, each side considers it essential to develop and produce
whatever is technologically possible. R&D is the instrument through which
'antagonistic co-operation' between the two leading adversary nations ensures a
never-ending escalation of arming.

3

Economic and social consequences of the arms race

United Nations Group of Consultant Experts

Dynamics of the arms race

The arms race is increasingly a worldwide phenomenon and, although its intensity varies markedly between regions, few countries and no major region has stayed out of it. The competition in armaments between the largest military powers is by far the most important. It involves the greatest diversion of resources, the greatest inherent dangers and constitutes the principal driving force of the worldwide arms race. This competition is even more intense than is suggested by the immense size and the rapid expansion of their arsenals, because it takes place primarily in a qualitative rather than a quantitative dimension, each new generation of weapons being more complex and more destructive than the systems it replaces.

The primary engine of this worldwide arms race is constituted by the qualitative arms race among the largest military powers. This is due chiefly to the virtual monopoly of these powers in development of advanced military technology, to their overwhelmingly large share of world production and world exports of advanced weaponry, and to the global character of their interests, politically and militarily. The six main military spenders not only account for three-quarters of world military spending, but for practically all military research and development (R&D) and for practically all exports of weapons and military equipment.[1]

The past decade has seen a continuous stream of new developments in the sphere of nuclear and conventional means of warfare. Because these technological and qualitative changes have not displayed the spectacular, eye-catching qualities which characterized some earlier developments, such as the advent of the atom bomb or of space technology, there is a danger that it may seem as though military technology has remained relatively unchanged. Such complacency would be

---

Excerpts from *Economic and Social Consequences of the Arms Race and of Military Expenditures*, updated report of the United Nations Secretary-General prepared by a Group of Consultant Experts, New York, 1978 (Publication sales No. E.78.IX.1). Members of the Group of Consultant Experts: S. A. Consalvi (Venezuela), H. de Haan (Netherlands), D. Djokic (Yugoslavia), G. Dolgu, Chairman (Romania), V. S. Emelyanov (USSR), P. G. Reynoso (Mexico), S. M. Hashmi (India), R. H. Huisken (Australia), L. Matajka (Czechoslovakia), I. M. Randolph (Liberia), K. W. Rothschild (Austria), Y. Ullmo (France), United Nations Secretariat: R. Björnerstedt, Assistant Secretary-General, L. Bota, Secretary of the Group, A. Boserup, University of Copenhagen, Consultant.

entirely unjustified. Recent developments have profoundly influenced military capabilities, worldwide destructive potentials and strategic conditions, possibilities and doctrines.

The most important and spectacular aspect of the arms race in the 1960s was the development and the full-scale deployment of intercontinental ballistic missiles (ICBMs) and of submarine-launched missiles (SLBMs), and the associated deployment of satellite surveillance and communication systems. By the end of that decade there was widespread concern that a new arms-race spiral might result from the development of anti-ballistic missile systems (ABMs) and from countermeasures in the form of increasing numbers of launchers and, more particularly, of increasing numbers of warheads per launcher to saturate ABM systems. The technical form for the latter development is multiple and independently targetable re-entry vehicles (MIRVs).

Moreover, a major post-MIRV innovation is already at an advanced stage of development. This is a manœuvrable re-entry vehicle (MARV) which can change direction in the terminal stages of its trajectory. This could make defence against ballistic missile attack more difficult, but in particular, if combined with developments now taking place in terminal guidance systems, it can provide MARVed missiles with pinpoint accuracies of a few tens of metres instead of current accuracies of somewhat less than one kilometre. With such accuracies, the silos now protecting the land-based ICBMs can be destroyed with near certainty with a single warhead at the first attempt. As a result it becomes possible to consider using 'strategic' nuclear weapons in new ways. In addition to being a means of massive reprisals against centres of population and industry to serve as a basic deterrent, it becomes possible to think of using ballistic missiles in 'counterforce' roles to gain military advantage at the outset of a war by striking at the weapons and military installations of the opponent, or to use them to conduct supposedly 'limited' nuclear war. The adoption of doctrines of this kind could greatly enhance the probability of nuclear war.

No less significant are the implications of the deployment of long-range cruise missiles. These weapons, now under development, are best described as small, highly manœuvrable, low-flying pilotless aircraft. They can be equipped with a nuclear as well as a conventional warhead. Current models have ranges of several thousand kilometres and accurate guidance systems, which readjust the trajectory at intervals by comparing terrain features with a map. The accuracy is therefore independent of the range. It will be impossible to determine from its geometry alone whether a cruise missile carries a nuclear or a conventional warhead and, within wide limits, what range it may have. Moreover, it is a small and easily concealed vehicle. Future agreements on strategic weapons may thus become very difficult to negotiate because they would be difficult to verify.

Developments in nuclear weapons technology proper are equally ominous, particularly the development of small, low-yield nuclear weapons, of enhanced radiation weapons and of tactical concepts for their use in battle. Delivered with higher accuracy and causing less collateral damage per warhead, their use on the battlefield may seem more acceptable, so that the step from non-nuclear to nuclear war may be more readily taken. Once they are used on the battlefield, escalation towards full-scale nuclear war becomes a dangerous possibility.

The importance of the changes now under way in the field of nuclear armaments and their carriers is not that their performance in missions tradition-ally assigned to them is improving year by year, but that essentially new types of missions are becoming possible. New technologies open the way for new doctrines. These in turn give an appearance of rationality to the deployment of weaponry embodying these technologies. At the same time they increase the dangers of war and alter the terms of the disarmament equation, rendering it more complex and more intractable.

The proliferation of nuclear technologies continues at an accelerating pace. France and China acquired a nuclear weapons capability in the 1960s. In 1974, India, which is not a party to the Non-Proliferation Treaty, conducted a nuclear explosion experiment underground. It was officially termed a peaceful nuclear explosion experiment. This explosion demonstrated how readily and cheaply a small nuclear weapons capability could be derived from a major civilian nuclear programme. In other cases a nuclear weapons capability could have been acquired without being demonstrated in a nuclear explosion. Civilian nuclear programmes, and with them, to a variable degree, the technical expertise and the fissile material required for military programmes, have spread all over the world during the 1970s. In 1975, nineteen countries had nuclear power plants in operation, and another ten countries will have them by 1980. Experimental reactors are now in operation in well over fifty countries. As far as most industrialized and several developing countries are concerned, there are no longer serious technological or economic barriers against initiating a nuclear weapons programme.

Also, as regards conventional weapons, developments have been far-reaching. Throughout the 1960s conventional weapons systems underwent continual and rapid refinement in terms of size, speed, propulsion, fire-power, accuracy and so forth. Unit costs for major weapons systems typically doubled in real terms during this period. For aircraft it was noted they doubled about twice as fast. Sophisticated weaponry, including supersonic aircraft, became commonplace in the armouries of industrialized as well as less developed countries.

New precision-guided munitions (PGMs), remotely piloted vehicles (RPVs) and other devices have been developed to carry a conventional warhead to its target with hit probabilities close to '1', or, in the case of RPVs, for reconnaissance and similar missions. This group of weapons is a whole family of devices using the latest developments in such fields as laser technology, microelectronics, electro-magnetic sensors in the radar, infra-red and optical ranges and wide-band data links for a variety of remote automatic guidance and/or homing devices. A first generation of PGMs made their appearance in the Indo-China war. In the Middle East in 1973, the enormous potential of such weapons against tanks and aircraft was demonstrated. Both the type of technology involved and their cost make PGMs accessible to many countries, and, indeed, many have them now in their inventories.

The new weapons, together with developments in such areas as night-vision devices, battlefield surveillance and communications, are likely to accelerate the pace of modern warfare and to place a still higher premium on standing military forces. Last but not least, with dramatic improvements in accuracy, the yield of the explosive charge becomes a less important parameter in performance. There have been suggestions, for example, that some of the missions now assigned to 'tactical' nuclear weapons could be performed by precision-delivered weapons with a conventional warhead. In principle this could mean that military planners would be more willing to dispense with the use of nuclear weapons in a limited conflict, but in practice it could equally well have the effect of blurring the distinction between the use of nuclear and non-nuclear weapons, thus enhancing the risk of an armed conflict developing into nuclear war.

A range of new weapons and munitions based on blast, fragmentation and incendiary effects has been developed, and was used, notably during the Indo-China war, for saturation bombing over large areas. Such carpet-bombing techniques approach nuclear weapons as regards the blind, indiscriminate destruction they cause, the long-term ecological effects to which they give rise, and the high proportion of wounded and maimed among casualties. Other weapons of massive and indiscriminate destruction have not lagged behind. The effectiveness of incendiary weapons has been considerably increased, and the development of binary nerve gases and their munitions (which are relatively innocuous to handle as the nerve gas is only assembled in flight) could seriously weaken the remaining technical and operational constraints on the deployment of chemical weapons.

Significant developments have also taken place in a number of other fields such as radar technology, anti-submarine warfare techniques, low-altitude interceptor aircraft, laser-guided cannon and many more.

The strong qualitative momentum of the current arms race has a number of important consequences for the way it develops, the insecurity it generates and in terms of the possibilities for disarmament. In an arms race where the emphasis is on quantity, where technological development is slow and of little consequence, countries may be expected to match their armament efforts to the stocks or the growth rates of the military forces of their opponents. There is room for saturation levels or for mutually agreed ceilings and reductions. Under conditions of rapid military innovation, on the other hand, the decisive factor in the military procurement plans of countries at the forefront of the technological arms race is not so much the actual military strength of their opponents but rather those technological advances which opponents might be able to achieve over the next decade or so (ten years being the typical gestation period for a major technological advance). Inevitably, as the apprehensions of military planners shift from the force levels towards the R&D efforts of their opponents, it is increasingly on the R&D efforts of their own country, which are known, that they will have to base their plans.

In an arms race where the stress is on technological advances the process of weapon and counter-weapon development therefore tends to become in some measure an *intra*-national process, in some cases only marginally related to the stages actually reached by other countries. Each country is actively seeking means of defeating its own most advanced weapons and of neutralizing its own most recent defences, thus conferring on the development of military technology a momentum and a rate of obsolescence much greater than in comparable civilian applications. A qualitative arms race with its long lead time and its emphasis on future possibilities rather than current realities tends to move in one direction only: one country's advances in weaponry will be emulated by others, but its self-restraint need not be. Similarly an increase in international tension may accelerate the arms race, but an improvement of the international climate will not necessarily suffice to slow it down.

The arms race is not only becoming more dangerous; it is also becoming more complex and more firmly entrenched. It is sustained by a variety of forces acting together, and it must be expected that to remove one of them is not sufficient to reverse its course. In fact, it may be assumed that it is not one or a few single factors but precisely their multiplicity which confers upon the arms race its great inertia and which has rendered it so intractable from the point of view of disarmament, any limited successes in one field tending to be offset very quickly by developments in other sectors of the arms race.

The commitment to incessant qualitative change is deeply embedded in the inner logic of the arms race. Agreements on qualitative and technological restrictions are not easily reached, not least because of difficult verification problems. But if the difficulties of securing some measure of control over this dimension of the arms race are particularly great, so too is the urgency of the need to take determined steps in this direction. Each passing year sees the initiation of a spate of new weapons, and existing programmes become more deeply entrenched in the military and political systems of countries and thus more difficult to stop.

In the light of the developments described above, it is necessary to expound openly the dangers of the continuation of the arms race, and to dispel illusions that lasting peace and security can coexist with huge accumulations of means of destruction. The adoption and implementation of resolute measures in the field of disarmament and particularly nuclear disarmament, ultimately leading to general and complete disarmament, has become imperative. At the same time it is necessary to intensify efforts for the adoption of partial measures of military disengagement and disarmament that can contribute to the achievement of that goal.

The arms race in terms of resources

The arms race, with its economic costs and social and political effects, nationally and internationally, constitutes an important obstacle to effective progress in establishing a new international economic order. Resources now being absorbed by the arms race are scarce and needed for socially constructive ends. Every year military activities throughout the world absorb a volume of resources equivalent to about two-thirds of the aggregate gross national product of those countries which together comprise the poorest half of the world's population.

Since the Second World War none of the major military powers have been at war with one another, but world military expenditure has been rising steadily. Over the past half century it has increased in real terms by a factor of 10, corresponding to an annual increase of nearly 5 per cent. Since the Second World War the direct costs of the arms race have exceeded $6,000 billion (in 1975 prices) or about as much as the aggregate GNP of the entire world in 1975.

Public expenditures for health services have expanded rapidly in recent years. Nevertheless, public health expenditures (to which privately financed medical care should be added to complete the picture) only amount to about 60 per cent of military expenditure on a world basis. Again differences between countries are very large. Even greater imbalances exist in the critical field of research funding. The resources devoted to medical research worldwide are only one-fifth of those devoted to military research and development. In all cases the resources consumed in the military sector are very large compared with the social expenditures of governments, even in such important fields as education and health, indicating the unfortunate priorities that govern the allocation of public funds throughout the world. In the world as a whole there are almost as many soldiers as there are teachers.

Such comparisons of gross expenditure for wholly incommensurate ends are, however, relatively meaningless as they stand. They give only a crude indication of the sacrifices in terms of social and economic progress that the arms race entails. A more adequate assessment would require a survey of the needs for increased resources for social and other non-military purposes, and a comparison of the costs of meeting those needs with the costs of military programmes.

The most alarming situation of all is in the area of nutrition. Half a billion people throughout the world are severely malnourished and millions more subsist on diets that are far below minimal needs. A large proportion of young children in developing countries are blocked in their physical and mental development because of diet deficiencies, which entails incalculable consequences for the next generation. In recent years famine has struck entire regions of the world, and on a per capita basis food production in the developing countries as a whole has been declining. Yet the poorest countries, those with per capita incomes below $200, generally countries whose military expenditures are modest in relation to GNP, nevertheless spend (on average) about as much for military activities as they spend on agricultural investment.

The vast benefits which could result from even trifling cuts in military expenditures, and the reallocation of the funds thus saved, are particularly obvious in the field of health. The World Health Organization (WHO) spent around $83 million over ten years to eradicate smallpox in the world. That amount would not even suffice to buy a single modern strategic bomber. The WHO programme to eradicate malaria in the world, estimated at a cost of some $450 million, is dragging on owing to lack of funds. Yet its total cost over the years is only half of what is spent every day for military purposes, and only a third of what will be spent, strictly for procurement, for each of the new Trident nuclear-missile submarines.

Moreover, the potential benefits of a transfer of resources from the military to the health sector reach far beyond the immediate humanitarian aspect. The implementation of such eradication programmes would by itself release important resources in the medical sector for new tasks, and, improving the general health standard in affected areas, would enhance the ability of people to improve their social and economic conditions in other respects. Such cumulative benefits are indeed a general feature of many development programmes, particularly of those which are directed towards the most destitute sectors of the population. In this respect as well expenditures for development purposes stand in stark contrast to military expenditures, which are a waste in themselves, which induce other countries to similar wastage, and which undermine the potential for future growth.

It is in the field of scientific and technological capability that the diversion of resources to military ends is most massive. It is estimated that at the present time some 25 per cent of the world's scientific manpower is engaged in military-related pursuits. In the past the fraction has been even higher. Indeed, it has been estimated that of total cumulative R&D spending since the Second World War some 40 per cent has been directed at achieving military ends. By far the largest part is spent on the development of equipment which has no conceivable civilian use.

As already noted, military research and development is overwhelmingly concentrated in the six main military spenders. Together they are reported to account for 96 to 97 per cent of world military R&D. As only a small percentage of the world's scientific and technical manpower is found in the developing countries, it follows that military research and development in the world absorbs perhaps ten times the entire scientific and technological capabilities available in developing countries. Moreover, technological innovation has been very rapid in the military field. One important consequence is that as high-technology weaponry spreads from the technologically leading countries to countries where the technical and industrial base is narrower, and as these countries engage in the production of advanced weapons themselves, military requirements take an increasing toll of already scarce technical skills and equipment. The civilian spin-offs from military research, if not in all cases negligible, have been trifling in comparison with the resources with which they were bought and with the results that could have been achieved if the efforts had been aimed directly at the civilian application.

Manpower is another one of the very large drains on resources which the arms race entails. The armed forces around the world total approximately 22 million people. The total manpower absorption by the military, direct and indirect, can only be guessed at. For the United States there is for every three persons in the armed forces another four in military-related employment. Military and military-related activities everywhere absorb a much higher proportion of the most qualified categories of persons than the share of the military budget in the gross national product might lead one to expect. This is obviously true of research personnel, engineers and technicians. It is also true in the field of administrative and managerial skills. In some cases the proportion of industrial employment directly or indirectly engaged in military-related production seems to be much higher than the proportion of GNP diverted to military ends. In any case it is evident that the overall drain on highly qualified manpower resources is often larger than either military budget figures or overall figures for military-related employment suggest.

The protection of the environment is an important part of the resource problem. Military activities impact in several ways on the task of repairing the environmental damages of the past and preventing or minimizing further degradation. One factor, perhaps in the long term the most important of all, is simply the diversion of financial and scientific resources involved in the arms race. Effective solutions to environmental problems will in many cases require large research and development efforts and considerable investments for reprocessing, for air and water purification and for many other tasks. Effective action in this field, not least where large-scale international co-operation is required, would be greatly facilitated by the abatement of the arms race and, not least, by the release of important scientific and technical resources which this would bring about.

The world's armed forces are also major consumers of a wide range of nonrenewable resources, both energy and raw-material reserves, though statistical information on this is fragmentary or non-existent. Extrapolating from United States figures, world military consumption of liquid hydrocarbons (excluding petroleum products used in the production of weapons and equipment) has been estimated to be about 700 to 750 million barrels annually. This is twice the annual consumption for the whole of Africa and corresponds to approximately 3.5 per cent of world consumption. For jet fuel, on the other hand, military consumption (in peacetime) is reportedly one-third of total consumption for the United States. Even though information is mostly lacking, it is evident that the military contribution to the depletion of natural resources is substantial in many cases.

Judging by the figures for the latest years, the share of output wasted on armaments is rising again for the world as a whole and for a majority of countries. This reflects the slower rate of growth of world output in recent years and the continued rise of military expenditure in most countries. Moreover, there has not been, of course, any long-term redeployment of resources away from the military at all. The long-term transfer has been entirely the other way: from the civilian economy where growth is generated, to the military sector which has appropriated a substantial part of that growth, increasing in absolute terms (and in constant 1973 prices) by almost 80 per cent from $150,000–160,000 million in 1960 to $270,000–280,000 million in 1977.

The arms race and economic and social development

One aspect of the economic and social impact of the arms race is the constraining effect on consumption, private and public, and on growth.

In the period under review, the economic outlook for the world has darkened considerably. This has underlined the intolerable character of the waste of resources and has added to the urgency of the many social and economic problems facing the world, problems whose effective alleviation would be greatly facilitated by the reallocation to socially constructive ends of the resources now spent on the arms race. In the 1970s inflation of a magnitude unprecedented in post-war history hit many countries.

The high level of military spending in the world not only diverts resources that are urgently needed for dealing effectively with these problems, but also helps to exacerbate these problems. Large military expenditures contribute to the depletion of natural resources, tend to aggravate inflationary tendencies and add to existing balance-of-payments problems. In this way, they have contributed to economic disruption and political instability in some countries. Even so, the implications of an arms race and of military expenditures on the scale typical of the post-war period are much more pervasive than mere economic considerations would suggest. Being one of the main factors shaping the international context, the arms race exerts a profound influence on the politics, economy and society of many countries.

So far, the high levels of military expenditure have not been noticeably affected by the economic recession which hit many countries after 1973. In some countries there is a marked contrast between a still buoyant military sector on the one hand and a depressed civilian economy and tightening or downright austere government budgets on the other. In some limited aspects of the arms race, one can even register a new impetus directly related to features of the present economic crisis: some countries have been able to improve their balance-of-payments position by increased arms exports.

One of the main economic problems of the first half of this decade was the accelerating inflationary process in many countries of the world. Theory and data are not at the point where the role of military expenditure in stimulating inflation can be qualified, but consideration of the various ways in which it can have an effect suggests that its contribution is not inconsequential. High military expenditures sustained over a long period of time are likely to aggravate upward pressures on the price level in several ways. First, military expenditures are inherently inflationary in that purchasing power and effective demand is created without an offsetting increase in immediately consumable output or in productive capacity to meet future consumption requirements. This excess demand creates an upward pressure on prices throughout the economy.

Second, there are reasons to believe that the arms industry offers less resistance to increases in the cost of labour and of the other factors of production than do most other industries, partly because of its highly capital- and technology-intensive character, and partly because cost increases in this sector can more readily be passed on to the customer. These increases in the cost of the other factors of production then spread to other sectors of the economy, including sectors where the rate of growth of productivity is lower, forcing up their prices as well. Finally, and more generally, the diversion of substantial capital and R&D resources away from the civilian sector impedes the long-term growth of productivity and thereby renders the economy more vulnerable to inflationary pressures. Inflationary trends, whatever their origin, tend to be exported, affecting other countries in the form of price increases, scarcities or in other ways, depending on the circumstances. The inflationary impact of military expenditure on the prices of exported military goods to developing countries results in a deterioration of their terms of trade.

As regards economic development and growth in particular, the maintenance and arming of large standing military forces absorbs a volume of resources substantial enough to affect all the basic parameters involved: the volume and structure of investment, the size and composition of the work force and the rate of technological change. Some 20 per cent of total world output is devoted to fixed capital formation, world military expenditures being equivalent to 25 to 30 per cent of this.

In most countries, therefore, there is scope for significant rises in investment if military budgets are reduced. Even crude calculations indicate that the potential effects of this on growth could be substantial. If the greater part of world military expenditure could, instead, be allocated to investment, growth rates might be expected to increase by 1 or 2 per cent. This is in fact very large.

If half the funds spent on armaments throughout the world in the period 1970–75 had instead been invested in the civilian sector, annual output at the end of the period could have been perhaps $200,000 million larger than it was. The sum of $200,000 million is somewhat more than the aggregate GNP of southern Asia and the mid-African region, the two large regions of acute poverty and slow growth in the world, with a total population of over 1,000 million people. Over a longer period the effects on world output of the reallocation of part of world military expenditures to investment purposes would be even more spectacular.

The glaring investment needs throughout the world in housing, urban renewal, health, education, agriculture, energy, environment and many other fields need no further emphasis. Continued economic growth presupposes increasing investments in energy and raw materials extraction, both from traditional sources and from new ones. Estimates of the costs of combating pollution indicate requirements of the order of 1.4 to 1.9 per cent of GNP under moderate assumptions and of the order of 2.5 to 4 per cent in a more maximalist version. To eliminate extreme poverty and to diminish the gap between developing and developed countries, developing countries need to increase investments very considerably. To reduce by half before the end of the century the gap in per capita incomes between rich and poor countries, currently of the order of 13:1, the same calculations indicate among other things that the rate of investment in poor countries would have to be raised to 30 to 35 per cent of GNP, and in some cases 40 per cent. World agricultural production would have to increase three or fourfold as compared with 1970. This would require substantial investment in opening up new land, in irrigation and in the institution of high-yield techniques. It is hard to imagine that such programmes would be at all possible without radical cuts in military budgets.

Manpower is another major factor in the growth equation where a massive diversion to military ends is taking place. It is still a widespread belief today that disarmament or discontinuation of some specific weapons programme would swell the ranks of the jobless, particularly when unemployment is already high. It should be stressed that such conceptions are wrong. Military outlays are not unique in their ability to generate employment. In fact, whereas military expenditures obviously create jobs in the industries supplying the armed forces, the growing high-technology component in military expenditures has eroded their direct and their overall job-creating potential. Today there is rapidly accumulating evidence that high military budgets instead of alleviating overall unemployment contribute substantially to it. According to the United States Government estimates (and only for this country do figures seem to be available) $1,000 million of military expenditure creates 76,000 jobs. But if the same amount is spent for civilian programmes of the federal government it creates an average of over 100,000 jobs, and many more than this if channelled into activities that are particularly labour-consuming. Calculations indicate that if the same $1,000 million were released for private consumption by means of tax cuts it would create 112,000 new jobs. In other words, a 10 per cent cut in the military budget, that is to say a cut of $8,000–9,000 million and a corresponding tax reduction, could diminish unemployment by 0.3 million, and more than this if cuts and alternative programmes were selected with a view to maximizing the effect on employment. Thus, the proposition that military expenditure generates employment at least effectively as, if not more than, non-military expenditure is demonstrably false.

The third major factor in the growth equation is technological change. Throughout the world an estimated 400,000 engineers and scientists are working on military projects. The opportunity cost of this diversion of resources is impossible to quantify. Its magnitude is suggested by recalling that, while scientific and technological advances have yielded enormous benefits for mankind, some 40 per cent of the financial resources devoted to R&D since the Second World War have been used in the military field. Military technology is moving further and further away from any conceivable civilian use, and is anyway focusing on fields which are mostly irrelevant for the solution of the more important present and future problems of the world. There can be no doubt that, in the final analysis, technological innovation in the civilian sector and, with it, growth are not furthered by military research and development but are greatly impaired by it.

It has often been pointed out that in some developing countries the military sector has contributed substantially to technological training and has helped to raise the level of technical skills, providing partial compensation for the resources spent on military activities. It is clear, however, that programmes of industrial development, civilian community projects and the like can achieve those results in a more direct, pertinent and cost-effective way.

The international sale of arms, or, more precisely, of military goods and services, today by far the most important part of arms transfers, is an aspect of the arms race which also has direct and indirect implications for the economies of the countries involved. For all those countries which are not major weapons producers themselves, an increase in military expenditures will normally mean increased imports and will result in a deterioration of the balance of trade. The fact that imports for military purposes generate no income and no exports with which to service the added debt further aggravates the longer-term effect on the balance of payments. For some developing countries facing acute debt-servicing problems, the balance of payments aspect of the costs which the worldwide character of the arms race imposes on all countries is particularly salient.

The trade in arms has opposite effects on the economies of importing and exporting countries. What is involved is a highly unequal exchange, detrimental in particular to efforts to bridge the gap between poor and rich countries. For the importer of arms it is in economic terms a pure waste of surplus which could have been used productively. Even when weapons are provided as gifts there are maintenance, operation and infrastructure costs to be included on the debit side. In contrast to the import of civilian goods these outlays raise neither consumption nor production and generate no future output from which to pay for them. Not so for the exporting country. That part of its arms production which is destined for its own armed forces again figures at a first approximation simply as an economic loss. But its production of weapons for export is no different in economic terms from any other export production. Importing countries are subsidizing military R&D in the arms-exporting countries. This also applies when, instead of importing weapons, countries produce them under licence. In a very real, although often marginal, way importing countries are thus helping to perpetuate the lead in military technology of the main arms-exporting countries and to sustain the rate of innovation and obsolescence in weaponry.

In the countries with a centrally planned economy the negative consequences of military expenditures are in principle of the same character as in other economic systems, but they make themselves felt in a different socio-economic context. Also for these countries military expenditures represent lost opportunities for economic and social development. Military expenditures are a drain on resources which could have been used for civilian purposes, either to accelerate growth and modernization in such fields as industry, agriculture and transport or to raise the standard of living and improve the quality of life.

Certain additional comments can be made with respect to the developing countries. In many of these countries, economic and social development programmes are largely determined and financed by the government. Military expenditure and development programmes appear as direct alternatives for the allocation of government resources. In recent years military expenditure in many of these countries has been growing faster than the civilian economy, thus narrowing the scope for effective development programmes. More specifically, the general negative effects of resource diversion to military uses tend to be aggravated in developing countries because modern armed forces make heavy demands on many of the resources which are most needed for development and which constitute severe bottle-necks in many cases: foreign exchange, skilled technical and managerial manpower and maintenance, repair and industrial production capacity.

The continuation of the arms race tends to draw all countries along with greater or lesser delays. In the process the limited strength of smaller countries and of countries with a limited industrial and technological base is undermined. These countries find themselves in a situation where the rate of innovation in military technology is set by countries with much greater resources. Under these conditions, merely keeping abreast in the arms race will require ever greater sacrifices. An ongoing arms race with its inherent tendency to spread and intensify in geographical, technological and economic terms will constitute an ever greater obstacle to social and economic progress in all countries and to the urgent development tasks of developing countries in particular. No task is more urgent than to stop this technological spiral at the centre of the world arms race where it originates, and through substantial disarmament in the leading military powers to pave the way for major reductions in arms expenditures throughout the world.

The domestic consequences of involvement in the arms race cannot be reduced to the economic costs and to the direct social consequences of diminished civilian production and growth. To regard it thus is to miss one side of the picture altogether. Contemporary military institutions are often such powerful and pervasive parts of society that they can have a considerable impact on political and social conditions and perceptions and can place important constraints on the evolution of societies. In this sense they can represent a major social force, influencing the social, political and ideological development of a country. It should be recognized that the military institution in the wide sense (including such institutions as paramilitary forces or secret services which may be formally independent of it) enjoys a unique position of strength in many societies. This is due to a variety of factors. First, there is its sheer mass combined with a centralized organization. Second, there are the privileged relations which the armed forces may entertain with key sectors of industry, being at once a customer and a link to government. Third, there is a privileged relation to the state and many areas of government policy (foreign, industrial, infrastructural, regional and others, depending on the circumstances). Fourth, the military institution can, to a varying degree, protect its operations from public scrutiny, and conduct a variety of activities under the label of national security. These may range from the establishment of a full-fledged covert foreign service or the covert conduct of foreign wars to moderate or more comprehensive surveillance of categories of political opponents. Last, but of course not least, the armed forces enjoy a monopoly of physical force and a position of instrument of ultimate recourse, *vis-à-vis* other states and internally.

It is the integration of this social force with industry and government which has been described as the 'military-industrial complex', whose 'total influence—economic, political, even spiritual—is felt in every city, every statehouse, every office of the Federal Government'.[2]

Such interpenetration is in no sense an exclusively American phenomenon. Wherever they occur, military-industrial or military-economic-political complexes have a self-preserving and self-reinforcing character. They are powerful, resourceful and pervasive coalitions that have developed around one common purpose: the continued expansion of the military sector, irrespective of actual military needs. In those countries where their influence is strong, such complexes are obviously an important factor in the perpetuation of the arms race. Many studies of the military-industrial complex in the United States (but their results can to a greater or lesser degree be generalized to other countries) have shown its ability to keep fears alive, to stimulate them when needed, and to initiate compensating activities to offset the effects of more marginal types of arms-control measures. Disarmament efforts, if they are to be successful, will have to take account of this.

In most cases one may assume that the military institution and the armed forces have a double role. They are at once an ultimate recourse in external affairs and an ultimate arbiter in internal affairs. These roles are not always unrelated. In an environment of external confrontation the limits of tolerated dissension get narrowed down, and the real or supposed external threat could become an argument for increased repression. Conversely, when internal dissension transgresses these limits, and when means for satisfying basic needs and aspirations are scarce, there could be a temptation to seek temporary refuge in domestic repression or in the escalation of foreign confrontation. Here governments can get trapped in an impossible situation where an increasing burden of military expenditures further delays economic and social progress, freezes social structures and exacerbates social tension, while other policies seem to be precluded by the context of confrontation and arms race with neighbouring countries. The conjunction of external and domestic confrontation, both of them temporarily stabilized through military buildup but ultimately exacerbated by it, can give rise to a particularly precarious situation.

The arms race not only entails heavy economic sacrifices. It also threatens and perverts democratic processes, and weakens those processes of social evolution which provide the only real hope for the future of mankind.

International implications of the arms race

The arms race represents a waste of resources, a diversion of the economy away from its humanitarian purposes, a hindrance to national development efforts and a threat to democratic processes. But its most important feature is that in effect it undermines national, regional and international security. It involves the constant risk of war engaging the largest powers, including nuclear war, and it is accompanied by an endless series of wars at lower levels. It raises an ever-greater barrier against the development of an atmosphere in which the role of force in international relations may be downgraded. In addition, it impedes relations between countries, affecting the volume and direction of exchanges, diminishing the role of co-operation among states and obstructing efforts towards establishing a new international economic order on a more equitable basis.

The international consequences of the arms race may be grouped under three headings, even though in practice these effects are in many ways interrelated. First and foremost, there is the strictly military aspect: on the one hand, a long series of wars, some of them of extreme destructiveness, seldom caused in any strict sense by the arms race, but very often inflamed by it; on the other hand, an ever-present possibility of nuclear conflagration.

Second, there are the economic effects (and, by implication, social effects) in the widest sense: the effects of the arms race and military expenditures on trade, on aid, on technological and scientific co-operation and on other kinds of exchange between countries. By diverting vast resources away from production and growth, and by contributing to inflation and the economic crisis which have affected many countries, the arms race directly and indirectly impedes the full development of international exchanges.

Third, there is the impact of the arms race on international political conditions. In an environment characterized by high military preparedness on all sides, conflicts, even minor ones, tend to be exacerbated and security considerations become salient in the policies of countries. This is an environment conducive to the creation of spheres of influence, in which local conflicts tend to become linked to regional or global confrontations and in which social and political developments are likely to be resisted if they seem to call existing alignments into question. The frictions arising from this rigidity at a time when the relative economic, political and military weight of countries changes more rapidly than ever are themselves possible sources of conflict.

One point most persistently stressed in documents and analyses pertaining to the new international economic order is the need for increasing development assistance in all its forms, not only in the form of official grants and loans on concessional terms, but also in the form of development-promoting measures with a concessionary component in such fields as trade in food and industrial goods, transfer of technology and many more. The arms race has not only diminished the priority given to aid in the policies of donor countries, it has also distorted the flow of bilateral assistance, in some cases to a marked degree.

Present levels of development assistance are clearly inadequate measured against the needs, and they even fall far short of the targets, not overly ambitious, set in the International Development Strategy for the Second Development Decade. During the first half of the decade, from 1971 to 1975, official development assistance from the developed market economies amounted to 0.32 per cent of their combined gross national product, reaching not even half of the strategy target, 0.7 per cent. Transfer to development assistance of funds equivalent to a mere 5 per cent of their current military expenditures would have been sufficient to meet the target fully.

Disarmament and development are by far the most urgent problems facing the world. It is therefore with good reason that the General Assembly and other United Nations bodies have repeatedly stressed the connection between them: the fact that these two tasks are likely to succeed together, or else to fail together.

A major aspect of the arms race in terms of the international system is its political effects in general, and its effect in fostering and exacerbating conflict in particular. In an international environment dominated by an arms race on the scale of the last decades, military-strategic considerations tend to shape the overall relations between states, affecting to a greater or lesser extent all other relations and transactions. Foreign policy and international exchanges generally tend to become subordinated to 'security' considerations in the widest sense. But there is no natural limit to the precautions that may seem necessary. In this way, the creation of spheres of influence, local, regional or global, and sometimes interference, direct or roundabout, in the domestic affairs of other states becomes a natural corollary of a worldwide arms race.

While it is probably not true to say that the arms race causes conflicts in any strict sense—the causes of conflicts are ultimately political, economic, etc.—a context of intense military preparedness can, of course, greatly enhance them, cause them to erupt into war, to spill over into neighbouring countries and block their peaceful settlement. The arms race produces a political climate in which minor incidents can be blown up to international crisis proportions and in which even insignificant disputes which under other circumstances could have been easily settled by negotiation become matters of great principle and the object of armed clashes.

The arms race tends to render the international political environment more rigid and more resistant to change. It fosters concern for the political and social options chosen by other countries, in particular by those countries that are deemed to have strategic importance, and it promotes a pattern of alliances and alignments that may reinforce confrontation and, in some cases, domination. Under such conditions processes of social transformation or emancipation are likely in many cases to be resisted. They become painful processes, postponed for too long, and they may end in protracted and destructive conflict, as several of the longest and most painful wars of the recent past have shown.

The preparation and implementation by all countries of a comprehensive programme of disarmament, and first of all nuclear disarmament, is an urgent necessity to avert the danger of nuclear war, foreclose use of force or the threat of the use of force, establish a lasting peace, eliminate the factors opposing the democratization of international relations and build step by step a new international economic, political and social order.

Conclusions

The main task of this report has been to analyse the social and economic consequences of the arms race. What emerges with particular force is the multiplicity of those consequences, not only in the field of security proper, but in all aspects of civil life. The social, political, technological and industrial options of countries are affected by their participation in the arms race. International policies, not only in the military field, but also in the fields of international trade and of co-

54

operation and exchanges generally, are influenced by the climate of confrontation and apprehension engendered by the arms race. Many of the major problems faced by the world community, problems of development, economic imbalance and inflation, pollution, energy and raw materials, trade relations and technology, and so forth, are enhanced and exacerbated by the arms race. Progress in other areas such as health, education, housing and many more is delayed owing to lack of resources.

Discussion of the consequences of the arms race—social, economic and military-political—presupposes some conceptual view of the phenomenon itself. Likewise, effective progress towards disarmament presupposes some understanding of the forces and processes that drive the arms race along. There is a growing body of literature on this question, but it is mainly confined to consideration of one or a few countries and to exposition of the one or the other particular model of the armaments process. The impact on disarmament efforts has therefore been virtually non-existent. What seems to be needed is not only an elaboration or integration of these several approaches to obtain a clearer understanding of the interplay of forces that sustain the arms race, but the gathering together of these separate strands in a way that could inform and guide action. What is needed even more is a clear outline of the views of different countries and groups of countries as to what constitutes the fundamental mechanisms of the arms race. Effective action to reverse it would seem to presuppose some agreement as to where the problem lies and what it consists of.

It has been stressed throughout this report that the two most important goals of the international community, disarmament, on the one hand, and development, on the other, which the States Members of the United Nations are committed to pursue vigorously, each in its own right, are in fact intimately linked. Development at an acceptable rate would be hard if not impossible to reconcile with a continuation of the arms race. Research and development is one area where the misdirection of efforts is glaring. In this as in other respects, vast resources, badly needed for development, are being consumed as countries make ever-greater sacrifices for military purposes.

Substantial progress in the field of disarmament would represent a decisive turning point as regards development, imparting new momentum to efforts in this direction and greatly facilitating progress in this field. Progress towards disarmament would release internal material, financial and human resources both in developed and in developing countries and would permit their redeployment to purposes of development. In fact, disarmament should be so designed that this close connexion between disarmament and development gets full recognition. Provisions to ensure the transfer to development purposes of part of the resources released, provisions to ensure that measures of armaments limitation are so designed that they do not impede the transfer of technology for peaceful ends and other similar provisions must be an integral part of disarmament measures.

Effective progress towards disarmament presupposes the elaboration of an overall plan, persuasive in concept and workable in application, a 'Strategy for Disarmament' as it were. This must be based on a thorough assessment of the problems involved, the forces propelling the arms race and the experience of the past. It should involve specification of priorities, decision on targets and adoption of programmes and, where appropriate, timetables. This strategy must be comprehensive enough to ensure a fair and equitable response to the concerns of every country, and flexible enough to permit taking realistic and concrete steps in the immediate future, in intermediate stages and in the final stage. In short, a framework is needed within which endeavours can be co-ordinated and against which progress can be measured. This is no less essential in the field of disarmament than it is in the field of development, or in any other field where a multiplicity of efforts is to lead effectively to a common goal.

To impart a new momentum to disarmament efforts it seems necessary not only to engage all countries in these endeavours on a basis of equality, but also to involve the peoples of all countries more actively and in a more coherent and organized fashion than has been the case hitherto. A variety of movements and organizations—political, professional, religious and others—can play an important role in this respect, and have in fact done so in the past. The negative consequences of the arms race, in terms of endangering their existence and in terms of social and economic sacrifices, affect all peoples of the world. They have an obvious right to information about the military policies and programmes of governments and their implications. Much of the secrecy in this field is not justified by military requirements. In some cases it results from mere tradition, in others it serves such purposes as shielding questionable or unnecessary armaments programmes from public scrutiny and public criticism. Without endangering the security of any country much greater openness of information could and should be applied in this field.

Given the character of the present arms race, effective disarmament will presuppose progress in two directions simultaneously: curtailment of the qualitative arms race, and reductions of military budgets. The first involves the erection of boundaries against further developments in weaponry. The agreements on biological weapons and on anti-ballistic missile systems are steps in this direction. Responsibility for continued and more rapid progress in this respect overwhelmingly rests with the main military powers and with the two largest powers in particular, which are alone in producing the full range of modern weapons and where most innovations in military technology and all innovation in nuclear weapons and their means of delivery originate.

Progress towards disarmament, it has been indicated, will require systematic co-ordination and planning with the participation of all states. This points, on the one hand, to the need for more effective means at the international level for information, research and evaluation on questions of disarmament to enable all Member States, not only the largest ones, to obtain effective insight and to take initiatives in questions of disarmament. On the other hand, the United Nations, and first of all its plenary organ, the General Assembly, whose task it is to harmonize the efforts of states in the attainment of their common goals, should be able to fulfil its role of overall guidance in the field of disarmament more effectively than it has been able to do in the past.

Notes

1. Reference here and elsewhere to the 'six main military spenders'—the United States of America, the Union of Soviet Socialist Republics, China, France, the United Kingdom of Great Britain and Northern Ireland and the Federal Republic of Germany—should not be allowed to conceal the very large differences within this group. Not all of these countries are leading in the process of arms innovation or in the production and export of arms; military expenditure (even more so military expenditure per capita) differs widely within this group of countries; and not all of them have military capabilities that give them a global military-strategic importance.
2. President Eisenhower, Farewell Speech to the Nation.

4

Worldwide effects of nuclear war— some perspectives

United States Arms Control and Disarmament Agency (ACDA)

Evolving knowledge

Much research has been devoted to the effects of nuclear weapons. But studies have been concerned for the most part with those immediate consequences which would be suffered by a country that was the direct target of nuclear attack. Relatively few studies have examined the worldwide, long-term effects.

Realistic and responsible arms-control policy calls for our knowing more about these wider effects and for making this knowledge available to the public. To learn more about them, the Arms Control and Disarmament Agency has initiated a number of projects, including a National Academy of Sciences study, requested in April 1974. The academy's study, *Long-term Worldwide Effects of Multiple Nuclear Weapons Detonations*, a highly technical document of more than 200 pages, is now available. This chapter seeks to include its essential findings, along with the results of related studies of this agency, and to provide as well the basic background facts necessary for informed perspectives on the issue.

New discoveries have been made, yet much uncertainty inevitably persists. Our knowledge of nuclear warfare rests largely on theory and hypothesis, fortunately untested by the usual processes of trial and error; the paramount goal of statesmanship is that we should never learn from the experience of nuclear war. The uncertainties that remain are of such magnitude that of themselves they must serve as a further deterrent to the use of nuclear weapons.

It has now been two decades since the introduction of thermonuclear fusion weapons into the military inventories of the great powers, and more than a decade since the United States, the United Kingdom and the USSR ceased to test nuclear weapons in the atmosphere. Today our understanding of the technology of thermonuclear weapons seems highly advanced, but our knowledge of the physical and biological consequences of nuclear war is continuously evolving.

Only recently, new light was shed on the subject in a study which the Arms Control and Disarmament Agency had asked the National Academy of Sciences to undertake. Previous studies had tended to focus very largely on radioactive fall-

Excerpts from *Worldwide Effects of Nuclear War . . . Some Perspectives*, Report of the United States Arms Control and Disarmament Agency, Washington 1975 (subtitles added).

out from a nuclear war; an important aspect of this new study was its inquiry into all possible consequences, including the effects of large-scale nuclear detonations on the ozone layer which helps to protect life on earth from the sun's ultraviolet radiations. Assuming a total detonation of 10,000 megatons—a large-scale but less than total nuclear 'exchange', as one would say in the dehumanizing jargon of the strategists—it was concluded that as much as 30–70 per cent of the ozone might be eliminated from the Northern Hemisphere (where a nuclear war would presumably take place) and as much as 20–40 per cent from the Southern Hemisphere. Recovery would probably take about three to ten years, but the academy's study notes that long-term global changes cannot be completely ruled out.

The reduced ozone concentrations would have a number of consequences outside the areas in which the detonations occurred. The academy study notes, for example, that the resultant increase in ultraviolet would cause 'prompt incapacitating cases of sunburn in the temperate zones and snow blindness in northern countries'.

Strange though it might seem, the increased ultraviolet radiation could also be accompanied by a drop in the average temperature. The size of the change is open to question, but the largest changes would probably occur at the higher latitudes, where crop production and ecological balances are sensitively dependent on the number of frost-free days and other factors related to average temperature. The academy's study concluded that ozone changes due to nuclear war might decrease global surface temperatures by only negligible amounts or by as much as a few degrees. To calibrate the significance of this, the study mentioned that a cooling of even 1 °C would eliminate commercial wheat-growing in Canada.

Thus, the possibility of a serious increase in ultraviolet radiation has been added to widespread radioactive fall-out as a fearsome consequence of the large-scale use of nuclear weapons. And it is likely that we must reckon with still other complex and subtle processes, global in scope, which could seriously threaten the health of distant populations in the event of an all-out nuclear war.

Discoveries by accident

Up to now, many of the important discoveries about nuclear-weapon effects have been made not through deliberate scientific inquiry but by accident. And, as the following historical examples show, there has been a series of surprises.

Castle/Bravo was the largest nuclear weapon ever detonated by the United States. Before it was set off at Bikini on 28 February 1954, it was expected to explode with an energy equivalent of about 8 million tons of TNT. Actually, it produced almost twice that explosive power—equivalent to 15 million tons of TNT.

If the power of the bomb was unexpected, so were the after-effects. About six hours after the explosion, a fine, sandy ash began to sprinkle the Japanese fishing vessel *Lucky Dragon* some ninety miles downwind of the burst point, and Rongelap Atoll, 100 miles downwind. Though forty or fifty miles away from the proscribed test area, the vessel's crew and the islanders received heavy doses of radiation from the weapon's 'fall-out'—the coral rock, soil, and other debris sucked up the fireball and made intensively radioactive by the nuclear reaction. One radioactive isotope in the fall-out, iodine-131, rapidly built up to serious concentration in the thyroid glands of the victims, particularly young Rongelapese children.

More than any other event in the decade of testing large nuclear weapons in the atmosphere, Castle/Bravo's unexpected contamination of 7,000 square miles of the Pacific Ocean dramatically illustrated how large-scale nuclear war could produce casualties on a colossal scale, far beyond the local effects of blast and fire alone.

A number of other surprises were encountered during thirty years of nuclear-weapons development. For example, what was probably man's most extensive modification of the global environment to date occurred in September 1962, when a nuclear device was detonated 250 miles above Johnson Island. The 1.4-megaton burst produced an artificial belt of charged particles trapped in the earth's magnetic field. Though 98 per cent of these particles were removed by natural processes after the first year, traces could be detected six or seven years later. A number of satellites in low earth orbit at the time of the burst suffered severe electronic damage resulting in malfunctions and early failure. It became obvious that man now had the power to make long-term changes in his near-space environment.

Another unexpected effect of high-altitude bursts was the blackout of high-frequency radio communications. Disruption of the ionosphere (which reflects radio signals back to the earth) by nuclear bursts over the Pacific has wiped out long-distance radio communications for hours at distances of up to 600 miles from the burst point.

Yet another surprise was the discovery that electromagnetic pulses can play havoc with electrical equipment itself, including some in command systems that control the nuclear arms themselves.

Much of our knowledge was thus gained by chance—a fact which should imbue us with humility as we contemplate the remaining uncertainties (as well as the certainties) about nuclear warfare.

Radioactive local fall-out

Most of the radiation hazard from nuclear bursts comes from short-lived radionuclides external to the body; these are generally confined to the locality downwind of the weapon burst point. This radiation hazard comes from radioactive fission fragments with half-lives of seconds to a few months, and from soil and other materials in the vicinity of the burst made radioactive by the intense neutron flux of the fission and fusion reactions.

It has been estimated that a weapon with a fission yield of 1 million tons TNT equivalent power (1 megaton) exploded at ground level in a 15 miles-per-hour wind would produce fall-out in an ellipse extending hundreds of miles downwind from the burst point. At a distance of 20–25 miles downwind, a lethal radiation dose (600 rads) would be accumulated by a person who did not find shelter within twenty-five minutes after the time the fall-out began. At a distance of 40–45 miles, a person would have at most three hours after the fall-out began to find shelter. Considerably smaller radiation doses will make people seriously ill. Thus, the survival prospects of persons immediately downwind of the burst point would be slim unless they could be sheltered or evacuated.

It has been estimated that an attack on population centres in the United States by 100 weapons of one-megaton fission yield would kill up to 20 per cent of the population immediately through blast, heat, ground shock and instant radiation effects (neutrons and gamma rays); an attack with 1,000 such weapons would destroy immediately almost half the United States population. These figures do not include additional deaths from fires, lack of medical attention, starvation, or the lethal fall-out showering to the ground downwind of the burst points of the weapons.

Most of the bomb-produced radionuclides decay rapidly. Even so, beyond the blast radius of the exploding weapons there would be areas ('hot spots') the survivors could not enter because of radioactive contamination from long-lived radioactive isotopes like strontium-90 or cesium-137, which can be concentrated through the food chain and incorporated into the body. The damage caused would be internal, with the injurious effects appearing over many years. For the survivors of a nuclear war, this lingering radiation hazard could represent a grave threat for as long as one to five years after the attack.

Worldwide effects of fall-out

Much of our knowledge of the production and distribution of radionuclides has been derived from the period of intensive nuclear testing in the atmosphere during the 1950s and early 1960s. It is estimated that more than 500 megatons of nuclear yield were detonated in the atmosphere between 1945 and 1971, about half of this yield being produced by a fission reaction. The peak occurred in 1961–62, when a total of 340 megatons were detonated in the atmosphere by the United States and the Soviet Union. The Partial Test-Ban Treaty of 1963 ended atmospheric testing for the United States, the United Kingdom and the Soviet Union, but two major non-signatories, France and China, continued nuclear testing at the rate of about 5 megatons annually. (France now conducts its nuclear tests underground.)

A United Nations scientific committee has estimated that the cumulative per capita dose to the world's population up to the year 2000 as a result of atmospheric testing to 1970 (cut-off date of the study) will be the equivalent of two years' exposure to natural background radiation on the earth's surface. For the bulk of the world's population, internal and external radiation doses of natural origin amount to less than one-tenth of a rad annually. Thus nuclear testing to date does not appear to pose a severe radiation threat in global terms. But a nuclear war releasing 10 or 100 times the total yield of all previous weapons test could pose a far greater worldwide threat.

The biological effects of all forms of ionizing radiation have been calculated within broad ranges by the National Academy of Sciences. Based on these calculations, fall-out from the 500-plus megatons of nuclear testing to 1970 will produce between two and twenty-five cases of genetic disease per million live births in the next generation. This means that between three and fifty persons per 1,000 million births in the post-testing generation will have genetic damage for each megaton of nuclear yield exploded. With similar uncertainty, it is possible to estimate that the induction of cancers would range from 75 to 300 cases per megaton for each 1,000 million people in the post-test generation.

If we apply these very rough yardsticks to a large-scale nuclear war in which 10,000 megatons of nuclear force are detonated, the effects on a world population of 5,000 million appear enormous. Allowing for uncertainties about the dynamics of a possible nuclear war, radiation-induced cancers and genetic damage together over 30 years are estimated to range from 1.5 to 30 million for the world population as a whole. This would mean one additional case for every 100 to 3,000 people or about 0.5 per cent to 15 per cent of the estimated peace-time cancer death rate in developed countries. As will be seen, moreover, there could be other, less well understood effects which would drastically increase suffering and death.

The ozone layer in the stratosphere

A nuclear war would involve such prodigious and concentrated short-term release of high-temperature energy that it is necessary to consider a variety of potential environmental effects.

It has been estimated that a 10,000-megaton war with half the weapons exploding at ground level would tear up some 25,000 million cubic metres of rock and soil, injecting a substantial amount of fine dust and particles into the stratosphere. This is roughly twice the volume of material blasted loose by the Indonesian volcano, Krakatoa, whose explosion in 1883 was the most powerful terrestrial event ever recorded. Sunsets around the world were noticeably reddened for several years after the Krakatoa eruption, indicating that large amounts of volcanic dust had entered the stratosphere.

Subsequent studies of large volcanic explosions, such as Mt Agung on Bali in 1963, have raised the possibility that large-scale injection of dust into the stratosphere would reduce sunlight intensities and temperatures at the surface, while increasing the absorption of heat in the upper atmosphere.

The resultant minor changes in temperature and sunlight could affect crop production. However, no catastrophic world-wide changes have resulted from volcanic explosions, so it is doubtful that the gross injection of particulates into the stratosphere by a 10,000-megaton conflict would, by itself, lead to major global climate changes.

More worrisome is the possible effect of nuclear explosions on ozone in the stratosphere. Not until the twentieth century was the unique and paradoxical role of ozone fully recognized. On the other hand, in concentrations greater than one part per million in the air we breathe, ozone is toxic; one major American city, Los Angeles, has established a procedure for ozone alerts and warnings. On the other hand, ozone is a critically important feature of the stratosphere from the standpoint of maintaining life on the earth.

The reason is that while oxygen and nitrogen in the upper reaches of the atmosphere can block out solar ultraviolet photons with wavelengths shorter than 2,420 ångströms (Å), ozone is the only effective shield in the atmosphere against solar ultraviolet radiation between 2,500 and 3,000 Å in wavelength. Although ozone is extremely efficient at filtering out solar ultraviolet in 2,500–3,000 Å region of the spectrum, some does get through at the higher end of the spectrum. Ultraviolet rays in the range of 2,800–3,200 Å cause sunburn, prematurely age human skin and produce skin cancers. As early as 1840, arctic snow blindness was attributed to solar ultraviolet; and we have since found that intense ultraviolet radiation can inhibit photosynthesis in plants, stunt plant growth, damage bacteria, fungi, higher plants, insects and animals, and produce genetic alterations.

Despite the important role ozone plays in assuring a livable environment at the earth's surface, the total quantity of ozone in the atmosphere is quite small, only about three parts per million. Furthermore, ozone is not a durable or static constituent of the atmosphere. It is constantly created, destroyed, and recreated by natural processes, so that the amount of ozone present at any given time is a function of the equilibrium reached between the creative and destructive chemical reactions and the solar radiation reaching the upper stratosphere.

The mechanism for the production of ozone is the absorption by oxygen molecules (O_2) of relatively short-wavelength ultraviolet light. The oxygen molecule separates into two atoms of free oxygen, which immediately unite with other oxygen molecules on the surfaces of particles in the upper atmosphere. It is this union which forms ozone, or O_3. The heat released by the ozone-forming process is the reason for the curious increase with altitude of the temperature of the stratosphere (the base of which is about 36,000 feet above the earth's surface).

While the natural chemical reaction produces about 4,500 tons of ozone per second in the stratosphere, this is offset by other natural chemical reactions which break down the ozone. By far the most significant involves nitric oxide (NO) which breaks ozone (O_3) into molecules. This effect was discovered only in the last few years in studies of the environmental problems which might be encountered if large fleets of supersonic transport aircraft operate routinely in the lower stratosphere. According to a report by Dr Harold S. Johnston, University of California at Berkeley (prepared for the Department of Transportation's Climatic Impact Assessment Program) it now appears that the NO reaction is normally responsible for 50 to 70 per cent of the destruction of ozone.

In the natural environment, there is a variety of means for the production of NO and its transport into the stratosphere. Soil bacteria produce nitrous oxide (N_2O) which enters the lower atmosphere and slowly diffuses into the stratosphere, where it reacts with free oxygen (O) to form two NO molecules. Another mechanism for NO production in the lower atmosphere may be lightning discharges, and while NO is quickly washed out of the lower atmosphere by rain, some of it may reach the stratosphere. Additional amounts of NO are produced directly in the stratosphere by cosmic rays from the sun and interstellar sources.

It is because of this catalytic role which nitric oxide plays in the destruction of ozone that it is important to consider the effects of high-yield nuclear explosions on the ozone layer. The nuclear fireball and the air entrained within it are subjected to great heat, followed by relatively rapid cooling. These conditions are ideal for the production of tremendous amounts of NO from the air. It has been estimated that as much as 5,000 tons of nitric oxide is produced for each megaton of nuclear explosive power.

What would be the effects of nitric oxides driven into the stratosphere by an all-out nuclear war, involving the detonation of 10,000 megatons of explosive force in the Northern Hemisphere? According to the recent National Academy of sciences study, the nitric oxide produced by the weapons could reduce the ozone levels in the Northern Hemisphere by as much as 30 to 70 per cent.

To begin with, a depleted ozone layer would reflect back to the earth's surface less heat than would normally be the case, thus causing a drop in temperature—perhaps enough to produce serious effects on agriculture. Other changes, such as increased amounts of dust or different vegetation, might subsequently reverse this drop in temperature—but on the other hand, it might increase it.

Probably more important, life on earth has largely evolved within the protective ozone shield and is at present adapted rather precisely to the amount of solar ultraviolet which does get through. To defend themselves against this low level of ultraviolet, evolved external shielding (feathers, fur, cuticular waxes on fruit), internal shielding (melanin pigment in human skin, flavenoids in plant tissue), avoidance strategies (plankton migration to greater depths in the daytime, shade-seeking by desert iguanas) and, in almost all organisms but placental mammals, elaborate mechanisms to repair photochemical damage.

It is possible, however, that a major increase in solar ultraviolet might overwhelm the defences of some and perhaps many terrestrial life-forms. Both direct and indirect damage would then occur among the bacteria, insects, plants, and other links in the ecosystems on which human well-being depends. This disruption, particularly if it occurred in the aftermath of a major war involving many other dislocations, could pose a serious additional threat to the recovery of post-war society. The National Academy of Sciences report concludes that in twenty years the ecological systems would have essentially recovered from the increase in ultraviolet radiation—though not necessarily from radioactivity or other damage in areas close to the war zone. However, a delayed effect of the increase in ultraviolet radiation would be an estimated 3 to 30 per cent increase in skin cancer for forty years in the Northern Hemisphere's mid-latitudes.

. . . as unpredictable as deadly

We have considered the problems of large-scale nuclear war from the standpoint of the countries not under direct attack, and the difficulties they might encounter in post-war recovery. It is true that most of the horror and tragedy of nuclear war would be visited on the populations subject to direct attack, who would doubtless have to cope with extreme and perhaps insuperable obstacles in seeking to re-establish their own societies. It is no less apparent, however, that other nations, including those remote from the combat, could suffer heavily because of damage to the global environment.

Finally, at least brief mention should be made of the global effects resulting from disruption of economic activities and communications. Since 1970, an increasing fraction of the human race has been losing the battle for self-sufficiency in food, and must rely on heavy imports. A major disruption of agriculture and transportation in the grain-exporting and manufacturing countries could thus prove disastrous to countries importing food, farm machinery, and fertilizers—especially those which are already struggling with the threat of widespread starvation. Moreover, in virtually every economic area, from food and medicines to fuel and growth-engendering industries, the less-developed countries would find they could not rely on the 'undamaged' remainder of the developed world for trade essentials: in the wake of a nuclear war the industrial powers directly involved would themselves have to compete for resources with those countries that today are described as 'less-developed'.

Similarly, the disruption of international communications—satellites, cables and even high-frequency radio links—could be a major obstacle to international recovery efforts.

In attempting to project the after-effects of a major nuclear war, we have considered separately the various kinds of damage that could occur. It is also quite possible, however, that interactions might take place among these effects, so that one type of damage would couple with another to produce new and unexpected hazards. For example, we can assess individually the consequences of heavy worldwide radiation fall-out and increased solar ultraviolet, but we do not know whether the two acting together might significantly increase human, animal, or plant susceptibility to disease. We can conclude that massive dust injection into the stratosphere, even greater in scale than Krakatoa, is unlikely by itself to produce significant climatic and environmental change, but we cannot rule out inter-actions with other phenomena, such as ozone depletion, which might produce utterly unexpected results.

We have come to realize that nuclear weapons can be as unpredictable as they are deadly in their effects. Despite some thirty years of development and study, there is still much that we do not know. This is particularly true when we consider the global effects of a large-scale nuclear war.

Part II. Studying the past

5

The historical perspective

Bert V. A. Röling
Professor of International Law
and Polemology

In the past man has based his hopes for peace on very different things: democracy, industry, commerce (especially free trade), disarmament, and even the possible emergence of extremely destructive arms. Nobel wrote to Bertha von Suttner, 'Perhaps my factories will put an end to war even sooner than your congresses; on the day when two army corps may mutually annihilate each other in a second, probably all civilized nations will recoil with horror and disband their troops.' Nobel realized that, at the time of his writing (1890), weapons might still have a too limited destructive power: 'To remedy this defect war must be made as death-dealing to the civil population at home as to the troops at the front . . . all war will stop short instantly, if the weapon is bacteriology.'*

This basic idea that people might be scared into peace was even shared by peace societies. But strong protest against it did always exist. 'To strew gunpowder on all sides may, no doubt, produce caution, but it is not the best way of preventing an explosion,' wrote W. E. H. Lecky in 1896. He also perceptively predicted: 'In the present condition of the world, it would be quite possible for the folly of a single ruler to bring down calamities upon Europe that might transfer the sceptre of civilization to the other side of the Atlantic.'

In the atomic era all the conditions have been fulfilled to make the civilian population the victim of any nuclear war. No doubt, the present nuclear-weapon states are indeed cautious. But only a few people trust that nuclear weapons would eliminate war, and many experts came to the conclusion that we are, as a result of the present arms race, on the road to certain disaster.

The official attitudes of governments, nowadays, do not differ much from the attitudes in the nineteenth and the first half of the twentieth century. Freezing propositions were resented by states aiming at less unequal positions of power. Proposals for substantial disarmament met the opposition of dissatisfied powers, striving for a change of the status quo, and not wanting to exclude the possibility that military power might play a role in achieving that change. Satisfied powers, enjoying a privileged position, were reluctant to give up the armed might that provided them with that cherished primacy. The rising state feared disarmament

---

* Bertha von Suttner won the Nobel Peace Prize in 1905, but the warning she gave in her Nobel lecture of that year went unheeded. The lecture is significant for the historical perspective it gives, and an extract from it is reproduced in an appendix to this chapter.—Ed.

because it would mean continuance of the resented status quo. The old rich, satisfied states feared that disarmament, through reduction of the power-distance on the contrary might contribute to unfavourable changes. Hence, the negative result in all the endeavours to arrive at arms reduction. The most spectacular failure was the Hague Conferences on disarmament to which most powers sent as delegates their notorious 'hawks'.

The League of Nations took an exceptional attitude with respect to national military power, recognizing that reduction of armaments was a condition of peace (Covenant, Art. 8). At the same time the peace treaties imposed on the vanquished Central Powers the obligation to disarm, as a first step to the general limitation of armaments. Elaborate provisions in the Covenant aimed at the realization of that general limitation. But nothing was achieved, except the checking of the naval race by the Washington Conference, 1922. There were endless discussions, endless conference proposals which mostly favoured one of the parties, and refusals often based on arguments which were contrary to standpoints maintained by the same state at another occasion.

The Soviet Union made its first proposal for general and complete disarmament in 1928. It was the first clash between the radical and the incremental approach. Doubts existed about the sincerity of the former, and the feasibility of the latter. In short: the same differences of official attitudes, then as now; attitudes behind which real intentions and opinions were hidden.

As a matter of fact, one may doubt whether the official standpoint, as formulated in the Covenant was sincere. The amendments on the Wilsonian proposals already give reason to doubt that sincerity. But more important, perhaps, was the inherent incompatibility of general disarmament on the one side, and the maintenance of the colonial system on the other. The colonial system meant domination of one nation by another. That domination was achieved, and maintained by military power. Abolishing military power, and maintenance of the colonial dominance is contradictory.

This aspect of things has great significance for our time. The colonial system disappeared in the fifteen years following the Second World War. But economic predominance continued. A minority of mankind is prosperous, and consumes a disproportional part of the fruits of the earth. Does it want to continue that consumption? Does it want to assure the constant flow of goods, if necessary by military means? If that is the case, we might as well stop thinking and talking about disarmament. A close relation exists between the prospects of arms reduction and the realization of a new international economic order.

Disarmament is rightly understood as meaning arms reduction to a specific level. In the Covenant that level was the compatibility with national safety. The discussion during the last 150 years on this point still deserves attention. It is significant when military power is considered to have as its primary, if not only, function to provide for the national safety, peace and security, and peace and independence. It means that all acquisitive functions are abolished. In other words, it means that armed power has as its primary function the neutralization of the armed power of the opponent. In this opinion the defensive quality of military power is stressed. The defensive function—that is the function to deter by the prospect of unacceptable resistance—may find expression in the weapons posture: unable to conquer, but strong in defence.

J. S. Mill, stressing that fear was the cause of armaments and of war, wrote that defensive measures should be limited to the lowest possible rather than always raised to the highest possible terms. 'As the highest possible terms, the provision for defence really does all the mischief to a community which a foreign enemy could do.' From what we now know about 1914, it is probable that there would have been no war if the states had been armed only for defence.

In conclusion, it is worth while to study the past, and to analyse the motives beyond the rejection of quite reasonable proposals for arms reductions. At the present time, more than ever, there is a need for substantial disarmament.

The sword shall not be the arbiter among nations

Bertha von Suttner
Nobel Peace Prize Winner, 1905

Let us look round us in the world of today. . . . A terrible war [the Russo-Japanese War (1904–05)], unprecedented in the world's history, recently raged in the Far East. This war was followed by a revolution [the Russian revolution of 1905], even more terrible, which shook the giant Russian empire, a revolution whose final outcome we cannot yet foresee. We hear continually of fire, robbery, bombings, executions, overflowing prisons, beatings, and massacres; in short, an orgy of the Demon Violence. Meanwhile, in Central and Western Europe which narrowly escaped war, we have distrust, threats, sabre-rattling, press-baiting, feverish naval buildup, and rearming everywhere. In England, Germany, and France, novels are appearing in which the plot of a future surprise attack by a neighbour is intended as a spur to even more fervent arming. Fortresses are being erected, submarines built, whole areas mined, airships tested for use in war; and all this with such zeal—as if to attack one's neighbours were the most inevitable and important function of a state. . . .

Well, we must not be blinded by the obvious; we must also look for the new growth pushing up from the ground below. We must understand that two philosophies, two eras of civilization, are wrestling with one another and that a vigorous new spirit is supplanting the blatant and threatening old. No longer weak and formless, this promising new life is already widely established and determined to survive. Quite apart from the peace movement, which is a symptom rather than a cause of actual change, there is taking place in the world a process of internationalization and unification. Factors contributing to the development of this process are technical inventions, improved communications, economic interdependence, and closer international relations. The instinct of self-preservation in human society, acting almost subconsciously, as do all drives in the human mind, is rebelling against the constantly refined methods of annihilation and against the destruction of humanity. . . .

However clearly envisaged, however apparently near and within reach the goal may be, the road to it must be traversed a step at a time, and countless obstacles surmounted on the way. . . .

From the Nobel lecture, 18 April 1906, Oslo, Norway.

This question of whether violence or law shall prevail between states is the most vital of the problems of our eventful era, and the most serious in its repercussions. . . .

On the solution of this problem depends whether our Europe will become a showpiece of ruins and failure, or whether we can avoid this danger and so enter sooner the coming era of secure peace and law in which a civilization of unimagined glory will develop. The many aspects of this question are what the second Hague Conference should be discussing rather than the proposed topics concerning the laws and practices of war at sea, the bombardment of ports, towns and villages, the laying of mines, and so on. The contents of the agenda demonstrate that, although the supporters of the existing structure of society, which accepts war, come to a peace conference prepared to modify the nature of war, they are basically trying to keep the present system intact. The advocates of pacifism, inside and outside the Conference, will, however, defend their objectives and press forward another step toward their goal—the goal which, to repeat Roosevelt's words, affirms the duty of his government and of all governments 'to bring nearer the time when the sword shall not be the arbiter among nations'.

6

Modern disarmament efforts before the Second World War

Stanford Arms Control Group

Historical perspective regarding the arms control and disarmament negotiations of the post-Second-World-War period can be gained by examining several of the attempts made to limit and reduce the levels of armaments prior to the Second World War. Although most of these attempts were failures, there were major developments in the naval area; these developments will be emphasized in this chapter.

Almost every advance in weaponry, from the crossbow to the bomber, has been accompanied by calls for its abolition. Attempts to abolish particular weapons played a not unimportant role at the end of the Middle Ages, but they were abandoned, until very recent times, as unproductive. There was, for example, fairly widespread revulsion against the introduction of firearms. Throughout Europe, laws were issued against their employment, and in some cases gunners when taken by the enemy were not treated as prisoners of war, but were executed as outlaws. Not surprisingly, these prohibitions failed; the problem of balancing force levels among different nations proved as difficult in the early modern period as today, and the prohibitions were soon renounced.

In the seventeenth and eighteenth centuries several European treaties contained specific proposals for disarmament. For example, one of the treaties of the 1648 Peace of Westphalia stipulated that all of the existing fortifications were to be demolished and that no new fortifications were to be erected. This provision was, however, never observed, let alone enforced.

In 1766 Prince Kaunitz, the Austrian Chancellor, offered Frederick the Great of Prussia a proposal for the limitation of national armaments. Kaunitz proposed a 75 per cent reduction of the forces of both Austria and Prussia, but this offer was rejected by the Prussians. Joseph II's renewal of the suggestion in 1769 was also refused.

A similar initiative was taken in 1816 by Tsar Alexander I of Russia, a mystical and aristocratic figure, who addressed a note to his fellow sovereigns proposing the negotiation of a reduction in the level of military forces. The first

Stanford Arms Control Group, 'Modern Disarmament Efforts Before the Second World War', in: John H. Barton and Lawrence D. Weiler (eds.), *International Arms Control, Issues and Agreements*, Stanford, Calif., Stanford University Press, 1976. (Reproduced with permission.)

reaction in London was deep suspicion, based on the fact that Russia, alone of the members of the victorious coalition against Napoleon, had as yet taken no steps to reduce its forces. After reflection, the Foreign Secretary, Lord Castlereagh, ordered his minister in Petersburg to inform the Russians that he believed every nation was the best judge of its own military needs, and that, although the British Government was always willing to let friendly powers know the extent of British armaments, it was not prepared to make them dependent upon international agreement. The continental powers were not even as accommodating as the British. Speaking for Austria, Prince Metternich showed no interest in the arms-reduction proposal at all, arguing that the size of a nation's forces must necessarily be determined by its geographic situation, its resources, its domestic situation, and other parochial factors. Metternich would not even agree to furnish information concerning Austrian armaments to other governments, least of all to Russia.

The outstandingly successful disarmament effort of the nineteenth century was the American-British attempt to reduce naval forces on the Great Lakes. The War of 1812, with its spectacular naval battles on the Great Lakes, had clearly demonstrated the importance of naval control of the Lakes, and there was concern in both Great Britain and the United States that a costly and dangerous naval arms race could begin between the two countries on the Great Lakes, increasing the chance of another Anglo-American confrontation similar to the War of 1812. The United States' concern increased in August 1815 when Great Britain announced its intention to increase its armed forces on the Lakes, and in November John Quincy Adams, the United States Minister to London, was authorized to begin negotiations with the British on limiting armaments on the Lakes. These negotiations continued intermittently until April 1817, when a formal agreement was enacted by an exchange of notes. The Rush-Bagot Agreement, which is still in force, limited the naval forces of the United States and Great Britain on the Great Lakes and Lake Champlain and required a substantial act of disarmament, since those vessels that exceeded the agreed-upon limits were too large to be sailed down the St Lawrence River and therefore had to be dismantled. On entering the agreement, the British overrode Canadian objections but avoided an arms race that would have been costly and would not have contributed to overall security.

Later in the nineteenth century, reduction of arms was usually proposed by governments when they were feeling at a disadvantage. Self-reliant or ambitious powers never seemed to be moved by any desire to have limits set to their armed forces. Thus, for example, in 1859 Lord Palmerston suggested disarmament to Napoleon III, but the Emperor (already contemplating a war against Austria in Italy) simply looked the other way. Ten years later, however, when Napoleon III was having financial difficulties and could not match the military expenditures of his fast-growing rival, Prussia, he was of a different mind and asked the British Government whether it would suggest a general arms reduction to the Prussians. The British agreed and the Foreign Secretary, Lord Clarendon, instructed his minister in Berlin to approach Prince Bismarck on the subject. Bismarck, knowing perfectly well that French financial difficulties lay behind the proposal for force reductions, refused even to lay the British proposal before his sovereign, explaining that the King would regard this as an attempt to weaken the striking power of Prussia at a critical time. Not long thereafter, France and Prussia were at war.

In the last decade of the nineteenth century, as relative military advantage grew in importance in the minds of military planners and a sort of 'arms race' psychosis began to emerge, there was a revival of interest in arms limitation and war prevention.

The most famous instance of this was the proposal that eventuated in the peace conference at The Hague in June 1899. The initiative, as in 1816, came from Russia. In August 1898, without preliminary consultations with other governments, the Russian Government issued and published a circular note, calling upon other governments to join it in a general conference to discuss the reduction of armaments. The foreign reaction to the Tsar's proposals was generally unfavourable. Some governments doubted the Tsar's sincerity; others felt that any reduction of armaments would tend to freeze the status quo to their disadvantage. In any event, all governments stalled, and no arms-control limitations were reached at the Hague conference. The conference did, however, succeed in some of the areas that are less directly related to arms control. An international court was established, arbitration was discussed, and the law of war was amended to provide for better treatment of prisoners. Declarations were developed prohibiting the use of expanding bullets and asphyxiating gases and the dropping of explosives from balloons.

Provision was made at this first Hague conference for a second one, which was to meet in 1907. When it did so, the atmosphere was more intense than in 1899, for the balance-of-power system that had worked reasonably well since 1815 had more clearly broken down and Europe was divided into two opposing coalitions, all members of which were heavily armed. Even so, when invitations went out, limitation of armaments was not mentioned among the subjects to be discussed, and when the conference convened, the limitations issue was bypassed. Again, however, the law of war was expanded, with prohibitions of arms 'calculated to cause unnecessary suffering' and of poison or poisoned weapons. Moreover, the rules for blockades were tightened and the requirement of a declaration of war was laid down.

A special case: attempts to control the Anglo-German arms race before the First World War

During this era, Great Britain and Germany were locked in an expensive naval arms race. Although negotiations to control the race were unsuccessful, the example deserves attention. It weighed heavily on the minds of negotiators after the First World War and contributed to success in concluding naval arms-control agreements at that time. Moreover, this arms competition is one of history's closest analogues to today's United States-USSR arms competition. The weapons involved were major technological systems that had never been tested. They were based on a doctrine very close to today's strategic theory. Their construction was supported by military-industrial complexes on each side. And the naval race may have been one of the substantial causes of the First World War.

An influential doctrine for sea power had been put forward in 1890 by Captain Alfred T. Mahan, an American naval officer, in the book *The Influence of Sea Power upon History, 1660–1783*. His argument, based on the simultaneous rise of the British Navy and the British Empire, was that international trade, especially with imperial possessions, was essential to national greatness and that protection of both trade and possessions required a strong navy. Otherwise, the nation would be cut off and vulnerable to blockade. But it would be impractical to control all oceans. The navy, therefore, would have to be designed to destroy other navies in line-of-battle, fleet-against-fleet combat. Mahan's argument was also being made by others such as Alfred von Tirpitz, who was then a captain, appointed to the German naval staff in 1892. It gained strength from the interest of the major European nations in expanding and protecting their own imperial possessions. Naval leagues were created in both Great Britain and Germany to lobby for larger fleets.

At the same time, the technology of naval forces was changing rapidly. Wooden construction was being replaced by metal construction; sails by steam, and smooth-bore cannon firing solid shot by torpedoes and rifled cannon firing explosive projectiles. Maintenance of a navy required construction of fleets of new battleships optimized for line-of-battle action, cruisers for speed, and torpedo boats and destroyers for delivery of and protection from torpedoes.

Enormous construction programmes were then necessary. Because it had an existing empire and was an island, Great Britain had long relied heavily on the navy for defence. In 1889, it authorized construction of seventy ships, including ten battleships, over the next decade, affirming the principle that its fleet should be at least equal to those of its next two competitors combined (then France and Russia).

Germany felt insecure, remembering that Great Britain had destroyed the Danish fleet at Copenhagen by surprise in 1807. It moved in 1898, with plans for nineteen new battleships and many lesser ships to be built over six years. A new law in 1900 raised the goal to thirty-eight by 1920. These laws were supported by Tirpitz and Emperor Wilhelm II, and by the iron and naval-construction industries. The laws passed through the Reichstag by the use of all sorts of manoeuvring. In 1908, Tirpitz even secretly allotted the construction contracts for two ships which were not to be authorized until 1909. The strategic mission of the fleet was unclear, even to the German Admiralty. Tirpitz's original argument was a deterrence argument: the fleet could be used for diplomatic bargaining, though smaller than the British fleet. The British would not risk an attack on it, because their losses, even after victory, would leave them too weak compared with Russia and France. This rationale failed when Russia and France became aligned with Great Britain; no substitute was developed and the German construction can be explained only by inertia and the political position of the pro-naval forces.

Great Britain responded to German construction by diplomacy to allow it to concentrate its forces at home where it could face the German fleet. Thus, it signed an Anglo-Japanese alliance in 1902, giving Japan its first equal treaty with a Western nation and permitting Great Britain to bring home its Far East Squadron. Similarly, as the entente patterns were built up before the First World War, and France became more closely associated with Great Britain, defence of the Mediterranean was assigned to the French fleet.

Great Britain also sought technological improvement, laying down the *Dreadnought*, the first of a new, more advanced battleship, in 1905. The technological advance was important, because the victor in a line-of-battle action was expected to be the side whose armour and guns permitted it to choose a range at which it could harm the opposing fleet but not be harmed. Tirpitz responded in 1907 with a programme for many dreadnought-class battleships. There were further escalations: by the outbreak of war in 1914, Great Britain had twenty dreadnoughts to Germany's thirteen, and forty older battleships to Germany's twenty. Britain maintained superiority, but in 1911 it had had to reduce its two-power standard to a standard of 60 per cent superiority over the German fleet in dreadnoughts.

Many efforts were made to stop the race, but all failed. Naval arms control came up at the Hague conferences of 1899 and 1907. Even the weak proposal of agreeing to state a budget level and not exceed it for three years failed at the first conference, whereas the still weaker proposal of exchanging information on construction plans failed at the second conference. When Edward VII of Great Britain visited Wilhelm II in 1908, the British proposed that Germany voluntarily slow its rate of building. The answer was no, although there were hints that Germany might do so in return for unstated British concessions. The incident was used by British officials to obtain political support for the naval programme.

New efforts were made in 1909, following the revelation of the advance allocation of German construction contracts, an action that frightened the British public because of its suggestion of secret German construction. The British proposed neutral inspection of dockyards, but got nowhere. At a broader level, the Germans offered to restrain their construction in return for a political accord that would amount to an alliance. The British rejected this as destructive of its entente with France and Russia. Bernhard von Bülow, the German Chancellor, dared not offend Wilhelm or the Reichstag by offering more. He made a last unsuccessful effort to obtain concessions from Tirpitz shortly before being defeated in the Reichstag.

By 1912, the new Chancellor, Bethmann Hollweg, was practically begging the British to make concessions so he could resist Tirpitz's plans for new construction before they were presented to the Reichstag. Lord Haldane visited Germany, offering political and colonial concessions in return for a German commitment not to increase its naval programme Tirpitz insisted on British neutrality and on including its as yet unpublished naval expansion programme in defining the baseline. Bethmann Hollweg wanted a weaker position. He and Tirpitz both threatened to resign; Wilhelm sided with Tirpitz. The German expansion programme was published and negotiations faded away. In 1913, Churchill twice offered a one-year naval holiday, but his offers were ignored.

Ironically, the elaborate fleets were hardly used in the war. Nearly all the German ships were tied down in their ports by British ships, which were equally tied down by this task. The net effect was that Germany could not employ surface raiders. There was only one large-scale surface-ship battle during the war: the submarine combat and land combat proved much more significant.

Nevertheless, the arms-race did contribute to the outbreak of war. Both Germany and Great Britain were paranoid about the other's fleet. Tirpitz clearly wanted naval war with Great Britain. Others on the German side may have hoped that its fleet would deter Great Britain from entering the war. This hope was dashed by the German violation of Belgium's neutrality, which swayed a wavering British public opinion. The arms-race background may also have contributed to that opinion change. It certainly helped provoke public tensions during the years before the war and helped lead Great Britain to an alliance against Germany.

The League and the interwar period

Long before the First World War ended, there was in every country touched by the conflict a strong sentiment that nothing of the kind should ever be permitted to happen again, and the Allied governments began to draft plans and proposals for the time when war was over. These had to do with the territorial reorganization of Europe that would follow the war, with the establishment of an international organization that would regulate relations and obviate friction among the powers, and with the question of armed force.

The security arrangements, including the creation of the League of Nations were quite creative. The Covenant of the new League showed the extent to which that organization was to be oriented toward disarmament:

The Members of the League recognize that the maintenance of peace requires the reduction of national armaments to the lowest point consistent with national safety and the enforcement by common action of international obligations.

The Council, taking account of the geographical situation and circumstances of each State, shall formulate plans for such reduction for the consideration and action of the several governments.

Such plans shall be subject to reconsideration and revision at least every ten years.

After these plans shall have been adopted by the several governments, the limitations of armaments therein fixed shall not be exceeded without the concurrence of the Council.

The Members of the League agree that the manufacture by private enterprise of munitions and implements of war is open to grave objections. The Council shall advise how the evil effects attendant upon such manufacture can be prevented, due regard being had to the necessities of those Members of the League which are not able to manufacture the munitions and implements of war necessary for their safety.

The Members of the League undertake to interchange full and frank information as to the scale of their armaments, their military, naval and air programmes and the condition of such of their industries as are adaptable to war-like purposes.

The major effects of this Covenant provision were the World Disarmament Conference of 1932 (discussed below) and a continuing, but unsuccessful, series of efforts to restrict trade in arms and munitions.

But assigning disarmament responsibility to the League was partly a way to put off hard issues, perhaps until they could be forgotten. Among the victorious powers that met in Paris in 1919, there was no desire for a radical agreed reduction of their own armed forces. Despite the feelings of the public on this score, the statesmen and soldiers who made up the Allied delegations believed this to be unrealistic. The armed might of the Central Powers had been destroyed, but peace had not descended on the world. There was civil war in Russia and communist armies were fighting in Finland, the Baltic states, and the Caucasus; there were small wars on the frontiers of Poland; and the Middle East, the Arab lands, and the Far East were in turmoil. The Allied Powers had no way to assess their future military needs in the face of these problems, and were unwilling to bind themselves to any specific provision for control of their armaments. Moreover, there were major differences in viewpoint between the United Kingdom and France. The former rapidly demobilized its land army. The latter was deeply concerned about defence against Germany and wished both guarantees and a favourable balance of military force.

The Allies were, of course, perfectly ready to be specific with respect to their enemies, and the most drastic provisions of the peace treaties signed with the former enemy states in 1919 were the so-called arms clauses, which provided for the disarmament of those states. The Treaty of Versailles, for example, prescribed that the German army of the future should be limited to 100,000 officers and men, denied Germany the possession of armour and military aircraft, placed severe limitations on its naval armaments, and ordered destruction of the industry that had supported the German war effort. (Germany later built 'pocket battleships' designed around the treaty restrictions and devised an army readily expanded to a much larger force.) In the Treaty of Saint Germain, similar provisions were made binding on the Austrian army; and the armies of other enemy states—Hungary, Bulgaria and Turkey—were treated the same way (although the restrictions on Turkey were lifted in the 1923 Treaty of Lausanne).

In addition to the naval accords discussed below, the 1920s saw several less far-reaching agreements. In 1923, for example, the Central American Disarmament Convention resulted in an agreement by Guatemala, Honduras, El Salvador, Nicaragua and Costa Rica to limit their armed forces, military aircraft and war vessels.

A more important and still relevant agreement, the Geneva Protocol, prohibiting the use of poisonous gas and also the use of chemical and biological weapons was signed by forty-six countries in 1925. The protocol successfully passed a major test during the Second World War, which saw no significant use of chemical or biological weapons, despite the fact that neither Japan nor the United States was a party to the treaty. Questions exist, however, on whether the belligerents were restrained by the force of the protocol or, instead, by the mutual fear of retaliation and the unpredictable tactical consequences of unleashing chemical and biological warfare on a large scale. Many weightier and equally solemn agreements, e.g. those relating to the protection of non-combatants, were systematically violated.

In February 1932 the League of Nations members and the United States and the Soviet Union assembled in Geneva for the World Disarmament Conference. During this conference it became immediately apparent that the key to the situation was France. A disarmament scheme that meant anything would be possible only if the French were willing to scale down their armaments, sacrificing the military superiority over Germany that they had won at Versailles. The French insisted that they could make such concessions only if other nations, particularly the United Kingdom, would give them guarantees of aid in case war should come again. The commitments of Locarno* were not strong enough for

---

* The Pact of Locarno, signed in 1925, contained a series of agreements whereby Belgium, France, Germany, Italy and the United Kingdom mutually guaranteed peace in Western Europe.— Ed.

France. In the conditions of 1932, the British did not feel that they could take on commitments stronger than the ones already made. At the same time, the British were afraid that the fragile democratic government in Germany would be ousted by its extremist opponents unless its leaders were given a diplomatic victory to show to the electorate. The best diplomatic victory would be an arms agreement to end the inferior armaments position that so many Germans felt to be injust and humiliating. The British wanted to give the Germans arms equality—that is, equality of status—and then to have each nation scale down its armaments and military budget.

The British used every kind of pressure they could think of, and the French stalled, finally accepting equality for Germany. At the same time, however, events were moving swiftly in Germany. During 1932 three German governments fell, and in January 1933 Adolf Hitler became Chancellor of Germany. In May 1933 Hitler unexpectedly announced his support of the British proposals, but this was largely a tactical move to give him time to consolidate his position on the home front. He had no intention of allowing himself to be bound by an international agreement on arms. In October, he announced that Germany was withdrawing from both the Disarmament Conference and the League of Nations, to which it had belonged since 1926.

This was the end of any hope of land disarmament in the interwar period. It is barely possible that *if* the conference had met sooner and *if* the French had not been so stubborn and *if* an agreement had been found to satisfy German feelings on the equality issue, a general agreement on reduction of land armaments might have been worked out that no one would have dared to refuse to sign. After October 1933 no such agreement would become possible until Hitler had been met militarily and defeated.

Naval arms control in the interwar period

The exception to the dismal picture just described is the effort to control naval arms. This effort began at the Washington Conference of 1921–22, a major diplomatic event that for better or worse put temporary limitations on what might otherwise have been a costly and dangerous arms race. In the years immediately preceding the conference, the United States, the United Kingdom and Japan had all announced major new naval construction programmes. The three major powers seemed to be on the verge of bitter and unnecessary competition in naval armaments.

In the United States, Woodrow Wilson had argued forcefully for naval preparedness during his administration, calling for a navy that would be 'second to none'. The Naval Appropriation Act of 1916 had approved the largest construction programme ever proposed at one time by any nation. By the end of the war Wilson was calling for further naval building which by 1925 would have given the United States a navy more powerful than that of all the other great nations combined.

Just how serious Wilson was about all this shipbuilding is debatable. He publicly recommended the 'uninterrupted pursuit' of the building programme because 'it would clearly be unwise for us to attempt to adjust our programme to a future world policy as yet undetermined'. With the Paris Peace Conference in session and the League of Nations looming large in his image of the post-war world, Wilson's motives may legitimately be questioned. He may have been the first American President to use the construction of military weapons as a bargaining chip for negotiations.

Warren G. Harding was elected in 1920, and said shortly before his inauguration that he saw 'no reason to look for a cessation of American naval increase'. While not exactly a ringing endorsement of Wilson's navy second to none, this did put Harding down on the side of big-navy enthusiasts.

Shortly before Harding's inauguration, Congress began debating a new naval appropriation bill. Public pressure was growing in the United States for curtailment of naval construction, and for some form of disarmament as an alternative to further expenditures for ships. Senator William Borah of Idaho proposed an amendment to the naval bill requesting the President to convene a meeting of the United States, the United Kingdom and Japan to consider ways of reducing the naval construction programmes of the three governments. Harding opposed the amendment, considering it an infringement on his executive prerogatives. But public sentiment was so overwhelmingly in support that Harding had no choice but to go along with it. The result was a compromise: the Borah resolution was approved, and in return Congress granted the administration's full request for naval construction.

The British were concerned over Harding's apparent commitment to naval pre-eminence. Prime Minister Lloyd George had engineered a dramatic reduction in British naval strength since the end of the First World War, and hoped to maintain the navy on this peacetime footing. The Royal Navy, however, had expressed serious concern about the impact of the American construction programme. By 1921 the pro-navy forces in the British Government had grown in number and strength, and were finally able to force the Prime Minister's hand. In March 1921, Lloyd George proposed a plan for construction of four new capital ships. Many British naval authorities had serious doubts about the future of capital ships in general, believing that the submarine and aeroplane had virtually negated the effectiveness of ships as weapons of war. Moreover, in the early 1920s, the United Kingdom was in the midst of an economic recession. Unemployment was rising, personal income was falling, and there was widespread support for a reduction in income tax. The United Kingdom was also saddled with a tremendous war debt, much of it payable to the United States. The government hoped this debt would either be reduced or eliminated, but care had to be taken to avoid antagonizing the United States. Any British naval build-up also ran the risk of stimulating American naval construction, the result of which might be to leave the United Kingdom worse off than before.

Japan had not stood idly by during the years of Anglo-American naval competition. It, too, had begun a process of naval expansion. In 1920 the Japanese Diet approved a programme calling for the construction of two new capital ships per year for eight years. By 1927 the Imperial Navy was to have a force of twenty-five modern capital ships.

Domestic pressures similar to those in the United Kingdom were beginning to build up in Japan. A serious recession had gripped the country by the end of 1920, and in those pre-Keynesian days recessions were thought to be cured by cutting back government spending rather than by increasing it. The naval building programme was a likely candidate for the fiscal scalpel. Naval construction was the largest item in the defence budget, and the defence budget itself was over half of total government expenditures. This was an enormous investment in naval might for a relatively small nation. Japan's population was only half that of the United States and Japanese per capita income was only one-tenth of the American. In spite of this disparity, Japan was planning to spend as much on its navy as the United States.

It was in this context that President Harding made his call for a conference to consider the limitation of naval armaments. It seemed a perfect case for arms control—three countries, each embarking on a course of naval expansion, two in direct and reluctant response to the naval construction of the third. It appeared to be a classic example of an arms race that could be halted by joint agreement.

The Washington Conference convened in November 1921 for what most observers thought would be a protracted negotiation. Secretary of State Charles Evans Hughes, however, dramatically announced specific figures for reductions of the United States' battleship fleet as well as those of the United Kingdom and Japan—an announcement that stunned the other delegations and, because of the support it evoked from public opinion, left them no way of refusing. Within a month, all the essential points were agreed upon. Under the final terms of the Five-Power Treaty, all signatories agreed to stop construction of capital ships for ten years, and to limit their total tonnage in capital ships. For the United States and the United Kingdom the limitation was 500,000 tons; for Japan, 300,000 tons. France and Italy were limited to 175,000 tons each. The three major powers were reasonably satisfied with the outcome, although the Japanese delegation was heard to grumble that the 5:5:3 ratio sounded a bit like Rolls-Royce, Rolls-Royce, Ford. In order to comply with the terms of the treaty, the leading powers had initially to scrap sixty-eight ships already built or under construction (twenty-eight for the United States, twenty-four for the United Kingdom and sixteen for Japan).

For the United Kingdom the agreement confirmed a new reality—parity with the United States. The argument made in the United Kingdom at the time was that the famous two-power standard had never been applied against the United States; instead it applied only against European powers. And, although neither the United States nor the United Kingdom wanted a naval arms race, the British held to a position that they ought to maintain parity with the United States. This led to restriction of the Washington Agreement to capital ships and aircraft carriers. The United Kingdom wanted a large number of small cruisers for commerce protection; the United States wanted fewer large cruisers, because it had fewer distant bases. A trade-off was not possible, because the cruisers the United States wanted could have outfought the small cruisers in a theoretical battleline engagement, violating the parity concept. Similarly, control of submarines effectively failed. The United Kingdom sought to ban submarines, viewing them useful only as commerce raiders. To the lesser naval powers, especially France, submarines appeared as a cheap counterbalance to large fleets. The United Kingdom had to content itself with a treaty that never came into force. This treaty would have required a submarine to warn a merchant vessel and make provisions for the safety of its crew before torpedoing it.

For Japan, the Washington Agreement was far more than an arms-control treaty. It was also a replacement of the Anglo-Japanese alliance of 1902 and a guarantee of Japan's predominance in the north-west Pacific. With the new European balance of power, the alliance was no longer so useful to the United Kingdom, and the United States objected to it, fearing that the United Kingdom and Japan might combine against it in the Pacific. There were war scares between the United States and Japan at the time, based on a possible naval arms race and on conflicts over China policy. Japan naturally opposed a combination of changes that would deprive it of its alliance and keep its fleet inferior as well. Part of the response was a four-power treaty of general and mutual respect for Pacific possessions among Great Britain, the United States, Japan and France. This treaty replaced the alliance by a commitment to talk in the event of difficulty. The other part of the response was commitments by the United States and the United Kingdom not to fortify certain Pacific outposts. Japan would then be geographically protected, because the United States and the United Kingdom would be unable to bring their forces to bear on Japan without bases. The immediate effect of the conference was a relaxation of United States-Japanese tensions.

The first effort to extend the treaty framework to cruisers and auxiliary vessels—which were being laid down in large numbers—failed at Geneva in 1927. The problems were both those between the United States and the United Kingdom and those between the United Kingdom and the continental European powers, particularly France, which hoped to obtain additional security guarantees in return for its commitment not to build ships.

The Anglo-American difficulty was finally worked out by negotiation of a 'yardstick' by which one United States eight-inch-gun cruiser would be considered the equivalent of nearly two British six-inch-gun cruisers. Following this side negotiation, limited success was reached at a new five-power conference held in London in 1930. France and Italy refused to adhere fully, so an 'escalator' clause was included, effectively ending the treaty if a non-party should build enough to threaten a party. The ratios were also adjusted slightly in favour of Japan.

After London, the situation rapidly worsened. No agreements were possible at the 1932 World Disarmament Conference at Geneva. Late in 1934, Japan, facing serious domestic backlash at the inferior position assigned to it by the agreement, formally abrogated the 1922 agreement, effective two years later. A second London Naval Conference in 1935, in which Japan did not participate, produced a treaty whose primary effect was to dismantle much of the elaborate limitation structure of the previous treaties. The United Kingdom entered several side agreements with Germany and the USSR during this era. By 1938, both the United Kingdom and the United States were embarked on major naval construction programmes, and the obligations of the side agreements were denounced by Germany and 'indefinitely suspended' by the United Kingdom during 1939.

Possible lessons

Although lessons drawn from history are always arguable, several speculations based on the 1890–1940 period seem warranted. The first is the role of individuals—much hung on the individual judgements and actions of men such as Tirpitz and Hughes.

The second is that military-industrial complexes have existed and have been influential as they were in Germany before the First World War, where the Chancellor's hands were effectively tied. Pressures for economy, working in the opposite direction, were clearly influential at the Washington Naval Conference. A good case can be made that that conference was merely an agreement not to build ships that would not have been built anyway.

Third, arms races have in some cases contributed to the outbreak of war, as did the pre-First-World-War Anglo-German race. And the Washington naval treaty, whether or not it prevented an arms race, did bring an era of good feeling between the United States, the United Kingdom and Japan. Again, however, the point must be balanced; resentment at the inferior position imposed on Japan by the naval agreements was later one of the factors contributing to the rise of Japanese militarism in the 1930s. Similarly, resentment at the one-sided disarmament provisions of Versailles contributed to Hitler's domestic support in much the same way. Any treaty that establishes several classes of nations is likely to provoke difficulty.

Fourth, the naval example makes one doubt the step-by-step theory of arms control. All the easy areas of naval agreement were found at Washington in 1922. What was left for Geneva and London were the hard problems; it is not surprising that they were not easily solved.

Finally, and most important, one must be struck by a sense of the irrelevance of the doctrines that moved both force planners and arms controllers. The battle fleets so expensively accumulated before the First World War were barely used in that war, although their existence did limit use of surface commerce raiders. Yet control of battle fleets was the goal of arms controllers during the 1920s. In spite of the agreement to control aircraft carriers and the abortive efforts to control submarines, the negotiators concentrated their attention on subtle battleship versus battleship calculations. These calculations were irrelevant to the next war, whose naval actions were to be fought in large part with submarines and aircraft carriers. And, as a final paradox, the arms races and agreements on weapons that proved useless may have been illusions, but they were illusions that helped bring good feelings in the 1920s and perhaps contributed to war in the eras immediately preceding the First and Second World Wars.

7

Conditions for successful disarmament

Quincy Wright
Former Professor of International
Law, University of Chicago

Even if there were a general conviction that the nuclear arms race makes for increasing insecurity in the age of rapid technological change, there is little likelihood, if statesmen continue to make policy as they have in the past, of ending that race. Lewis Richardson's simultaneous equations have demonstrated that when war is highly mechanized, arms races are more likely to end in war than in equilibrium if, as he says, statesmen 'do not stop to think'.[1]

There seems little likelihood that guided by 'realists' they will stop long enough to rid themselves of their obsessions. The lion, suggested Salvador Madariaga from his long experience as head of the disarmament section of the League of Nations Secretariat, wants to eliminate all weapons but claws and jaws, the eagle all but talons and beaks, and the bear all but an embracing hug.[2] Nuclear powers will probably be unwilling to eliminate nuclear weapons, the present insignia of greatness, but will increase their capability in nuclear-headed missiles and in technical capacity to make even more destructive instruments, and may even force non-nuclear powers to reduce their security by installing weapons which will make them targets of attack.

We must, therefore, expect tensions to increase as the technologists and arms controllers take over from politically oriented statesmen, until, by accident, miscalculation of a 'fail-safe' mechanism, escalation of 'nibbling aggression', or sheer desperation of a public overwhelmed by fears, there will be a nuclear holocaust.

History of disarmament

The forty years' history of disarmament negotiations under the League of Nations and the United Nations, interrupted by ten years of preparation for and waging of the Second World War, gives little ground for expecting disarmament by agreement. In 1942, after considering the possibility of peaceful co-operation under the League of Nations, or of a world empire by successful conquest, I wrote:

From J. David Singer (ed.), 'Weapon Management and World Politics. Proceedings of the International Arms Control Symposium, December 1962', *The Journal of Conflict Resolution*, No. 7, September 1963. (Reproduced with permission.)

The trend of military history since 1932 has looked toward a third alternative. On the one hand, states adopted more extensive conscription laws, maintained larger standing armies, voted larger military appropriations, provided more efficient frontier defenses, and strove for a higher degree of economic self-sufficiency. On the other hand, they utilized centralized propaganda instruments and economic controls to develop in each population a more fanatical and aggressive national spirit. The combination of these policies precipitated the Second World War, and may tend toward frequent general wars on a gigantic scale, with the eventual destruction of civilization.[3]

There are, however, historical instances of disarmament. What have been the conditions of these successes? They appear to have been the conclusion of a war, the technological obsolescence of weapons, the diversion of political animosities, or a sense of security. Let us consider these conditions in succession.

The termination of a war. This has sometimes led to compulsory disarmament of the defeated power, as of Prussia in 1807 and Germany in 1919 and 1945. Such disarmament, however, has usually been of short duration because the victors have been divided or lethargic in imposing it and the vanquished have been anxious for revenge, as was Germany in the 1930s, or because the victors have desired to re-arm the vanquished against a new enemy, even though the vanquished at first wished to retain the economic and political advantages of its disarmament, as in the case of Germany and Japan in the 1950s.

The termination of a war may also lead to voluntary disarmament of the victors because they feel secure and prefer to spend resources for productive purposes. Thus, the United States greatly reduced its armaments after the Civil War and after the First World War, as evidenced by the percentage of military expenditures to total federal expenditures and to total national income, as well as by per capita costs of military preparation. The United Kingdom, France, Italy and the Soviet Union similarly reduced military expenditures in the 1920s. The United States reduced its land and naval armaments for a few years after the Second World War, while it had a monopoly of the atomic bomb. The post-First-World-War reduction, however, ended in the 1930s with the rise of the Axis, and the United States began rebuilding armaments after the Second World War with the Korean War of 1950 and the Soviet acquisition of atomic weapons.

There have also been instances of agreements to disarm after a stalemated war. The Rush-Bagot Agreement of 1817 between Great Britain and the United States disarmed the Great Lakes and by implication the entire United States-Canadian frontier. This agreement was concluded after the War of 1812 and the agreement to accept the pre-established Canadian-American boundary in the Treaty of Ghent. The Rush-Bagot Agreement is still in effect and appears to have been the most enduring of all disarmament agreements. Stalemated hostilities, however, are by no means certain to bring about disarmament, as witness the present cease-fire lines in Palestine, Korea, Kashmir, Viet Nam, and Germany, on either side of which hostile forces confront each other.

While the termination of war may bring about temporary unilateral disarmament and often induces efforts to disarm by agreement, as it did after the Napoleonic and the world wars, and while it has in a few instances led to agreements for boundary disarmament, or limitation of particular types of armament, it has not in the past led to general disarmament.

Obsolescence. Advances in technology have sometimes led to the obsolescence of particular weapons and their abandonment unilaterally or by agreement. The crossbow, use of which continued, and was indeed increased, after its prohibition by the Lateran Conference of 1215, was abandoned when the development of firearms made it obsolete. The St Petersburg Convention of 1868 eliminated explosive bullets of under 400 grams, considered to cause unnecessary suffering, after the development of shrapnel and machine guns made such bullets less useful. The Washington Conference of 1922 limited the number of battleships after many naval experts advised that they were obsolete, though the inequality of the 5:5:3 ratio so wounded the pride of Japan that it refused to continue the agreements after 1936. The use of poison gases was prohibited by a Hague declaration of 1907, but gas was used in the First World War. The Convention of 1925, again prohibiting gas, was observed in the Second World War because its use was not sufficiently effective to compensate for the burden of providing gas masks when both sides had it. Italy, however, used gas in the 1930s against Ethiopians who could not retaliate.

It is conceivable that states may eventually regard nuclear-headed missiles as too dangerous to use and the threat to use them as incredible, and may therefore agree to abandon them. The problems of prestige and inspection are, however, likely to prevent such action. The Baruch proposal for internationalization of all nuclear materials and installations was initiated by the United States when it had a monopoly of the atomic secrets but was rejected by the Soviet Union which presently produced nuclear weapons itself.

Diversion. Great Britain and France abandoned a naval arms race in the late nineteenth century when they began to fear Germany more than they feared each other, and entered into the entente in 1904. The Anglo-American naval arms race, which began mildly in the 1890s and accelerated when in 1916 President Wilson declared a policy of 'a navy second to none', was ended by American entry into the First World War and by the Washington Conference Treaties of 1922 in which the United Kingdom agreed to equality when the attention of both was directed to the problem of Japan. Franco-German military rivalry was ended with the alliance of these states against the USSR in NATO and by the treaty of 1963. Shifts in the balance-of-power situation, in these and in other instances, have stopped one arms race by beginning another. This condition, however, does not assist in general disarmament.

Security. The most important condition for disarmament has been a sense of security eliminating any apparent need of arms for defence and permitting economic interests and taxpayers' pressure to exert influence. Such security may arise from geographical conditions, which in the case of the United States induced a low level of armaments from 1814 to 1890 except for the brief period of Civil War. Great Britain maintained insignificant land armaments at home during much of its history because it felt adequately defended by its navy. Such security may arise, as previously suggested, from the defeat and disarmament of an aggressive power. After the First World War the average arms expenditures of all the great powers combined decreased on average from 31 per cent to 18 per cent of the national budgets and the per capita expenditures from $6.16 to $5.47.

A sense of security may also arise from general confidence in the stability of the balance of power, as seems to have been the case in the generation after the Napoleonic Wars. Such reductions of armaments have usually been by voluntary unilateral action. Certain areas, such as Latin America, Asia and Africa, have, at times, because of the Monroe Doctrine, or agreements among colonial powers, been kept out of power politics and arms in these areas have been at a low level. Regional disarmament agreements have been made, for example those relating to Pacific bases at the Washington Conference of 1922.

Agreements, such as the naval disarmaments between Chile and Argentina in 1902, and among the great Naval Powers in 1922 and 1930, have been concluded to last for only a few years and have included escape clauses, thus manifesting fear that the stable balance may be short-lived. This caution suggests that disarmament agreements have been more a consequence than a cause of a sense of security. The rarity of disarmament agreements indicates that a general sense of security has been a rarity in the history of the state system. It can hardly exist when some powerful states make it clear that they are less interested in the security of their present possessions than in radical changes of territory or status and, therefore, threaten the security of others, nor can it exist when major political disputes exist between powerful states. Calling the Washington Conference in 1921, President Harding said, 'The prospect of reducing armaments is not a hopeful one unless this desire [for peace] finds expression in a practical effort to remove causes of misunderstanding and to seek grounds for agreement as to principles and their application.'

This review of the history of disarmament indicates that the problem is political and psychological more than it is military and technological. Moral disarmament or limitation of the will to fight must precede military disarmament or limitation of the instruments of fighting. This was recognized in the Hensley Amendment to the United States Naval Appropriation Act of 1916 and in the call for the Washington Conference in 1921 which was concerned with the serious Far Eastern problems as well as disarmament. The League of Nations recognized this relationship in its formula adopted in 1922, that peace rested on the three legs of security, arbitration and disarmament. Only after collective security had established confidence that states would not be victims of aggression, and a system of peaceful settlement had established confidence that disputes, whether legal or political, would be settled justly, was it thought that disarmament could be tackled effectively. On 27 March 1933, the representatives of Great Britain, Germany, and the United States in the League of Nations Disarmament Conference replied to the representative of the USSR (Litvinov), who had urged 'immediate, complete and general disarmament', that 'a will for peace must first be established', and went on to indicate the measures that they considered necessary to create this will. The existence of dissatisfied, crusading or revenge-seeking powers makes it difficult to establish that will for all states capable of disturbing the peace. It has even been suggested that 'the threat of violence and the occasional outbreak of real violence—which gives the threat credibility—are essential elements in peaceful social change not only in international but also in national communities'.[4]

The history of disarmament efforts under the United Nations has been a repetition of that under the League of Nations, in spite of vast, but probably still unappreciated, changes in the situation wrought by the development of nuclear-headed missiles. In 1942, I wrote:

It has been said that states will not reduce armaments unless they are given an equivalent in political guarantees of security. Under the pressure of taxpayers, governments, it is supposed, maintain armaments at no greater level than they consider necessary for security, or, if they are dissatisfied with the *status quo*, at no greater level than they consider necessary to effect the changes desired. They will not, therefore, agree to disarm until assured of a substitute method of security or of change. There is certainly evidence to support this contention. Successful disarmament treaties have always been accompanied by political arrangements which were believed by the parties to augment their political security or to settle their outstanding political problems. The two have gone hand in hand, and considering the conditions of successful negotiations, it is unlikely that agreements will ever be reached on the technical problems of disarmament unless the parties have lessened tensions by political settlements or by general acceptance of international procedures, creating confidence that such settlements can be effected peacefully.

It is however clear that the armament required by one country for security is a function of the armament of others, though statesmen have more easily perceived the influence of foreign increases upon their own needs than the influence of their own measures upon foreign needs. Theoretically, therefore, it is possible to conceive a self-executing treaty which would stabilize the balance of power and reduce the probability of war, although it dealt with nothing but the armament programs of the states and a system of inspection.[5]

Moral disarmament

Following this, I discussed the prospects of armament-building holidays, quantitative disarmament, rules of war, and finally, moral disarmament. Discussion of moral disarmament has included consideration of the regulation of international propaganda and of the political problems of security on the one hand, and the possibility of modifying the international status quo on the other.

Moral disarmament, from the standpoint of those countries satisfied with their present possessions, means genuine belief that they will be able to retain them without resort to arms. But from the standpoint of those that are anxious to modify the territorial *status quo*, it means genuine belief that they will be able to acquire what they want by peaceful procedures. The problem lies in the realm of international law, organization, and public opinion. . . . It is, however, related to the problem of material armament, in that the statistics of the latter provide evidence of the former, and reciprocally effective regulation of material armament influences moral attitudes. When armament budgets, personnel and materiel are rising at an accelerating rate, it may be assumed that international tensions are increasing and that states are morally as well as materially rearming. Armament races evidenced by such statistics constitute a form of international relations closely related to war, and often ending in war itself.[6]

Now, as in the League period and the post-Napoleonic period, the problem of disarmament is the problem of creating conditions giving general confidence that international peace and security, including a rectification of injustices, will prevail for a long future. If that confidence is limited, not more than an armament-building holiday of short duration can be agreed upon. In proportion as confidence grows, general and complete disarmament will be possible. Salvador Madariaga remarked: 'The problem of disarmament is not the problem of disarmament. It really is the problem of the organization of the world community.'[7]

It would appear that among activities useful for developing a stable and a just world creating such confidence, consideration should be given to education, law, policy, power and organization in the international field.

Education. People and governments should be educated to accept a general picture of the world which is both feasible and desirable. A world empire, a world federation, or a world united by a single value system are not feasible in any foreseeable future because of the present variety of cultures and ideologies, the present intense sentiments of national independence among peoples, and the present distribution of power among states with conflicting policies. The system of diplomacy, national armaments and an international law which recognized war as a legitimate act of state, although it has at times sustained a military balance of power giving moderate stability to Europe, as it did in the nineteenth century, is not now desirable. Such a system, under present conditions, leads to the extreme instability of a bipolarized world in which military actions may proceed with a speed far greater than the possibilities of diplomatic adjustment, to the extreme destructiveness of nuclear weapons and nuclear fallout, and to the extreme probability that war will occur, as it has in the past, in balance-of-power systems. Furthermore, it is difficult, if not impossible, to construct a mechanical system of mutual deterrence which will, on the one hand, make deliberate war incredible by assuring unbearable second-strike capability and, on the other hand, make threats of such a war credible as instruments of diplomacy for maintaining the political balance. Such a system, in proportion as it succeeds in making deliberate war incredible, tends to make accidental, escalated, pre-emptive, or irresponsible war inevitable.

The only world which seems both feasible and desirable is that pictured in the League of Nations Covenant and in the United Nations Charter. The statesmen of 1919 and 1945 agreed on a world of peaceful coexistence and co-operation among sovereign states under law. While this system includes aspects of federation, common values, and equilibrium, it differs from the others in its emphasis upon coexistence, co-operation, and competition among sovereign states and the peaceful solution of their conflicts through the organization of procedures and measures of collective security sustained by a universal opinion opposed to war.

Law. To clarify this image of the world and to maintain opinion in its support of the rules of order and principles of justice on which it rests, it should be better understood by both peoples and governments. Such key terms as recognition, aggression, defence, territorial integrity, political independence, and collective security should be better defined. Such principles as self-determination of peoples, respect for human rights, non-intervention in domestic jurisdiction, co-operation for economic and social progress, and the practice of tolerance should be elaborated. Continuous development of international law and its incorporation in national legal systems is essential in order to identify the national interest and national security of each state with the firm establishment of such a world, and to assure effective participation of all the nations in its activities.

Policy. Continuing effort should be made by governments to reduce international tensions, especially by eliminating false images of other nations and exaggerated views of alien ideologies. Suitable to this end are policies of defence without provocation, conciliation without appeasement, and utilization of United Nations procedures to deal with threats to peace, and to settle controversies when diplomacy, mediation, conciliation, and utilization of regional agencies have failed. National policy directives and legislation should continually be guided by such considerations, and particular attention should be given to the elimination of false fears. Professors Charles McClelland and C. A. W. Manning have pointed out, following the psychological findings of Kurt Lewin,[8] that men act, whether making personal or governmental decisions, from their perceptions of the situation, not from the actual situation as it might be viewed by an omniscient being. Perceptions of international situations are often distorted because of the inadequacies of communication. International relations are not, in fact, about relations between nations but relations between distorted images of nations. Is Soviet policy motivated mainly by fear of attack from the West or by ambition to spread communism? Does Khrushchev mean it when he says communist policy is directed toward economic development and peaceful competition between different systems in the improvement of standards of living? Is he so convinced that communism will win in such peaceful competition that he is ready to abandon the use of force and to disarm if the 'capitalist' states will do likewise? These questions, and similar questions about the beliefs and objectives of Western statesmen, would receive different answers, at different times, from different persons on both sides of the East–West divide.

Power. Efforts should be made to stabilize the power situation in the world by increasing the military capability of the United Nations, the small states, and certain regional groups, other than the present great alliances; by demilitarizing, denuclearizing, or neutralizing certain regions, states, and frontiers; by moderating the mutual fear, which each of the great alliance systems now has of the other, through internal checks in each alliance giving assurances against its use for aggression but retaining its defensive potentialities; and similarly by developing in each great power legal, political and military checks and balances designed to increase its defensive and reduce its aggressive capabilities.

Organization. Finally, continuing efforts should be made to strengthen the United Nations: (a) its system of collective security should be improved to assure prompt intervention in situations threatening international peace in order to avoid hostilities, to bring about a cease-fire preventing the escalation of hostilities, to mobilize collective action to frustrate aggression, or to organize the policing of cease-fire lines, and disturbed frontiers and areas; (b) procedures for dealing with disputes should be made more available and reliable and more effective in assuring just settlements. Procedures for keeping international law up to date and for assuring its observance should be developed. International co-operation should be encouraged to promote economic development, cultural exchange, scientific advance, transnational communications, health, education, and other matters within the competence of the Economic and Social Council and the Specialized Agencies.

Conclusion

It is to be hoped that persistent efforts by governments, international organizations and private agencies in these directions may, in time, create conditions in which disarmament agreements to strengthen defensive power, weaken offensive power, save national resources for productive purposes and reduce tensions can be negotiated. With the growth of confidence that all states have renounced war in fact as well as in theory, have accepted the image of a United Nations world, are anxious to realize that world in practice, and believe that necessary changes can be effected by peaceful means, the problem of inspection to assure observance of disarmament agreements may be soluble and agreements general or regional, comprehensive or partial, qualitative or quantitative may be accepted.

History does not give too much support for the attainment of this achievement but the new technology may bring statesmen to realization of its expediency.

Notes

1. Lewis Richardson, *Arms and Insecurity*, Pittsburgh, Pa., Boxwood Press, 1960, pp. 12, 75.
2. Salvador de Madariaga, *Disarmament*, New York, Coward-McCann, 1929.
3. Quincy Wright, *A Study of War*, Chicago, Ill., University of Chicago Press, 1942, p. 328.
4. Harold L. Nieburg, 'The Threat of Violence and Social Change', *American Political Science Review*, Vol. 61, December 1962, p. 865.
5. Wright, op. cit., p. 800.
6. Ibid., p. 813.
7. De Madariaga, op. cit., p. 56.
8. Charles A. McClelland, 'The Function of Theory in International Relations', *The Journal of Conflict Resolution*, Vol. 4, September 1960; C. A. W. Manning, *The Nature of International Society*, London, G. Bell & Sons, 1962; Kurt Lewin, *Field Theory in Social Science*, New York, Harper, 1951.

Part III. Armament dynamics

8

The dynamics of the arms race

Marek Thee
International Peace Research Institute, Oslo

Theorems of arms races

A number of theorems set out to explain the motivation, causation and dynamics of arms races. Different models emphasize particular aspects and driving forces that animate the armaments rivalry. Stress is laid, depending on specific approaches, on the political, economic, technological or psychological aspects and elements of given situations and structures. Five sets of explanations are most current: (a) imperial and national rivalries, power politics, expansionist schemes; (b) security dilemmas caused by the aggressive and rapacious policies of neighbours or other powers; (c) system competition and ideological or religious conflict (crusades, cold war); (d) profit or other vested interests of industry, the military, state bureaucracy and technological establishment (the military-industrial-bureaucratic-technological complex); (e) the momentum set up by scientific and technological pressures, their impact on the art of warfare and on weapon modernization.

In real life, we are liable to discover a combination of all these acting to stimulate the arms race. Such a complex and broad phenomenon as the current arms race cannot be adequately explained in terms of one or two motivating forces only. In different contexts and circumstances the prime causation may be attributed to a specific set of determinants. But to some extent, all five generating forces coexist and are complementary.

Obviously, there are also restraining factors. In a dialectical way, we find these in parallel political, social, economic, technological and psychological parameters. Among them are political rationality, resistance to violence, economic curbs and expediency, strategic caution and prudence, ethical inhibitions and moderation, or the very limits of current technological capabilities. It is certainly important to keep in mind these constraining elements, especially in attempting to devise strategies for arms control and disarmament. However, in analysing the current arms race we must also remain vividly aware of the striking asymmetry between the driving and restraining forces, and concentrate upon the stimulants and energizers of armament, which are vastly stronger than the elements of restraint.

Shortened version of 'The Dynamics of the Arms Race, Military R&D and Disarmament', *International Social Science Journal*, Vol. XXX, No. 4, 1978.

At a more basic level, the motivating and invigorating factors behind the arms race may be reduced to two main categories; externally and internally impelled. This simple classification is especially meaningful for the design of basic paradigms of arms races on the one hand, and for evolving checks on them on the other. Although elements and extensions of both these categories can be found to varying degrees under all the five groups of stimulants, and though both categories tend to interact and overlap, the three first categories may essentially be classified as externally, and the last two as internally, stimulated arms races. The 'external' pattern is mostly associated with the internationally animated action-reaction model of inducing and energizing the race, while the 'internal' pattern is mainly related to socio-economic and self-sustaining models rooted in the structures and operation of the national war machine, and the reinforcing behaviour of particular domestic actors.

Over the past century, and especially after the Second World War—with the unfolding of industrial society and the advent of the second technological revolution—the trend moved from mainly internationally induced to predominantly internally energized arms races. The recent acceleration of the arms race despite détente and the relaxation of international tension, and despite the conclusion of a number of arms-control agreements, may serve to confirm this trend. Its explanation lies in the growth of corporate constituencies with vested interests in military production and strength, and in the powerful impetus given to armaments by technological rivalry. The outcome is a momentum which takes less account of external factors and assumes a life of its own. We will return to these issues later.

Contemporary armaments dynamics

With specific reference to the current armament dynamics, we may single out four factors: (a) the high intensity of the action-reaction and over-reaction impulses at the international level; (b) the threat postures inherent in the dominant military-strategic doctrines and their autistic reinforcement; (c) the role, size, structure and mode of operation of military research and development, i.e. the technological momentum; and (d) the enlarged coalition of economic, military, political and technological forces forming the military-industrial-technological-bureaucratic complex.

These varied factors can be related either to the material base or to the political and ideological superstructure in society, and the way they interact. Together they form the structural framework, environment and climate that set the pace for armament dynamics. What follows is a short review of these four main components of contemporary armament dynamics.

The action-reaction-over-reaction pattern

Historically, the mutually stimulating action-reaction pattern is the most common explanation of the arms race. Driven by rivalry for territory and wealth, by security dilemmas, ideological fervour, suspicion and fear, pairs of contending nations or alliances steadily build up their arsenals. In the process they not only react to the real moves of the adversary but also raise the stakes as a response to his imaginary moves—to what they perceive as measures or intention by the opponent to bolster his military strength and drive for supremacy. The final outcome is frequently an over-response by both sides. A chain reaction of spiralling armament is set into motion.

At present, with the focus less on quantities and more on technological advances, the action-reaction effect has a much stronger and wider impact than in the past. The two main traditional assumptions of the action-reaction theory were (a) that an increase in a nation's armaments is positively proportionate to its opponent's armaments expenditures, and (b) that the rate of arms acceleration is negatively proportionate to the level of existing arsenals. Because of the technology race, both these assumptions are losing their validity today. In order to meet expected breakthroughs by the adversary, the technology race creates a propensity to project far into the future. By advanced planning, it tries to match the long lead-times required for the development of new weapons. Such postures naturally stimulate over-response—a reaction out of proportion to real challenges. Consequently, overreaction becomes a permanent condition. At the same time, the rate of technological innovation tends to subdue inhibitions that may arise in view of the attained level of armament. The quick sequence of development and deployment in recent years, of new and more advanced weapon systems by the United States and the Soviet Union despite the awareness of escalation effects (e.g. inter-continental ballistic missiles, new generations of nuclear warheads, multiple independently targetable re-entry vehicles (MIRVs), laser-guided weapons, etc.) serves to prove the point.

An integral ingredient of the action-reaction dynamic is the exaggerated atmosphere of secrecy surrounding security and military affairs. This has tightened since the Second World War, as attested by the mushrooming activities of the various intelligence services. Introduced as a matter of principle and accepted by a meeting of minds as a rule of behaviour, secrecy generates a propensity to 'worst-case' analyses, i.e. contingency planning based on pessimistic assumptions ascribing to the adversary intentions and capabilities far in excess of what reliable intelligence would suggest. Worst-case analysis, in fact, means the institutionalization of overreaction. Secrecy undermines confidence and breeds mistrust. It also helps to whip up hawkish opinion behind armament, and to invent 'weapon gaps' to fuel the arms race. This was the case with the famous 'bomber gap' in the mid-1950s and the 'missile gap' in the 1960s in the United States. Thus, inordinate secrecy helps invigorate the action-reaction effect. It has become a formidable motive power behind armaments.

Since the Second World War, the action-reaction dynamic has been reinforced by ideological polarization and socio-political systemic confrontation. Much of the atmosphere of suspicion and fear comes from encapsulation into a Manichean mentality, from the ever greater intrusion of the state into the life of citizens, and from political dogma. All this has a divisive effect, tending to produce exaggerated images of the enemy that serve to sustain conflict postures. In such a climate, the armaments curve reacts nervously to any crisis and moves only along one plane: upward, never returning to its bases.

In sum, the action-reaction armaments dynamic is animated by political, ideological and psychological determinants. To the extent that international polarization—systemic, political and ideological—has become more intense the dynamics generated by action-reaction-overreaction has equally increased. One of the most deplorable consequences has been a climate that facilitates the abuse of the action-reaction pattern to mobilize public opinion to support the arms race.

Let us add a final remark concerning the action-reaction effect in a triangular constellation, the direction in which the situation is now evolving, with China entering the arms race as a potential superpower. Such triangular dynamics tend to have a much more energizing effect than bilateral rivalry. It seems plausible that if a party to the arms race must take account of not one but two adversaries, his reaction and over-reaction will enhance accordingly. The threat from the third party serves as a catalyst for the race between the other two antagonists. It was precisely the triangular dynamics between the Soviet Union, the Western powers and Nazi Germany that exploded into the Second World War. It was also the triangular dynamics between the United States, the Soviet Union and China that contributed to the protraction of the Indo-China war. Thus, considering the growing role of China in international affairs, as well as the sensitivity of military relations between China and the Soviet Union on the one hand, and of Sino-American relations on the other, we may assume a further intensification of the action-reaction effect and its increasing impact on the current arms race.

Military doctrines, threat postures and autistic pressures

The discussion of the political and ideological climate in contemporary international relations, in its military context, leads us to a central concept in current armament dynamics: the autistic effect. 'Autism' refers to the hardening, under specific circumstances, of hostile impulses and motives into obstinate and persistent attitudes. Such a process becomes self-sustaining and impervious to changes in the environment as well as to possible alterations in the postures of the adversary. A penetrating study of the behavioural consequences of contemporary international polarization has revealed that autism—self-reproduced hostility—plays an important role in impelling the current arms race. Catalysed by the doctrine of deterrence and threats as reflected in the balance of terror, autistic pressures or bilateral autism reinforce political antagonism and the rush to arm.

The doctrine of deterrence has a special place in contemporary armament dynamics. Devised to fit the emergence of nuclear weapons, deterrence has become paramount in current military thinking and great-power strategies. Its main premise is that the foe can be held in check by the threat of nuclear retaliation. It thus requires a constant increase in armaments, to enhance retaliatory power and inflict potentially ever greater damage on the enemy. Consequently, the doctrine of deterrence has become a compelling prescription for moving up the ladder of armament. Presented to the general public as a formula to preserve peace, deterrence has in fact meant the establishment of a threat system, the constant perfection of the tools of war, and the perpetuation of a state of continuous bellicose preparation. As nuclear arms have improved and have been made more operational, the concept of retaliation has been widened, finding reflection in ever more refined war strategies. It started with the crude 'massive retaliation' threat, moved on to the concept of mutual assured destruction (MAD), which made the populations of large cities hostages to nuclear attack, to end up with counterforce strategies directed mainly against targets of military significance.

No other element of the political and ideological superstructure of contemporary international relations has had a greater impact on armament than the doctrine of deterrence; it locks the contending parties in an open-ended arms race. It both stimulates military R&D and the war industry to ever greater efforts, and tends to petrify structured hostility to the point of no return.

It is in this context that autistic pressures become evident. Threats originally directed at the adversary and designed to deter his military ambitions turn inward, generating security fears and a quest for stronger retaliatory power. External threats enter the internal security debate mainly as legitimation for arming. In the process, preoccupation with the enemy fades into a self-centred and inner-directed security psychosis, laden with images of the foe and manifested in an urge for yet more arms. The consequences are far-reaching. The traditionally tension-producing postures of *para bellum* or 'peace through strength' harden and petrify. No level of armaments seems satisfactory. In relation to the strategic-arms limitation talks between the United States and the USSR, we observe that, though the talk is of 'parity', the race is for superior strength—for strategic superiority. Growing military capability by one side is interpreted by the other as political and military intent, and the race for strategic superiority becomes a permanent condition. In fact, at the centres of power, strategic superiority is believed to have an essential political utility. The national security adviser to President Carter, Zbigniew Brzezinski, put it this way:

I don't consider nuclear superiority to be politically meaningless. . . . The perception by others or by oneself of someone else having 'strategic superiority' can influence political behaviour. In other words, it has the potential for political exploitation even if in an actual warfare situation the differences may be at best or at worst on the margin.[1]

The race for strategic superiority is also one of the reasons for the failure of SALT to halt strategic armament. Despite arms-control negotiations, it is becoming evident that we have now reached a stage where the pursuit of strategic superiority and, indeed, efforts to achieve first-strike capability have become the focal point of the arms race.

New technology and military research and development

The horizons opened by the findings of nuclear physics and the second technological revolution are essential for the current race for strategic superiority and first-strike capabilities.

Military R&D today absorbs the talents of about half a million scientists and engineers around the globe, 85 per cent of this effort being undertaken in the United States and the Soviet Union. The present size of military R&D is a recent international phenomenon. It grew rapidly after the Second World War, reflecting the shift in the arms race from quantity to quality. Whereas before the Second World War military R&D consumed less than 1 per cent of armaments expenditures, it now absorbs 10 to 15 per cent. Investment in military R&D has increased four to five times faster than the general rate of growth of global armaments expenditures.

Historically, we seem now to be at a turning-point that is similar, albeit at a higher level, to the revolutionary change in military technology that occurred in the late 1950s and early 1960s with the launching of Sputnik, the development of intercontinental ballistic missiles, of the nuclear-powered strategic submarine, of the supersonic bomber and the high-speed re-entry missiles. At that time, the technological breakthrough radically changed the strategic scene, making nuclear weapons more operational and extending their reach to all continents, including the national territories of the United States and the Soviet Union. Today, the perils loom even larger. Both the cumulative improvement in military technology of the last decade in accuracy, reliability and manoeuvrabiiity and the new weapon systems developed, produced and deployed or in the stage of development—the MIRVs, the MARVs (manoeuvrable re-entry vehicles), long-range cruise missiles, mobile intercontinental ballistic missiles (ICBMs), satellite hunter killers, en-hanced-radiation and enhanced-blast nuclear warheads, etc.—immensely in-crease the nuclear warfare potential and make first-strike capabilities a feasible proposition.

Forces impelling military R&D

An important aspect in the operation of military R&D is what may be called the 'Frankenstein drive': an autonomous impulse which Robert McNamara has pointedly defined as 'a kind of intrinsic, mad momentum of its own'. In fact, we may speak of forces—structural, institutional and operational—that impel military R&D and that act as a powerful drive behind armaments. Four of these forces are of basic significance: (a) the impulse to technological competition, (b) the stabilizing and invigorating effects of the long lead-times, (c) the follow-on imperative and growth propensity, and (d) the block-building and cross-fertilization effect.

The impulse to technological competition derives from the very size, expansion and goal-setting of military R&D. Military research has spread into a large number of industrial enterprises, laboratories, universities, special research institutes and centres of learning. As modern warfare encompasses all aspects of human life and invades all environments—land, sea, deep-sea, space, jungles and deserts—so also has military R&D penetrated almost all scientific disciplines —natural, social, medical or behavioural. It is only natural that the hundreds of thousands of scientists and engineers dispersed in thousands of research plants, and working on parallel problems, should be competing among themselves in inventing, developing and perfecting new arms and weapon systems. Moreover, in order to stimulate results and achieve optimum efficiency, 'healthy' competition is consciously sustained by the authorities through the allocation of funds, the structured rivalry between different services (army, air forces, navy) and various laboratories, and the procurement policy.

Thus, competition in military R&D is no casual phenomenon. It is a built-in structural feature complemented for the same purpose of efficiency, by interaction and co-ordination.

The rivalry within the military R&D network is partly comparable to the competition in other socio-economic domains, where prestige, material interests and group pressures are vital. However, the scientists' motivation has additional incentives in the shape of scientific curiosity and the prestige attached to the work. Secondly, competition is tougher both because of the size of the venture and because the end-product can never be allowed to fall below the highest technological standards. By definition, new weapons must be better and more efficient than the previous generation, and of course better than those in the hands of the adversary. Certain criteria of cost-efficiency must also be observed. Though military R&D is probably one field where economic factors play a minimal role, instances arise where the abundance of new weapon systems with similar applications pose problems of competition in production and deployment. Such a case was the recent rivalry in the United States between the B-1 bomber and the long-range cruise missiles. The choice fell to the cruise missiles, and Secretary of Defense Harold Brown was quick to point to cost-effectiveness as the crucial criterion for the selection.

The outcome of this rivalry is a race at the national level that reinforces the race at the international level. In fact, researchers in the military R&D network are more often preoccupied with the better-known exploits of fellow researchers in rival institutions in their own country than with the details of the less-known achievements abroad. Consequently, the autonomous domestic dynamic of the race tends to exceed its international momentum.

One may point incidentally to the extremely detrimental effects on national and international development of the commanding role of military R&D in science and technology. Not only does it absorb the best scientific and technological talents, and thus represent a misallocation of human and material resources, but it also distorts priorities in research and development. It distorts the direction of research and corrupts scientific activity which could be basic for human welfare. The spill-over effects into civilian fields are negligible in comparison with the investments.[2] The loss is particularly great considering the requirements of the Third World.

The second force listed is linked to the long lead-times needed for the development of modern arms. It takes up to ten years, or more, to complete a cycle from the initial stages of discovery to the mastering of technology and the production of new weapon systems. This has several consequences. First, it assures stability, constancy and continuity both to military R&D and the armaments momentum. Secondly, long lead-times intertwine with bureaucratic inertia, infusing additional vigour into the armaments process. It is difficult to withdraw from a commitment to a specific weapon system once an initial investment has been made, a decision taken, and the development effort set in full motion. Thirdly, long lead-times influence the decision-making process in armaments, by exerting pressure for early decisions in order to pre-empt the adversary and make the new weapons available on time. The technological imperative weighs both on the situational judgements and the choice of arms. Fourthly, long lead-times also stimulate the efficiency of military R&D. As the race in technology aims to close or widen the technological gap between the contending parties, the urge emerges to shorten the lead-times for the development of new weapons. This, in turn, contributes, to the domestic dynamics of military R&D and the arms race as a whole.

In the context of the long lead-times in military R&D we may also point to an important side-effect: the negative impact on arms control. While arms-control negotiators discuss the limitation of known and existing weapon systems, military R&D, protected by secrecy, proceeds with the development of new weapons, which undermines both the negotiations and the agreements concluded. The pace of weapon innovation generally moves faster than the pace of arms-control negotiations. And as certain categories of arms become obsolete, so do agreements that refer to them. Thus, in addition to being a driving force behind armaments, military R&D also obstructs arms-control and disarmament negotiations.

A third force in military R&D is the 'follow-on' imperative—the urge to go ahead and expand. Under conditions of an arms race with the focus on the qualitative improvement of weapons, it becomes vitally necessary to maintain and expand military R&D. Preservation or gaining the lead in technology is today crucial for the goals of the military establishments, and positions of power on the international scene. The more advanced the technological race, the greater the reliance on military R&D. The urge is to step up the technological effort. The completion of one weapon system requires a follow-up by a new one, the development of offensive arms requires a response in the development of new defensive weapons and vice versa. The highly specialized manpower mobilized for military R&D must be retained and protected, and the entire enterprise be kept on a constant footing of readiness and alertness. Moreover, the involvement in ever-new research projects and directions calls for a steady extension of facilities and for increasing manpower. Thus, military R&D tends to swell and, in turn, to invigorate the arms race. It has become force in its own right, and its capabilities and readiness weigh heavily in the balance of power. As a technological, military and political asset, military R&D has become an instrument of diplomacy, adding force to negotiating positions.

The fourth force in the operation of military R&D that contributes to its effectiveness is what Kosta Tsipis[3] has called the building blocks of weapon development, or cross-fertilization effect. He remarks: 'Quite often a major military system grows out of the maturing of several seemingly unrelated technologies—the building blocks—which, when pulled together, form a new and often unexpected system or make technically possible a system envisioned years before.'[4] Many projects initially moving in different directions converge later to result in a new system, as was the case with strategic reconnaissance-satellite programmes. The great variety of research projects and the mass of scientists involved allow for a high cross-fertilization of ideas and projects. But at the same time the building-block force generates pressures that evade control. In his *Origins of the MIRVs*, Herbert York has emphasized this aspect: 'Programmes evolving from many independent and seemingly unrelated purposes and decisions, cannot be controlled or stopped by directly confronting them. They can only be slowed or stopped by slowing or stopping the arms race as a whole.'[5] This is but one indication of the complex problems we may encounter in trying to bring military R&D under control.

Destabilizing effects, arms control and irrationality

The race in arms technology has a pervasively destabilizing effect on the world military balance. Each new discovery, in offence or defence, contributes to instability because it gives advantages to one side, which is often perceived as intending to use its advantage to strike first. From a more general perspective, the technological race promotes instability in two ways: through real advances and through psychological effects. Real advances in technology tend to destroy whatever stability in the balance of forces may be apparent, while psychological effects intensify the race, by reinforcing responses enhanced by secrecy—worst-case planning and over-reaction. The higher the spiral and the more complex the technology, the more difficult it is to judge and control the balance; hence, the more shaky any position of stability.

Thus, the race in military technology increases and amplifies elements of uncertainty in the military environment. As it spreads and acquires global dimensions adding fuel to local conflicts and regional arms races, it also contributes to the growth of international tension.

For arms control, the effect of the race in military technology is devastating, for the former cannot keep pace with the latter. The technological race wrecks the main purpose of arms control, to arrive at some military stability by steered balanced armaments. Faced with failure because of technological dynamics, some arms controllers believe that stability can be achieved only by adjusting to the very highest level of weapon perfection, which, obviously, is a prescription for even fiercer rivalry.

The focus on high military technology affects arms control in an even more immediate way. It corrupts the negotiating process, introducing elements into the talks themselves which accelerate armament dynamics. Efforts to attain quantitative limitations in armaments generate pressures for qualitative compensation. While the negotiators are trying to agree on a quantitative ceiling, innovations are in the meantime being introduced which make even smaller arsenals more efficient and destructive. The SALT exercise serves as a good example. This practice has gone hand in hand with another device—the bargaining-chip method—which consists in the development, parallel to the negotiations, of new weapon systems supposed initially to force the adversary's hand during the talks, but which in the process are absorbed into the military inventory. This was the case with the MIRVs which, we were told, were first developed as a bargaining chip in the SALT negotiations, but finally became a key strategic weapon in the arsenals of both the United States and the USSR.

An effect similar to the quantity/quality compensation is achieved by the passage from simple first-generations testing methods to more advanced and sophisticated techniques. Thus, the 1963 Partial Test Ban Treaty moved nuclear tests underground, and the 1974 Threshold Test Ban Treaty was designed for a continuation of tests at a lower threshold but with improved techniques. Finally confronted with different force structures and levels of equipment in the United States and the USSR, the SALT negotiations succumbed to reconciling the specific requirements of both military establishments by accepting ceilings which made allowances for their actual force levels and existing weapon programmes. Thus, under pressure of technology, arms control turned into a collaborative exercise in mutual armament.

The current stalemate in arms control reflects the dilemmas created by the explosion of military technology. The accelerated rate of military technological innovation further exacerbates the crisis.

No element in contemporary armament dynamics has assumed such a central position, with such a profound impact on the arms race, as military R&D. The core and nerve centre of the race in technology, it is the mainstay and most energizing factor in the arms race, operating so as to tie armament dynamics organically to economic and production structures, to the military establishment, the state bureaucracy and the innovative drive of the second technological revolution. As such it escapes social control and tends to become ungovernable.

An air of irrationality and absurdity underlies the hasty and nervous exertions of military R&D. There is little sense to the accumulation of overkill capabilities and the deployment of ever-more advanced nuclear arms around the world. Europe is a point in case. Its nuclear arsenals grew erratically as newly perfected warheads were made available, the latest being the neutron bomb. Foe and friend alike fall victim to the terror of the robot-like military R&D production line. The very pace of the arms race is largely decided within the military R&D network through autonomous technological drift.

The alliance of establishments

The autonomous domestic armaments drive impelled by military R&D finds powerful social support through the alliance between the military, industrial, state bureaucratic and scientific-technological establishments. It was Dwight D. Eisenhower who, in his farewell Presidential address, drew attention to the phenomenon of the 'military-industrial complex' as a mighty influence within society. He said:

This conjunction of an immense military establishment and a large arms industry is new in the American experience. The total influence—economic, political, even spiritual—is felt in every city, every State House, every office of the Federal government. . . . In the councils of government, we must guard against the acquisition of unwarranted influence, whether sought or unsought, by the military-industrial complex. The potential for the disastrous rise of misplaced power exists and will persist.[6]

These were not casual remarks. They reflected a deeply felt reality and growing anxiety not only about armament lobbies but also about the democratic fabric of society. In the context of the Indo-China adventure, these words had a prophetic ring. 'We must never let the weight of this combination endanger our liberties and democratic processes,' Eisenhower emphasized.[7] Professor George Kistiakowsky, the President's Special Assistant for Science and Technology, notes in his memoirs that the President 'had talked to me more than once about his concern with what the speech called *the military-industrial complex*'.[8] Eisenhower was unhesitatingly in favour of basic academic research, Kistiakowsky reports the President as saying, but he 'feared only the rising power of military science'.[9] As research has become central to the technological revolution—Eisenhower stressed in his message—we must also be alert to the 'danger that public policy could itself become the captive of a scientific-technological élite'.[10]

Yet almost two decades later we still do not take this authoritative warning seriously.

Though Eisenhower referred to the 'military-industrial complex', he was evidently concerned not only about the alliance between the military and arms industry, but also about the role of the state political bureaucracy in 'every State House, every office of the Federal government', and the position of power captured by the military 'scientific-technological élite'.

Thus, by identifying the internal social forces behind armaments—'the web of special interest', in Eisenhower's words[11]—we may speak of the military-industrial-technological-bureaucratic complex (MITBC), which wields formidable power. It reflects an organic unity of both the strongest elements in the economic base of the society, and the most potent elements in the political and ideological superstructure. All four establishments have developed, for reasons of their own—profits, professional engagement, lucrative positions, the satisfaction of personal and group interests, diplomatic usefulness, etc.—a vested interest in military strength, and they exert their influence to enhance these interests by separate action and co-operative undertakings. Their horizontal reach in society has spread constantly since the Second World War, and their vertical influence on the decision-making processes has grown sharply with the explosion in military technology in recent years. It is not necessary to study the inside stories of governments, such as the *Pentagon Papers*, to pin-point the facts. We know only too well that armaments, power structures and power politics have a decisive influence on the formation of governments, external and internal politics, and the way our world is steered.

The MITBC is by no means an exclusively Western phenomenon. We lack sufficient studies concerning the Soviet Union, but this does not mean that such social forces do not exist there. Certainly, the MITBC, set in a society with state-owned industry and the prevalence of the state in all spheres of social and economic life, operates in a different way than in a society with privately owned industry and a different socio-political complexion. Yet the motivation springs from similar roots, the inner dynamics moves along related lines and the effects are the same.

Indeed considering its socio-economic structure and the broad dominance of the state, we may ask if the MITBC in the Soviet Union does not have an even more pervasive influence than the corresponding corporate constituencies in the West. Without detailed study and research, it is difficult to give a ready answer. There is, however, one fundamental element in the structure of the Soviet economy and state management which may allow for some tentative conclusions. Official economic theory and praxis in the Soviet Union, as well as in China, adheres to the orthodoxy which asserts that heavy industry, the mainstay of arms manufacture, must have absolute priority over other industrial branches, including light industry and the production of consumer goods. However great the share of civilian production in the heavy industrial sector, this is highly indicative of the weight of military considerations in the management of the state as a whole. To this we may add that military, industrial, technological and bureaucratic interest groups are prominently represented at all levels of the party and government hierarchy. It may be difficult to ascertain just where the main lines of influence lie. Are they with the generals, the bureaucrats, the technocrats or the industrial managers? But it is hard to deny that they carry important weight, or even dominate the decision-making processes, judging from the composition of the leadership in the party and state bodies and organizations, and from a simple reading of the East European press.

In the context of the special position of the MITBC in the councils of the state, and its influence on politics, the economy and social affairs, a number of broader societal and systemic problems emerge. Considerable evidence points to processes which generate malfunctions of society and structural distortions of a fundamental nature both in national and international life. Eisenhower was concerned, and rightly so, with the impact on liberties and the democratic processes. With military interests gaining prevalence in state affairs, there is reason to fear that participation in, and democratic control over, public matters will diminish and authoritarian trends increase. Such basic human values as peace, the sanctity of human life and non-violence must suffer.

Parallel problems are posed by the seizure of controlling positions by the military in science and technology. The socio-economic consequences are far-reaching. Acquiring the highest competence in modern technology, the military demands not only a decisive voice in the choice of arms, but aspires also to predominance in determining priorities in other crucial spheres of economic activity and human development. This is most evident in the Third World countries where, in the wake of the world arms race, militarism and militarization have spread alarmingly.

There are other economic, social and political outgrowths. One, of basic significance, is the waste of resources. Another is the global proliferation of arms promoted by the pursuit of economies of scale. A third is the gravitation of investments, because of attractive conditions (profit incentives, less public control, state support, elimination of rational economic calculus) away from civilian projects and into military production. Finally, under the pressure of the different corporate MITBC constituencies, basic human needs are degraded, the system becomes rigid through a proliferating bureaucracy and loses flexibility to respond in a human way to human affairs.

Many other instances of critical detrimental effects of the MITBC impact in national and international affairs could be mentioned. They all have one crucial feature in common: in a dialectical way they all sustain and accelerate armament dynamics and the arms race.

Notes

1. Cf. Zbigniew Brzezinski in an interview with Jonathan Power, *International Herald Tribune*, 10 October 1977.
2. Cf. Seymour Melman, 'Twelve Propositions on Productivity and War Economy', *Armed Forces and Society*, Vol. 1, No. 4, August 1975.
3. Kosta Tsipis, 'The Building Blocks of Weapon Development', *The Bulletin of the Atomic Scientists*, April 1977.
4. Ibid.
5. Herbert York, *The Origins of MIRV*, Stockholm, SIPRI Research Report No. 9, 1973, p. 23.
6. Dwight D. Eisenhower, *Waging Peace, The White House Years 1956-1961, A Personal Account*, p. 616, New York, Doubleday & Co., 1965.
7. Ibid.
8. George B. Kistiakowsky, *A Scientist at the White House*, p. 425, Cambridge, Mass., Harvard University Press, 1976.
9. Ibid.
10. Ibid.
11. Eisenhower, op. cit., p. 615.

On the theory of armaments dynamics

Gert Krell
University of Frankfurt am Main
Peace Research Institute, Frankfurt

In political and scholarly debates on the causes of the armament dynamics in the East-West conflict, three models are generally offered, with several variants.

The nationalistic model

On both sides the nationalistic interpretation of the arms race still looms large in public opinion and in official statements. It is always the enemy who has aggressive intentions or at least bears responsibility for the rivalry and the conflict. Both sides pretend that their own arms efforts are purely defensive. In the extreme variant, this asymmetry is explained by a fundamental aggressiveness of the other system.

However, recent political debate has tended to become more differentiated. Most politically relevant forces in the West have acknowledged the existence of an at least partial interest of the Soviet Union in détente and arms control, while the Soviet leadership has long distinguished between 'aggressive' and 'realistic' forces in the West.

The systemic model

In the systemic model the causes of the conflict and the arms race are not seen as being located on one side only. The arms race appears rather as a consequence of structural problems of the international system.

The variant 'competition of interests'. Those who hold to this variant emphasize the real conflicts of interest and values between the superpowers and their alliances. In its most radical form this variant is articulated by the People's

Paper published in *Bulletin of Peace Proposals*, Vol. 10, No. 1, 1979. Abridged from Gert Krell, 'Zur Theorie und Empirie der Rüstungsdynamik', in Klaus-Dieter Schwarz (ed.), *Sicherheitspolitik. Analysen zur politischen und militärischen Sicherheit*, 3rd ed., Bad Honnef, 1978 (the empirical chapter on United States defence policy is not included here). Translated by Gert Krell.

Republic of China, which simply combines the two extreme nationalistic positions of the other side's fundamental aggressiveness. As recently as in early 1977 Hua Kuo-feng stated that 'imperialism' and 'social imperialism' both by their very nature represented war.[1]

In a more moderate form, the concept of competing claims and interests in the East-West conflict—without the nationalistic interpretation—has since détente become a part of the diplomatic vocabulary. This no longer aims at the dissolution of or a unilateral accommodation by the opposing system, but rather at a limitation and regulation of the competitive relationship.

'North-South conflict within the East-West conflict'. In this variant the October revolution and the building-up of 'socialism in one country' are interpreted as the dissociation of an underdeveloped society from the dominating influence of and exploitation by Western capitalism: accordingly, the East-West conflict is seen as a kind of hidden North-South conflict. There can be no doubt that the Soviet Union even after its 'dissociation' has for decades been inferior to the capitalist West in its economic development, military strength, and diplomatic weight, and some after-effects of this inferiority can still be seen today. It is also true that the foreign policy interests of the Soviet Union have sometimes combined with national revolutionary movements, while the West has often tried to secure its colonial possessions with military force and in doing so has supported privileged and conservative élite groups.

But this model of an internationalized class conflict has lost much of its appeal with the emergence of a rough military balance between both alliance systems, with secure second-strike capabilities, and with 'overkill' potentials for mutual annihilation. The conflict of the two social systems in East and West has always contained a large portion of power politics. Soon after the Second World War one could speak of a 'cold war' between two socialist countries (USSR-Yugoslavia), and by now the Sino-Soviet split has led to an export of arms races and to proxy wars.

'Security dilemma'. In this theorem, too, the two nationalistic positions are combined, but this time not the enemy images but the self-images. John Herz, who developed the theorem of a 'security dilemma', proceeded on the assumption that the political intentions of both superpowers were more or less defensive. Because of the anarchic structure of the international system, with independent units capable of using force and not subordinated to a superior authority, a race for security ensued. Fearing attack, conquest or destruction, every state in its pursuit of security accumulated and armed forces in order to be able to counter the power of its 'opponent'.[2] Referring to the arms race, the United States diplomat George F. Kennan once defined the security dilemma in the following words:

Today the military rivalry, in naval power as in nuclear weaponry, is simply riding along on its own momentum, like an object in space. It has no foundation in real interests—no foundation in fact, but in fear, and in an essentially irrational fear at that. It is carried not by any reason to believe that the other side *would*, but only by an hypnotic fascination with the fact that it *could*. . . . There is a Kafkaesque quality to this encounter. We stand like two men who find themselves confronting each other with guns in their hands, neither with any real reason to believe that the other has murderous intentions towards him, but both hypnotized by the uncertainty and the unreasoning fear of the fact that the other is armed. The two armament efforts feed and justify each other.[3]

Approaches emphasizing domestic variables

Maintaining peace by military means (we here accept the official legitimization on both sides) requires apparatuses, institutions, and ideologies that sustain this policy in the individual societies; it requires a military bureaucracy, and a political, propagandistic, technological, and economic infrastructure. It is this infrastructure and it is the social functions of arms production and defence policy that the 'critical' approaches are mainly concerned with. (Some systemic approaches also include domestic variables.) Three main areas of research can be discerned: conflict strategies and ideologies, arms interests, and the social and economic structure of a society.

Conflict strategies and ideologies

The fallacies of deterrence strategy. There is good reason to suppose that the system of nuclear deterrence in the East-West conflict has reduced the risk of war between countries members of the two different alliances, and also between countries within an alliance; though at the price of increasing the risk of war in the less clearly defined peripheral regions.[4] But—and this is often overlooked—the system of nuclear deterrence cannot even in the central conflict area reduce the risk of nuclear war to zero, and that means that over a long period of time this risk will increase to 1: one day nuclear war will occur. Although the risks of the deterrence system can be influenced, deterrence policy by necessity produces instabilities.

A major requirement of successful deterrence is the rational behavior of the actors. In reality, societies and governments often behave far less rationally than is asked for in the theory. History is full of examples of states that have engaged in suicidal adventures. Of all governmental decisions leading to big wars after 1910, about 60 per cent turned out to be wrong—and that concerns the estimate of the capabilities and intentions of the other graat povers at the time when the war began, as well as the assessment of the actual course of the war and its consequences. We know from many studies and simulations of the decision-making process that the number of misperceptions and mistakes tends to increase in crisis situations. Dtress, threats, insecurity, and time pressure reduce the capabilities for a rational processing and evaluation of information.

Deterrence policy not only strains the rationality of the individual systems and their decision-making processes, it also results in a continuous competition for security with its attendant risks for international stability. The United States social scientist Anatol Rapoport has used the example of a fire in a theatre to explain the difference between individual and collective rationality: if a fire breaks out in a theatre, then individual rationality recommends every single visitor to try to reach the exit as fast as he can. Irrespective of the other visitors' behaviour, this is the 'optimal' strategy for everyone. But if everybody hurries to the exit, only a few will succeed in reaching it in time. A more disciplined audience, however, has a far greater chance of leaving the theatre at short notice.

Correspondingly, attempts by nation states or alliances to optimize their security interests individually by no means lead to more security for both sides. One side's deterrent is the other side's terror; and a spiral of threats, fears and counter-threats develops. The dynamics of technological invention figure large in this process; for in a technology-intensive environment, when positive and reliable information about the other side is scarce, one's own technological research becomes a measure for present and possible future threats. Charles Schultze, budget director under Kennedy and Johnson, and one of President Carter's economic advisers, described this technological 'autism' as follows:

As we learn about new technology, *we project it forward* into the Soviet arsenal, thereby *creating new potential contingencies* to be covered by our own forces. . . . Continually advancing technology and the risk aversion of military planners therefore combine to produce ever more complex and expensive weapons systems and ever more contingencies to guard against.[5]

But when each side thinks that its security needs do not permit it to forgo important new defence technologies, then both will always want to balance (or anticipate) the other side's possible advantages. Thus a basic principle of stable deterrence, the elimination of arms-racing tendencies, will be violated again and again through technological progress.

Enemy images. Mutual fear is a main element of the conflict between East and West and one of the foundations of the arms race. But threat analysis is based on information which is often incomplete or selected. Evaluation and judgement are unavoidable. Now, obviously, the term 'enemy image' refers to an analysis that departs from reality. But this criterion cannot be sufficient for a definition. First of all, there is a legitimate margin for controversies about what information and which interpretations most closely reflect reality. Secondly, one can also have a 'friend image', i.e. an image of the other side that is too optimistic and minimizes real dangers. And finally, neither anti-communism nor anti-imperialism is simply a product of propaganda by dominating interest groups: these enmities have also developed historically from the personal experiences of groups and individuals which do not at all belong to the ruling classes.

Thus, it would be an undue simplification to reduce the East-West conflict to irrational or manipulated images of the enemy; but there has been an excess of hostility until this day, an unnecessary amount of tension. It appears in more subtle forms of black-and-white thinking, when in the assessments and interpretations of conflicts the other side is systematically and one-sidedly incriminated—by omitting information which would reflect on one's own side or by a double-standard evaluation of equal or similar behaviour. These subtle forms of 'enemy images' can be found in Western views of the Korean War, for instance, or more recently in comments on political developments in Africa.

Arms interests

Bureaucratic politics. The theorem of bureaucratic politics is based on the assumption that defence decisions come about not in a rational process of information-gathering and debate but by compromises between various organizations that follow standard operation procedures and develop individual 'department ideologies'. Thus the interaction among states would only have the function of legitimizing the internal dynamics *(Eigendynamik)* of these bureaucratic interests. Allison and Morris have explained this theorem in a classic statement:

> While actions of foreign governments and uncertainty about the intentions of other countries are obviously important, the analysis above suggests that the weapons in the American and Soviet force postures are *predominantly* the result of factors *internal* to each nation. Not only are organizational goals and procedures domestically determined, but the resulting satisfactions of political officials are to be found overwhelmingly at home.[6]

Obviously the defence bureaucracy is important in this bureaucratic decision-making process. The defence bureaucracy is in charge of large and expensive programmes; it regards the fight for hardware and its share of the budget as essential. The military leadership stands under constant organizational pressure. As for the United States, Morton Halperin—another pioneer of the theorem of bureaucratic politics—once pointed out that the army always wanted the latest tank and the latest helicopter, the air force the latest aeroplane, and the navy the latest naval aircraft and the latest aircraft carrier.[7]

It is the rationale of the defence bureaucracy—as of every other organization—to maintain and improve its autonomy and morale, its central mission, its role, and its budget. These bureaucratic interests are reflected in the views of the military about the defence budget, and about the relationship between defence and the economy and between armaments and foreign policy. It is an empirical question whether and to what extent these bureaucratic interests will prevail. The specific conservatism of the military bureaucracy may in some constellations be an obstacle to innovations in defence technology; it is not at all certain that the military will always demand huge increases in defence spending or fight for all kinds of new weapons systems and/or military missions. Also, inter-service rivalry may often reduce rather than increase the influence of the military. It is also doubtful if the military will support the more dangerous and aggressive political decisions. In the United States, the military on the average have not adopted a more aggressive stance compared to the civilian decision-makers, in internal debates about interventions. But they have asked for military escalation and the full commitment of military force, once the decision to intervene has been made.[8] Finally, in all their demands the military and the defence bureaucracy—and this is true at least for the states relevant to the East-West context—depend on support from important parts of the other civilian decision-making bodies; and thus the reference to the interests of *the* military and *the* defence bureaucracy alone does not explain too much.

The 'military-industrial complex': combined defence interests. The concept of the military-industrial complex is probably the most common of those that concentrate on domestic factors of the arms race. The theoretical and political debate has one of its origins in Eisenhower's famous and often—although usually selectively—quoted farewell address of January 1961; the concept gained in significance during the course of the Viet Nam War and the ABM-debate towards the end of the 1960s. Eisenhower warned not only of the defence industry, but of a combination of influences that could be felt at various stages:

The Congressman who seek a new defense establishment in his district; the company in Los Angeles, Denver or Baltimore that wants an order for more airplanes; the services which want them; the armies of scientists who want so terribly to test out their newest views. Put all these together, and you have a lobby.[9]

This original meaning of the MIC-concept, which referred to the combined effects of a military bureaucracy and an industrial arms production as significant factors in the decision-making process and in the social and economic structure of a society, has been fundamental to this day Ideally we may distinguish between four positions:

The conservatives support the military-industrial complex, because they look upon it as a safeguard of security and an instrument of foreign-policy interests.

The technocrats criticize defects in military procurement such as cost overruns, excess profits, corruption, dual programming, and poor efficiency on the supply and the demand side.

The liberals criticize the MIC's political influence on defence policy and the influence of the 'war system' on the economy.

The radicals regard the United States and correspondingly the Soviet Union as a whole as one huge military-industrial complex.

The concept of the military-industrial complex has repeatedly been criticized as a conspiracy 'theory', and some authors actually use it in this sense. More serious representatives of the MIC-concept, however, do not proceed from the image of an obscure, yet well-organized military-industrial mafia; but are more concerned about the militarization of traditional group interests, such as the interests of large organizations in survival and expansion, the sales interests of industry, technocratic interests of researchers and inventors, and employment interests of workers and trade-unionists. More important may be a critique that does not deny the many empirical details of the MIC-debate, but challenges the range and explanatory value of the concept. The variety of terms such as 'political-military-industrial complex', 'administrative-military-industrial-scientific complex', 'political-ideological-scientific-technological-industrial complex', 'military-industrial-feudal-clerical complex', or 'military-industrial-West-Point complex' certainly demonstrate how shaky the foundations of this debate often are. Nobody will doubt that some kind of a military-industrial complex exists, but the 'definition' of this phenomenon seems difficult. In all highly industrialized countries that maintain armed forces, there has to be some kind of co-operation between the military and the defence industry. We should also bear in mind that cost-overruns and inefficiencies are not confined to the field of military procurement. Finally, we must remember that the military-industrial complex is not a monolith. There is competition among the services, the defence industry, and among defence-dependent regions for defence expenditures and weapons programmes; also, different parts of the MIC serve different functions and pursue interests that may be mutually exclusive.[10]

Objections to the MIC-concept may also be raised from a leftist viewpoint. In one of the few systematic studies of the military-industrial complex in the United States (covering the period 1963 to 1972), Czerwick and Mueller found that participation in the defence market, yielded only short-time advantages, if any, in the profit/sales and also the profit/capital rate. There has been a strong trend towards diversification, which makes use of the term 'defence industry' problematic: the defence market is only one of several markets even for the 'defence corporation'. Many of the symptoms usually criticized in studies of the military-industrial complex were found to be typical of organized capitalist economics as a whole. The often quoted 'Great Wall of China' between civilian and defence production was out of the question. Thus, 'in order to explain the pressures on domestic and foreign policy . . . the MIC cannot be isolated as a scapegoat. The social system as a whole is not to be excused at its expense'.[11]

The social and economic system

Class and armaments. Egbert Jahn, who regards the MIC—whatever part of reality it may explain—as a minor or a secondary phenomenon, proceeds on the assumption that defence policy is generally based on very real and recognizable contradictions of interests in the international system:

Defence policy is basically determined by the interests of the ruling classes in capitalism and the dominating social groups in bureaucratic socialism. . . . These dominating interests are in conflict with each other (conflicts between several national and subnational groups of the capitalist class and the socialist bureaucracy) as well as with the interests of the dominated classes and main social groups.[12]

This sociological approach wihch includes class relations emphasizes the relationship between internal and external conflicts. The research results of F. Hoffmann, who found that at various times in several European countries the dividing line between arguments for and against armaments always ran between the conservative and the progressive parties respectively, seem to support Jahn's assumption.[13] But it certainly would be ra rash conclusion to infer that the lower classes as a whole have always supported disarmament and the upper classes rearmament. Interests in domestic stability are compatible with different kinds of defence policy. There are significant differences among Soviet and United States élites about the sense and purpose of the nuclear arms race. Jahn replaces the utopian idea of proletarian internationalism, whose failure he describes in detail, with the utopian idea of a pacifistic internationalism which will rise to power worldwide and throw all weapons away. With that he remains within the constraints of the classic dilemma of Marxist theory and practice: the problem of simultaneous abolition of domination throughout the world.

But it is well justified in principle to include questions of social class interests in an analysis of arms-race dynamics. The determination of the contents of 'security', for instance, is influenced by social relations and background. The following statement by Senator Edward Kennedy in a hearing in 1972 may be illuminating in this context:

115

I agree with you, Mr Chairman, that the security interests of the people of my city of Boston are more threatened by violence in the streets of Boston than they are by 17 million peasants in North Vietnam.[14]

As for the East European countries of 'real socialism', Rudolf Bahro has written of groups that 'need the atmosphere of a besieged fortress to support their rule'. He points to the domestic risks which a reduction of troops and armaments would present to the conservative bureaucracy.[15]

Defence production as economic policy. To this day no systematic comparative studies exist on the economic impact of defence production in capitalist and socialist countries. The question about the relationship between the capitalist mode of production (or between capitalist development) and armaments, however, is often raised, although answers are highly divergent. The textbook version about Western capitalist economies (only fully developed capitalist economies are under discussion here) can be found in Samuelson's well-known *Economics*:

If there is a political will, our mixed economy can rather easily keep C[onsumption] + I[nvestment] + G[overnment] spending up to the level needed for full employment *without armament spending.*[16]

In 1943, Natalie Moszkovska had come to quite the opposite conclusion:

As the production of consumption goods cannot expand adequately due to the restricted purchasing power of the people, capital must increasingly turn to the manufacture of murderous weapons—even if it were otherwise peaceful. As matters stand it does not find any other field of application.[17]

Albert Szymanski has demonstrated that one should be very careful with general statements about the connection between capitalism and defence demand. He found that high defence expenditures do not necessarily correlate with low unemployment rates, and that growth rates in capitalist countries with low defence expenditures were higher on an average than in countries with larger defence expenditures.[18] Other social scientists, also using statistical methods, came to simular conclusions. Jong Ryool Lee found a strong negative correlation between defence expenditures as a percentage of GNP and the real growth rate in the United States from 1946 to 1969. Nardinelli and Ackermann's results also show a significant negative effect of defence expenditures on the growth of the civilian national product (real GNP minus defence expenditures) in the United States for the period 1946 to 1973.[19]

However, it would certainly be premature to conclude—as is sometimes done—that these statistical results once again demonstrate the follies of Marxist approaches. There are many (non-Marxist) capitalists who see a positive correlation between defence demand and prosperity, and there are many Marxists who do not agree with Baran/Sweezy's or Michael Reich's more orthodox findings. As far as the Federal Republic of Germany is concerned, Peter Schlotter and Manfred Schmidt have shown that one cannot speak of a permanent guarantee by the state for the accumulation of capital in the defence sector.[20] There can be no doubt, on the other hand, that defence demand in some cases has encouraged growth, at least regionally, and the validity of the above-quoted statistical analyses may have to be examined more thoroughly.

Armament dynamics in the United States (conclusions)

Finally, we want to consider how far the empirical results can be integrated and generalized.[21] The assumption that the arms race is predominantly determined by domestic factors certainly cannot be sustained throughout. At least, some ideas about the influence of domestic factors on defence policy have to be modified. The significance of domestic economic factors and of the military-industrial complex has sometimes been overrated, while the role of basic foreign policy and arms-control attitudes (including enemy images) has been underestimated. And one cannot simply speak of *the* interests of the defence bureaucracy. It is true that the Pentagon leadership of the Nixon era came very close to the cliché of 'bureaucratic interests' and 'bureaucratic truths'; but in the late McNamara period there was a core group in the Pentagon strongly committed to arms control. And finally, although United States conservatives preferred defence increases to defence cuts during 1971–74, a conservative position cannot be generally identified with expansions in the defence budget. In the 1950s, it was the conservative Eisenhower administration which, against Democratic objections, tried to keep the defence budget within certain limits, and that for economic reasons.

On the other hand, the analysis has shown that only in a very narrow sense can one speak of an action-reaction process between 'the' United States and the Soviet Union, at least as far as the period of détente around SALT I is concerned. The international level certainly forms a general background for and sets limits to interpretations and political actions—but there is a broad spectrum of perceptions of the threat, and there exist totally different views about the necessity and the use of certain reactions. Moreover, these reactions are influenced by many factors that have little or nothing to do with international politics.

No one can say with certainty how the Soviet Union would have 'reacted' to a more restrained United States defence and arms-control policy. But it seems conceivable that in Moscow the position of the supporters of détente and arms limitation would have been strengthened. With ABM there has been such a process of mutual learning. But ABM remains the only weapons system of significance to be effectively limited in the arms-control negotiations; and that not least because of the domestic opposition. The power of this opposition against ABM in the United States, however, was based on a very favourable and probably rare constellation. ABM met almost all criteria which make a weapons system 'vulnerable'. Not too many jobs were involved at the time of the decision; opposition against the project and sometimes very strong opposition came from the peace movement and the arms-control community and the civilian leadership in the Pentagon and from large sections of Congress, and—which is very rare—from unorganized public opinion. ABM was extremely expensive and highly questionable technologically.

If in the administration Kissinger's position had alone been relevant, or especially if the political views of the liberals—their perception of the conflict and their understanding of the many dimensions of security—had been representative of arms-control policy (which would require an analogous distribution of opinions in the electorate, of course), then despite economic defence interests the United States would have given clearer signals of restraint and made several attempts to transfer the learning process of ABM to other weapons systems and the dynamics of the arms race as a whole. In this respect one might call the arms race 'autistic'.

Inasmuch as enemy images, bureaucratic, economic and class interests prevent a more restrained armaments policy on the other side, too one might as well speak of an action-reaction process, because defence interests and ideologies mutually support each other. But it is an interaction process which should be characterized as 'mutual political interdiction'.[22] Political interdiction exists when the conflict constellation within one coalition—the current state of the internal debates and confrontations—shifts in reaction to signals that indicate changes in the actions and intentions of the coalition on the other side. Deliberate as well as incidental actions by or within a coalition may influence the 'correlation of forces' between those arguments supporting détente and those hostile to détente as they are advanced by the contending actors in the other camp.

From this follows that those groups who are interested in détente and arms limitations must support their domestic positions mutually by signals of restraint and a willingness to co-operate. If arms control remains confined to the level of international diplomatic negotiations, it will constantly be jeopardized by the nationalistic interpretation of the arms race and by a security policy which narrowly focuses on nation-state or alliance interests. Although it does not end there, effective arms control begins at home.

Notes

1. *Süddeutsche Zeitung*, 16 May 1977, p. 7.
2. John H. Herz, *International Politics in the Atomic Age*, New York and London, Columbia University Press 1967.
3. 'Interview with George F. Kennan', *Foreign Policy*, No. 7, Summer 1974, p. 39.
4. Cf. Erich Weede, *Weltpolitik und Kriegsursachen im 20. Jahrhundert. Eine quantitativempirische Studie*, Munich (Oldenbourg) 1975.
5. 91/1 US Congress, Joint Economic Committee, Subcommittee on Economy in Government, Hearings: *The Military Budget and National Economic Priorities*, Part 2, Washington, D.C., 1969, p. 552.
6. Graham Allison and Frederic A. Morris, 'Armaments and Arms Control. Exploring the Determinants of Military Weapons', in: Franklin Long and George Rathjens (eds). *Arms, Defence Policy, and Arms Control*, New York, Norton, 1976, p. 126.
7. Morton Halperin, 'Why Bureaucrats Play Games', *Foreign Policy*, No. 6, Spring 1972, pp. 69–83.
8. Cf. Richard K. Betts, *Soldiers, Statesmen, and Cold War Crises*, Cambridge, Mass., and London, Harvard University Press, 1977.
9. Speech at the Naval War College, 3 October 1961; excerpts reprinted in the *New York Times*, 13 June 1971, p. 67.
10. For a critique of the MIC-concept cf. Monika Medick, 'Das Konzept des "Military-Industrial Complex" und das Problem einer Theorie demokratischer Kontrolle', *Politische Vierteljahresschrift*, Vol. XIV, No. 4, December 1973, pp. 499–526. Morton Halperin, 'The Limited Influence of the Military-Industrial Complex', in Halperin, Stockfish and Weidenbaum (eds.), *The Political Economy of the Military-Industrial Complex*, Berkeley, Calif. 1973, pp. 1–20; Jerome Slater and Terry Nardin, 'The Military-Industrial Complex Muddle', *The Yale Review*, Vol. LXV, No. 1, 1975, pp. 1–23.

11. Edwin Czerwick and Harald Mueller, 'Rüstungskonzerne, ökonomisches Interesse und das Konzept des "militärisch-industriellen Komplexes" ', *Friedensanalysen*, No. 6, 1977, p. 171.
12. Egbert Jahn et al., 'Probleme der Analyse der sowjetischen Sicherheitspolitik', *Forschungsberichte der HSFK* (Frankfurt), No. 6, 1973, pp. 3–8.
13. Frederik Hoffmann, 'Arms Debates A "Positional Interpretation" ', *Journal of Peace Research*, Vol. VII, 1970, pp. 219–28.
14. 92/2 United States Congress, Senate Committee on Foreign Relations, Hearings: *Strategic Arms Limitation Agreements*, Washington, 1972, p. 256.
15. Rudolf Bahro, *Die Alternative. Zur Kritik des real existierenden Sozialismus*, Cologne and Frankfurt, EVA, 1977, pp. 515–16.
16. Paul A. Samuelson, *Economics*, 8th ed., New York, McGraw Hill, 1970, p. 803.
17. Quoted in Ernest Mandel, *Spätkapitalismus. Versuch einer Erklärung*, Frankfurt, Suhrkamp, 1972, p. 280.
18. Albert Szymanski, 'Military Spending and Economic Stagnation', *American Journal of Sociology*, Vol. 79, No. 1, July 1973, pp. 1–14.
19. Jong Ryool Lee, 'Changing National Priorities in the United States', in Bruce M. Russett and Alfred Stepan (eds.), *Military Force and American Society*, New York, Harper & Row, 1973, pp. 61–105; Clark Nardinelli and Gary B. Ackerman, 'Defense Expenditures and the Survival of American Capitalism', *Armed Forces and Society*, Vol. 3, No. 1, November 1976, pp. 13–16.
20. Peter Schlotter, *Rüstungspolitik in der Bundesrepublik. Die Beispiele Starfighter und Phantom*, Frankfurt, Campus, 1975; Manfred Schmidt, 'Staatliche Ausgabenpolitik und Akkumulationsentwicklung im Rüstungssektor der Bundesrepublik', *Gesellschaft. Beiträge zur Marxschen Theorie*, Vol.5, 1975, pp. 10–67.
21. A more detailed study analysing political, ideological, bureaucratic, and economic factors is Gert Krell, *Rüstungsdynamik und Rüstungskontrolle. Die gesellschaftlichen Auseinandersetzungen um SALT in den USA 1969–1975*, 2nd ed., Frankfurt, Haag & Herchen, 1978.
22. The concept was taken from Franklyn Griffiths, 'Transnational Politics and Arms Control', *International Journal*, Vol. XXVI, Fall 1971, p. 667.

10

Arms-race dynamics and arms control

Dieter Senghaas
Professor of Political Science,
University of Bremen

The nature of the contemporary arms race

Détente and armaments

The political élites in East and West so far have pursued their strategy of détente only in conjunction with a policy of unceasing armamentism. Also the Government of the Federal Republic of Germany has continued to emphasize that it cannot carry out détente and *Ostpolitik* without reaffirming a deterrence strategy based on a traditional military alliance framework.

What circumstances today essentially determine the dynamics of armament developments, i.e. the growth of armaments and the trend of the international arms race?

External and internal impulses to armaments

When the Cold War was still in full swing, it was comparatively simple to legitimize armament policies and the international arms race. The traditional explanation of the arms-race dynamics has been based on the simple assertion that armament policies can only be interpreted as reactions to actions of the opponent. This action-reaction theorem conceives armament policies as being dictated from the opponent, or as 'other-directed'. It is asserted that particular armament measures of one side are directly geared to the armament measures of the opponent. Since both antagonists behave (at least according to the self-image they propagate) equally other-directedly, it may be assumed that a reciprocal escalation spiral necessarily emerges, in the process of which weapon systems are invented, numerical plateaux fixed, and in which the supersession of old systems by qualitatively higher ones is determined.

As much research on the biography of weapon systems has shown, we can clearly state on the basis of the known evidence that the action-reaction scheme is at least highly dubious, if not completely false. The main trends of the

Shortened version of 'Arms Race Dynamics and Arms Control in Europe', *Bulletin of Peace Proposals*, Vol. 10, No. 1, 1979.

international arms race between East and West have developed quite differently from what has been asserted in the action-reaction theorem.

In the last twenty years the main antagonists—the big powers and their allies—have been, on the average, more autonomous in the self-determination of their specific armament policies than most commentators usually assume. Their main decisions have been far more geared to the needs of various segments of their societies, to be specified later on in this chapter. They have been mainly 'inner-directed' and less dictated by external forces. The self-centred imperatives of national armament policies have been far stronger than those which have resulted from the reciprocal interaction with the so-called 'potential' enemy.

This alternative theorem can be empirically verified. Our observations refer particularly to the nuclear-strategic area of the present arms race. The reason for this emphasis is not that the nuclear-arms race and nuclear weapons have been and still are the most dangerous and potentially most destructive war potentials; our emphasis on the nuclear-strategic arms race is of paradigmatic value since certain key aspects of contemporary types of arms races can be particularly well analysed in that area. But at the same time we have to emphasize the very characteristics of the strategic arms race which cannot be transferred to an analysis of other types of arms races and weapon systems.

The race in technology

The most outstanding characteristic of the present arms race between East and West consists in the fact that this arms race has been more than any one before a continuously qualitative one. Most of the arms races before 1945 were primarily quantitative races. Although there have been many qualitative innovations in weapon technology during the last two centuries, the life cycles of weapon systems were considerably longer than the case after 1945.

The basic characteristic of the present arms race shows up in a permanent stream of technological innovations which, besides other causes, set the pace for contemporary armament policies. The reverse of this continuous innovation consists in the tremendous propensity to obsolescence of weapon systems, once prodced. The many abortive weapon systems of the last twenty years are another sign of the same trend. In contradistinction to the armament policy of previous decades, the present arms race extends not only to one type of weapon system or to a few, but rather to the entire spectrum of destruction potentials in the possession of the political and military apparatus today. The range of this spectrum begins with the subversive activities of intelligence agencies; it comprises types of counter-insurgency warfare, conventional war potentials, tactical and strategic nuclear-weapon systems, as well as instruments of political propaganda and psychological warfare. The spectrum reaches out into a variety of new horrendous weapon programmes related to types of war theatres so far unknown in warfare, like laser weapon systems.

All these programmes are subject to what can be particularly observed on the nuclear strategic level: the continuous modernization of existing systems and the forced innovation of new ones. Both measures, the modernization of old systems and the elaboration of new ones, aim at the improvement of the quality of weapon systems: the improvement of their precision, their reliability, their invulnerability.

The lead-time requirements of contemporary weapon-systems planning—the time from research and development to the implementation of new systems—turn the future into history: as in very few segments of highly industrialized societies, the range of options for decisive political action in the future is continuously narrowed down by decisions in the present.

Doctrines, interests and technologies

Deterrence and worst-case scenarios

The intensity of technological innovations has been speeded up by the prevailing security doctrine of mutual deterrence. This doctrine is based on the paradoxical, yet traditional, premise that the outbreak of violence and wars in international politics can be prevented with the help of deterrence policies by the continuous improvement of the means of warfare. Under present conditions, the attempt to prevent war by deterrence policies, however, leads not only potentially or with high probability but rather with necessity to its very extensive preparation, simply to guarantee mutual retaliation.

In this connection, the so called worst-case doctrine—a fundamental strategic orientation motivating the variegated contingency planning of the political and military apparatus—has functioned as a speeding-up mechanism for national armament policies. This doctrine is oriented towards future potential 'catastrophic gaps' in the weapon arsenals and is based on the combined assertion of the worst possible intention of the enemy and its best ability to develop new military strategies and weapon technologies. The unprecented differentiations in political and military contingency planning, a result of a deterrence policy pursued for twenty years, are no random product but the combined result of this doctrine and the social forces fixated to it. The same can be said about the propensity to overperception, overreaction, and overdesign in contemporary military strategy. As long as deterrence policies are pursued, the military contingency planning will be geared to the expectation of the worst possible. As a consequence the image of the enemy becomes a functional value in this policy, although the degree of fixation to the enemy is quite variable.

Socio-political interests

It has been asserted that the intensity of technological innovations has been speeded up, though probably not exclusively caused, by the specific security policy doctrine of mutual deterrence. Other factors have been equally responsible for the maintenance of this policy and the perpetuation of the arms race.

One important factor seems to be the proliferation of armament-oriented interests, with respect both to numbers and to segments of the societies affected by contemporary armament policy. The political and social interests on which deterrence policies are based are as much differentiated as the existing weapon systems and the contingency planning related to prevailing escalation doctrines. Specific military missions of the armed forces are institutionally co-ordinated with administrative segments of the civil and military administration, with research and development laboratories, and with the production plants for weapon systems. There is presently much talk about a military-industrial complex, the existence of which can hardly be denied in highly industrialized capitalist and socialist societies, particularly in the United States and the USSR. However, the infrastructure of this complex is composed rather of a series of important partial alliances, sometimes mutually exclusive, and sometimes highly interlocked. Therefore it makes more sense to talk about the existence of administrative-military-industrial-scientific complexes.

This interest-structure of contemporary armament policy has led to a militarization of international politics, since the vested interests of those social groups and politicalinstitutions which participate in the planning and production of software and hardware devices for the military have generally been far better organized and stronger than the activities of other groups with a stake in foreign policy. The only really relevant exception to this, at least in capitalist countries, is represented by the socio-economic groups involved in foreign economic policy.

In order to understand the impetus of the contemporary international arms race, we have, in the first instance, to recognize this particular kind of interest-basis of armament policies. To put emphasis on the manifold interests, including psychological interest fixations, is vitally important in the evaluation of this decisive factor on which arms races are built up and which contributes to the speeding-up of the international arms race. But we must equally emphasize the tremendous hierarchization of decision-making processes related to armament policies, which justifies speaking of the existence of a security policy oligarchy or an armament policy power élite, respectively. Despite this incontestable hierarchization of the political deliberation and decision processes in the area of security policies, we must understand the incrementalist basis of the political deliberation process by which certain aspects of the momentum built into military apparatus can be explained. The latter aspect particularly holds for Western countries in which well-known rivalries between administrative organizations, military services, scientific laboratories and the production plants of weapon systems have been quite openly fought through. But such conflicts do not end up in an inroad into the various activities of the military apparatus: rather, they contribute to their inflation. It is far easier for interest groups and interest coalitions intrinsically involved in national armament policies to agree on the largest common denominator than on the smallest. In the representation of their collective interests (for example, with respect to an increase of the share of military expenditures from public budgets) all these groups tend to agree, despite their rivalries, about the modalities of how to implement basic policy postures. The interpenetration of those interest groups and their tight co-ordination justify our calling these a security policy power élite.

Technological momentum

The second essential factor which helps explain the innovation intensity of the contemporary qualitative arms race could be termed the impulse resulting from technology (technology-impulse) and those organizational imperatives which emerge from it. The direction and the speed of technological innovation processes do not represent autonomous data which could be adequately analysed apart from the concrete interest-configuration from which innovation processes emerge.

The direction of technological research and the intensity in which innovations have developed are essentially dependent upon particular political premises, which are givens for a natural science and weapon technology research within the context of predetermined political and budgetary priorities. Within such a context, innovation processes might assume a life of their own which, in the last instance, leads to the strange fact (so congenial to all weapons designers) that the so-called threat to the nation tends to be measured by the development stage and at the technological levels of one's own armaments or by the potential technological progress of one's own weapon technology, and far less by armaments and technologies of the opponent.

In military-technological research and innovation programmes, the action-reaction theorem particularly fails as an explanatory device. Let us here refer to a report of the United Nations Secretary-General in October 1971:

On the surface it would seem that the effort to improve the quality of armaments, or to defend against them, follows a logical series of steps in which a new weapon or weapon-system is devised, then a counter-weapon to neutralize the new weapon, and then a counter-counter weapon. But these steps neither usually nor necessarily occur in a rational time sequence. The people who design improvements in weapons are themselves the ones who as a rule envisage the further steps they feel should be taken. They do not wait for a potential enemy to react before they react against their own creations.

Organizational imperatives

Organizational imperatives are particularly developed by those apparatuses which, on the basis of an exclusive specialization (as in the case of the aerospace industry), have been active at the most advanced front in the development of improved armament technologies. As has been proved by empirical analyses, the research, development, experimenting, production and implementation phases of major weapon systems follow a rigid sequential scheme within given research and production plants, not affected by vicissitudes in the development of international politics. The theorem of the so-called follow-on imperative attempts to circumscribe this fact; it explicitly states what has been taken for granted in the context of the prevailing security policy and what has led to a forced arming of the participants, respectively: namely, that defence administrations and those social forces involved in the security and defence business put much effort into the maintenance of keeping established research and production plants going, since any interruption of the work in these institutions is considered intolerable by the political and military élites, due to the long lead-time requirements of modern weapon technology.

The interdependence of interest alliances and technological innovation impulses, which are largely predetermined by those interests, has to be interpreted as the most decisive link in the configuration of social forces, political institutions and publically relevant ideologies—which all together considerably determine armament dynamics today. The order of magnitude of armament policies in highly industrialized societies has led in many instances to an auto-dynamic growth of the security apparatus to a degree which frequently does not even make any more sense within the conventional security policy rationales. The problem of overspending and underaccomplishing is, apart from the general cost explosion, intrinsic to the military apparatus of given size: this does not lead so much to a problem in civil-military relatinships but rather to the impossibility of any effective control of organizations whose size is, in budgetary terms, often larger than the GNP of many countries. This can also be clearly seen in an analysis of contemporary defence planning. The latter tends today to be fairly reactive to developments which result from the interconnections between interest alliances and technological progress; it has hardly any operative function in such rational discussions of security policy options in which the substance of the discussion would deliberately not remain fixated to the premises of the conventional doctrines of mutual deterrence and threatened retaliation. As long as segments of the military apparatus are not going to be completely eliminated under an increasing cost pressure, and manifold missions of the armed services will be perpetuated also in middle-sized states, defence planning necessarily leads to a policy of 'muddling through'. Also in Europe such a costly muddling through can be increasingly observed in the existing apparatus. It will be intrinsic to them as long as there is no incisive reorientation both in missions and in the organization of the military build-up from the Cold War.

Psychostrategies

In the past twenty years the inflationary growth of the military apparatus has been legitimized by general doctrines supposed to represent a common denominator of many specific strategic programmes. Essential parts of these programmes have been motivated, apart from the already-mentioned doctrine of deterrence, by so-called balance-of-power doctrines and the doctrine of stability, and in the West particularly by the doctrines of superiority and most recently of parity and sufficiency. To a large extent, these doctrines are not new; they have already been common frames of legitimization of national military policies before 1945. The partially operative function they had before the Second World War has, however, been lost in the face of tremendously increasing overkill capabilities in the last decade and a half. So the attempt to reach some level of superiority has become, even in terms of contemporary military strategy, irrational. None the less, the continuous arming and rearming has been legitimized by simple rationalizations; for instance a once-achieved position of strength and superiority should not be given up; and numerical inferiority cannot be tolerated (which is absurd on the given level of overkill capabilities).

We must note that the doctrines of military balance and military stability have, at various points in the last twenty years and under most different contexts, justified completely different, concrete security policy measures. This can easily be understood if we consider these doctrines as psychostrategies and not so much as strategies related to precise hardware calculations. Strategic doctrines are best understood as political weapons. So nuclear-strategic superiority has in the West been assumed as the basic criterion for stability and balance, which has then turned the United States into an oversophisticated pacemaker of the international arms race for nearly twenty years; otherwise the many laments of representatives

125

from Western defence administrations in the face of massive Soviet nuclear strategic and navy deployment programmes after 1967 cannot be understood. The achievement of a kind of numerical-quantitative nuclear strategic balance between East and West in the late 1960s and early 1970s has been thus in the West quite consistently criticized as a serious undermining of 'stability' and 'balance'. Other examples could be added. They all show that those doctrines do not have, in any strict sense of the term, an operative meaning; they rather represent *ex post facto* rationalizations of those situations which favour, either numerically or politically, the very side which happens to propagate these doctrines. They thus represent instruments of propaganda and means of legitimization, not guidelines for a rational argumentation about security problems.

Application to East and West

We tend to assume that these phenomena can at present be equally observed both in capitalist and in socialist countries. These factors are quite clearly not system-independent in their origin, but their practical consequences and implications, in the frame of an ongoing political, ideological, and socio-economic antagonism between East and West, can be labelled as system-neutral. As long as there is a heated qualitative arms race, their effects are independent of different socio-economic orders; concretely speaking, they are independent of certain basic premises of capitalist and socialist social orders, as can quite clearly be empirically observed.

There are certain important specific impulses of armament dynamics which cannot be compared across the borders of different social orders and which constitute additional, perhaps basic momenta of inertias in the growth patterns of armament policies. For example, there has been much discussion on the socio-economic functions of armaments in capitalist states, and such functions have been well documented; there has been also some discussion on the rule-preserving and disciplining functions of military apparatuses in capitalist states. Rule-preserving and intrasocietal and international disciplining functions of military apparatuses in socialist countries have been observed in many instances, as well as the particular interests of the party personnel in power to use the military apparatus for their own aims. An empirical approach to further analyses of such societal (manifest and latent) functions of military apparatus could start with a functional analysis of armament expenditures and with a discussion of the actual use as well as the threatened use of the military under certain conditions. Postwar history offers rich intrasocietal and international materials for such analyses.

A detailed analysis of these functions of armaments is not the object of our present study, since we are more interested in the analytical elaboration of congruent and less in the analysis of specific impulses of armament dynamics. This limited orientation can be particularly justified by the fact that the defence apparatuses in all major societies have become impervious to the undeniable political changes in the East-West conflict. We know very well that such a substantive restriction in our arguments is very problematic, but we would like to emphazise that it is not at all arbitrary. Inasmuch as conflict potentials with warlike implications have also developed among socialist states, this type of analysis merits also special attention in studies with a Marxist approach.

Essential features of armament dynamics

Internal and international interaction

Let us summarize our observations so far. First, the international arms race is much less induced by external reasons than commonly assumed. Essentially the international arms race has been inner-directed: it has been fuelled more by internal than by external forces. Thus, the arms race is not so much one between interacting antagonistic powers with a reciprocal escalation, as it is a competition of the various states within their own boundaries. The competitors within the scope of national armament policies are civilian, military, industrial, administrative, and scientific groupings. The 'action-reaction' scheme in armament policies is far more evident within nations of alliances than with respect to their interaction.

Action-reaction processes, which have been the core of so many arms-race models, do exist, but not in the context in which they have usually been assumed so far. The action-reaction scheme rather characterizes the development of certain types of weapons systems (bombers versus missiles) or the development of individual armament technologies within certain weapon systems. The action-reaction-scheme also characterizes the manifold political, military, strategic, administrative, and industrial processes which can be observed within military alliances. To summarize, this scheme characterizes such types of internal interaction patterns far more than the transnational or international interaction patterns between the antagonists.

Redundant causation and configurative causality

The second observation which can be formulated about the present international arms race consists in its redundant causation. The emphasis on such redundant causation is of great importance, since redundantly caused phenomena cannot be altered by working on one or only a few of their constitutive causal impulses. Transformation strategies which aim at overcoming the present arms race have therefore to be more broadly conceptualized than conventional arms-race-control measures. Inasmuch as the loosening up of enemy fixations does not at present lead to an inroad into the growth patterns of defence apparatuses, conventional arms-control measures are not apt to restrict the qualitative growth of these apparatuses.

Aside from this type of redundant causation, a further notion has to be mentioned: the configurative causality of the growth patterns of defence apparatuses (and thus, by implication, of arms-race dynamics). Conventional causal schemes have conceptualized causality in terms of the sequential inter-action of independent, intervening and dependent variables. Configurative causality is quite different from that type of one-dimensional causality, inasmuch as synchronous and diachronous analyses of total phenomena, like the contemporary defence apparatuses, show that all possible causal interactions and causal sequences can be observed simultaneously with no clear-cut, one-dimensional rigid sequential patterns prevailing. (For example, this applies between the three decisive variables of armament policies like armament interests, armament technologies and armament ideologies). Naturally, in the biography of individual weapon systems a clear weighting of these factors in terms of conventional bi- or multivariate causal models can nevertheless be determined. So it can be clearly shown in the biography of some weapon systems that industrial interests were decisive in initiating a new weapon programme and that the technological innovation has been the result of such lobbying pressures from the side of those groups interested in such a development; whereas in the development of other weapon systems often just the contrary can be observed, namely that a once-achieved technological innovation will be occupied by specific armament interests which then formulate certain contingency plans with the result that such a programme looks indispensable to fill certain 'gaps' in the existing weapon arsenals. The fact that all of these types of interactions do take place at one and the same time and over time between the political and military administrations, the armed services, the armament industries, technology, and scientific laboratories represents a real challenge for any conventional causal explanation of armament dynamics. We try to come to grips with these phenomena by the notion of configurative causality, the understanding of which is decisive for an adequate analysis of the growth patterns of armament policies, as well as for the understanding of the inertias and momenta built into these apparatuses taken as a whole.

Consequences for arms control

Technological impulses and diplomacy

These conclusions are of immediate practical value for the evaluation of a strategy of arms control. If it is true that armament dynamics is redundantly caused and if major reasons for armament policies are rooted in societal configurations (within societies and within alliances) rather than in rational reactions to actions of the so-called potential enemy, then we are confronted with specific consequences: a strategy of arms control has to be based on a multiplicity of measures if armament dynamics is to be limited and curtailed effectively.

The question with regard to the true intervention function of arms-control agreements in, and their inroad into, the autonomous probability of armament development trends is decisive. In the past years, the control function of arms-control agreements with regard to their intervention in existing armament-technology trends has been practically nil.

The enormous discrepancy between the massive inner-societal impulses for further growth of armaments and for re-armament and the ritual of diplomatic negotiations is characteristic of arms-control negotiations. This ritual begins with deplomatic soundings as to whether such negotiations are desired by all sides; it is continued by determining the participants, the place where the negotiations will take place, the preliminary negotiations, the long discussion on the agenda, and then, finally, perhaps the beginning of the negotiations—which may last for several years. While all this is being done in a rather spectacular way, entering the headlines of daily newspapers, the national or alliance-pledged armament policy is quietly but in a far more momentous way taking a new step towards the future.

Political options in matters of arms control and disarmament are then restricted by actual armament developments.

While diplomatic delegations discuss a subject for many years in laborious sessions, this subject is often already outdated from a military-technological viewpoint at the beginning of the negotiations, and/or it is superseded by new armament-technological developments in the course of the protracted negotiations.

Arms-control policies could constitute one of several direct strategies for the solution of imminent armament and security problems, if they would really reach a dynamics of their own within a policy of peace promotion deliberately aspired to. Under present conditions this would be possible only with the help of massive interference in the research-and-development programmes by which so far the arms race has been continuously pushed ahead. One could talk about successful arms-control measures only if these qualitative dimensions of the contemporary arms race could be really controlled with the final result of a containment and cutdown of national armament policies. That is to say, arms-control measures have to be evaluated not on the basis of their symbolic value, but by the degree to which they really represent an effective inroad into those factors analysed in the previous paragraphs, particularly into manpower and investment (procurement) and research and development.

Even in that instance, arms-control policies will overstep decisive thresholds only if such a strategy is part of a comprehensive peace policy composed of many components, containing, among others, so to speak, round-about strategies. By these the armament sector will not be affected directly; they rather aim at the build-up of peace-promoting structures without which a distargeting of the defence apparatuses will not come about. In this respect we particularly think about peace-promoting measures in the area of socialization processes and about reorientations in the allocation of social resources geared to newly defined societal priorities.

11

The military innovation system and the qualitative arms race

Harvey Brooks
Gordon McKay Professor
of Applied Physics,
Harvard University

A limitation on the rate of technological progress in weapons systems is emerging as a central problem for the future of arms control. In SALT I, technological progress threatened to overtake the slow pace of the negotiations. At the start of the negotiations, for example, the multiple independently targetable warhead (MIRV) was in its later development stages, but by the time the agreement had been concluded, it was a fairly well-tested weapon, ready for full-scale deployment in the Minuteman system and in the Poseidon missile for the Polaris submarines. MIRV potentially multiplied the destructiveness carried in a single missile to the point where any agreement to limit the deployment of offensive strategic missiles was made much more difficult. Fortunately, technological progress in ballistic-missile defence did not make obsolete an agreement on ABM limitation, but even here the emergence of possible exotic ballistic-missile defences (such as high-power lasers) almost threatened agreement and did complicate the negotiations. Since SALT, a whole panoply of new weapons possibilities has emerged into public view and is being vigorously pursued in the United States: the Trident submarine, the B-1 bomber, the long-range cruise missile, the manoeuvrable re-entry vehicle (MARV), a programme for increased missile accuracy. Meanwhile the Soviet missile programme has also made great progress.

After the Partial Test-Ban Treaty, and again after SALT I, it was necessary to assuage domestic critics of these treaty agreements by promising a vigorous research-and-development programme. Indeed, the partial test ban apparently resulted in very little limitation on weapons progress, as both the United States and the Soviet Union pursued increasingly elaborate and sophisticated underground testing. The SALT agreement was used in part to justify new weapons programmes in the United States, while the vigour of the Soviet missile test programme suggests that this may have been the price paid for the agreements by the Soviet leadership to its military critics within the Soviet Union. There are indications that both sides intended to utilize some of the resources that would be saved by the agreements not to deploy ABM in order to accelerate research on new

Shortened version from *Daedalus*, Summer 1975.

offensive systems. These could then be substituted for existing systems within the quantitative limits set by SALT. In fact SALT, by permitting the substitution of qualitatively improved weapons for older ones, provided a powerful incentive for weapons-system innovations on both sides.

The testing or demonstration of new technological weapons can be politically as destabilizing as their actual deployment, especially in the absence of reliable intelligence. Thus the projected bomber gap of the mid-1950s and the alleged missile gap of the early 1960s were inferred from Soviet capabilities that had only been demonstrated on the level of research and development or prototype testing. The inferences proved unfounded, since there was no major deployment of either bombers or ICBMs. But the United States had in the meanwhile launched a major build-up of bombers and ICBMs, which gradually acquired a justification of its own, independent of the hypothesized but non-existent threat that had originally inspired it. Similarly the mere possibility that the Soviet Union was about to demonstrate an ABM capability around Moscow was used to justify the vigorous pursuit of a MIRV programme in the United States and ultimately the deployment of MIRVs on both the sea-based and the land-based forces.

This chapter will be concerned with the impact of qualitative progress in weapons technology and with some possible means of controlling it. We will first deal with the impact of technology on the stability of the strategic deterrent and with the potential political effects of qualitative progress in conventional weapons. We will then consider several types of proposals that have been made for slowing the rate of technological progress in weapons development, with emphasis on strategic weapons. The final section will discuss the overall system of weapons development and procurement and will analyse those parts of the system that appear to generate pressures and incentives to perpetuate it.

Prospects and impact of the qualitative arms race

How do qualitative changes in weapons affect the world military balance, and what does 'stability' mean in the military situation? Clearly any change that increases the advantage of the side attacking first contributes to instability, and any change that reduces this relative advantage is stabilizing. This is true at both the 'strategic' and 'tactical' levels. Thus the development of invulnerable retaliatory systems, such as Polaris, has contributed to stability because these systems guarantee the destruction of the side that attacks first; the first attack would scarcely attenuate the completeness of the retaliatory strike. An increase in the relative effectiveness of anti-tank weapons would also tend to reduce the incentives for a first strike in land warfare. Improved strategic intelligence, that is, instant knowledge of the opponent's deployments, is also generally stabilizing, especially if the intelligence capability of each side is fully known to the opponent. The ABM, on the other hand, was considered destabilizing because it presented the possibility of limiting the damage from a retaliatory strike. MIRV was also considered destabilizing because it potentially limited the effectiveness of a land-based ICBM system deployed in a retaliatory mode. Forward-based nuclear weapons in Europe are destabilizing to the extent that they might be immobilized by surprise attack, especially a conventional one. Finally, conventional weapons whose effectiveness in an initial attack can be greatly enhanced by time for mobilization are destabilizing because they provide an incentive for the opponent to counterattack before mobilization can be effected; the classic example of this can be found in the outbreak of the First World War.

Stability is a political as well as a military concept. It is in its political aspect that technological innovation is particularly important because of the long time lapse between a demonstrated capability and full deployment of the corresponding weapons system. Thus any technological achievement that becomes known to the other side and which, when fully deployed, would jeopardize the effectiveness of retaliation (whether at the strategic or tactical level) is bound to create apprehension about the future and stimulate counteraction. The result is a spiral of technological innovations. The principle of overreaction or 'worst-case analysis' generally guarantees that the reaction to a revelation of technological innovation in weapons exceeds what was justified by the actual situation.

Technology and military equilibrium

In the past twenty years, technological change has sometimes increased and sometimes decreased the stability of the strategic deterrent. For example, the first liquid-fuelled ICBMs contributed to instability because they were not 'hardened' and could not be made instantly ready to fire. This would have provided an incentive for the other side to launch its weapons first, in order to destroy the vulnerable weapons before they were functional. On the other hand, the development of solid-fuelled ICBMs, and especially of submarine-launched ballistic missiles, resulted in a less vulnerable retaliatory capability; this reduced or eliminated the incentive for pre-emptive strike and thus improved strategic stability. Similarly, the development of satellite surveillance decreased the likelihood that either side could deploy strategic weapons secretly. Satellites with infra-red detection ensured immediate warning of a missile attack launched from anywhere in the world, which reduced the likelihood of successful pre-emptive attack. It also decreased the instability that results from exaggeration of enemy capabilities or a misinterpretation of enemy intentions stemming from unreliable intelligence.

When the ABM emerged as a technical possibility in the 1960s, its technological threat to strategic stability was immediately recognized because it cast doubt on the effectiveness of a retaliatory strike. In principle, the development of MIRV similarly threatens stability, as the ratio of the number of independently targetable re-entry vehicles to the number of missile launchers increases the likelihood of success of a pre-emptive strike against the enemy's land-based launchers. The prospect of anti-submarine detection technology, which could make impossible the concealment of sea-based missile forces, would also be a potentially destabilizing development.

If neither the ABM nor MIRV had been developed, the strategic situation at the end of the 1960s would probably have been at its most stable. Both sides possessed land-based and sea-based missiles, which were virtually certain to survive any initial attack with undiminished effectiveness, while the cities and industrial capacity of each superpower were defenceless against retaliatory strikes. A basic objective of the SALT negotiations would then have been to freeze—or at least prolong—this balance. The ABM treaty contributed greatly towards this end, but the other developments mentioned earlier worked against it. What now are the prospects for the future?

The revolutionary 1950s and 1960s were made possible by the confluence of several basic technological advances which came to maturity at more or less the same time—solid-fuel rocket propulsion, high yield-to-weight thermonuclear warheads, inertial guidance, compact solid-state electronics and computers, MIRV and re-entry technology. With the possible exception of the application of laser techniques in missile defence and ground warfare, comparable technological developments that promise the sort of qualitative leaps we witnessed then are not now on the horizon. We ought, however, to remind ourselves that the rapid advances from 1950 to 1060 were not anticipated until they were almost upon us, even though they may appear in retrospect to have been foreseeable. Scientists and technologists, in trying to foresee the state of the art more than five years into the future, have been notoriously myopic—conservative as to actual possibilities and inaccurate in their anticipation of the direction of development. Thus, it would be injudicious to hope that the posture of mutual assured destruction is proof against technological change for more than five, or at most ten, years. We cannot reliably see that far into the future, given past rates of technological progress in military weapons systems.

Invulnerability of the sea-based deterrent

Perhaps the most serious question for the stability of mutual deterrence is whether any technical changes are in prospect that might compromise the invulnerability of the submarine missile forces of either side, and thus undermine the certainty of retaliation. An anti-submarine-warfare (ASW) system that could compromise the deterrent effect of the submarine-based missile force would have to meet very stringent requirements. It would have to be able to make a surprise pre-emptive attack simultaneously on all the enemy's submarine missile forces, including those in port. Such an attack would have to be made with close to 100 per cent confidence, for if even one submarine escaped destruction it would have the capacity for inflicting serious and probably unacceptable retaliatory damage on cities and population. Furthermore, any action against the submarine force short of pre-emptive attack would provide strategic warning and hence would risk drawing some form of counter-attack.

A war of attrition against the sea-based deterrent would be technically somewhat more feasible and could be imagined as a form of political backmail. Unless the nation attacked were in a position to retaliate without at the same time destroying itself, this form of political blackmail is risky, but barely credible. In practice, however, there are too many options for a less drastic response, including a retaliatory campaign of attrition against the enemy's sea-based forces. Nevertheless, belief that an opponent had the capability of conducting such a war of attrition could contribute greatly to tensions and produce political instability. Thus the demonstration of certain qualitative capabilities in ASW, without any evidence of deployment, might provide incentives to accelerate the arms race, much as the mere hint of a possible Soviet ABM system contributed to the deployment of MIRV.

Returning to the question of pre-emptive attack, the difficulties seem almost insurmountable. It would require detection, positive identification, and close and continuous tracking of all missile-firing submarines, plus the ability to launch simultaneously a lethal ASW weapon at each submarine on command from a central point. The requisite assured destruction could probably be achieved only with nuclear underwater weapons fired from vehicles that could carry sonar tracking gear close to the target, while remaining relatively immune to the effects of nearby underwater nuclear explosions. Hydrofoils, hovercraft, helicopters or similar exotic vehicles might be made to have these characteristics. However, the tactics for such an operation could not be developed without a great deal of rehearsal and training, probably including the fairly routine practice tracking of potential targets. Such exercises could hardly be ignored by an alert opponent.

One could also imagine the disposition of passive and active sonars over the oceans, which could be monitored by satellite and would assist tracking operations, but the necessary dispositions would be very costly and would have to be in place continuously and be highly reliable. As sophisticated signal-processing electronics and information storage become more compact and inexpensive, worldwide monitoring of submarines, closely co-ordinated with trailing vessels, becomes conceivable, though still very costly. For this reason, there are arms-control incentives for trying to inhibit such developments, whose mere demonstration would stimulate doubts about the future invulnerability of the deterrent. The nation under threat could also develop decoy vehicles to confuse both the trailing vessels and any ocean-wide surveillance system designed to assist them. The same electronic sophistication that facilitated ocean surveillance would make possible relatively inexpensive decoys against tracking techniques that could simulate the characteristics of submarines. Even a small number of sufficiently realistic decoys could confuse the would-be attacker and greatly increase his uncertainty as to whether some part of the retaliatory force might have survived his attack.

A careful consideration of possible technical threats to the sea-based deterrent therefore forces the conclusion that they do not reveal a clear-cut technical advantage either to ASW or to the survival of the deterrent. The launching of a major ASW programme would most likely simply trigger a race between measure and countermeasure, ending in an expensive stalemate similar to that which probably would have resulted from an ABM versus land-based missile race.

Conclusion

In the foreseeable future, the qualitative arms race is not likely to lead to major strategic instabilities, provided the ABM treaty remains in force. Nevertheless, continued innovation could lead to wasteful and expensive deployments of weapons, and it could offer many opportunities for internal bureaucratic manoeuvre aimed at exaggerating technological breakthroughs in order to justify new programmes. One counter to this is certainly more open discussion and criticism of weapons proposals in a wider arena of opinion. By carefully considering the reaction to, and possible countermeasures for, the next generation of systems, such discussion would have the effect of deflating the benefits claimed for the development and deployment of proposed new systems.

Potentials for curbing the qualitative arms race

In the past it has often been assumed that limitation of progress in weapons technology was rendered impossible by the difficulties inherent in verifying such limitations, especially in the research-and-development stage. Thus, arms-control discussions have tended to concentrate on agreements for numerical limitations to the deployment of certain classes of weapons that can be verified with reasonable confidence through unilateral intelligence means. However, even the Partial Test Ban (PTB) was an attempt to limit technological progress in the sense that it was expected, through the prohibition of atmospheric tests, to inhibit the development of high-yield nuclear weapons and to make all weapons-testing more costly and thus slow it up. In fact, the PTB did not prove to be as inhibiting as expected. Its main benefit was the reduction of atmospheric contamination. But driving tests underground made them publicly less visible, and thus reduced the pressure of world opinion for further damping the qualitative race in nuclear arms.

The SALT agreements did include a specific prohibition of the testing of certain kinds of ABM components of satellite-based ABM development. Less than complete confidence in verification was accepted in these agreements, which seem to have set a precedent for other possible limitations without insistence on verification. That verification is as much a political as a technical matter, that perfect verification is impossible, and that it is also unnecessary if there is some measure of political trust, are also increasingly accepted ideas. The terms of an arms-control agreement are sufficiently interconnected to allow each element to affect the others, and hence not every element has to be verifiable with complete confidence so long as some parts of the agreement can be tested on a sample basis.

Obviously, the closer a weapons system is to deployment the more readily can its progress be verified. The final proof-testing of a weapon, necessary to demonstrate sufficient confidence in its reliability to warrant deployment, is a large, complex process, and it is difficult to conceal. On the other hand, once a weapon has reached that stage, bureaucratic vested interests have usually consolidated to insure its further development, so that ease of verification is offset by greater internal bureaucratic momentum. In what follows, we shall examine a series of proposals, starting with those that aim at inhibiting innovation nearest to the final deployment stage and ending with attempts to limit innovation at earlier stages of the process. The object of all these proposals is to prohibit or retard developments that are politically or militarily destabilizing or that simply add to the costs of maintaining a military posture on both sides without contributing to the security of either.

Comprehensive nuclear test ban (CTB)

The prohibition of all nuclear testing has been an important aim for arms control from the very beginning. Its importance derives from the belief that no nation will place a new type of weapon in inventory if its properties cannot be realistically tested or its reliability verified by proof testing. It is theoretically possible to develop and deploy a nuclear weapon on the basis of scaled laboratory tests alone, but confidence in the reliability and the characteristics of such a weapon would probably be too low for use in a crisis.

135

The past obstacles to conversion of the limited test-ban treaty of 1963 into a permanent comprehensive test ban (CTB) have been American insistence on the need for on-site inspection for suspected underground nuclear tests and the alleged value of underground nuclear explosions for peaceful purposes, such as large earthworks or the stimulation of natural-gas sources. On the Soviet side, a desire not to subject itself to limitations not enforceable against the Chinese was probably also an important factor. More generally, neither side was prepared to accept constraints that would decisively impair its subsequent freedom of action. The PTB was acceptable precisely because it contained no real constraint on innovation in nuclear weapons or peaceful uses.

Since 1963, the technology of detection and identification of underground tests by unilateral means has advanced rapidly, more rapidly than most scientists then expected it could. It is now doubtful that significant weapons advances can be made using tests that are small enough to escape detection with certainty. Even if progress could be made with such small tests, reliable warheads would probably not be placed in inventory without conducting many proof and training tests, a few of which are likely to be detected and to provoke suspicions. The non-adherence of other powers to a CTB could be handled by an agreement of finite duration, subject to reopening if a universal ban were not achieved within a specified period of time. Such an interim agreement would probably increase the pressure on all nations to adhere formally to the ban. Unlike the situation in the Non-Proliferation Treaty, the superpowers would be taking the lead in forgoing their freedom of action, as opposed to demanding a forbearance from others that they were unwilling to impose upon themselves.

Limitation on the number of missile launchings

Experimental launchings are an essential part of missile development and are at the same time readily detectable by unilateral methods, using observation from satellites as well as electronic monitoring of communications and telemetering. In addition, training and confidence missile firings are necessary to keep a weapons inventory in readiness. Therefore, limitation of the number of test firings is a potential means for retarding innovations in missiles that can be verified unilaterally. The limitation that would be most practical to enforce would be one on the total annual number of firings, whether for research and development, proof-testing, or training. The difficulty is that the number of launchings permitted would have to be sufficient to allow each side to retain confidence in the readiness of its deterrent, but that this number, if entirely diverted to research purposes, might permit one side to achieve a dangerous technological advantage. Separate limits on confidence firings and on research-and-development launches would be a preferable alternative, but they would be much harder to enforce because of the difficulties involved in distinguishing experimental from proof launches. For this reason, a limitation on total number of launches, combined either with agreements or with mutual declarations foregoing specific kinds of research, development, testing, and evaluation, would be more practicable.

Restrictions to permit international observation on the location of target areas
As pointed out by Herbert York,[1] the SALT agreements included a provision for

restricting ABM tests to specified test ranges. This stipulation suggests an excellent precedent for a restriction on all kinds of missile testing to specified ranges and for a restriction on down-range impact areas to locations that can be fairly easily observed by other countries, for example, international waters, or land sites close to international boundaries, or coastlines. Such mutually agreed-upon restrictions would improve ability to distinguish between experimental and proof tests, and they might thus make separate limits on the number of such tests more feasible. Furthermore, the SALT agreements have established a precedent for prohibiting interference with unilateral means of observation, either directly or through attempted concealment of certain classes of activities, such as construction of missile silos. The reaffirmation of this concept in the case of missile testing would clearly be desirable.

The limitation of military budgets

There are two main arguments for limiting military expenditures. The first is that it is the most direct means for slowing the arms race without having to conduct endless technical bargaining over the equivalence of specific weapons systems. The second is that the resources thus saved could then be devoted to the solution of other basic international problems. Indeed, to the extent that military expenditures divert the world's resources from economic development, they become major contributors to world political instability, quite apart from the more direct effects of the 'toys' on which the money is spent.

Two ways of approaching reduction of military budgets are: (a) reduction of the total military budget by mutual agreement of the superpowers (with the intention also of constricting military research and development); or (b) direct reduction of military research-and-development budgets only. Either of these methods presents problems because a great deal of military-related research is supported from outside the formal military budget. In the United States, the AEC and NASA budgets include a large military component, and some military research and development is probably hidden in other appropriations (e.g. recently highly publicized technological expenditures of the CIA). Early exploratory research is especially easy to bootleg under other categories of expenditure. In the Soviet Union a great deal of military research is apparently part of the 'science budget', and it is not included in reports of military expenditure.

Another difficulty is that what the United States calls 'test and evaluation' and what the Soviet Union calls 'assimilation into production' are excluded from research and development in the Soviet system, though included as such in American expenditures. On the other hand, a considerable amount of 'independent R&D' by industry in the United States is not treated as military, although it is indirectly financed out of military-procurement appropriations. There are also important differences in the cost factors for military research and procurement between the United States and the Soviet Union, so that direct comparison of any military budget is exceedingly difficult. Although salaries of technical personnel are lower in the Soviet Union, the rate of 'productivity' in technical work is almost certainly much lower as well. For example, the Soviet Union lacks a high-quality instrument industry, with the result that much experimental equipment is made and maintained by individual scientists.

Nevertheless, even recognizing these difficulties, the possibilities of mutually agreed limitations in military budgets should not be dismissed completely, especially if they could be coupled with agreements to deploy the skilled manpower thus released for some more beneficial purpose, such as the development of new energy resources related to world development.

Demobilization of manpower and facilities devoted to military research and development

York[2] has proposed a plan for the gradual removal of secrecy from research, so that scientific findings may ultimately be redirected to other purposes, and he cites the conversion of the Fort Detrick biological-warfare facility to cancer and related biological research as a precedent for what might be achieved on a larger scale in other areas of military-related technology. He proposes the annual transfer of 5 to 10 per cent of the people now working on secret projects to 'non-secret projects conducted in open facilities'. Since this would result in a much more rapid increase in non-secret publishable research than could be accomplished through the normal growth of the scientific community, the transfers could be readily monitored, especially if the United States and the Soviet Union would also agree to an exchange of statistics on scientific and technical personnel, including the occupations and organizational affiliations of new university graduates.

There is no question that secrecy in research has contributed greatly to the mutual suspicions and the apprehensions about 'technological surprise' that have characterized so much Cold War thinking. The monitoring of the transfer proposed by York would be facilitated by the natural inclination of scientists and engineers to disseminate their work among their peers and thus gain public credit for priority in discovery or invention. It might even be possible to organize official international meetings dealing with military technology, its progress, and the assessment of its broader effects and socio-political implications. Eventually an authoritative public literature on military technology might appear, open to criticism and evaluation by the international technological community.

This greater openness in military technology may not only reduce apprehensions about 'technical surprise', but also make it more difficult for the 'hawkish' experts in any country to use selective release of information about an opponent's technical capabilities as an argument for large new weapons programmes. On the other hand, too much publicity may stimulate irresponsible 'gadgeteering' and unreasonable public fears about weapons possibilities that are in fact impractical.

There are also those who would argue that secrecy encourages inefficiency and 'boondoggling' with resources that might be used much more effectively if the public were really privy to what was going on. While this is certainly a possibility, we believe that the advantages of publicity and open criticism outweigh the dangers of accelerated progress in politically perilous directions.

Unilateral action of scientists as a worldwide community to withhold their services from military research and development

It has been argued that, were scientists simply to refuse to participate in military research, the qualitative arms race could be slowed and the 'technological imperative', which drives advances in military technology, could be dampened. A frequent proposal has been for a kind of Hippocratic Oath of scientists (and presumably also engineers) not to engage knowingly in research whose purpose is to facilitate the destruction of human life or the injury of fellow human beings. Another similar proposal is for a professional 'code of ethics' among scientists, which would be made prerequisite to membership in a professional society and would necessarily be combined with some licensing system. Sanctions could then be applied, after the manner of disbarment proceedings in medicine or law, which would effectively prevent individuals who violated the code from earning a living in their profession. Still other proposals have included forms of strike or boycott against organizations engaged in military research. These, however, are effective weapons only if the decision of a majority of members of an occupational group can be enforced on the entire membership. They are ineffective unless employment in a profession can be given some attribute that the entire group can benefit from collectively, or not at all.

Perhaps the most obvious point to be made in connection with all these suggestions is that, to be effective, they would have to involve sanctions against individuals that could reach across national lines. A code of ethics enforced effectively in one nation and not in another would not much inhibit military technological progress, and it could well lead to alterations in the military balance that would increase rather than decrease the likelihood of conflict. It would also be enforceable only in a world already largely disarmed, i.e. in which the overwhelming number of technical people were engaged in non-military research. At present, a quarter of all technologists derive some support for their work, if not their livelihood, from military research, and—in the absence of realistic employment alternatives for these people—the 'code-of-ethics' idea does not appear very practical. A partial adoption of such a code would only tend to isolate military scientists from the moral climate of the majority of their fellow professionals, thus making military development less rather than more sensitive to broader human implications.

A second and perhaps more fundamental point is that the distinction between 'good' and 'bad' research is much more difficult to draw in practice than the simplifications required for collective action can accommodate. Except in the final stages of development, most technical progress has manifold implications. Furthermore, so long as the use of force or the threat of force is an accepted instrument of international politics or domestic security, the line between 'good' and 'bad' research will remain obscure. Is it evil to work on temporarily disabling chemicals when the alternative may be thoroughly lethal bullets? By what logic is tear gas a legitimate police weapon in domestic disorders, but an illegal weapon in international conflict? If the use of conventional air-dropped bombs is a legitimate form of warfare, is research directed towards improving their ability to discriminate more accurately between military and non-military targets to be regarded as aimed at the destruction of human life or at its protection? Is research directed at improving intelligence gathering about military matters stabilizing of destabilizing? Will research on body armour for infantry and police be condemned or condoned by a 'Hippocratic oath'? What is the moral status of research directed at better care of war casualties? These examples just begin to indicate the complexity of the issues. Codes of ethics usually break down when applied to such complex moral questions, as we already know from modern medical practice.

One could, of course, take the position that any research whose results are likely to be used primarily in a military setting is morally suspect because its ultimate purpose is to facilitate the killing or injuring of fellow human beings. One could even argue in favour of allowing military action to become more lethal for the sake of making force ultimately less acceptable as a means for settling political conflict. Such subtleties, however, do not lend themselves to the kind universal moral consensusessential to the enforcement of a professional code of ethics.

The final argument is essentially a political one. If the majority in a nation decides that a cetain course of action is legitimate and desirable, does some small group have the right or duty to withhold its special skills as a means of enforcing its own political value judgements on the majority? Most of us would agree, I think, that the individual has the right and duty to follow the dictates of his own conscience, and that he should be afforded some protection by society in doing so. However, in an organization where the views of a majority are enforced on all members and in a situation where membership is a precondition for practising one's profession, the problem becomes more complicated. For then one is opening up the possibility that national policy will be determined not by a majority of citizens, but by, for example, a majority of physicists or electrical engineers. Is this compatible with a democratic polity?

So long as war and preparation for the possibility of war are generally regarded as legitimate, if regrettable, national activities, it is difficult to see how collective unilateral action on the part of selected occupational groups can be either effective or politically legitimate. However, an entirely different situation would obtain with respect to activities that had been outlawed by mutual agreement of governments. Once agreements have been reached to prohibit or limit certain kinds of research, collective actions of scientists or engineers can become a legitimate and useful tool in enforcing their observation by organizations. Under such circumstances, it might even be legitimate for the majority in a professional group to enforce its views on a minority, if the action thus enforced prevents, for example, the violation of a treaty.

Conclusion

To summarize, the most promising lines of action for controlling the qualitative arms race probably lie in mutually agreed limitations on testing, including limits on the number of permissible missile launches, and on a comprehensive nuclear-test ban. Agreements to refrain from research are often difficult to monitor, though they may have considerable value if accompanied by well-publicized commitments to refrain from actions that would jeopardize the stability of mutual deterrence. In fact, such general declarations may be more useful than attempts to negotiate highly detailed prohibitions, since they can shift the balance of the internal bureaucratic debate on whether to go forward with a given weapons development. The ban in the ABM treaty on the testing of exotic ABM techniques in space provided a precedent, though it fell short of clearly limiting research and development. Attempts at unilateral action by professional groups, such as 'codes of ethics' forbidding participation in research aimed at injury to or destruction of human life, are likely to be ineffective because of the ambiguity and lack of consensus regarding what constitutes 'good' and 'bad' research. However, professional self-discipline that is legitimized by official mutual weapons-control declarations provides some hope.

Cutting back on military research: opportunities and problems

In 1970, the total research funds in the world devoted to military efforts were estimated at $25,000 million, about 40 per cent of the world total for research generally. Some 25 per cent of the world's scientific and technical manpower was engaged in research, which, however general its potential application, had been originally justified primarily on military grounds. This 25 per cent probably represents the most sophisticated and highly trained segment of the technical community. The military devotes much more money than other economic enterprises do to research and development: it accounts for one-eighth of all world expenditures for military purposes, whereas in manufacturing industries in the United States, for example, it accounts for only about 4 per cent of sales. From 1958 to 1965, 80 per cent of the personnel additions to research and development occurred in just two industries, aerospece and electrical equipment, i.e. those most heavily involved in government-financed defence research. In 1968 roughly, 43 per cent of the physicists in the United States with doctoral degrees were at least partially dependant on military budgets for support of their scientific effort. Moreover, a significant fraction, perhaps 20 per cent, of the scientific recruitment in the 1960s was accomplished through a 'brain drain' of trained people from the rest of the non-communist world, including the less industrialized countries. These immigrants were either employed directly in the American military space effort, or, probably more frequently, replaced native Americans in less technically glamorous civilian occupations. During this period, some of the less fashionable fields of engineering attracted up to 50 per cent of foreign graduate students, many of whom remained in the United States

There is now fairly wide agreement among economists that the American concentration on space defence in the early 1960s had a depressing effect on innovation in the private economy, as well as on efforts for public improvement in such areas as pollution control, public transportation and housing.

If one looks at the technical component of the many complex challenges facing our interdependent world in the remainder of this century, one has a sense that humanity can ill afford the diversion of talent represented by its military effort. These considerations also suggest that efforts to control military research expenditures for arms-control reasons should be accompanied by vigorous efforts to redeploy the resources thus liberated to priority civilian tasks. This may prove difficult to do, but such an effort is needed, not so much to cushion the impact of unemployment as to insure the fullest possible use of resources and capacities. These will be badly needed, especially during the last two decades of this century, when the supply of new graduates in science and engineering will be declining. It would be hoped that a significant part of the technical resources liberated from military technology could be devoted to problems related to economic development in deprived parts of the world, although this is the most difficult kind of reconversion.

The longer the world postpones tackling the problem of technological reconversion, the more difficult and intractable will it become. As military space technology advances, it tends to become increasingly remote from potential civilian applications. In the 1950s military aircraft became prototypes for civilian jets, and military and intelligence computers contributed to the data-processing market. But today the sophisticated equipment required for an ABM system goes far beyond what is needed for anything but the tiny scientific computing market, e.g. in numerical weather modelling. The attempt to transfer the technology of supersonic bombers and fighters to a civilian SST is proving much more expensive and of more dubious benefit than was the case with subsonic aircraft. After some early enthusiasm, it does not appear that space vehicles offer much promise for delivering the mail, or carrying intercontinental passengers, or even disposing of radio-active wastes. The booster technology required for communications satellites or earth-resource survey satellites is largely of early-1960s vintage. There are still some generic technologies, such as lasers or large-scale computer memories, which have major civilian applications, but these items are mostly at the research end of the development spectrum; they do not benefit much from the large sums spent on end-item military developments. Such civilian benefit as derives from military research expenditures comes largely from the relatively inexpensive background and exploratory research that precede systems development.

Thus, even if the American military space effort did result in useful economic 'spin-off' in the past—a proposition that is increasingly being called into question—it is less likely to do so in the future. The benefits that derive from military research are greatly attenuated when classified and disseminated only within a restricted community. Studies indicate that the number of patents per dollar of research-and-development expenditure is much smaller for military and space efforts than for industrially sponsored research. In consequence, space and military research must be justified primarily on its own merits and not on the basis of any benefits alleged for the rest of the economy. If the alternative were not to make use of the ressources or skills at all, perhaps there would be some slight justification for the 'spin-off' argument, but it certainly has no merit when one takes into consideration all of the other needs of society.

Some of the economic adjustments occasioned by decline in military expenditures might be handled more easily on a multinational basis. Many of the serious problems facing the world in resources, energy, environment, population, food, or economic development lend themselves to co-operative efforts among countries, and the political appeal of such co-operation would help to neutralize the negative economic effects of declining defence expenditures. The incentives for military innovation might decline if the alternative uses of technical manpower could be made more tangible through multinational action.

Conclusion

Our discussion has shown that new technology has helped to fuel the arms race, though not all technological developments are potentially destabilizing to the military balance. Without doubt, a less frenetic research effort in military technology would reduce the pressures for deployment of the resulting, often unnecessary, weapons systems. It would also decrease the likelihood of still more new technological development that would give an important military or political advantage to one side, or create a situation in which safety was perceived to lie in attacking first. Any reduction in the rate of military innovation would be most valuable if it were selective, but selectivity will necessitate a system of assessment that assures consideration in a context broader than immediate political or military advantage. The notion of an 'impact statement' to be required before each major decision about new weapons development might be useful, especially if it could be broutht within an international or at least a multinational framework.

We have considered a number of proposals for limiting the rate of military technological innovation, with special emphasis on forestalling those that might be threatening to the stability of the military balance. Among the most useful are a comprehensive ban on nuclear testing and a limit on the number of missile tests. The political value should be stressed of mutual declarations of policy, foreswearing either development or deployment actions that would jeopardize confidence in each side's retaliatory capability. Such declarations could help to set in motion internal forces which would insure that proposed military developments are looked at more critically. The case of ASW development poses an especially difficult problem because of the ambiguity between ASW for the protection of sea communications and ASW for compromising the sea-based deterrent. However, the increasing ability of nations to cut off vital natural resources at their source without fear of military reprisal may now be fundamentally changing the role of sea communications and naval power in this equation.

Limitations on military research and development are also increasingly required to conserve technical resources for the urgent problems facing humanity. There is a growing divergence between trends in military technology and the technological needs of the rest of the world's economy. The longer the attempt is delayed to convert some military technical resources to other ends, the more difficult will this conversion become. As time goes on, swords will look less and less like ploughshares.

Notes

1. H. York, 'Some Possible Measures for Slowing the Qualitative Arms Race', *Proceedings of the 22nd Pugwash Conference on Science and World Affairs, Oxford, England, September 7-12, 1972*, pp. 228–35, Oxford, 1973.
2. *Ibid.*, p. 232.

12

Arms control and technological change

Christoph Bertram
Director, International Institute of Strategic Studies, London

For the past two decades, the control of arms through mutual agreement has seemed one of the most promising ways to pursue stability and rational accommodation between East and West in the nuclear age. The concepts of arms control, articulated and refined in the late 1950s and early 1960s, were soon tried out in practice. In 1969 the Soviet-American talks on the limitation of strategic arms (SALT) got under way, leading to a series of treaties and agreements in 1972 and 1974. Since 1973, delegations from member states of the two East-West military alliances, the Warsaw Pact and NATO, have met regularly to seek agreement on the reduction of theatre forces in Europe, so far without result. However slow the process, advocacy of arms control remains the symbol with which politicians in East and West seek to demonstrate the sincerity of their desire for peace.

After almost four years of negotiation, the Soviet Union and the United States now seem on the threshold of a SALT II agreement. Yet one should be careful not to hail the new agreement too enthusiastically as evidence of successful arms control. It is more the result of the determination of both sides to overcome that major obstacle to agreement that has, in recent years, increasingly tended to render compromise more and more difficult: the dynamics of technological change in modern arms competition.

At first glance, this is no more than a banality. After all, there has rarely been a period in which the characteristics of weapons have remained unchanged. The dynamics of military technology have often exceeded and even defined those of civilian industrial technology; they have never stood still. Arms-controllers have always been familiar with this problem, and when they have negotiated quantitative restrictions on weapon systems, they have defined them not just in terms of numbers but in qualitative terms as well: battleships. ICBMs, MIRV launchers, etc. This measure is adequate at times when the dynamics of technological change are relatively restrained, but it ceases to be sufficient when military technology undergoes major qualitative changes, when the performance of weapon systems alters so drastically that the categories of agreement can no

Introductory chapters from *The Future of Arms Control. II: Arms Control and Technological Change: Elements of a New Approach*, London, IISS, 1978. (Adelphi Papers, 146.)

longer embrace them and when all consensus on quantities of weapons inherent in a mutual arms-limitation accord is jeopardized by performance improvements on one side which are not matched by equivalent advances on the other.

The dilemma

Technological change has characterized much of the competition in arms between East and West over the past three decades. Sometimes new technologies were the result of major breakthroughs, in concept at least, if not always in implementation: reliable intercontinental delivery systems carrying nuclear weapons against far-distant targets; multiple and independently targetable warheads which increased the destructive capability of each missile launcher; antiballistic missile technology; sea-based missile launchers; satellite reconnaissance—to name a few in the strategic nuclear field. Others were the result of a cumulation of evolutionary improvements; much of the technology of precision guidance and target acquisition which will considerably affect the performance of both strategic and conventional weapons belongs in this category. Yet the problem of technological change, while always present, did not seem to worry arms controllers unduly until very recently. They felt that priority had to be given to restricting the numbers of specific weapon systems and that this would also restrict the weapon technologies that went with them. Qualitative arms control was, in this sense, a byproduct of quantitative arms control.

This approach was never satisfactory, thouth perhaps the best available. Today it is in danger of becoming inadequate for three reasons, one political, the other two technical.

Political strains

Politically, arms control has been seen as a symbol of East-West détente, perhaps the most tangible and unambiguous of all such symbols. If East and West are able to agree on limiting or reducing the forces they have available to pit against each other, this will indeed be one token of their sincere commitment to peace and accommodation. But arms-control agreements will only acquire this politically important symbolic significance if they are regarded both in East and West as fair and equitable: if not—if public or official opinion on one side feels 'we have been had'—an agreement will not be interpreted as a genuine gesture towards détente but as a confirmation of long-held suspicions.

The trouble is that, because of technological change and the difficulty of incorporating it in an agreement, it has become almost impossible for arms-control negotiators to produce treaties which will be unequivocally fair and equitable. A bargain struck on the basis of the technological characteristics of specific weapons existing at the time of agreement will become inequitable as one side or the other introduces qualitative improvements which have not been ruled out, or deploys alternative weapon systems which bypass the restrictions agreed upon. Theoretically, it might be possible to resolve this problem by entering into new negotiations once the base of the old agreement shows signs of erosion. However, given both the inherent speed of technological innovation and the widespread tendency of politicians, analysts and the media to speed it up further in their minds by assuming that a known technology is already a deployed one, the intervals between agreements would have to be very brief indeed. The complexity of negotiating new, or renegotiating old, quantitative restrictions would undermine the hope that new and more durable results could be achieved in time. As a result, arms-control treaties and agreements which consist of striking numerical balances are drawn into inevitable political controversy, generating doubts over, rather than promoting confidence in, détente and increasing the political risk for the leaders on both sides.

The fate of the Soviet-American Interim Agreement on the Limitation of Offensive Strategic Weapons of 1972 is a case in point. The numerical balance struck in the agreement soon appeared, rightly or wrongly, to many in the United States to give a one-sided advantage to the Soviet Union, as Soviet weapons developments were catching up with American qualitative superiority. Rapid renegotiation became necessary, not least for domestic political reasons, which gave rise to the Vladivostok Accord only thirty months later. But even this compromise, which granted MIRV parity to the Soviet Union in exchange for an equal ceiling of total strategic forces, did not remove SALT from political controversy in the American debate. The dynamics of technological change eroded not only the basis of the original agreement, but also—and more importantly—eroded much of the desired political effect which both sides had sought to achieve. Rather than being a promoter of détente and political trust, inadequate arms control has become a consumer of trust.

Limits to verification

The second reason why technological change is rendering inadequate the current practice of negotiating quantitative restraints is the increasing difficulty of verification. That agreements on arms limitation must be adequately verifiable has been accepted wisdom for a long time, and technological inventiveness has indeed made this a realistic and unobtrusive principle in permitting the detailed observation of the military effort of another country through satellite reconnaissance. But verification depends on what is observable. Today, significant improvements in military forces and weapons are becoming less and less observable and may be concealed altogether. This poses an awkward dilemma: if a major determinant for arms control is verifiability, and verifiability is less and less assured, then fewer and fewer arms can be covered by agreement, and arms control becomes more and more irrelevant. But, without adequate verification, how can even the most promising arms-control agreement provide both sides with the trust in compliance by the other?

Neither of the two techniques for solving this dilemma suggested in recent arms-control negotiations justify much optimism. The first is to verify compliance to qualitative arms restrictions—for example, which missiles are equipped with MIRV—through the observation of weapons tests. This is based on two questionable assumptions: first, that responsible governments and cautious generals will not entertain the idea of deploying new weapons technology without thorough testing; second, that all tests will be adequately observable. While adequate testing is desirable, it would scarcely be undertaken if camouflage were seen to be of higher importance, particularly since military planners are used to living with a high degree of uncertainty anyway. In addition, many of the more important new weapons technologies in command, control and communications, guidance and target acquisition elude observation altogether.

The other technique for rendering accountable the unobservable characteristics of weapons is the 'counting as if' method: a weapon system (say, an intercontinental missile of uncertain performance) is regarded, for assessment's sake, as if its performance were certain. The SALT II negotiations have already provided one such example: since the Soviet ICBM SS-18 had been tested both with MIRV and with a single warhead, the United States declared that within the Vladivostok limit of 1,320 MIRV launchers, it would count each Soviet SS-18 as if it carried more than one independent warhead. This may be helpful in specific cases, but as a general device its efficacy is more than doubtful. Elevated to a standard measure for assessing qualitative, non-observable weapons improvements, 'counting as if' is a positive stimulus to maximum exploitation of qualitative advances and hence to qualitative arms competition: why should either side maintain a single warhead on a missile if it is counted as a multi-warhead missile anyway? Moreover, it only makes sense if the weapons characteristics are known and form the subject of agreed numerical limitations. 'Counting as if' is at best an auxiliary device, but it is not a satisfactory answer to the verification problem at a time of technological change.

Multi-mission weapons

It might still be possible to make do with a less than satisfactory answer if it were not for another, and probably the most important, feature of current weapons technology: the defiance of traditional categories of weapons definition. Not only does technology improve performance within existing and defined weapons categories; it also makes possible multi-category and multi-mission weapons. The distinction between nuclear and non-nuclear systems, or strategic and theatre weapons, was never absolutely clear-cut but it was sufficiently precise to allow arms-control negotiators to operate with it, incorporate it in treaty language and provide governments with a relatively unambiguous notion of their mutual obligations. It was possible, by restricting certain weapon systems, to restrict certain military missions: a limit on battleships limited also the amount of firepower a navy could project beyond the shores; a ceiling on offensive intercontinental missiles also restricted the ability to launch a first strike against the other side; a freeze on theatre nuclear delivery vehicles also curtailed the destruction of specific theatre targets beyond the range and yield of conventional systems.

The trend towards multi-category and multi-mission systems is rapidly eroding this link between restrictions by category and curtailment of military performance. Limitation of the numbers of a particular category of weapon system no longer restricts the military mission the system used to support, since that mission can be allocated, albeit sometimes less effectively, to other, unrestricted systems. The particular feature of technology that makes this possible is the interchangeability of those factors which define weapon performance: range, yield and accuracy. In the past, a weapon of intercontinental range had to have a warhead which was both nuclear and high-yield, in order to make up for the inaccuracy caused by distance, and both features were more or less rigid requirements: there was no way of replacing the nuclear by a conventional explosive, since the weight differential would significantly reduce the range of the delivery system, and no way of substituting the high nuclear yield by a lower one, since this would drastically reduce destructive efficiency. But increasingly over the past years these absolute thresholds for performance requirements have become relative, largely as a result of the dramatic improvement in missile accuracy. Accuracy is no longer a function of range, as inter-continental delivery systems can attain Circular Error Probability (CEPS) as low as 100 metres over thousands of kilometres. Low accuracy no longer has to be offset by high explosive yields, and conventional explosives, guided to the heart of a point target, can sometimes produce destructive effects of a kind previously reserved for certain nuclear missions.

The initial motivation for these performance improvements was to render delivery systems more effective, i.e. to produce better strategic or better theatre weapons. Their real and long-term significance, however, lies elsewhere: the visible size and configuration of a weapon system are no longer reliable indicators of its performance and mission, as performance elements within the same shell can be allocated differently and can even be changed rapidly to produce a wide range of mission capabilities.

The most obvious example of this development is the modern cruise missile: it can be a tactical or a theatre weapon, but with a smaller warhead load and the resulting increase in range, the same system can also be turned into a long-range weapon, capable of reaching strategic targets deep inside enemy territory. It can, at least theoretically, carry a nuclear or a conventional warhead. Cruise missile ranges can be as high as 4,000 kilometres and as low as desired, and their mode of launch—from the air, from sea-based launchers or from the ground—is equally variable.

Variability is also the feature of another weapon system, the Soviet SS-20 IRBM. Its booster consists of the last two rocket stages of the three-stage ICBM SS-16. By adding the third stage, an intermediate-range ballistic missile targeted on Europe or China can be turned into an ICBM targeted on the United States. The time required for conversion is estimated by some to be no more than a few hours.

It would, of course, be an exaggeration to claim that this trend towards multi-category, multi-mission weapons is entirely new. Theatre arms, like artillery, air-defence systems or tactical aircraft, have for long been 'dual-capable', i.e. able to deliver both nuclear and conventional explosives with resulting variations in range and destructiveness. Manned bombers often span strategic and non-strategic missions if their range permits. The American B-52 force has today a primary strategic nuclear mission, but many of the aircraft were used during the Viet Nam War for conventional area-bombing against targets in South-East Asia. The Soviet Backfire bomber, although probably not intended for use against strategic targets in the United States, has caused problems of definition and accountancy in the SALT negotiations because of its theoretical ability to reach American territory on some missions with in-flight refuelling. Equally, shipbased delivery systems have enjoyed considerable variability—witness the decision of NATO's Nuclear Planning Group in May 1976 to include Polaris/Poseidon SLMB in the theatre nuclear forces assigned to the Supreme Commander in

Europe (SACEUR). So the multi-mission phenomenon is, indeed, not entirely new. But while it had seemed relatively marginal during the development of inter-continental missile systems, it is now becoming much more central, challenging notions that have been essential to arms-control policies of the past twenty years. It is blurring the distinction between strategic and non-strategic weapon systems and making the verifiability of agreements uncertain.

The answer to the problem cannot lie in singling out the latest and most obvious of these new systems, the cruise-missile, and trying to find ways of making it conform to familiar arms-control definitions (for instance, by prohibiting all cruise-missiles, or by so restricting cruise missile sizes that trade-offs between range, guidance, nuclear and non-nuclear use have little or no relevance to the performance). The inapplicability of the approaches of traditional arms control to the cruise missile is a product not so much of any particular characteristic of this specific weapon system as of the technological elements that are responsible for its performance: the miniaturization of guidance and engine, the increased accuracy of delivery, the development of explosives tailored to specific targets and the relatively low cost which allows production in large numbers. If the cruise missile were banned altogether or in specific configurations, other combinations of these elements would still be conceivable and conceived, and would pose the same problem again, possibly within a short time.

Nor can the answer to the erosion of existing weapons categories—strategic/theatre, nuclear/non-nuclear—lie in the setting up of a third or fourth category or of a new arms-control forum designed to cover systems below SALT and above regional negotiations such as MBFR. These systems have often been referred to as 'grey-area weapons', but this is a misleading term, since it suggests that defining the 'grey area' between strategic and regional arms control would make it possible to subject them to a specific arms-control regime. The particular significance of multi-mission weapons is precisely that they cannot be pinned down in any category; they can span the whole spectrum. Attempts to deal with them with the help of a new category or a new arms-control forum will, therefore, be irrelevant to the problem they pose.

For the same reason, the answer to the challenge of the new technologies is also unlikely to lie in an attempt to squeeze them into the framework of existing arms-control negotiations. Splitting up the 'grey area' between the more SALT-related systems (such as long-range nuclear cruise missiles or versatile medium-range ballistic missiles of the SS-20 type) and systems more related to regional security concerns and regional arms-control forums (such as the short-range cruise missile or the Backfire bomber) can be no more than a temporary and makeshift measure. Not only would verification—which is which in what context?—soon prove frustrating but, even if verification were attainable, any arrangement in one forum would deeply affect and disturb the considerations of the other. A severe restriction on cruise missiles in SALT would not only curtail the ability of the superpowers to carry out other military tasks with these systems that they would not want to forgo, but it would also, at least indirectly, circumscribe the use of these weapons by their allies (a problem peculiar to allies of the United States) in purely regional roles and would cause strains in the alliance. Conversely, the inclusion of theatre cruise missiles in MBFR, even if compliance were verifiable, is bound to affect the balance of strategic forces discussed in SALT and with it political relations between the super-powers as well as between the United States and her allies. Much of the 'grey-area weapons' technology is not exclusive to the super-powers; refusal by their allies to conform to rules framed by Soviet and American negotiators (leading perhaps to national development of cruise missiles) would limit the scope of super-power agreement while potentially undermining cohesion within the Western alliance.

These, then, are the three problems that technological change poses for the future of East-West arms control: first, the speed of technological change injects a high degree of ambiguity into restrictions directed primarily at quantitative levels of forces, and not only complicates the negotiations but, more important, endangers the political acceptability of their outcome; second, qualitative improvements are often more significant and less verifiable than quantitics of weapons, so that arms-controllers have to choose between agreements that are fully verifiable but increasingly irrelevant for the control of military potential and agreements that may be relevant but cannot be adequately verified; and third, the trend of technological change is towards multi-mission weapons which undermines the definitional categories which have, in the practice of East-West negotiations, been a primary 'organizing principle'. If arms control continues to encompass only the existing categories, it will fail to cover much of the new weaponry, which, as a result, will acquire increasing importance in the arsenals of both sides and will reduce the relevance of existing and future control agreements; if new categories were defined, these would prove equally elusive.

Attempts to cover the whole range from strategic-nuclear to regional-conventional weapons in one framework of negotiation and agreement could scarcely be promising: not only would the process of negotiation be even more cumbersome and agreement delayed beyond relevance but, more important, the wider framework would not do away with the problem of comparing categories and numbers of weapons. The search for strategic stability would be frustrated by the specific concerns of regional security. In this situation the United States may well decide that the former is more important than the latter; that if the security of the regional alliance were to interfere with the Soviet-American strategic relationship, then the alliance would have to take second place. It is a choice which the United States has so far refused to accept.

This analysis of the dilemma is, of course, based on two assumptions: first, that the dilemma matters and that arms control remains an important instrument in the search for East-West security; second, that technological change, which has largely caused the dilemma, cannot be effectively controlled.

Why arms control?

The traditional objectives of East-West arms control have been three: to reduce the likelihood of war by increasing stability; to reduce the damage of war if war does break out; and to reduce the economic cost of preparing for war. If arms control today has lost much of its initial popularity, this is due not only to a greater recognition of the complexities involved, but also to doubts about whether arms control can realistically achieve these objectives.

Stability?

Current East-West arms-control negotiations—SALT and MBFR—are concerned with aspects of the strategic and theatre balance, both of which have, after all, enjoyed a relatively high degree of stability in the past. The major change in the strategic relationship between the United States and the Soviet Union has been Soviet accession to parity. But that, it can be argued, is a condition for stability. In spite of the introduction of new weapons on both sides, in spite of a multiplication of deliverable warheads, a dramatic increase in the precision of delivering destructive power and a combination of symmetries and asymmetries in the force posture of both the Soviet Union and the United States, the post-1970 balance has shown remarkable resilience.

Although a very great deal of thought and diplomatic effort, hard bargaining and political courage has been invested by both sides in the process of strategic arms control, it is difficult to prove that without any of it—with the possible exception of the Anti-Ballistic Missile (ABM) Treaty—the stability of the central balance would by now be seriously undermined. The current discussion on limited strategic options, scenarios of limited first strikes against vulnerable ICBMs and the inadequacies of 'mutual assured destruction' concepts for deterrence indicates that the stability of the balance is under strain, and no more. The fact that much of this discussion fails to excite fears and concerns beyond the small society of strategic analysts rather confirms the resilience of the existing strategic relationship between the two superpowers, arms control or no arms control.

The European theatre balance, now the subject of East-West negotiation on force reductions, has shown an equally impressive degree of stability, in spite of the absence of any arms-control agreement. This is not to say that the balance is perfect in all respects, nor that there are not very real and sincere doubts over its future in the light of a continuous Soviet build-up which exceeds NATO efforts. But it does indicate that, in spite of changes in force ratios, political crises and the impact of technological innovation on the military arsenals of both sides, relative stability has in the past been obtained without arms control.

That is, of course, not really surprising. After all, there are other means for obtaining and maintaining stability than arms control, in particular that of offsetting through military efforts any threats to the balance as each side perceives it. The test for arms control is, therefore, not whether stability has been present without it but whether it has contributed to more stable military relationships. Here the record is at least ambiguous. Arms control has made the military relationship between East and West more calculable, and therefore stable, when it has been preclusive in character, i.e. when its aims have been to restrict the emplacement of weapons on the seabed, to prohibit the development and deployment of biological weapons, to reduce anti-ballistic-missile defences to the point of insignificance, as in the 1972 Soviet-American treaty. However, where negotiators have sought not preclusive arrangements but quantitative limitations and reductions of existing arsenals, the contribution to stability has been less evident. Details of military-force relationships have often received emphasis beyond their real strategic significance; reductions seem to have been contemplated primarily in connection with older and more obsolete weapon systems, and

151

new programmes have been entertained both to provide a card in the bargaining with the opponent and to mollify domestic political and military opposition. In this respect, the relevance of arms control to strategic stability has been doubtful. While it is impossible to judge with any certainty what would have been the state of the strategic balance without SALT, it is clear that the negotiations and the political ambiance they have created have generated at least some dynamics that have favoured arms competition rather than control.

In the European context, the effect of quantitative, systems-orientated arms limitation on stability is equally ambiguous. While reductions of arms and forces in the potential conflict area of Central Europe might make war preparations more visible and therefore perhaps less likely, they could weaken political stability in a continent where military and political relationships are so closely intertwined: in Eastern Europe, where Soviet political control is underpinned by military presence, and Western Europe, where the strain of negotiations could emphasize differences between allies at the cost of alliance cohesion, and where the establishment of certain arms-control zones could lead to political divisions. This need not be so—but the contribution of arms control to stability is not so clear-cut and obvious as to warrant, for this reason alone, a major political effort.

Damage limitation?

Nor is the need for arms control all that obvious when it comes to the second objective: reducing the damage if war should break out. Paradoxically, the introduction of new weapons technology has sometimes been more successful in this respect than have efforts at controlling arms. The increased accuracy of delivery systems, both for strategic and theatre use, means that collateral damage (that is, unintended damage) can be considerably reduced. New precision-guided weapons with conventional warheads may, in the European theatre, be able to perform tasks that before had been allocated to nuclear weapons, thus raising the 'nuclear threshold'. As strategic systems can be used more selectively, because of refinements in command and control as well as accuracy, the threshold of all-out nuclear war is further removed from regional conflict, and military installations replace urban centres as the primary targets in the echelon of escalation below that upper threshold. These technologies may well be 'destabilizing', in that they remove one barrier against their employment, that of uncertainty of effect; as the effect of weapons becomes more calculable, the decision to go to war may also. But if war does break out, the new technologies allow for a more discriminating and controlled use—an important objective of arms control. This, again, is not an argument *against* arms control; efforts at damage limitation, like the current Red Cross talks on incendiary and other weapons, or the negotiations of the United Nations Disarmament Conference in Geneva on chemical weapons, weather modification and weapons of mass destruction, may also contribute to making war less indiscriminately destructive. The point is merely that arms control, contrary to the beliefs and hopes of some, is not the only, and often not the most effective, way of achieving this goal.

Reducing military costs?

The third objective, that of reducing the economic burden of the military effort, has been both the most pragmatic and the least successfully attained to date in East-West arms-control negotiations and agreements. The promise of savings in defence expenditure has been offered by political leaders in East and West every time they have embarked on negotiations over the limitation of arms. Yet the results have rarely matched the promises. In connection with the SALT I experience, Allison and Morris have noted :

After a decade of steady decline in [American] strategic expenditures—in the absence of a SALT Treaty and attendant principles and agreements—defence budgets submitted to the Congress [after the 1972 SALT Agreements] . . . called for a levelling off of that decline and indeed, for increasing strategic expenditures.[1]

On the Soviet side, judging by the range of new deployments and newly started strategic programmes, the discrepancy between expressed economic hopes and actual expenditure, although less verifiable, has been no less and probably much greater than in the United States. Even if future SALT negotiations should produce sizeable reductions, as opposed to ceilings without cuts, in the strategic arsenals of both sides, these are not likely to produce major economies but would probably involve the phasing out of old systems in favour of new and more expensive ones. The major exception to the rule has been the ABM Treaty, in which both sides agreed not only to limit, but in reality to forgo the investment for, a functioning ballistic-missile defence, an example to which we shall return later.

No practical experience with mutual arms limitation has so far been gained in the European theatre. The MBER negotiations have been accompanied by publicly expressed hopes that they would result in the maintenance of security at lower costs. This might be the case if negotiations were to lead to a sizeable cut in military manpower; but the Western reductions envisaged by NATO's proposals—20,000 United States forces in the first phase and a further 53,000 United States and allied in the second—would not go far in producing savings for the six NATO forces involved in the prospective reduction area (even assuming reductions would lead to the units being disbanded rather than redeployed elsewhere). Savings would certainly be much less than the $20,000 million per annum which, it has been argued, could result from NATO weapons standardization. Where not manpower but weapons cuts are considered, as in the December 1975 NATO proposal to withdraw from West European territory 1,000 nuclear warheads with launchers in exchange for a withdrawal of 1,700 Soviet tanks from Eastern Europe, any savings are likely to be largely offset by the cost of modernizing those that remain.

This assessment is, of course, open to the criticism that it concentrates on savings against actual, but not against potential, expenditure. In the absence of negotiated restrictions, it has been argued, the arms race would have continued unabated and major new weapon investments would have been necessary to keep ahead in the race. This might well be true but it is not self-evident. For one thing, the contention rests on a hypothetical comparison—between that which is and that which might have been. As the point raised by Allison and Morris makes clear, it is by no means certain that the absence of arms control would have promoted arms competition more than has the negotiation of formal agreements. For another, it assumes that the primary driving force of the arms race is the action-reaction process by which the weapons procurement of each side is a response to that of the other. However, this is an assumption that has been increasingly and persuasively challenged by recent academic studies; at worst it is erroneous, at best too simple.

If the economic rewards of arms control have generally been disappointing, some kinds of arms control seem to have yielded more tangible results. The ABM example is, after all, impressive as a preclusive arms-control agreement which rules out of the legitimate arsenals of both sides the specific military mission of ballistic missile defence and prohibits investment on production and deployment (not research or development) of weapons designed to provide it. Quantitative limitations, however, if they imply reductions at all are likely to produce only marginal savings, because in the bargaining of mutual concessions both sides will tend to seek the smallest common denominator, which often means retention of the largest force. It is also easier to agree on phasing out obsolete weapons which are obsolete precisely because new and more expensive systems have superseded them, thus offering economies in maintenance but not in investment as the most likely saving. Moreover, quantitative restrictions of specific systems encourage the search for alternative, non-restricted systems in a world of technological change. It is therefore not surprising if the economic advantages of quantitavive arms control have been less than impressive and represent, by themselves, an insignificant dividend for the effort invested.

Has East-West arms control then outlived its usefulness? The balance in the strategic Soviet-American relationship and in the European theatre is not ideal but it is still relatively stable. Potential damage in war could be reduced with the help of some of the new military technologies that are being introduced over the next few years. The tangible economic dividends of arms control have generally been meagre.

And yet the reasons why, in spite of doubts, disappointments and disillusionment, attempts at arms control between East and West must be continued remain powerful, perhaps more powerful than in the past.

Arms control as conflict management

Much of the original American enthusiasm for arms control was shaped in a period of clear American superiority, and more recent disappointments may have much to do with the difficulties of living in a state of nuclear strategic parity. Both the Soviet Union and the United States face a tough learning process. The Soviet Union must learn that catching up with the leader is one thing, gaining superiority over him quite another. The United States must learn that parity is a combination of asymmetries and that marginal advantages on one side or the other do not undermine stability. This learning process will be made even more difficult by the fact that some of the basic elements of nuclear deterrence will be called into question by technological change and will require careful deterrence management. The most important and potentially the most disturbing of these changes is the vulnerability of second-strike forces to strategic counter-force action. With growing missile accuracy, land-based ICBMs (even those in hardened silos) will become, sooner for the United States or later for the Soviet Union, targets that can be destroyed by the other side with a relatively high degree of reliability. As to sea-based nuclear-missile forces, the anti-submarine warfare (ASW) effort continues and may, over time, decrease the margin of invulnerability which they enjoy today. These developments will not only raise the general level of strategic nervousness; they may also reopen the question of ballistic-missile defence which has been presumed closed since the ABM Treaty of 1972. The degree of strategic turbulence will therefore be considerable over the next decade; probably much greater than that provoked by the relatively simple process of adjustment to the Soviet-American parity of secure second-strike forces which has marked the previous one. During this period of pronounced sensitivity, with its concomitant risks of miscalculation and misinterpretation, arms control will provide an essential framework of management.

Nuclear proliferation

The other development which will confront the two strategic superpowers in the decade ahead is nuclear proliferation. As other countries demonstrate their real or potential status as nuclear-weapons powers, the need is becoming manifest for the Soviet Union and the United States to keep their strategic relationship clear of the impact of third-party proliferation. Not that, in the foreseeable future, there will be serious rivals to the status of the superpowers, nor that the next decade is likely to see the emergence of many fully fledged nuclear-weapons states; the situation will be much less clear-cut. Some states will visibly invest in a nuclear-weapons option without proceeding to its implementation; others will set up a minimum force, primitive by superpower standard but nevertheless frightening to neighbours; other states again will keep the world guessing as to whether or not they have acquired the capability to deliver nuclear weapons against an enemy; and a further group will make their continued non-nuclear status dependent on the co-operative behaviour of others, including the adequate supply of conventional weapons. As a result, nuclear power will be brought into international politics much more actively than before, in spite of the continued military pre-eminence of the United States and the Soviet Union. It is against this background that the superpowers must seek to protect their relationship of mutual deterrence through the continued process of dialogue which is arms control.

Finally, the arms-control process between East and West should be sustained in order to constrain the use of force in the period of international change, potential conflict and gradual adjustment which the world will be facing over the next decade or two. There is a risk that wars in the Third World could embroil the Second and First Worlds as well, that domestic change in East and West European countries could blur the European dividing line and introduce, into a continent which has owed much of its stability of the last thirty years to the predictability of alliances, a degree of unpredictability which could jeopardize security in the short run. And there is a risk that the Soviet Union, faced at home with the dilemma of the continued postponement of needed modernization of her political system for fear of its survival, and abroad with her inability to influence events other than by military force, might seek via the active employment of military resources an expansion of her influence and release from internal deadlock. Arms-control negotiations and agreements will not be capable of repressing the use of force on their own, but they may contribute to restraint, however modestly, in a period when the world will need all the barriers against conflict it can construct.

The requirement for arms control follows, therefore, from the need to manage and control military competition between East and West in the years ahead. Can this not be done adequately by dialogue, by discussion and by the explanation of respective doctrines—in other words, without specific agreements on subjects which, like force reductions and weapons deployment, are affected by technological change? Dialogue and discussion are, no doubt, an important ingredient of the management of arms competition, but they must be expressed in agreements in order that their success can be assessed and so that they may receive and maintain political support. Results mean visible restrictions, reductions and constraints. As these will be affected by changes in military technology, arms control will either have to develop the means to slow down and control technological change, or it will have to devise other methods of restraint which are less subject to the dynamics of technological innovation and change than the existing method of primarily quantitative limitation.

Note

1. G. T. Allison and F. A. Morris, in Long and Rathjens (eds.), *Arms, Defence Policy and Arms Control*, pp. 99–100, New York, Norton, 1976.

Part IV. Arms control and disarmament

13

Review of arms-control agreements

Jozef Goldblat
Stockholm International Peace Research Institute

Introduction

The practice of negotiating disarmament in an international forum with a view to making the measures adopted applicable to many nations is relatively recent. Apart from the 1899 and 1907 Hague conferences, which made an attempt to codify the laws of war, only one conference was held prior to the Second World War to discuss the universal reduction and limitation of armaments: the World Conference convened on 2 February 1932, under the auspices of the League of Nations, and attended by representatives from more than sixty states. After several years of work, general agreement seemed to exist on the following principles: (a) prohibition of certain methods of war; (b) qualitative and quantitative limitation of armaments; (c) supervision of the manufacture of and trade in arms; (d) publicity of national defence expenditure; (e) supervision of the implementation of the obligations; and (f) guarantees of the implementation. However, agreement could not be reached as regards the application of these principles, and on 22 January 1936 the Council of the League of Nations decided to postpone the work of the conference.

The League conference never reconvened. International efforts to regulate armaments on a worldwide scale resumed only after the Second World War, within the framework of the United Nations Organization which was created 'to save succeeding generations from the scourge of war'.

A multitude of proposals related to international disarmament, including proposals for a complete elimination of armed forces and armaments, have been made in various forums, both within and outside the framework of the United Nations. But so far, only a few so-called arms-control measures have been agreed upon, imposing certain, not particularly burdensome restrictions on the armament policies of states. Originally, the term 'arms control', coined in the United States, was meant to denote measures regulating the arms race rather than stopping it; it had a connotation clearly distinct from that of the reduction of

Excerpts from *Arms Control, A Survey and Appraisal of Multilateral Agreements,* Stockholm, International Peace Research Institute (SIPRI) and London, Taylor & Francis Ltd, 1978 (the volume also contains a comprehensive collection of texts of multilateral arms-control agreements concluded after the Second World War and relevant documents from before 1939).

armaments or disarmament. Subsequently, however, diverse measures intended to freeze, limit or abolish certain categories of weapons; to prevent certain military activities; to regulate the deployment of forces; to proscribe transfers of certain militarily important items; to reduce the risk of an accidental war; to constrain or prohibit the use of certain arms in war; or to build up international confidence through greater openness in the military field, have come to be included under the rubric of arms control. It is in this broad sense that the term 'arms control' will be used here.

Multilateral arms-control agreements

The main undertakings assumed in the multilateral arms-control agreements already in force, or about to enter into force, include: (a) prevention of militarization or of military nuclearization of certain areas or environments; (b) restrictions on weapons tests; (c) prevention of the spread among nations of specified weapons; (d) prohibition of production as well as elimination of stocks of certain types of weapons; (e) prohibition of the use of certain methods of warfare; (f) observance of the rules of conduct in war; (g) notification of certain military activities; and (h) verification of obligations contracted under previously signed treaties.

The 1959 Antarctic Treaty

This declared that the area south of latitude 60° S. shall be used exclusively for peaceful purposes. The treaty prohibits any measures of a military nature, such as the establishment of military bases or fortifications, the carrying out of military manoeuvres or the testing of any type of weapons. There is also a ban on nuclear explosions in the Antarctic, whatever their nature, as well as on the disposal of radioactive waste material, subject to possible future international agreements on these subjects.

The Antarctic Treaty is an important preventive measure, the first of its kind to be concluded after the Second World War. Its denuclearization clause, which has helped to prevent the use of the empty expanses of the Antarctic as a nuclear testing ground or a nuclear weapon base, is particularly significant.

The 1963 Partial Test-Ban Treaty

The PTBT prohibits any nuclear explosions (that is, also those which are intended for peaceful purposes) in the atmosphere, outer space or under water, or in any other environment if the explosion would cause radioactive debris to be present outside the territorial limits of the country conducting it.

The PTBT has helped to curb the radioactive pollution caused by nuclear explosions, but it could not stop it altogether: non-party nuclear powers (France and China) continued testing in the atmosphere, and underground explosions, permitted under the treaty, often also release radioactive products into the air. Moreover, the arms-control objectives of the treaty have not been even partially achieved.

By the time the PTBT was concluded, the two main testing states, the United States and the USSR, had already carried out extensive series of explosions in the atmosphere and knew that this activity could be continued underground. In fact, since 1963 they have carried out more nuclear explosions than during the period preceding the signing of the PTBT. This has enabled them to develop new generations of nuclear warheads and of related delivery vehicles. In other words, the nuclear arms race has been allowed to continue unhampered. The pledge given by the United Kingdom, the United States and the USSR in the preamble and Article I of the PTBT—to achieve the discontinuance of all nuclear-weapon test explosions for all time—has not as yet been fulfilled.

Limitations on the size of nuclear explosions, which were included in the 1974 United States-USSR Threshold Test-Ban Treaty (TTBT), may constrain the development and testing of high-yield warheads and bombs. But the yield threshold, 150 kilotons, is so high (ten times higher than the yield of the bomb dropped on Hiroshima in 1945) that the parties cannot be experiencing onerous restraint in continuing their nuclear-weapon programmes.

The 1967 Outer Space Treaty

This lays down principles governing peaceful activities of states in outer space. The follow-up agreements—namely: the Agreement on the Rescue of Astronauts, the Return of Astronauts and the Return of Objects Launched into Outer Space; the Convention on International Liability for Damage Caused by Space Objects; and the Convention on Registration of Objects Launched into Outer Space—address themselves to technical and legal aspects of international co-operation in the exploration and use of outer space for peaceful purposes. Only one clause of the Outer Space Treaty itself (Article IV) is directly related to arms control: it elaborates on a United Nations General Assembly resolution, unanimously adopted in 1963, and prohibits the placing in orbit around the earth of any objects carrying nuclear weapons or any other kinds of weapons of mass destruction, the installation of such weapons on celestial bodies, or the stationing of them in outer space in any other manner. The establishment of military bases, installations and fortifications, the testing of any type of weapons and the conduct of military manœuvres on celestial bodies are also forbidden.

However, the outer-space environment has not been denuclearized. The flight through outer space of ballistic missiles carrying nuclear weapons from one point to another on the earth's surface has not been forbidden. Even nuclear weapons placed in orbit but flying less than one full revolution round the earth, the so-called fractional orbital bombardment systems (FOBS), seem to have escaped proscription. Moreover, the deployment in outer space of weapons not capable of mass destruction is subject to no restriction whatever. This has left a wide margin for permitted military activities, an opportunity which is being taken advantage of by the United States and the USSR and perhaps other states. In addition to space-based anti-missile defences not prohibited by the 1972 United States-USSR ABM Treaty, both sides are engaged in developing devices capable of intercepting, destroying or disabling satellites in orbit, adding a new dimension to the arms race.

Complete demilitarization of outer space is probably unattainable so long as ballistic missiles exist in weapon arsenals. But, given this situation, an agreement safeguarding satellites would be necessary to avoid war in space, to preserve strategic stability and to ensure that arms control treaties verified from space are being complied with.

The 1967 Treaty of Tlatelolco

This treaty prohibits the testing, use, manufacture, production or acquisition by any means, as well as the receipt, storage, installation, deployment and any form of possession of nuclear weapons in Latin America. The extracontinental or continental states which are internationally responsible for territories lying within the limits of the geographical zone established by the treaty (that is, France, the Netherlands, the United Kingdom and the United States) undertake to apply the statute of military denuclearization to these territories by adhering to Additional Protocol I annexed to the treaty. Under Additional Protocol II the nuclear-weapon states undertake to respect the statute of military denuclearization of Latin America, and not to contribute to acts involving a violation of the treaty, nor to use or threaten to use nuclear weapons against the parties to the treaty.

The Treaty of Tlatelolco is now in force for an area of more than 8 million square kilometres and inhabited by some 150 million people, the ultimate goal being to cover an area of 20 million square kilometres with a population of around 280 million. The importance of this nuclear-weapon-free zone in a populous region of the world in undeniable. Nevertheless, the treaty contains ambiguous points which may weaken its 'non-armament' impact. One of them is related to so-called peaceful nuclear explosions.

Explosions of nuclear devices for peaceful purposes are allowed under the treaty and procedures for carrying them out are stipulated. Some countries interpret these provisions as prohibiting the manufacture of nuclear explosive devices for peaceful purposes unless or until nuclear devices are developed which cannot be used as weapons. So formulated, the condition can hardly be fulfilled because nuclear explosives, irrespective of the objective pursued, contain identical nuclear components, and their production requires essentially the same technology. Other countries consider that the treaty has sanctioned peaceful explosions involving devices used in nuclear weapons. Thus, the important problem of compatibility of an indigenous development of nuclear explosive devices for peaceful purposes with participation in this nuclear-weapon-free zone agreement has remained unresolved.

Another controversial point is the geographical extent of the Latin American nuclear-weapon-free area. The zone of application of the treaty embraces the territory, territorial sea, air space and any other space over which the zonal state exercises sovereignty in accordance with 'its own legislation'. The broad definition of the zone, as contained in the treaty, is not acceptable to all the nuclear-weapon powers called upon to respect its denuclearized status.

And, finally, since neither transport nor transit of nuclear weapons has been explicitly prohibited by the treaty, the question has arisen whether these activities are actually permitted. Once nuclear weapons are allowed to be in transit in Latin America, even if such transit is limited to port visits or overflights, it will be impossible to maintain that the zone has been totally and effectively denuclearized.

The Treaty of Tlatelolco is significant as the first agreement restricting the use of nuclear weapons. But not all assurances of non-use, so far obtained, have been unconditional. The United States and the United Kingdom have reserved the right to reconsider their obligations with regard to a state in the nuclear-weapon-free zone in the event of any act of aggression or armed attack by that state, carried out with the support or assistance of a nuclear-weapon power. Whether or not such a hedged guarantee conforms to the spirit of Additional Protocol II is open to question.

The Treaty of Tlatelolco was specifically intended to preclude the emergence of nuclear-weapon powers in Latin America. This goal has not been achieved, in spite of the fact that the treaty is in force for the overwhelming majority of the states in the region. In 1977, ten years after the signing of the treaty, several countries of Latin America were still not bound by its provisions.

Cuba, which in 1962 allowed Soviet nuclear weapons to be stationed on its territory, has refused to join the treaty. Argentina has so far only signed the treaty, while Brazil has signed and ratified it but, unlike most other parties, has not waived the requirements that are to be met before the treaty enters into force for any given country (this is also the case with Chile). However, even if the latter two countries became party to the Treaty of Tlatelolco, they might still insist, as they have repeatedly done in the past, that they had the right to carry out their own nuclear explosions for peaceful purposes. And since peaceful explosions are essentially indistinguishable from military tests, any of these countries exploding a nuclear device would become, *de facto*, a nuclear power, which would defeat the purpose of the treaty.

It is of interest to note that there have also been attempts to limit conventional armaments in Latin America. In the 1974 Declaration of Ayacucho, the six members of the so-called Andean Group (Bolivia, Chile, Ecuador, Peru and Venezuela) plus two non-members (Argentina and Panama) undertook to create conditions permitting an effective limitation of armaments and putting an end to their acquisition for offensive purposes. The stated aim of these measures was to devote all possible resources to the economic and social development of the countries in Latin America. Several meetings have taken place since the signing of the declaration with a view to translating its provisions into an internationally binding instrument.

An agreement on conventional-weapon restraints in Latin America could have a positive impact on peace and security in the area. However, the prospects for such an agreement are not bright due to the following circumstances: political as well as territorial disputes continue to exist in Latin America; the chronic instability of regimes in many Latin American countries creates a constant demand for arms for internal purposes; the major arms-exporting countries do not seem to be willing to forgo whatever advantages they may draw, political or economic, from continued weapon supplies to Latin America; and, in addition, the agreement envisaged by the Andean states falls short of the requirement that, to be effective, regional arms limitation must apply to all militarily significant countries of the region.

The 1968 Non-Proliferation Treaty

This treaty prohibits the transfer by nuclear-weapon states to any recipient whatsoever of nuclear weapons or other nuclear explosive devices or of control over them. The NPT also prohibits the receipt by non-nuclear-weapon states from any transferor whatsoever, as well as the manufacture or other acquisition by those states, of nuclear weapons or other nuclear explosive devices. (Unlike the Treaty of Tlatelolco, the NPT has not defined a nuclear weapon or a nuclear explosive device.) In addition, the nuclear-weapon states are not allowed to assist, encourage, or induce any non-nuclear-weapon state to manufacture or acquire the devices in question. There is no express prohibition for non-nuclear-weapon states party to the NPT to provide such assistance, encouragement or inducement to other non-nuclear-weapon states which are not party to the NPT. But the United States and the USSR, the powers that were responsible for the formulation of the relevant provisions, have made it clear that such a case would be regarded as a violation of the treaty.

The need to halt a wider spread of nuclear weapons grew out of the realization that the possession of these weapons by many countries would increase the threat to world security. But the concept of a treaty prohibiting the acquisition of weapons by an overwhelming majority of states, while tolerating the retention of the same weapons by a few, has given rise to controversies relating to the balance of rights and obligations of parties under international agreements.

To attenuate the asymmetries inherent in the NPT, the nuclear-weapon powers have undertaken to facilitate the exchange of equipment, materials and scientific and technological information for the peaceful uses of nuclear energy, with due consideration for the needs of the developing areas of the world (Article IV); to make available their services, at low cost, for peaceful applications of nuclear explosions (Article V); to pursue negotiations on measures relating to the cessation of the nuclear arms race and to nuclear disarmament and on a treaty on general and complete disarmament (Article VI); and, under a separate arrangement, to provide security guarantees to non-nuclear weapon states. But all these 'compensatory' provisions have proved to be of little consequence.

Assistance in the development of nuclear energy for peaceful purposes could have been a powerful inducement to join the NPT if it had been reserved only for the parties. But nuclear transactions have continued to be conducted according to the rules and customs of commercial competition and in keeping with the political interests of the supplier states rather than in conformity with the international non-proliferation strategy. Non-parties have not been excluded from participation in international co-operation in the nuclear field. In some instances they have even managed to secure more material supplies and technical aid than have the parties. The most striking case is that of India, which, notwithstanding its official statements that it would not subscribe to the NPT and that it was preparing a nuclear explosion, received nuclear material and associated equipment.

The NPT provision dealing with disarmament was included at the insistence of non-nuclear-weapon states, with a view to matching the cessation of 'horizontal' proliferation with the cessation of 'vertical' proliferation. The idea was that the NPT should become a transitional stage in a process of nuclear disarmament. But it soon became clear that the nuclear-weapon powers considered it an end in itself. In fact, the obligation undertaken was not to disarm, but to negotiate. Moreover, the term 'cessation', as applied to the nuclear arms race, does not convey the same meaning for all states. For example, the United States-

USSR Interim Agreement of 1972, which allowed an unlimited multiplication of nuclear warheads, and which placed no restrictions on the qualitative improvement of weapons, has often been described by the two sides as a measure meeting the requirements of the NPT, while others have seen in it an encouragement to further competition in arms.

Under a 1968 United Nations Security Council resolution the states forgoing the acquisition of nuclear weapons under the NPT received a pledge of immediate assistance, in accordance with the United Nations Charter, in the event that they became 'a victim of an act or an object of a threat of aggression in which nuclear weapons are used'. But the value of this pledge is questionable. The resolution and the associated declarations by the United Kingdom, the United States and the USSR merely reaffirm the existing United Nations Charter obligation to provide assistance to a country attacked, irrespective of the type of weapon employed. Since all the nuclear-weapon powers are now also permanent members of the Security Council, a decision concerning military or non-military measures against a delinquent state could not be taken if any one of them cast a negative vote, inasmuch as it is inconceivable that a nation which had used nuclear weapons would consent to a collective action being taken against itself. Moreover, immediate active intervention, as envisaged by the resolution, is deemed unacceptable by some non-aligned and neutral states, unless assistance has been specifically requested by them. However, the most serious deficiency of the resolution resides in the fact that it provides for action only when a threat of nuclear attack has been made or an attack has already occurred. It does not offer assurance for the prevention of the use or threat of use of nuclear weapons. In other words, states which have decided not to acquire nuclear weapons have received no guarantee that nuclear weapons possessed by others would not be used against them.

The 1971 Sea-Bed Treaty

This prohibits emplanting or emplacing on the sea-bed and the ocean floor and in the subsoil thereof beyond the outer limit of a sea-bed zone (coterminous with the 12-mile outer limit of the zone referred to in the 1958 Geneva Convention on the Territorial Sea and the Contiguous Zone) any nuclear weapons or any other types of weapons of mass destruction as well as structures, launching installations or any other facilities specifically designed for storing, testing or using such weapons.

Even the denuclearization undertaking is only partial: the portion of the sea-bed which is adjacent to the coast of nuclear-weapon states, and which is therefore more suitable for the emplacement of nuclear weapons than are outlying areas, has been excluded from the prohibition. Neither does the treaty prevent the great powers from installing nuclear weapons beneath the territorial waters of other states, if those states authorize such installation, and if the operation is carried out within the 12-mile sea-bed zone. The United States, which together with the USSR sponsored the treaty, also explained that submersible vehicles carrying nuclear weapons on board, and able to navigate in the water above the sea-bed, would be viewed as any other ship and not as violating the treaty when they are anchored to, or resting on, the ocean bottom.

Only fixed nuclear installations or bottom-crawling vehicles which can navigate exclusively when in contact with the sea-bed, and which, moreover, are specifically designed to use nuclear weapons, have been banned. But such devices, being very vulnerable, appear not to be militarily attractive. Thus the treaty has prohibited something which was in any case not likely to be developed. And since it permits the use of the sea-bed for facilities which service free-swimming nuclear-weapon systems, it presents no obstacle to a nuclear arms race in the whole marine environment.

The 1972 Biological Weapons Convention

This convention prohibits the development, production, stockpiling or acquisition by other means, or retention of biological agents or toxins, of types and in quantities that have no justification for peaceful purposes, as well as weapons, equipment or means of delivery designed to use such agents or toxins for hostile purposes or in armed conflict.

Because of their uncontrollability and unpredictability, biological weapons have always been considered of little utility. But, in prohibiting the further development of biological weapons, the Biological Weapons (BW) Convention has aimed at eliminating the possibility that scientific advances modifying the conditions of production, stockpiling and use of these weapons could make them militarily more attractive. The convention is also meant to prevent the spread of biological and toxin weapons to countries which do not possess them. However, its most remarkable feature consists in the requirement to destroy the agents and toxins, as well as related weapons, equipment and means of delivery which are in the possession of the parties, or to divert them to peaceful purposes. This is the first international agreement since the Second World War which, by abolishing an entire class of weapons, involves some measure of 'sacrifice'.

It is regrettable that chemical weapons were not prohibited at the same time. Since 1925 these weapons had been considered together with biological weapons, and have been associated with them in the public mind. Indeed, chemical weapons may be potentially more attractive to the military than biological weapons: they are more predictable and can produce immediate effects, which are important qualities in actual combat; and they are maintained in the arsenals of certain states and have already been used on a large scale in war with disastrous consequences to the attacked nations. For these reasons, the parties to the BW Convention had to recognize that the convention was only a step towards an agreement effectively prohibiting also the development, production and stockpiling of chemical weapons, and providing for their destruction. They have undertaken to continue negotiations with a view to reaching such an agreement.

The 1975 Final Act of the Conference on Security and Co-operation in Europe (Helsinki) contains a 'Document on Confidence-building Measures and Certain Aspects of Security and Disarmament'. The rationale for adopting the document was formulated as follows:

To contribute to reducing the dangers of armed conflict and of misunderstanding or miscalculation of military activities which could give rise to apprehension, particularly in a situation when the participating states lack clear and timely information about the nature of such activities.

The only provision stated in concrete terms concerns the notification of major military manoeuvres in Europe, to be given at least twenty-one days in advance or, in the case of a manoeuvre arranged at shorter notice, at the earliest possible opportunity prior to its starting date. The term 'major' means that at least 25,000 troops are involved. Manoeuvres with fewer troops can also be considered as major if they involve 'significant numbers' of troops especially trained for invasion purposes (amphibious or airborne).

The preamble of the document states that the notification of manoeuvres 'rests upon a voluntary basis'; it is, therefore, not a legally binding commitment. None the less, it is a declaration of intent solemnly adopted by the representatives of the participating states at the highest possible level; and since the parties expressed their conviction of the political importance of prior notification of major military manoeuvres for 'the promotion of mutual understanding and the strengthening of confidence, stability and security', and accepted the 'responsibility of each of them' to implement this measure, the document carried a potential for exerting pressure on non-observing states.

In spite of these deficiencies, the undertaking to notify signifies a step, though a modest one, towards openness in military affairs. Moreover, the document contains a promise that consideration will be given to the question of notification of major military movements.

The Environmental Modification Convention, 1977

The Environmental Modification Convention, opened for signature in 1977, prohibits military or any other hostile use of environmental modification techniques.

The negotiations on the ENMOD Convention were motivated, *inter alia*, by concern that environmental forces could be used for military ends, and that environmental manipulation could have serious consequences for human welfare. But the resulting agreement has not entirely allayed this concern since it has not banned all environmental modification techniques for hostile purposes. Only the use of those techniques which have widespread, long-lasting or severe effects as the means of destruction, damage or injury to states party to the convention has been prohibited.

According to an understanding reached during the negotiations (but not written into the convention), the term 'widespread' means encompassing an area on the scale of several hundred square kilometres; 'long-lasting' refers to a period of months, or approximately a season; while 'severe' is to be interpreted as involving serious or significant disruption or harm to human life, natural and economic resources or other assets. Exempted from the prohibition are non-hostile uses of modification techniques, even if they produce destructive effects above the threshold described above. Equally permissible are hostile uses which produce destructive effects below the threshold.

According to another understanding, the hostile use of techniques which produce earthquakes, tsunamis, an upset in the ecological balance of a region, changes in weather patterns (clouds, precipitation, cyclones of various types and tornadic storms), changes in climate patterns, changes in ocean currents, changes in the state of the ozone layer, and changes in the state of the ionosphere, is unconditionally prohibited. However, none of these phenomena seems likely to be caused through deliberate action for rational warlike purposes, that is, in such a way that the effects would be felt only, or primarily, by the enemy. Techniques that can produce more limited effects—such as precipitation modification (short of changing the weather patterns), or formation or dissipation of fog—and are likely to be used to influence the environment with hostile intent in a selected area, especially in tactical military operations (facilitating the effectiveness of other weapons), have escaped proscription. And it is precisely such techniques that may enter the sphere of military competition.

The humanitarian laws of war

Efforts to reduce brutality in war have a long history. They have been motivated by ethical and religious as well as practical considerations. Of special significance was the Declaration of St Petersburg of 1868. It proclaimed that the only legitimate objective which states should endeavour to accomplish during war is to weaken the military forces of the enemy, and that the employment of arms which uselessly aggravate the suffering of disabled men, or render their death inevitable, would be contrary to the laws of humanity.

Following the spirit of the St Petersburg Declaration, Declaration IV, 3 of the Hague Conference, held in 1899, prohibited the use of so-called dum-dum bullets, which expanded or flattened easily in the human body and caused more serious wounds than other bullets.

The Second Hague Conference, held in 1907, adopted a Convention on Laws and Customs of Land Warfare, Convention IV, which confirmed the principles of the St Petersburg Declaration. It stated that the right of belligerents to adopt means of injuring the enemy is not unlimited, and it prohibited the employment of arms, projectiles, or material calculated to cause unnecessary suffering. In particular, the convention prohibited the use of poison or poisoned weapons, the treacherous killing or wounding of individuals belonging to the hostile nation or army, or the killing or wounding of an enemy who had laid down his arms or surrendered. The same conference restricted and regulated, in Convention VIII, the use of automatic submarine contact mines; prohibited, in Convention IX, the bombardment by naval forces of ports, cities, villages, habitations or buildings which were not defended; and proclaimed, in Declaration XIV, a prohibition on the discharge of projectiles and explosives from balloons or by other methods of a similar nature.

In addition to attempting to codify the laws of war on a worldwide scale, the two Hague conferences brought advances in establishing institutions and procedures for settling international disputes. Plans for a third conference had to be abandoned in view of the intensified interstate antagonisms that preceded the First World War.

After the war, on 17 June 1925, the Geneva Protocol was signed, prohibiting the use of asphyxiating, poisonous or other gases, and of all analogous liquids, materials or devices, as well as the use of bacteriological methods of warfare. In the part dealing with gases, the protocol actually ratified a prohibition previously declared in international documents. These included the 1899 Hague Declaration IV, 2, under which the contracting powers had agreed to abstain from the use of projectiles for the diffusion of asphyxiating or deleterious gases, as well as the 1907 Hague Convention IV, mentioned above. The need to restate the prohibition of acts already held in abhorrence and condemned by world opinion was prompted by the experience of the First World War, during which the extensive use of poisonous gas resulted in as many as 1.3 million casualties.

As a legal constraint, the Geneva Protocol has been weakened by the reservations made by a number of states which limit its applicability to nations party to it, and to first use only. The danger that the weapons prohibited by the protocol may, under certain circumstances, be resorted to (as has occurred on several occasions since its adoption) will remain as long as these weapons are retained in the military arsenals of states. None of the existing international instruments proved sufficient in providing humanitarian safeguards during the Second World War. Indeed, the shock of the discovery of mass crimes committed during that war led to the 1948 Convention on the Prevention and Punishment of the Crime of Genocide—the so-called Genocide Convention. This convention declares genocide, defined as the commission of acts intended to destroy, in whole or in part, a national, ethnical, racial or religious group, as such, to be a crime to be prevented and punished. Further rules were worked out at a conference held in Geneva in 1949, and were included in the following four conventions: Convention (I) for the Amelioration of the Condition of the Wounded and Sick in Armed Forces in the Field; Convention (II) for the Amelioration of the Condition of the Wounded, Sick and Shipwrecked Members of Armed Forces at Sea; Convention (III) Relative to the Treatment of Prisoners of War; and Convention (IV) Relative to the Protection of Civilian Persons in Time of War.

The Geneva Conventions of 1949 were conceived primarily as a code of behaviour in wars of the traditional type, conducted between states and between regular armies. However, since the Second World War most armed conflicts have been civil wars. Guerrilla warfare has been the prevalent type of such conflicts and has complicated the application of the principle that a distinction must be observed between the civilian and the military. As a result, the protection of civilians has weakened considerably. Furthermore, the laws of war which relate directly to the conduct of hostilities by banning or restricting the use of a specific weapon or type of weapon, as distinct from rules designed to accord protection to certain persons, places or objects in armed conflicts, had not developed since the 1907 Hague Conventions, with the sole exception of the above-mentioned 1925 Geneva Protocol. In particular, air warfare had remained to a great extent uncodified; aerial bombardment, which caused the destruction of many cities in the Second World War, was not expressly forbidden; and weapons that had come into existence during the past decades and which were of an especially cruel or inhumane nature had not been specifically prohibited.

To deal with all these matters, a Diplomatic Conference on the Reaffirmation and Development of International Law Applicable in Armed Conflicts was convened in Geneva in 1974. In 1977, at the end of the fourth session of the conference, two protocols were adopted: Protocol I, relating to the Protection of Victims of International Armed Conflicts; and Protocol II, relating to the Protection of Victims of Non-international Armed Conflicts. Both were signed on 12 December 1977.

Protocol I reiterates and expands the traditional rules regarding the protection of the civilian population. The prohibition against indiscriminate attacks now covers attacks by bombardment by any methods or means which treat as a single military objective a number of distinct objectives located in a city, town, village or other area containing a similar concentration of civilians or civilian objects; as well as attacks expected to cause incidental losses or injuries to civilians, which would be excessive in relation to the direct military advantage anticipated (Article 51, paragraph 5). Reprisals against the civilian population are forbidden (Article 51, paragraph 6). It is furthermore prohibited to destroy foodstuffs, agricultural areas for the production of foodstuffs, crops, livestock, drinking-water installations and supplies and irrigation works, for the specific purpose of denying the civilian population those objects that are indispensable for their survival (Article 54). Dams, dykes and nuclear electric-power generating stations have been placed under special protection, and shall not be attacked, if an attack on them may cause severe losses among civilians (Article 56). (This protection will, however, cease if the installations in question are used in significant and direct support of military operations and if an attack on them is the only feasible way to terminate such support.) The prohibition also applies to the attack, by any means, of non-defended localities, declared as such by the appropriate authorities of a party (Article 59), or to the extension of military operations to zones on which the parties have conferred by agreement the status of demilitarized zone (Article 60).

A special provision is devoted to the protection of the natural environment against widespread, long-term and severe damage. It includes a prohibition on the use of methods and means of warfare that are intended or may be expected to cause such damage to the natural environment and thereby to prejudice the health or survival of the population (Article 55).

Protocol I is applicable not only to interstate armed conflicts, but also to conflicts in which peoples are fighting against colonial domination and alien occupation and against racist regimes in the exercise of their right to self-determination (Article 1). In this way, guerrilla fighters have been covered by international protection. In particular, they have been given the right to prisoner-of-war status if they belong to organized units under a command responsible to the party concerned, and if they carry their arms openly during each military engagement, and during such time as they are visible to the adversary before launching an attack (Articles 43 and 44). On the other hand, mercenaries, as defined in the protocol, have no right to combatant or prisoner-of-war status (Article 47).

Several articles dealing with relief actions in favour of the civilian population have strengthened the corresponding clauses of the 1949 Geneva Convention IV. The duties of the occupying power include the provision, to the fullest extent of the means available, of supplies essential to the survival of the civilian population of the occupied territory (Article 69).

Protocol II develops and supplements Article 3, which appears in all the four

Geneva Conventions of 1949, and which deals with armed conflicts not of an international character. It prescribes humane treatment of all the persons involved in such conflicts, care for the wounded, sick and shipwrecked, as well as protection of civilians against the dangers arising from military operations. It does not apply to internal disturbances, such as riots, sporadic acts of violence and similar acts.

The two protocols of 1977 constitute a step forward in the development of the humanitarian laws of war, even though some of their provisions lack clarity and certain definitions are imprecise. Their greatest shortcoming, however, is that they have not forbidden any specific weapon which is excessively injurious or has indiscriminate effects. Nuclear or other weapons of mass destruction, which clearly fall under this category, were not even considered at the Geneva Diplomatic Conference. The question of conventional weapons of a particularly cruel nature was discussed but has not been resolved. The weapons most often mentioned in this context are incendiaries, including napalm, small-calibre, high-velocity projectiles, certain blast and fragmentation weapons, including weapons the primary effect of which is to injure by fragments not detectable by X-ray, as well as mines and booby-traps.

Bilateral arms-control agreements (summaries)

The 1963 United States-Soviet Memorandum of Understanding regarding the Establishment of a Direct Communication Link (United States-Soviet 'Hot Line' Agreement)

Establishes a direct communications link between the governments of the United States and the USSR for use in time of emergency. An annex attached to the memorandum provides for two circuits, namely a duplex wire-telegraph circuit and a duplex radio-telegraph circuit, as well as two terminal points with telegraph-teleprinter equipment between which communications are to be exchanged.

The 1971 United States-Soviet 'Hot Line' Modernization Agreement (amended in 1975)

Establishes, for the purpose of increasing the reliability of the direct communications link set up pursuant to the Memorandum of Understanding of 1963, two additional circuits between the United States and the USSR, each using a satellite communications system, and a system of terminals (more than one) in the territory of each party. Matters relating to the implementation of these improvements are set forth in an annex to the agreement.

The 1967 British-Soviet Agreement on the establishment of a Direct Communication Line (British-Soviet 'Hot Line' Agreement)

Establishes a direct teletype communications line between the Kremlin, Moscow, and 10 Downing Street, London, for contacts at government level.

The 1971 Agreement on Measures to Reduce the Risk of Outbreak of Nuclear War between the United States and the USSR (United States-Soviet Nuclear Accidents Agreement)

Provides for immediate notification in the event of an accidental, unauthorized incident involving a possible detonation of a nuclear weapon (the party whose nuclear weapon is involved should take necessary measures to render harmless or destroy such weapon); immediate notification in the event of detection by missile warning systems of unidentified objects, or in the event of signs of interference with these systems or with related communications facilities; and advance notification of planned missile launches extending beyond the national territory in the direction of the other party.

The 1972 United States-Soviet Agreement on the Prevention of Incidents on and over the High Seas

Provides for measures to assure the safety of navigation of the ships of the armed forces of the United States and the USSR on the high seas and flight of their military aircraft over the high seas, including rules of conduct for ships engaged in surveillance of other ships as well as ships engaged in launching or landing aircraft. The parties also undertake to give notification of actions on the high seas which represent a danger to navigation or to aircraft in flight, and to exchange information concerning instances of collisions, instances which result in damage, or other incidents at sea between their ships and aircraft.

The 1973 Protocol to the United States-Soviet Agreement on the Prevention of Incidents on and over the High Seas

Provides that ships and aircraft of the parties shall not make simulated attacks by aiming guns, missile launchers, torpedo tubes and other weapons at non-military ships of the other party, nor launch nor drop any objects near non-military ships of the other party in such a manner as to be hazardous to these ships or to constitute a hazard to navigation.

The 1972 Agreement on Basic Principles of Relations between the United States and the USSR

States that the United States and the USSR will proceed from the common determination that in the nuclear age there is no alternative to conducting their mutual relations on the basis of peaceful coexistence. They will do their utmost to avoid military confrontations and to prevent the outbreak of nuclear war. The prerequisite for maintaining and strengthening peaceful relations between the United States and the USSR are the recognition of the security interests of the parties based on the principle of equality and the renunciation of the use or threat of force. The parties will continue their efforts to limit armaments on a bilateral as well as on a multilateral basis. They will continue to make special efforts to limit strategic armaments. Whenever possible, they will conclude concrete agreements aimed at achieving these purposes. They regard as the ultimate objective of their efforts the achievement of general and complete disarmament and the establishment of an effective system of international security in accordance with the purposes and principles of the United Nations.

The 1972 United States-Soviet Treaty on the Limitation of Anti-Ballistic Missile Systems (SALT-ABM Treaty)

Prohibits the deployment of ABM systems for the defence of the whole territory of the United States and the USSR or of an individual region, except as expressly permitted. Permitted ABM deployments are limited to two areas in each country—one for the defence of the national capital, and the other for the defence of some intercontinental ballistic missiles (ICBMs). No more than 100 ABM launchers and 100 ABM interceptor missiles may be deployed in each ABM deployment area. ABM radars should not exceed specified numbers and are subject to qualitative restrictions. National technical means of verification will be used to provide assurance of compliance with the provisions of the treaty.

The 1974 Protocol to the United States-Soviet Treaty on the Limitation of Anti-Ballistic Missile Systems

Provides that each party shall be limited to a single area for deployment of anti-ballistic missile systems or their components instead of two such areas as allowed by the SALT-ABM Treaty (see above). Each party will have the right to dismantle or destroy its ABM system and the components thereof in the area where they were deployed at the time of signing the protocol and to deploy an ABM system or its components in the alternative area permitted by the ABM Treaty, provided that, prior to initiation of construction, notification is given during the year beginning on 3 October 1977, and ending on 2 October 1978, or during any year which commences at five-year intervals thereafter, those being the years for periodic review of the ABM Treaty. This right may be exercised only once. The deployment of an ABM system within the area selected shall remain limited by the levels and other requirements established by the ABM Treaty.

The 1972 United States-Soviet Interim Agreement on Certain Measures with Respect to the Limitation of Strategic Offensive Arms (SALT Interim Agreement)

Provides for a freeze for up to five years of the aggregate number of fixed land-based intercontinental ballistic-missile launchers and ballistic-missile launchers on modern submarines. The parties are free to choose the mix, except that conversion of land-based launchers for light ICBMs, of for ICBMs of older types, into land-based launchers for modern 'heavy' ICBMs is prohibited. National technical means of verification will be used to provide assurance of compliance with the provisions of the agreement.

The SALT Interim Agreement (SALT I) was followed by the 1974 Vladivostok Joint United States-Soviet statement on the question of further limitation of strategic offensive arms, and by the SALT II Agreement signed in Vienna, on 18 June 1979 but not yet ratified by the end of 1980.

The 1972 United States-Soviet Memorandum of Understanding regarding the Establishment of a Standing Consultative Commission

Establishes a Standing Consultative Commission to promote the objectives and implementation of the provisions of the SALT/ABM Treaty and Interim Agreement, of 1972, and of the Nuclear Accidents Agreement of 1971. Each government shall be represented by a commissioner and a deputy commissioner, assisted by such staff as it deems necessary. The commission is to hold at least two sessions per year.

The 1973 United States-Soviet Agreement on the Prevention of Nuclear War

Provides that the parties will act in such a manner as to exclude the outbreak of nuclear war between them and between either of the parties and other countries. Each party will refrain from the threat or use of force against the other party, against the allies of the other party and against other countries in circumstances which may endanger international peace and security. If at any time relations between the parties or between either party and other countries appear to involve the risk of a nuclear conflict, or if relations between countries not parties to this agreement appear to involve the risk of nuclear war between the USSR and the United States or between either party and other countries, the Soviet Union and the United States, acting in accordance with the provisions of this agreement, shall immediately enter into urgent consultations with each other and make every effort to avert this risk.

The 1974 United States-Soviet Treaty on the Limitation of Underground Nuclear Weapon Tests (Threshold Test Ban Treaty—TTBT)

Prohibits from 31 March 1976 the carrying out of any underground nuclear-weapon test having a yield exceeding 150 kilotons. Each party undertakes to limit the number of its underground nuclear weapon tests to a minimum. The provisions of the treaty do not extend to underground nuclear explosions for peaceful purposes which are to be governed by a separate agreement. National technical means of verification will be used to provide assurance of compliance and a protocol to the treaty specifies the data that have to be exchanged between the parties to ensure such verification.

Since by 31 March 1976, the agreed cut-off date for explosions above the established threshold, the treaty was not yet in force, the parties stated that they would observe the limitation during the entire pre-ratification period.

The 1976 United States-Soviet Treaty on Underground Nuclear Explosions for Peaceful Purposes (Peaceful Nuclear Explosions Treaty—PNET)

Prohibits the carrying out of any individual underground nuclear explosion for peaceful purposes, having a yield exceeding 150 kilotons, or any group explosion (consisting of two or more individual explosions) with an aggregate yield exceeding 1,500 kilotons. The treaty governs all nuclear explosions carried out outside the weapon test sites after 31 March 1976. The question of carrying out individual explosions with a yield exceeding 150 kilotons will be considered at an appropriate time to be agreed. In addition to the use of national technical means of verification, the treaty provides for an exchange of information and, in certain specified cases, access to sites of explosions.

The 1976 French-Soviet Agreement on the Prevention of the Accidental or Unauthorized Use of Nuclear Weapons (French-Soviet Nuclear Accidents Agreement)

Provides that the parties will maintain and, possibly, improve their organizational and technical arrangements to prevent the accidental or unauthorized use of nuclear weapons under their control. They will notify each other immediately of any accidental occurrence or any other unexplained incident that could lead to the explosion of one of their nuclear weapons and could be construed as likely to have harmful effects on the other party. In the event of an unexplained nuclear incident, each party will act in such a manner as to avoid the possibility of its actions being misinterpreted by the other party. For transmission of urgent information, primary use will be made of the direct communications link between the Elysée Palace, Paris, and the Kremlin, Moscow. (The link has been established following an accord of 9 November 1966 between France and the USSR.)

The 1977 British-Soviet Agreement on the Prevention of an Accidental Outbreak of Nuclear War (British-Soviet Nuclear Accidents Agreement)

Provides that the parties will maintain and, whenever necessary, improve their organizational and technical arrangements for guarding against the accidental or unauthorized use of nuclear weapons under their control. They will notify each other immediately of any accident or other unexplained or unauthorized incident which could result in the explosion of one of their nuclear weapons or could otherwise create the risk of the outbreak of nuclear war, and the party whose nuclear weapon is involved will immediately take the necessary measures to render harmless or destroy such a weapon without causing damage. Each party will act in such a manner as to reduce the possibilities of its action being misinterpreted. For transmission of, or requests for, urgent information, the parties will use the direct communications link between their governments.

Conclusions

The idea of controlling the weapons of war has a strong appeal in a world troubled by tension, insecurity and the growing threat of annihilation. In and of itself, arms control cannot remove the motives for acquiring arms, but it may help to reduce suspicion and improve relations among states; to minimize the risks of war by accident or miscalculation, or even by design; to narrow the disparity between heavily and lightly armed states; to mitigate the scope of destruction and suffering in armed conflicts; to save resources for economic and social development; to diminish the dangers to the human environment; and to pave the way towards a more secure world. For these reasons arms control has become part and parcel of multilateral diplomacy and a focus of international attention.

It is sometimes argued that unilateral cuts or restraints in the acquisition of arms are preferable to formal international agreements. The arguments run as follows: unilateral decisions arouse less bureaucratic opposition within the countries concerned than do interstate treaties; in the process of negotiations each side usually tries to improve its bargaining position through the development or deployment of weapons that it would not otherwise have undertaken, thereby stimulating arms competition rather than abating it; and arms-control agreements may sometimes provide justification or an excuse for embarking on new weapon programmes which are not covered by the agreements.

Unilateral measures are certainly feasible where states perceive no specific military threat and can take action without requiring reciprocity. Unilateral cuts in arms could also be made by states with substantial 'over-kill' capacity, which would apply, in the first place, to the United States and the USSR. However, significant unilateral cuts are politically unlikely for most nations. Normally, a country embarking on arms reductions would expect similar responses from other nations. Reciprocal restraints assumed without formal treaty commitments—and there are many areas where this could be done without risk to the security of respective nations—would usefully supplement the present more conventional means of achieving arms control, but could not replace them. Limitations resulting from parallel moves would need to be codified in treaties to become durable and enforceable. A treaty defines the range of prohibited activities and gives the prohibition the force of law. It inhibits certain government decisions and neutralizes those forces within each state which would otherwise urge new arms acquisitions. Moreover, abrogation of a legally binding commitment is more complicated and hazardous than reversing a unilateral undertaking.

The arms-control treaties hitherto reached have made a contribution to better understanding among nations, but have failed in a most essential respect: they have not halted the arms race or reduced the military potential of states. The choice of arms-control measures has been haphazard; in many cases, the weapons prohibited have had little, if any, military importance, and the outlawed activities have never been seriously contemplated as methods of war. Negotiations have not kept pace with advancing military technology and rising levels of armaments. It may well be that the very tactic of discussing small, 'easy-to-achieve', unrelated steps meant to produce incremental effects, is fallacious and needs to be revised in favour of a more integrated approach.

14

The achievements
of arms control

George Ignatieff
University of Toronto, Canada

A discussion of the achievements of arms control, however modest these may have been, is relevant to an assessment of the dangers of nuclear war. While arms-control or arms-regulation measures cannot of themselves assure peace, their connections with the whole diplomatic process known as détente makes them an important aspect of any speculation about the dangers of nuclear war.

Indeed, arms-control talks have largely reflected the efforts of the super-powers to moderate their enmity in the interests of survival in the nuclear age. The resulting measures, as will be seen, come closer to 'crisis management' than to 'arms control'. The word 'control' may be taken to imply an international authority exercising the powers of verification and inspection. Such a body does not exist except in the limited function of the International Atomic Energy Agency with the consent of the state to be inspected. This semantic problem with the use of the word 'control' has provided a fertile field for misunderstanding in all disarmament debates. There has been very little progress towards disarmament, and the Soviet Union, for one, denounces in principle the idea of control being exercised over armaments and will accept control only over measures of disarmament.

Arms control in effect has as much to do with political relationships as with strategic-military relationships. This holds true particularly between the nuclear-weapon powers, whether the discussion is bilateral as in the Strategic Arms Limitation Talks (SALT) or multilateral as at the Geneva Disarmament Conference or the United Nations.

At the dawn of the nuclear age some of the best minds believed that if this supertechnology were applied to war it would produce such catastrophic results that all preparation for war would be rendered utterly obsolete. This belief has not prevailed. Instead, the relationship between the superpowers has proceeded on the assumption that the military-political-economic survival of the United States, the USSR, and other nuclear-weapon states requires a capability to survive a nuclear first strike and to inflict unacceptable damage on the attacker in retaliation. This

Slightly abridged version of *The Dangers of Nuclear War*, edited by Franklyn Griffiths and John Polanyi, University of Toronto Press, 1979.

doctrine is put forward on both sides as justification for the continuing reliance on deterrence, rather than disarmament, to ensure security.

Proposals for the elimination of nuclear weapons

Within months of the dropping of the only two atomic bombs used in war, an imaginative proposal was put forward by the United States for the elimination of nuclear weapons from the armoury of nations. In 1946, Dean Acheson, then American Under-Secretary of State, in association with David Lilienthal, head of the Tennessee Valley Authority, proposed 'a plan under which no nation would make atomic bombs or the material for them. All dangerous activities would be carried on—not merely inspected—by a live, functioning international authority.'

The Baruch Plan, as it came to be known when Bernard Baruch presented it to the Atomic Energy Commission of the United Nations, represented a far-reaching disarmament as well as arms-control proposal. It would have eliminated the atomic bomb monopoly then enjoyed by the United States and it would also have transferred all national privileges in the field of atomic energy to the control of an international authority. It included Baruch's controversial proposal that there should be 'condign punishment' for violation of a United Nations treaty banning atomic weapons and controlling the production and use of fissionable materials.

This plan proved too much to accept even in the aftermath of the most destructive war yet experienced by mankind. The Soviet counter-proposal took the form of a draft convention simply calling for a ban on the production and use of atomic weapons within three months of the entry into force of the convention, and for the destruction of existing stockpiles. The United States was not willing to give up its monopoly in atomic weapons without the adoption of its proposed far-reaching assurances against the danger that these weapons would be developed by its rival.

The question of the elimination or even the reduction of nuclear weapons has remained ever since on the agenda of all arms-control discussions, both bilateral and multilateral, without coming any closer to a solution. This failure meant that nuclear-weapon proliferation, with all its attendant risks, was not contained at a time when there was only one stockpile to eliminate, that of the United States. Since then, the USSR, the United Kingdom, France, China and more recently India have been added to the list of those possessing a nuclear capability or thermonuclear fission for military purposes.

In these circumstances, those involved in the negotiations for the elimination of nuclear weapons began to devote their efforts to the reduction of the threat of nuclear war, especially of surprise attack. Efforts to prevent a surprise attack were succeeded by efforts to place international restraints upon nuclear proliferation, especially through the Non-Proliferation Treaty and the international safeguards system of the International Atomic Energy Agency.

Reduction of the possibility of inadvertent war

In the early 1960s, progress was made in reducing the risk of nuclear war by accident, miscalculation or failure of communication. As one means of accomplishing this objective, the establishment of rapid communications by direct link in case of emergency was proposed and accepted. A memorandum of understanding (the 'Hot-Line' Agreement) was signed by the United States and the USSR in June 1963. This was updated by the 'Accidents Measures' Agreement of 1971 and the 'Hot-Line' Modernization Agreement as well as by 'hot-line' agreements between the USSR and France, as well as the USSR and the United Kingdom. Thus crisis management became essential in reducing the risk of nuclear war by the superpowers.

But the acceptance of the necessity of crisis management carries the disquieting connotation that the nuclear-arms race continues, and that there will be crises. It is important to recognize the limitation as well as the potential of such arms-control measures. The potential includes diplomatic contact and communication at all levels. Since the root causes of war lie in international anarchy, that is to say the prevalence of national sovereignty and interests over the common interest and international law, the development of lines of communication was critical.

In addition to communication between the superpowers over crises such as the successive confrontations over Berlin, the Cuban missile crisis, and the Middle East, we have had the European Security Conference which culminated in the Helsinki Agreement of 1975 and the ongoing Conference in Vienna on the Mutual Reduction of Forces and Armaments and Associated Measures in Central Europe. These are multilateral negotiations involving the participation of all those powers concerned with the security of Europe, including Canada and the United States. The Helsinki Final Act, signed in the summer of 1975, in particular represented a kind of codification of the various ideas embodied in détente, including such arms-control measures as reciprocal observation of manoeuvres by representatives of NATO and the Warsaw Pact to reduce the possibilities of war by miscalculation.

Détente, however, has not led to a reversal or even a slowing down of the arms race. Moreover, it is largely confined to understandings about the reduction of the possibility of nuclear war in Europe. There, the NATO doctrine of 'flexible response' assumes the use of tactical nuclear weapons in response to Soviet attack with conventional weapons, without Soviet prior agreement to refrain from escalating hostilities to total war. Those who have been left out of the superpower consultative process have denounced détente as an exercise by the superpowers in hegemony. China, indeed, has insisted that a pledge of no 'first use' of nuclear weapons by the United States and the USSR is a condition of its participation in any arms-control negotiations. Furthermore, when the North-South confrontation intersects with the East-West confrontation, détente has not prevented superpower intervention in local wars in Indo-China, Angola or the Middle East and other local wars which also involve the risk of nuclear confrontation.

Newly independent and economically underdeveloped countries have increasingly been drawn into the orbit of superpower hegemony and away from their traditional 'uncommitted' role in world affairs. The superpowers and their allies are involved in the supply of weapons, training, and other military assistance, tending to add fuel to the arms race and increasing the risk of limited nuclear conflict. Thus the arms-control measures so far undertaken to reduce the possibility of war have hardly had the desired effect. Instead, they have added fuel to the arms race between the United States and the USSR and their respective allies, and have involved them in Third World problems. Those who believe that deterrence with its costs and risks cannot match the advantages which might be obtained in improved collective security and reduced expenditures on defence as a result of real disarmament argue that the arms-control measures associated with détente have in fact institutionalized the arms race.

The case made by these critics of arms control is persuasive, especially when one considers the problem of overcapacities for fighting a war of 'overkill'. Bringing the nuclear capacities of the superpowers down to a minimum necessary to deter war is a reasonable objective, but one which has certainly so far not been brought any nearer to realization by SALT.

There are certain aspects of SALT and other bilateral contacts and negotiations that undoubtedly are of value. For one thing, the capabilities of the nuclear arsenals of the superpowers are no longer secret, even though secrecy shrouds plans for their use. Knowledge of the circumstances under which they would be prepared to use nuclear weapons would provide the key to assessing the dangers of nuclear war.

Another benefit of SALT, as of other methods of communicating between the superpowers, is the machinery of constant contact and negotiation which to a considerable extent reduces the risk of nuclear war by design or intention. SALT has proved a certain measure of effectiveness in arriving at agreements to restrict the building of defences against ballistic missiles and in dealing with the nuclear equation by which nuclear parity is determined.

The negative result of institutionalizing the arms race is that the superpowers have become prisoners of their own various industrial, military and scientific interests, and of their tendency to match every move of the adversary, as essential to parity and ultimately to survival. It should be noted that, so far, all tactical nuclear weapons remain totally outside the regulations of arms-control agreements and that delivery vehicles, which can be used for conventional (as well as nuclear) weapons, are also regulation-free.

The risk inherent in the present open-ended competition between the superpowers is evident. Even what has been agreed to date does not provide any barrier against qualitative improvements of existing nuclear-weapons systems, nor against innovations introduced to keep pace with advancing technology through research and testing. Experts dispute, for example, whether the new generations of weapons systems—the improvements in bombs (like the neutron bomb) or in the means of delivery (like the American long-range cruise missile or the Soviet SS20)—represent a legitimate development of new capabilities to keep pace with advancing technology, or whether they have a destabilizing effect which increases the risk of nuclear war.

There can be no doubt that, unless some new approach to arms control is attempted, the present dynamic elements in the situation will promote an ever-increasing overkill capacity, as each side strives to retain what is considered to be a 'safe margin' of parity. Such a new approach must at the very least include the total prohibition of nuclear testing and of flight testing of delivery vehicles as the first steps in an effort to scale down to some agreed minimum deterrent. A further exchange of information should be possible now that the governments of the two superpowers have derived sufficient knowledge of each other's capabilities from satellite surveillance. With the reduction of the barriers of secrecy, one could see arms-control measures serving to reduce the possibilities of nuclear war.

General and complete disarmament

While all the wars waged since the Second World War have been local wars fought with conventional weapons, almost all the discussion and all the measures of arms control agreed to have related to nuclear weapons. This preoccupation is understandable since the use of nuclear weapons constitutes a threat to civilization and even to human survival.

But from the outset, the aims of arms control were defined at the United Nations in comprehensive terms, inclusive of all arms and armed forces. The Charter of the United Nations gave primary responsibility for the maintenance of international security to the Security Council, which was to act on behalf of the world community in dealing with international disputes and any threats to peace. National armaments and armed forces were to be subordinate to the authority of the Security Council, through agreements to be negotiated with that body, and all arms were to be subject to regulation, i.e. arms control. The permanent members of the Security Council were the superpowers and when their wartime alliances broke down the basis of the world security system collapsed. Consequently, the agreements which were to have subordinated national armaments and armed forces to the world organization fell by the board and the Security Council in effect ceased to exercise any jurisdiction in the matter of arms control.

When the General Assembly of the United Nations took over the responsibility for providing a forum for the discussion of disarmament and arms control in 1959, it set general and complete disarmament as the goal to be pursued. In the course of resuming negotiations on disarmament, the Soviet Union and the United States agreed to a set of principles as a basis for renewed negotiations. These principles specifically related the problem of disarmament to the problem of preventing war. Thus, the goals of the negotiations were stated to be: (a) that disarmament is general and complete and war is no longer an instrument for settling international problems; and (b) that such disarmament is accompanied by the establishment of reliable procedures for the peaceful settlement of disputes and effective arrangements for the maintenance of peace in accordance with the principles of the Charter.

Although in the prior negotiations both sides had submitted the outlines of draft treaties on general and complete disarmament, the two superpowers soon disagreed on the important, substantive issue of whether nuclear delivery weapons should be eliminated in the first stage as desired by the Soviet Union, or retained for later disposal as preferred by the United States. In other words, differences over the strategic balance between the superpowers prejudiced the possibility of progress in any comprehensive approach towards disarmament. In order to escape from this impasse which threatened to bring disarmament talks to a standstill, the negotiations turned to consideration of partial or collateral arms-control measures.

Meanwhile, the winds of change of decolonization were blowing away the remnants of empire in the West. Scores of countries in Africa and Asia had found independence under conditions that involved them or their previous colonizers in a series of wars. The proliferation of states and of weapons went hand in hand. The fact that they were conventional weapons seemed to have made them exempt from any restraints except those that might be adopted by individual exporting countries. The question of restrictions on the sale of conventional arms remains an important item on the agenda of any conference attempting to curb the danger of nuclear war, especially with the growing automaticity, lethality and sophistication of conventional weapons.

The concern that local wars fought with conventional weapons might turn into nuclear confrontation arises from the fact that the nuclear-weapon powers, especially the superpowers, have all at one time or another intervened in the affairs of Third World countries. In this way, the North-South confrontation tends to intersect with the East-West, and local wars, if allowed to spread, could get out of hand, risking the threat of nuclear war. To reduce that risk, consideration needs to be given to measures of arms control of conventional weapons. Such measures would include indirect methods, such as publishing and monitoring military expenditures and international arms sales, and direct methods, such as prohibiting export of certain categories of weapons to areas of conflict, as well as strengthening the peace-keeping and peace-making capacities of the United Nations.

Collateral measures of arms control

After the failure of talks on general and complete disarmament, the Geneva Disarmament Conference wanted to avoid a similar breakdown in negotiations. To this end, it introduced the consideration of various ways of lowering international tensions, building up confidence and preventing the extension of the arms race to new environments. The discussion of such measures was not intended to prejudice the negotiation of agreements on conventional or nuclear disarmament, nor any confidence-building arrangements discussed bilaterally, such as the 'hot-line' between Washington and Moscow. In fact, these collateral measures have proved to be the only area in which some progress was registered at Geneva in the 1960s and early 1970s.

Among the collateral measures favoured by the Soviet Union and its allies have been: the reduction of military budgets; a non-aggression pact between NATO and the Warsaw Pact powers; the prohibition of the use of nuclear weapons; the establishment of nuclear-free zones; the reciprocal withdrawal of foreign troops from the territories of other countries; the elimination of foreign military bases and the reduction in the number of armed forces; the Partial Test Ban; and the Non-Proliferation Treaty.

The United States and its allies, for their part, singled out the most urgent arms-control measures relating to nuclear activities, particularly the test ban and the issue of non-proliferation. They have also given priority to the cessation (cut-off) or limitation (cut-back) in the production of fissionable material, the transfer of agreed stocks to peaceful uses, a freeze on strategic delivery vehicles, and the reduction of bombers.

At the height of the Sputnik period when the United States and the USSR were competing as to who would put the first man on the moon, Canada, supported by Italy and Mexico, had pressed for a commitment to ensure the peaceful uses of outer space. Nuclear weapons and other weapons of mass destruction were subsequently banned from outer space on the recommendation of the General Assembly in 1963, and by a treaty signed by the United States and the USSR in 1967.

The most important collateral measures to date have, however, been the Partial Test Ban of 1963 and the Non-Proliferation Treaty of 1968. These were addressed to vertical and horizontal nuclear proliferation, respectively. The Partial Test Ban, by putting restraints on the environment in which testing could take place and limiting testing to underground explosions, was intended to restrict the development of new weapons by the nuclear powers. In effect, since the signing of the treaty, testing has steadily increased both in the United States and the USSR, while China and France have so far refused to accept this restraint. The most that can be said about this agreement is that it has become a sort of environmental measure, reducing the fall-out effects of massive explosions that the two superpowers indulged in on land and at sea before the ban went into effect.

The Non-Proliferation Treaty (NPT) was intended to prevent the spread of nuclear weapons to non-nuclear countries; however, the obligations of this treaty proved unbalanced. The nuclear powers undertook to negotiate, in good faith, the cessation of the nuclear arms race. This they have failed to carry out—or, if they have, there is little to show for it! The non-nuclear powers were obliged to accept international controls over their nuclear fuel and installations, and the International Atomic Energy Agency (IAEA) and its safeguards were used to implement this undertaking.

The weakness in mutuality and balance was noted when the General Assembly voted in June 1968 to recommend the conclusion of the NPT. France and a number of potential nuclear countries abstained, including Argentina, Brazil, India, Israel, Pakistan, South Africa, Spain, Switzerland and several other African countries. India flatly refused to join the NPT during the negotiations, arguing that the treaty was discriminatory. India's acquisition of a plutonium separation plant, leading subsequently to a test explosion, points up the inevitable conclusion that what is needed now is not another 'paper' arms-control measure dependent upon good faith for its implementation. Rather, we need agreement on comprehensive, universal, and vigilant controls, especially of the critical elements in the fuel cycle.

In order to obtain agreement to these kinds of controls from countries like India, it may be necessary for the nuclear-weapons powers to carry out their previous pledge at least to begin to cease and reverse the arms race, and to submit their non-military nuclear facilities to inspection and verification by the IAEA.

This kind of mutuality of commitment might then open the door to better understanding with non-nuclear countries with regard to the supply of nuclear technology and materials. It must be recognized that the developing countries' seeking of nuclear sources of energy is an integral part of their demand for a fair share of the world's resources in order to raise the standard of living of their peoples. Thus, to control nuclear proliferation, measures preventing the diversion from peaceful uses to nuclear weapons or other nuclear explosive devices must be improved. In order to achieve this goal of peaceful nuclear development, however, there must also be inducements to join the NPT and to accept a universally acceptable system of safeguards under the IAEA. To provide such inducements, the nuclear developed countries must be ready to accept the same controls as those seeking development, and they must be willing to transfer nuclear technology and materials to developing countries.

The remaining collateral measures agreed to at Geneva and elsewhere were the Biological Weapons Convention of 1972, outlawing germ warfare and eliminating toxic weapons; the Treaty of Tlatelolco, prohibiting nuclear weapons in Latin America; the Sea-Bed Treaty of 1972, prohibiting the emplacement of nuclear weapons and other weapons of mass destruction on the sea-bed or ocean floor; and the Environmental Modification Treaty, prohibiting some forms of environmental warfare. These measures of arms control are even more marginal in their impact on the possibilities of nuclear war than the other measures we have considered.

The Biological Weapons Convention at least can be said to be the only measure of actual disarmament agreed to since the Second World War, since it involved the destruction of existing stockpiles. In any case, bacteriological and biological weapons as well as environmental warfare must surely be the least significant addition to the military capabilities of any powers large or small. No adequate control provisions were adopted and the convention simply amended the Geneva Protocol of 1925, outlawing chemical warfare by adding another group of noxious and lethal agents to the ban. Moreover, ambiguities remain regarding the precise definition of prohibition by the Geneva Convention and the negotiation of an effective total ban on the use of chemical and biological weapons remains on the agenda.

The Treaty of Tlatelolco was in large part due to Mexico's reaction to the Cuban missile crisis, and was an attempt to keep nuclear weapons out of Latin America. It also debarred the testing, use, manufacture, production, or acquisition of nuclear weapons by its signatories. Unfortunately, the treaty is not yet in force. Three important nations of the hemisphere—Argentina, Brazil and Chile—have signed but either not ratified or not waived the requirements that are to be met before the treaty enters into force. Despite these gaps in its implementation, the treaty is a first step towards the denuclearization of the area and provides a possible model for the denuclearization of other areas in the world where the possibilities of war are more evident, like the Middle East or South-East Asia.

The most that can be said about the Sea-Bed Treaty is that it bars the establishment on the sea-bed or ocean floor of stationary bombardment systems armed with nuclear weapons, in the event that any power should wish to resort to this method for purposes of concealment. What the Sea-Bed Treaty is supposed to prevent, however, has never been of military interest. In any case, submarines do a better job of providing underwater cover for the discharge of nuclear weapons. This arms-control measure did keep the Geneva disarmament negotiators busier for a while than they would have been otherwise, but it did not really contribute to what is a desirable objective: the complete demilitarization of the oceans to permit their unrestricted economic development and exploitation. This question is now engaging the attention of the Law of the Sea Conference at the United Nations. The Sea-Bed Treaty was a 'non-armament' measure, extremely difficult to control, and its signing might be termed a 'non-event'.

The urgent need for progress

From this discussion of 'achievements' in arms control to date, it is obvious why there is a growing demand for some dramatic happening to highlight public concern about the lack of progress towards disarmament. At the United Nations, this clamour has found expression in the form of support for a special session of the General Assembly, which took place in 1978, or of a World Disarmament Conference. The latter would direct attention to disarmament as urgent and essential, if we are to reduce the possibility of war and husband scarce resources for peaceful uses.

Progress toward disarmament has been virtually nil. None the less, some progress in measures of partial arms control has been achieved, especially in areas where the two superpowers and their respective allies have tried to reduce the possibilities of surprise attack by improving communications to facilitate crisis management, increasing contacts at all levels of government, and exchanging more information. It can be argued that these kinds of measures, including satellite surveillance, have had the effect of reducing the possibility of nuclear war by increasing the ability to detect preparations for such a war in advance.

The possibility of nuclear war through accident or miscalculation is not, however, ruled out. Especially dangerous is the potential for escalation of violence arising from a limited war, and the proliferation of nuclear capabilities to still more countries. These will not have the benefit of an invulnerable retaliatory capacity for deterrence, and among them conventions of communication and reciprocity in matters of crisis management either will not exist, or will not be as elaborate as those between NATO and the Warsaw Pact. The most promising motivation for more effective action in the field of arms control and disarmament is the widespread, virtually universal, craving for peace in a world in which there are relatively few nations that have not in recent years experienced the ravages of war.

In order to give expression to this craving and clamour for effective action, it is essential to avoid the impasse of all or nothing which was the fate of the discussion of general and complete disarmament based upon the Zorin-McCloy Principles in the 1960s. Crucial to any progress in reducing the possibilities of nuclear war are: (a) certain prior agreements among the superpowers; (b) agreements by the other nuclear-weapons powers; and (c) curbs on non-nuclear weapons.

Agreements among the superpowers

In order to reduce the possibility of nuclear war and open the way for China to enter into commitments similar to the arms-control measures accepted by the superpowers, the United States and the USSR should first be prepared to moderate their nuclear hegemony by an unconditional pledge not to be the first to initiate any act of nuclear warfare—i.e. to renounce the option of 'first use'.

The other commitment which the superpowers should undertake is not to attack any nuclear-weapons-free country with nuclear weapons. The resolution passed by the Security Council on this matter in 1968 took the form of offering assistance in the event of attack. What is needed is the outlawing of any attack with nuclear weapons on a nuclear-weapons-free country.

The superpowers should also make a special effort to stop and reverse the gushing stream of nuclear overkill. This goal could be achieved by following up the SALT I and Vladivostok agreements not only with quantitative reductions, but also with an agreement curbing qualitative competition, by not seeking to develop new nuclear weapons or new generations of existing weapons systems. Unless both stop the development of new weapons, the game of 'catch-up' will never stop.

Agreements by other nuclear-weapon powers

It behoves all nuclear-capable powers, which are supplying non-nuclear-capable countries with nuclear fuel and technology, to agree on ways of strengthening international safeguards under IAEA. The processing and distribution of nuclear fuels and reactors must be regulated so that competition does not contribute to nuclear proliferation.

All nuclear-weapons powers should be urged to participate in arms-control and disarmament negotiations. The first agreement that should be sought is for the banning of all nuclear-weapons tests. Previously, those nuclear powers who have participated in arms-control negotiations have argued that it would be prejudicial to their security if a comprehensive test ban went into effect but were not accepted by all nuclear-weapons powers. This vicious circle has to be broken. Moreover, arguments that control of a test ban is impossible no longer hold water since sensitive seismological instruments, as well as satellite surveillance, now provide adequate means of verification.

Once a way is found to curb nuclear-weapon development, by a comprehensive test ban and by stopping flight testing of new delivery vehicles, attention should be focused on trying to fix the parameters and rules for a minimum deterrent. It is difficult to conceive of the nuclear powers agreeing to a gradual scaling down of their respective capabilities unless they know what the size and composition of a minimum deterrent force might be at the end of the process. It is also difficult to conceive that the nuclear powers will not insist on retaining some 'nuclear shield', so long as they remain dependent for their security on national armaments and armed forces, rather than upon international authority backed by forces like the United Nations.

Curbs on non-nuclear weapons

We have already noted that the issue of curbing the proliferation of conventional arms has been overshadowed by the discussion of nuclear-arms control. Because conventional weapons have a relatively limited range of threat and their effects are less destructive, they have been used in innumerable wars, while nuclear weapons have only been stockpiled. It is recognized, however, that wars starting with conventional weapons could possibly escalate to nuclear war, if the confrontation of nuclear-weapons powers were involved. Such a threat has been considered more likely in Europe where superpower confrontation arises from treaty obligations, but it could conceivably occur elsewhere by accident or miscalculation.

The other factor bearing upon the control of conventional weapons is that only the two superpowers are entirely self-sufficient in arms production. All other countries are more or less dependent on imports of certain weapons, parts and equipment, or on licences needed for the domestic production of arms, especially as these become even more automatic, lethal and sophisticated. This dependence applies to industrially advanced countries; conventional arms sale are even more important for the developing countries. International transfer of conventional weapons is constantly increasing.

In order to institute curbs on the sale of conventional arms, the first step is to lay bare the facts. Arms-control measures might then be sought, either indirectly or directly. Indirectly, one way of curbing conventional arms production and transfer would be to curb military expenditures by international agreement. Military expenditures might be required to be reported to a United Nations agency and monitored by it. Registration of weapons production or transfer might also be required.

A more direct approach might involve invoking the Hague Convention of 1907 prohibiting the transfer of arms from outside states, presumed to be neutral, to any state taking part in warfare. The fact that such transfers take place and are not discussed at the United Nations, points to a need to focus on the problem.

In addition to curbing the transfer or sale of conventional arms to certain areas of hostility, it should be possible to outlaw or curb the production and transfer of certain non-nuclear, i.e. biological and chemical, mass-destruction weapons, whose use is already supposed to be curbed by the Geneva Convention and the Biological Weapons Convention. As conventional weapons become increasingly automatic, lethal and sophisticated, consideration should also be given to placing restraints on the production and transfer of specific arms more suited to total war (leading to the use of nuclear weapons) than to purely defensive purposes.

Further efforts are also required for regional arms-control and disarmament arrangements. A case in point is the proposal which has been under consideration for some time at the United Nations for an agreement to limit military activity in the Indian Ocean. By the same token, an essential element of any Middle East settlement must surely be to provide local restraints on military activity as well as guarantees for the observance of the settlement from outside powers. In this way, beginning with joint efforts to restrain the possibility of nuclear-weapons proliferation (on the model of the Tlatelolco Treaty) wider demilitarization could be built up in regions where neighbouring countries have an obvious mutual interest in arms limitation as a means of promoting confidence and peace.

Conclusion

Finally, it must be admitted that the 'achievements of arms control' to date have yet to come to grips with the central and basic problem of drastic reductions in nuclear weapons and systems, and an effective cessation of the technological or qualitative arms race. All that is necessary to prove this is the continuing escalation of military expenditures by the superpowers and the development of new weapons. It can be argued that international anarchy, as it prevails today despite the United Nations and its Charter, is the root cause of the possibility of war. The strengthening of international organization and the building up of a respect for international law, to which all countries must contribute, has to go hand in hand with arms control, if we are truly to reduce the possibilities of war. Whether the countries possessing or capable of developing a nuclear capability decide to exercise it within the next few years will depend mainly on consideration in each country of its security requirements as well as the international climate affecting international co-operation. The workability of arms control depends on the example and the standard of international relations set by the two superpowers who at present set the pace in the arms race. Only by their leadership and example can we hope to succeed in having any de-escalation of the arms race and any control of the proliferation of nuclear weapons.

If the United States and the USSR continue to set the pace in militarization in both nuclear and conventional weapons, relying on national armaments rather than international peace-keeping forces for the maintenance of national peace and security, it cannot be expected that other countries will accept the legitimacy of nuclear restraint and arms control.

15

Disarmament and détente

Evgeni M. Primakov
USSR Academy of Sciences

Mankind has entered an extremely important stage of development. A number of objective reasons and the purposeful policy of the socialist countries, as well as the realistic attitude of the leaders of some capitalist states, have stimulated the movement from the Cold War to a 'new international order' based on the principles of peaceful coexistence between countries with two opposing socio-political systems. The essence of this movement is the relaxation of international tension.

However, the path of relaxation is not straight. The resistance of the militarist circles and difficulties of a political, psychological and scientific and technological nature complicate the process of détente, making it zigzag. In these conditions political détente must be complemented by military détente.

Stages in the disarmament struggle

Throughout its entire history the Soviet Union has been working tirelessly for a halt to the arms race and for disarmament.

The attitude of the United States and other NATO countries towards curtailing the arms race after the Second World War should be viewed in relation to three stages, characterized by changes in the correlation of the military strategic forces of the states belonging to the two opposing systems and by shifts in the international situation.

The first stage

The period from the end of the war to the early 1950s was highlighted by the 'atomic monopoly' of the United States, the beginning of the Cold War in relations between the states of the two systems and, as a result, the completely negative attitude of the United States and other capitalist countries to measures on disarmament.

Indicative in this respect was the so-called Baruch Plan, submitted by the

Abridged version of 'Political Détente and the Problem of Disarmament', *International Détente and Disarmament*, Tampere Peace Research Institute, Helsinki, 1977; and 'The Outlook on Disarmament', *International Social Science Journal*, Vol. XXVIII, No. 2, 1976.

United States in 1946 to the United Nations Disarmament Commission. The Baruch Plan did not in fact envisage the prohibition of atomic weapons, but it guaranteed American corporations access to sources of nuclear raw materials, control over the economies of other countries and the opportunity to produce atomic bombs for an indefinite period of time. At the time the United States subordinated all measures, even for a reduction of conventional armaments, to the adoption of the Baruch Plan or the consolidation of the United States monopoly on atomic weapons. Subsequently, the Western powers, while concentrating attention on the question of control, in fact aimed at collecting information about the armed forces of the socialist countries. All initiatives of Western states at that stage actually boiled down to attempts to retain the monopoly on atomic weapons and to talk with the Soviet Union from a position of strength.

The second stage

This lasted from the early 1950s to the late 1960s. It was characterized on the one hand by the liquidation of the United States monopoly on atomic weapons, by the creation, for the first time, of thermonuclear weapons in the USSR, by the launching in a near-earth orbit of the world's first Soviet satellite and by the balancing of Soviet-United States military-strategic forces; and on the other by the continuing Cold War, which often put world peace in jeopardy. Under these circumstances the United States began to deviate somewhat from its stubborn negative position with regard to disarmament measures; however, it continued to strive for one-sided advantages from these measures, which were not always possible due to the changed correlation of forces in the world.

Compelled by peace-loving public opinion to demonstrate its desire to solve the disarmament problem, the United States and some other leading capitalist powers still proceeded from the idea of forming and consolidating their military-strategic superiority over the world of socialism. Most weight was placed on the preservation of American advantages in the nuclear field. Indicative in this respect was the 'Outline of Basic Provisions of a Treaty on General and Complete Disarmament in a Peaceful World', submitted by the United States to the 18-Nation Disarmament Committee in April 1962, to counterbalance Soviet proposals. This outline did not envisage any obligation to destroy all nuclear weapons, without which general and complete disarmament is out of the question.

The third stage

This stage, from the early 1970s on, is keynoted not only by the establishment of a military-strategic balance between the two systems, which had already taken place in the 1960s, but also by the reluctant acceptance of this fact by the leaders of the United States and other capitalist countries. A difficult process has begun of a gradual break with the Cold War and the introduction of the principles of peaceful coexistence into relations between the states of the two opposing systems.

The third stage could become exceptionally important, a turning point, in fact, for disarmament prospects.

First, an essential condition that makes it possible to implement measures for the limitation of the arms race and for disarmament is that a strategic balance ('strategic nuclear parity', as it is sometimes termed) has come into being between the socialist and capitalist countries, first and foremost between the USSR and the United States—the two most powerful states which shoulder the greatest responsibility for the maintenance of peace and international security. In these conditions each side is capable of delivering a devastating nuclear-missile attack on the other.

The arms race was forced on the Soviet Union by the United States, which was the first to have created and used nuclear weapons. Another example: the United States was also the first to equip ballistic missiles with multiple independently targeted re-entry vehicles (MIRVs).

Thus the Soviet Union and other socialist countries were compelled to increase their military power and they were ultimately able, through the enormous efforts of their peoples, to reach a strategic balance, whose principal distinctive feature is that it is in a dynamic state. In this state the quantitative and qualitative levels of all types of strategic armaments of the two sides are not constant but are changing and developing all the time.

Secondly, the peace-loving forces have scored deep-rooted, positive political shifts in world development during the 1970s, which are of enormous significance for the disarmament struggle. One needs only to point to the noticeable general improvement in the international political climate. The process of political relaxation has opened up great opportunities for strengthening universal security on the basis of the implementation of measures limiting armaments. Owing to the relaxation of tension, the strengthening of trust and a greater co-operation between states with different social systems, a real opportunity has emerged to solve the problems of stopping the arms race and eliminating the threat of a nuclear war, problems that only recently many people thought insoluble.

Thirdly, as a result of scientific and technological progress, not only has the destructive potential of various types of weapons enormously increased and the reliability of their accurate delivery become greater, but also major successes and 'breakthroughs' in quite different fields—seismology, radar, space, etc.—have been achieved, thus making it possible to remove in many instances the question of control, which for many years was used by the Western powers as an argument against many initiatives proposed with a view to reducing armaments and effecting disarmament.

These three factors of paramount importance—the mutually recognized military-strategic equivalence of the forces of the states belonging to the two opposing systems, political détente, and scientific and technological achievements permitting reliable supervision of disarmament—have emerged for the first time. The combined impact of these factors on historical developments creates conditions for bringing nearer the solution of the problem of armaments reduction and a stop to the arms race.

Naturally, these conditions alone do not automatically lead to a successful reduction of armaments and to disarmament. There are still forces in the world responsible for the trends and processes that are actively hampering disarmament. The bellicose circles of militarist reaction continue, though on a much narrower scale, to exert influence, sometimes quite strongly, on policy-making in the imperialist countries. This is the main reason why it has not yet been possible to stop the arms race and thwart, or curtail, material preparations for war, despite the unquestionable successes of the peace-loving forces that are largely due to the active struggle of the USSR and other socialist states for the relaxation of international tension and the emergence of a realistic approach in the policies of a number of the principal capitalist countries.

Significantly, there has not yet been a radical turn in the minds of the American scholars studying the problems of the arms race, and many representatives of American academic circles still adhere to their old positions. In this connection, an article by F. A. Long, Professor of Cornell University, entitled 'Arms Control from the Perspective of the Nineteen-seventies', published in the United States in 1975, may well be of interest. He writes:

Even the 1960 definition of 'arms control' remains entirely adequate today; paraphrasing Thomas Schelling slightly, it is: (a) to reduce the probability of war, (b) to reduce the costs of preparations for war, and (c) to reduce the death and destruction if control fails and war comes.[1]

It is quite clear that such a definition leaves a wide scope for using the process of the limitation of the arms race not to stop it altogether, but to make it less costly.

Apart from the direct opposition to disarmament on the part of the forces of reaction and militarism, there are objective difficulties engendered by the complex nature of the very process of the international limitation of armaments (implementing the principle of the protection of security, working out criteria for the comparison of the limitation of the arms systems, questions of control, etc.). To solve all these problems is not an easy matter from both the purely technical and the psychological point of view, all the more so since the Cold War lasted for two decades and the traditions it engendered are still alive, while the period of détente covers only a few years.

But it is precisely because of the new historical conditions that the drive to halt the arms race has become the principal task and has acquired a special, even decisive, importance.

The proposals submitted in September 1976 by the Soviet Union point out major directions in the struggle to end the arms race and for disarmament.[2] These are: conclusion of the world treaty on the non-use of force in international relations, cessation of the nuclear arms race, reduction and subsequent elimination of nuclear weapons, prohibition of nuclear-weapon tests, consolidation of the regime of non-proliferation of nuclear weapons, prohibition and destruction of chemical weapons, prohibition of the development of new types and new systems of weapons of mass destruction, reduction of armed forces and conventional armaments, creation of peace zones, reduction of military budgets, convocation of a World Disarmament Conference.

'Impulse' for further advance needed

The essence of military détente lies in a guaranteed repudiation of the use of force in inter-state relations, and the implementation of measures to limit, and ultimately to stop, the arms race. This would involve the reduction of armaments, the armed forces and military expenditures, and subsequent disarmament. In other words, it envisages a gradual reduction in military preparations by means of measures dealing ever more profoundly with the sphere of armaments and undertaken by an increasing number of states.

Universal and complete disarmament would indeed make military détente irreversible. Agreement on universal and complete disarmament would be the most radical way of solving the problem. However, taking into account the obtaining situation, the problem of military détente can and must be solved by reducing and stopping the arms race, that is, before reaching an agreement on universal and complete disarmament. The gradual reduction of military preparations should not necessarily be carried out in strict hierarchical sequence, that is, when approaches and solutions to one problem are not sought until another one is solved. On the contrary, the movement to disarmament through partial measures can and must proceed on a broad scale, dealing simultaneously with many relevant problems. Such a movement is necessary, above all, because when it is virtually impossible to reach the ultimate goal at one go, the road to this goal lies through partial measures, implemented step by step.

Soviet-American undertakings in the field of limitation of strategic arms are of a historic significance from the viewpoint of reducing the threat of a nuclear war and limiting and stopping the arms race. Among them are the treaty between the USSR and the United States on the Limitation of Anti-Ballistic Missile Systems and the Protocol to it, the Interim Agreement on Certain Measures with Respect to the Limitation of Strategic Offensive Arms, as well as SALT II. Further steps for subsequent limitations and a possible reduction of strategic arms would make it possible to preclude the opening up of new channels for the arms race.

Any radical approach to a solution of the problem of limiting and stopping the arms race would be impossible without political détente. At the same time, the course of events has confirmed that the political relaxation of international tension cannot automatically lead to military détente. It only creates favourable conditions for it. On the other hand, without military détente, without radical measures contributing to the reduction of the arms drive, the process of political relaxation of tension cannot proceed successfully. Consequently, the dialectic of the interaction and interdependence of political and military détente is as follows: military détente is impossible without political détente, but the latter cannot be stable and reliable enough if it is not confirmed and complemented by concrete measures diminishing the level of military confrontation of the two systems.

After the first successes in the political sphere the further relaxation of international tension became dependent, to a decisive degree, on the implementation of military détente, which directly rests on the need for agreed measures on the discontinuation of the arms race. It is important that the process of the relaxation of tension as a whole should develop and should not be allowed to turn back.

For some time already the process of détente has been proceeding parallel with the arms race, under conditions of a constant mounting of the military potentials of states and the perfection and accumulation of weapons. According to estimates made by Professor E. H. S. Burhop, Chairman of the Executive Council of the World Federation of Scientific Workers, the total military stockpiles of states by the mid-1970s amounted to approximately four tons of explosives per person. It was also estimated that the United States possessed at the time 30,000 units of nuclear weapons, which in explosive yield exceeded 600,000 times the yield of the atomic bomb dropped on Hiroshima during the Second World War. In many countries military budgets are growing, arsenals are being increased with various ultra-modern weapons which are constantly being perfected, the earth's atmosphere is still being polluted by nuclear explosions, costly research is being done in order to enhance the destructive potential of nuclear weapons, the accuracy of strategic rockets and their nuclear warheads in hitting small targets is being improved, and research and development work on creating various systems of anti-submarine warfare is noticeably growing in scope. New states are drawn into military preparations and the threat of the proliferation of nuclear weapons has not been removed.

'Parallelism' in the development of political relaxation and the arms race cannot proceed for any length of time without causing irreparable harm to international détente. Consequently, the possibility of the reorganization of international relations on the principles of peaceful coexistence of states belonging to the two opposing socio-political systems directly depends on whether this 'parallelism' is eradicated or not.

An end to the arms race and measures on disarmament are the most important means of neutralizing the two principal causes of the threat of a world war in our time, namely, the attempts of the imperialist circles to destabilize the military-strategic balance of forces of the two opposing systems and a dangerous development in a number of international 'outlying' conflicts. The bellicose forces of imperialism continue to pursue their course aimed at obtaining military superiority over the Soviet Union and other socialist countries and liquidating the military-strategic equivalence brought about by the change in the correlation of forces between the two systems; this course is fraught with serious military danger.

It should be said quite unequivocally that recognition of the military-strategic equivalence as a factor stabilizing peaceful relations between states belonging to opposing socio-political systems is by no means identical with, and is even directly opposed to, the Western concept of 'balance of power'. The Soviet Union's course is aimed at lowering the level of the strategic balance that has taken shape, with the preservation and consolidation of the mutual security of the parties concerned. In the conditions of a divided world this is the only possible road leading to a halt to the arms race. Realistically minded politicians in the West also speak in favour of lowering the level of the existing military-strategic balance. At the same time, the supporters of the 'balance of power' concept have as their aim the ensuring of constant 'breakthroughs' in the military sphere; they are trying to destabilize strategic equivalence and to upset it in their favour. They do not conceal the fact that these violations give one-sided advantages which can be used by capitalist countries in their attempts to force on the Soviet Union and other countries of the socialist community decisions favourable to them.

The aim of destabilization of the existing military-strategic parity is often presented as the 'concept of deterrence'. A theory has emerged in the Pentagon, according to which the relaxation of international tension, both in the political and military spheres, is not the only alternative to the Cold War, and international security can be safeguarded by perfecting the 'deterrence systems'. Along with this concept various theories have been elaborated about the 'acceptability' of limited nuclear wars with 'counterforce', 'selective' use of strategic and tactical nuclear weapons. Such concepts become especially dangerous to the cause of peace when they are used as the foundation for concrete, costly programmes aimed at the intensification of the quantitative and qualitative arms race; they serve as a means to justify and speed it up.

It is hard to believe that the initiators of the 'selective' arms race do not understand that under present conditions it is impossible to force the opponent unilaterally not to perfect its corresponding counter-systems. Even if the adherents of the 'selective' accumulation of armaments wished to contain the arms race within certain limits, they would be unable to do so. The 'selective' accumulation of weapons is not only incapable of ensuring a stable peace, but, on the contrary, is fraught with the threat of war, for it can lead to a definite temporary destabilization of the military-strategic balance, which could strengthen the hand of the bellicose circles that still considerably influence the shaping of policy in the imperialist countries. Only disarmament and a stop to the arms race can eliminate this danger.

A similar conclusion applies to the threat to universal peace stemming from international conflicts. This threat is caused by the fact that great powers are drawn into some of these conflicts to a sufficiently high degree. While the United States and other capitalist countries deliver arms to states pursuing an aggressive course or to subversive extremist elements that are fanning international conflicts, the Soviet Union and other members of the socialist community supply arms to the countries that are victims of aggression.

The expanding trade in armaments stimulates the arms drive in individual regions and throughout the world. For instance, the United States is known to have assumed the obligation of supplying Israel with samples of the most up-to-date aviation technology which is still at the stage of research and development. This spurs on the work and shortens the production period. According to American experts, the enormous arms deliveries to Israel and other 'clients' lead to the commissioning of additional capacities in military production in the United States, to say nothing of the fact that individual types of weapons are often tested and perfected on the field of international conflict, and this, too, contributes to the arms race.

The Soviet Union has time and again put forward the idea of creating regional systems of collective security, turning individual regions into zones of peace and stopping arms deliveries in connection with the developing process of a peaceful settlement of conflicts. The initiative for stopping the arms race in the regions of military conflicts becomes especially vital today, when there is a danger of certain participants in international conflicts coming close to the production of nuclear weapons. Co-ordination of measures in the limitation of the arms race and in disarmament, accompanied by the further normalization of international relations, would contribute to the neutralization of the consequences of international military-political conflicts that are dangerous to universal peace.

The most important trends

In existing circumstances, two aspects of the drive to prevent further stockpiling and refinement of armaments are of particular importance: first, renunciation of the right to develop new forms and systems of mass destruction weapons likely to upset the present strategical balance; and, second, the introduction of limitations on the further refinement of existing weapons.

As at the outset of the nuclear age, it now seems likely that we are on the verge of major scientific discoveries which may be used for military purposes. What once occurred in the nuclear field may be repeated now in other advanced fields of science and technology, the present level of which is such that there is a serious danger that weapons even more terrible than nuclear ones may be developed. A consequence of this may be the emergence of qualitatively new means of waging war, the use of which would threaten the world's population with an irreversible catastrophe.

Reason and conscience make it a human duty to do everything possible to prevent the emergence of such weapons. The qualitative refinement of existing weapon systems warrants particular concern in present circumstances. Its immense practical importance stems above all from the fact that refinement of this kind is the prevalent current feature of the arms race, on which militaristic circles pin their chief hopes of gaining unilateral strategic advantages. It is, in fact, in the process and as a result of the qualitative refinement of strategic armaments that the most dangerous destabilizing tendencies in the military field arise and develop. Moreover, this is precisely the area in which the latest scientific and technological innovations are most actively used and in which the most complex and costly military research and experimental development takes place.

To make progress towards disarmament, it is essential to work out and apply effective measures for progressive limitation of the qualitative arms race. Though complex, difficult and urgent, it is perfectly feasible to solve this problem step by step, particularly as the first steps have already been taken. One possible way of limiting the arms race would be to end all test explosions of nuclear weapons (including underground tests), which would make it much more difficult to refine existing strategic-missile and nuclear-weapon systems and develop new ones, and would also be conducive to a more favourable political climate. At present, the political, scientific and technical situation is such that it would be possible to achieve complete prohibition of nuclear tests, which can be done only if all nuclear powers are parties to the agreement.

The question of qualitative limitation of the arms race is not, of course, merely a question of renouncing nuclear-weapon tests. Unfortunately, it has not so far been possible to make progress towards slowing down and limiting military scientific research and experimental development. Possible measures in this connection range from complete prohibition to partial limitation of the most dangerous forms, for example by reducing the resources set aside for this purpose.

One other important aspect of the arms race must not be passed over: the manufacture of small nuclear weapons equipped with small-calibre nuclear warheads of relatively low power (of the order of 1 kiloton), delivered to their target by missiles of relatively short range. It is by no means fortuitous that the creation of such weapons is advocated with particular insistence by those military and political circles which at the same time proclaim the 'acceptability' and 'controllability' of so-called 'small' or 'limited' nuclear wars. In fact, such ideas and the arguments which accompany them ultimately serve only one purpose: gradually to accustom world public opinion to the view that it is acceptable to use nuclear weapons. Such a view is indefensible. Nuclear weapons, however 'miniature' they may be, remain weapons of mass destruction.

If plans to develop small-calibre nuclear weapons are put into practice, this will not reduce the threat of global thermonuclear war but, on the contrary, make it a great deal more likely. Even the use of such weapons in carefully calculated 'doses' could in certain circumstances lead to the subsequent use of strategic nuclear missiles, in other words to the escalation of a 'limited' nuclear war into a general thermonuclear holocaust. This makes it even more important to put into effect the decision of the United Nations General Assembly on the non-use of force in international relations and permanent prohibition of the use of nuclear weapons.

One part of the disarmament problem is the reduction of conventional weapons. In this connection, steps designed to reduce armed forces and armaments in specific regions are highly important. The negotiations taking place in Vienna on the reciprocal reduction of armed forces and armaments in Central Europe are particularly significant. Such a reduction should not have the effect of impairing the security of any party and should indeed be for the advantage of all; and it should be extended to nuclear weapons.

It would be a very opportune step towards limiting the arms race to take immediate specific measures to reduce the military expenditure of the major world powers with the prospect of using part of the resources released in order to meet the urgent needs of developing countries. The solution of existing difficulties would undoubtedly be facilitated if rapid effect were given to the Soviet proposal for the military budgets of all permanent members of the United Nations Security Council to be reduced by 10 per cent and part of the funds thus saved used to provide assistance to developing countries.

Notes

1. F. A. Long, 'Arms Control from the Perspective of the Nineteen-seventies', *Daedalus* (Arms, Defence Policy, and Arms Control), Summer 1975, p. 1.
2. United Nations Doc. A/32/232, 28 September 1976.

16

Third World and disarmament: shadow and substance

M. Azim Hussain
Third World Foundation, London

For Third World countries the most pressing problem is the widening gap between the rich and the poor nations of the world and, therefore, the need for a new international economic order to prevent further economic dislocation at the international level and human decay at the national level. For most Third World countries hunger and poverty are aggravated by the pressures to divert their resources to armaments. It has been universally recognized since the Second World War that disarmament, development and security are interrelated. The United Nations General Assembly proclaimed the First Disarmament Decade and the Second Development Decade, which are now drawing to a close, but there are no signs of progress toward disarmament, and as a consequence little has been achieved to fortify either security or development.

Mirage of disarmament

Security and disarmament, such vital and imminent issues at the end of the Second World War, and espoused year after year with growing eloquence, remain elusive. Within a few weeks of the signing of the United Nations Charter, the Hiroshima and Nagasaki bombs dealt a blow to the new world organization. At its first General Assembly in 1946, the very first resolution recognized by unanimous decision the close connection between problems of security and disarmament and asked the newly established United Nations Atomic Energy Commission urgently to make specific proposals for 'the elimination from national armaments of atomic weapons and of all other major weapons adaptable to mass destruction'. Since then and up to 1978, when the United Nations Special Session Devoted to Disarmament was held, 228 resolutions urging disarmament and international security have been adopted without any serious breakthrough.

The pattern of superpower posturing was set from the very beginning; both sides would present comprehensive proposals for disarmament but would be careful to see to it that these would contain conditions which the opposite side was

Shortened version from *Third World Quarterly*, Vol. II, No. 1, January 1980.

unlikely to accept. At the first meeting of the United Nations Atomic Energy Commission, the United States presented the Baruch Plan for the prohibition of the manufacture of atomic bombs and for placing all phases of the development and use of atomic energy under an international authority, but this seemingly magnanimous plan contained provisions which the Soviet Union could not accept. Moreover, the United States immediately demonstrated its unwillingness to sacrifice its advantage by conducting its first post-war atomic test seventeen days after Baruch had presented his plan to the commission and before its relevant technical committee had met. In 1949 the Soviet Union exploded its first atomic bomb. After three years of inactivity the United Nations Atomic Energy Commission was formally dissolved in 1952 and, with the explosion of a hydrogen bomb by the United States later that year and by the Soviet Union in 1953, the idea of international custody of nuclear weapons disappeared from superpower proposals.

The first fifteen years of the United Nations—the years of the Cold War—were dominated by the debate as to whether conventional or nuclear disarmament should come first until an approximate nuclear balance was established between East and West. As a result of this, in the early 1960s nuclear disarmament assumed primary importance and the focus shifted towards general and complete disarmament (GCD). In 1962 the United States and the USSR submitted to the Geneva Disarmament Committee draft treaties for GCD which included establishment of a United Nations peace-keeping machinery. But after a debate over the first few clauses, and within a year, the holistic approach of GCD was given up. The moral imperative and sense of urgency on the part of the major powers towards disarmament has been declining ever since, while the clamour for it, particularly by the Third World countries, has become increasingly vociferous.

With every major advance in nuclear weapons technology and their systems of delivery there have been changes in strategies of nuclear warfare and in the interrelationship of the superpowers. Whatever the nature of the competition for hegemony in the name of their respective ideologies, and whatever the acrimonious polemics over regional conflicts and peripheral world issues, there has been seen in recent years a measure of understanding between them of the fundamental issues of war and peace and of 'spheres of influence'. The doctrine of 'massive retaliation' and 'roll back' was not applied to the uprisings in the German Democratic Republic (1953), Poland and Hungary (1956), and Czechoslovakia (1968). The United States accepted the *de facto* division of Europe into East and West, just as the Soviet Union respected the hegemony of the United States over Latin America, as evidenced in 1962 by their avoidance of a clash over Cuba. In other areas such as the Middle East and certain parts of Africa and Asia, where distant countries have been brought into alliances, or had influence otherwise exerted over their policies, they have avoided a head-on clash, notwithstanding the militarization of aid and the politicization of development aid.

The nature of the relationship of the superpowers and their respective alliances is well reflected in the achievement or lack thereof in the whole field of disarmament generally, and more specifically during the last two decades. During this period the measures adopted were marginal, partial or non-armament ones. There were no arms-reduction, limitation or disarmament measures. The aim of the superpowers is to regulate the danger of unlimited competition among themselves rather than to reduce their arsenals. These partial measures have not led to arms reductions or to savings in military budgets of a kind to have any measurable economic implications. On the contrary, the superpowers have achieved a staggering overkill capacity.

United Nations Special Session Devoted to Disarmament

With a dismal record in the field of disarmament for over thirty years, Third World countries asked for the holding in 1978 of a Special General Assembly Session where they expressed profound regret that there was agreement neither on a comprehensive test ban (CTB) nor SALT II, and the two military alliances were unwilling to incorporate the principle of incompatibility between the maintenance of military bases and the presence of troops in foreign territories, on the one hand, and international peace and security on the other. At least four of the five nuclear-weapon states would not agree to renounce the first use of nuclear weapons or to give assurances that they would not use or threaten to use such weapons against non-nuclear-weapon states.

The superpowers and their respective alliance partners resisted the efforts of Third World countries on the grounds that to move too far and too fast would create instability in view of the imbalance in conventional forces in Europe, which made it necessary that nuclear and conventional disarmament go hand in hand. They stressed the importance of limiting conventional arms by showing that 133 wars involving eighty countries and killing millions of people had been fought with conventional weapons since 1945. This ploy of bringing up the question of imposing control and effecting reduction in the transfer of conventional arms to Third World countries has been brought up several times when the nuclear-weapon powers and their allies have been pressed hard on nuclear disarmament. However, led by India, the Third World countries resisted the emphasis proposed on the limitation of transfers of conventional arms by arguing that such limitations would not affect arms transfers within alliances; in their view, it was precisely such alliances which were the main threat to world peace. The Chinese expressed Third World views when they said that 'for the sake of strengthening their national defence, safeguarding their national independence and security, all countries have the right to acquire the necessary conventional weapons on an equitable basis'.

Conventional arms transfers

Despite their public postures the superpowers and the major arms-supplier countries, except in Europe between the two alliances, seem to have no intention to limit transfers of conventional weapons in relation to the rest of the world, in the foreseeable future. The interests of the arms suppliers are commercial, political and strategic. Arms sales abroad are encouraged, since greater sales reduce the per unit cost of weapons for the country which manufactures them; often R&D costs are recovered from the sale of new weaponry abroad. Large-scale arms transfers to particular countries also take place for political and strategic purposes; in many cases it is the result of great-power rivalry over the extension of their influence or the gaining of a strategic advantage. Sometimes major powers see arms sales as a means of freezing a conflict or maintaining a balance of confidence in situations where political solutions continue to elude the parties. Since the Second World War the major military powers have not been at war with one another, but they still wish to keep in readiness to go to war. The technological advance in the field of armaments is very rapid, weapons becoming quickly obsolete; hence a constant supply of second-hand and surplus equipment has become an important feature of the arms trade. Arms transfers are now not exclusively a function of the pattern of alliances and alignments as most of them were in the 1960s and earlier. There has been a major shift towards transactions on a commercial or near-commercial basis. Of the world arms trade, 75 per cent is with Third World countries; this represents nearly 80 per cent of military expenditure on conventional armaments.

It is estimated that the current arms trade to developing countries is about $20,000 million of which 86 per cent is divided thus: 36 per cent United States, 30 per cent USSR, 10 per cent France and 10 per cent United Kingdom. Other substantial suppliers are the Federal Republic of Germany, Israel and Sweden. Following commercial and foreign policy interests the United States is willing to sell almost anything short of nuclear weapons. The 1979–83 backlog of United States orders for delivery was $32,000 million. Under its Military Assistance Programme the United States supplied arms to fourteen Third World countries in 1950 and to seventy in 1978. For the USSR, the export of arms is central to its foreign policy. France has always promoted sales uninhibited by restraints. The United Kingdom established in 1966 the Defence Ministry's sales organization, which has compiled a 734-page catalogue of almost every item from Corvettes to combat socks.

Though Western powers have stressed the need for parallel progress in conventional and nuclear disarmament, and have set up a United Nations committee to discuss limitations on the transfer of conventional weapons, the prospects of the limitation or reduction on a multilateral basis are somewhat remote because of the vested interests, both strategic and commercial, of arms suppliers, and the obligations of many Third World countries stemming from bilateral and regional security problems and, in many areas, internal and security needs. In 1976 when the issue was raised by the United States, United Kingdom and Japan in the General Assembly, Argentina objected to their suggesting to developing countries what level of military equipment they needed for their defence needs. India successfully argued that the proposal would restrict the freedom of small states, leaving the major powers free to increase their arsenals. In the absence of other disarmament measures, including nuclear disarmament, it would be discriminatory against smaller and less developed countries as well as liberation movements.

Disarmament and development

Another issue which attracted great attention at the United Nations Special Session Devoted to Disarmament was that of the link between disarmament and development.

The United Nations had asked the developed countries to devote 1 per cent of their GNP to the Third World. This figure was later reduced to 0.7 per cent. NATO and the Warsaw Pact countries, whose military expenditure represented 85 per cent of the world total, devoted only 0.25 per cent and 0.04 per cent respectively to development assistance while military expenditures continued to increase. During the 1950s and 1960s a salient feature of aid was that much of it was devoted to armaments. In the past decade, the poor nations have financed over 80 per cent of their development out of their own meagre resources.

The linkage of disarmament and development has been seen by developing countries as far back as 1950, when India submitted a draft resolution to the General Assembly recommending the establishment of a United Nations Peace Fund, to be financed out of the money saved through disarmament, for the development of Third World countries. Little notice was taken of this until two decades later when in 1970 the General Assembly called for a close link between the Second Development Decade and the First Disarmament Decade.

To bridge the gap between developed and developing countries, Kurt Waldheim suggested the diversion of one-tenth of military expenditure to development efforts. President Leopold Senghor of Senegal suggested a 'War Tax' of 5 per cent of armament budgets which would yield $20,000 million annually for development assistance. France proposed the establishment of an International Fund for Disarmament and Development derived from tax on 'excessive arms expenditure'. As far-reaching proposals for disarmament were being formulated by developing countries, they saw the prospect of increasingly vast resources for their social and economic progress falling into their laps. But the militarily significant powers managed to modify or qualify most of the proposals and the issue of the linkage of disarmament and development was shelved by the United Nations Special Session Devoted to Disarmament, the Secretary-General being requested to undertake a three-year study on the link between disarmament and development.

Future prospects

It was understandable that at the United Nations Special Session Devoted to Disarmament there was among Third World countries almost universal dissatisfaction with the results achieved by the Geneva Disarmament Committee as well as by the various bilateral and regional agreements during the last three decades. There was a great disparity between the approach and the objectives of the superpowers and their allies and those of the Third World countries. Inevitably, grandiose objectives and programmes were formulated, mostly by Third World countries. These the superpowers and their allies grudgingly accepted, making reservations after the adoption of the Final Document. They gave their own interpretations, no doubt having even greater unexpressed reservations about their actual intentions than about many parts of the Final Document. In these circumstances, it was inevitable that the workmen should find fault with their tools and a great deal of time was spent on improving the machinery, qualitatively and quantitatively, for achieving disarmament.

The existing United Nations membership machinery consisted of the deliberative annual sessions of the General Assembly and, within the General Assembly, the Assembly's First Committee, which dealt with disarmament and related international security questions. Hereafter it was to deal exclusively with disarmament. Secondly, the Disarmament Commission, established in 1952, was revived and entrusted with the task of making recommendations annually to the General Assembly and to the disarmament negotiating body. Thirdly, the Special Session of the General Assembly Devoted to Disarmament, again consisting of all United Nations membership, was to meet in 1981, to evaluate the work done in the three preceding years. Fourthly, there was to be a World Disarmament Conference at 'the earliest appropriate time' with 'universal participation', which meant again United Nations membership and a few countries not members of the United Nations. Thus instead of one there are now four deliberative bodies with practically the same membership.

The existing negotiating body, the Geneva Conference of the Committee on Disarmament, of thirty-one members, with the United States and USSR as co-chairmen, was enlarged to forty members, including all the five nuclear-weapon states with a monthly rotating chairmanship.

The nature of the changes to the machinery was regarded by Third World countries as their signal achievement, perhaps the only item of success during the whole session; the new machinery would offer more frequent opportunities for them to exercise greater pressure for more rapid progress. But the truth of the matter is that what is needed is not an ever-increasing number of organs, forums and conferences, but the will on the part of the superpowers and their allies to bring about genuine disarmament. Should this will on the part of the nuclear-weapon states not be forthcoming, the Third World countries—being concerned more with change than with the status quo and with the freezing of the power relations and the authority structure that flows from the rights and special responsibility of the superpowers—would feel just as frustrated as they do with regard to the resistance in developed countries to a new international economic order.

17

The nuclear arms race: an alternative perspective

K. Subrahmanyam
Institute for Defence Studies and Analyses, New Delhi

Introduction

The nuclear arms race over the last three decades has imposed its culture on large sections of mankind. The pressures on the élites of the nuclear-weapon countries to justify to their own populations the enormous expenditures involved in sustaining the nuclear arms race have led to their mobilizing consciously not only their industrial and military establishment in favour of the nuclear arms race, but also their academic, political and information establishments to propagate the virtues of the interminable arms race.

A national constituency for the arms race has developed in the nuclear-weapon states. The armament industries deal with frontier technologies and attract the best talents available in the country. They provide employment to highly skilled categories of workers who are vocal and effective in their political influence. The multiplier effect of the armaments industry is felt all over the country and by a wide cross-section of the population. No politician can easily ignore it and no political party can turn its back on it. Currently, sales of sophisticated arms and technical services to oil-rich countries are justified in terms of redressing the balance-of-payment deficits and absorbing the surplus petro-dollars.

While information about the pressures in the Soviet Union is not available to the same extent as in the United States, there is no reason to believe that the situation in the USSR is very different. In the case of the Non-Proliferation Treaty (NPT), SALT and the current negotiations on armaments, there appears to be considerable congruence in the strategic theologies of the United States and the USSR.

The nuclear theology

The core doctrine of this theology is deterrence. It is argued that the United States

Shortened version of a working paper prepared for the International Workshop on Disarmament, Delhi (India), March 1978, *Bulletin of Peace Proposals*, Vol. 9, No. 3, 1978.

initially needed to have nuclear weapons to counter the enormous conventional superiority of the USSR. Once the Soviet Union developed nuclear weapons, the United States had to keep ahead in weapons technology to deter it. Deterrence has been institutionalized and enshrined as the first principle of international relations, especially between the two great powers. Since the need to do away with deterrence is not foreseen, the arms race will be interminable. The only agreement possible is for the two countries to agree to conduct the arms race at a mutually acceptable pace and to outdistance all others. This is what SALT and NPT are about.

The fact, however, is that the nuclear arms race was triggered off, not by the need for deterrence, but by the attempt to freeze the international hierarchical power structure. The very first use of the atom bomb to destroy Hiroshima and Nagasaki was a demonstration of the nuclear weapon as the new symbol and currency of international power. Japan was already offering to surrender, and the destruction of the two cities was unnecessary from either a military or a political point of view. They were destroyed to impress upon the world, and particularly the Soviet Union, that the United States had inherited the mantle of the British Empire as the foremost power of the world.

Even today, the justification for development and deployment of enhanced radiation weapons is in terms of deterring a possible Soviet armour attack. At one point, tactical nuclear weapons were advocated as an effective deterrent against the Soviet armour, but the advocates of such a strategy did not bother to explain how deterrence would operate when the other side also developed tactical nuclear weapons, just as they do not bother to explain what advantage the enhanced radiation weapon would bestow on one side when the other side also developed it. Or worse still, whether the enhanced radiation weapons give any advantage at all even if the other side is bound to use its nuclear weapons, whether clean or not. Collateral property damage and civilian casualties cannot be avoided once nuclear weapons start getting introduced into the battle. These kinds of argument in support of the deterrence thesis carry no conviction.

In fact, the net effect of the deterrence thesis appears to have been to the detriment of its advocates. As the United States got involved in the costly Viet-Nam War, the Soviet Union was able to build up a nuclear arsenal to match that of the United States and was able to compel the acceptance of real mutual deterrence in SALT I. Meanwhile, the Soviet Navy too was built up as a seven-ocean blue-water navy. The deterrer has been deterred, and the Soviet Union today seeks to have the same flexibility of options as the United States enjoyed between 1945 and 1970. In this analysis, no value judgement in favour of one or the other dominant nuclear power is implied. It is offered only to expose the fallacies in the doctrine of deterrence as practised by its ardent proponents.

Murphy's Law

The doctrine of deterrence, in the form of a posture adopted by a nation to communicate to a potential adversary that aggression against the country concerned would not be cost-effective, had been practised long before Hiroshima. The doctrine of deterrence in the pre-nuclear era did not always succeed in preventing the outbreak of war. Miscalculations in some cases, and correct calculations in certain others as to the cost-effectiveness of armed action, did lead to wars. Nothing that has happened in the nuclear era leads to the conclusion that miscalculations will not be made or that the doctrine of deterrence, as practised today by the nuclear powers, has any inbuilt safeguards against such miscalculations that are likely to prove more effective in preventing wars than was the case with comparable doctrines in the pre-nuclear era. The wars in the Indo-Chinese peninsula are too recent to warrant any faith in the view that miscalculations by nuclear powers are not likely to occur. The law of probability (Murphy's Law) maintains that if in any system something can go wrong, then some time or other it is bound to go wrong. Therefore, with the growing stockpiles of nuclear weapons and their increasing dispersal, the probability of their use is increasing day by day.

In the nuclear era, three crucial dimensions have emerged which have a vital bearing in the calculus of deterrence. These are (a) the enormity of the destructive power of nuclear weapons; (b) the extremely short time-frame within which enormous damage can be inflicted; and (c) the vast uncertainty surrounding the likely extent of ecological and societal damage that may result from large-scale use of nuclear weapons. Though there is considerable literature on the subjects of limited nuclear wars, counterforce strikes and demonstration strikes against superior conventional forces, it has not been credibly established that once the nuclear threshold was crossed it would be feasible to limit the scope, extent or manner of weapon usage. The time factor, the deep reach of the weapons and their wide dispersal appear to rule out the possibility of any realistic limitation.

Though the nuclear theology has been propagated for nearly a quarter of a century, no detailed and credible scenarios are available of how the nuclear war will be fought between the two major nuclear powers, except as a spasmic one, how command and control will be maintained during the nuclear exchange, how exactly the war will be brought to an end and how a settlement will be negotiated thereafter. In the absence of such a detailed and credible scenario, the arguments for a nuclear war-winning capability and a disarming first-strike capability have gained ground. Such arguments and the acquisition of such capabilities have become the basis for intensifying further the nuclear arms race.

The MAD doctrine and freedom of intervention

One would expect that the main thrust of the doctrine of deterrence would be to highlight the high degree of uncertainty relating to the outcome of a nuclear war in terms of strategic objectives and the certainty that the nuclear exchange would not be commensurate with any rational political goal. If these postulates had been widely understood and disseminated, the interminable nuclear arms race would not have taken place, and it would have been appreciated that beyond a point the piling up of nuclear arms was not a cost-effective proposition.

But the proponents of the nuclear theology gave a different twist to the doctrines. They brought in the issue of 'credibility'. According to this doctrinal refinement, it is not enough if uncertainty is created in the mind of the adversary with regard to the outcome of nuclear exchange. It is essential to impress upon the adversary the certainty that in any nuclear exchange the organized society of the adversary nation will be destroyed, although, as a corollary, one's own organized society may be destroyed as surely. This is the MAD (Mutual Assured Destruction) doctrine.

The purpose of the high priests of nuclear theology is not merely to achieve mutual deterrence. If that were so, proliferation would be encouraged rather than frowned upon: for a multinuclear world would only increase the deterrence on every nuclear power. What they aim at is not total nuclear deterrence, but a kind of deterrence that would allow them freedom of intervention at the non-nuclear level. Therefore, the doctrine of deterrence is further refined as credible deterrence in the interest of achieving stability. The acquisition of nuclear weapons by other nations is deemed to contribute to instability because it would complicate the operation of the two major nuclear-weapon powers at the non-nuclear level.

The struggle for domination

What is sought for under this doctrine, then, is not just the capability of deterring an adversary, but the projection of an image of nuclear superiority and the capability of intervening militarily with conventional forces in various areas of the world, masked by the rhetoric of stability. This motivation became clear when the practitioners of nuclear theology rejected the no-first-use doctrine and declined to pledge themselves to non-use of nuclear weapons against non-nuclear-weapon states. The real objective of the arms race is to sustain the capability of military dominance, using the doctrine of deterrence to provide a plausible rationalization. And military dominance has become an end in itself, or at best the most reliable form of global dominance.

It is of interest to note here that when the stronger of the two dominant nuclear-weapon powers resorted to the strategy of credible deterrence by publishing figures of the missiles deployed, the weaker power resorted to the strategy of deterrence through uncertainty. Up to this point, the nuclear theologians had not raised the issue of destabilization of the nuclear balance of terror. When the stronger side had raced ahead and completed its silo-based solid-fuelled missile programmes and was far ahead in submarine-based missile programmes, it was not considered destabilizing, in spite of the immense superiority of one side over the other. Nor was the development of MRV technology or, in our day, the development of the neutron bomb or cruise missile. But as soon as the other side developed the ABM technology, it was announced that the nuclear balance had been destabilized. At one point, when the development and deployment of ABM was accepted as feasible and desirable, a case was made out (in 1967) for a light ABM coverage against a possible Chinese ICBM threat. The Chinese have yet to fire an ICBM. This is an example of how the doctrine is tailored to meet the needs of decisions taken on considerations other than those avowed. The undue concern of the USSR regarding the enhanced-radiation weapon also seems to fall into this category. It is not unlikely that, once the USSR develops its own weapon, its condemnation of it will cease. One may recall what happened to the Stockholm Appeal in the 1950s after the USSR developed its nuclear arsenal.

First-strike capability and counterforce

In assessing nuclear-war fighting capability, the number of launchers and warheads, the throw-weight, the accuracy and the survivability are all relevant factors. Yet very often the nuclear theologians tend to emphasize one factor to the complete exclusion of all others. One usual argument is that a particular side is developing the first-strike capability. While making this point, the availability of the second-strike capability in a submarine-borne missile force is wholly ignored and a seemingly plausible case is made for the development of new weapon systems, such as mobile missiles and manned bombers.

The doctrine of counterforce strike is one of the most specious pieces of logic even for the nuclear theology; it is not distinguished for the rigour demanded by logic. It has been argued by very responsible people that it would be possible to fight a nuclear war with minimum casualties by aiming very accurate missiles on the adversary's missile silos. The proponents of this doctrine are unable to explain how the adversary would know that the warheads were being aimed only at his silos and not on his population centres, especially when he must launch his missiles on receiving the warning even before his silos were struck. Secondly, the adversary's missiles may not be very accurate. Thirdly, adapting the mimimax rule, the uncertainty of a nuclear exchange, the adversary who received the warning of incoming warheads would have to presume the worst—that his population centres were being destroyed—and aim his missiles at the population centres of the country striking first. At that stage, with nuclear warheads hurtling down towards a nation, any hot-line communication on one's limited intentions would carry little credibility.

The role of NPT

The same dubious theology has converted the NPT into a treaty to license unlimited proliferation of nuclear weapons by the five nuclear-weapon powers. The title of the treaty held out the promise that its objective was to ensure non-proliferation of nuclear weapons, whether by the two nations already proliferating or by new nations wanting to join the proliferating game. The Preamble and Article VI of the treaty lay down the obligation to pursue negotiations, 'in good faith', on effective measures relating to the cessation of the nuclear arms race at an early date and to nuclear disarmament, as well as to a treaty on general and complete disarmament under strict and effective international control. Since the NPT was signed in 1968, the proliferating nations have multiplied the number of their weapons and have thereby violated the treaty they themselves sponsored. They have brusquely turned down all pleas of other non-proliferating signatories to the treaty to abide by the letter and spirit of the treaty.

The NPT of nuclear weapons, as implemented to date, has created a category of crypto nuclear-weapon nations passing for non-nuclear-weapon nations. Most of the alliance partners of the dominant nuclear powers resort to the doctrines of nuclear war to ensure their security. They are members of nuclear planning groups which carry out detailed contingency plans for nuclear war. They permit nuclear-weapon stockpiling on their soil, extend home-port facilities to nuclear-weapon carriers, train their troops in the use of nuclear weapons and develop contingency plans to get nuclear weapons transferred to them for use in the event of a nuclear war; and yet they pose as non-nuclear-weapon nations. This is like a person calling himself a teetotaller because he never drinks at his own expense. The number of nuclear-weapon nations is not just five; the allies of the dominant nuclear-weapon powers should also be counted among them.

The NPT, if serious in its avowed purpose, should have denigrated nuclear weapons. Instead, it has sought to confer prestige on the possession of nuclear weapons—even by forces which are thoroughly non-credible as deterrents according to nuclear theology itself, and has therefore exempted such nations from international inspection of their nuclear facilities. Instead of obliging the nuclear-weapon powers to discourage the trend towards proliferation, the treaty has imposed all the obligations on the non-nuclear-weapon powers. The nuclear-weapon powers would not even accept the obligation of no-first-use; they would not even guarantee to spare non-nuclear-weapon countries. The treaty was therefore seen as a clear demonstration of the dominance of the nuclear-weapon powers over the non-nuclear-weapon powers.

Arms race and arms control

The most blatant exercise in subterfuge indulged in by the nuclear theologians is to present the continuing arms race among the dominant nuclear powers as an arms control or limitation measure. After signing the so-called Non-Proliferation Treaty, two of its sponsors increased the number of launch vehicles, warheads and throw-weights, and the accuracy and sophistication of delivery vehicles. Yet an inventory of the arsenals of both sides in terms of launch vehicles only (without taking into account all the other factors involved in accelerating the arms race) and the agreement not to proceed with the ABM systems (which had been found technologically not cost-effective) were hailed as great arms-limitation measures. After the agreement was signed, both sides proceeded to increase the number of warheads with multiple independent re-entry vehicles, to develop cruise missiles, neutron bombs, SS-20 missiles, Delta and Trident submarines with longer-range missiles, manoeuvrable re-entry vehicles (MARVs), and, on top of it, to increase the accuracy of their missiles. Let us hope that the next enumeration of the arsenals of both sides is not hailed as yet another arms-control measure.

The entire history of the so-called arms-control agreements reveals that they relate to deployment of armaments of uncertain military advantage which are not likely to be cost-effective in the perception of the military planners of the dominant powers. The Antarctica Treaty, the Outer Space Treaty, the Treaty on Placing Weapons of Mass Destruction on the Sea Bed and Ocean Floor, the Convention on Bacteriological and Toxic Weapons and the Convention on the Prohibition of Military or any other Hostile Use of Environmental Modification Techniques, all fall into this category. The so-called NPT and SALT I are not arms-control measures but armament legitimation measures. They have all served as soporifics to lull the world into a sense of forward movement in arms limitation and, in a few cases, have even served to mislead the world into accepting arms-legitimization measures as arms-limitation measures.

The irony is that the dominant nuclear-weapon powers are themselves caught in a tragic dilemma. The more the stability of mutual deterrence is emphasized, the less usable and relevant the vast nuclear stockpiles become in international relations. Their obsession with power and domination blinds them to the risk of nuclear war through strategic miscalculations, possibilities of seizure of nuclear weapons and fissile materials by terrorist and secessionist groups, clandestine acquisitions leading to irresponsible use for narrow political or racial ends, and, above all, the ever-present danger of joint domination degenerating into a struggle for total domination.

The three worlds in the nuclear stratarchy

The nuclear arms race has led to three worlds in the global nuclear stratarchy. The First World consists of the United States and other industrialized countries allied and associated with it. The Second World includes the two socialist nuclear-weapon powers (USSR and China) and countries allied and associated with them. The Third World consists mostly of non-aligned and non-nuclear-weapon nations. The first two worlds are characterized by their reliance on nuclear weapons and nuclear-weapon doctrines to ensure their security; they have a relationship of mutual deterrence. This may not preclude schisms and contradictions among them, even an eventual conflagration. None the less, both share the belief in nuclear theology. The Third World does not accept it. The resistance of some Third World countries to signing the NPT or accepting full-scope safeguards without their being accepted by the nuclear-weapon states arises from their desire not to be subjected to a nuclear-weapons culture. For them to accept these pressures will not be just humiliating: it will mean their acceptance of the legitimacy of nuclear weapons as a mode of power, segregation and dominance.

The first two worlds are not in a position to break out of the bonds of the nuclear-weapons culture. Hence the non-aligned and developing countries have a new role to play in countering this culture. In the 1950s and early 1960s, the non-aligned movement was able to constrain the operation of the doctrine of deterrence which sought to convert the whole world into a bipolar system. Now the task before the non-aligned world is to resist the transformation of the latent power of nuclear-weapon stockpiles into usable political and economic power.

18

The competition in the stockpiling of weapons: a way out

Oleg Bykov

Institute for World Economics and International Relations, Moscow

The tremendous danger and heavy burden of the arms race which is engulfing the world are sufficiently clear. Mankind is faced with the choice either to stop stockpiling the means of self-destruction or to subject its own existence to the most serious threat, but the tempo of the arms race is not only not slowing down but even accelerating. There continues to be a qualitative refinement in weapons of mass destruction, incorporating the latest advances in science and technology, and their quantity is being continually increased.

There is an increase in the number of states which are becoming involved in competition in the stockpiling of weapons. Following in the footsteps of the major powers in amassing considerable military arsenals we find many medium-sized and small countries, even developing countries. Is there a way out of this situation? We are firmly convinced that there is.

A comprehensive analysis of world development today has led research workers in our institute to the scientific and well-founded conclusion that the necessary objective possibilities exist for halting the arms race and bringing about disarmament. Primarily, there has been a perceptible change in the socio-political picture of the world. There has been a strengthening of the world positions of socialism and other progressive forces which have a vital interest in averting a universal military conflict. There is an increase in the role in international affairs of the developing countries and the non-aligned states. There is an intensification of their positive influence on the solution of the problems of disarmament. The effectiveness of the efforts of all peace-loving states and peoples aimed at disarmament depends on those efforts being organically incorporated in the historic process of the consistent limitation and subsequent total elimination of the very possibility of military solutions of controversial international problems. This policy of stopping the arms race is in keeping with the interests of the whole of mankind. The general course of contemporary international events makes the whole problem of war and peace a different one. Gone for ever are the times when military solutions to international problems were quite often viewed from the

From the statement at the Special Session of the United Nations General Assembly Devoted to Disarmament, June 1978, *Disarmament from the Aspect of Peace Research*, International Institute for Peace, Vienna.

standpoint of obtaining specific advantages or of losing certain positions. In our nuclear age, global military conflict gambles with the lives of hundreds of millions of people and with the fates of whole countries, and, to a large extent, with the whole future of mankind.

It is vain to suppose that it is possible to provoke the outbreak of a world conflagration and then stand aside and warm one's hands at the fire. We are convinced that the collective political will of the peoples and states of the world, the vital interests of the whole human species, should be able to prevail over the selfish calculations of those amateurs of military adventures.

A new and important factor in international development in the 1970s has been the positive change in the world situation. The advent of détente has opened up favourable political prospects for progress in disarmament, and the first, but very modest, measures in limiting arms have served as a stimulus for the further improvement of the political climate in the world. The arms race has begun to lose one of its sources of momentum; I refer to tension in relations between states with opposing social systems. An important objective prerequisite for the conclusion of agreements on the reduction of armaments is the current approximate balance of forces between the USSR and the United States of America and between the Warsaw Pact countries and the North Atlantic Alliance. This is one of the major realities of contemporary international relations, and consistent progress towards disarmament can be brought about only by taking it into account and, of course, by observing strictly the principle of equality and safeguarding the security of all parties.

Of course, the balance of military power, particularly the balance of terror, is no substitute for sound and solid international security. This would be true even given a gradual reduction, instead of an increase, in the level of this balance. In the contemporary world, in the final analysis, the expansion of military arsenals does not strengthen, but actually weakens, general security. At the same time the strategic balance which has developed is the only possible starting point for a consistent, stage-by-stage process of reducing armaments, right up to, and including, their elimination. These objective factors of the contemporary international scene should also include recognition of the urgent need to resolve, by concerted efforts on the part of the whole of mankind, the most important global problems of the last quarter of the twentieth century.

Much has been said at this Special Session about the arms race putting a brake, throughout the world, on the solution of these problems. Studies undertaken by our institute have produced convincing evidence that it will hardly be possible to solve such global problems as the need to provide the whole population of the planet with food, medical care and housing, to provide industry with raw materials and energy, and to preserve the natural environment, if we continue to spend such colossal sums of money for military purposes.

Furthermore, the arms race poisons the political climate in the world and makes more difficult the broad international co-operation which is so necessary to the solution of the global problems of our time. The Institute for World Economics and International Relations is doing a great deal of research work in its attempts to find real possibilities for constructive international co-operation. We see a restraint of the arms race as providing encouraging prospects for the solution of general human problems, for the equitable restructuring of international economic relations, for the earmarking of the funds saved for the purpose of meeting the needs of Third World development, and for converting military industries to peaceful production. According to our calculations such a transfer would restrain, rather than fuel, inflation and reduce unemployment in Western countries.

While speaking of the objective factors which, in the final analysis, will determine the solution to the disarmament problem, I should point out that to a considerable extent the process is hindered by inertia and by the accelerating pace of the armaments-producing machine. It is impossible to stop that machine overnight. It is not easy, even during the initial stages of the development of systems of modern weapons, to devise large-scale long-term programmes to slow down and restrict their development, and it is even more difficult at later stages. Differences between the existing structures of military forces have an effect, as has the parties' lack of synchronization in the development of various types of new weapons. When it comes to proposing specific ideas for the limitation of armaments and for disarmament, all of this must be given due weight. However, it is not because of these difficulties that it has not been possible, so far, to stop the military preparations that are under way. The pattern of technological development in the production of weapons, and the political-strategic realities of our time, do not constitute the major hindrance to military détente. The real hindrance lies in the narrow, selfish interests and subjective attitudes of those who bank on the continuation and intensification of the arms race. The cause of disarmament cannot advance if it continues to be guided by the political stereotypes of the past. It will be impossible to stop the arms race if stopping it is linked with the aim of obtaining one sided advantages, detrimental to the interests of others and detrimental to peaceful international co-operation. History has demonstrated cogently the ineffectiveness of attempts to halt the impetuous development of the social progress of mankind by force of arms. Yet there remain in the West politicians and strategists who think in terms of curbing the social and national liberation of the peoples of other countries, and that leads inevitably to a complication of the international situation, and speeds up the arms race. Of course, there are other people who obstruct the curbing of the arms race. I refer to those who preach the inevitability of world nuclear war and who approach the problem of disarmament in a neolithic fashion. They replace the concept of real disarmament—that is the disarmament of all states, without exception—with their formula of disarmament on the part only of the two so-called superpowers. Despite all their words about the desirability of disarmament they call openly for a stepping up of the armaments and military preparations of other states, primarily themselves.

Let us suppose for a moment that, instead of making concerted efforts to curb the arms race as a whole, we achieved disarmament only of the two major powers. Who would stand to win? Obviously it would be only those who refused to associate themselves with any practical disarmament measures and who developed major military potential, intending to use it to implement their expansionist policies. If the arms race is to be limited it is necessary to have political realism and to take fully into account the objective realities of our time. All states must always be ready to attempt to arrive at mutually acceptable and effective decisions that are not detrimental to the security of any of them, and will strengthen international security. The Soviet Union has always been, and remains, a staunch champion of disarmament. The purpose of its proposals is to achieve a merging of political détente with military détente, and to start all-embracing talks on disarmament, including nuclear disarmament.

The breadth and constructiveness which distinguishes the policy of the Soviet Union in curbing the arms race is obvious. In that policy the primary, most topical problems are linked with long-term prospects for general and complete disarmament.

The realistic nature of the Soviet proposals as they are constantly being developed takes into account both the new political, strategic and military-technical elements and also the constructive initiatives of other countries. The Soviet Union, as we know, has introduced a whole series of concrete proposals designed to ensure a decisive breakthrough in the struggle for the cessation of the arms race.

No one, of course, can claim a monopoly in putting forward proposals on disarmament. All initiatives are good, no matter where they come from. The only important thing is that they should be constructive in character and should be conceived in a sincere desire to spare the world the threat of military disaster.

Part V.   The United Nations and disarmament

The United Nations has the constitutional purpose of maintaining international peace and security, which, it is widely agreed, requires an active and even central role in promoting not only arms control but more particularly disarmament. Since the founding of the United Nations, the promotion of disarmament has been a major task of the Organization. (For a detailed account of the work of the United Nations in this field, the reader may consult The United Nations and Disarmament: 1945–1970 (United Nations publication, Sales No. 70.IX.1) and The United Nations and Disarmament: 1970–1975 (United Nations publication, Sales No E.76.IX.1).)

The Tenth Special Session of the General Assembly (the first Special Session Devoted to Disarmament), held in 1978, marked a new beginning for these efforts. Because it constituted a milestone, the Final Document of that Special Session will be the first reading in this part. Two appendices provide clarification on two matters mentioned in the Final Document.

19

Final Document of the Special Session of the United Nations General Assembly Devoted to Disarmament

I. Introduction

1. The attainment of the objective of security, which is an inseparable element of peace, has always been one of the most profound aspirations of humanity. States have for a long time sought to maintain their security through the possession of arms. Admittedly, their survival has, in certain cases, effectively depended on whether they could count on appropriate means of defence. Yet the accumulation of weapons, particularly nuclear weapons, today constitutes much more a threat than a protection for the future of mankind. The time has therefore come to put an end to this situation, to abandon the use of force in international relations and to seek security in disarmament, that is to say, through a gradual but effective process beginning with a reduction in the present level of armaments. The ending of the arms race and the achievement of real disarmament are tasks of primary importance and urgency. To meet this historic challenge is in the political and economic interests of all the nations and peoples of the world as well as in the interests of ensuring their genuine security and peaceful future.

2. Unless its avenues are closed, the continued arms race means a growing threat to international peace and security and even to the very survival of mankind. The nuclear and conventional arms build-up threatens to stall the efforts aimed at reaching the goals of development, to become an obstacle on the road of achieving the new international economic order and to hinder the solution of other vital problems facing mankind.

3. The dynamic development of détente, encompassing all spheres of international relations in all regions of the world, with the participation of all countries, would create conditions conducive to the efforts of states to end the arms race, which has engulfed the world, thus reducing the danger of war. Progress on détente and progress on disarmament mutually complement and strengthen each other.

4. The Disarmament Decade solemnly declared in 1969 by the United Nations is coming to an end. Unfortunately, the objectives established on that occasion by the General Assembly appear to be as far away today as they were then, or even further because the arms race is not diminishing but increasing and

United Nations General Assembly resolution S-10/2.

outstrips by far the efforts to curb it. While it is true that some limited agreements have been reached, 'effective measures relating to the cessation of the nuclear arms race at an early date and to nuclear disarmament' continue to elude man's grasp. Yet the implementation of such measures is urgently required. There has not been any real progress either that might lead to the conclusion of a treaty on general and complete disarmament under effective international control.* Furthermore, it has not been possible to free any amount, however modest, of the enormous resources, both material and human, which are wasted on the unproductive and spiralling arms race and which should be made available for the purpose of economic and social development, especially since such a race 'places a great burden on both the developing and the developed countries'.

5. The members of the United Nations are fully aware of the conviction of their peoples that the question of general and complete disarmament is of utmost importance and that peace, security and economic and social development are indivisible, and they have therefore recognized that the corresponding obligations and responsibilities are universal.

6. Thus a powerful current of opinion has gradually formed, leading to the convening of what will go down in the annals of the United Nations as the first Special Session of the General Assembly devoted entirely to disarmament.

7. The outcome of this Special Session, whose deliberations have to a large extent been facilitated by the five sessions of the Preparatory Committee which preceded it, is the present Final Document. This introduction serves as a preface to the document which comprises also the following three sections: a declaration, a programme of action and recommendations concerning the international machinery for disarmament negotiations.

8. While the final objective of the efforts of all states should continue to be general and complete disarmament under effective international control, the immediate goal is that of the elimination of the danger of a nuclear war and the implementation of measures to halt and reverse the arms race and clear the path towards lasting peace. Negotiations on the entire range of those issues should be based on the strict observance of the purposes and principles enshrined in the Charter of the United Nations, with full recognition of the role of the United Nations in the field of disarmament and reflecting the vital interest of all the peoples of the world in this sphere. The aim of the declaration is to review and assess the existing situation, outline the objectives and the priority tasks and set forth fundamental principles for disarmament negotiations.

9. For disarmament—the aims and purposes of which the declaration proclaims—to become a reality, it was essential to agree on a series of specific disarmament measures, selected by common accord as those on which there is a consensus to the effect that their subsequent realization in the short term appears to be feasible. There is also a need to prepare through agreed procedures a comprehensive disarmament programme. That programme, passing through all the necessary stages, should lead to general and complete disarmament under effective international control. Procedures for watching over the fulfilment of the obligations thus assumed had also to be agreed upon. That is the purpose of the programme of action.

---

* For text on agreed principles, see Appendix I—Ed.

10. Although the decisive factor for achieving real measures of disarmament is the 'political will' of states, and especially of those possessing nuclear weapons, a significant role can also be played by the effective functioning of an appropriate international machinery designed to deal with the problems of disarmament in its various aspects. Consequently, it would be necessary that the two kinds of organs required to that end, the deliberative and the negotiating organs, have the appropriate organization and procedures that would be most conducive to obtaining constructive results. The last section of the Final Document, Section IV, has been prepared with that end in view.

II. Declaration

11. Mankind today is confronted with an unprecedented threat of self-extinction arising from the massive and competitive accumulation of the most destructive weapons ever produced. Existing arsenals of nuclear weapons alone are more than sufficient to destroy all life on earth. Failure of efforts to halt and reverse the arms race, in particular the nuclear arms race, increases the danger of the proliferation of nuclear weapons. Yet the arms race continues. Military budgets are constantly growing, with enormous consumption of human and material resources. The increase in weapons, especially nuclear weapons, far from helping to strengthen international security, on the contrary weakens it. The vast stockpiles and tremendous build-up of arms and armed forces and the competition for qualitative refinement of weapons of all kinds to which scientific resources and technological advances are diverted, pose incalculable threats to peace. This situation both reflects and aggravates international tensions, sharpens conflicts in various regions of the world, hinders the process of détente, exacerbates the differences between opposing military alliances, jeopardizes the security of all states, heightens the sense of insecurity among all states, including the non-nuclear-weapon states, and increases the threat of nuclear war.

12. The arms race, particularly in its nuclear aspect, runs counter to efforts to achieve further relaxation of international tension, to establish international relations based on peaceful coexistence and trust between all states, and to develop broad international co-operation and understanding. The arms race impedes the realization of the purposes, and is incompatible with the principles, of the Charter of the United Nations, especially respect for sovereignty, refraining from the threat or use of force against the territorial integrity or political independence of any state, the peaceful settlement of disputes and non-intervention and non-interference in the internal affairs of states. It also adversely affects the right of peoples freely to determine their systems of social and economic development, and hinders the struggle for self-determination and the elimination of colonial rule, racial or foreign domination or occupation. Indeed, the massive accumulation of armaments and the acquisition of armaments technology by racist regimes, as well as their possible acquisition of nuclear weapons, present a challenging and increasingly dangerous obstacle to a world community faced with the urgent need to disarm. It is, therefore, essential for purposes of disarmament to prevent any further acquisition of arms or arms technology by such regimes, especially through strict adherence by all states to relevant decisions of the Security Council.

13. Enduring international peace and security cannot be built on the accumulation of weaponry by military alliances nor be sustained by a precarious balance of deterrence or doctrines of strategic superiority. Genuine and lasting peace can only be created through the effective implementation of the security system provided for in the Charter of the United Nations and the speedy and substantial reduction of arms and armed forces, by international agreement and mutual example, leading ultimately to general and complete disarmament under effective international control. At the same time, the causes of the arms race and threats to peace must be reduced and to this end effective action should be taken to eliminate tensions and settle disputes by peaceful means.

14. Since the process of disarmament affects the vital security interests of all states, they must all be actively concerned with and contribute to the measures of disarmament and arms limitation, which have an essential part to play in maintaining and strengthening international security. Therefore the role and responsibility of the United Nations in the sphere of disarmament, in accordance with its Charter, must be strengthened.

15. It is essential that not only governments but also the peoples of the world recognize and understand the dangers in the present situation. In order that an international conscience may develop and that world public opinion may exercise a positive influence, the United Nations should increase the dissemination of information on the armaments race and disarmament with the full co-operation of Member States.

16. In a world of finite resources there is a close relationship between expenditure on armaments and economic and social development. Military expenditures are reaching ever higher levels, the highest percentage of which can be attributed to the nuclear-weapon states and most of their allies, with prospects of further expansion and the danger of further increases in the expenditures of other countries. The hundreds of billions of dollars spent annually on the manufacture or improvement of weapons are in sombre and dramatic contrast to the want and poverty in which two-thirds of the world's population live. This colossal waste of resources is even more serious in that it diverts to military purposes not only material but also technical and human resources which are urgently needed for development in all countries, particularly in the developing countries. Thus, the economic and social consequences of the arms race are so detrimental that its continuation is obviously incompatible with the implementation of the new international economic order based on justice, equity and co-operation. Consequently, resources released as a result of the implementation of disarmament measures should be used in a manner which will help to promote the well-being of all peoples and to improve the economic conditions of the developing countries.

17. Disarmament has thus become an imperative and most urgent task facing the international community. No real progress has been made so far in the crucial field of reduction of armaments. However, certain positive changes in international relations in some areas of the world provide some encouragement. Agreements have been reached that have been important in limiting certain weapons or eliminating them altogether, as in the case of the Convention on the Prohibition of the Development, Production and Stockpiling of Bacteriological (Biological) and Toxin Weapons and on Their Destruction and excluding

particular areas from the arms race. The fact remains that these agreements relate only to measures of limited restraint while the arms race continues. These partial measures have done little to bring the world closer to the goal of general and complete disarmament. For more than a decade there have been no negotiations leading to a treaty on general and complete disarmament. The pressing need now is to translate into practical terms the provisions of this Final Document and to proceed along the road of binding and effective international agreements in the field of disarmament.

18. Removing the threat of a world war—a nuclear war—is the most acute and urgent task of the present day. Mankind is confronted with a choice: we must halt the arms race and proceed to disarmament or face annihilation.

19. The ultimate objective of the efforts of states in the disarmament process is general and complete disarmament under effective international control. The principal goals of disarmament are to ensure the survival of mankind and to eliminate the danger of war, in particular nuclear war, to ensure that war is no longer an instrument for settling international disputes and that the use and the threat of force are eliminated from international life, as provided for in the Charter of the United Nations. Progress towards this objective requires the conclusion and implementation of agreements on the cessation of the arms race and on genuine measures of disarmament, taking into account the need of states to protect their security.

20. Among such measures, effective measures of nuclear disarmament and the prevention of nuclear war have the highest priority. To this end, it is imperative to remove the threat of nuclear weapons, to halt and reverse the nuclear arms race until the total elimination of nuclear weapons and their delivery systems has been achieved, and to prevent the proliferation of nuclear weapons. At the same time, other measures designed to prevent the outbreak of nuclear war and to lessen the danger of the threat or use of nuclear weapons should be taken.

21. Along with these measures, agreements or other effective measures should be adopted to prohibit or prevent the development, production or use of other weapons of mass destruction. In this context, an agreement on elimination of all chemical weapons should be concluded as a matter of high priority.

22. Together with negotiations on nuclear disarmament measures, negotiations should be carried out on the balanced reduction of armed forces and of conventional armaments, based on the principle of undiminished security of the parties with a view to promoting or enhancing stability at a lower military level, taking into account the need of all states to protect their security. These negotiations should be conducted with particular emphasis on armed forces and conventional weapons of nuclear-weapon states and other militarily significant countries. There should also be negotiations on the limitation of international transfer of conventional weapons, based in particular on the same principle, and taking into account the inalienable right to self-determination and independence of peoples under colonial or foreign domination and the obligations of states to respect that right, in accordance with the Charter of the United Nations and the Declaration on Principles of International Law concerning Friendly Relations and Co-operation among states, as well as the need of recipient states to protect their security.

23. Further international action should be taken to prohibit or restrict for

humanitarian reasons the use of specific conventional weapons, including those which may be excessively injurious, cause unnecessary suffering or have indiscriminate effects.

24. Collateral measures in both the nuclear and conventional fields, together with other measures specifically designed to build confidence, should be undertaken in order to contribute to the creation of favourable conditions for the adoption of additional disarmament measures and to further the relaxation of international tension.

25. Negotiations and measures in the field of disarmament shall be guided by the fundamental principles set forth below.

26. All States Members of the United Nations reaffirm their full commitment to the purposes of the Charter of the United Nations and their obligation strictly to observe its principles as well as other relevant and generally accepted principles of international law relating to the maintenance of international peace and security. They stress the special importance of refraining from the threat or use of force against the sovereignty, territorial integrity or political independence of any state, or against peoples under colonial or foreign domination seeking to exercise their right to self-determination and to achieve independence; non-intervention and non-interference in the internal affairs of other states; the inviolability of international frontiers; and the peaceful settlement of disputes, having regard to the inherent right of states to individual and collective self-defence in accordance with the Charter.

27. In accordance with the Charter, the United Nations has a central role and primary responsibility in the sphere of disarmament. In order effectively to discharge this role and facilitate and encourage all measures in this field, the United Nations should be kept appropriately informed of all steps in this field, whether unilateral, bilateral, regional or multilateral, without prejudice to the progress of negotiations.

28. All the peoples of the world have a vital interest in the success of disarmament negotiations. Consequently, all states have the duty to contribute to efforts in the field of disarmament. All states have the right to participate in disarmament negotiations. They have the right to participate on an equal footing in those multilateral disarmament negotiations which have a direct bearing on their national security. While disarmament is the responsibility of all states, the nuclear-weapon states have the primary responsibility for nuclear disarmament and, together with other militarily significant states, for halting and reversing the arms race. It is therefore important to secure their active participation.

29. The adoption of disarmament measures should take place in such an equitable and balanced manner as to ensure the right of each state to security and to ensure that no individual state or group of states may obtain advantages over others at any stage. At each stage the objective should be undiminished security at the lowest possible level of armaments and military forces.

30. An acceptable balance of mutual responsibilities and obligations for nuclear and non-nuclear-weapon states should be strictly observed.

31. Disarmament and arms limitation agreements should provide for adequate measures of verification satisfactory to all parties concerned in order to create the necessary confidence and ensure that they are being observed by all parties. The form and modalities of the verification to be provided for in any

specific agreement depend upon and should be determined by the purposes, scope and nature of the agreement. Agreements should provide for the participation of parties directly or through the United Nations system in the verification process. Where appropriate, a combination of several methods of verification as well as other compliance procedures should be employed.

32. All states, in particular nuclear-weapon states, should consider various proposals designed to secure the avoidance of the use of nuclear weapons, and the prevention of nuclear war. In this context, while noting the declarations made by nuclear-weapon states, effective arrangements, as appropriate, to assure non-nuclear-weapon states against the use or the threat of use of nuclear weapons could strengthen the security of those states and international peace and security.

33. The establishment of nuclear-weapon-free zones on the basis of agreements or arrangements freely arrived at among the states of the zone concerned, and the full compliance with those agreements or arrangements, thus ensuring that the zones are genuinely free from nuclear weapons, and respect for such zones by nuclear-weapon states, constitute an important disarmament measure.

34. Disarmament, relaxation of international tension, respect for the right to self-determination and national independence, the peaceful settlement of disputes in accordance with the Charter of the United Nations and the strengthening of international peace and security are directly related to each other. Progress in any of these spheres has a beneficial effect on all of them; in turn, failure in one sphere has negative effects on others.

35. There is also a close relationship between disarmament and development. Progress in the former would help greatly in the realization of the latter. Therefore resources released as a result of the implementation of disarmament measures should be devoted to the economic and social development of all nations and contribute to the bridging of the economic gap between developed and developing countries.

36. Non-proliferation of nuclear weapons is a matter of universal concern. Measures of disarmament must be consistent with the inalienable right of all states, without discrimination, to develop, acquire and use nuclear technology, equipment and materials for the peaceful use of nuclear energy and to determine their peaceful nuclear programmes in accordance with their national priorities, needs and interests, bearing in mind the need to prevent the proliferation of nuclear weapons. International co-operation in the peaceful uses of nuclear energy should be conducted under agreed and appropriate international safeguards applied on a non-discriminatory basis.

37. Significant progress in disarmament, including nuclear disarmament, would be facilitated by parallel measures to strengthen the security of states and to improve the international situation in general.

38. Negotiations on partial measures of disarmament should be conducted concurrently with negotiations on more comprehensive measures and should be followed by negotiations leading to a treaty on general and complete disarmament under effective international control.

39. Qualitative and quantitative disarmament measures are both important for halting the arms race. Efforts to that end must include negotiations on the limitation and cessation of the qualitative improvement of armaments, especially weapons of mass destruction and the development of new means of warfare so

that ultimately scientific and technological achievements may be used solely for peaceful purposes.

40. Universality of disarmament agreements helps create confidence among states. When multilateral agreements in the field of disarmament are negotiated, every effort should be made to ensure that they are universally acceptable. The full compliance of all parties with the provisions contained in such agreements would also contribute to the attainment of that goal.

41. In order to create favourable conditions for success in the disarmament process, all states should strictly abide by the provisions of the Charter of the United Nations, refrain from actions which might adversely affect efforts in the fields of disarmament, and display a constructive approach to negotiations and the political will to reach agreements. There are certain negotiations on disarmament under way at different levels, the early and successful completion of which could contribute to limiting the arms race. Unilateral measures of arms limitation or reduction could also contribute to the attainment of that goal.

42. Since prompt measures should be taken in order to halt and reverse the arms race, Member States hereby declare that they will respect the objectives and principles stated above and make every effort faithfully to carry out the programme of action set forth in Section III below.

III. Programme of Action

43. Progress towards the goal of general and complete disarmament can be achieved through the implementation of a programme of action on disarmament, in accordance with the goals and principles established in the declaration on disarmament. The present programme of action contains priorities and measures in the field of disarmament that states should undertake as a matter of urgency with a view to halting and reversing the arms race and to giving the necessary impetus to efforts designed to achieve genuine disarmament leading to general and complete disarmament under effective international control.

44. The present programme of action enumerates the specific measures of disarmament which should be implemented over the next few years, as well as other measures and studies to prepare the way for future negotiations and for progress towards general and complete disarmament.

45. Priorities in disarmament negotiations shall be: nuclear weapons; other weapons of mass destruction, including chemical weapons; conventional weapons, including any which may be deemed to be excessively injurious or to have indiscriminate effects; and reduction of armed forces.

46. Nothing should preclude states from conducting negotiations on all priority items concurrently.

47. Nuclear weapons pose the greatest danger to mankind and to the survival of civilization. It is essential to halt and reverse the nuclear arms race in all its aspects in order to avert the danger of war involving nuclear weapons. The ultimate goal in this context is the complete elimination of nuclear weapons.

48. In the task of achieving the goals of nuclear disarmament, all the nuclear-weapon states, in particular those among them which possess the most important nuclear arsenals, bear a special responsibility.

49. The process of nuclear disarmament should be carried out in such a way, and requires measures to ensure, that the security of all states is guaranteed at progressively lower levels of nuclear armaments, taking into account the relative qualitative and quantitative importance of the existing arsenals of the nuclear-weapon states and other states concerned.

50. The achievement of nuclear disarmament will require urgent negotiation of agreements at appropriate stages and with adequate measures of verification satisfactory to the states concerned for: (a) cessation of the qualitative improvement and development of nuclear-weapon systems; (b) cessation of the production of all types of nuclear weapons and their means of delivery, and of the production of fissionable material for weapons purposes; (c) a comprehensive, phased programme with agreed time-frames, whenever feasible, for progressive and balanced reduction of stockpiles of nuclear weapons and their means of delivery, leading to their ultimate and complete elimination at the earliest possible time. Consideration can be given in the course of the negotiations to mutual and agreed limitation or prohibition, without prejudice to the security of any state, of any types of nuclear armaments.

51. The cessation of nuclear-weapon testing by all states within the framework of an effective nuclear disarmament process would be in the interest of mankind. It would make a significant contribution to the above aim of ending the qualitative improvement of nuclear weapons and the development of new types of such weapons and of preventing the proliferation of nuclear weapons. In this context the negotiations now in progress on 'a treaty prohibiting nuclear-weapon tests, and a protocol covering nuclear explosions for peaceful purposes, which would be an integral part of the treaty', should be concluded urgently and the result submitted for full consideration by the multilateral negotiating body with a view to the submission of a draft treaty to the General Assembly at the earliest possible date. All efforts should be made by the negotiating parties to achieve an agreement which, following endorsement by the General Assembly, could attract the widest possible adherence. In this context, various views were expressed by non-nuclear-weapon states that, pending the conclusion of this treaty, the world community would be encouraged if all the nuclear-weapon states refrained from testing nuclear weapons. In this connection, some nuclear-weapon states expressed different views.

52. The Union of Soviet Socialist Republics and the United States of America should conclude at the earliest possible date the agreement they have been pursuing for several years in the second series of the strategic arms limitation talks. They are invited to transmit in good time the text of the agreement to the General Assembly. It should be followed promptly by further strategic arms limitation negotiations between the two parties, leading to agreed significant reductions of, and qualitative limitations on, strategic arms. It should constitute an important step in the direction of nuclear disarmament and, ultimately, of establishment of a world free of such weapons.

53. The process of nuclear disarmament described in the paragraph on this subject should be expedited by the urgent and vigorous pursuit to a successful/ conclusion of ongoing negotiations and the urgent initiation of further negotiations among the nuclear-weapon states.

54. Significant progress in nuclear disarmament would be facilitated both by parallel political or international legal measures to strengthen the security of states and by progress in the limitation and reduction of armed forces and conventional armaments of the nuclear-weapon states and other states in the regions concerned.

55. Real progress in the field of nuclear disarmament could create an atmosphere conducive to progress in conventional disarmament on a worldwide basis.

56. The most effective guarantee against the danger of nuclear war and the use of nuclear weapons is nuclear disarmament and the complete elimination of nuclear weapons.

57. Pending the achievement of this goal, for which negotiations should be vigorously pursued, and bearing in mind the devastating results which nuclear war would have on belligerents and non-belligerents alike, the nuclear-weapon states have special responsibilities to undertake measures aimed at preventing the outbreak of nuclear war, and of the use of force in international relations, subject to the provisions of the Charter of the United Nations, including the use of nuclear weapons.

58. In this context all states, in particular nuclear-weapon states, should consider as soon as possible various proposals designed to secure the avoidance of the use of nuclear weapons, the prevention of nuclear war and related objectives, where possible through international agreement, and thereby ensure that the survival of mankind in not endangered. All states should actively participate in efforts to bring about conditions in international relations among states in which a code of peaceful conduct of nations in international affairs could be agreed and which would preclude the use or threat of use of nuclear weapons.

59. In the same context, the nuclear-weapon states are called upon to take steps to assure the non-nuclear-weapon states against the use or threat of use of nuclear weapons. The General Assembly notes the declarations made by the nuclear-weapon states and urges them to pursue efforts to conclude, as appropriate, effective arrangements to assure non-nuclear-weapon states against the use or threat of use of nuclear weapons.

60. The establishment of nuclear-weapon-free zones on the basis of arrangements freely arrived at among the states of the region concerned constitutes an important disarmament measure.

61. The process of establishing such zones in different parts of the world should be encouraged with the ultimate objective of achieving a world entirely free of nuclear weapons. In the process of establishing such zones, the characteristics of each region should be taken into account. The states participating in such zones should undertake to comply fully with all the objectives, purposes and principles of the agreements or arrangements establishing the zones, thus ensuring that they are genuinely free from nuclear weapons.

62. With respect to such zones, the nuclear-weapon states in turn are called upon to give undertakings, the modalities of which are to be negotiated with the competent authority of each zone, in particular: (a) to respect strictly the status of the nuclear-weapon-free zone; (b) to refrain from the use or threat of use of nuclear weapons against the states of the zone.

63. In the light of existing conditions, and without prejudice to other measures which may be considered in other regions, the following measures are

especially desirable: (a) adoption by the states concerned of all relevant measures to ensure the full application of the Treaty for the Prohibition of Nuclear Weapons in Latin America (Treaty of Tlatelolco), taking into account the views expressed at the Tenth Special Session on the adherence to it; (b) signature and ratification of the Additional Protocols of the Treaty for the Prohibition of Nuclear Weapons in Latin America (Treaty of Tlatelolco) by the states entitled to become parties to those instruments which have not yet done so; (c) in Africa, where the Organization of African Unity has affirmed a decision for the denuclearization of the region, the Security Council of the United Nations shall take appropriate effective steps whenever necessary to prevent the frustration of this objective; (d) the serious consideration of the practical and urgent steps, as described in the paragraphs above, required for the implementation of the proposal to establish a nuclear-weapon-free zone in the Middle East, in accordance with the relevant General Assembly resolutions, where all parties directly concerned have expressed their support for the concept and where the danger of nuclear-weapon proliferation exists. The establishment of a nuclear-weapon-free zone in the Middle East would greatly enhance international peace and security. Pending the establishment of such a zone in the region, states of the region should solemnly declare that they will refrain on a reciprocal basis from producing, acquiring or in any other way possessing nuclear weapons and nuclear explosive devices, and from permitting the stationing of nuclear weapons on their territory by any third party, and agree to place all their nuclear activities under International Atomic Energy Agency safeguards. Consideration should be given to a Security Council role in advancing the establishment of a nuclear-weapon-free zone in the Middle East; (e) all states in the region of South Asia have expressed their determination to keep their countries free of nuclear weapons. No action should be taken by them which might deviate from that objective. In this context, the question of establishing a nuclear-weapon-free zone in South Asia has been dealt with in several resolutions of the General Assembly, which is keeping the subject under consideration.

64. The establishment of zones of peace in various regions of the world under appropriate conditions, to be clearly defined and determined freely by the states concerned in the zone, taking into account the characteristics of the zone and the principles of the Charter of the United Nations, and in conformity with international law, can contribute to strengthening the security of states within such zones and to international peace and security as a whole. In this regard, the General Assembly notes the proposals for the establishment of zones of peace, *inter alia*, in: (a) South-East Asia where states in the region have expressed interest in the establishment of such a zone, in conformity with their views; (b) the Indian Ocean, taking into account the deliberations of the General Assembly and its relevant resolutions and the need to ensure the maintenance of peace and security in the region.

65. It is imperative, as an integral part of the effort to halt and reverse the arms race, to prevent the proliferation of nuclear weapons. The goal of nuclear non-proliferation is on the one hand to prevent the emergence of any additional nuclear-weapon states besides the existing five nuclear-weapon states, and on the other progressively to reduce and eventually eliminate nuclear weapons altogether. This involves obligations and responsibilities on the part of both nuclear-

weapon states and non-nuclear-weapon states, the former undertaking to stop the nuclear arms race and to achieve nuclear disarmament by urgent application of the measures outlined in the relevant paragraphs of this Final Document, and all states undertaking to prevent the spread of nuclear weapons.

66. Effective measures can and should be taken at the national level and through international agreements to minimize the danger of the proliferation of nuclear weapons without jeopardizing energy supplies or the development of nuclear energy for peaceful purposes. Therefore, the nuclear-weapon states and the non-nuclear-weapon states should jointly take further steps to develop an international consensus of ways and means, on a universal and non-discriminatory basis, to prevent the proliferation of nuclear weapons.

67. Full implementation of all the provisions of existing instruments on non-proliferation, such as the Treaty on the Non-Proliferation of Nuclear Weapons and/or the Treaty for the Prohibition of Nuclear Weapons in Latin America (Treaty of Tlatelolco) by states parties to those instruments will be an important contribution to this end. Adherence to such instruments has increased in recent years and the hope has been expressed by the parties that this trend might continue.

68. Non-proliferation measures should not jeopardize the full exercise of the inalienable rights of all states to apply and develop their programmes for the peaceful uses of nuclear energy for economic and social development in conformity with their priorities, interests and needs. All states should also have access to and be free to acquire technology, equipment and materials for peaceful uses of nuclear energy, taking into account the particular needs of the developing countries. International co-operation in this field should be under agreed and appropriate international safeguards applied through the International Atomic Energy Agency on a non-discriminatory basis in order to prevent effectively the proliferation of nuclear weapons.

69. Each country's choices and decisions in the field of the peaceful uses of nuclear energy should be respected without jeopardizing their respective fuel cycle policies or international co-operation, agreements and contracts for the peaceful uses of nuclear energy, provided that the agreed safeguard measures mentioned above are applied.

70. In accordance with the principles and provisions of General Assembly resolution 32/50 of 8 December 1977, international co-operation for the promotion of the transfer and utilization of nuclear technology for economic and social development, especially in the developing countries, should be strengthened.

71. Efforts should be made to conclude the work of the International Nuclear Fuel Cycle Evaluation strictly in accordance with the objectives set out in the final communiqué of its Organizing Conference.

72. All states should adhere to the Protocol for the Prohibition of the Use in War of Asphyxiating, Poisonous or Other Gases, and of Bacteriological Methods of Warfare, signed at Geneva on 17 June 1925.

73. All states which have not yet done so should consider adhering to the Convention on the Prohibition of the Development, Production and Stockpiling of Bacteriological (Biological) and Toxin Weapons and on Their Destruction.

74. States should also consider the possibility of adhering to multilateral

agreements concluded so far in the disarmament field which are mentioned below in this section.

75. The complete and effective prohibition of the development, production and stockpiling of all chemical weapons and their destruction represents one of the most urgent measures of disarmament. Consequently, conclusion of a convention to this end, on which negotiations have been going on for several years, is one of the most urgent tasks of multilateral negotiations. After its conclusion, all states should contribute to ensuring the broadest possible application of the convention through its early signature and ratification.

76. A convention should be concluded prohibiting the development, production, stockpiling and use of radiological weapons.

77. In order to help prevent a qualitative arms race and so that scientific and technological achievements may ultimately be used solely for peaceful purposes, effective measures should be taken to avoid the danger and prevent the emergence of new types of weapons of mass destruction based on new scientific principles and achievements. Efforts should be appropriately pursued aiming at the prohibition of such new types and new systems of weapons of mass destruction. Specific agreements could be concluded on particular types of new weapons of mass destruction which may be identified. This question should be kept under continuing review.

78. The Committee on Disarmament should keep under review the need for a further prohibition of military or any other hostile use of environmental modification techniques in order to eliminate the dangers to mankind from such use..

79. In order to promote the peaceful use of and to avoid an arms race on the sea-bed and the ocean floor and the subsoil thereof, the Committee on Disarmament is requested—in consultation with the states parties to the Treaty on the Prohibition of the Emplacement of Nuclear Weapons and Other Weapons of Mass Destruction on the Sea-Bed and the Ocean Floor and in the Subsoil Thereof, and taking into account the proposals made during the 1977 Review Conference of the parties to that treaty and any relevant technological developments—to proceed promptly with the consideration of further measures in the field of disarmament for the prevention of an arms race in that environment.

80. In order to prevent an arms race in outer space, further measures should be taken and appropriate international negotiations held in accordance with the spirit of the Treaty on Principles Governing the Activities of States in the Exploration and Use of Outer Space, including the Moon and Other Celestial Bodies.

81. Together with negotiations on nuclear disarmament measures, the limitation and gradual reduction of armed forces and conventional weapons should be resolutely pursued within the framework of progress towards general and complete disarmament. States with the largest military arsenals have a special responsibility in pursuing the process of conventional armaments reductions.

82. In particular the achievement of a more stable situation in Europe at a lower level of military potential on the basis of approximate equality and parity, as well as on the basis of undiminished security of all states with full respect for security interests and independence of states outside military alliances, by agreement on appropriate mutual reductions and limitations would contribute to

the strengthening of security in Europe and constitute a significant step towards enhancing international peace and security. Current efforts to this end should be continued most energetically.

83. Agreements or other measures should be resolutely pursued on a bilateral, regional and multilateral basis with the aim of strengthening peace and security at a lower level of forces, by the limitation and reduction of armed forces and of conventional weapons, taking into account the need of states to protect their security, bearing in mind the inherent right of self-defence embodied in the Charter of the United Nations and without prejudice to the principle of equal rights and self-determination of peoples in accordance with the Charter, and the need to ensure balance at each stage and undiminished security of all states. Such measures might include those in the following two paragraphs.

84. Bilateral, regional and multilateral consultations and conferences should be held where appropriate conditions exist with the participation of all the countries concerned for the consideration of different aspects of conventional disarmament, such as the initiative envisaged in the Declaration of Ayacucho subscribed to by eight Latin American countries on 9 December 1974.

85. Consultations should be carried out among major arms suppliers and recipient countries on the limitation of all types of international transfer of conventional weapons, based in particular on the principle of undiminished security of the parties with a view to promoting or enhancing stability at a lower military level, taking into account the need of all states to protect their security as well as the inalienable right to self-determination and independence of peoples under colonial or foreign domination and the obligations of states to respect that right, in accordance with the Charter of the United Nations and the Declaration on Principles of International Law concerning Friendly Relations and Co-operation among States.

86. The United Nations Conference on Prohibitions or Restrictions of Use of Certain Conventional Weapons Which May Be Deemed to Be Excessively Injurious or to Have Indiscriminate Effects, to be held in 1979, should seek agreement, in the light of humanitarian and military considerations, on the prohibition or restriction of use of certain conventional weapons including those which may cause unnecessary suffering or have indiscriminate effects. The conference should consider specific categories of such weapons, including those which were the subject-matter of previously conducted discussions.

87. All states are called upon to contribute towards carrying out this task.

88. The result of the conference should be considered by all states, and especially producer states, in regard to the question of the transfer of such weapons to other states.

89. Gradual reduction of military budgets on a mutually agreed basis, for example, in absolute figures or in terms of percentage points, particularly by nuclear-weapon states and other militarily significant states, would be a measure that would contribute to the curbing of the arms race and would increase the possibilities of reallocation of resources now being used for military purposes to economic and social development, particularly for the benefit of the developing countries. The basis for implementing this measure will have to be agreed by all participating states and will require ways and means of its implementation acceptable to all of them, taking account of the problems involved in assessing the

relative significance of reductions as among different states and with due regard to the proposals of states on all the aspects of reduction of military budgets.*

90. The General Assembly should continue to consider what concrete steps should be taken to facilitate the reduction of military budgets, bearing in mind the relevant proposals and documents of the United Nations on this question.

91. In order to facilitate the conclusion and effective implementation of disarmament agreements and to create confidence, states should accept appropriate provisions for verification in such agreements.

92. In the context of international disarmament negotiations, the problem of verification should be further examined and adequate methods and procedures in this field be considered. Every effort should be made to develop appropriate methods and procedures which are non-discriminatory and which do not unduly interfere with the internal affairs of other states or jeopardize their economic and social development.

93. In order to facilitate the process of disarmament, it is necessary to take measures and pursue policies to strengthen international peace and security and to build confidence among states. Commitment to confidence-building measures could significantly contribute to preparing for further progress in disarmament. For this purpose, measures such as the following, and other measures yet to be agreed upon, should be undertaken: (a) the prevention of attacks which take place by accident, miscalculation or communications failure by taking steps to improve communications between governments, particularly in areas of tension, by the establishment of 'hot lines' and other methods of reducing the risk of conflict; (b) states should assess the possible implications of their military research and development for existing agreements as well as for further efforts in the field of disarmament; (c) the Secretary-General shall periodically submit reports to the General Assembly on the economic and social consequences of the armaments race and its extremely harmful effects on world peace and security.

94. In view of the relationship between expenditure on armaments and economic and social development and the necessity to release real resources now being used for military purposes to economic and social development in the world, particularly for the benefit of the developing countries, the Secretary-General should, with the assistance of a group of qualified governmental experts appointed by him, initiate an expert study on the relationship between disarmament and development. The Secretary-General should submit an interim report on the subject to the General Assembly at its thirty-fourth session and submit the final results to the Assembly at its thirty-sixth session for subsequent action.

95. The expert study should have the terms of reference contained in the report of the Ad Hoc Group on the Relationship between Disarmament and Development appointed by the Secretary-General in accordance with General Assembly resolution 32/88 A of 12 December 1977. It should investigate the three main areas listed in the report, bearing in mind the United Nations studies previously carried out. The study should be made in the context of how disarmament can contribute to the establishment of the new international economic order. The study should be forward-looking and policy-oriented and

---

* For United Nations action on the standardization of military budgets, see Appendix II—Ed.

place special emphasis on both the desirability of a reallocation, following disarmament measures, of resources now being used for military purposes to economic and social development, particularly for the benefit of the developing countries and the substantive feasibility of such a reallocation. A principal aim should be to produce results that could effectively guide the formulation of practical measures to reallocate those resources at the local, national, regional and international levels.

96. Taking further steps in the field of disarmament and other measures aimed at promoting international peace and security would be facilitated by carrying out studies by the Secretary-General in this field with appropriate assistance from governmental or consultant experts.

97. The Secretary-General shall, with the assistance of consultant experts appointed by him, continue the study of the interrelationship between disarmament and international security requested in Assembly resolution 32/87 C of 12 December 1977 and submit it to the thirty-fourth session of the General Assembly.

98. At its thirty-third and subsequent sessions the General Assembly should determine the specific guidelines for carrying out studies taking into account the proposals already submitted including those made by individual countries at the Special Session, as well as other proposals which can be introduced later in this field. In doing so, the Assembly would take into consideration a report on these matters prepared by the Secretary-General.

99. In order to mobilize world public opinion on behalf of disarmament, the specific measures set forth below, designed to increase the dissemination of information about the armaments race and the efforts to halt and reverse it, should be adopted.

100. Governmental and non-governmental information organs and those of the United Nations and its Specialized Agencies should give priority to the preparation and distribution of printed and audio-visual material relating to the danger represented by the armaments race as well as to the disarmament efforts and negotiations on specific disarmament measures.

101. In particular, publicity should be given to the Final Document of the Tenth Special Session.

102. The General Assembly proclaims the week starting 24 October, the day of the foundation of the United Nations, as a week devoted to fostering the objectives of disarmament.

103. To encourage study and research on disarmament, the United Nations Centre for Disarmament should intensify its activities in the presentation of information concerning the armaments race and disarmament. Also, the United Nations Educational, Scientific and Cultural Organization is urged to intensify its activities aimed at facilitating research and publications on disarmament, related to its fields of competence, especially in developing countries, and should disseminate the results of such research.

104. Throughout this process of disseminating information about developments in the disarmament field of all countries, there should be increased participation by non-governmental organizations concerned with the matter, through closer liaison between them and the United Nations.

105. Member States should be encouraged to ensure a better flow of information with regard to the various aspects of disarmament to avoid

dissemination of false and tendentious information concerning armaments, and to concentrate on the danger of escalation of the armaments race and on the need for general and complete disarmament under effective international control.

106. With a view to contributing to a greater understanding and awareness of the problems created by the armaments race and of the need for disarmament, governments and governmental and non-governmental international organizations are urged to take steps to develop programmes of education for disarmament and peace studies at all levels.

107. The General Assembly welcomes the initiative of the United Nations Educational, Scientific and Cultural Organization in planning to hold a World Congress on Disarmament Education and, in this connection, urges that Organization to step up its programme aimed at the development of disarmament education as a distinct field of study through the preparation, *inter alia,* of teachers' guides, textbooks, readers and audio-visual materials. Member States should take all possible measures to encourage the incorporation of such materials in the curricula of their educational institutes.

108. In order to promote expertise in disarmament in more Member States, particularly in the developing countries, the General Assembly decides to establish a programme of fellowships on disarmament. The Secretary-General, taking into account the proposal submitted to the Special Session, should prepare guidelines for the programme. He should also submit the financial requirements of twenty fellowships to the General Assembly at its thirty-third session for inclusion in the regular budget of the United Nations, bearing in mind the savings that can be made within the existing budgetary appropriations.

109. Implementation of these priorities should lead to general and complete disarmament under effective international control, which remains the ultimate goal of all efforts exerted in the field of disarmament. Negotiations on general and complete disarmament shall be conducted concurrently with negotiations on partial measures of disarmament. With this purpose in mind, the Committee on Disarmament will undertake the elaboration of a comprehensive programme of disarmament encompassing all measures thought to be advisable in order to ensure that the goal of general and complete disarmament under effective international control becomes a reality in a world in which international peace and security prevail and in which the new international economic order is strengthened and consolidated. The comprehensive programme should contain appropriate procedures for ensuring that the General Assembly is kept fully informed of the progress of the negotiations including an appraisal of the situation when appropriate and, in particular, a continuing review of the implementation of the programme.

110. Progress in disarmament should be accompanied by measures to strengthen institutions for maintaining peace and the settlement of international disputes by peaceful means. During and after the implementation of the programme of general and complete disarmament, there should be taken, in accordance with the principles of the Charter of the United Nations, the necessary measures to maintain international peace and security, including the obligation of states to place at the disposal of the United Nations agreed manpower necessary for an international peace force to be equipped with agreed types of armaments. Arrangements for the use of this force should ensure that the United Nations can

effectively deter or suppress any threat or use of arms in violation of the purposes and principles of the United Nations.

111. General and complete disarmament under strict and effective international control shall permit states to have at their disposal only those non-nuclear forces, armaments, facilities and establishments as are agreed to be necessary to maintain internal order and protect the personal security of citizens and in order that states shall support and provide agreed manpower for a United Nations peace force.

112. In addition to the several questions dealt with in this programme of action, there are a few others of fundamental importance, on which, because of the complexity of the issues involved and the short time at the disposal of the Special Session, it has proved impossible to reach satisfactory agreed conclusions. For those reasons they are treated only in very general terms and, in a few instances, not even treated at all in the programme. It should be stressed, however, that a number of concrete approaches to deal with such questions emerged from the exchange of views carried out in the General Assembly which will undoubtedly facilitate the continuation of the study and negotiation of the problems involved in the competent disarmament organs.

IV. Machinery

113. While disarmament, particularly in the nuclear field, has become a necessity for the survival of mankind and for the elimination of the danger of nuclear war, little progress has been made since the end of the Second World War. In addition to the need to exercise political will, the international machinery should be utilized more effectively and also improved to enable implementation of the programme of action and help the United Nations to fulfil its role in the field of disarmament. In spite of the best efforts of the international community, adequate results have not been produced with the existing machinery. There is, therefore, an urgent need that existing disarmament machinery be revitalized and forums appropriately constituted for disarmament deliberations and negotiations with a better representative character. For maximum effectiveness, two kinds of bodies are required in the field of disarmament—deliberative and negotiating. All Member States should be represented on the former, whereas the latter, for the sake of convenience, should have a relatively small membership.

114. The United Nations, in accordance with the Charter, has a central role and primary responsibility in the sphere of disarmament. Accordingly, it should play a more active role in this field and, in order to discharge its functions effectively, the United Nations should facilitate and encourage all disarmament measures—unilateral, bilateral, regional or multilateral—and be kept duly informed through the General Assembly, or any other appropriate United Nations channel reaching all members of the Organization, of all disarmament efforts outside its aegis without prejudice to the progress of negotiations.

115. The General Assembly has been and should remain the main deliberative organ of the United Nations in the field of disarmament and should make every effort to facilitate the implementation of disarmament measures. An item entitled 'Review of the implementation of the recommendations and decisions

adopted by the General Assembly at its Tenth Special Session' shall be included in the provisional agenda of the thirty-third and subsequent sessions of the General Assembly.

116. Draft multilateral disarmament conventions should be subjected to the normal procedures applicable in the law of treaties. Those submitted to the General Assembly for its commendation should be subject to full review by the Assembly.

117. The First Committee of the General Assembly should deal in the future only with questions of disarmament and related international security questions.

118. The General Assembly establishes, as successor to the commission originally established by resolution 502 (VI) of 11 January 1952, a Disarmament Commission, composed of all States Members of the United Nations, and decides that: (a) the Disarmament Commission shall be a deliberative body, a subsidiary organ of the General Assembly, the function of which shall be to consider and make recommendations on various problems in the field of disarmament and to follow up the relevant decisions and recommendations of the Special Session Devoted to Disarmament. The Disarmament Commission should, *inter alia,* consider the elements of a comprehensive programme for disarmament to be submitted as recommendations to the General Assembly and, through it, to the negotiating body, the Committee on Disarmament; (b) the Disarmament Commission shall function under the rules of procedure relating to the committees of the General Assembly with such modifications as the commission may deem necessary and shall make every effort to ensure that, in so far as possible, decisions on substantive issues be adopted by consensus; (c) the Disarmament Commission shall report annually to the General Assembly and will submit for consideration by the Assembly at its thirty-third session a report on organizational matters; in 1979, the Disarmament Commission will meet for a period not exceeding four weeks, the dates to be decided at the thirty-third session of the Assembly; (d) the Secretary-General shall furnish such experts, staff and services as are necessary for the effective accomplishment of the commission's functions.

119. A second Special Session of the General Assembly Devoted to Disarmament should be held on a date to be decided by the Assembly at its thirty-third session.

120. The General Assembly is conscious of the work that has been done by the international negotiating body that has been meeting since 14 March 1962 as well as the considerable and urgent work that remains to be accomplished in the field of disarmament. The Assembly is deeply aware of the continuing requirement for a single multilateral disarmament negotiating forum of limited size taking decisions on the basis of consensus. It attaches great importance to the participation of all the nuclear-weapon states in an appropriately constituted negotiating body, the Committee on Disarmament. The Assembly welcomes the agreement reached following appropriate consultations among the Member States during the Special Session of the General Assembly Devoted to Disarmament that the Committee on Disarmament will be open to the nuclear-weapon states, and thirty-two to thirty-five other states to be chosen in consultation with the President of the thirty-second session of the Assembly; that the membership of the Committee on Disarmament will be reviewed at regular intervals; that the Committee on Disarmament will be convened in Geneva not later than January

1979 by the country whose name appears first in the alphabetical list of membership; and that the Committee on Disarmament will: (a) conduct its work by consensus; (b) adopt its own rules of procedure; (c) request the Secretary-General of the United Nations, following consultations with the Committee on Disarmament, to appoint the Secretary of the committee, who shall also act as his personal representative, to assist the committee and its Chairman in organizing the business and timetables of the committee; (d) rotate the chairmanship of the committee among all its members on a monthly basis; (e) adopt its own agenda taking into account the recommendations made to it by the General Assembly and the proposals presented by the members of the committee; (f) submit a report to the General Assembly annually, or more frequently as appropriate, and provide its formal and other relevant documents to the States Members of the United Nations on a regular basis; (g) make arrangements for interested states, not members of the committee, to submit to the committee written proposals or working documents on measures of disarmament that are the subject of negotiation in the committee and to participate in the discussion of the subject-matter of such proposals or working documents; (h) invite states not members of the committee, upon their request, to express views in the committee when the particular concerns of those states are under discussion; (i) open its plenary meetings to the public unless otherwise decided.

121. Bilateral and regional disarmament negotiations may also play an important role and could facilitate negotiations of multilateral agreements in the field of disarmament.

122. At the earliest appropriate time, a World Disarmament Conference should be convened with universal participation and with adequate preparation.

123. In order to enable the United Nations to continue to fulfil its role in the field of disarmament and to carry out the additional tasks assigned to it by this Special Session, the United Nations Centre for Disarmament should be adequately strengthened and its research and information functions accordingly extended. The centre should also take account fully of the possibilities offered by specialized agencies and other institutions and programmes within the United Nations system with regard to studies and information on disarmament. The centre should also increase contacts with non-governmental organizations and research institutions in view of the valuable role they play in the field of disarmament. This role could be encouraged also in other ways that may be considered as appropriate.

124. The Secretary-General is requested to set up an advisory board of eminent persons, selected on the basis of their personal expertise and taking into account the principle of equitable geographical representation, to advise him on various aspects of studies to be made under the auspices of the United Nations in the field of disarmament and arms limitation, including a programme of such studies.

125. The General Assembly notes with satisfaction that the active participation of the Member States in the consideration of the agenda items of the special session and the proposals and suggestions submitted by them and reflected to a considerable extent in the Final Document have made a valuable contribution to the work of the special session and to its positive conclusion. Since a number of those proposals and suggestions which have become an integral part of the work

of the special session of the General Assembly, deserve to be studied further and more thoroughly, taking into consideration the many relevant comments and observations made in both the general debate in plenary meeting and the deliberations of the Ad Hoc Committee of the Tenth Special Session, the Secretary-General is requested to transmit, together with this Final Document, to the appropriate deliberative and negotiating organs dealing with the questions of disarmament all the official records of the Special Session Devoted to Disarmament, in accordance with the recommendations which the Assembly may adopt at its thirty-third session. Some of the proposals put forth for the consideration of the special session are listed below:

(a) Text of the decision of the Central Committee of the Romanian Communist Party concerning Romania's position on disarmament and, in particular, on nuclear disarmament, adopted on 9 May 1978;

(b) Views of the Swiss Government on problems to be discussed at the tenth special session of the General Assembly;

(c) Proposals of the Union of Soviet Socialist Republics on practical measures for ending the arms race;

(d) Memorandum from France concerning the establishment of an International Satellite Monitoring Agency;

(e) Memorandum from France concerning the establishment of an International Institute for Research on Disarmament;

(f) Proposal by Sri Lanka for the establishment of a World Disarmament Authority;

(g) Working paper submitted by the Federal Republic of Germany entitled 'Contribution to the seismological verification of a comprehensive test ban';

(h) Working paper submitted by the Federal Republic of Germany entitled 'Invitation to Attend an International Chemical-weapon Verification Workshop in the Federal Republic of Germany';

(i) Working paper submitted by China on disarmament;

(j) Working paper submitted by the Federal Republic of Germany concerning zones of confidence-building measures as a first step towards the preparation of a worldwide convention on confidence-building measures;

(k) Proposal by Ireland for a study of the possibility of establishing a system of incentives to promote arms control and disarmament;

(l) Working paper submitted by Romania concerning a synthesis of the proposals in the field of disarmament;

(m) Proposal by the United States of America on the establishment of a United Nations Peace-keeping Reserve and on confidence-building measures and stabilizing measures in various regions, including notification of manoeuvres, invitation of observers to manoeuvres, and United Nations machinery to study and promote such measures;

(n) Proposal by Uruguay on the possibility of establishing a polemological agency;

(o) Proposal by Belgium, Canada, Denmark, Germany, Federal Republic of, Ireland, Italy, Japan, Luxembourg, the Netherlands, New Zealand, Norway, Sweden, the United Kingdom of Great Britain and Northern Ireland and the United States of America on the strengthening of the security role of the United Nations in the peaceful settlement of disputes and peace-keeping;

(p) Memorandum from France concerning the establishment of an International Disarmament Fund for Development;

(q) Proposal by Norway entitled 'Evaluation of the Impact of New Weapons on Arms Control and Disarmament Efforts';

(r) *Note verbale* transmitting the text, signed in Washington on 22 June 1978 by the Ministers for Foreign Affairs of Argentina, Bolivia, Chile, Colombia, Ecuador, Panama, Peru and Venezuela, reaffirming the principles of the Declaration of Ayacucho with respect to the limitation of conventional weapons;

(s) Memorandum from Liberia entitled 'Declaration of a New Philosophy on Disarmament';

(t) Statements made by the representatives of China, on 22 June 1978, on the draft Final Document of the Tenth Special Session;

(u) Proposal by the President of Cyprus for the total demilitarization and disarmament of the Republic of Cyprus and the implementation of the resolutions of the United Nations;

(v) Proposal by Costa Rica on economic and social incentives to halt the arms race;

(w) Amendments submitted by China to the draft Final Document of the Tenth Special Session;

(x) Proposals by Canada for the implementation of a strategy of suffocation of the nuclear arms race;

(y) Draft resolution submitted by Cyprus, Ethiopia and India on the urgent need for cessation of further testing of nuclear weapons;

(z) Draft resolution submitted by Ethiopia and India on the non-use of nuclear weapons and prevention of nuclear war;

(aa) Proposal by the non-aligned countries on the establishment of a zone of peace in the Mediterranean;

(bb) Proposal by the Government of Senegal for a tax on military budgets;

(cc) Proposal by Austria for the transmission to Member States of working paper A/AC.187/109 and the ascertainment of their views on the subject of verification;

(dd) Proposal by the non-aligned countries for the dismantling of foreign military bases in foreign territories and withdrawal of foreign troops from foreign territories;

(ee) Proposal by Mexico for the opening, on a provisional basis, of an ad hoc account in the United Nations Development Programme to use for development the funds which may be released as a result of disarmament measures;

(ff) Proposal by Italy on the role of the Security Council in the field of disarmament in accordance with Article 26 of the Charter of the United Nations;

(gg) Proposal by the Netherlands for a study on the establishment of an international disarmament organization.

26. In adopting this Final Document, the States Members of the United Nations solemnly reaffirm their determination to work for general and complete disarmament and to make further collective efforts aimed at strengthening peace and international security; eliminating the threat of war, particularly nuclear war; implementing practical measures aimed at halting and reversing the arms race; strengthening the procedures for the peaceful settlement of disputes; and reducing military expenditures and utilizing the resources thus released in a manner which

will help to promote the well-being of all peoples and to improve the economic conditions of the developing countries.

127. The General Assembly expresses its satisfaction that the proposals submitted to its Special Session devoted to disarmament and the deliberations thereon have made it possible to reaffirm and define in this Final Document fundamental principles, goals, priorities and procedures for the implementation of the above purposes, either in the declaration or the programme of action or in both. The Assembly also welcomes the important decisions agreed upon regarding the deliberative and negotiating machinery and is confident that these organs will discharge their functions in an effective manner.

128. Finally, it should be borne in mind that the number of states that participated in the general debate, as well as the high level of representation and the depth and scope of that debate, are unprecedented in the history of disarmament efforts. Several heads of state or government addressed the General Assembly. In addition, other heads of state or government sent messages and expressed their good wishes for the success of the Special Session of the Assembly. Several high officials of Specialized Agencies and other institutions and programmes within the United Nations system and spokesmen of twenty-five non-governmental organizations and six research institutes also made valuable contributions to the proceedings of the session. It must be emphasized, moreover, that the Special Session marks not the end but rather the beginning of a new phase of the efforts of the United Nations in the field of disarmament.

129. The General Assembly is convinced that the discussions of the disarmament problems at the Special Session and its Final Document will attract the attention of all peoples, further mobilize world public opinion and provide a powerful impetus for the cause of disarmament.

Twenty-seventh plenary meeting
30 June 1978

The President of the General Assembly subsequently informed the Secretary-General that the Committee on Disarmament, referred to in paragraph 120 of the above resolution, would be open to the nuclear-weapon states and to the following thirty-five states: ALGERIA, ARGENTINA, AUSTRALIA, BELGIUM, BRAZIL, BULGARIA, BURMA, CANADA, CUBA, CZECHOSLOVAKIA, EGYPT, ETHIOPIA, GERMAN DEMOCRATIC REPUBLIC, GERMANY, FEDERAL REPUBLIC OF, HUNGARY, INDIA, INDONESIA, IRAN, ITALY, JAPAN, KENYA, MEXICO, MONGOLIA, MOROCCO, NETHERLANDS, NIGERIA, PAKISTAN, PERU, POLAND, ROMANIA, SRI LANKA, SWEDEN, VENEZUELA, YUGOSLAVIA and ZAIRE.

Appendix I. General and complete disarmament

Joint Statement on Agreed Principles for Disarmament Negotiations of the Soviet Union and the United States (the McCloy-Zorin Agreement) made on 20 September 1961, unanimously endorsed by the United Nations General Assembly in resolution A/RES/ 1722 (XVI) of 20 December 1961[1]

Having conducted an extensive exchange of views on disarmament pursuant to their agreement announced in the General Assembly on 30 March 1961,

Noting with concern that the continuing arms race is a heavy burden for humanity and is fraught with dangers for the cause of world peace,

Reaffirming their adherence to all the provisions of the General Assembly resolution 1378 (XIV) of 20 November 1959,

Affirming that to facilitate the attainment of general and complete disarmament in a peaceful world it is important that all states abide by existing international agreements, refrain from any actions which might aggravate international tensions, and that they seek settlement of all disputes by peaceful means,

The United States and the USSR have agreed to recommend the following principles as the basis for future multilateral negotiations on disarmament and to call upon other states to co-operate in reaching early agreement on general and complete disarmament in a peaceful world in accordance with these principles.

1. The goal of negotiations is to achieve agreement on a programme which will ensure that (a) disarmament is general and complete and war is no longer an instrument for settling international problems, and (b) such disarmament is accompanied by the establishment of reliable procedures for the peaceful settlement of disputes and effective arrangements for the maintenance of peace in accordance with the principles of the United Nations Charter.

2. The programme for general and complete disarmament shall ensure that states will have at their disposal only those non-nuclear armaments, forces, facilities and establishments as are agreed to be necessary to maintain internal order and protect the personal security of citizens; and that states shall support and provide agreed manpower for a United Nations peace force.

3. To this end, the programme for general and complete disarmament shall contain the necessary provisions, with respect to the military establishment of every nation, for: (a) disbanding of armed forces, dismantling of military establishments, including bases, cessation of the production of armaments as well as their liquidation or conversion to peaceful uses; (b) elimination of all stockpiles of nuclear, chemical, bacteriological and other weapons of mass destruction and cessation of the production of such weapons; (c) elimination of all means of delivery of weapons of mass destruction; (d) abolishment of the organization and institutions designed to organize the military effort of states, cessation of military training, and closing of all military training institutions; (e) discontinuance of military expenditures.

4. The disarmament programme should be implemented in an agreed sequence, by stages until it is completed, with each measure and stage carried out within specified time-limits. Transition to a subsequent stage in the process of disarmament should take place upon a review of the implementation of measures included in the preceding stage and upon a decision that all such measures have been implemented and verified and that any additional verification arrangements required for measures in the next stage are, when appropriate, ready to operate.

5. All measures of general and complete disarmament should be balanced so that at no stage of the implementation of the treaty could any state or group of states gain military advantage and that security is ensured equally for all.

6. All disarmament measures should be implemented from beginning to end under such strict and effective international control as would provide firm assurance that all parties are honouring their obligations. During and after the implementation of general and complete disarmament, the most thorough control should be exercised, the nature and extent of such control depending on the requirements for verification of the disarmament measures being carried out in each stage. To implement control over and inspection of disarmament, an International Disarmament Organization including all parties to the agreement should be created within the framework of the United Nations. The International Disarmament Organization and its inspectors should be assured unrestricted access without veto to all places as necessary for the purpose of effective verification.

7. Progress in disarmament should be accompanied by measures to strengthen institutions for maintaining peace and the settlement of international disputes by peaceful means. During and after the implementation of the programme of general and complete disarmament, there should be taken, in accordance with the principles of the United Nations Charter, the necessary measures to maintain international peace and security, including the obligation of states to place at the disposal of the United Nations agreed manpower necessary for an international peace force to be equipped with agreed types of armaments. Arrangements for the use of this force should ensure that the United Nations can effectively deter or suppress any threat or use of arms in violation of the purposes and principles of the United Nations.

8. States participating in the negotiations should seek to achieve and implement the widest possible agreement at the earliest possible date. Efforts should continue without interruption until agreement upon the total programme has been achieved, and efforts to ensure early agreement on and implementation of measures of disarmament should be undertaken without prejudicing progress on agreement on the total programme and in such a way that these measures would facilitate and form part of that programme.

Letter from Presidential Adviser McCloy to Deputy Foreign Minister Zorin: verification of retained forces and armaments, 20 September 1961[2]

Dear Mr Zorin·

At the 18 September 1961 session of our bilateral discussions on disarmament you indicated that the draft of a joint statement of agreed principles which I submitted to you on behalf of the United States Government on 14 September 1961 would be acceptable to the Government of the Soviet Union provided the following clause were omitted from paragraph 6:

'Such verification should ensure that not only agreed limitations or reductions take place but also that retained armed forces and armaments do not exceed agreed levels at any stage.'

This sentence expresses a key element in the United States position which we believe is implicit in the entire joint statement of agreed principles that whenever an agreement stipulates that at a certain point certain levels of forces and armaments may be retained, the verification machinery must have all the rights and powers necessary to ensure that those levels are not exceeded.

It appears from your statements that the Soviet Union will be unwilling to agree to a joint statement of agreed principles unless the above-mentioned clause is omitted therefrom. My government has authorized me to inform you that, in the interest of progress toward resuming disarmament negotiations, it is willing to remove the above-mentioned sentence from paragraph 6 of the joint statement of agreed principles since it is an item to which the Soviet Union has not agreed.

This is done upon the express understanding that the substantive position of the United

States Government as outlined in the above-quoted sentence and in our memorandum of 14 September 1961 remains unchanged, and is in no sense prejudiced by the exclusion of this sentence from the joint statement of agreed principles.

The United States continues to adhere to and will continue to advance the principle contained in the omitted sentence as a necessary element in any comprehensive disarmament negotiations or agreement.

Very truly yours,

John J. McCloy

Letter from Deputy Foreign Minister Zorin to Presidential Adviser McCloy, 20 September 1961[3]

Dear Mr McCloy,

I have received your letter of 20 September 1961, in which you express a reservation with regard to the position which the United States of America intends to adopt in subsequent negotiations on disarmament.

According to the agreement which we reached in the course of a bilateral exchange of views, the United States agreed not to include, in the joint statement by the Governments of the USSR and the United States on the principles for disarmament negotiations, the proposal with which you are conversant and the adoption of which would imply acceptance of the concept of the establishment of control over armaments instead of control over disarmament. In your letter you say that this proposal 'expresses a key element in the United States position'.

In this connection I must state that, as you know, the position of the USSR on the question of control over general and complete disarmament has been thoroughly and clearly explained in the statements of the Soviet Government and its leader N. S. Khrushchev. The Soviet Union favours the most thorough and strict international control over the measures of general and complete disarmament. While strongly advocating effective control over disarmament and wishing to facilitate as much as possible the achievement of agreement on this control, the Soviet Union is at the same time resolutely opposed to the establishment of control over armaments.

It appears from your letter that the United States is trying to establish control over the armed forces and armaments retained by states at any given stage of disarmament. However, such control, which in fact means control over armaments, would turn into an international system of legalized espionage, which would naturally be unacceptable to any state concerned for its security and the interests of preserving peace throughout the world. The position of the United States on this question, if it insists on the proposal described above, will inevitably complicate agreement on a programme of general and complete disarmament, on the general principles of which we have agreed.

The Soviet Union will continue to make every effort towards the earliest preparation of a treaty on general and complete disarmament under effective international control.

I have the honour to be, . . .

V. Zorin
Permanent Representative of the USSR
to the United Nations

Notes

1. From official records of the General Assembly, Fifteenth Session, 20 September 1961 (A/4879).
2. From United Nations document A/4880, 20 September 1961.
3. From United Nations document A/4887, 25 September 1961.

Appendix II. United Nations action on the standardization of military budgets (Editor's note)

In 1973, the Soviet Union proposed a one-time reduction of the military budgets of the permanent members of the Security Council by 10 per cent and the diversion of 10 per cent of the funds thus saved to development assistance. The hope was expressed that other major economic and military powers would also follow suit. By a vote of 83 in favour, 2 against (China and Albania) and 38 abstentions (*i.a.* all NATO countries), the United Nations General Assembly endorsed the Soviet proposal (resolution 3093A of 7 December 1973). There was greater support for a second resolution adopted the same day (3093B) requesting the Secretary-General to prepare a report on the feasibility of the reduction of military budgets and the utilization of funds thus saved to provide international assistance to developing countries. Here the outcome was 93 votes in favour, 2 against and 26 abstentions. The United States, United Kingdom and France abstained, although they welcomed the suggested study.

Thus, the Soviet proposal won the support of the developing countries but was not accepted by the other members of the Security Council. China considered it unjust to demand that all great powers reduce the military budgets by the same proportion. All the other members of the Security Council doubted the practicability of the proposal because no agreed-upon method of calculating military budgets exists. Moreover, the United States questioned the very concept of linking the reduction of military budgets with development assistance.

There was, however, one positive result from the Soviet initiative. At the request of the United Nations General Assembly, three consecutive expert reports on the standardization of military budgets were prepared (1974, 1976, 1977). These three reports focused on a mutually acceptable conceptual definition of the scope and content of military budgets and on ways to standardize reporting of military expenditures so as to arrive at a universally agreed system to measure, compare and verify reductions of military budgets. The Soviet Union and its allies abstained in voting on resolutions seeking to establish and improve standardized systems of reporting military expenditures. Such votes have in recent years generally received the support of about 120 Western and developing countries. Controversy has persisted between East and West on two issues:

First, the West considered the acceptance of a standardized, verifiable reporting system for military expenditures as a prerequisite for possible reductions in military budgets, while the Soviet Union has favoured 'concurrent unilateral reductions' based on official budget figures without international scrutiny. Implicit in this Soviet position—apart from the intense secrecy which surrounds Soviet military affairs—is the realization that different methods of accounting exist in East and West and that this difference makes comparisons very difficult. Added to this is the controversial dollar/rouble conversion rate.

Second, East and West still maintain somewhat diverging views concerning the link between reduction of military budgets and channelling part of the funds saved for development assistance. The Soviet Union insists on the materialization of the link: implementation—according to its view—being dependent not on budgetary technicalities but on political negotiations. The United States, on the other hand, while insisting on budget standardization, still maintains that disarmament and development are separate issues and should be considered on their own merits.

20

Taking stock of the United Nations Special Session Devoted to Disarmament

Sverre Lodgaard
International Peace Research Institute, Oslo

The arms race: eluding man's grasp

At the United Nations Special Session Devoted to Disarmament, leaders from all over the world for the first time after the Second World War gathered to discuss ways and means of turning the arms-ridden history of mankind towards disarmament. During the general debate, more than twenty heads of state or government and about 100 Foreign Ministers made it plain, in more or less outspoken language, that the real issue at stake was the survival of mankind. The final declaration was very clear-cut: 'Mankind is confronted with a choice: we must halt the arms race and proceed to disarmament or face annihilation' (para. 18 of the Final Document).

It is widely acknowledged that the Tenth Special Session met to discuss the most important of all questions. Yet the session first of all reaffirmed one of the most puzzling facts about contemporary arms build-up: that it is virtually out of control. Even with the best of intentions, political leaders do not seem to be in a position to stop the arms race. Their interventions, frequently of the highest order both in substance, style and oratorical presentation, have but marginal effects on military realities. During one of the most difficult periods in United States–Soviet relations in more than fifteen years, and in the midst of another wave of arms build-ups, the discrepancy between intention and action, words and deeds, was unmistakable. With an abundance of top-level oratory for more than two weeks, the session vigorously demonstrated this deplorable state of affairs. As realistically assessed in the Final Declaration, the arms race outstrips by far the efforts to curb it and continues to elude man's grasp.

The arms race: eluding man's attention

The strength of the forces sustaining the arms race is far out of proportion to that of any movement for disarmament. Symptomatically, the arms manufacturers did not even have representatives on the spot: they have more direct and far more effective ways of influencing the political systems than by lobbying at the United

Adapted from a paper published in the *Bulletin of Peace Proposals*, Vol. 9, No. 3, 1978.

Nations. For them as well as for the mass media in many parts of the world, the session obviously looked impotent: nothing to fear, not much to report.

To some extent, however, the mass media may also have been discouraged from reporting on the session by hawks in the governments, and by armament firms doing so much advertising that pressure could be brought to bear on opposition to disarmament. In the industrialized world, where military establishments are generally well developed and entrenched and for the time being profiting also from heightened East-West tension, vested arms interests could probably restrict themselves to the control of 'noise' in generally well-oiled war machines. In developing parts of the world, where many new nations are in the process of expanding and consolidating their military forces, the scope for information about the dangers of arms build-up is limited as well. China, while taking a more active part in disarmament discussions than ever since it took its proper place in the United Nations in 1971, is giving high priority to military build-up in an effort to make up for the time lost during the political turmoil after Mao's death. The Chinese population is uniformly geared to an arms build-up in preparation for the inevitable Third World War.

The arms race not only eludes man's grasp, but its dangers also elude man's attention.

Programme without action

The Final Document consists of an introduction, a declaration containing: (a) a review and appraisal of disarmament efforts made so far; (b) an outline of goals and priorities; and (c) basic principles to guide future disarmament efforts, a programme of action, and a section on the machinery of international disarmament negotiations.

The weakest part of the document is undoubtedly the programme of action. It enumerates a number of measures and negotiations which have been contemplated and pursued for some time, without offering anything significantly new. This applies above all to the nuclear issues, which were declared to have the highest priority. While the threat of nuclear war is recognized as increasing, the programme of action contains few, if any, new measures to curb the nuclear arms race.

One exception deserves notice. For the first time, it proved possible to consider the problems relating to the worldwide accumulation of conventional armaments and the international transfer of such arms in a constructive way in the United Nations. As a result of the Special Session, a consensus has been achieved to the effect that the limitation and gradual reduction of such weapons and transfers should be resolutely pursued. The issue has now been firmly established as one of the priority items in United Nations disarmament deliberations.

Other issues may, or may not, be followed up in more resolute ways after the session. Negative security guarantees are a case in point. Following a declaration on non-use of nuclear weapons by the Soviet Union, all nuclear-weapon states except China—which made an unconditional non-use pledge at the time of its first nuclear test in 1964—made partly new declarations. The programme of action contains but a vague appeal to the nuclear-weapon states to pursue efforts to conclude, as appropriate, effective arrangements to assure non-nuclear-weapon states against the use or threat of use of nuclear weapons (para. 57). Whether the unilateral declarations nevertheless provided new impetus to the demand for an international convention on the non-use of nuclear weapons remains to be seen.

Since consensus was not achieved on new proposals and initiatives, the programme of action mainly wraps existing political differences in consensual language. In that process, the overall balance of views was by and large preserved. With the partial exception of some paragraphs on non-proliferation, where the inalienable rights of all states to develop nuclear-power programmes in conformity with their own priorities, interests and needs (eventually including reprocessing and recirculation of plutonium) are strongly underlined, and the reference to the Non-Proliferation Treaty, the programme of action is so weak as to question its importance; new points of balance were not introduced.

Generally, the programme of action bears the mark of the status quo.

Accomplishments

The session nevertheless made a number of achievements which may seem small and uninteresting at first glance, but which may stimulate disarmament work in a number of ways that may later prove significant. We shall therefore spell them out at some length here—for their potential long-term value.

First, the session defined a comprehensive approach for further pursuit of arms restraint and disarmament. Usually, a General Assembly debate has 120 items, some fifteen to twenty of them devoted to disarmament. Close to twenty resolutions are usually passed concerning disarmament measures. The Special Session had only one item: this permitted a general debate solely on disarmament, and the pursuit of disarmament questions in a coherent fashion. In this regard, the session set an important precedent that may prove to be the first step towards an effective comprehensive programme of disarmament. The elaboration of such a programme will be a top priority issue for the new disarmament machinery and will be conducted concurrently with negotiations on partial disarmament measures.

Second, the international disarmament machinery was strengthened—at the United Nations by establishing a successor to the Disarmament Commission (which never met after 1965) and by devoting the work of the First Committee of the General Assembly entirely to disarmament and related international security questions; in Geneva by replacing the present Conference of the Committee on Disarmament with a new Committee on Disarmament, where the chairmanship rotates among its members and the representative of the United Nations Secretary-General acts as the Secretary of the committee. The Disarmament Commission will meet as a deliberative body. Its recommendations will be submitted to the General Assembly, and through it to the Committee on Disarmament, which will be the negotiating forum. While considering the elements of the comprehensive disarmament programme, the Disarmament Commission may also consider draft treaties that are submitted to the United Nations. So far, drafts have been submitted on a 'take-it-or-leave-it' basis. For the future, more thorough assessments can be made, and amendments undertaken.

Third, the session may have fostered a clearer sense of urgency in governmental circles as to the necessity of achieving real arms restraint and disarmament.

246

Above all, the relationship between disarmament and international security may be better understood. In preparation for the session, there has also been a great deal of thinking about the ways and means of achieving disarmament as well. The Final Document does not fully reflect this: a number of proposals are mentioned in general terms—or not at all. However, governments now have a greater stake in disarmament proposals than before, and will follow them up in New York, Geneva and other contexts as appropriate. The session thus had an educational effect, which has given rise to political commitments and obligations that may in turn be reinforced by intensified activities in the new disarmament machinery.

Machinery improvements are not basic to progress in disarmament: the essential factor is political will and political support. However, governments will have to pay more attention to disarmament, and the negotiations may become more efficient. This is likely to carve out some more space for disarmament issues in the mass media. The plenary meetings of the Committee on Disarmament will be open to the public unless otherwise decided, and so will deliberations of the Disarmament Commission. Altogether, this will make it easier and more attractive for the public to follow international disarmament activities, and to plan and target disarmament actions. Upgraded governmental efforts in combination with a stronger and better organized and targeted disarmament movement may bring greater progress in the future.

Fourth, the session did much to forge new links between disarmament and several other global issues, including development and environment if not human rights. This may bring new groups and movements into the quest for disarmament.

The recognition of incompatibility between arms build-up and the realization of a new international economic order, and the universal acceptance of the principle that resources released as a result of disarmament should be devoted to economic and social development and to the bridging of the economic gap between developed and developing countries (para. 35), may bring the arms race under stronger attack from social and economic points of view. Furthermore, a number of national environmental movements are stepping up their protests against military activities. Growing militarization is, moreover, increasingly recognized as a threat to democratic government and an encroachment upon human rights, although for obvious reasons these aspects of arms build-up will not easily find their way into United Nations documents. Evidence of such links is, however, abundant, and concern is growing first of all regarding political developments in the Third World. Altogether, the evolving multi-pronged attack on arms build-up improves the prospect for effective action against the arms race.

Fifth, the United Nations Centre for Disarmament will intensify its study programme. The Secretary-General shall, *inter alia,* continue the study of the interrelationship between disarmament and international security (para. 95), and initiate an expert study on the relationship between disarmament and development (para. 92). The latter study will place special emphasis on reallocation of resources now being used for military purposes to economic and social development, aiming at results that can effectively guide the formulation of practical conversion measures (para. 93). An advisory board will be established to assist the Secretary-General in elaborating a more coherent study programme (para. 121).

To turn the arms race into disarmament, arms restraint has to be more vigorously pursued as an integral part of national security considerations. Concrete proposals to this effect were put forward at the session. States were asked to assess the possible implications of their military research and development for existing agreements as well as for further efforts in the field of disarmament (paras. 91 and 92). A proposal that budget requests for new weapons be accompanied by an evaluation of their arms-control impact, so as to allow arms restraint and disarmament objectives to have a stronger impact on national decision-making, did not obtain the necessary support at this stage. The study of disarmament and international security may, however, improve the ground for structural representation of arms-restraint objectives in national decision-making processes, and bring concrete ideas to this effect a step further.

By designing the reports in such a way that the main results are accessible also to people without prior special knowledge of the issues involved, the study programme may have a considerable educational effect. This applies not least to the study on disarmament and development. This study may have a great public impact in conveying a better idea of the present respective flows of resources to military and civilian ends, and in showing what can be achieved in civilian realms by reallocation of resources, and how it can be done.

Unesco is also asked to step up its educational activities (paras. 101 and 105).

Sixth, the Final Document addresses itself to some specific measures designed to increase the dissemination of information about the arms race and the efforts to halt and reverse it (para. 98).

Dissemination of information is not only a question of making scientific results available in popular form. It is at the same time a political activity. Scientifically sound and reliable information is sometimes made suspicious and illegitimate by forces sustaining an arms build-up, while false and tendentious information is allowed to flourish. 'The fact that men have become accustomed to war preparations has so corrupted their mentality that objective and humane thinking becomes a virtual impossibility; such thinking will even be regarded and suppressed as unpatriotic.'[1]

As a source of information, United Nations documents have often proved to be useful instruments. The United Nations may at times seem disconnected from the main centres of political power. This is often to the bad, but in some respects also to the good: precisely for this reason, governments can sometimes afford to use a vocabulary which is less defensive of political realities and more straightforward in assessing international problems than usual. Transplanted back to the national constituencies, United Nations resolutions and studies have therefore proved to be instrumental in legitimizing arguments for arms restraint—and the Final Document is no exception.

Public opinion and political will: did the session live up to its task?

Today's young people have no assurances that they will live out their lives. . . . The young today are living the lives of condemned people.[2]

Removing the threat of a world war—a nuclear world war—is rightly recognized in the Final Document to be the most acute and urgent task of the present day (para. 18). Nevertheless, people are largely alienated from the horrors of nuclear weapons, and have so far gone along with the steady accumulation of ever more effective means of mass destruction with only sporadic protests. The increasing technological complexity of the arms race, and the deliberate habit of élites of keeping the ordinary man guessing with technicalities, has produced a feeling of helplessness which is hard to get rid of. Mobilization of public opinion—a *sine qua non* for halting and reversing the arms race—therefore faces both psychological and political hindrances.

The session took some steps to improve the situation. Its main significance lies in the education of the public. It also gave governments a greater stake in disarmament measures, and stimulated international negotiations by having a more efficient disarmament machinery embark upon the elaboration of a comprehensive disarmament programme. The arms situation remains frightful, but without the session it would have been worse. Seen against the gloomy military-political background that obtains at present, the consensus document finally arrived at was no negligible achievement.

However, the standard of judgement has to be more ambitious than this. To come to grips with the arms race is to shoot at a rapidly moving target. The question is: are the above-mentioned accomplishments initiating new trends which can bring the arms race back under control? Full judgement naturally has to be reserved, but the fight for disarmament seems to be an uphill fight even after the session, and so far the goal is not significantly closer. Given the catastrophic nature of failure to halt the arms race, far more needs to happen.

Notes

1. From Otto Nathan and Heinz Norden (eds.), *Einstein on Peace*, New York, Simon & Schuster, 1960.
2. Dr George Wald in *Disarmament Times*, Friday, 16 June 1978.

21

An integrated approach to disarmament

Frank Barnaby
Stockholm International Peace Research Institute (SIPRI)

Global militarization

The conclusion of the Partial Test-Ban Treaty on 5 August 1963 can be regarded as a turning-point in post-Second-World-War disarmament negotiations. Although its arms-control value is low, the treaty has been interpreted as the first proof, after years of the Cold War, that restrictions on the military activities of states can be agreed upon. It is fitting, therefore, to match the post-1963 developments in armaments against the hopes held at that time that the arms race would be brought under control. Moreover, by 1963 most of the large colonies had become independent and could themselves decide on their future military activities.

Since 1963 world military expenditures have increased by about 40 per cent, to reach the current figure of about $400,000 million a year. The Third World share of the total has increased from about 4 per cent in 1963 to about 15 per cent today.

In the past fifteen years the world's armed forces have increased by nearly 30 per cent, to about 26 million persons. An even more serious waste of resources may be the waste of talent. Many of those engaged in military activities are highly skilled technicians and scientists.

Militarization has assumed a global character mainly due to the arms trade. Since 1963, the trade in major weapons—aircraft, missiles, armoured vehicles and ships—has increased more than fivefold. The bulk of these weapons were sold to Third World countries. And, since 1973, the arms trade has escalated, increasing at the unprecedented annual rate of 15 per cent.

More and more countries are producing their own weapons. Fifteen years ago only a handful of industrialized countries were weapon producers. Today about fifty countries—of which about one-half are in the Third World—are producing major weapons. Thus a constantly increasing number of nations are investing large amounts of resources in domestic arms industries at the expense of the civilian sectors of their economies.

Although about 80 per cent of military money is spent on conventional

SIPRI statement to the Special Session of the United Nations General Assembly Devoted to Disarmament, *Statement on World Armaments and Disarmament*, Stockholm, SIPRI, 1978.

armaments and forces, the greatest single threat to mankind is that of nuclear war. In 1963, the nuclear arsenals contained about 4,000 relatively primitive warheads. These were enough to destroy our civilization. But today, nuclear arsenals contain tens of thousands of sophisticated nuclear weapons, with a total nuclear explosive power equivalent to that of about one million Hiroshima bombs.

Qualitative improvements in nuclear weapons continue virtually without restraint. Between the signing of the Partial Test-Ban Treaty and the end of 1977, 629 nuclear explosions were carried out, mainly to improve the efficiency of nuclear weapons. The nuclear-weapon powers party to the treaty are responsible for 86 per cent of these explosions. The rate of testing has been much higher after the treaty than before it (forty-five per year as against twenty-five per year, on average).

The capability to produce nuclear weapons is spreading worldwide through peaceful nuclear programmes. In 1963 only nine countries had significant peaceful nuclear programmes. Today the number is nearly thirty.

Militarization does not stop with the earth's land mass. The oceans and outer space are becoming increasingly militarized. Since 1963, 1,536 satellites serving military purposes and representing an important part of the qualitative arms race have been launched into space. This number is about 75 per cent of all satellites launched. So far as the marine environment is concerned, in 1963 less than a dozen nuclear-powered submarines, for example, were operated by the world's navies. Today there are more than 250 such submarines.

The adverse effects of warfare and other military activities on the human environment are generally incidental to the many activities associated with maintaining armies. In some wars, however, they can be an intentional and integral component of the military strategy being used. There is a noticeable trend for modern warfare to become increasingly destructive of the environment. Man may soon be able to manipulate certain forces of nature. If these abilities were to be employed for hostile purposes, their environmental impact could be disastrous.

No one can be sure that mankind would, in the long term, survive a general nuclear war.

New approach of disarmament

The arms-control treaties now in force have had little or no effect on the military potential of states. The choice of measures adopted has been haphazard. In several cases, the outlawed activities have never even been seriously considered as methods of war. It is now obvious that the method of negotiating small, unrelated steps cannot produce meaningful arms reductions. Insignificant restraints are bound to lag behind the rising levels of armaments and advances in military technology. SIPRI is convinced that a new approach is required.

We have in mind an integrated approach to disarmament, as opposed to piecemeal arms control. Large 'packages' of measures—comprising quantitative reductions and qualitative restrictions to be carried out simultaneously—should be negotiated. This would allow a margin for any trade-offs necessary to take into account the different security needs of states. The wider the range of weapons covered, the greater would be the value of each package. Nuclear weapons and other weapons of mass destruction (particularly chemical warfare agents) must obviously have top priority. But it seems important to us that conventional disarmament should proceed in parallel—not only because conventional armaments account for the bulk of world military expenditures, but also because the very possession of nuclear weapons has been justified by a perceived need to deter aggression started with conventional weapons. Indeed, conventional armed conflict might well escalate into a nuclear war.

Quantitative reductions and qualitative limitations should be accompanied by restrictions on the production, deployment and transfer of weapons. The significance of arms-control packages would be further enhanced if they provided for prohibitions of certain specific categories of weapons. Undertakings not to use certain means of warfare might also usefully be included since there is less incentive to develop or maintain weapons with an uncertain future. Cuts in military budgets could be linked to cuts in arms manufacture or other military activities.

The integrated approach places the main emphasis on multilateral negotiations involving all militarily important states, and all participants should be prepared to make certain equitably balanced contributions to disarmament. But the integrated approach is not incompatible with bilateral talks dealing with the United States–Soviet arms race or with regional disarmament negotiations, which should be encouraged.

The use of force in international relations should be abolished by eliminating the instruments of war. But complete worldwide disarmament would require an adequate international security system—a workable machinery for the peaceful settlement of disputes and effective peace-keeping arrangements. Our approach of integrated disarmament measures would facilitate the creation of such a security system.

22

The United Nations Special Session: two years after

Homer Jack
World Conference on Religion and Peace, New York

The Tenth Special Session of the United Nations General Assembly Devoted to Disarmament 'marks not the end but rather the beginning of a new phase of the efforts of the United Nations in the field of disarmament'. So stated the penultimate sentence in the long Final Document of the Special Session. This ended with the assertion that the conference 'will attract the attention of all peoples, further mobilize public opinion, and provide a powerful impetus for the cause of disarmament'.

Two years after the Tenth Special Session was held, and two years before the announced convening of the next Special Session, this is an appropriate time to begin to assess the results of this first event. Despite the grim atmosphere for disarmament negotiations today, is there some good news about the implementation of the Tenth Special Session?

There may be tiny bits of 'progress', but the bad news is that this session did not attract the attention of all peoples—before, during or after—and it did not further mobilize public opinion and it did not provide a powerful impetus for the cause of disarmament. What, then, did it accomplish?

Rather than indulge in speculation, let us scan the Final Document and evaluate its implementation.

Programme of action

The introduction of the Final Document and the declaration are not relevant here, but the programme of action constitutes a check-list for the next steps along the road leading eventually to general and complete disarmament. There has been very little substantive progress all along the way. There is no nuclear disarmament. The United States and the USSR did, to be sure, conclude—since the Tenth Special Session—the SALT II Treaty in June 1979, but this has yet to be ratified. In the meantime, there is no assurance that the intent of that treaty will be implemented by both parties until such time as it might enter into force.

There is no cessation of nuclear-weapons tests by the five nuclear-weapon

From a paper published in *Arms Control Today*, June 1980.

states, either through a moratorium or otherwise. Indeed, Sweden reported in the new Committee on Disarmament at Geneva that during 1979, the first full year after the Tenth Special Session, the Soviet Union conducted twenty-eight nuclear-weapons tests, the United States fifteen, France nine, the United Kingdom one, and the Chinese apparently none. There is no comprehensive test-ban treaty, although trilateral negotiations (among the USSR, United Kingdom and United States) have continued for almost three years. An ad hoc working group of the Committee on Disarmament devoted to a CTB has been advocated by the Group of 21 (independent and non-aligned members of the Committee on Disarmament), but this has not yet been established.

No new arrangements have been made to ensure non-nuclear-weapon states against the use or threat of use of nuclear weapons, although the Committee on Disarmament established in July 1979 an ad hoc working group to negotiate effective international arrangements on the strengthening of security guarantees. This group was extended in March 1980. No new nuclear-free zones have been established, despite repeated United Nations encouragement for their creation in Africa, the Middle East and South Asia. The Latin American zone (Treaty of Tlatelolco) has been inching towards completion. The only progress made in implementing the decision to make the Indian Ocean a zone of peace was a meeting held of the littoral and hinterland states in July 1979. Indeed, the Indian Ocean is fast becoming a zone of warships.

No new success has been registered to prevent the proliferation of nuclear weapons—horizontally or vertically. Since the Tenth Special Session, several states have been added to the informal list of those which allegedly may possess untested nuclear weapons. The study of the International Nuclear Fuel Cycle Evaluation (INFCE) has been concluded, but no negotiations associated directly with it were ever contemplated.

More states have adhered to the Biological Weapons Treaty, and its first Review Conference was held in March 1980, but not without allegations that some states may be holding back information. The conference did approve by consensus a Final Declaration. No treaty has yet been concluded for the complete prohibition of all chemical weapons and their destruction, although negotiations began in 1971. The Committee on Disarmament has, however, established an ad hoc working group towards completing a treaty. (Despite the 1925 Protocol, allegations about the use of chemical weapons have continued.)

A proposal on major elements of a treaty prohibiting the development, production, stockpiling and use of radiological weapons was submitted by the United States and the USSR in July 1979 to the Committee on Disarmament. The latter is seeking agreement on a radiological weapons convention in an ad hoc working group. No results have been achieved to prohibit the development and manufacture of other new types of weapons of mass destruction, either through a general agreement on specific weapons or particular types of such weapons. Also no efforts have been made to add to the existing treaties to prevent an arms race on the sea-bed and ocean floor, and in outer space.

If there has been no nuclear disarmament, there has been little reduction, and much increase, in armed forces and conventional weapons. If the Soviet Union took 1,000 tanks and 20,000 troops out of Central Europe in 1979, that state introduced more of both into Central Asia in 1980. The proposed quick-strike rapid deployment force of the Carter Administration with 110,000 troops is also hardly a step towards conventional disarmament.

The first session of the 1979 United Nations Conference on Prohibition of Inhumane and Indiscriminate Weapons was held last September. No treaty was completed. However, a second session will be held in Geneva beginning in September 1980. Allegations of the continued use of napalm have been made. Military budgets have not been gradually reduced, but rather steeply increased.

There have been numerous studies. The expert research on the relationship between disarmament and development, under the creative leadership of Inga Thorsson of Sweden and with twenty-seven experts, is continuing. By 1981 it might produce several dozen major research papers quite apart from a series of conclusions and recommendations. The study on the relationship between disarmament and international security, involving ten experts, under the chairmanship of Carlos Romulo of the Philippines, will also be finished by 1981.

Many other studies, either launched by the Tenth Special Session or the two sessions of the General Assembly held since, are also in progress and include the following topics: (a) a comprehensive test-ban treaty; (b) an international satellite monitoring agency (to be completed in 1981 with the help of eleven experts); (c) confidence-building measures based on positive experiences in Europe (to be completed in 1981 with the help of thirteen experts); (d) institutional arrangements for disarmament within the United Nations (to be completed in 1981 with the help of twenty experts); (e) Israeli nuclear armament (to be completed in 1981); (f) South Africa's capability in the nuclear field (to be completed in 1980 with the help of four experts); (g) various aspects of nuclear weapons, updating the earlier United Nations study on 'Effects of the Possible Use of Nuclear Weapons. . .' (to be completed in 1980 with the assistance of twelve experts); (h) aspects of regional disarmament (to be completed in 1980 with the assistance of ten experts); (i) a practical test involving a range of states of an instrument for standardized reporting on military expenditures and refinements based on that test.

The Tenth Special Session asked the United Nations, governments, and non-governmental organizations (NGOs) to prepare and distribute materials on the arms race and disarmament. All continue to issue such information, but not noticeably in greater amounts. *The United Nations Disarmament Yearbook*, created before the Special Session, and compiled by the United Nations Centre for Disarmament, has completed its third volume. The latter is a 535-page assessment of events during the calendar year 1978, including the Special Session. The United Nations Centre for Disarmament also publishes the twice-yearly periodical *Disarmament*, issued in the six working languages of the United Nations.

For two years Disarmament Week (the seven-day period beginning each 24 October) has been observed. This is a direct result of the Special Session and there is increasing participation by governments, NGOs, and the general public. The United Nations Centre for Disarmament has so far been prevented, partly by the general fiscal conservatism at the United Nations of both the USSR and the United States, from being able to 'intensify its activities in the presentation of information'. NGOs have continued, but hardly increased, their participation in disarmament affairs, although closer relations between them and the centre began in 1980 with the appointment of an NGO staff liaison officer. Unesco convened its World Congress on Disarmament Education in Paris in June 1980.

One exciting result of the Special Session was the inauguration of a programme of fellowships in disarmament, especially for young diplomats from Third World countries. Twenty fellows participated in the first class during 1979, while the second group has just been notified of its appointment.

No measures have been taken, as requested by the Special Session, in the United Nations system to strengthen institutions for maintaining peace and settling disputes.

Disarmament machinery   *resulting from* F.D

The Final Document spelled out the need for revitalizing existing disarmament forums, both of a deliberative and negotiating character, and for creating new ones. The First Committee of the General Assembly—a deliberative body—has increasingly become 'The Disarmament Committee', with other items (e.g. Korea) relegated to other committees. (The United Nations Centre for Disarmament has issued, beginning with the thirty-fourth General Assembly (1979), a computerized index to the debate in the First Committee and disarmament items in the plenary.) Each session of the General Assembly has had an agenda item entitled 'Review of the implementation of the recommendations and decisions adopted by the General Assembly at its Tenth Special Session'.

A new Disarmament Commission has been established. Also a deliberative body, it is composed of all Member States. Its second session began in mid-May 1980. As requested by the Tenth Special Session, the Disarmament Commission at its first session elaborated the elements of a comprehensive programme of disarmament. With the 1979 General Assembly declaring the 1980s the Second Disarmament Decade, it also asked the Disarmament Commission in 1980 to elaborate a draft declaration giving targets for accomplishing the major disarmament goals. The Disarmament Commission could yet develop into a major disarmament organ.

The next Special Session on disarmament has been scheduled for 1982 at United Nations Headquarters. The comprehensive programme of disarmament is likely to be the centre-piece of this event.

The Conference of the Committee on Disarmament meeting at Geneva has been transformed, at the suggestion of the Special Session, into the Committee on Disarmament. The membership has increased from a total of thirty-one states to thirty-five non-nuclear-weapon states plus all five permanent members of the United Nations Security Council. France joined the Committee on Disarmament in January 1979 and the People's Republic of China joined in February 1980. The co-chairmanship by the USSR and the United States has been abandoned for a monthly rotation among all members. The Committee on Disarmament adopted its own rules of procedure and appointed former Indian Ambassador to the United Nations, Rikhi Jaipal, as its Secretary. It opened its plenary meetings to public, press, and NGOs adopted an agenda and has formed ad hoc working groups. One of the latter is to work further on the comprehensive programme of disarmament, since the Disarmament Commission in 1979 elaborated its elements.

The Ad Hoc Committee on the World Disarmament Conference has continued to meet. With China and the United States resisting a World

Disarmament Conference—perhaps rightly so—one will not take place at least until after the next Special Session.

The United Nations Centre for Disarmament with its new mandate after the Special Session has been somewhat strengthened through reorganization and a small budget increase. Given the needs of the Second Disarmament Decade of the 1980s, the United Nations Centre may yet give the executive leadership necessary for an implementation of the Final Document and the contemplated comprehensive programme of the next Special Session.

The Secretary-General appointed certain eminent persons to constitute an Advisory Board on Disarmament Studies. This comprises thirty individuals—some have already had to be replaced—and has met four times. Its first report recommended that a United Nations Institute for Disarmament Research be established within the framework of the United Nations Institute for Training and Research (UNITAR). This may begin operation this year in Geneva.

The 1979 General Assembly adopted a lengthy Declaration on International Co-operation for Disarmament, but this is unlikely to hasten negotiations since it is mostly a quick rehash of the Final Document.

United Nations Secretary-General Kurt Waldheim predicted that the Special Session would be 'the largest, most representative gathering ever convened to consider the question of disarmament'. It was. Despite its large and representative nature, the Special Session only barely fulfilled the minimum hopes of its advocates.

The Introduction of the Final Document affirmed that the 'decisive factor for achieving real measures of disarmament is the "political will" of states'. Nevertheless, it also affirmed that 'a significant role can also be played by the effective functioning of an appropriate international machinery designed to deal with the problems of disarmament'. The appropriate international machinery for disarmament is now in place, Lacking still is that factor called 'political will' and this seems more evanescent than ever, 'especially of those possessing nuclear weapons'.

Thus, nothing has happened in the two years since the Tenth Special Session adjourned to question the truth of the most-quoted paragraph in the Final Document.

Removing the threat of a world war—a nuclear war—is the most acute and urgent task of the present day. Mankind is confronted with a choice: we must halt the arms race and proceed to disarmament or face annihilation.

23

Comprehensive programme of disarmament

United Nations
Department of Public Information

The goal of general and complete disarmament under effective international control has been proclaimed by the United Nations since 1959 as the ultimate aim of disarmament efforts. Many countries have offered detailed proposals for reduction of armaments in stages, with variations as to which types of arms or forces would be reduced first, numerical limits to be set, time-limits and methods of control. Despite discussions in the General Assembly, in the Geneva negotiating bodies and elsewhere, no agreements have been reached on an all-inclusive plan for disarmament.

In a Joint Statement of Agreed Principles on Disarmament set forth by the United States and the Soviet Union in 1961, the two powers said that a programme for disarmament applying to all countries should provide for disbanding of armed forces, dismantling of military establishments including bases, cessation of arms production, liquidation of armaments or conversion to peaceful purposes, elimination of all stockpiles of nuclear, chemical, bacteriological and other weapons of mass destruction as well as their means of delivery, abolition of military institutions and cessation of military training, and discontinuance of military expenditures. The statement called for creation of an international disarmament organization within the framework of the United Nations, whose inspectors would have unrestricted access to all places as necessary for verification of disarmament measures, and it envisaged arrangements for a United Nations peace force.

The elaboration of a comprehensive programme dealing with all aspects of the problem of the cessation of the arms race and general and complete disarmament under effective international control was proposed by the General Assembly in 1969. The Conference of the Committee on Disarmament held discussions concerning a comprehensive programme, as requested by the Assembly, but was unable to produce an agreed text.

Today, general and complete disarmament is no longer regarded as an objective to be achieved through a single and comprehensive instrument which would embody various timetables for nuclear and conventional disarmament or define the final status for the remaining forces and armaments. It is seen as a goal

From *The United Nations versus the Arms Race*, New York, United Nations, 1980.

to work towards in the expectation that one achievement may follow upon another, in accordance with certain logical priorities, with each stage of success creating increased mutual confidence and adding to the chances of success in the next phase.

General and complete disarmament under effective international control, the Special Session declared, remains the ultimate goal of all efforts exerted in the field of disarmament. When this is finally achieved:

General and complete disarmament under strict and effective international control shall permit states to have at their disposal only those non-nuclear forces, armaments, facilities and establishments as are agreed to be necessary to maintain internal order and protect the personal security of citizens and in order that states shall support and provide agreed manpower for a United Nations peace force.[1]

At the 1978 Special Session, the new Disarmament Commission was given the task of considering the elements of a comprehensive programme of disarmament to be submitted to the Assembly; the programme is then to be elaborated by the Committee on Disarmament. The Assembly said:

Negotiations on general and complete disarmament shall be conducted concurrently with negotiations on partial measures of disarmament. With this purpose in mind, the Committee on Disarmament will undertake the elaboration of a comprehensive programme of disarmament encompassing all measures thought to be advisable in order to ensure that the goal of general and complete disarmament under effective international control becomes a reality in a world in which international peace and security prevail and in which the new international economic order is strengthened and consolidated.[2]

Elements of programme

In 1979, the Disarmament Commission outlined the elements of a comprehensive programme, a package of interrelated measures to be carried out in stages. The commission agreed:

That the comprehensive programme should be based principally on the Final Document of the Special Session.

That it should lay down an agreed framework for sustained international action, including negotiations at different levels (i.e. multilateral, regional and bilateral) on specific disarmament measures.

That elaboration of the comprehensive programme should take place urgently and parallel with negotiations on concrete disarmament measures.

That the comprehensive programme should contain a phased programme which, in its first stage, should give special attention to cessation of the nuclear arms race and removal of the threat of a nuclear war.

That it should be elaborated and implemented on the basis of the priorities set forth in paragraph 45 of the Final Document:

Priorities in disarmament negotiations shall be: nuclear weapons; other weapons of mass destruction, including chemical weapons; conventional weapons, including any which may be deemed to be excessively injurious or to have indiscriminate effects; and reduction of armed forces.

259

That the process to be outlined should take place in an equitable manner ensuring the right of each state to security, and should take into account the importance of both nuclear and conventional disarmament, as well as 'the special responsibility of the states with the largest military arsenals and the necessity for adequate measures of verification'.

The Disarmament Commission said the comprehensive programme should encompass the following measures:

Disarmament measures

Nuclear weapons

Nuclear-test ban.

Cessation of the nuclear arms race in all its aspects and nuclear disarmament, which will require urgent negotiation of agreements at appropriate stages and with adequate measures of verification satisfactory to the states concerned for: (a) cessation of the qualitative improvement and development of nuclear-weapon systems; (b) cessation of the production of all types of nuclear weapons and their means of delivery, and the production of fissionable material for weapons purposes; (c) reduction of stockpiles of nuclear weapons and their means of delivery, leading to their ultimate and complete elimination at the earliest possible time.

Effective international arrangements to assure non-nuclear-weapon states against the use or threat of use of nuclear weapons.

Continuation of the strategic arms limitation negotiations between the two parties concerned.

Further steps to prevent the spread of nuclear weapons, in accordance with the provisions of paragraphs 65 to 71 of the Final Document.

Establishment of nuclear-weapon-free zones.

Other weapons of mass destruction

Prohibition of the development, production and stockpiling of all chemical weapons and their destruction.

Prevention of the emergence of new types of weapons of mass destruction and new systems of such weapons.

Prohibition of the development, production and use of radiological weapons.

Conventional weapons and armed forces

Cessation of the conventional arms race.

Agreements and measures, multilateral, regional and bilateral, on the limitation and reduction of conventional weapons and armed forces.

Prohibitions or restrictions of use of certain conventional weapons, including those which may cause unnecessary suffering or which may have indiscriminate effects, taking into account the result of the 1979 United Nations Conference on Prohibitions or Restrictions of Use of Certain Conventional Weapons Which May Be Deemed to Be Excessively Injurious or to Have Indiscriminate Effects.

Consultations among major arms suppliers and recipients on the international transfer of conventional weapons.

Military expenditures

Reduction of military expenditures.

Verification

Verification methods and procedures in relation to specific disarmament measures, to facilitate the conclusion and effective implementation of disarmament agreements and to create confidence among states.

Related measures

Further steps to prohibit military or any other hostile use of environmental modification techniques.
Consideration of further steps to prevent an arms race on the sea-bed and the ocean floor and the subsoil thereof.
Further steps to prevent an arms race in outer space.
Establishment of zones of peace.

Other measures[3]

Confidence-building measures, taking into account the characteristics of each region.
Measures aimed at achieving relaxation of international tension.
Measures aimed at preventing the use of force in international relations, subject to the provisions of the Charter of the United Nations.
Implementation of the provisions contained in the Final Document intended to mobilize world public opinion in favour of disarmament.
Disarmament studies under the auspices of the United Nations.

Disarmament and development

Bearing in mind the close relationship between disarmament and development and taking into account the United Nations studies carried out in this field, the comprehensive programme of disarmament should include measures aimed at ensuring that disarmament makes an effective contribution to economic and social development and, in particular, to the full realization of the new international economic order through:
Reallocation of resources from military purposes to economic and social development, especially for the benefit of the developing countries.
Savings from the reduction of military expenditures, particularly by nuclear-weapon states and other militarily significant states, should increase the flow of resources to economic and social development, especially for the benefit of the developing countries.
Strengthening of international co-operation for the promotion of the transfer and utilization of nuclear technology for economic and social development, especially in the developing countries, taking into account the provisions of paragraphs 68 to 70 of the Final Document.

Disarmament and international security

Strengthening of international procedures and institutions for:
Maintenance of peace and security in accordance with the Charter of the United Nations.
Peaceful settlement of disputes.
Effectiveness of the security system of the Charter of the United Nations.
United Nations peace-keeping in conformity with the Charter of the United Nations.
The Disarmament Commission agreed that the Committee on Disarmament should commence work on the elaboration of the comprehensive programme at the earliest possible date. It is hoped that the comprehensive programme can be adopted no later than 1982, at the next Special Session on disarmament.

Notes

1. Final Document, para. 111.
2. Final Document, para. 109.
3. In this context, mention was made in commission discussions of the following United Nations declarations: (a) Declaration on Principles of International Law concerning Friendly Relations and Co-operation among States; (b) Declaration on the Strengthening of International Security; (c) Declaration on the Preparation of Societies for Life in Peace.

24

Elements of a comprehensive programme of disarmament: a proposal by China

Chinese Delegation
United Nations Disarmament Commission, Geneva

Objective of the comprehensive programme of disarmament

The objective of the comprehensive programme of disarmament is, by formulating reasonable principles and practical and effective measures for disarmament, to promote real progress in disarmament, oppose a new world war and all armed aggression and safeguard international peace and security.

The main principles of the programme

The programme should include the following main principles:

For the purpose of safeguarding international peace and security, relations between states must be based on the principles of mutual respect for sovereignty and territorial integrity, mutual non-aggression, non-interference in each other's internal affairs, equality and mutual benefit and peaceful coexistence. No state may seek hegemony in any form and in any part of the world or subject other states to aggression, interference, subversion, expansion or control. No disarmament measure may impair the sovereignty, independence and security of any state.

In order to safeguard the security of all states, the two states with the largest nuclear and conventional arsenals have the primary responsibility for disarmament and should be the first to reduce their armaments. When they have drastically reduced their nuclear and conventional armaments and closed the huge gap between them and the other nuclear states and militarily significant states, the other nuclear states and militarily significant states should join them in reducing armaments according to reasonable ratios.

It is imperative to bring about the complete prohibition and total destruction of nuclear weapons so as truly to eliminate the danger of nuclear war. While nuclear disarmament is being considered, equal importance should be given to the question of reducing the superpowers' ever-growing arsenals of conventional armaments, and disarmament in these two fields should be carried out in

Proposal presented by the Chinese Delegation at the United Nations Disarmament Commission on 15 May 1980, *Beijing Review*, 1 June 1980.

conjunction. Full attention should also be paid to the prohibition and destruction of biological and chemical weapons and other weapons of mass destruction.

The actual process of disarmament should benefit the economic and social development of states. The superpowers are spending huge sums on the arms race, which not only increases the danger of war and jeopardizes international peace and security, but also hinders the establishment of a new international economic order. Their military expenditures account for two-thirds of the military budgets of all countries put together, so it is only natural that they should be called on first of all to reduce greatly their military expenditures and to make real contributions to aiding the developing countries.

No disarmament measure may prejudice the right of states to make use of modern scientific and technological achievements to promote their economic development. The superpowers must be prevented from using disarmament and the non-proliferation of nuclear weapons as pretexts to deprive other states of their right to use nuclear energy and develop their nuclear industries for peaceful purposes.

While formulating more comprehensive disarmament measures, importance should be attached to limited-scope measures, including regional measures. Zones of peace or nuclear weapon-free zones shall be established in the light of the specific conditions prevailing in different parts of the world and the desire of the states in the regions concerned. These zones shall be free from rivalry for hegemony between the superpowers, foreign military presence in all its forms, all armed occupation of other countries' territory and direct or indirect armed intervention and the threat of force. All nuclear states shall unconditionally undertake not to use or threaten to use nuclear weapons against these zones.

The question of disarmament concerns the security and interests of all states and should be discussed and settled by all states on an equal footing. The organization and procedures of the disarmament machinery should be democratized; they should be free from superpower manipulation and control and should fully reflect the demands and wishes of all states in the world.

The role of the United Nations in the field of disarmament should be strengthened. The United Nations General Assembly shall be kept informed of progress in all bilateral and multilateral disarmament negotiations. All parties to disarmament negotiations should earnestly consider and respect the recommendations and calls made by the General Assembly.

Disarmament agreements should provide for strict and effective measures of international control to ensure their effective implementation. No control or verification measure may prejudice the sovereignty and security of any state.

The people of the world should be fully informed about the intensification of the arms race between the superpowers, the increasing danger of war and the lack of progress in disarmament in order to get active mass participation in the struggle for disarmament and the defence of world peace.

Main measures

The comprehensive programme of disarmament should provide for the following main measures:

Nuclear disarmament

The ultimate aim of nuclear disarmament is the complete prohibition and total destruction of nuclear weapons and their means of delivery.

Pending agreement by the nuclear states on the non-use of nuclear weapons, all nuclear states, the two states with the largest nuclear arsenals in particular, shall unconditionally undertake not to use or threaten to use nuclear weapons against the non-nuclear-weapon states and nuclear-weapon-free zones.

The two states with the largest nuclear arsenals shall immediately stop their nuclear arms race, cease all activities aimed at improving the quality and increasing the quantity of their nuclear weapons and begin to reduce and destroy their nuclear weapons by stages. When substantial progress has been made in the destruction of their nuclear weapons, thus closing the huge gap between their nuclear arsenals and those of the other nuclear states to the satisfaction of the majority of states, the other nuclear states shall then join them in negotiations for the total destruction of nuclear weapons.

Reduction of conventional weapons

As a step preceding the reduction of conventional weapons, the two states with the largest conventional arsenals shall renounce military intervention in and threat of force against other states, both direct and indirect, withdraw all their troops stationed abroad and dismantle all their military bases on foreign soil.

The two states with the largest conventional arsenals shall first greatly reduce their conventional weapons and equipment. They can start by reducing the number of such heavy weapons as tanks, aircraft, warships and artillery. When substantial progress has been made in this regard, the other militarily significant states shall join them in reducing conventional armaments according to reasonable ratios.

Prohibition of chemical and biological weapons

All chemical and biological weapons shall be completely prohibited and totally destroyed. Pending the attainment of this goal, all states shall unequivocally undertake not to use any chemical or biological weapons.

A convention on the complete prohibition and total destruction of all chemical and biological weapons shall be negotiated and concluded as soon as possible.

Prohibition of all new weapons of mass destruction

The two superpowers shall immediately stop the research, development and production of all new weapons of mass destruction and renounce their use.

Establishment of zones of peace

At the request of the states in the region, South-East Asia should be declared a zone of peace, freedom and neutrality. All attempts by any state to seek any form of hegemony in this zone are prohibited, all foreign troops shall be withdrawn, all foreign military bases dismantled and all foreign aggression, expansion, interference and control eliminated.

The position of declaring the Indian Ocean a zone of peace should be respected by all states, the two superpowers in particular. Activities of rivalry for hegemony between the superpowers must be stopped. The independence and sovereignty of the littoral and hinterland states there should be strictly respected. There must be no military threat, aggression or expansion in any form directed against these states.

In conformity with the desire of the countries in the region, the Mediterranean should be declared a zone of peace.

Nuclear-weapon-free zones

All nuclear states shall respect the status of the nuclear-weapon-free zones and unconditionally undertake not to use or threaten to use nuclear weapons against these zones.

The status of the nuclear-free zone in Latin America shall be respected by all states.

In conformity with the common desires of the states in the respective regions, nuclear-weapon-free zones shall be established in the Middle East, Africa, South Asia, etc.

25

The disarmament process: where to begin

Robert C. Johansen
Institute for World Order, New York

Banning all nuclear tests

The purpose of a comprehensive test ban is to close completely the door on nuclear testing, a door left open in the 1963 Partial Test-Ban Treaty and the 1974 Threshold Treaty. The former allows underground tests of any size; and the latter, which is not yet ratified, permits underground weapons tests up to 150 kilotons. A treaty banning all tests, if universally accepted, would prevent additional countries from developing their own weapons. Even if only the nuclear powers ratified such a ban, it would inhibit the further sophistication of nuclear explosives for weapons purposes.

The negative consequences that would flow from not having a comprehensive nuclear test ban are more clear. Many of the non-nuclear-weapon countries which signed the 1968 nuclear Non-Proliferation Treaty (NPT) will not accept indefinitely a situation in which the nuclear powers continue to test, refine and deploy new weapons that are prohibited for non-nuclear powers. If one wants to prevent the spread of nuclear weapons to additional countries, a ban on tests in present nuclear-weapon countries is the essential place to begin.

Establishing nuclear-weapon-free zones

A nuclear-weapon-free zone protects states within a region from the potential threat posed by one of them acquiring nuclear weapons. For such a zone to be most effective, all states of an area must agree to the prohibition.

Nuclear-free zones do offer flexibility not present in the NPT. First of all, they may cover regions of the globe, such as the Indian Ocean, where no state exercises sovereignty. Second, in nuclear-weapon-free zones, states may undertake obligations they refused in the NPT. For example, in the Treaty of Tlatelolco, which prohibits nuclear weapons in the Latin American states that have ratified it, the United States and the United Kingdom both agreed not to use or to threaten to use nuclear weapons against any countries in the zone, a provision they refused to

Shortened version from an essay published by the Institute for World Order in 1977.

include in the NPT. China and France have also agreed to this provision even though they are not parties to the NPT.

The main virtue of a nuclear-weapon-free zone is to discourage non-nuclear countries within a region from acquiring nuclear weapons, and to prevent stationing, transport, or deployment of nuclear weapons by nuclear countries within the territories of signatories.

There is important political mobilizing appeal in the idea that large sections of the globe can become sanctuaries where no nuclear weapons exist and where nuclear powers commit themselves never to use nuclear weapons. A majority of states support nuclear-free zones. In recent years the United Nations General Assembly has endorsed the idea in Africa, South Asia, the Middle East, and the South Pacific. In addition, without mentioning nuclear weapons specifically, the General Assembly in 1971 declared the Indian Ocean a 'zone of peace' where foreign military deployments should be prohibited. This declaration, which has yet to be made legally binding in a treaty, received the support of China, India and Japan. France, the Soviet Union, the United Kingdom and the United States opposed it as violating the freedom of the seas.

Prohibiting tests of new missiles

A useful proposal for strategic arms limitation would be a ban on missile flight testing for vehicles with a range beyond 600 kilometres. This would prevent the development of new types of multiple warheads and the manoeuvring re-entry vehicle. Verification is possible through aerial surveillance by satellites and other means of inspection not requiring foreign inspectors on any country's territory.

Stopping the proliferation of nuclear weapons

Nuclear proliferation is widely discussed as a problem by strategic experts in the nuclear-weapon countries. It would be a mistake, however, to separate the spread of nuclear weapons to new governments from the continued possession of nuclear weapons by old members of the nuclear club. The poor and at present less powerful countries will not be inclined to give up access to nuclear weapons permanently without a reciprocal prohibition against the right of nuclear-weapon countries to retain them indefinitely. Even a universally applied comprehensive test ban would be inequitable in its political consequences unless accompanied by nuclear disarmament. In short, there is no reasonable or politically feasible means for preventing the spread of nuclear weapons to additional countries without drastic changes in the policies of the nuclear-weapon countries themselves.

The important issue here is the continued existence of nuclear weapons in any national government's hands, not the potential possession of nuclear weapons by additional governments. Although the proliferation issue is seldom viewed in this light, non-proliferation proposals become realistic and politically attractive only when combined with a broad policy of denuclearization that includes all present nuclear-weapon countries and perhaps even civil nuclear-power installations from which materials may be taken to make bombs. Indeed, the question must be raised: can an effective non-proliferation policy be decoupled from complete nuclear disarmament or from the curtailment of civilian uses of nuclear power? Despite the unbalanced obligations of the NPT for the nuclear 'haves' and 'have-nots', the overriding importance of discouraging nuclear wars is sufficient to justify continued efforts to gain universal adherence to the NPT if at the same time the nuclear-weapon countries are pressed to move towards nuclear disarmament. The latter do not favour placing the non-proliferation issue in this broader context, but the non-nuclear-weapon states generally do.

Restricting the use of nuclear weapons

The first steps towards nuclear disarmament should be aimed at the most heavily armed nuclear powers. A campaign could be initiated to call into question the right to use nuclear weapons under any circumstances. Insofar as nuclear weapons are indiscriminate in their destructive consequences, they are genocidal, and hence illegal under international law. Moreover, they threaten unfathomable destruction to the environment and to unborn generations.

As a first step toward discouraging the use of nuclear weapons, all nuclear-weapon states could be asked to accept a pledge never to launch nuclear weapons against non-nuclear-weapon countries. A second pledge could be given by all nuclear powers never to use nuclear weapons first. This might produce a national self-restraint similar to the prohibition against poisonous gas. The first commitment would help prevent the spread of nuclear weapons, while the second would help stabilize relations during a possible war between nuclear powers. These steps would also provide an incentive for non-nuclear states to sign the NPT because they would have an assurance that their security would not be undermined by their giving up the chance to obtain nuclear weapons.

A no-first-use pledge is significant because it would be a first step in the process of delegitimizing nuclear weapons in general. If taken seriously, it would immediately dampen nuclear-arms competition between the superpowers because there would be no point in developing a nuclear warfighting capability beyond a minimal deterrent—something that existed more than a decade ago. More importantly, a commitment never to be the first to use nuclear weapons is a logical prerequisite to universal commitments never to use them at all and eventually to remove them from national arsenals.

Reducing military expenditures

If nations agreed to reduce their military expenditures by a given percentage each year, this could become an effective means for disarming. At the point where annual expenditures would pass below the amount needed for simple maintenance of existing weapons, they would be effectively reduced because of obsolescence and decay. Budget cuts avoid the loopholes present in limited arms-control agreements that restrict one type of weapon while allowing new deployments of other weapons. Thus the chief virtue of this approach is that it is comprehensive and comprehensible.

269

If public pressures for budget cuts are strong enough, a programme of reductions could be begun even before the establishment of any alternative, transnational means for providing security.

Initiating general and complete disarmament

General and complete disarmament is a policy recommendation that has received little attention in recent years because it lacks sufficient support to make it appear even remotely feasible politically. This position calls for comprehensive arms reduction by all national governments, according to a specific timetable, to a minimal level consistent with the need for police forces to maintain domestic tranquillity.

Pressing consistently for general disarmament may eventually build the necessary climate of support to make it politically feasible. Although small steps toward a disarmed world appear to be politically easier to take than large ones, thirty years of negotiations of partial measures offer little hope that they will achieve a reversal of the increase in arms. Perhaps disarmament will be achieved only when it is placed in a broad political context that includes strengthening transnational means for peaceful change and security maintenance. To the extent that this is true, advocating general and complete disarmament—rather than partial steps—reminds us of the need to consider fundamental institutional change. In addition, such a posture underscores the need to measure the presently armed world against the goal of a disarmed world, rather than against small steps of arms control which, even if achieved, seem to legitimize the weapons that remain.

Establishing a transnational peace force

Reducing national arms to the minimal level necessary for maintaining internal order probably cannot be achieved without constructing some alternative mechanisms for protecting security. Thus the creation of a permanent transnational peace force, individually recruited and responsible to a global authority, takes on genuine importance. Even though a disarmed world lies some distance in the future, it would be useful to begin the incremental process of legitimizing a transnational force as soon as possible.

Establishing a United Nations centre for analysis and monitoring of disarmament

Since the obligations eventually established for achieving disarmament must be universally applied and impartially verified, only a global agency can adequately and authoritatively perform this task. The necessary monitoring function could be given to an expanded and strengthened Disarmament Centre within the United Nations Secretariat. It could supplement the efforts of existing private and governmental agencies by providing global assessments of present arms trends and suggesting areas for arms reductions, as well as monitoring disarmament agreements. The sooner that such an agency begins to operate, even if by inspecting existing arms-control agreements that are bilateral or regional in scope, the more likely that such an agency will gain the experience and legitimacy necessary in time to facilitate and monitor more comprehensive arms reductions among all states.

26

The international law of arms control and disarmament

Bert V. A. Röling
Professor of International
Law and Polemology

The function of national armed forces

Because of the emergence of atomic weaponry, Albert Einstein and Bertrand Russell declared in their famous Manifesto, issued in London on 9 July 1955: 'We have to learn to think in a new way.'

'To think in a new way', first, with respect to weaponry, with respect to the function of national armed power.[1] The advent of atomic weapons and rocketry has confronted us with a paradoxical dilemma: technology gave birth to weapons which cannot be used at least between nuclear powers because their use would mean mutual destruction. Limited wars between such powers might easily escalate to nuclear war, and tactical nuclear warfare might escalate into strategic nuclear war. But the consequences of the use of strategic weapons—the 'central systems' in the United States and the Soviet Union—are so destructive[2] that the superpowers will not dare activate them. Reasonably speaking, they neutralize each other.[3] They no longer deter war, but do deter the use of the strategic central systems.

War between a nuclear power and a non-nuclear-weapon state is still thinkable—for example, a war between one of the superpowers and a Third World country. But there exist high risks, indeed macro-risks, that such a war would draw the other superpower into the conflict. Even wars between Third World states risk involving the nuclear powers. According to Karl Deutsch, war has become the privilege of the underdeveloped and poor states.[4] But he neglects the tendency of the great powers to intervene. The research concerning those Third World conflicts has shown that, in most cases, the great powers have been involved.[5]

Because of the introduction of nuclear weapons, conflicts, wherever they may take place, must not be resolved by war. That was the main conclusion of the Einstein-Russell manifesto. Weapons have become unusable. But until mutual disarmament is achieved, armed power is still indispensable. One-sided, unilateral disarmament would make the weapons of the other party usable again. We have to face the dilemma of unusable but indispensable weapons.

What is the function of national armed power in such a situation? Historically, armed power has had an acquisitive function: conquest through war, or the extraction of concessions by threat of war, the latter now called 'coercive diplomacy'.[6] The acquisitive function also characterizes the military role in a 'total strategy' or *stratégie d'ensemble*: conquering by economic or ideological means, and defending the newly won interests against possible military action of the injured party by deterring such action.[7]

It seems to me that in the age of unusable weapons it is no longer reasonable to use weapon power for acquisitive aims. The macro-risks involved are too high. Since modern technology has made defence, at least between nuclear powers, almost impossible, the use of the weapons would destroy what was to be defended—the only rational function of armed power is negating: in a word, deterrence. It means that a country is willing and able to resist attack. If a country does not have this will and this capacity (whether or not in combination with other countries), it is more or less at the mercy of every powerful neighbour. It must make concessions to maintain the peace. 'Coercive diplomacy' may compel it to do so. Blainey[8] correctly stated that a balance of power is not a precondition of peace but of independence.

If the function of national military power is considered to be a negating function—aimed at preventing damage to our interests—a distinction must be drawn as to the means by which these interests can be violated. The term 'military security' is used to indicate a nation's security, peace and independence with respect to the military might of an opponent. But national interests can be damaged by other means such as economic or ideological action. In this instance the function of national armed power would be to forestall 'indirect aggression' or to take military action if that deterrence failed. The establishment of the American 'rapid deployment forces' is an example of the former, the Soviet action in Afghanistan of the latter.

One very disturbing feature of our times is that providing for 'economic security' or 'ideological security' is considered a military responsibility. It is disturbing because the great powers have become vulnerable: the United States particularly in the economic field, because of growing economic interdependence (which for the United States means dependence on raw materials, especially oil, in other countries), the Soviet Union in the ideological field because of religious revivals such as the Muslim renaissance and the growing demands for political freedom in Eastern Europe.

Rationally speaking, the unusability of armed power should lead to the restriction of the military function to what is absolutely indispensable, and the conclusion should be that national armed power can be no longer considered an instrument for the preservation of economic or ideological security. The function of deterring damaging non-violent action through the threat of the use of force can no longer be regarded as a reasonable weapon function in the hands of national states. The only reasonable function of the military is to provide for 'military security'. 'Peace is our profession', now the motto of the American Strategic Air Command, expresses what should be considered the real aim of the military profession: preventing the use of force.

Prohibition of the use of force

The only reasonable function of national armed power appears to be also its only legitimate function. According to Article 51 of the United Nations Charter, the use of armed force in self-defence is allowed only in case of armed attack, and even in that case only as long as the Security Council has been unable to take effective measures. Article 2, paragraph 4, forbids the use of force and the threat of the use of force. The view of the Charter is clear; it amounts to the prohibition of the first use of national military power. This view is also stressed by the definition of aggression, adopted on 14 December 1974 by the General Assembly (Res. 3314 [XXIX]). Article 5, sub-paragraph 1 of that definition expressly states: 'No consideration of whatever nature, whether political, economic, military or otherwise, may serve as a justification of aggression'.[9]

This strict interpretation has been rejected by many scholars.[10] The traditional view that armed power has a function in the case of violation of so-called 'vital interests' prevails in many circles. According to that view 'armed attack' is one of several means of legitimate self-defence. But the ban on the use of force loses its meaning if every state is allowed to use armed force when convinced that its vital interests are endangered. Some lawyers go so far as to maintain that 'the extreme coercion of the concerted oil measures probably constituted a threat or use of force, forbidden by Article 2, paragraph 4 of the UN Charter'.[11]

General acceptance of the crucial United Nations principle concerning the use of force is blocked not only by interpretations of the Charter that run counter to its history, its wording and its purpose. This basic tenet is also undermined by proposals or treaties which seem to assume that a general prohibition of the use of force does not yet exist. In the Declaration of the States Parties to the Warsaw Treaty,[12] it is proposed to initiate 'negotiations on the following urgently needed measures to stop the arms race and avert the threat of war'. One of these measures is the 'conclusion of a world treaty on the non-use of force'. But such a treaty would make sense only if there were no treaty forbidding the use of force! Such a treaty does exist—the Charter, the most important treaty, which takes precedence over every other treaty that might conflict with it (Article 103).

There exist other treaties with provisions that implicitly refute the general rule prohibiting the use of force. According to the American-Soviet Agreement on the Prevention of Nuclear War (22 June 1973) 'each party will refrain from the threat or use of force against the other party, against the allies of the other party and against other countries in circumstances which may endanger international peace and security'. Does this mean that the threat or use of force is allowed in circumstances which do not endanger international peace and security? It seems to me that sloppy drafting is the explanation of this confusing text. Such proposals and treaties, however, cannot change the existence of the provision of the Charter. The legal situation with respect to the use of national armed force is clear.

To rely on law in arguments concerning international relations is at best a precarious business. Law is only one of the factors which play a role in determining the actions of nations, and it is not the strongest one. But we must not forget that the fate of our culture, if not humanity, rests on the validity of the prohibition of the use of force. This ban is not a luxury which makes life more tranquil or pleasant. It is the precondition of life itself. It is a rule which follows directly from the present weapon dilemma: that our weapons are unusable but still indispensable. The prohibition of the first use of force is the logical consequence of that dilemma.

Role of international law

As law plays only a relative role in international relations, a legal prohibition of the use of force is not enough. States have no confidence that other states will always respect the prohibition, hence the build-up of national military strength. The right to possess arms has always been one of the principal prerogatives of sovereignty. In traditional international law this right was unlimited. Proposals concerning disarmament, such as those put forward at the Hague peace conferences, came to naught. After the First World War, reduction of national armaments was considered a condition of peace (Covenant of the League of Nations, Article 8), and Germany was disarmed *en vue de rendre possible la préparation d'une limitation générale des armements de toutes les nations* (Treaty of Versailles, Part V, Preamble). After the Second World War, too, the rights of the vanquished to possess arms were restricted. In most peace treaties the possession of A-, B- and C-weapons was prohibited.

In the inter-bellum only one treaty concerning arms control, the Washington Treaty of 1922, was concluded. After the Second World War the concept of arms control and disarmament came to the fore. Numerous negotiations took place and some treaties were concluded. A treaty of 1972 prohibits the possession of biological weapons. Non-nuclear weapon states, parties to the Non-Proliferation Treaty (1968) and parties to the Tlatelolco Treaty (1967), are forbidden to obtain and possess nuclear weapons. The United States and the USSR are forbidden, by the SALT I ABM Treaty, to build up an effective ABM.

Weapon freedom may be restricted by treaty provisions forbidding possession of more than a specified number of weapons of a specific kind. SALT I restricts the quantity of offensive ballistic missiles (the 'central systems'). Other treaties forbid the placement of weapons in specific regions (Antarctica, 1959, Outer Space 1967, the Sea-Bed 1971). The Convention on the Prohibition of Military or Any Other Hostile Use of Environmental Modification Techniques (ENMOD), which came into force in October 1978, forbids in advance the possession of specific kinds of weapons which do not yet exist.

States that adhere to such treaties may then be said to have recognized the rule that 'the right of states to possess arms is not unlimited'. But treaties are binding only on the states which have ratified them. However, treaties can be denounced. Consequently, progressive development of international law should lead to the basic rule which limits this traditional right of states.[13]

If the only legitimate function of national armed power is to deter other states from using their armed power, then the logical consequence would be that the possession of arms which can perform illegitimate functions should be forbidden. Missions or functions of national armed power, describing the specific tasks for which military capabilities can be used, should be made the primary focus of agreement. Some capabilities, such as launching a disarming pre-emptive first strike or a successful surprise attack, should be forbidden by treaty.[14] The logical consequence of the ban on the use of force, except to resist armed attack, is a further ban on the possession of offensive arms. In this respect the distinction between offensive and defensive weapons and weapon systems will take on a new meaning. This distinction has specific significance with respect to the premeditated war—war as defined by von Clausewitz, the continuation of national policy by military means.

Another type of war exists: the inadvertent, accidental war. This is a concept of fundamental significance in the era of unusable weapons. Because this kind of war stems from misperception, miscalculation or a local crisis, another weapon distinction deserves attention: the distinction between stabilizing and destabilizing weapon systems.

The Einstein-Russell manifesto recognized that 'the abolition of war will demand distasteful limitations of national sovereignty'. One of these undoubtedly is the restriction of national weapon freedom. A new chapter of international law concerning the law of arms control and disarmament should be added to the existing limitations of national sovereignty. Such a set of all-embracing rules could only gradually be established. The development might start with the formulation of guiding principles for disarmament negotiations, based on the concept of the functional approach. A beginning might be made with guidelines for the prevention of new offensive or destabilizing weapon systems. Gradually, we might reach the stage at which the guiding principle would be the ban on the possession of excessive armaments.[15] From these guidelines, rules concerning the legitimate possession of armed power should be formulated, based on the principle that the possession of arms designed for illegitimate functions is forbidden.

It is amazing that the Special Session of the General Assembly Devoted to Disarmament paid so little attention to the role of international law in this field. In its Final Document the function of law is slighted. Some guidelines are formulated, especially concerning 'the right of every state to security'. 'At each stage [of disarmament] the objective should be undiminished security at the lowest possible level of armaments and military forces' (para. 29).[16] But no link is recognized between the legitimate function of national military power—the right to use the national armed forces, on the one hand, and on the other the restriction of national weapon freedom to the right to possess national armed forces. The former should condition the latter. Unesco, in this respect, has gone further than the United Nations. Peace experts, meeting on the occasion of the Pope's visit to Unesco in June 1980, stressed the need for a new chapter of international law concerning arms control and disarmament. They solemnly declared: 'We affirm as a consequence of the prohibition of war, that the right of states to arm is not unlimited and that the restrictions of this right should be developed under a new branch of international law.'

Mission of small countries

Arms control and disarmament are a must that we all recognize. But we also know that thirty-five years of negotiations have failed to produce significant results.

Who is to blame for this disastrous failure? According to Alva Myrdal, the main responsibility rests on the superpowers, who have dominated the negotiations. She suggests that they were unwilling to engage in genuine disarmament; it would touch upon their superpower status. Their agreements are instead aimed at 'balancing' each other, at preventing either from becoming superior, especially with respect to obtaining a disarming first-strike capability. Their other dominant interest is the maintenance of their power-distance relative to the rest of the world.[17] She also blames the smaller states: 'all nations sin by their silence on the madness of the arms race and by participating in the militarization of the world in their humble way'.[18]

But it cannot be denied that the world, the vast majority of states, is becoming impatient. The Special Session of the General Assembly Devoted to Disarmament was one of the first symptoms of that impatience. The smaller nations requested the session and are largely responsible for its Final Document, which establishes an institutional framework for continued discussion in which these very nations can play a role. They want to raise their voices because they will be the first victims if a war should occur.

In those discussions, guidelines should be developed for arms-control negotiations, guidelines prohibiting offensive-weapon systems and destabilizing innovations which put a premium on haste—systems which might induce states to initiate hostilities (such as a disarming first-strike capability) or to escalate the fighting (as would be the case, for instance, with the Euro-strategic weapons).

The General Assembly is not a world legislature. It cannot establish binding rules. But its resolutions can gradually change the moral climate in the world. This has happened with respect to decolonization, to the universal applicability of human rights, to the new international economic order—all areas in which its resolutions played a role in changing attitudes. Its guidelines can buttress the action of disarmament movements in every state and thereby have great influence.

It seems to me that the small nations of the world have a historic mission in this field.

They should assert their right to participate in world affairs, be it in the General Assembly or in a European security conference. This amounts to an appeal to the small partners in military alliances and to non-aligned and neutral countries. The great exhortation of the nineteenth century to the powerless may be revived in a new form: 'Nuclear proletarians of the world, unite!'

Let there be no misunderstanding. This is not a plea for dissolving NATO or the Warsaw Pact. These alliances have an indispensable function. They contributed in the past to the Cold War climate and to the arms race. Their historical function now is to be instruments of détente and effective arms control. But to achieve just that, the smaller partners must become active in that direction.

Military security and weapon security

Until the present, negotiations have approached the disarmament problem from its periphery, so to speak, concentrating on quantities of manpower or of specific weapons. Negotiations were based on the distinction between categories of weapons. But the systemic innovations brought about by technology have blurred these distinctions and led to what was called 'a conceptual crisis in disarmament doctrine'. Existing categories, on which negotiations were based, proved to be obsolete.[19] Bertram suggested that a new approach was needed, based on the mission of weapons and weapon systems, 'missions' being understood as 'the specific tasks to which military capabilities can be put'. It is these missions or functions that should be made the primary focus of agreement.

277

If a link is established between the only legitimate function of national armed power—the neutralization of the armed power of the possible opponent—and the rights of a state to possess arms, the question arises: 'How much is enough?' The prevailing military answer might well be: 'So much that we can win the war.' It means that striving for superiority which is now so evident. The correct answer should be: 'So much that the war will not occur.' A 'calculated inferiority' is then sufficient—less weaponry and weaponry of another kind. The calculation concerning the desirable degree of inferiority should be based on the concept of non-offensive deterrence:[20] an armed power which is visibly incapable of attack and conquest, but offers the deterring prospect of formidable resistance in case of foreign aggression.

In this respect the distinction between 'military security' and 'weapon security' may clarify the issue. Military security is security with respect to the use of armed power by a possible opponent. It concerns fear of 'the Russians', 'the Americans', 'the Germans', 'the Chinese'. Sufficient deterring power provides for this security.

'Weapon security' has to do with the danger inherent in the weapon situation, the danger stemming from the weapons themselves. If, for instance, both superpowers had a 'disarming first-strike capability', war would be inevitable, human nature being what it is. 'Weapon security' does not concern only a bilateral relationship. The impact of the ongoing arms race on the global weapon situation cannot be ignored: the local arms races, the proliferation of nuclear weapons. It seems to me that the arms race, especially the technological arms race, that has gone on for decades has brought us to a point at which 'the weapons' are more to be feared than 'the Russians' or 'the Americans'.

A strategy of non-offensive deterrence would provide for 'military security', but, at the same time, would have a considerable—and very favourable—impact on 'weapon security'. Adoption of that strategy by both superpowers and both military alliances would open the road to real disarmament, to elimination of the existing overkill, to abolition of the destabilizing weapon systems which at present endanger peace.

Non-offensive deterrence: the European theatre

A final observation: the superpowers will probably refuse, for the time being, to adopt a strategy of non-offensive deterrence. It is incompatible with their global military imperial policy, especially with their intention to react globally with military means to economic challenges and ideological developments. A special advantage of the strategy of non-offensive deterrence is the possibility of its local application. The strategy might be tried out in Europe, where borders are recognized and where the main policy aim of both blocks is to prevent a military confrontation. A European security conference might consider the feasibility of non-offensive deterrence in the European theatre. In so doing, the most threatened continent might show the way by which the world could solve its weapon dilemma. Here also it may be the historic mission of the smaller states—the smaller members of the alliances, the non-aligned and neutral European states—to bring about a fundamental transformation in NATO and the Warsaw Pact—from products of the Cold War to instruments of détente and disarmament.

Notes

1. I leave aside the domestic function of military power, related to domestic safety, and the United Nations function of national military power in a system of collective security or as part of United Nations peace-keeping forces.
2. See the report of the Office of Technology Assessment to the American Congress: *The Effects of Nuclear War*, published in book form by Croom Helm, London, 1980.
3. This was clearly stated by Henry Kissinger in his Brussels speech, September 1979: 'The Future of NATO', *Washington Quarterly*, Autumn 1979, Vol. II, No. 4, pp. 3–17, and more or less confirmed by Brezhnev's speech in Berlin the same year.
4. Karl W. Deutsch, 'Der Stand der Kriegsursachenforschung', *DGKF-Hefte* (Bonn), No. 2, 1973, p. 20.
5. See Istvan Kende, '116 Wars in 30 Years', in Carlton and Schaerf (eds.), *Arms Control and Technological Innovation*, pp. 303–21, London, Croom Helm, 1977.
6. The name was coined by Thomas W. Schelling, *Arms and Influence*, Yale University Press, 1966. He wrote frankly: 'The power to hurt is bargaining power. To exploit it is diplomacy—vicious diplomacy, but diplomacy' (p. 2).
7. The *stratégie totale* was developed by the French general André Beaufre. In his *Stratégie de l'action* (Paris, 1966), he considers this strategy *'la stratégie de l'avenir'* (p. 128). It was applied to the European situation by Franz Joseph Strauss. Strauss aims at a United Europe extending to the borders of the Soviet Union. The 'satellite states' should be seduced into coming over to the West by the latter's wealth and liberty. The military might of a united Western Europe—*'die Kraft eines integrierten Grossraumes'*—should be great enough to deter the Soviet Union from militarily retaking what it lost in a non-military manner, as it did in 1968. See his *Herausforderung und Antwort*, Stuttgart, 1968.
8. Geoffrey Blainey, ('The Abacus of Power', *The Causes of War*, pp. 108–26, Macmillan, 1973, Book II, Chapter 8) maintains that if a country is aware of its inferior power position, it will prefer to give in to the demands of its more powerful neighbour rather than fight and lose.
9. For further elaboration of the legal situation concerning the prohibition of the use of force, I may refer to my publications: 'Aspects of the Ban on Force', in 'Essays on International Law and Relations in Honour of A. J. P. Tammes', *Netherlands International Law Review* (Special Issue), 1977, pp. 242–59, and 'Die Definition der Aggression', *Recht im Dienst des Friedens*, pp. 387–403, Festschrift für Eberhard Menzel, Berlin, Dunker & Humblot, 1976.
10. See Yehuda Melzer, *Concepts of Just War*, Leiden, Sijthoff, 1975; D.N. Bowett, *Self Defence in International Law*, New York, Praeger, 1958, who states: 'The cases in which self-defence would justify the use of force against a delict not involving force would be extremely rare' (p. 110). The traditional opinion is clearly expressed in Martin Wright, *Power Politics*, edited by Hedley Bull and Carsten Holbread, Pelican Books, 1979: 'Powers will continue to seek security without reference to justice, and to pursue their vital interests irrespective of common interests' (p. 293). For the interpretation of the Charter provisions, as given in the text, with extensive argumentation, see Jan Brownlie, *International Law and the Use of Force by States*, Clarendon Press, 1963, which concludes: 'Threats to security not involving the use of force do not justify forcible measures of self-defence' (p. 433); and Michael Akehurst, *A Modern Introduction to International Law*, 3rd ed., pp. 240–51, London, 1980.
11. So Julius Stone in his 'Israel, the United Nations and International Law. Memorandum of Law', submitted to the Security Council (A 35–316. S. 14045 of 3 July 1980, para. 22). In his 'Force and the Charter in the Seventies', *Syracuse Journal of International Law and Commerce*, 1974, pp. 1–17, Stone confronts the vulgar understanding 'about a new era' in which all threat or use of force between states is virtually outlawed as an instrument of policy with 'the actualities that the threat or use of force continues to be a main instrument of policy between states'.
12. Transmitted to the United Nations, 19 May 1980 (Dec. A. 35–237. S. 13948).
13. The ground rule with respect to the *use* of weapons in an armed conflict is to be found in Article 22 of the Hague Rules: 'The right of belligerents to adopt means of injuring the enemy is not unlimited.'
14. According to the 'Joint Statement of Principles and Basic Guidelines for Subsequent Negotiations on the Limitation of Strategic Arms', signed at Vienna, 18 June 1979, by Carter and Brezhnev, 'the parties will continue, for the purposes of reducing and averting the risk of outbreak of nuclear war, to seek measures to strengthen strategic stability by, among other things, limitations on strategic

offensive arms most destabilizing to the strategic balance and by measures to reduce and to avert the risk of surprise attack'.

15. In this respect it is worth while to consider that the concept of disproportionate or excessive damage was accepted as a valid criterium for legal prohibitions in Protocol I to the four Red Cross Conventions of 1949.

16. The same thought is expressed in paras. 1, 19, 22, 29, 49, 50, 82 and 83.

17. Alva Myrdal, *The Game of Disarmament, How the United States and Russia Run the Arms Race*, New York, Pantheon Books, 1976, p. 22 et seq.

18. Ibid., p. 318.

19. Compare Christoph Bertram, *The Future of Arms Control. II: Arms Control and Technological Change: Elements of a New Approach*, London, IISS, 1978. (Adelphi Papers, No. 146.) In an earlier Adelphi Pape (No. 126, 1976), 'New Weapons Technologies, Debate and Directions', Richart Burt came to the conclusion: 'To be effective against a background of the vertical and horizontal proliferation of new technologies in the 1980s arms control may have to shift away from controlling delivery vehicles numbers towards mutual understandings about the deployment and operational use of the new systems' (p. 32).

20. For further elaboration of this concept, see: Horst Mendershausen, *Inoffensive Deterrence*, Santa Monica, Rand Corporation, 1975; and Bert V. A. Röling, 'Feasibility of Inoffensive Deterrence', *Bulletin of Peace Proposals* (Oslo), Vol. 9, No. 4, 1978, pp. 339–47.

Part VI.   Some alternative peace strategies

27

Graduated and reciprocated initiatives in tension-reduction (GRIT)

Charles E. Osgood
University of Illinois, United States of America

My own area of specialization has been, broadly speaking, in the area of human communication, and my research has been, at the macro-level, on how nations perceive each other's intentions and mutually create escalations and de-escalations of conflicts. The focus of my concern at the inter-nation level has been the rationalization of a strategy alternative whose technical name is *graduated and reciprocated initiatives in tension-reduction*. While doodling at a conference in the early 1960s, I discovered that the initials of this mind-boggling phrase spelled GRIT—and, although I generally take a dim view of acronyms, this one not only was easy for people to remember but also suggested the kind of determination and patience required to successfully apply it. I will outline the general nature and rationale of this strategy.

General nature and rationale of GRIT

GRIT is a form of calculated de-escalation of tensions. It is the mirror-image of calculated escalation of tensions—described by Herman Kahn (1965) as 'a competition in resolve' and 'a competition in risk-taking' designed to push an opponent beyond his risk ceiling before we reach ours. Calculated escalation has four salient features: first, the steps are unilaterally initiated (we did not negotiate with the North Vietnamese about increasing the tempo of our bombing or moving it closer to Hanoi, we simply did it); second, each such step propels the opponent into reciprocating if he can, with more aggressive steps of his own (development of multiple nuclear warheads propels the Soviet Union into analogous developments); third, such steps are necessarily graduated in nature—by the unpredictability of technological breakthroughs, by limitations imposed by logistics, and by the oscillating level of perceived threat. But calculated escalation is obviously a tension-increasing process, the termination of which is a military resolution (victory, defeat or, in our time, even mutual annihilation).

Shortened version of 'GRIT for MBFR: A Proposal for Unfreezing Force-level Postures in Europe'—an expansion of testimony given before the Sub-committee on Europe of the House Committee on Foreign Affairs, 23 June, 1973.

Grit: Tension re-duction to cure [handwritten]

Charles E. Osgood

tension in duction [handwritten]

⎧ If we change this last feature—shift it from tension-induction to tension-⎫
⎩reduction—we have the essence of GRIT as a strategy in conflict situations. It is⎭
one in which nation A devises patterns of small steps, well within its own limits of
security, designed to reduce tensions and induce reciprocating steps from nation B.
If such unilateral initiatives are persistently applied, and reciprocation is obtained,
then the margin for risk-taking is widened and somewhat larger steps can be
taken. Both sides, in effect, begin edging down the escalation ladder, and both are
moving, within what they perceive as reasonable limits of national security,
towards a political rather than a military resolution. Needless to say, successful
application of such a strategy assumes that both parties to a conflict have strong
motives for getting out of it. ← *motives of mutual enlightened intrest* [handwritten]

One of the aims of GRIT is to reduce and control international tension levels.
Another is to create an atmosphere of mutual trust within which negotiations on
critical military and political issues can have a better chance of succeeding; in other
words, GRIT is not a substitute for the more familiar process of negotiation, but
rather a facilitative, parallel process. Yet another aim of GRIT is to enable a nation
to take the initiative in a situation where an unsatisfactory status quo has become
frozen—which is precisely the situation in Europe today as far as the confrontation of the military forces of East and West is concerned. And I might add one
other aim of GRIT: it is, I believe, a kind of inter-nation behaviour that is
appropriate in a nuclear age—when the use of calculated escalation may be an
open invitation to mutual disaster.

However, being unconventional an international affairs, the GRIT strategy is
open to suspicion abroad and resistance at home. Therefore, it is necessary to spell
out the ground-rules under which this particular 'game' should be played and
demonstrate how national security can be maintained during the process, how the
likelihood of reciprocation can be maximized, and how the genuineness of
initiations and reciprocations can be evaluated. These 'rules' are spelt out in detail
in *An Alternative to War or Surrender* (Osgood, 1962) and applied to the
Vietnamese and Chinese situations in *Perspective in Foreign Policy* (Osgood,
1966). At this point I will merely list some guidelines for applying GRIT to a
conflict situation.

Maintaining security

The question here is whether reasonable margins of security can be maintained
while at the same time risking enough of it by degrees to induce reciprocation from
an opponent. Although I would be the first to agree that mutual nuclear deterrence
does not provide any real security in the long run, it does provide a temporary
shield under which moderate risks can be taken.

1. *Unilateral initiatives must not reduce our capacity to inflict unacceptable
   nuclear retaliation should we be attacked at that level.* However, deliberate
   (and necessarily 'surprise') nuclear attack by one superpower upon another is
   most unlikely, given the near-certainty of devastating retaliation. Therefore:
2. *Unilateral initiatives must not cripple our capacity to meet conventional
   aggression with appropriately graded responses using conventional weapons.*
   These two capacities on both sides define the balance, or status quo, at any
   given point in time; but it is a status quo susceptible to modification in absolute

level. However, changes in level should not abruptly destabilize the balance.

3. *Unilateral initiatives must be graduated in risk according to the degree of reciprocation obtained from an opponent.* This is the essential self-regulating (feedback) characteristic of GRIT. The relative risk remains roughly constant throughout the process. In order to keep applying pressure upon an opponent to reciprocate, and yet not weaken ourselves progressively in any one area:

4. *Unilateral initiatives should be diversified in nature, both as regards sphere of action and geographical locus of application.* This also provides for maximum flexibility in applying GRIT.

Inducing reciprocation

GRIT strategy presupposes that the opponents in any conflict have certain motives, whether shared or not, for avoiding the consequences of escalating it—if nothing more than the costs in human lives and fortunes. However, given the mutual perceptions of threat that the conflict has already generated, the major factor determining the success or failure of GRIT is the sophistication with which we utilize what we think we know about human nature in the execution of this strategy. This is where all that the behavioural and social sciences can tell us should be brought to bear—but, being comparatively youthful sciences, what they can tell us with assurance is not as much as would be desired. Since it is by no means obvious to the other party, particularly in the early stages, that our initiatives are other than ploys in a cold war:

1. *Unilateral initiatives must be designed and communicated so as to emphasize a sincere intent to reduce tensions.* In this connection, 'atmosphere-setting' public statements by the heads of state involved, including explicit outlining of the tension-reducing policy, are advisable. Since it is important that the opponent has time to evaluate the significance of our initiatives and the advantages (or disadvantages) of reciprocating:

2. *Unilateral initiatives should be publicly announced at some reasonable interval prior to their execution and identified as part of a deliberate policy of reducing tensions.* This also minimizes the potentially unstabilizing effects of unexpected unilateral moves, and it can influence interpretation of our actions when they come. Further, without specifying the exact form or magnitude:

3. *Unilateral initiatives should include in their announcement explicit invitation to reciprocation in some form.*

These three rules have a cumulative value in enlisting pressures of world opinion on the side of continuing participation in the de-escalating of tensions.

[handwritten margin note: 3 rules of GRIT]

Demonstrating and evaluating the genuineness of initiatives and reciprocations

From the beginning of the GRIT process, evaluation of the genuineness of the moves of the opponent is steadily going on on both sides. And, of course, once the process is well under way, the distinction between who is 'initiator' and who is 'reciprocator' tends to become blurred. Thus the factors influencing evaluation of unilateral actions apply to both parties. Since initiatives are liable to the charge of 'propaganda', particularly in the early stages:

1. *Unilateral initiatives that have been announced must be executed on schedule*

285

regardless of any prior commitments to reciprocate by the opponent. Observed commission of the promised action is strong evidence for the genuineness of the intent. Unlike traditional bargaining and negotiating procedures, GRIT substitutes *post* commitment (via reciprocation) for *prior* commitment, thereby breaking the chains of mutual-agreement-before-action and freeing both sides for taking the initiative. However, because early actions necessarily entail low risk, and therefore may often have low apparent significance:

2. *Unilateral initiatives should be continued over a considerable period, regardless of the degree or absence of reciprocation.* Like the steady pounding of a nail, pressure towards reciprocating builds up as announced act follows announced act of a tension-reducing nature, even though the individual acts may be small in magnitude. However, to contribute to a cumulation of pressure:

3. *Unilateral initiatives must be as unambiguous and as susceptible to verification as possible.* Although overt deeds are also liable to misinterpretation, actions still speak louder than words.

A few questions and answers

I will conclude by trying to answer some of the questions that are most often put to me when I talk about GRIT. But in doing so I will have to question some of the traditionally unquestioned assumptions made about national defence (Osgood, 1963). GRIT is an attempt to apply in international relations some of the principles of communication and learning that have been found to hold in interpersonal relations—where the communication is more by deeds than by words and where what is learned is mutual understanding, trust and respect.

The rules we want any opponent to learn are these: (a) if he tries to change an unsatisfactory existing status quo by force, we will firmly resist and restore the status quo; (b) if he tries to change the status quo by means which reduce tensions, we will reward him by steps having similar intent; (c) if he tries to take advantage of our conciliatory initiatives, we will shift immediately to firm and punishing resistance; (d) if, on the other hand, he reciprocates our initiatives with steps of his own having similar intent, we will reward him with somewhat larger steps designed to reduce tensions.

My colleagues in psychology would recognize this strategy as the familiar process of deliberately shaping behaviour. Needless to say, we have to practise what we preach—follow the same rules—if we expect others to learn them. Since the existing status quo is reasonably stable and clear in Europe, it would seem to be a good place in which to try out such a mutual learning process. But the novelty of the GRIT process raises shrieks of incredulity from hawks, and clucks of worry even from doves. Here are some of the questions I am most often asked.

What reason do you have to believe that your 'rules'—which you admit are anchored in individual behaviour—would apply to the 'behaviour' of nations? It is certainly true that nations are not individuals, physically or behaviourally. In only the grossest use of analogy does a nation have an integrated communication system that organizes its activities the way the human nervous system does. And the nation, given all of its interest groups competing to influence policy, would have to be treated as a case of split (indeed, multiple) personality. Nevertheless, political scientist Karl Deutsch was able to write a book entitled *The Nerves of Government* (1963) which explores even this gross analogy fruitfully.

But the critical point is that the decision-making of nations is a distillation of the thinking of individual human minds, and GRIT is designed to influence how individuals in nations think about people in other nations in terms of their likely attitudes and motives. The mass media, of course, facilitate this process. Applicability of principles of interpersonal behaviour is further enhanced by the fact that individuals in nations do tend to think about nations in human terms—i.e. tend to personify them—and this includes statesmen and political scientists, as even a casual reading of the literature on international relations will testify. Nations are identified with personal pronouns (we, they and even him in the military jargon); relations between nations are described with interpersonal verbs (nation A trusts, aids, confronts or threatens nation B); and even purely human mental states are attributed to nations (which can have motives, attitudes, emotions and intentions). It therefore seems reasonable to apply the principles of interpersonal behaviour to international behaviour—and by so doing, try to influence the latter by operating on the former.

Wouldn't any conciliatory gestures on our part destroy the credibility of our resolve and invite further aggression? The usually unquestioned assumption being made here is that the opponent shares our own perception of ourselves as being peaceful in intent, and therefore his blustering words, his military build-ups, and so on *must* be based on aggressiveness rather than on fear. How can *they* be afraid of peaceful, benignly intentioned *us*? From such reasoning it follows that we must maintain a threatening image of ourselves, lest we be taken advantage of. But there are two ways of creating and preserving credibility. Maintaining a stance of implacable hostility is one way; it is consistent with an escalation strategy, and it is what we find practised between rival gangs in our city ghettos. Maintaining a stance of firmness but potential co-operation is another way; this is consistent with a de-escalation strategy, and it is the way police have found most effective in deterring juvenile delinquency.

Calculated de-escalation employs both the 'stick' and the 'carrot'—not as threats and promises, but as precise responses to aggressive or conciliatory actions by the opponent. At each stage we retain appropriately graded nuclear and conventional forces to resist effectively military escalation by an opponent. But we think of these capabilities not simply as a deterrent but rather as a security base from which to take calculated steps towards a political resolution of the conflict. If any opponent misinterprets our initiatives as a sign of weakness, and makes an aggressive probe to test his interpretation—as the Soviets did in Cuba after the Bay of Pigs fiasco—then we shift promptly to the 'stick'. We resist firmly, and punishingly if necessary, but calculatedly, applying precisely that level of force required to restore the status quo existing prior to his aggression. We do not ourselves escalate beyond this level, and, while applying the 'stick', we keep communicating that our intent is explicitly to restore the prior status quo (i.e. that there has been no shift in our basic policy).

Such probes—if they occur on a tentative basis (which is likely, given the nuclear possibility in the background)—can provide a most effective kind of learning experience for both parties to the conflict. I have reason to believe that this was precisely what happened in the Cuban missile crisis: the naval blockade of Cuba was a level-of-force action appropriate to the intensity of the Soviet probe; it indicated firmness of intent and was accompanied by a demand (appropriate when using the 'stick') that the missiles be removed; when Khrushchev began dismantling and removing the missiles (a process which we could verify, by the way), Kennedy praised him for his dedication to world peace; and the 'Experiment' began in the summer of the next year.

One can imagine similar scenarios in the European theatre, should GRIT be applied—for example, a Soviet probe into Thrace—and hopefully a similarly calculated response sequence that could be used to restore the status quo without shifting de-escalation into a new spiral of escalation. If my assumption about fear rather than aggression being the prime mover in the confrontation with the Soviet Union is correct, then the prior application of GRIT strategy should reduce Soviet threat perceptions, and hence their felt need for aggressive probing.

Doesn't GRIT strategy require that goodwill already exist between the parties in conflict if it is to succeed? Not at all. What is required is sufficient self-interest on both sides. I have tried to demonstrate that in the European situation there exist both shared and unique motivations towards reducing military forces for all parties. If opponents in a conflict situation can be induced, because of their own self-interest, to keep on behaving *as if* they believed and trusted each other, then a general psychological principle of congruence between acting and believing will cause their beliefs to fall in line with their acts. In other words, mutual goodwill can literally be created in the service of mutual self-interest.

Doesn't any novel approach like this involve too much risk? Anything we do in the nuclear age means taking risks. Escalating conflicts which involve, directly (as in Europe) or even indirectly (as in the Middle East), another nuclear power unquestionably carry the greatest risk. Simply doing nothing—remaining frozen in a status quo that is already at much too high a level of force and tension—is certainly not without risk in the long run. And surrender, whether by abrupt withdrawals that presage a new period of isolationism or by 'the instalment plan', would eliminate our influence on the future, unstabilize the present political situation, and ultimately threaten our own way of life.

GRIT also involves risk. But if carefully planned, the risking comes in small packages and, in a sense, carries insurance by virtue of the nuclear and graded conventional capabilities we retain throughout the process. But what if—given the gap between our technological know-how and our know-how about ourselves—this strategy fails? I think we would be pretty much back where we are right now—still the most powerful nation on earth without the slightest idea of how to use our power in our own self-interest.

The Conference on Security and Co-operation in Europe and the negotiations on mutual and balanced force reductions represent a prime opportunity for the two nuclear superpowers to reduce the tensions that exist between them. If I am right, because of the complexities of the issues and the number of interested parties, both of these negotiation processes are liable to be difficult and drawn out. I have outlined a strategy which, by operating directly on the perceived levels of mutual threat in a calculated fashion, may make it possible to reduce perceived threats and thereby facilitate these negotiations.

Looked at in broader perspective, the European confrontation has many positive elements in it, many motivations on all sides that favour détente, and it therefore offers itself as a potential proving ground for a strategy that is novel but yet appropriate to the nuclear age in which we are trying to survive. The alternative assumption of mutual nuclear deterrence—that we can go spinning forever into eternity, poised for mutual annihilation and kept from it only by fragile bonds of mutual fear—is untenable. The ultimate goal must be to get out from under the nuclear Sword of Damocles by eliminating such weapons from the human scene.

References

DEUTSCH, K. W. 1963. *The Nerves of Government*. New York, The Free Press of Glencoe.
KAHN, H. 1965. *On Escalation: Metaphors and Scenarios*. New York, Praeger.
OSGOOD, C. E. 1962. *An Alternative to War or Surrender*. Urbana, Ill., University of Illinois Press.
——. 1963. Questioning some Unquestioned Assumptions about National Defense. *The Journal of Arms Control*, No. 1, pp. 2–13.
——. 1966. *Perspective in Foreign Policy*. Palo Alto, Cal., Pacific Books.

28

Strategies for peaceful change

Ernst-Otto Czmpiel
Peace Research Institute, Frankfurt am Main
Federal Republic of Germany

Strategies of 'risk-free induction'

The set of strategies labelled 'risk-free induction' has been formulated primarily to make members of the system reduce the tension of conflicts. Generally, this also affects the conflict itself in so far as its manifestation is transformed. Consequently, there appear chances for conflict solution which were not previously visible.

Concerning the East-West conflict this means: we need strategies which allow a certain unit (e.g. the Federal Republic of Germany) to induce its allies as well as its opponents to strive for reduction of conflict tension. The territorial, social, economic, and ideological elements of the conflict as a whole are not dependent on a deterrent system based on a high level of armaments. They could easily be transformed into some sort of competition or judicial dispute. This would neither solve the conflict, nor could one speak of a real peaceful policy; nevertheless, much progress would have been made. In addition to lessening the danger of war, both sides could save a large amount of armaments costs. Mutual communication could be increased, perhaps even partial co-operation could be initiated. Chances for conflict solutions would result which are not visible at present, and which would not emerge at all without such a transformation. If the past twenty-five years have proved anything at all, it is the fact that dissociative threat systems are basically incapable of solving conflicts.

This experience, as well as the lack of alternatives due to the state of weapons technology, suggests the remaining strategy on induction, whose innovative and emancipative content can politically and practically be secured in this way. As dissociation has failed, induction remains the sole alternative. The strategy must certainly be risk-free. Consequently, induction is not identical with unilateralism, the one-sided attempt to break away from the system. Rather, it is a strategy which decisively aims at effecting changes which involve the system as a whole. It will not destabilize the system, but transform it. To accomplish this, innovations are required, not risks. Armaments are the simplest example we can use to

Shortened version from 'Peace as a Strategy for Systemic Change', *Bulletin of Peace Proposals*, Vol. 10, No. 1, 1979.

demonstrate the absence of risks: we need a strategy which, without endangering the security of the initiating country, tries to induce all members of the system to reduce their armaments. The demand for the absence of any risk in no way curtails the inductive capacity of this strategy. Because of the traditional value-maximizing strategies, the area of behaviour which lies before the area of risks has been expanded so far that its decomposition in itself would mean a substantial change of the state of the system.

Gradualism

Similar strategies for change have certainly been devised in the past; peace research, however, has to date not extensively taken note of them. As early as 1962, Charles Osgood set forth the concept of 'gradualism' as 'an alternative to war or surrender'. Its core is the theory of graduated reciprocation in tension-reduction (GRIT).

Gradualism represents a generally applicable de-escalation strategy by which tension processes can be interrupted and reversed. Escalations which are increased step by step can be diminished in the same manner.

But gradualism is not related only to the armaments sector, although it is mainly applied there. Its mechanisms can certainly be used for a general reduction of tensions. In the first place, the 'artificial tension' could be affected, then the actual subject-related tension itself. The artificial tension is an epiphenomenon which ensues from consensus building, rule stabilization, or simply habit. To the extent that these processes develop a life of their own, become autistic, they create a meta-conflict by provoking corresponding reactions on all sides of the conflict. This meta-conflict is certainly connected with the factual conflict; it could, however, be easily separated from it. This is the direction in which a gradualistic strategy would have to proceed. It would have to correct stereotyped enemy images by revealing their psychological structure and their role in the manipulation of consensus. Factual and well-founded analysis would have to take the place of defamation and slander of the opponent. This could be supplemented by a whole range of positive gestures and offers which would sever the totality of the conflict without any risk and reduce it to a level arising out of factual divergencies. Official visits, cultural exchanges, and reciprocal actions of the same type in no way interfere with conflicting relations, they only delimit them.

It is conceivable that such gradualistic strategies may not release corresponding reactions from the addressee. This does not constitute an objection in principle, however. First of all, the time-span over which these strategies will be applied has to be extended—the more, the longer the threat system has existed and the more intensive it has been. Secondly, as there exists no alternative to these strategies, they must be applied without limit. If they fall short of success, they should not be abandoned but intensified. Their final success can be taken for granted, hypothetically at least, to the extent to which the alternative strategies of threat and deterrence can be unequivocally considered to have failed.

Gradualism and disarmament

The gradualistic strategy becomes especially obvious with regard to the neuralgic sphere of disarmament. At this point it can be shown that it is neither unilateral nor affirmative. On the one hand, gradualism must not lead to unilateral destabilization, especially because the symmetry of mutual deterrence has had a stabilizing effect since 1949. On the other hand it is possible, because of the resulting absence of risk, to effect considerable disarmament steps. Over-capacities have emerged with all parties to the East-West conflict, for reasons mentioned above.

The dialogue of the superpowers, which is directed only at arms control anyway, is related to those over-capacities alone and is restricted to their comparison. The SALT agreement is confined to this area; the discussion has excluded as irrelevant the question of how much deterrence is really necessary.

Obviously, the amount of destructive capacity which the opponent has at his disposal signifies an important factor in this two-man situation which is also characterized by the security dilemma. It is equally obvious that by hinting at the security dilemma and its anticipative possibilities for justification, any amount of armaments could be internally justified. We know that this amount is determined by other factors, too, and is only verbally declared to be exclusively a foreign policy necessity. The military-industrial complex considerably determines the amount of armaments with its syndrome of institutional and individual interests. Also in the Federal Republic of Germany one can already identify such a complex; its consequences can be clearly perceived with regard to arms sales. We may take for granted that there exists a corresponding ideological-military complex in the Soviet Union.

The influence of these factors on the size of the defence capacity can only be hinted at here. The most prominent feature is provided by the indisputable statement that armaments are not kept at the lowest level necessary for deterrence, but are determined by factors in no direct relation to this deterrence. To reduce the amount of armaments by this superfluous amount would not affect security, it would actually be risk-free. The scope within which United States armaments expenditures could be reduced without any security risk lies between $10,000 and $30,000 million.

Such a reduction would be of immense benefit to the United States itself—as to any country which reduces armaments—because considerable sums would be released for domestic needs. Above all, the induction potential of such a reduction would be significant. It could be taken as a signal of rational behaviour, and could strengthen forces in the Soviet Union interested in similar reductions. If the other Western European countries followed such a United States example, the Warsaw Treaty Organization would be confronted with the problem of either following suit or further neglecting domestic problems for the sake of unnecessary defence expenditures. Conditions are reversed at present, to be sure: the Western powers have been leading the armaments escalation and the socialist countries are now close at their heels. This quite large area which comes before the real defence needs could be exploited to diminish, without any risk, the economic strains, convert arms control into disarmament, and in this way reduce tensions. Gradualistic strategies can therefore be considered as a relatively risk-free undertaking and as a valuable, important, and pre-eminent concept which would render possible the risk-free abolishment of major tensions.

Induction for conflict solution

The strategy of risk-free induction is of larger scope. Disarmament in that area which has been built up in excess of actual defence needs provides an ideal example of this strategy. In its core, it is certainly devised to provide conflict solutions and to bring about substantial détente through the lessening and dissolution of political differences and the resulting tensions. This core of risk-free induction is the political-practical result of a foreign policy which, instead of interest-maximizing, is satisfied with their optimizing and is therefore prepared to see the opponent as a potential future co-operator and to respond to him accordingly.

Even with regard to this core, the strategy is risk-free. It does not sell off the interests but it expresses the fact that their realization is possible exclusively through compromise. The theoretical problems which confront us were hinted at earlier. Strategically, the question arises of how compromise readiness can be converted into an attitude comprising the whole system. Peace research has in the past largely neglected these strategical problems. It has distinguished associative from dissociative strategies which it assigned to symmetrical or asymmetrical conflicts. It has differentiated in principle between various conflict types and their solutions.

In these terms, risk-free induction could be described as procedural, associative solution of symmetrical conflicts, at least with regard to the East-West conflict. What is decisive is that strategy research must proceed from this differentiation between single conflict types and the corresponding solutions to generation of concrete and practical plans.

Mankind does not lack instructions for such a strategy. Christ's Sermon on the Mount provides the radical precept: love your enemies. Interestingly, it is confirmed by a secular theory, game theory. Although its rules in no way fill the humane depth of the Christian love principle, they do confirm that core which has always troubled *homo politicus* most of all. Towards the enemy—that is the external confronting position, to which aggression and liquidation tendencies can be imputed—only an associative strategy will be successful. It is the sole strategy which can substitute and replace the temporarily effective, but in its long-term prospects ineffective, expensive and dangerous strategy of deterrence.

A strategy is called 'associative' if two opponents both profit. Game theory provides an example with the prisoner's dilemma: both sides win if they co-operate. This classical example also shows that the two sides do not reach co-operation in a conflict constellation because each worries about the other side's lack of reaction. This co-operation has to be reached through induction. In contrast to the example of prisoner's dilemma, this is possible in international relations, because of existing communication possibilities and extended time-spans. Experimentally, it has been proved by game theory that the dilemma can be solved and co-operation effected, if the following strategy is applied: (a) start of co-operation; (b) continuation of co-operative tendencies, as long as the opposing side joins in; (c) immediate reaction if there is repeated or frequent refusal by the other side; but (d) partial insertion of a succession of two or three unilateral co-operative impulses in order to give the opponent a chance to decide for a succession of mutual co-operative impulses, too. This result has been confirmed in several

293

variants by various game and simulation experiments. They have also demonstrated that the main obstacle towards such a strategy is the desire to maximize profit.

Some results of behavioural research point in the same direction: 'The open secret of human communication is to treat one's partner in a way which is more valuable to him than it is expensive for oneself, and to be treated by him in a way which is more valuable to oneself than it is expensive for him.'[1] Although this result is generally related to interpersonal relations and the outcomes of game-theoretical attempts cannot be transferred—at present—into the international arena as reliable strategies, the facts are certainly sufficient to underline the heuristic value of associative induction. It represents a specific reduction of the precept of the Sermon on the Mount, as its normative magnitude, which reaches beyond man's actual capabilities, is reduced to a practical dimension which can make it acceptable, as it is inevitable anyway.

What is decisive is conformity with the direction which the strategy must be devised to take. It has to be inductive. Led by Christ's Sermon on the Mount and game theory respectively, the strategical discussion should try to extend risk-free induction beyond the outlined scope of application. Thereby it can proceed to the centre of the conflict and the tension which originates there.

It is quite simple to determine the thrust of this strategy: continuous compromise-readiness. It is more difficult to point out this meaning precisely. Some general rules can be given and a few examples listed. First, the offer of compromise-readiness has to be sharply distinguished from a concrete offer of a compromise. The actual shaping of the compromise can be left quite open. What the strategy requires is compromise-readiness in principle. This may, in extreme cases, be simply negatively defined as an explicit, unequivocal renunciation of value-maximizing strategies, although this has to be restricted to extreme cases. The *Ostpolitik* of the Federal Republic of Germany had been obscure until 1969, because renunciation of the application of military force had been combined with a refusal to compromise. Such a contradiction is naturally interpreted by the opponent as an attempt to effect maximization of one's own interests, which is only verbally concealed. The *Ostpolitik* of the Socialist-Liberal coalition with its Moscow and Warsaw agreements contains, on the other hand, much more than a plain signal of compromise-readiness. It concludes the process which we have called inductive strategy. To continue our example, a strategy could have consisted of continuous offers to the Soviet Union and Poland since 1949, regarding negotiations about renunciation of military force and about the Oder-Neisse borderline. The readiness for compromise would thus have been definitively visible, without the compromise itself being anticipated.

One further example which points out the positive effect of the strategy of risk-free induction is President Nixon's policy towards China in 1971–72. The communiqué issued during Nixon's visit to Peking can be called the paradigm of mutual offers of compromise-readiness and simultaneous refusal to reach actual compromise. Neither of the two sides withdrew from one of its positions. The differences were written into the communiqué by both sides through the precise formulation of the different points of view. Together, both sides only stated their intention to 'keep contact through various channels . . . to promote the normalization of relations between the two countries and continue the exchange of opinions about matters of mutual interest'. These rather vague agreements were, however, quite clearly directed towards the hope that the 'accomplished success will open new perspectives for the relations between the two countries'. Antagonisms were therefore not touched at all, only the perspective of handling them in a violent manner was replaced by one of possible compromise. The content of the compromise remained unclear, even doubtful for a long time. What is decisive is that compromise has become the sole method of conflict solution that will be used in the future.

A fundamental change in foreign-policy orientation, expressed in practical terms by the strategy of risk-free induction, has thus become more evident. It is based on removing from the antagonisms the perspective of possible violent conflict and of incorporating them strongly into modes of compromise in principle. In this context, the continuous offer to negotiate is but a tactical variant of this strategy. There are others—participation with opponents in international organizations and co-operation within this framework, for example. The offer to participate in economic co-operation could be another instrument to proceed through risk-free induction. Although economic relations cannot necessarily be considered inductive as such—the Federal Republic of Germany has for years conducted its economic and political relations with the Soviet Union in completely separate ways—offers to co-operate economically can highly increase the induction potential. To be sure, mutual gains must be distributed so that a real inductive factor is created. Even with regard to conflicts between developed and developing countries, the strategy of risk-free induction could be important, perhaps through attempts to induce the developing countries to align their internal organization in a democratic manner. The big effort of Western development assistance could, if adjusted correspondingly, become an effective instrument to promote democratization (and industrialization) of the Third World. After multilateralization of the distribution, such an incentive would not contradict advantage-free enlistment. Because development assistance is still far from this function, strategy research should be especially concerned with it.

Risk-free induction is consequently emerging as a vital peace strategy. It is positioned between long-range strategies of advantage-free enlistment,[2] the effects of which will appear only after decades, and strategies with short-range effects which can do little more than prevent the worst. Risk-free induction, on the other hand, decisively influences those processes in which conflicts are being formed. Although it cannot proceed to the core of these processes and prevent conflict formation itself—as advantage-free enlistment can—it can influence them relatively early and direct them towards co-operative ways of handling.

Even if advantage-free enlistment should succeed in bringing about systemic change, induction strategies would not become superfluous. Conflicts would lose the perspective of violence, but they would still require handling to organize their solution. Until systemic change can be accomplished, however, these strategies could decisively change the configuration of international conflicts. They could actually realize peace with regard to any single case, before it has been institutionalized through the societal organization of the system members. Because such strategies contribute to the solution of present conflicts in an emancipative manner, they also become functional for the situation which they anticipate. To the same degree that risk-free induction changes the perspective of conflict solution and directs it towards compromise, it reduces system tension. System-change through the strategy of advantage-free enlistment is in this way directly promoted. With their intermediate position, strategies of risk-free induction emerge as those concepts which should attract the attention of strategy research. Their importance for mastering present conflicts is as great as it is for the preparation of systemic change.

Notes

1. G. C. Homans, 'Social Behavior. Its Elementary Forms' (New York, 1961), cited in Herbert C. Kelman (ed.), *International Behaviour. A Social Psychological Analysis*, p. 470, New York, 1965.
2. Advantage-free enlistment as a medium of peaceful systemic change denotes a long-range concept. The strategy starts on the assumption that one country begins to initiate systemic change. Its theory can be described quite easily. If the said progressive order, which may be described as political, economic, and societal democratization, is established in one unit—e.g. if the Federal Republic of Germany realized optimum societal progress—then an impetus with considerable system effect would result. This impetus is based on the attraction inherent in problem solutions. There is a parallel with regard to technology. Any invention which satisfies a human need is—wherever possible—either directly taken over or at least imitated. It never remains isolated. Correspondingly, one may expect that any progress which concerns the emancipation of man—as long as it is 'real', which means that it must affect the individual and be felt by him—will activate forces and generate processes which cause repetition in the whole system. Advantage-free enlistment as a long-term—oriented strategy for systemic change expresses the worthiness of imitating the example, and equally the fact that the attractiveness of the strategy rests inclusively in itself and not in its presentation, be it through propaganda or the export of ideology.

29

Confidence-building as an approach to co-operative arms regulations in Europe

Karl E. Birnbaum
Austrian Institute for International Affairs

General considerations

In political debates and diplomatic negotiations 'confidence-building measures' (CBMs) has recently become an increasingly popular term. This chapter attempts to clarify some of the general problems encountered in efforts to promote confidence between East and West in Europe. In particular, the chapter addresses three major issues that would seem to be of crucial importance in this context: (a) the reasons for the emergence of the 'CBM philosophy' as an approach to arms control in Europe; (b) the nature of confidence-building processes between adversary partners in East and West; and (c) the negotiability of CBMs. The analysis is concluded with a discussion of the requirements for making progress in this field and a plea for recognizing its urgency in the face of an escalating arms build-up and a generally deteriorating international situation.

The emergence of the confidence-building approach to arms control

Over the last few years several factors in combination have tended to push the confidence-building approach to arms control into the foreground. First and foremost among them are the difficulties and frustrations of what could be termed the 'conventional approach' to arms control.

The impasse of these efforts aiming at agreements imposing quantitative restrictions on discrete weapon systems and force levels has been only too obvious. Arms-control negotiations and agreements stipulating such quantitative restrictions have had the effect of mobilizing and activating bureaucratic élites and other groups with vested interests in sustaining high or even rising levels of military expenditure. For this and other reasons they have not been conducive to greater stability and the lowering of force levels. In addition the rapid pace of technological change has confronted parties to arms-control agreements and negotiations with increasingly intractable problems of definition and verification. Two characteristics of modern weaponry, in particular, have tended to block prospects for making significant progress towards co-operative arms regulations:

Slightly shortened version from Karl E. Birnbaum, *Arms Control in Europe: Problems and Prospects* (The Laxenburg Papers, No. 1, 1980).

(a) the multi-purpose nature of recent additions to or improvements in the armoury of the major powers; and (b) the quick-reaction properties of modern weapon systems. The first has implied a loss of predictability in the behaviour of a potential adversary, the second more immediately devastating effects if these weapon systems were actually used. As a consequence weapon-acquisition processes have tended to consume the minimum level of mutual confidence achieved through declaratory policy, high-level diplomacy or other largely political means.

Against this background of distrust fed by ideological and political conflicts, but more particularly by the uncertainties resulting from the ambiguous nature of recent weapons developments, the 'philosophy of confidence-building' has emerged as a possible way to overcome the deadlock in arms-control efforts.

In as far as both sides displayed a credible preoccupation with stabilizing the arms environment, it seemed plausible to assume a common interest in clarifying *intentions* by mutual reassurance. In the context of the Conference on Security and Co-operation in Europe (CSCE) different schemes to achieve such reassurance have been negotiated and partly implemented.

As the 1970s drew to a close the increasing interest in the CBM approach to arms control could also be attributed to an awareness of the fact that the rhetoric of détente and the stark evidence of an accelerated arms build-up on both sides could no longer be kept apart and were perceived by an increasing number of people as patently incompatible. Hence, one could register a growing recognition in East and West that a minimum of joint management in the realm of arms policies was a necessary precondition for the continuation of détente and of mutually beneficial co-operation in different fields. The experience with CBMs in the context of the CSCE was not altogether discouraging and suggested that these or similar schemes might provide a framework for more effectively managed co-operative arms regulations in Europe.

The nature of confidence-building between antagonistic partners

Trust can be conceived as an attitude based on a mixture of knowledge and uncertainty between interdependent parties, whose potential to harm and help each other is mutually recognized.

The risk of betrayal is thus inherent in the very concept of trust. The aim of confidence-building therefore must be to reduce the perceived risks of such a betrayal. The assessment of these perceived risks in turn is influenced by two sets of factors: (a) the amount of verifiable information about motives and intentions as well as capabilities of an adversary partner; and (b) the physical constraints circumscribing his behaviour. Technological developments in the arms field that tend to make available evidence regarding military capabilities more ambiguous have put a premium on credible information about intentions and on verifiable measures that imply effective constraints on the military dispositions of a potential opponent. While it is notoriously difficult to ascertain political intentions with any degree of confidence—particularly between ideological adversaries—the post-Helsinki experience would seem to suggest that some improvement with regard to practices providing for the exchange of reliable information about operational guidelines for military dispositions in East and West is attainable. Similarly, the

Vienna negotiations on troop reductions in Central Europe indicate that there may be some opportunity for introducing mutually reassuring constraints by negotiating limitations on military options without jeopardizing fundamental security arrangements deemed to be essential by the members of NATO and the Warsaw Treaty Organization (WTO).

Given residual and recurring manifestations of deep distrust between Eastern and Western governments, progress can at best be achieved by small steps and over a long period of time. But while confidence-building between antagonistic partners must be conceived as a gradual process, it is equally important that all involved recognize the dynamic nature of trust-building between East and West: confidence is liable to falter unless it is sustained by reassuring evidence. Johan Holst and Karen Melander have correctly observed that 'confidence-building involves the communication of credible evidence of the absence of feared threats'.[1] This effort must be both continuous and cumulative.

The negotiability of CBMs

Any attempt to promote confidence between East and West must take into account the principal difficulties encountered in this field. A fundamental one arises from the fact that the requirements for deterrence and for confidence-building are inherently irreconcilable. Parties that threaten each other with ever more deadly weapons for the sake of mutual deterrence will obviously find it hard to convince one another of their benign intentions—which is the essence of confidence-building. Yet, to the extent that the major powers in NATO and WTO perceive their mutual relations as a mixture of hostility, competition and limited co-operation—for which there is some evidence—they should be inclined to view neither deterrence nor confidence-building in absolute terms. Hence, even in a situation where the basic deterrence structures between East and West continue to prevail, it should at least be possible to dispel mutual distrust by such steps as the exchange of information, explanations of procurement and deployment decisions, and verifiable agreements limiting military options.

A second difficulty in terms of negotiability derives from the nature of CBMs comprising a wide variety of steps—including both 'subjective' and 'objective' elements;[2] progress in this realm on the other hand presupposes a comprehensive approach. In particular it is important to recognize that (as Jonathan Alford has pointed out)[3] two types of confidence are involved in this context: on the one hand self-confidence in the ability to defend oneself, if threatened or attacked, and on the other hand mutual confidence, implying the notion that neither side is in fact intending to threaten or to attack. Self-confidence is best served by verifiable agreements or 'objective' measures limiting military options of potential opponents and is thus mainly based on considerations of capability. Such measures may also be conducive to enhancing mutual confidence but fostering the latter in addition requires willingness to divulge guidelines for military dispositions in order to affect 'subjective' perceptions regarding intentions. While the aim must be to engender a mutually reinforcing interaction between the two types of confidence-building by a combination of 'objective' and 'subjective' steps, the parties face a basic dilemma in terms of the negotiability of agreements in this area. In the present period of considerable mutual suspicion—residual as well as recurring—there is a particularly urgent need for tangible, 'objective' measures. Yet, in a climate of acute mutual distrust such steps, implying the denial of some physical options, are hard to negotiate—as suggested by the discussions on 'associated measures' in the context of the Vienna negotiations on troop reductions in Central Europe. The CSCE experience indicates that it is easier to start at the soft, 'subjective' end of CBMs. But it must be realized that if confidence-building as an approach to co-operative arms regulations is to have a future, the process will have to entail verifiable constraints as well. The fact that some measures such as the prior notification of military exercises and movements comprise 'subjective' as well as 'objective' elements may facilitate the implementation of a comprehensive strategy of confidence-building.

A final difficulty in terms of negotiability stems from the fact that CBMs have been discussed in several diplomatic forums: mainly the CSCE and the Vienna negotiations on troop reductions in Central Europe but also SALT. While each forum has concentrated on different types of measures, such fragmentation tends to complicate the co-ordination of efforts, not to speak of the difficulties of sustaining a continuous, comprehensive and cumulative process. A high-level consultative body with a mandate to review the whole field might conceivably ameliorate the situation.

The case for a double approach to CBMs

CBMs are well entrenched in existing and proposed negotiating forums dealing with European security issues. These negotiations may well survive or come into being in spite of the recent deterioration of the relations between the superpowers. But if CBMs are to become more than cosmetics to appease an alarmed public, a forum for a continuous high-level dialogue between East and West would seem to be required. An effective body of this kind would be needed to ensure proper co-ordination, to overcome bureaucratic inertia and to keep up the necessary momentum. More importantly, however, only a high-level consultative committee could initiate a process that would enable the participants to conceive confidence-building as an integral part of a comprehensive effort to achieve co-operative arms regulations in Europe and elsewhere. If over a longer period of time government representatives from East and West met regularly to compare overall assessments, to exchange information on weapon acquisition and force deployments, to communicate concerns and preoccupations, etc., the resulting learning process might eventually affect subsequent weapons acquisition decisions on both sides. Since the latter have tended to erode and to nullify the results of arms-control agreements, it should be clear that this learning process is of crucial importance. It would seem to offer at least some hope that the vicious circle bedevilling arms-control efforts could one day be broken.

The double approach to CBMs proposed here would thus imply that a high-level confidence-building dialogue in combination with extended CBMs of the kind negotiated in the CSCE be viewed as an integral part of a comprehensive strategy aimed at managing arms competitions and political conflicts. The confidence-building component can never substitute arms-control agreements freezing or limiting force levels. But it is a necessary forerunner and supplement of such agreements.

The confidence-building approach has registered some modest success in Europe. In order to be effective in terms of co-operative arms regulation this approach will have to be adapted to the particular conditions prevailing in different regions. But at the same time its globalization appears to be particularly urgent in view of the deterioration of the international situation.[4] While peace has been divisible, all assertions to the contrary notwithstanding, confidence between the major powers is surely not. To restore at least a minimum of mutual trust between them and thus make their behaviour mutually more predictable and calculable would seem to be urgently required in the present dangerous period of world politics. The realities of the nuclear age make it imperative that the dialogue between the major powers never stops, if only to avoid a disastrous military conflagration. Crisis management is the most elementary level of confidence-building. The comprehensive confidence-building approach suggested in this chapter offers the prospect of moving beyond crisis management into a more stable relationship, where crises and arms build-ups could be avoided and continued competition regulated to the advantage of both sides.

Notes

1. Johan Holst and Karen Melander, 'European Security and CBM', *Survival*, July/August 1977.
2. Cf. Jonathan Alford (ed.), *The Future of Arms Control. III: Confidence-building Measures*, pp. 5-6, London, IISS, 1979. (Adelphi Papers, No. 149.)
3. Cf. ibid. p. 3.
4. Both requirements are reflected in a resolution on confidence-building adopted by the United Nations General Assembly on 11 December 1979.

30

A political design for world disarmament

Yoshikazu Sakamoto
University of Tokyo

Introduction

Thirty years after Hiroshima and Nagasaki, despite the tortuous but unmistakable progress of 'détente' in the arena of international politics, the nuclear arms race goes on unabated and the world's military expenditure continues its upward spiral. Why is this so?

One reason lies in the development of military technology, which has triggered the vertical nuclear arms race and horizontal nuclear proliferation. The endless arms race appears to be the inevitable product of the progress of military technology. In fact it is said that, in the process of developing new technology, the United States, for instance, having developed a new weapon, often proceeds to develop counter-weapons independent of the actual development of counter-weapons by the USSR. Here is a manifestation of the self-perpetuating chain reaction of military technological development.

Has the progress of military technology, then, of necessity produced today's arms race? Obviously it has not. It is by humans, organizations and society that technology is developed and employed; technology does not develop by itself.

It is true that improved accuracy of missile delivery systems may bring about a shift to counter-force strategy; on the other hand, precisely because of the danger that the improved accuracy may create an extremely unstable military balance of power, it can equally lead to a redirection of policy from continuing arms race to disarmament. Which direction to take is a matter of political choice, not a matter dictated by technology. The same can be said about nuclear proliferation. Political choice, not technology, determines whether the United States and the Soviet Union, in view of the technological feasibility of nuclear proliferation, would attempt to solidify their nuclear superiority and virtual monopoly or would take the initiative for global nuclear disarmament.

The issue of the arms race must, therefore, be considered in its political context. What political conditions provide the basis for today's arms race? What political conditions are obstructing disarmament? What are the political conditions that can promote and bring about disarmament? By formulating the problem

Shortened version from *Peace Research in Japan 1974-75.*

in the context of political choice we shall be able to identify the implications of the disarmament question for individual humans as political actors. Let us then make analytical observations of the political context of the disarmament problem.

Disarmament is not only an end that ought to be attained; it must also be a goal that can be attained. This does not mean that it is attainable without changing the existing international system. It means that disarmament, while calling for a transformation of the existing international political system, presupposes that kind of transformation of which the origins and causes are inherent in the present international political system.

In the light of present international behaviour, our primary concern has to be focused on the military power of the United States and the USSR of the 'First World', associated with their 'spheres of influence'. This is not to neglect the problems of the 'Second World' or especially of the 'Third World', which is in flux. But unless the problem of 'big-power hegemonism' of the First World is first taken up, it will be difficult to proceed to the problems of the other three worlds (the Fourth World comprising poor countries with very low military expenditures).

How, then, is it possible to achieve the reduction of the military capabilities of the United States and the USSR? To answer this question we have to identify the conditions that generate and promote the arms race between the superpowers.

Political structure of the arms race under détente

The arms race between the United States and the Soviet Union has continued uninterrupted for nearly three decades since the late 1940s. Even though the arms race as a military phenomenon has been constantly under way, however, its political context has undergone a significant alteration.

The most important motivating factor of the arms race up to the early 1960s, which we will call the 'Cold War arms race', was the mutual distrust and fear between the United States and the USSR. It was a vicious circle of actions and reactions which, under conditions of a shortage or absence of crucial information about the intention and capabilities of the adversary, were taken to mean the worst. Consequently, the strategy for moving from the Cold War to détente focused on efforts to increase and improve political communications.

Notwithstanding that, the arms race is not over. On the contrary, the arms race between the United States and USSR, particularly on the level of nuclear-weapon systems, has assumed the character of an even sharper qualitative contest. In other words, in place of the Cold War arms race a new type of arms race under conditions of political détente, what might be called a 'détente arms race', has emerged. But why, if political distrust between powers is the primary cause of the arms race, does détente not lead to its end? What indeed are the causes of the détente arms race?

Three interpretations have been put forward with regard to this point. The first is the view that, even under 'détente', there still remain distrust and conflict between the United States and the Soviet Union. This view holds that essentially the Cold War has not come to an end. In fact there is still a strong distrust of the Soviet Union on the part of conservatives in the United States, and the same is probably true of the distrust of the United States among conservatives in the Soviet Union.

The second interpretation, in contrast, maintains that the arms race by the United States and the USSR is a means of establishing and perpetuating the hegemony of the two superpowers and has its foundation in their common interest. If one holds the view that the United States and the USSR seek their condominium over the world, the fact that the United States-USSR détente and the arms race between them are proceeding simultaneously is not in the least surprising, because their military power can be considered to be directed not so much at each other as at their own allies and neutral countries.

The third interpretation takes the view that the primary cause of the arms race by the United States and the USSR does not lie in inter-nation relations but stems from internal political structures, particularly the military-industrial-bureaucratic complex. From this viewpoint it is equally not surprising to see that the arms race is continuing in spite of the relaxation of political tension between powers.

As mentioned above, an awareness of the role played by the military-industrial complex is not new; however, two significant developments have taken place in today's intellectual context of the discourse. First, against the background of the continuing arms race under conditions of détente, a view has gained prominence that attributes, unlike in the Cold War period, primary importance to the domestic political structure. As reflected in such concepts as 'bureaucratic politics' (G. Allison and M. Halperin) and 'bureaucratic revolution' (R. Barnet), the approach that emphasizes the bureaucratic system as an independent variable in the context of foreign policy-making has recently gained wide currency in the United States.

Secondly, in contrast to the Cold War period, the view has become increasingly common that points out the correlation between the arms race and the domestic structure, not only as regards the United States or a capitalist system but also with respect to the Soviet Union. Under socialism, although the 'industrial' sector obviously plays a different political role from that in a capitalist society, it can hardly be denied that there are problems created by the system of military bureaucracy.

These are the three interpretations regarding the détente arms race. To sum up, the first interpretation concedes the contradiction between political détente and the arms race and goes on to explain the arms race by pointing to the persistent political tension. The second interpretation is based on the view that détente and the arms race are mutually compatible and even complementary. From this standpoint, in order that the United States and the USSR may justify to the rest of the world the enormous military power they deem necessary to consolidate their hegemonic position, it is to their advantage that, to the extent conformable to this purpose, conflicts persist—or appear to persist—between the two. The third interpretation takes the view that détente and the arms race are unrelated, as it were, and that even with a relaxation of tension between states domestic factors can still lead to an arms race. This view also holds that the military-bureaucratic systems in the United States and the USSR share a common interest in the sense that they both have vested interests in the arms race.

Which of the three interpretations is valid? Probably such a question is in itself not pertinent. It is more accurate to say that each of the three contains an element of truth, and that is why the détente arms race has its unique complexity in comparison with the Cold War arms race.

The problem then is to explore how this détente arms race with its threefold character can be transformed into disarmament, and to identify the conditions of such a transformation and the motive force for disarmament dynamics.

Counter-trends towards disarmament

A key to the transformation of the détente arms race into disarmament dynamics can be found precisely in the counter-trends inherent in each of the three aspects of the détente arms race referred to above. That is to say, today's arms race is a composite of three factors—the trend towards continuing tension among powers, the trend towards maintenance of superpower dominance, and the trend towards preservation of internal vested interests in the arms race. What is extremely important is the fact that each of these trends generates within itself a counter-trend in favour of disarmament.

First of all the arms race that is intended to pursue 'security' in the context of international conflict is bringing about, due to increased accuracy of the missile delivery systems and various other reasons, extremely insecure and unstable conditions. In order to attain and maintain their own security, therefore, the United States and the USSR must seek a change of course away from the arms race. This is the first counter-trend inherent in the current trends.

Second, if the two superpowers agree to solidify their hegemony and to take concerted action, this fact itself erodes the unity within the two blocs and inevitably promotes a counter-trend towards global multipolarization and decentralization of international political power, extending to the developing areas as well.

Third, the growth of a huge bureaucratic system at home has fostered a sense of political alienation in society and created the counter-trend towards erosion of authority and belief-system supporting the polity. Evidently, the decline of military values and symbols in the West is a case in point, as is reflected in the lowering morale and discipline among soldiers of NATO forces or in the shift of many countries from conscription to voluntary enlistment.

These contradictions and challenges inherent in the détente arms race are quite serious, so serious that the parties to the arms race themselves have begun to deal with the dilemmas. Hence the 'arms control' approach. This approach is characterized by attempts to minimize the contradictions and disruptions within the existing system without altering its fundamental structure. Herein lies its limitation.

In contrast to 'arms control', the 'disarmament' approach faces the issue more squarely and endeavours to solve the problem at its root. Further, the goals and rationale of the disarmament approach are also related to the three trends and counter-trends mentioned above. That is to say, disarmament is better suited than either the détente arms race or arms control (a) in overcoming the danger of the arms race to achieve international peace and security; (b) in transforming the structure of big-power dominance to establish international democracy and well-being; and (c) in altering the giant bureaucratic system to ensure democratic participation and well-being on the domestic level.

Inception of nuclear disarmament

What steps, then, should be taken to go beyond the détente arms race and arms control in the direction of disarmament? As stated earlier, a design for this process must take the existing contradictions and counter-trends as its point of departure.

Thus the first stage for redirecting the arms race towards disarmament can properly be envisaged from the perspective of the superpowers pursuing their own security. The dilemma that the arms race and weapons development today threaten the security of the superpowers is best exemplified by the fact that both the United States and the USSR possess more than sufficient nuclear arms for 'overkill'. This refers not only to the quantitative excess that enables each to destroy the other more than ten times. The existence of excessive nuclear weapons in itself gives rise to a shift from counter-city to counter-force strategy, which is more aggressive and requires a greater number of warheads and missiles. At the same time the adoption of counter-force strategy makes it easier to rationalize *post factum* the possession of surplus weapons already manufactured. In this sense, the quantitative excess of arms leads to a qualitative change in strategy. It is therefore not surprising that some of the policy-makers in the big powers have suggested that first of all the excessive weapons be eliminated. Former science adviser to the President of the United States, Herbert York, for one, has made the following proposal.

In his view, cities in the Soviet Union that can be regarded by the United States as significant targets for nuclear attack number at most 100. If we suppose for the moment that the number is 200, and further that there are also 200 similar targets for attack in China, the total comes to 400. Even if we assume that each of these targets is double-targeted to allow for possible missile failure, the total number does not exceed 800. On the other hand, even subtracting a certain percentage of nuclear warheads that are not available for launching at all times, the United States still possesses no fewer than 5,300 nuclear warheads ready for instant launching. Thus the difference of 4,500 constitutes the excess, which must have been targeted on military installations.[1]

The number 800 in York's proposal constitutes the level of 'minimum deterrence', but it is not necessary to attach positive significance to this specific figure. What should be stressed here are the following three points. The first relates to the fact that the number of excess weapons that can be abolished is extremely large. Therefore, if even the proponents of 'deterrence' strategy can agree to such a large-scale reduction, and if in fact the United States and the USSR destroyed such a large number of excess weapons, that in itself would be a beginning of considerable significance. At the same time, if those who subscribe to the doctrine of nuclear deterrence agreed to this large-scale reduction, it would amount to an admission of how imprecise the concept of 'deterrence' is and how 'deterrence' strategy itself has contributed to the production of over-kill capabilities.

Second, what is most important here is not the figure 800 nor 'minimum deterrence' as such, but the very *process* of abolishing a large quantity of nuclear weapons and the pattern of behaviour involved in the process. If, for example, the United States, which has nuclear superiority, unilaterally eliminates several hundred of its most modern missiles, and calls on the Soviet Union to reciprocate for a similar reduction, thus eliciting positive reaction from the Soviet Union, it will succeed in starting a cycle of disarmament dynamics as well as a process of political 'confidence-building'. This will mitigate the distrust between powers that is one of the causes of the détente arms race. And, what is more important, if this process of confidence-building continues and generates a momentum, political conditions can be created which permit a continued arms reduction not only to the 'minimum deterrence' level of 800 but way beyond. Furthermore, since the act of unilaterally eliminating the most modern missiles means in fact a declaration to end the contest for weapons development, it will be possible, along with arms reduction, to accede to a total nuclear test-ban agreement.

Third, what has always constituted an obstacle to arms reduction is the issue of inspection and verification. However, in the case of nuclear-weapon delivery systems, and large missiles in particular, it is not difficult to dismantle and eliminate them openly and with advance notice, allowing inspection and verification by reconnaissance satellites of the other side. Further, it is quite conceivable to use this dismantling operation for the purpose of a political demonstration of the goodwill and peace-oriented policy of the disarming nations.

Two paths to world decentralization of power

Thus, the initiation of nuclear disarmament will meet the first requirement of ensuring the security of the United States and the Soviet Union. Similarly, the third requirement, that of securing democracy and well-being at home—both or at least one of them—is a demand that can and should be accommodated by the two superpowers. Consequently, the greatest remaining possible obstacle to nuclear arms reduction will be the expected resistance of the two superpowers to a voluntary relinquishment of the military superiority that they enjoy *vis-à-vis* other countries. Viewed from this perspective alone, it would seem unrealistic to expect the United States and the Soviet Union to undertake nuclear disarmament. But what other alternatives do the two superpowers have?

One alternative is to proceed with the détente arms race. However, if the arms race continues while political conflict and distrust between the United States and the Soviet Union persist, their own security is bound to be jeopardized. If, on the other hand, the arms race continues while political relaxation progresses between the United States and the Soviet Union, military dissociation of the allies from the two superpowers and proliferation of military power including nuclear arms are likely to ensue, inevitably undermining the dominant position of the superpowers. Another alternative that would permit the United States and the Soviet Union to escape this dilemma would be to maintain their dominance through a joint United States-USSR arms development. The kind of joint enterprise already undertaken in the area of space exploration might be applied to the military field to establish a global 'condominium' by the United States and the Soviet Union. However, a difficulty also arises here, because a United States-USSR condominium is likely to generate common resistance by other nations and encourage their nuclear development, including nuclear-arms proliferation.

In short, the policy of perpetuating the dominance of the superpowers contains a fundamental dilemma. The only remaining alternative, then, is clear. It is for the United States and the Soviet Union to recognize the fact that, in the long run, an international system dominated by superpowers cannot be beneficial even to themselves. On top of that, it is in their interest to seize the initiative for disarmament of their own accord, and thus to opt for the establishment of a global system of disarmament before it is too late.

Two important points should be stressed in this connection. First, we must not fail to recognize that, in the course of history from the present to the future, there will be a mounting demand for dispersion of power as an almost irreversible current. This is reflected in the trend toward multipolarization on the international level and decentralization on the domestic level—namely, the growing demand in both international and domestic spheres for a greater extent of participation in the decision-making process. This does not always mean that units of political and economic life are becoming smaller. There are also moves for larger units, such as the European Community.

The demand for and trend towards decentralization can go in two diametrically opposite directions. On the one hand, there is a possibility that the demand for political decentralization may lead to military proliferation, accelerating the proliferation of nuclear arms. Obviously, this would create an extremely insecure and dangerous world. There is, however, another possibility—namely, political decentralization will be achieved without being accompanied by military proliferation. This would be a world in which more equal and democratic international relations have been established. In such a world it would be possible to maintain the minimum level of peace and order with a moderate-scale United Nations police force. Which of these two models will be realized depends on whether political decentralization can be successfully separated from military proliferation, and this, in the final analysis, depends on whether global disarmament can be achieved. Consequently, if the United States and the Soviet Union are to choose the second model, it is obvious that they must begin by taking the initiative for disarmament.

Second, once the United States and the Soviet Union have accomplished large-scale nuclear arms reduction, we must proceed to the next stage by placing on the agenda for disarmament reduction of nuclear arms by China, France and the United Kingdom. Judging from the posture of China and France to date, this may appear to be a terribly difficult task. The conflict between China and the Soviet Union is particularly bitter and entangled. If the Soviet Union were to choose voluntarily to reduce its nuclear arms and to cut down its own position as a superpower, however, it would serve as powerful evidence of its rejection of 'hegemonism' and undoubtedly contribute to the relaxation of tension between the USSR and China. The creation of such a political climate would in turn facilitate China's participation in nuclear disarmament at the next stage.

The 'three worlds' and disarmament

It follows from the above analysis that the second stage of disarmament following the large-scale reduction of nuclear arms by the United States and the Soviet Union would have to meet the following conditions. First, it must be a global disarmament involving not only the First World, but the Second and Third as well. Second, it must be a general disarmament including both nuclear and conventional weapons. Third, parallel to the progress of disarmament, an international peace-keeping machinery to maintain the minimum level of world order must be established. This must be a peace-keeping machinery compatible with political decentralization, and it is neither necessary nor desirable to make it anything more than a reinforced United Nations police force and the stand-by forces earmarked for the use of the United Nations, both consisting of contingents from medium-sized and smaller countries. Proponents of world federalism often advance a blueprint for a unified peace-keeping force more powerful than the armed forces of any Member States. However, such an overwhelmingly powerful machinery has the danger of itself generating conflicts over the issue of who should control it.

It is not necessary to argue in detail the measures, steps and arrangements that are conducive to the fulfilment of these three conditions. For one thing, various possibilities with respect to the details of the second stage will open up in the course of progress of the first stage, and it is rather futile to try specifically to predetermine what the second stage should be like. Here, we would do no more than suggest some basic ideas regarding the first condition. The first condition is being singled out because, as global disarmament involves three worlds with their different structures and standpoints, each of the three worlds can be expected to take its own unique approach to disarmament.

Accordingly, in the second stage of disarmament, the First World (including France and the United Kingdom) must see to it that, while their own disarmament programme is under way, they also cease arms exports to other countries. This is one of the essential conditions for separating political multipolarization from military proliferation. Until now, the emerging nations have been opposed to the idea of banning arms exports, chiefly because it was considered to lead to the perpetuation of the gap between North and South in the form of the monopoly of modern weapons by the highly industrialized countries. If, however, industrialized countries themselves that have the capacity to export weapons take steps towards disarmament, this objection will eventually lose its grounds. Today, the arms race and arms exports by industrialized countries, particularly the First World, are going hand-in-hand; what is needed is precisely the opposite—to let disarmament and the ban on arms exports proceed hand-in-hand. The ban on arms exports may create certain temporary problems regarding employment and balance of payments; however, the First World must recognize that this is a matter of long-term security for itself as well as for others.

As for the Second World, consisting of highly industrialized countries which are allies of the United States (including Japan), they are historically endowed with the conditions favourable to creating, as they curtail armaments, advanced welfare states surpassing the United States and the Soviet Union. That is to say, they are capable of building a model society on the basis of a more progressive disarmament programme than others, giving an impact to the First and the Third Worlds by serving as an example, and thus encouraging disarmament by these two worlds. It goes without saying that it is not an easy task to create a model society today where not merely a high level of consumption but also material and cultural conditions for the self-fulfilment of humans must be realized. But it is a challenge worth accepting. In other words, the Second World nations should not be content with symmetric disarmament, responding in kind to arms reduction by other countries; they should proceed with disarmament at a faster pace than the superpowers, and promote global disarmament through the asymmetric response in the form of building a model society.

Such a policy may appear at times to the superpowers as a 'free ride'. In fact, Japan has been a case in point. Had disarmament been an impossible goal, there might be some justification for Americans in criticizing as a 'free ride' Japan's policy of spending relatively little on armaments. But, inasmuch as disarmament is possible, post-war Japan, whose military expenditure has not exceeded 1 per cent of GNP in the last two decades, can be considered a society that acted in anticipation of world disarmament. The low military expenditure of post-war Japan has not only contributed to her economic growth, but, coupled with the decline in value of military symbols in the wake of Japan's defeat in 1945, no doubt made a significant contribution to the transplantation on to Japanese soil of democratic values on the political, cultural and educational levels. In this sense, the 'free ride' itself can serve as a model.

Next, from the standpoint of the Third World, and the developing countries in particular, the existing global system of military power serves above all as a pillar of the system of control by the North over the South. One of the important differences between the Cold War arms race and the détente arms race is the following: the former, while containing in reality the element of the North's dominance over the South, was primarily conceived in terms of East-West conflict; in the case of the détente arms race, however, the fact that it performs the function of the mechanism of political control both on the international and domestic levels has unmistakably come to the surface. Many developing countries have a structure of dual control—namely, the international control of the South by the North and the domestic control of the masses by élites within countries of the South—and the world weapon system as a whole serves to sustain this dual structure of control. For the Third World, therefore, disarmament is not only a question of peace among the big powers, but should mean above all a precondition for liberation of oppressed peoples.

Nevertheless, arms are frequently purchased from the North by the South with a view to attaining liberation and independence from the North. However, such action has generally resulted in promoting the North's arms race, increasing the South's technological dependence on the North, and exacerbating armed disputes among the countries of the South. This by no means is the road to liberation and independence from the North. The proper course for the emerging nations should be precisely the opposite.

The first thing that the developing countries must do in order to attain autonomy is to solve conflicts and disputes among themselves through their own efforts by non-military, peaceful means. Armed conflicts between countries of the South only increase their dependence on military supplies from the North as well as the danger of military intervention by the North. A surer way to liberation and autonomy for the emerging nations is to achieve non-military resolution of their conflicts, to neutralize thereby the weapons of the North, and furthermore to promote disarmament by the North through a boycott of the weapons of the North. It is through such a reduction of military dependence that the South can increase its ability to gain more effectively concessions and co-operation from the

North for bridging the economic gap between the North and South. And this, in turn, will promote disarmament by the North, and the transfer to the South of the well-being that disarmament in the North will yield.

The second step that the Third World countries must take to attain autonomy is to achieve the liberation of the masses at home and to eliminate oppression by the privileged military regimes. Obviously not all military regimes in developing countries are to be repudiated. However, the more a military regime is removed from the people, the greater its degree of dependence on military assistance or the purchase of arms from the North. Therefore, it is through establishment of political authority rooted in the people that the developing countries can acquire freedom from military dependence on the North and, through this, contribute to promoting disarmament in the North.

Basic model of disarmament

These are the points we must take into account in regard to the actions the three worlds should take at the second stage of disarmament. Needless to say, global disarmament must continue to go forward. It is not necessary here, however, to draw up a scenario for the ensuing stages, because what has been stated already points to the motive force and basic model for the process of disarmament. To sum up, it consists of a cycle in which big military powers which possess relative superiority take the first initiative for disarmament; this will result in the reduction of their military control over other countries; those other countries in turn will gain relatively increased political influence and put pressure on the big powers for arms reduction, thus promoting further disarmament by the big powers. This is a model representing a cycle where disarmament promotes political decentralization, and political decentralization in turn promotes disarmament. If this basic model of the disarmament process is continuously recreated, it should be possible to proceed ultimately to general and complete disarmament. The implications of this model are restated in Figure 1.

Patterns of behaviour in international relations can be classified in four categories: 'dominate', 'do not dominate', 'dominated', and 'not dominated'. Combination of these will make the following four types: (a) those that dominate but are not dominated, namely, the First World; (b) those that are dominated but also dominate, namely, the Second World and the Third World (particularly the bigger powers in the Third World); and (c) those that are dominated but do not dominate, namely, the Fourth World. Inter-nation relations of type (d) where

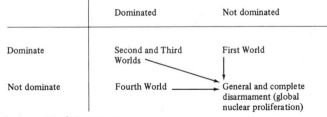

FIG. 1. Basic model of disarmament.

nations neither dominate nor are dominated will conceivably emerge under two different conditions. One is 'global nuclear proliferation', that is, the condition in which all countries are armed with nuclear weapons. At one point, China advocated this model, but it has not been heard recently to endorse it actively, probably because China, too, has recognized that this model, in which nuclear armament is introduced into a Hobbesian state of nature, will lead to an extremely insecure and dangerous situation. The other model is 'general and complete disarmament'. In essence, our analysis has been devoted to delineating the basic contours of a design whereby the worlds of (a), (b) and (c) converge on a world in which general and complete disarmament has been achieved, a world in which no one dominates and no one is dominated.

The road to this goal will not be an automatic, linear process. It will be a process which requires constant effort, pressures and unerring decisions in the direction of disarmament. It will also be beset by reactions and regressions. To repeat, however, the most fundamental choice comes down to the decision whether, on the basis of the recognition of political decentralization as an irreversible demand and trend, military proliferation is to be separated from it or not. The decision not to separate the two will move the world in the direction of 'global nuclear proliferation'. The choice for us is clear.

To be sure, 'general and complete disarmament' is not an objective that can be attained in the near future. This does not mean that it is an 'unrealistic' goal divorced from the present reality. Today, we have come to the realization, in connection with problems such as environmental pollution and depletion of resources, that 'we must not colonize our future generations'. This is a view based on the awareness that we today have the power to determine the fate of the world of tomorrow. True, 'general and complete disarmament' will not be attained in the very near future. On the other hand, probably no one believes that, fifty or a hundred years hence, United States-USSR and Sino-Soviet conflicts will remain unchanged, or that the nation-state system that has a history of no more than four centuries or so will continue to exist forever. If it can be conceived that the existing system of international politics will some day come to an end and the system of armament based on national territorial units will undergo a fundamental transformation, we should use our power to define and design the future in order to pre-empt such a future and to accelerate its attainment. Needless to say, we have the ability and responsibility not only to prevent the deterioration of the world from the present to the future; we also have the ability and responsibility to ensure, as soon as possible, that future generations will inherit a better world.

Note

1. H. York, 'Deterrence by Means of Mass Destruction', Pacem in Terris Paper, 1973, quoted in *SIPRI Yearbook*, 1974, pp. 58 et seq.

Part VII. Public opinion and education for disarmament

31

The role of the mass media in the search for peace

Séan MacBride[1]
International Peace Bureau, Geneva

The nuclear menace

Albert Schweitzer quite rightly warned that 'Man has lost the capacity to foresee and to forestall the consequences of his own acts'. The truth of this warning is only too obvious to everyone now. But in no area has man been more irresponsible than he has been in regard to nuclear weapons.

We all know that wars have been the rule rather than the exception. We all know that when there is a war armies do not hestitate to use all the weapons available to them, no matter how horrifying these weapons are. We all know that the militarists in every country always want more arms and more money. Now, however, a completely new dimension is facing humanity in regard to war. Man has acquired the capacity to destroy the entire human race.

As Arthur Koestler put it:

From the dawn of consciousness until 6 August 1945, man had to live with the prospect of his death as an individual.

Since the day when the first atomic bomb outshone the sun over Hiroshima, mankind as a whole had had to live with the prospect of its extinction as a species.

Oblivion is now the only alternative to world disarmament. Yet, in regard to nuclear weapons we have accepted quite a number of entirely irrational assumptions. First of all, it was said that the scientific method of making nuclear weapons could be kept a well-guarded secret and that not more than a few 'responsible' nations could ever discover how to make them, or could ever have the capacity of making them. This, of course, was a complete fantasy. It should have been obvious to everyone that it would be impossible to guard the secrets of nuclear weaponry in such a way as to prevent other nations from discovering how to make them.

But even if this had been possible, it would have served little purpose because it

---

Paper based on a statement made at the Peace Forum organized by Unesco in November 1979 ; also used as a document for the World Congress on Disarmament Education, Unesco, Paris, 9–13 June 1980. (Doc. SS-80/CONF.401/31.) © Unesco 1980.

is the major powers that have the capacity of making nuclear weapons and it is these very powers that are most likely to use them. But the fantasy that the manufacture of nuclear weapons could be limited to a few major powers persisted until a few years ago. Man has a capacity to push aside from his mind unpleasant problems; the more unpleasant and terrifying the problem is, the less inclined is man to face up to it. This has never been more clearly demonstrated than in the case of the attitude of society to the nuclear danger. Rational, sane, intelligent politicians and men of science have refused to face up to the dangers that confront humanity as a result of the nuclear menace.

Public opinion, disarmament and the media

In an otherwise dismal situation, there has been one hopeful development. By reason of higher standards of education on the one hand and on the other hand of the tremendous technological developments that have taken place in electronic communication, public opinion has acquired a new dimension. It is now at the centre of the power structure. No government can now act in defiance of its own public opinion—or indeed in defiance of international public opinion. Governments, as well as political parties, have therefore to organize public opinion polls in order to be sure that their policies conform with their own public opinion. This is a new development which underscores the importance of public opinion. Accordingly, there has been a shift in the centre of gravity of power from governments and secret diplomacy to the area of public opinion. These developments therefore make it possible for public opinion to play a much more important and decisive role in regard to world disarmament. But in order that public opinion may act decisively in regard to disarmament it must be fully and truthfully informed by the media.

Unfortunately, however, disarmament issues only receive the most inadequate coverage from the media. For example, the United Nations General Assembly Special Session Devoted to Disarmament was given only minimal coverage in the Western press; it received a much more extensive coverage in the socialist press. The inadequacy of the media coverage on disarmament issues stems from a number of different factors. The principal factor, is that governments are mostly interested in creating a climate of opinion which will be favourable to increased expenditure for military purposes and armament. Naturally, if they emphasized the irrationality and dangers of the arms build-up they would find it more difficult to obtain the funds which their militarists want for military purposes. Accordingly, in turn, they influence the media to play down the question of disarmament and to play up the need to increase armaments in order to meet a possible aggression.

Forces behind armaments

The forces in favour of increased armaments in the world are much more extensive and much more powerful than is usually appreciated. They include the following:

First, the military establishments that control the army, the air force and the navy. Their profession and their training is to build the biggest possible military machine and to be ready to make war. They invariably wish to have more arms and to have a more powerful military machine than that of any possible enemy they may have to face. Armament and war are their *raison d'être*. They regard the advocacy of disarmament as a form of treason. General and complete disarmament would involve the end of their profession, their status and privileges. War ministries, which are now euphemistically named 'defence' ministries, are regarded by their governments as the experts whose advice is to be taken in regard to all matters appertaining to disarmament. It is therefore axiomatic that the military establishments in every country use whatever influence they may have with the governments and with the mass media in order to justify increased armament and increased military expenditure. What they never tell their governments or the media is that no side can now win a nuclear war; they can merely create oblivion.

Second, the arms merchants and the industrial-military complex in the United States and in Western Europe are extremely powerful protagonists of the arms race. To them, of course, disarmament spells disaster. They campaign both at national and international levels. Some of them control, either directly or indirectly, some of the organs of the press. We know from the Muldergate scandal and also from the Lockheed scandal that they do not hesitate to bribe extensively in order to promote the sales of their arms, aircraft and chemicals. It is a sad commentary on the morality of this era that heads of state, prime ministers, ministers, generals, Members of Parliament and members of Congress have accepted bribes from such multinationals. It is also known that some of these multinationals employ high-powered lobbyists, journalists and PR experts and have acquired interests in some newspapers. It is not unreasonable to assume that these interests also seek to influence the media.

Third, international military organizations such as NATO and the Warsaw Pact have unlimited resources devoted to the promotion of armament propaganda. The Secretary-General of NATO, for example, and the Commander-in-Chief of the NATO forces have not hestitated to organize campaigns in the different NATO countries in order to promote an increase in armaments and an increase in military expenditure. The resources available to NATO for propaganda purposes are nearly unlimited. In addition to direct propaganda they also make use of so-called strategic research institutes to create a sense of alarm that will justify a military build-up.

Consciously or unconsciously, deliberately or not, information organs are used to generate a climate in which the arms race appears to be more acceptable. Deliberate misuse of information has on several occasions accelerated the arms build-up. Information is fed to the media which tends to encourage or justify the arms race.

For all these reasons it is of the utmost importance that all those involved in the media should exercise the utmost care in sifting the information which is fed to them in regard to the need for increased armament.

International broadcasting

I now wish to divert to another matter which may be of importance. There has been a phenomenal growth in the volume of international external radio broadcasting in the course of recent years. Originally these international radio broadcasts were developed in wartime as part of psychological warfare. However, now they constitute a major element in the opinion-forming process in the world of communications.

The phenomenal growth of international broadcasting is not yet fully appreciated. Some thirty countries now broadcast regular daily programmes intended for listeners in other countries. An idea of the magnitude and extent of these programmes may be gauged by the following broadcasting data from the top five states: USSR, 2,010 hours per week broadcast in over eighty languages; the United States, 1,813 hours in over sixty languages; the People's Republic of China, 1,436 hours in over forty-six languages; the Federal Republic of Germany, 789 hours in over thirty-nine languages; and the United Kingdom 711 hours in over thirty-nine languages.

Some twenty-five other states also have daily international radio broadcasts in a variety of languages.

While no accurate audience research in regard to international radio broadcasts has yet been carried out, it is generally agreed that these radio broadcasts have a very substantial audience and that this audience is increasing rapidly. At times of political crisis or of major news events there is a very considerable amount of 'cross-listening'. More interested and sophisticated listeners frequently listen to two or more foreign news broadcasts so as to form their own assessment of a given situation. Since jamming has virtually stopped there has been a healthy and a welcome competition in the quality and the standard of these international broadcasts. While, naturally, each of these services seeks to present its own country and policies in the best possible light, they provide a continuous source of information which is valuable. They often serve to correct the imbalance which sometimes is noticeable on some of the major international services.

My reason for drawing attention to the importance in development of the international radio broadcasts is twofold. In the first place, I would suggest that an effort should be made to get the national authorities responsible for these international broadcasts to devote a certain percentage of their broadcast time to news items and material intended to promote détente and general and complete disarmament. In the present climate it may not be easy to get agreement on this. But why not attempt it ?

I know that most governments thoroughly dislike the international radio broadcasts conducted by those to whom they are opposed. However, these external radio services have become a regular feature; they are a fact of life. Why not accept them and why not try to use them in order to promote the ideals of the United Nations, of Unesco and of world peace?

As I have pointed out, some thirty countries engage in international broadcasts. They broadcast in over 100 different languages at the rate of over

12,000 hours a week. This represents a tremendous output. It is, indeed, a measure of the recognition by the major countries of the importance of public opinion. It is the recognition by the governments concerned that the centre of gravity of power lies with public opinion and that in order to further their own policies and objectives they must inform public opinion and seek its support. If anything, it is likely that the extent of these services will continue to increase and that their quality will continually improve.

A United Nations broadcasting station

There is nothing that can be done to stop or to alter the course of these broadcasts. But is it not surprising that there is not one single station broadcasting in the name of the United Nations and Unesco, advocating an end to the arms race and urging the achievement of general and complete disarmament?

Has the time not come when the United Nations and Unesco should have their own radio station or possibly a radio satellite which would broadcast continuously twenty-four hours a day in at least twenty different languages ? I know that this would cost money and I know that it would present many difficulties. It would require considerable organization; the programmes would have to be exceedingly good. But there is no doubt that this would be the most effective way of creating a world public opinion in support of general and complete disarmament. It would also be the best way of securing public support for the United Nations and for Unesco. If we believe in the concept of world solidarity and of international peace we must be prepared to take bold initiatives, we must be prepared to fight for and capture the support of the people of the world. If Albania can transmit international radio programmes for 564 hours a week in many different languages, is there any reason why the United Nations and Unesco could not each run its own international broadcasting service?

Accordingly, my suggestion in regard to international radio broadcasting is twofold: in the first place efforts should be made to ensure that the existing services include programmes relating to world disarmament and secondly there should be at least one radio station transmitting twenty-four hours a day in support of the programme of general and complete disarmament decided upon.

A joint publishing venture

I would here like to single out for particular praise the recently launched international quarterly newspaper supplement focused on problems related to development, especially those dealing with the establishment of a new international economic order, which is being jointly published by sixteen major newspapers around the world. On the initiative of Unesco and the United Nations, a meeting of newspaper editors and directors of international agencies presided over by Kurt Waldheim agreed to the joint publication, with the following sixteen papers participating at the outset: *Asahi Shimbun*, Japan, which is generously providing support for newsprint costs where required; *Dawn*, Pakistan; *Excelsior*, Mexico; *Frankfurter Rundschau*, Federal Republic of Germany; *Indian Express*;

319

Jornal do Brasil; *Magyar Nemzet,* Hungary; *Le Monde,* France; *El Moujahid,* Algeria; *El Pais,* Spain; *Politica,* Yugoslavia; *Die Presse,* Austria; *Le Soleil,* Senegal; *La Stampa,* Italy; *Zycie Warszawy,* Poland; *Development Forum,* United Nations.

Each issue of the supplement, the first of which appeared in June and the second in September 1979, contains articles from the participating newspapers. Most noteworthy in this joint publishing venture is the variety of editorial, economic and ideological opinions represented, proving that differing viewpoints can be reconciled through co-operation and dialogue, that basic issues can be discussed without resorting to the usual blocs or simplified stereotypes. This achievement by such prominent representatives of the world press is expected to be expanded by additional participating newspapers and could well be extended to similar co-operation among broadcasters. I would urge that world disarmament become one of the principal objectives of this new endeavour. It is a significant example of international co-operation to support a common cause, as well as an indication of the aspirations that support the establishment of a new world communication order.

To conclude, may I suggest that the statement of the American Jesuit, Father T. McSorely, S.J., should be one of our slogans:

The taproot of violence in our society today is our intent to use nuclear weapons. Once we have agreed to that, all other evil is minor in comparison. Until we squarely face the question of our consent to use nuclear weapons, any hope of large-scale improvement of public morality is doomed to failure.

Notes

1. Séan MacBride, Nobel Peace Prize, 1974; Lenin International Prize for Peace, 1977; American Medal of Justice, 1978; Medal of the International Institute for Human Rights, 1978; President of the International Peace Bureau.

32

The imperative of disarmament education

Excerpts from the opening statements at the
World Congress on Disarmament Education,
Unesco, Paris, 9–13 June 1980

Education is basic to peace[1]

After the ending of the Second World War, Unesco's constitution declared that 'since wars begin in the minds of men, it is in the minds of men that the defences of peace must be constructed'.

Through education, through the spread of culture and through the broadest possible dissemination of information, Unesco's fundamental task is to work for peace, more especially by seeking to bring its influence to bear upon the conscience and intelligence of individuals and peoples so that they may overcome prejudice, misconceptions and the feelings of hatred and intolerance which give rise to aggressiveness and war. In order to achieve that end, we must first of all combat the injustices, inequalities and deep-rooted factors which strike at human dignity and create an atmosphere conducive to warfare, intolerance and misunderstanding.

I know that the idea of disarmament education is far from meeting with unanimous approval. I know, too, that many are still sceptical as to whether genuine disarmament is even a possibility. The debate on these issues has been going on for nearly a century. In the period between the two wars, what efforts were made in an attempt to secure from the great powers of the time a serious pledge to work towards genuine disarmament! We know what happened then. And since 1945, how many approaches have been made and constantly thwarted! How, then, can we fail to have misgivings about even the point of such action? Thirty-five years after the war, the arms race continues, acquiring ever more formidable proportions. The military blocs stand in defiance of one another, nuclear weapons develop and proliferate. At this very moment, as I speak to you, the world is spending a million dollars a minute to maintain military operations, while millions of human beings are suffering from hunger or starving to death, are the victims of diseases that accompany destitution, and are still illiterate. Surely we cannot fail to be staggered by the absurdity and the intolerable nature of the excessive arms build-up side by side with extreme poverty, ignorance and underdevelopment?

By proclaiming the decade starting in 1980 the 'Second Disarmament Decade', the General Assembly in effect conceded the failure of the First Decade announced in 1969. Although certain negotiations and agreements have given rise to mechanisms for monitoring the development of nuclear weapons, there has been no halt to the arms race and to its expansion.

It is vital, then, to find other ways whereby we may embark upon a genuine process of peace.

Education (genuine education, not merely instruction) is basic to justice; education is basic to peace; education is basic to the new order.

It is to build up the defences of peace in the minds of men that we must call on teachers, the mass media, parents, scientists and intellectuals. We must make clear that the aim is not to undermine national security or create antagonism in regard to the armed forces responsible for ensuring it, but to prevent force overriding reason, and weapons overriding dialogue.

It is increasingly clear that a genuine process of disarmament presupposes the development, within world opinion, of a new attitude, one that reflects a spirit of peace and co-operation.

It is here that Unesco's role can be decisive. By introducing education for disarmament, by the bold application of a policy of research on the socio-cultural factors conducive to the arms race, by disseminating reliable and objective information on all of its aspects, it is possible to create a new outlook which will gradually help to bring that race to a halt.

To learn to live peacefully[2]

Costa Rica decided to proscribe its army thirty years ago, as the debris of the Second World War still smouldered on the ground, thereby pledging to dedicate more of its resources to education and health.

We, in Costa Rica, wished to undertake a unique experiment. We asked ourselves if, in the end, it would be worth while, in terms of security or conquest, to maintain an army, or if, instead, and owing to man's rationality, it were possible to have greater trust in reason and the world than in weapons. The question seems naïve, but the answer has given us excellent results. Weapons do not offer security, and the most substantial and delightful victory is that which is attained without violence.

Humanity has tested the most varied prescriptions and formulae in order to stop war, hatred, and violence. Two alternatives are left for us: education and information. If we do not convert them into instruments of peace, there will not be a twenty-first century.

Is it possible to teach peace? Is it possible for man to learn to live peacefully? It is not necessary to return to Socrates' time, or to enter into Plato's Dialogues, in order to demonstrate that virtue is the object of knowledge, and that, through such learning, the society may be regenerated.

Disarmament is essentially a political decision, and we shall arrive at this goal when world pressure is so immense and overwhelming that politicians and the military are unable to oppose it. But this world force can only be attained, through education and information, as supplements of a great crusade of humanity that starts in school, continues in the home, and is then projected through information to the entire world.

United Nations called the 1970–80 period the Decade of Disarmament. The result of that decade is visible: an unprecedented expansion in the world's arms race, as though the dedication of humanity to a noble objective meant, in this era of the absurd and irrational, the attainment of the contrary. During this Disarmament Decade, military expenditures went up from $200,000 million in 1970 to more than $400,000 million in recent years.

The Report of the Club of Rome is clear on the subject. In the developing countries, there is one soldier for every 250 inhabitants, while there is only one physician for every 3,700. The industrialized nations have invested an annual average of $95 per person in their military forces, while they have only contributed an annual average of $5 per capita to the development of the poorer nations. With the estimated cost of an intercontinental ballistic missile, 50 million undernourished children in poorer countries could be adequately fed, 65,000 health care centres and 34,000 elementary schools could be built. In the developing countries, $230 are spent annually on each school-age child, and $14,800 are spent on each soldier.

For those of us who once decided to live without an army, without arsenals, and still strive to survive by the force of the world and reason, the law and freedom, this is a grotesque panorama.

A new international moral order

Novel forms and methods are needed in a changing and confusing world, seemingly content at remaining day and night on the verge of disaster. However, the true formulae are not the product of imagination, nor the fruit of novelty; rather, they are inside ourselves, and in the great cultural heritage of humanity. Let us promote reason through education, and let us announce, next to a new international economic order, a new moral order. Let us go back to the classroom, at the kindergarten, the primary and high school, and the university. Let us espouse without fear the greatness of absolute values, and the permanence of that which is essential. Let us preach a new humanism. Let us desperately cling, by conviction and desire to survive, to man's most effective instrument, education, in order for the subject of peace to invade the minds, hearts and consciences of children and young people from their infancy, since peace, like virtue, must also be the object of knowledge.

'The accumulation of destructive strength in the name of national defence is the main threat against international stability and human security,' and, as Einstein stated in 1950, 'the belief that it is possible to obtain security through weapons, under the present state of military technology, is a tragic illusion'. The reason for this fallacy or contradiction is found in an old Latin proverb, *'Si vis pacem, para bellum'*: if you desire peace, prepare for war. That is, peace has been conceived, throughout the history of humanity, as the preamble or prelude of war: not as a good in itself, and generator of other kinds of good for man, but as the lapse during which arms are polished, and strategies are revised for a new war. We live in the conviction that peace is only attainable by preparing ourselves for peace. *'Si vis pacem, para pacem.'* This is our principle. In other words, if we desire peace, there is but one way to fulfil our desire: educate for peace.

A radical departure from traditional concepts and values[3]

The General Assembly of the United Nations, at the Special Session Devoted to Disarmament in 1978, welcomed this initiative of Unesco and urged that disarmament education be developed as a distinct field of study. It is an initiative that has received unanimous and universal support and its realization will require manifold and concerted efforts.

At this stage, our task is to see how the writing of a new chapter in the long and creative history of education—a chapter on 'Disarmament Education'—can be started.

In taking these first steps, we should be fully aware of the fact that disarmament education not only represents a new field of activity, but that it also involves the promotion of a goal that is still far from fulfilment. Indeed, if one looks dispassionately at the present situation, one can see that, while it is fully recognized that war is not a rational instrument of policy, political ingenuity has thus far been unable to provide a real alternative to the system known as the balance of power or, in the language of our time, the balance of terror.

More than ever before states are seeking security through the accumulation of armaments. More than ever before, military considerations weigh heavily in national policies.

I mention these facts to stress that a programme on disarmament education will require a radical departure from traditional concepts and values.

In my view, the approach to disarmament education should be neither too narrow nor too technical. The approach should be such as to stimulate that attitude of mind that attaches primary importance to human development, aspirations and well-being. The problem of disarmament will always have to be kept in focus, but that should not exclude the setting of the problem in its historical and political context, nor the using of the experiences gained from other branches of knowledge and education.

On the financial aspects of information and studies concerning disarmament, the Secretary-General of the United Nations, Kurt Waldheim, made a concrete proposal at the Special Session of the General Assembly Devoted to Disarmament. Recalling the high investment that is devoted to research and development in the military field, he noted that nothing remotely comparable was devoted to research on how the arms race could be stopped and reversed. He, therefore, suggested that governments devote to national and international disarmament efforts $1 million for every $1,000 million currently spent on arms.

The Secretary-General, in his statement, also repeatedly stressed the need for increased emphasis on public education, if world public opinion was to be brought to bear effectively on disarmament.

May I be allowed, in this connection, to note that public opinion seems never to have been more perplexed and confused about security issues than it is at present. There may be many reasons for this, but one of them might be found in the existence of too many competing and contradictory strategic theories, which tend to obscure the issues rather than shedding light on them. This has contributed to forestaling an informed public debate. In other words, the public feels sometimes that the issues are too complex for it to try to understand them. And this is taking place at a time when there is an urgent need, more than ever, for public opinion to make its views clearly heard.

Re-ordering of priorities

The primary goal of a programme of disarmament education should be, therefore, to explain in clear and simple terms, to the largest possible number of people, what the realities of the present situation are and why in the nuclear age security is not to be found in an ever-expanding accumulation of arms, but in disarmament and in an ever-increasing degree of co-operation among nations. Co-operation, not confrontation, is the answer to the problems of a divided, crowded and restless world—a world that now possesses the means of total self-destruction.

To this effect, the programme should help disseminate authoritative information on world armaments and about the need for relentless international efforts to reduce them.

It should call attention to the fact that the problem of security cannot be narrowed down to one of increasing military expenditures.

It should call for a re-ordering of priorities, both national and international, to stop the further wastage of resources on the accumulation of weapons that can only bring ultimate destruction to mankind.

It should spread the message of the Final Document of the Special Session of the General Assembly of the United Nations, that the time has come to put an end to the arms race, to abandon the use of force an international relations and to seek security in disarmament, that is to say, through a gradual but effective process beginning with a reduction in the present level of armaments.

This is the only way we can avoid the appalling risks that threaten the future, and indeed the very survival, of the human family. In that regard, education can make a decisive contribution, because it is through education that any sensible human being develops an understanding of the need to coexist and co-operate with other human beings. If this implies a change of attitude, let us have a change.

Disarmament education as a democratization process[4]

The international community is increasingly coming to recognize the importance, as regards efforts in favour of disarmament, of fostering the *democratization* of the negotiations involved. In point of fact, it is imperative that not only the major powers but all countries should participate in the disarmament negotiation process, because the dangers of the arms race affect all nations alike. The threat of atomic war is lying in wait everywhere but, as we have also seen in the past decades, so-called conventional wars are being sparked off in various regions of the Third World and it is frequently the poorest and least developed countries which bear the brunt of those wars in terms of human and material losses and of the economic and social cost. Nor will it have escaped anybody that while the major powers avoid direct confrontation, they nevertheless come up against each other through the Third World countries which become embroiled in those conflicts and are powerless to avert them or solve them by themselves. World-wide concern over disarmament is accordingly bound to encompass all nations.

The second aspect of the democratization of disarmament negotiations is, to our mind, even more important. What somebody said about wars being too serious a matter to be left to generals is equally applicable to disarmament. Indeed, since people are, in the last resort, the main victims of the use of armed force, they ought also to take the most active part possible in the common effort in favour of disarmament. For this to come about, people have to be provided with information and education on disarmament, as they are in other spheres of knowledge.

This new stage in the democratization process is called 'disarmament education'.

A host of formidable obstacles

The task that has brought us together is not easy. Disarmament is not only a technical issue. If our children are to manage to live in a demilitarized world—and that is our most cherished hope—far-reaching changes are needed in international relations (including a new international order with all its economic, social and cultural implications), in social and political structures and in cultural values and personal attitudes. To achieve the ideals of a demilitarized world, from which the arms of mass destruction have been banished, a host of formidable obstacles will have to be overcome. Let us examine some of them.

It has frequently been pointed out how necessary it is to redirect the flow of economic resources earmarked for military purposes towards the socio-economic development of peoples. But there is also a general awareness of the difficulties involved in the redeployment of production for military purposes to production of goods and services for development, especially in times of recession and growing unemployment in many industrial economies, not to mention the powerful interests of all kinds that are vested in the production and sale of arms.

Discussion sometimes centres around who is more responsible for the arms race: those who export arms or those who buy them. The argument is a fallacious one, for the international arms trade which economically benefits sellers and buyers alike is an inseparable whole and action for disarmament must affect them both equally.

In recent decades there has been an abundance of different political and strategic doctrines concerning foreign or domestic security or the vital interests of such and such a state. This is due to the growing possibility of armed conflict entered into not for the purpose of repelling a military attack, but as an answer to an economic or political challenge. Furthermore, surveys have shown that in various regions of the world the acquisition of armaments more often serves for the maintenance of domestic peace than for defence against foreign aggression.

These processes, in turn, generate an atmosphere in which public opinion is conditioned to think that there is a certain kind of conflict which can only be resolved by the use of force or the threat of force; and this makes it difficult to increase the numbers of those who are in favour of a non-violent and peaceful solution to conflicts, and creates currents of opinion favourable to the continuation of the arms race.

As far as mass psychology is concerned, based on the spread of certain fashionable theories, it is often held that man is naturally aggressive and given to violence, and that recourse to arms consequently responds to certain innate tendencies in human beings and cannot be avoided.

Most of our school textbooks, history books and popular literature help to conjure up a glorified vision of military personalities, feats of arms, wars and conquests, to which children are conditioned from an early age.

The mass media bring grist to the mill in a wide variety of ways: films, television series and radio programmes, and the sale of games and toys of a military nature (from tin soldiers to electronic galaxy wars), all of which are mass-produced throughout the world by specialized industries, including a number of multinational corporations.

Faced as we are with this series of obstacles—among others which may truly appear to be insurmountable, there is a need for a global, multilateral effort to promote disarmament, with the active participation of peoples and not just governments, which would lead to a gradual demilitarization of our societies. In this collective effort, the great potential strength of a well-informed public opinion is of paramount importance. We may recall that since the end of the last world war, public opinion and non-violent action by peoples have contributed more than once to peaceful decolonization, to putting an end to colonial wars or those with no popular support, or to overthrowing anti-democratic dictatorships.

This is why disarmament education is of particular significance at the present time for the peoples of the world, especially for those of the developing countries which are seeking to emerge from hunger and poverty. At present, 100 times more is spent on every soldier than on every primary-school pupil in the world. How can that proportion and that trend be reversed? Grandiloquent or pious declarations are not enough, moralizing speeches are not enough, good intentions are not enough. What must be done is to develop specific programmes and projects consistent with the profound aspirations for peace and justice of all the peoples of the world.

Notes

1. From the address by Frederico Mayor, Deputy Director-General of Unesco.
2. From the opening address by Rodrigo Carazo, President of the Republic of Costa Rica.
3. From the statement by Jan Mårtenson, United Nations Assistant Secretary-General, United Nations Centre for Disarmament.
4. From the address by Rodolfo Stavenhagen, Assistant Director-General, Sector for Social Sciences and their Applications, Unesco.

33

Disarmament education as a distinct field of study

Alessandro Corradini
Former Director and Deputy to the Assistant Director-General,
United Nations Centre for Disarmament

The conceptual framework

At the Special Session of the General Assembly Devoted to Disarmament held in 1978, the members of the United Nations, in the Final Document of the session, urged Unesco to step up its programme aimed at the development of disarmament education as 'a distinct field of study'.

Developing a programme of disarmament education will undoubtedly prove to be a challenging task, as there are only a few clearly established points of reference on the subject and the subject itself calls for a deep reassessment of many traditional concepts and values, particularly with regard to peace and security.

In this connection, the first paragraph of the Final Document of the Special Session of the General Assembly Devoted to Disarmament offers a most eloquent example of the thinking which necessarily must inspire a programme of disarmament education. It may be useful, therefore, to quote the paragraph in its entirety:

The attainment of the objective of security, which is an inseparable element of peace, has always been one of the most profound aspirations of humanity. States have for a long time sought to maintain their security through the possession of arms. Admittedly, their survival has, in certain cases, effectively depended on whether they could count on appropriate means of defence. Yet the accumulation of weapons, particularly nuclear weapons, today constitutes much more a threat than a protection for the future of mankind. The time has therefore come to put an end to this situation, to abandon the use of force in international relations and to seek security in disarmament, that is to say, through a gradual but effective process beginning with a reduction in the present level of armaments. The ending of the arms race and the achievement of real disarmament are tasks of primary importance and urgency. To meet this historic challenge is in the political and economic interests of all the nations and peoples of the world as well as in the interests of ensuring their genuine security and peaceful future.

In this opening statement of the Final Document, the problem is not only clearly defined but also set in an historical context, and the element of change, which dominates the present course of human events, is rightly emphasized.

Shortened version from the *Bulletin of Peace Proposals*, Vol. 11, No. 3, 1980.

'The unleashed power of the atom', said Einstein, 'has changed everything except our way of thinking,' and he warned the peoples of the world and their governments that they would bring unprecedented disaster upon themselves 'unless there is a fundamental change in their attitudes towards one another as well as in their concept of the future'.

The implications of the 'unleashed power of the atom' and the need to evolve a new peaceful 'concept of the future' are, indeed, the core of any programme of disarmament education.

A philosophy of disarmament

Starting from the premise contained in paragraph 1 as quoted above, the Final Document examined the potentialities of disarmament in relation to international peace and security, in a comprehensive and detailed manner, and in so doing it established clear principles and guidelines for action.

Meaningful points can be found in each one of its 129 paragraphs, but the following, more than others, express the philosophy underlying the document:

(a) The existence of nuclear weapons and the continuing arms race pose a growing threat not only to international peace and security but to the very survival of mankind (paras. 1, 2, 11, 18, 47);

(b) The arms race is not diminishing but increasing and outstrips by far the efforts to curb it (para. 4);

(c) The present situation, marked as it is by the accumulation of vast stockpiles of arms and a tremendous build-up of armed forces, both reflects and aggravates international tensions, sharpens conflicts in various regions of the world, hinders the process of détente, exacerbates the differences between opposing military alliances, jeopardizes the security of all states and increases the threat of nuclear war (para. 11);

(d) Enduring peace and security cannot be built on the accumulation of weaponry by military alliances, nor be sustained by a precarious balance of deterrence or doctrines of strategic superiority (para. 13);

(e) Security must be sought in disarmament, i.e. through a gradual but effective process beginning with a reduction in the present level of armaments (para. 1);

(f) The adoption of disarmament measures should take place in such an equitable and balanced manner as to ensure the right of each state to security and prevent individual states or groups of states from obtaining advantages over others at any stage. At each stage the objective should be undiminished security at the lowest possible level of armaments and military forces (para. 29);

(g) Effective measures of nuclear disarmament and the prevention of nuclear war have the highest priority. To this end, it is imperative to remove the threat of nuclear weapons, to halt and reverse the nuclear arms race until the total elimination of nuclear weapons and their delivery systems has been achieved, and to prevent the proliferation of nuclear weapons (para. 20);

(h) Negotiations should also be carried out on the balanced reduction of armed forces and of conventional armaments, based on the principle of undiminished security of the parties with a view to promoting or enhancing stability at a lower level of armaments and forces (para. 22);

(i) There should also be negotiations on the limitation of international transfer of conventional weapons (para. 22);

(j) In general, priorities in disarmament negotiations should be: nuclear weapons; other weapons of mass destruction, including chemical weapons; conventional weapons; and reduction of armed forces. Nothing should, however, preclude states from conducting negotiations on all priority items concurrently (paras. 45 and 46);

(k) General and complete disarmament under effective international control is the ultimate objective of the efforts of states in disarmament (para. 20);

(l) All the peoples of the world have a vital interest in the success of disarmament negotiations (para. 28);

(m) All states have the duty to contribute to efforts in the field of disarmament and all states have the right to participate on an equal footing in those disarmament negotiations which have a direct bearing on their national security (para. 28);

(n) While disarmament is the responsibility of all states, the nuclear-weapon states have primary responsibility for nuclear disarmament and, together with other militarily significant states, for halting and reversing the arms race. It is therefore important to secure their active participation (para. 28);

(o) The arms race impedes the realization of the purposes, and is incompatible with the principles, of the Charter of the United Nations, especially respect for sovereignty, refraining from the threat or use of force against the territorial integrity or political independence of any state, peaceful settlement of disputes and non-intervention and non-interference in the internal affairs of states. It also adversely affects the rights of people freely to determine their systems of social and economic development, and hinders the struggle for self-determination and the elimination of colonial rule, racial or foreign domination or occupation (para. 12);

(p) Disarmament, relaxation of international tensions, respect for the right to self-determination and national independence, the peaceful settlement of disputes in accordance with the Charter of the United Nations and the strengthening of international peace and security are directly related to each other. Progress in any of these spheres has a beneficial effect on all of them; in turn, failure in one sphere has negative effects on others (para. 34);

(q) Progress in disarmament should be accompanied by measures to strengthen the institutions for maintaining peace and the settlement of disputes by peaceful means (para. 110);

(r) In a world of finite resources there is a close relationship between expenditure on armaments and economic and social development. The hundreds of billions of dollars spent annually for military purposes are in sombre and dramatic contrast to the want and poverty in which two-thirds of the world's population live. Resources released as a result of the implementation of disarmament measures should be used in a manner which will help to promote the well-being of all peoples and to improve the conditions of the developing countries (paras. 16, 35);

(s) The economic and social consequences of the arms race are so detrimental that its continuation is obviously incompatible with the implementation of the new international economic order based on justice, equity and co-operation (para. 16);

(t) The General Assembly of the United Nations should continue to consider what concrete steps should be taken to facilitate the reduction of military budgets (para. 90);

(u) In order to facilitate the conclusion and effective implementation of disarmament agreements and to create confidence, states should accept appropriate provisions of verification in such agreements (para. 91);

(v) Although the decisive factor for achieving real measures of disarmament is the 'political will' of states, and especially of those possessing nuclear weapons, a significant role can also be played by the effective functioning of an appropriate international machinery designed to deal with the problems of disarmament in its various aspects (para. 10);

(w) For maximum effectiveness two kinds of bodies are required in the field of disarmament—deliberative and negotiating. All Member States should be represented on the former, whereas the latter, for the sake of convenience, should have a relatively small membership (para. 113);

(x) The reduction of armaments and armed forces should be pursued both through international agreements and a policy of mutual example (para. 13);

(y) The United Nations, in accordance with its Charter, has a central role and primary responsibility in the sphere of disarmament. In order effectively to fulfil its responsibility, the United Nations should be active in the field, should encourage and facilitate all disarmament efforts—unilateral, bilateral, regional or multilateral—and be kept duly informed of their progress and results (paras. 27 and 114);

(z) The role and responsibility of the United Nations in the sphere of disarmament must be strengthened (para. 14).

Taken together, these views express a clear and coherent philosophy of disarmament and, as such, they provide a solid and valuable basis for the elaboration of a programme of disarmament education.

A definition of disarmament

There are numerous current definitions of disarmament and many, too many, concepts for a subject of such critical importance, among them 'regulation', 'limitation', 'reduction' and 'elimination' of armaments, as well as 'arms control'. It is difficult, therefore, to disagree with the suggestion that the concept of disarmament should be extricated from the 'terminological jungle' which has grown up around it, particularly since the introduction of the term 'arms control'.[1]

By taking an unambiguous position on the question of disarmament, the Final Document has contributed most significantly to bringing back the true meaning of disarmament, that is, the reduction and, ultimately, the elimination of armaments. It should also be clear from what has been said in the previous section of this chapter that the philosophy of the Final Document is a philosophy of disarmament, not of regulation of armaments or, what is the same, of arms control.

The expressions 'regulation of armaments' and 'arms control' do not appear anywhere in the document. It consistently takes the view that security in the nuclear age must be sought through the reduction and ultimate elimination of armaments. The Final Document sometimes refers to 'arms limitation', but even in those instances a reduction is implied, given the document's clear goal as set out in its very first paragraph and subsequent ones.

Even where the document refers to measures that do not call for reductions of armaments, such as 'collateral' and 'confidence-building' measures, it is made clear that they should be undertaken as a way of contributing to the creation of favourable conditions for the adoption of concrete disarmament measures (para. 24). The same applies to the cessation of nuclear-weapon tests by all states, a measure that is placed by the Final Document 'within the framework of an effective nuclear disarmament process' and is viewed, in particular, as a means of halting the qualitative improvement of nuclear weapons and the development of new types of such weapons and of preventing the proliferation of nuclear weapons (para. 51).

Even more important, the Final Document considered that SALT II should constitute a step in the direction of nuclear disarmament, i.e. it should be followed promptly by further strategic arms-limitation negotiations, 'leading to agreed significant reductions of, and qualitative limitations on, strategic arms' (para. 52).

Thus, no alternative to a policy of disarmament is envisaged in the Final Document. No plan is offered on 'how to live with the bomb'. On the contrary, what is repeatedly urged is the halting and reversing of the arms race, particularly the nuclear arms race, and the achievement of real disarmament.

This position of the General Assembly was, of course, the inescapable conclusion deriving from the recognition of the fact that 'the accumulation of weapons, particularly nuclear weapons, today constitutes much more a threat than a protection for the future of mankind'. Indeed, the Assembly went even further and warned that mankind today is confronted with 'an unprecedented threat of self-extinction arising from the massive and competitive accumulation of the most destructive weapons ever produced' (para. 11).

Under these circumstances, the General Assembly could offer only one strategy for survival, namely, the development of an effective alternative to the arms race that would ensure, through well-organized efforts by the international community, genuine security and a peaceful future for all the nations and peoples of the world.

Too often, the distinction between arms regulation and disarmament has been ignored and this has created much confusion about the very nature of the problems involved in the implementation of a disarmament policy.

In a programme of education for disarmament the distinction should be clearly maintained. Of course, the distinction does not imply incompatibility. This is reflected in the Charter of the United Nations, which in Article 11 associates disarmament with the regulation of armaments. Consequently, every possible effort should be made to explore whether in some cases measures of arms control could ultimately lead to concrete measures of disarmament. For instance, prohibition of use of certain categories of weapons could, under certain circumstances, become the starting-point for their ultimate elimination. This has happened in the case of biological weapons and it might happen again with regard to chemical weapons.

However, the record thus far has not been very encouraging.

As the General Assembly recognized in its Final Document, with regard to the agreements of the past two decades, 'the fact remains that these agreements relate only to measures of limited restraint while the arms race continues' (para. 17).

Similarly, the Secretary-General of the United Nations has on a number of occasions called attention to the fact that those agreements, while regulating to some extent the competition in armaments and proscribing certain particularly undesirable developments, have not resulted in any reduction of important weapon systems, nor have they restrained the pace of the arms race.

Disarmament education

Having clarified the meaning of the word 'disarmament', how should the expression 'disarmament education' be understood?

Here a distinction can be, and has been, drawn between education *about* disarmament and education *for* disarmament. The former, it has been said, concentrates on the reasons why disarmament should be sought and provides information on what is done and should be done to achieve disarmament. The latter aims at generating 'such attitudes, decisions and actions as will promote disarmament'.[2]

The ultimate goal of a programme of disarmament education is undoubtedly to promote disarmament. On this basis, the choice between education about disarmament and education for disarmament should not pose very serious difficulties. A commitment to education for disarmament, i.e. to developing attitudes that will help promote disarmament, should not exclude, however, the acquisition of a body of notions about disarmament. Undoubtedly, people must be convinced about the reasons why disarmament can contribute to national and international security and thus to peace. They must also be informed on present and past efforts to make progress towards disarmament and on the concrete results of those efforts.

What is most important is that the acquisition of such notions never be considered an end in itself. Disarmament education cannot consist only in reiterating what has been said and done (or has not been done) under the name of disarmament since the end of the Second World War, or even earlier. For, as Salvador de Madariaga said half a century ago, 'Understanding and not mere knowledge is what is needed if the problem of disarmament is to find a solution.' He also rightly stressed that of all the obstacles related to the question of disarmament, none was so difficult to overcome as the psychological obstacle, and this led him to offer a most valuable pedagogical approach. If the main obstacle is in the mind and soul of men, he said, we must try to reach the mind and soul by the most direct approach, i.e. 'through man's sensibility to events conveyed in vital form by aesthetic means'.[3]

Education for disarmament, therefore, should help people to understand, through an effective and judicious approach, why and how disarmament can contribute to the attainment of a stable and secure peace. It should also help develop attitudes that will promote disarmament, i.e. stimulate greater awareness of the need for a higher degree of co-operation. Indeed, the path of disarmament is most difficult to follow 'for men and women whose innermost texture has been woven with prejudices, traditions and feelings inimical to human co-operation'.[4]

Disarmament and the strengthening of national and international security

In a programme of disarmament education, the relationship between disarmament and security must necessarily occupy a prominent place.

The crucial role of disarmament for the strengthening of security in all its aspects has been emphasized in numerous documents and resolutions of the United Nations. Yet the relationship between disarmament and security still presents complex problems which require thorough and systematic consideration. In particular, a critical examination of the prevalent assumption that military power equals security appears to be urgently needed.

This is an area in which, one must admit, there is no uniformity of views, because security is an area that is dominated by the way in which nations visualize the attainment of their own goals, free from external threats.

It should be recognized, however, that the concept of national security—a concept in which many different elements coexist—has been unduly oversimplified, and that too often national security is identified exclusively with large military forces and the possession of sophisticated and costly weapons. In other words, the tendency has been to narrow down the problem of security to one of increasing spending for military programmes. Security, however, does not necessarily increase with large military investments and, as it has been noted, there is a point beyond which, even under conditions of military competition, expenditures on defence are not only wasted but will take away funds which are needed for other essential sectors such as education, health and economic development.

Other important points, which are of great relevance to a programme of disarmament education, have been made by the Secretary-General of the United Nations in a preliminary report on the relationship between international security and disarmament which he submitted to the Special Session of the General Assembly Devoted to Disarmament, in 1978.[5]

What is involved in this relationship was described by the Secretary-General as follows.

First, the process of continuous arms acquisition has in itself become a major source of insecurity. The emergence of new weapons systems, the refinement of old ones and their proliferation throughout the world, while often designed to redress or restore a military balance, in fact lead to military instability, rivalry and tension. Seen in perspective, the period since the Second World War has been one of continuing accumulation of weapons and, concomitantly, diminishing international security.

Second, progress in disarmament would vastly increase the scope for international co-operation in all fields, for in an international environment dominated by the arms race there is a heightening of mistrust and confrontation between nations and their political and economic relations tend to be subordinated to military-strategic considerations. The halting and reversal of the arms race would contribute to the consolidation of a policy of détente and its expansion in functional and geographical terms and would thus tend to ensure that relations among nations are conducted in accordance with the principles of national independence and sovereignty, equality of rights, non-resort to force or the threat of force and the right of every people to decide its own destiny.

Third, effective measures of disarmament would also facilitate the solution of a number of problems which are not only of critical importance in their own right, but constitute some of the most important facets of the security problems facing the world. Among these are the problem of development and the related task of establishing a new international economic order. Progress towards the solution of the problems of poverty, hunger, illiteracy and disease that afflict a large part of mankind would tend to create favourable conditions for order and stability and to eliminate situations conducive to conflict and disruption at the international and domestic levels.

The Secretary-General also noted that initially armaments may be a symptom of underlying political differences, but beyond a certain point the armaments programmes themselves, the tensions they cause in many parts of the world and the attitudes and institutions they give rise to, assume the character of independent forces propelling the arms race. In this situation, countries tend to view questions of international peace and security chiefly in terms of relationships of force and of military safeguards against any conceivable contingency. Therein lies a major obstacle to disarmament: the arms race fosters the very attitudes and institutions which perpetuate it.

To break that vicious circle, the Secretary-General pointed out, involved a two-fold task: the cessation of the arms race and disarmament, on the one hand, and the building up of a system of world order based on collective responsibility on the other. This might require greater efforts to seek a common understanding of the causes and mechanisms that sustained the arms race and, at an appropriate stage, the development of more reliable means for the maintenance of international peace and security. There was also a need for a more thorough exploration of the way in which the processes of disarmament and of strengthening international security are linked, and of the precise relationships that may exist between specific measures in these two fields.

Working and organizing for peace

The history of mankind, it has been said, *'est faite de guerres gagnées et de paix perdues'.*[6] Nothing bears witness to this state of affairs more than the many thousands of peace treaties that have been recorded since the dawn of human history.[7] Yet, if one single nuclear conflict were to break out, no peace treaty could ensure the continuation of life on earth. Consequently, in the nuclear age there is no real alternative to peace.

Obviously, this does not mean that the danger of war is no longer present in our time. Let us not forget that since 1945 there have been more than one hundred wars and other conflicts which have resulted in over 25 million casualties and widespread destruction. What is meant is that there is no assurance that mankind would survive a general nuclear war and that, therefore, the ultimate goal of all mankind must be the maintenance and strengthening of peace in the interest of present and future generations.

It was this thinking that inspired the recent Declaration of the Preparation of Societies for Life in Peace,[8] which was adopted by the General Assembly just a few months after the conclusion of the Special Session Devoted to Disarmament, on the initiative of Poland. In that declaration, the General Assembly, recognizing that peace among nations is 'mankind's paramount value', held in highest esteem by all principal political, social and religious movements, called upon all states to ensure that their policies, 'including educational processes and teaching methods as well as media information activities', would be compatible with the task of the preparation for life in peace of their respective societies. The declaration also underlined the fact that a prerequisite for the maintenance of peace is the elimination of the threat inherent in the arms race.

Indeed the most effective way to develop a policy of co-operation and peace would be for all states, and in particular the major powers, to engage themselves now in a gradual process of disarmament beginning with a reduction in their present level of armaments. This would have an immediate beneficial effect because, as the Final Document clearly recognized (para. 11), while the accumulation of arms and the build-up of armed forces reflects international tensions, it also aggravates them.

It must be recognized that, on this question of how to start a process of disarmament, two different schools of thought have confronted each other for a long time and the matter will, perhaps, never be definitively settled on a theoretical basis. First, there are those who, believing that armaments are the cause of war, are in favour of a direct or technical method, 'whereby a direct solution is sought in the examination of the technical means for reducing and limiting armaments at once'. Second, there are those who believe that wars are the cause of arms, and see the cure of war in the indirect or political method 'whereby the solution of the problem is sought in the creation of the political circumstances required for disarmament to take place, so to say, of itself'.[9]

The distinction is legitimate, but not such as to create an insurmountable obstacle to disarmament. As it has been rightly noted, progress in disarmament must be determined, in practice, by the interplay of those two approaches.[10] What is of crucial importance is that both elements—the political as well as the technical—be brought to bear on the solution of the problem.

In its Final Document the General Assembly agreed that progress in disarmament should be accompanied by measures to strengthen the institutions for maintaining peace and for the settlement of disputes by peaceful means (para. 110). Similarly, the Secretary-General of the United Nations, as indicated earlier in this chapter, has spoken of a two-fold task, namely, the cessation of the arms race and disarmament, on the one hand, and the building up of a system of world order, on the other.

Concluding remarks

As to the basic concepts of a programme of disarmament education, an attempt has been made to explore them. They can be summarized as follows:

1. The subject of disarmament should be placed in an historical context as there is nothing utopian about disarmament. While the common element of all utopias is the rejection of history, disarmament has been in the mainstream of history since 1919, and even earlier. Since the dawn of the nuclear age it has become a prerequisite for the survival of humankind.

2. The element of change, as represented by the 'unleashed power of the atom', has introduced an entirely new dimension into the relations between nations, which must necessarily be rethought in the light of the new realities. The role of disarmament—both nuclear and conventional—in relation to peace should be a major aspect of any such reassessment.

3. The Final Document of the Special Session of the General Assembly Devoted to Disarmament, a document that the whole membership of the United Nations adopted by consensus, provides the most complete set of principles and guidelines for disarmament.

4. The concept of disarmament, which is that of reduction and elimination of weapons, and the concept of regulation of armaments or arms control are not

incompatible, but moving from the one to the other implies a reversal in the direction of the arms race.

5. Disarmament education should help promote disarmament. It should develop greater understanding of what is needed if the problem of disarmament is to find a solution. It should make people aware of the need for a higher degree of co-operation at all levels.

6. The contents of the programme of disarmament education should in no way be confused or replaced with the contents of a programme of strategic studies.

7. The relationship between disarmament and security is an area that, thus far, has not received systematic consideration, even though it has been the subject of investigation. This relationship should be a focal point of a programme of disarmament education and efforts should be made to develop a coherent line of thought on this critical subject.

8. The development of disarmament education as a 'distinct' field of study should not imply treating the subject of disarmament in 'isolation' from other fields of human endeavour. Disarmament must be related first of all to peace, mankind's paramount goal.

9. It should also be recognized that disarmament has its roots in international politics and that, therefore, every possible effort should be made on all sides to create and maintain the political conditions that will facilitate the achievement of disarmament measures. In a process of disarmament, there are both technical and political problems to be solved and there is a constant interplay between the two.

10. A programme of disarmament education should include a study of how disarmament is related to the building up and strengthening of a system of world order. It should be understood that disarmament implies the progressive development of an organized peace system, but that disarmament should be pursued at every stage of the process of institution-building.

Notes

1. Alva Myrdal, *The Game of Disarmament*, p. xvi, New York, 1976.
2. Anatol Pikas, 'Disarmament Education through Teacher Training', *Bulletin of Peace Proposals*, Vol. 11, No. 3, 1980.
3. Salvador de Madariaga, *Disarmament*, pp. x–xi, London, 1929.
4. Ibid., p. xi.
5. United Nations Document A/S-10/7.
6. Gaston Bouthoul, *La Paix*, p. 21, Paris, 1974.
7. 'Un historien patient a compté entre 1500 avant J.-C. et 1860, c'est-à-dire en trois mille ans environ, plus de huit mille traités de paix connus, et qui, tous, devaient subsister éternellement. Ce chiffre considérable est certainement très inférieur à la réalité. . . .' Bouthoul, *Huit mille traités de paix*, p. 11, Paris, 1948.
8. General Assembly resolution 33/73.
9. De Madariaga, op. cit., p. 24.
10. Ibid.

34

Ten principles
for disarmament education

Extract from the Final Document of the World Congress
on Disarmament Education
Unesco, Paris, 9–13 June 1980

1. Relation of education to disarmament

Disarmament education, an essential component of peace education, implies both education about disarmament and education for disarmament. All who engage in education or communication may contribute to disarmament education by being aware and creating an awareness of the factors underlying the production and acquisition of arms, of the social, political, economic and cultural repercussions of the arms race and of the grave danger for the survival of humanity of the existence and potential use of nuclear weapons.

2. Definition of disarmament

For the purpose of disarmament education, disarmament may be understood as any form of action aimed at limiting, controlling or reducing arms, including unilateral disarmament initiatives, and, ultimately, general and complete disarmament under effective international control. It may also be understood as a process aimed at transforming the current system of armed nation states into a new world order of planned unarmed peace in which war is no longer an instrument of national policy and peoples determine their own future and live in security based on justice and solidarity.

3. Role of information

Disarmament education requires the collection and dissemination of reliable information from sources offering the highest degree of objectivity in accordance with a free and more balanced international flow of information. It should prepare learners, in the strictest respect for freedom of opinion, expression and information, to resist incitement to war, military propaganda and militarism in general.

4. Relation to economic and political realities

Disarmament education cannot, however, confine itself to the dissemination of data and information on disarmament projects and prospects nor even to commenting on the hopes and ideals which inspired them. It should recognize fully the relationship disarmament has with achieving international security and realizing development. To be effective in this regard, disarmament education should be related to the lives and concerns of the learners and to the political realities within which disarmament is sought and should provide insights into the political, economic and social factors on which the security of peoples could be based.

5. Research and decision-making

In addition to reaching the general public, disarmament education has a more specific and equally crucial task of providing rational arguments for disarmament based on independent scientific research which can guide decision-makers and, to the extent possible, rectify perceptions of a potential adversary based on incomplete or inaccurate information.

6. Substantive approaches

As an approach to international peace and security, disarmament education should take due account of the principles of international law based on the Charter of the United Nations, in particular, the refraining from the threat or use of force against the territorial integrity or political independence of states, the peaceful settlement of disputes, non-intervention in domestic affairs and self-determination of peoples. It should also draw upon the international law of human rights and international humanitarian law applicable in time of armed conflict and consider alternative approaches to security, including such non-military defence systems as non-violent civilian action. The study of United Nations efforts, of confidence-building measures, of peace-keeping, of non-violent conflict resolution and of other means of controlling international violence take on special importance in this regard. Due attention should be accorded in programmes of disarmament education to the right of conscientious objection and the right to refuse to kill. Disarmament education should provide an occasion to explore, without prejudging the issue, the implications for disarmament of the root causes of individual and collective violence and the objective and subjective causes of tensions, crises, disputes and conflicts which characterize the current national and international structures reflecting factors of inequality and injustice.

7. Links with human rights and development

As an integral part of peace education, disarmament education has essential links with human rights education and development education, in so far as each of the three terms peace, human rights and development must be defined in relation to the other two. Moreover, disarmament education offers an occasion to elucidate emerging concepts such as the individual and collective rights to peace and to development, based on the satisfaction of material and non-material human needs.

8. Pedagogical objectives

Whether conceived as education in the spirit of disarmament, as the incorporation of relevant materials in existing disciplines or as the development of a distinct field of study, disarmament education should apply the most imaginative educational methods, particularly those of participatory learning, geared to each specific cultural and social situation and level of education. It aims at teaching *how* to think about disarmament rather than *what* to think about it. It should therefore be problem-centred so as to develop the analytical and critical capacity to examine and evaluate practical steps towards the reduction of arms and the elimination of war as an acceptable international practice.

9. Values

Disarmament education should be based upon the values of international understanding, tolerance of ideological and cultural diversity and commitment to social justice and human solidarity.

10. Sectors of society concerned

Disarmament education should be the concern of all sectors of society and public opinion. Indeed, schools, non-formal and informal education circles such as the family, community organizations and the world of work, universities and other research centres and information media, all have a part to play in this task. Educators and communicators should strive to develop the most appropriate and effective language and teaching methods for each situation. The challenge is all the greater as the stakes are so high.

35

Secondary-school and teacher-training curricula for disarmament education: problems, needs and priorities

Betty Reardon, World Council for Curriculum
and Instruction

Introduction

In order to acquire information regarding the current status of curricula for disarmament education at the secondary-school and teacher-training levels, a simple survey questionnaire, calling for brief narrative replies, was circulated to around 1,000 educators in over sixty countries. Approximately 300 were sent with a cover letter to selected educators working in curriculum development and teacher education in some twenty countries in all world regions. Among this number were also about thirty peace educators and 200 people from the Unesco Associated Schools Projects and National Commissions. Over 500 were distributed with the WCCI *Newsletter* and 300 with the COPRED *Chronicle*.

While there is no assurance that the majority of these questionnaires were actually received by the individuals to whom they were addressed, the return, slightly over sixty responses from less than thirty countries, was extremely limited. Nor were there responses which indicated that the questionnaire itself, in form or content discouraged response (one respondant, who replied to almost all the questions, said it was difficult.) Several were returned with responses to the effect that 'there is no disarmament education in our country or institution'. Some curriculum experts wrote: 'I know of no curricula on disarmament.' The most common reply to the question on obstacles to disarmament education was: 'Lack of curriculum material'.

While these results may have been disappointing, considering the hopes of the reviewer that progress in the field had occurred in the two years since a preliminary survey on the topic had been conducted among a narrower sample of peace educators (Unesco SS/78 Conf. 603), they were not surprising, as those peace educators working on issues and topics related to the arms race and

Paper presented at the World Congress on Disarmament Education, Unesco, Paris, 9–13 June 1980.

disarmament are generally of the opinion that curricular materials dealing substantively and directly with these issues and topics are not available. There are a few scattered units, but no systematically fully developed curricula. This lack of material is the more to be deplored because it is equally evident that the field of peace education has developed adequate conceptual frameworks and appropriate pedagogical approaches for dealing with most other peace-related topics in a responsible and effective manner. What has been made even more evident by this recent survey is that disarmament is possibly the most complex and difficult of all subjects in the field of peace education. It presents unique and challenging needs in curriculum development and some distinct priorities for educational research. The two levels of education at which the needs are especially pressing and the priorities particularly urgent are teacher training and secondary schools.

Teacher training is vital because teaching *per se* is the single most influential factor in the entire process of formal education. Teachers profoundly affect not only substantive knowledge but also intellectual and analytical development and world-view and socio-political attitudes. These latter two affective matters are, according to the opinion of both educators and politicians, probably the most significant determinants of the conditions under which disarmament is sought. World-view is significant in that it determines to a large extent what is deemed to be important and worth struggling for, as well as attitudes towards allies and opponents in the struggle. Socio-political attitudes affect the limits of pragmatic possibilities for policy-making and the level of attention accorded to particular public issues. Few would argue that disarmament can be achieved without its coming to be perceived as important and worth struggling for and to be seen as a practical political possibility. Public attitudes in these areas are most deeply influenced by the media, political leadership and education. It is the latter influence which provides the specific intellectual and analytical skills which citizens bring to bear on the formation of opinion in public affairs. Education is, therefore, the most obvious channel through which the public can be prepared to think systematically and constructively about disarmament issues. Teachers as the agents for this preparation bear a great responsibility and possess an excellent opportunity to affect public information and opinion about the central question of our era: 'Can we put an end to the spiral of destructive capacity and overcome the threat to human survival posed by the arms race?' Teachers may be in as significant a position to influence the achievement of disarmament as are political leaders. The knowledge they have of the issues and problems related to disarmament and the skills of issues analysis and problem-solving that they are able to communicate to students are crucial to the success of any disarmament process. Teacher education should, therefore, be a top priority for disarmament education.

While it must be recognized that the majority of the earth's people, all of whom have a vital stake in the achievement of disarmament, are not able to attend secondary school, none the less this level of formal education is the next most important influence on widespread citizen education about disarmament. Several factors make secondary education extremely significant for substantive education about the arms race and disarmament. First, it is the level at which the specific subject-matter of citizenship education is taught, and students are introduced to social problems and public issues. The refinement of attitudes and beginning of systematic thinking about politics takes place during the secondary-school years. Many who later become active citizens and leaders in opinion formation begin to develop their interests and activities at this stage; some are guided in the cultivation of their analytical capacities and clarification of their world-views by well-prepared teachers who do not seek to inculcate a particular view, but to help students to develop the capacity to make their own analyses and formulate their own world-views. Finally, and maybe most important with regard to disarmament, the enrolment in secondary schools is highest in the industrial weapon-producing nations, especially 'the major powers' which have the greatest potential and responsibility for the achievement of disarmament. It is essential that the citizens of these nations be well educated in the problems of and prospects for disarmament.

Conceptual problems in curriculum development for disarmament education

The major problems of curriculum development are conceptual. To state the issue most succinctly: peace educators have failed to identify the basic concepts upon which to build curricula to teach specifically about disarmament as such. We do not have the conceptual tools with which to think about disarmament.

While the resolution of these conceptual problems alone will not overcome all the obstacles to disarmament education, their clarification is essential to fulfilling the need for curriculum development. To insist on their centrality is not to overlook the usefulness of existing materials and methods of peace education, many of which can be integrated into an adequate 'education *for* disarmament', by which is meant an education to cultivate an understanding of the necessity of disarmament, and to promote favourable attitudes towards disarmament. Indeed, there is every reason to encourage and initiate this form of disarmament education immediately, so that it provides the background and groundwork for that specific, substantive form, 'education *about* disarmament and how to achieve it'. This latter form is most suited to secondary education and should be a requirement of teacher education.

The conceptual problems and research requirements discussed in this chapter will derive primarily from 'education *about* disarmament'. While 'education *for* disarmament' comprises significant cognitive knowledge about facts related to the need for and the history of disarmament efforts, the main objectives are in the affective domain, particularly in those attitudes that have been identified as underlying a 'climate favourable' to disarmament. This field of disarmament education addresses itself especially to the psychological obstacles. 'Education *about* disarmament' comprises primarily cognitive objectives, knowledge and skills for dealing with the key concepts of disarmament and for the projection of potential institutional components of a disarmed world. As the former mode of disarmament education moves from the affective objectives of favourable attitudes as a basis for disposing learners to fulfil the cognitive objectives of acquiring information on the needs for and problems of disarmament, the latter provides cognitive skills and capacities which lead to the affective objective of a reasonable belief in the practical possibility of the achievement of disarmament. It is this objective, the educational *sine qua non* for the attainment of a disarmed world, which has been thwarted by the lack of conceptual tools for thinking about disarmament. These tools are essentially those necessary to planning and achieving a preferred future.

This assertion was supported by several of the responses to the questionnaire, especially by the pattern of topical content the survey revealed. The topics cited by those who replied that some level or form of disarmament education was included in the curricula of their countries or institutions indicated that most attention is given to diagnostic rather than prescriptive or preferred future aspects of the problems of peace and disarmament. Disarmament education in this respect is 'problem-centred', but not particularly 'solution-oriented'. Like the vast majority of curricula on social problems and human affairs it tends to deal only with what is and what has been rather than with what could or should be. The greater number of responses indicated curricular attention to the causes of war, which additional descriptive material revealed to be historical rather than contemporary. The lesser number noted some attention to the process of disarmament or the goal of general and complete disarmament. There were indications not only of avoidance, but of actual rejection of the serious consideration of disarmament. One director of a peace studies centre noted: 'I seek to show that historically arms control may be realistic, but disarmament is virtually impossible to attain.' While no detailed reasons were given for this, it is a sample of the prevailing conventional wisdom regarding the 'inevitability' of war and the 'utopianism' of disarmament. Rejection of 'utopianism' may be the most serious conceptual obstacle to education *about* disarmament, for utopias are probably the most useful conceptual tool for thinking about disarmament. What we need most is a repertoire of conceptual and analytic tools for thinking about change.

Among the major conceptual problems of disarmament education which point up the lack of educational objectives and teaching tools for institutional change are three which are especially acute. These problems have been identified less by the recent survey than by discussions among peace educators inspired by the preparation and follow-up of the United Nations Special Session Devoted to Disarmament.

First among these is the most widely recognized and the most challenging: disarmament as a negative concept. Not only is the word itself negative, connoting 'undoing' rather than doing, but nearly all the related processes discussed or explored are also negative (i.e. 'arms limitation', 'dismantling', 'reduction', 'de-escalation' refer to the reversal of negative dynamics); few, and those are seldom discussed, refer to the initiation of positive dynamics.

This problem of the negative concept is reinforced by the lack of positive points of reference. We are severely lacking, in spite of some fairly detailed proposals for general and complete disarmament and recommendations for economic conversion, in images of a disarmed world, images which could instruct us in the possibilities of carrying out necessary social, economic and political functions. To most people, even many of those committed to peace, disarmament within the context of present modes of carrying out those functions is simply impossible. Whether that perception is true or not, it seems likely that it will remain a major obstacle to disarmament until we have overcome this conceptual problem of lack of believable images of a disarmed world, images which some peace educators have referred to as 'relevant utopias' and 'preferred worlds'.

Finally, the prevalent conceptual structures for teaching about contemporary problems provide students with prepackaged content which requires them to learn previously derived answers to the questions posed by the curriculum. They are taught, primarily in the historic mode, about probable solutions based on the past. Few are given the opportunity to speculate on or invent futuristic solutions. The practice of building most curricula on the basis of preselected, sequentially presented historically derived knowledge tends to stifle the creative capacities necessary for projecting the needed images and for inventing positive processes for achieving a disarmed world.

The prevalence of the historical and sequential model for curriculum development presents a 'double bind' for disarmament education. Disarmament for the most part is conceived and presented as a goal in itself rather than as a means to the broader goal of world peace. As the concept of 'peace' has frequently been rejected as a serious subject of education not only for being 'utopian' but also for being 'too vague' and 'undefinable', and considering the difficulties of planning strategies for a goal which cannot be envisioned as is the case with disarmament, both disarmament and peace have been rejected as impossible, even by those who admit that human survival is placed in jeopardy by war. As with all double binds the 'peace and disarmament' restraints on constructive action lead to hopelessness and, among distressingly large numbers, to actual despair.

Some peace educators, however, have determined to confront these conceptual problems, to acknowledge the negative components of disarmament, to accept the challenge posed by the need for images and models, and to attempt to transcend the limits of a closed, sequential curriculum. The first steps in this confrontation are the identification of curricular needs and educational research priorities in education about disarmament. For the reasons cited in the introduction those exemplars of needs and priorities set forth below will relate to secondary education and teacher training.

Secondary education

Secondary education here refers to formal education provided for young people from approximately 14 to 18 years of age who have completed basic elementary education. The needs and priorities noted below refer to all secondary education, and would be the same for students receiving vocational education as for those preparing for university. It is assumed that all citizens have a fundamental stake in the attainment of disarmament and, therefore, all who have an opportunity to study the issues should be prepared and motivated to take part in making and carrying out policies to achieve a disarmed world.

Curriculum needs at the secondary level

While the survey responses indicated a generalized lack of materials of all kinds on the subject of disarmament, the needs identified here will relate exclusively to the specific conceptual problems cited in the foregoing section. Secondary-school curricula need to provide education to enable citizens to think constructively about disarmament, to define its operational and institutional requirements and to design strategies to fulfil the requirements.

The secondary-level curricular needs which arise from the negative nature of disarmament can be categorized in the areas of values and functions, the value issues which affect arms policy and the functions which are served by arms. As far as the reviewer was able to ascertain there are no curricular materials which provide bases for studying the value conflicts arising from the contradictory views of security inherent in the concepts of armament *v.* disarmament, nor are there materials designed to provide an understanding of the various economic and political as well as military functions which are provided by arms within the war system, the present institutional means for resolving conflicts among and between nations.

Curriculum materials are needed to enable students to explore the relative value priorities placed on economic and social security in relation to military security. Materials are also needed to clarify the fundamental values and world-views which espouse the need for armed force to protect national interests and maintain international order. Such exploration and clarification may enable students to see disarmament not only as the reduction of arms, but also as the rejection of armed force as an acceptable means of conflict resolution, a double negative, so to speak, out of which the positive concept of peace can be derived.

The various functions of arms and the military, from providing for national defence against external threats to offering employment and production, as well as serving as a means of domestic control and sometimes internal repression, need to be described simply and clearly in secondary curricula. Students need to understand that virtually all public functions can be performed in a variety of ways and that the modes chosen are determined by the society's value priorities. Such materials could also help students to see that different modes of performing public functions bear different costs, that military security is sometimes bought at the cost of social and/or economic security.

Curricula on these topics could introduce students to the concepts of economic conversion and alternative security systems as the means of achieving the functional equivalents of military production and protection in a disarming world. As both are positive concepts they can be used to counterbalance the negative aspects of economic dislocation and 'defencelessness' which characterize popularly held notions of what disarmament involves.

Secondary curricula also need to include materials for teaching about utopias as tools for transcending seemingly irresolvable problems and especially as a means of providing images of previously inexperienced states or totally new human institutions. While some literature courses include science fiction and some social science courses devote attention to futuristics, neither literature courses nor social science curricula have focused these perspectives on the issues of arms and security. Thus secondary education has not provided students either with models of a disarmed world designed by others nor helped them to develop the imaging skills necessary to invent their own images and models.

There is clearly a curricular need for materials which are based upon futuristics and utopias as heuristic devices to analyse, evaluate and learn from, not to be rejected as the useless fruit of purposeless imagination, nor to be unquestionably accepted as the dogmatic alternative to the war system. Political education, such as that required for disarmament, can make as constructive use of utopias as can philosophy. Most of all curricula need to encourage students themselves to exercise the same skills whose results they have studied in the works of Plato, Thomas More or Marx.

Curricula based upon the concept of social invention as a contemporary and participatory skill can help to overcome the conceptual obstacles to disarmament education posed by sequential historical-content arrangement and prepackaged problem solutions as the dominant mode of organizing curricula. The notion of social invention also calls for curricula based upon the concepts of simultaneous changes and multi-faceted problems. Curricula need, for example, to help students to understand that peace-keeping proposals must be dealt with in tandem with economic conversion programmes. Because the achievement of disarmament calls for system change rather than a sequential problem-by-problem approach, the present tendency to try to analyse and resolve security issues in a discrete one-by-one fashion needs to be changed towards instruction which provides an analytic framework illuminating the interrelationships among the multi-faceted issues of world security. Curricula on disarmament need to be developed in the holistic fashion now recommended for other global issues such as population and environment.

The foregoing needs, arising from the general conceptual problems of education about disarmament, have been expressed in terms of content and materials. Most of these content needs of secondary curricula can be readily met on the basis of the knowledge produced by peace research. While content needs do not necessarily demand special educational research, the development of more effective instructional modes for disarmament education does call for new pedagogical inquiries.

Research priorities for secondary level

One possible instructional mode for confronting the conceptual problem of negativity in relation to disarmament is values analysis and/or exercises in moral reasoning. Although educational research and curriculum development has explored the application of previous research in valuing and moral reasoning to various social issues and some global problems, none appears to have related them to security issues and arms problems. Research into how the cognitive content requirements of education about disarmament can be related to what has been learned about the means to teach the skills of values analysis could help to synthesize into a new and effective instructional mode former findings of peace research and educational research.

Some original educational research is required to devise teaching techniques to cultivate the balance between systematic discipline and creative imagination necessary to the development of constructive imaging skills.

Heuristic devices for identifying and analysing simultaneous social, political and economic processes should be researched as the basis for instruction about policy planning for system change.

Research is also needed into the possibility of integrating substantive disarmament education into the various subject-matter courses offered in secondary schools. In addition to the development of materials and techniques for use in citizenship and social education, it is equally important to place a high priority on inquiring into the possibilities for teaching about weapons develop-

347

ment and the consequences of weapons-use in courses in the natural sciences. Research should be conducted, not only into ways in which the scientific principles underlying modern weaponry can be taught, but also into ways in which the values and moral decisions made by scientists have affected the arms race and how they may affect the achievement of disarmament.

Teacher training

Given the previously cited importance of teachers in preparing the public to understand the need for disarmament, to confront the obstacles to it and to develop the capacities and motivation to achieve it, the training of teachers for all levels of formal (and, indeed, non-formal) education should include disarmament education. Since all teachers are to receive such instruction in their training for the full range of teaching possibilities, curricula for teacher training should include materials designed for education *for* disarmament as well as for education *about* disarmament.

The survey and other inquiries among peace educators revealed that there is even less attention to disarmament education in the field of teacher training than in secondary education. Virtually none of the training opportunities on the subject which are available are offered in the standard curricula and courses of the regular teacher-training institutions. In-service courses and irregular workshop offerings are provided in a very few instances by non-governmental and/or extra-curricular programmes. These programmes, like most teacher-training efforts in global issues, are designed and made available by private agencies.

A symposium on disarmament education in institutions of higher learning held at the International Institute for Peace in Vienna in January 1980 revealed that teacher training is not the only sector of higher education which suffers from a lack of teaching and curricula on disarmament. Disarmament education is not entirely unknown, but it is rare in universities. Teacher training is not a separate problem of disarmament education, but rather a component of the problem as it is manifest at the university level. As a matter of fact, as far as education *for* disarmament is concerned, teacher training offers more than other university courses. This is because elementary teachers are trained in issues and techniques for dealing with conflict and ethnic prejudice. Indeed, the existing training opportunities, curricula and teaching techniques in education *for* disarmament could be integrated into an immediately applicable programme of teacher training. However, as with other university courses, curricula on education *about* disarmament are severely lacking.

Curriculum needs for teacher training

Curriculum needs for teacher training are as closely and functionally related to the conceptual problems of disarmament education as are those at the secondary level. They are, however, more dependent upon the instructional mode needs than on content. Indeed, instructional mode itself becomes a significant form of content in teacher training. Materials needed for preparing teachers would also coincide to a large degree with those required for general university education, particularly as regards specific subject-matter or disciplines. But there are also some special needs in teacher education which require close and immediate attention if the general aims of disarmament education are to be met.

These aims are: first that the whole educational process should be conceived in the 'spirit of disarmament'; next that disarmament teaching should be introduced into those subjects which most lend themselves to it; finally, teaching disarmament as such should be initiated so as to confront obstacles to the goal and create innovations to overcome them. In the terms used in this chapter the first aim would be a means to education *for* disarmament, the second contains elements of education both *for* and *about* disarmament, and the third would be a means to education *about* disarmament in a perspective similar to that suggested for confronting the conceptual problems of disarmament education. As teacher-training needs and recommendations for education *for* disarmament are discussed elsewhere, and because a diagnosis and recommendations on the integration of disarmament education into those courses which most lend themselves to it will appear in the report on the Vienna symposium, the needs cited here will relate primarily to the third aim of disarmament education.

Given the urgency of the problem of disarmament and the need for disarmament education, there is a need for a separate and special course on disarmament education to be offered in all teacher-training institutions. This special course should include: concepts and definitions of terms related to disarmament and the arms race; a listing and description of the most widely recognized obstacles to disarmament; a general history of warfare, weapons development and efforts and landmarks in the struggle for peace and disarmament; current and futuristic proposals for disarmament and peace-keeping; and an introduction to curricular materials, teaching techniques and resources for teaching about disarmament.

This course could be complemented by special units or courses in other subject areas usually studied by pre-service teachers. These curricula should cover such other issues and topics as: ethical problems of war and disarmament, values questions raised by theories of security, analysis of the feasibility and desirability of proposals for disarmament and/or alternative security systems. Actual practice in innovative teaching techniques such as those derived from the research recommended for the secondary level should be offered as an addition to the traditional courses in teaching methods.

The goal of these units and courses should be the merger and incorporation of disarmament education as a special aspect of peace education into the total training programme of all teachers. Over the long term these special courses in disarmament would be absorbed into a regular ongoing focus on peace education, aimed not just at achieving peace, but more particularly at maintaining it. Thus peace education would become the core and basis of social education and the major component in the programme to prepare teachers for their roles of significant influence on the social order. All the standard education courses including foundations of education, school administration, curriculum development, teaching methods and subject-matter courses would have a focus on peace, so that ultimately the special course on disarmament could become an integrating summary course rather than a comprehensive emergency measure.

Countries responding to survey questionnaire

Africa:
Egypt, Kenya, Mauritius, Nigeria, Senegal, Sudan, Uganda, Zaire

Arab states:
Iraq

Asia and Oceania:
Australia, India, Japan, Sri Lanka, Taiwan

Europe:
Finland, Federal Republic of Germany, Ireland, Netherlands, Norway, United Kingdom

Latin America and the Caribbean:
Chile, Jamaica, Mexico

North America:
Canada, United States

36

Armament and disarmament in the teaching of economics

Pierre Fabre
Association Française de Recherches sur la Paix (ARESPA)

Today's world is characterized by the inflated role of the arms industry, and this situation has many repercussions on all attempts in favour of disarmament. Nevertheless this area has been excluded from most university economic studies.

For the industrialized countries disarmament raises the question of conversion of industrial capacities within the framework of new economic relations.

For the Third World countries the question raised is that of the dominating global development model, with an intensity strengthened by the fact that both industrialized 'models', the capitalist and the socialist ones, are characterized by a heavy concentration of economic resources for military ends.

In this paper we explain why we think it is urgent to introduce the armament/ disarmament dimension in the economic programmes.

Importance of the economy in the problems of disarmament

Global world military expenditure in 1978 was estimated at $400,000–450,000 million. In real terms this means that (with constant prices) these expenditures have quadrupled during the last thirty years.

If we confine ourselves to the activity of all armaments industries, there are only ten countries in the world that have a larger GNP than the world annual turnover of these industries ($120,000 million in 1978).

It is also possible to illustrate the size of the economic problems that a reduction in the level of forces or a partial disarmament would create with the mass of workers directly depending on armaments production in the three European countries with the biggest armament industries: 7 per cent of the industrial manpower in the United Kingdom, 4.5 per cent in France and 2 per cent in the Federal Republic of Germany. These figures include only workers employed directly in armament production, not those whose activity provides input used in the process of arms production.

But it is a qualitative analysis that gives its whole economic significance to the system of military production. It is well known that a large part of this production

---

Paper published in the *Bulletin of Peace Proposals*, Vol. 11, No. 3, 1980.

is concentrated in high-technology sectors, the ones in which the future of nations is dependent and which have very specific links and effects on the whole economy.

Besides this national level, we must emphasize the role of military transfers within international trade. They amounted globally to less than 2 per cent of international trade in 1977, but to more than 5 per cent of the imports of Third World countries and probably around 20 per cent of their imports of technological goods. The industrialized countries are using this kind of trade as a means towards fighting their balance-of-trade deficits. One should also remember that the transfers of military technology have increased tremendously. It is clear that the diversion of all kinds of resources creates an amplifying relation between the growth of military activities and the economic situation of the Third World.

These data show that disarmament (no matter to what degree) will raise economic questions which will be all the more intense because of the traditional use of the arms industry as a means of economic regulation, therefore consecrating a special place for this kind of activity within the national structure of production.

Thus, promoting education in favour of disarmament also means (at the university level) studying, teaching and researching on the real importance of the armaments economy within the whole productive structure and on the problems and new possibilities that would appear in the event of disarmament.

Educational interest of the economic study of armament and disarmament

To allow the economic study of armaments the place it deserves in the university would demystify a large number of currently accepted ideas and would shed light on one of the main common characteristics between centrally planned economies and market economies. The educational aspect of this process is theoretical as well as empirical.

We have classified the main pedagogical characteristics of this discipline in three categories.

Knowledge of the idiosyncrasies of the armaments economy

For an economist it is particularly important to know what are in reality the financial, productive and labour volumes covered by military activities. This knowledge must be the result of the 'inter-branch' approach we will suggest later.

This inter-branch approach should make it possible to evaluate the effects of armament production, up-stream and down-stream, on the rest of the production system at their correct levels. The nature of technological progress which characterizes this type of production and its diffusion within the industrial and economic fibre should be clarified.

The mechanisms that are specific to the military-industrial activity transform it into a 'sector' very different from other economic activities. The type of relations it establishes between the 'demand' (the state and more precisely the armed forces) and the 'offer' (the armaments managers) are qualitatively and quantitatively unique. The enormous financial resources required by military research and development are as much the consequence of the specificity of the equipment studied as a way of working.

As for employment, two main characteristics of the armaments economy seem to be fundamental, and are rarely known. On the one hand, this activity engages a much larger number of engineers and highly qualified technicians than any other production. This kind of labour would be released in the event of disarmament. On the other hand, the potential for creating jobs in this activity is rather poor because of the intensive use of capital that predominates.

The effects of armaments economy on the general level of prices and inflation are not too well known and it would be important to analyse them quantitatively.

Finally, it is urgent to arrange some courses around the theme 'armament and development'. Whether it is from the point of view of the structure of the international trade or of the effects of the transfers of military technology (armament factories, selling of production licences, etc.) or even of the shortage of available resources, there are certainly many links between the present economic situation of the Third World countries and military policies. Today this subject is neither covered by economic courses nor by economic and social-development studies.

Interest regarding the study of economic policies

Through the study of military expenditures the theme of state intervention in the economic life of liberal societies appears in one of its most widely known but seldom studied forms.

The feedback between the study of voluntary policies and theory naturally implies a very careful analysis of the Keynesian view of economics. Inversely, the study of Keynes's works—a university classic of political economy—should be more often and more accurately illustrated by the use of military expenditures as a means of economic regulation.

The alternatives that would be made possible by disarmament measures constitute also an important aspect of such courses because of the predominant role played by the state as the promotor of the economic redeployment which would have such a magnitude that prudent (and inventive) planning would be necessary.

The perspectives that disarmament would create lead also to considering the flexibility and adaptability of the production apparatus of modern economies. These considerations are increasingly necessary (even excluding any hypothesis of disarmament) because of the accelerating technological evolution, of the inclusion of new factors (quality of life, environment protection, etc.) and of the mutations that are linked with the present world crisis.

Disarmament implies the conversion of many production capacities and workers. Thus conversion is altogether a technical, labour and economic-policy problem.

Interest regarding the 'economic technique'

National military expenditures are being spent through defence budgets. Thus the economic study of military activities must include a training for budget reading.

To think of disarmament measures leads also to the problem of the availability of new resources and the necessity to plan new budgetary expenses in order to guarantee the transition.

The military procurement policy that exists in various countries makes it possible to analyse the link between a procurement policy and its realization over a period of time through the budgetary apparatus.

The 'armaments industry' is not precisely an economic branch or sector. It is oriented towards a single objective (the production of arms systems or of non-lethal military-oriented equipment) the products of many sectors and branches: aerospace, shipbuilding, electronics, nuclear activities, precision machine-tools, etc. Although it may strongly dominate and influence the production and the technological base of these branches, it is not individually included in any. The armaments industry is an actual inter-branch intersection which allows a multisector approach to reality. This type of analysis is not often seen in university studies but it shows the variety of technical processes which satisfy a specific form of need.

Furthermore, the multi-branch analysis makes it possible to raise the fundamental question of the definition of the economic categories and of their limits in its most general form and, particularly, for the national economic statistics. This way it is possible to introduce the idea of critics of statistical data, which is essential in the work of economic analysis.

The national armaments market is characterized by the existence of a single buyer: the state, equipping its armies—though the growth of international arms transfers limits this consideration. This situation, called 'monopsone', is relatively rare in liberal economies and it appears as an actual case to develop the study of this concept.

In countries where the sales to foreign armies have developed, or inversely where the non-existence of a military production apparatus leads to imports, an analysis of trade balances and of international trade could be carried out.

Research

Teaching structures in universities usually go along with research functions. Thus, effort concerning education would be followed by progress in the knowledge of armaments economy. As a matter of fact, there are few investigations in this field. The result is two-fold: on the one hand many myths exist about this sector and its positive economic impact; on the other, the very idea of disarmament is held back (without considering here the dominant political factors) by the lack of real knowledge of the economic consequences of such an action, of the perspectives it would open up or of the policies to initiate. A deeper knowledge of these possibilities would help to exert pressure in favour of disarmament measures.

Recommendations

From the economic nature of many problems linked with disarmament and from the educational interest for including armament studies in university, we recommend that:

A survey of programmes and manuals of economic courses be conducted by Unesco; it would summarize and bring up to date the consideration of armaments and disarmament in university and, eventually, suggest accurate measures.

The role of armaments industries during certain historical periods (the First World War, the Korean war, etc.) be introduced and explained in courses on economic history.

The analysis of the impact of the armaments industry illustrate the courses on the multi-sector approach.

Analysis on the flexibility of the production systems and of the possibilities of conversion of armaments industries be also undertaken (especially with the analysis of the distribution of the factors of labour and capital and with the study of 'growth models').

The study of state intervention policies and of the means of economic regulation it uses show the important role played by national defence budgets.

Courses on economic and social development should include a fundamental study of the role of armaments in the developing economies. Thanks to an open pedagogical process, it would be interesting to give the students of the Third World an opportunity to consider these problems in order to evaluate the link between armaments and development, and the validity of traditional schemes of growth and of implicit models of development that result from them.

In the areas of studies where research is encouraged (Master's degree, Ph.D.) the introduction of these considerations in previous-year studies would increase the themes of research susceptible to enrich the study of disarmament.

37

The flow of information and disarmament

Tapio Varis
University of Tampere, Finland

The traditional news value

It is very obvious that contemporary solutions of disarmament problems are not possible without wide support from the public, as well as from numerous non-governmental organizations and peace movements.

One can always ask the question whether the public is sufficiently aware of the situation and whether or not the general attitude of the people contributes to a constructive solution of the problems.

For example, public opinion and attitudes based on fear and tension do not compose a constructive element. While international tension and the Cold War created insecurity, fear and uncertainty, the process of détente has had the opposite effect.

For the practising journalist it is not too easy to report the progress in a process like détente because it is much easier to observe isolated and negative events than less 'visual' development in social processes.

When analysing the negatively shaped opinion of some Western mass media towards détente, some researchers have taken a critical look at the traditional news-value of the Western conception. It is known that many of the Western media find disagreements more important as 'news' than agreements. Johan Galtung and Mari Ruge stressed in 1965 that in the Western news approach foreign news is related to organizational and occupational factors—especially to such factors as are connected with the visibility and acceptability of various events to newsmen and organizations. News is made up of personalities or events rather than of less visible social structures and processes. Positive events are less visible than negative ones and news which is accepted has to come within the realm of the expected and the possible. Newsmen tend to see the world according to single events instead of long-term processes and historical trends.[1]

Galtung himself made some policy implications in his study. More emphasis on build-up and background material should be given and journalists should be better trained to capture and report long-term developments, and concentrate less on isolated events. Occasional reports on the trivial, even if it does not make news,

Shortened version of a paper prepared for a Unesco symposium in 1978.

should be presented to counterbalance an image of the world as composed of strings of dramatic events. Furthermore, as Galtung stressed, more emphasis should be given to complex and ambiguous events and culturally distant zones. It was also felt necessary to fight against easy stereotypes.

Although some later criticism of the theory has treated it as too psychological and would like to place it within a larger framework of a politico-economic theory, many of the ideas by Galtung and Ruge are particularly valid now, and their policy recommendations are as equally important now as they were ten years ago. Recent experience has suggested that more understanding is needed of the ownership structure of the transnational mass-media systems, as well as of the nature of information flows in international relations.

Consciousness-raising about the powers of defence

Some observations can be made of the development in Europe, although the period since the signing of the CSCE Final Act in Helsinki 1975 is too short to allow a comprehensive evaluation of such a long-term programme of action like the Helsinki agreements. The problems of journalism only form a part of 'co-operation in humanitarian and other fields', but they have been an area of most conflicting views. Compared with other forms of international co-operation, there are very few agreements and very little experience in co-operation in the field of information between countries with different social systems.

The theoretical assumptions on the role of information flow and cultural exchanges for peace and security are very different in the political philosophy of different systems. In the Western countries, the production, distribution and consumption of information (and mass culture) are approached as comparable to the commodity production of things. According to this thinking, international exchange should follow the laws of demand and supply, and allow the making of commercial profits. The socialist countries have followed a more reserved line in relation to the free flow of mass-circulated products of any kind, and have emphasized the responsibility of mass communication and mass media in the development of international relations.

The policy recommendations following these two approaches are basically opposite. The Western view maintains that in order to gain peace and security the flow of all kinds of information over the borders should be increased. This line has recently been made very complicated by making this kind of 'freedom' an absolute thing in an abstract form. The socialist countries have maintained the idea that increasing confidence and co-operation in all fields of human activity also contributes to the increased flow of information between countries and peoples.

Some researchers have pointed out that in the present international climate in Europe the mass media and public opinion have at least three general tasks. The first is consciousness-raising about the process of détente and efforts towards disarmament. The socialist and non-aligned countries have shown particular interest towards these issues in their information channels and public organizations. The second task is the promotion of new social relations to widen political détente to military détente. And the third task of the mass media is the promotion of a new information order in Europe. There is a need for a more balanced

357

exchange of information between countries of different social sytems in order to lessen military tension and increase confidence.

The global perspective

Another equally important dimension of détente is the global perspective for such an international climate and disarmament. One of the major international political movements for worldwide political, economic, military and cultural goals has been the movement of the non-aligned countries. These countries—mainly developing ones—have reached the conclusion at numerous international conferences that the stabilization of the world economy and the consolidation of world peace and security are mutually dependent, interrelated and only possible in a new system of international relations.

In the last few years the intellectuals, political movements and governments of the developing countries have found that the present unjust economic order is supported and maintained by an international information order which does not properly reflect the aspirations, achievements, and culture of the developing countries. Just as the transnational market economy is mainly controlled by a few global, transnational corporations, so is transnational information and news production and distribution in the hands of a few transnational agencies.

The non-aligned countries have agreed to improve their mutual information activity by strengthening self-reliance in information, by increasing the activity of their news-agency pools, and by applying the principles of the New Delhi declaration.[2] This declaration stresses the importance of ending transnational dependency in information in order to promote political liberation and economic progress.

It is also possible to improve education in global thinking on such problems as peace, disarmament and progress, which require a creative and unprejudiced attitude from all peoples. Although no major changes in the ownership patterns of the mass media would arise, there are a number of possibilities to improve the situation. These include a more democratic management of the mass media by means of editorial democracy through the staff, and systems of general self-management. More attention should be paid to the training of journalists, as Galtung proposed more than ten years ago, to choose and evaluate events and information in order to be able to follow such complex processes as disarmament, the arms race and détente. There is also a strong need for improving feature services on disarmament problems, and even of a peace press agency.

All parties have recognized that an informed public opinion is a vital ingredient in influencing foreign policy. Now it is extremely important to arm public opinion with facts to promote disarmament and to struggle against those power élites in the mass media whose influence prevents any honest and constructive dialogue between different parties which have the serious intention of ending the arms race.

Notes

1. Johan Galtung and Mari Holmboe Ruge 'The Structure of Foreign News', *Journal of Peace Research*, No. 1, 1965.
2. Conference of Ministerial Level Government Representatives and Heads of New Agencies of Non-aligned Countries, New Delhi, 8–17 July 1976.

38

The contribution
of public opinion
to international détente

Alexander Kalyadin
Institute for World Economy and International Relations, Moscow

Role of the public

Problems of the elimination of the danger of a new world war, of curbing the arms race, of disarmament have become the subject matter of discussions and serious studies not only on the governmental, but also on the public level.

World developments bear witness to the increasing importance of various types of public activity in curbing the inhuman and reactionary forces bent on preventing disarmament and keeping alive the threat of world war. This importance is due, first, to an intensification of those processes in world development which make it possible for the popular masses to play a growing role in shaping international relations and in influencing the making of foreign policies pursued by the respective states. Secondly, arms reduction and disarmament are by their very nature complex tasks involving not only inter-state relations but also the domestic political, social and economic climates of states. Specific social groups, organizations and individuals in capitalist society are known to favour the arms race and to be active in different ways and along different lines in support of these policies. The activities of the military-industrial complex are a typical and vivid example of the forces interested in carrying on unceasing preparations for war. Hence not only government efforts but also vigorous activity on the part of all those public forces in favour of peace and the unity of all such forces are needed to move ahead along the path to disarmament. Undoubtedly, governments and diplomats have a major role to play in making disarmament an effective reality. The public performs a useful service in helping settle problems under discussion at governmental levels. In addition, there are important issues which as a rule cannot be effectively dealt with in the framework of diplomatic negotiations. Public forces can greatly facilitate the resolution of such questions by exposing the myths continually spread by the champions of the arms race to deceive the people, by influencing public opinion in favour of disarmament and by launching mass campaigns to back specific anti-militarist demands.

Shortened version from the introduction to *Détente and Disarmament, Problems and Perspectives*, Vienna, Gazzetta Publishing House, 1976.

The Stockholm Appeal, dated 19 March 1950, started a worldwide mass campaign to ban nuclear weapons and made an invaluable contribution to lessening the immediate danger of world war. The Stockholm Appeal Signature-Raising Campaign (with over 500 million signatures collected throughout the world) served as evidence to the effect that the public has a growing role to play in reducing the danger of war and in maintaining and strengthening peace.

When the 'Cold War' was at its height, the peace movement initiated and actively promoted international mass campaigns to curb the arms race, ban nuclear testing and prevent nuclear proliferation, establish nuclear-weapon-free zones, dismantle foreign military bases and achieve other specific disarmament measures.

The broadly based mass peace movement has contributed to the initial adoption of international measures aimed at curbing some of the grave aspects of the arms race. In this connection special mention must be made of the very positive significance of the activity of public peace movements and organizations on the normalization of the international psychological climate which was poisoned by the Cold War, their contribution towards influencing world public opinion in favour of the conclusion of initial international disarmament agreements, their support for the proposals of the socialist governments and other peace-loving states, and for United Nations resolutions to limit war preparations. It should be added that public organizations have made proposals and taken initiatives which subsequently became the subject of negotiations at governmental level and were then formulated in international legal documents. To begin with, the public proposed the prohibition of nuclear-weapons testing, geophysical warfare and other bans which later resulted in a series of important multilateral agreements. It should be specifically emphasized that scientists, and scientists' organizations (the World Federation of Scientific Workers, the Pugwash Movement) have made a contribution of their own to the discussion and solution of such major problems as the nuclear-weapons test ban, the ban on bacteriological warfare, technical methods to control the observation of agreements limiting armaments, and determining those areas where steps to limit armament are urgent and feasible.

The public movements and organizations proved to be an effective force behind the Moscow Partial Test-Ban Treaty, banning nuclear-weapon tests in the atmosphere, outer space and under water (1963), the 1970 Non-Proliferation Treaty and their degree of effectiveness. Broad sections of the international public supported treaties prohibiting the stationing of nuclear and other weapons of mass destruction in outer space, on the sea-bed and ocean floor, and in the subsoil in some regions of the world, as well as the convention prohibiting the development, production and stockpiling of bacteriological (biological) and toxic weapons and their destruction, which was the first measure towards real disarmament in the history of international relations. The Geneva Protocol banning the use of chemical and bacteriological weapons is an internationally recognized instrument. The public supported the Soviet-United States negotiations conducted to limit stategic arms, and has helped to create an atmosphere of détente which has promoted Soviet-United States agreements limiting strategic weaponry and preventing nuclear war. All these very important treaties, agreements and understandings contribute towards reducing the danger of nuclear war and curbing the arms race to a certain degree and clearing the way towards the effective solution of major problems of political and military détente, including the aim of finally eliminating the danger of a world war.

Although armament continues and is heated up by imperialist circles, the initial agreements are ample proof that in the struggle against the arms race tangible results are possible and that the establishment of lasting peace is a very feasible aim. In turn, government-level agreements facilitate and encourage public activity in favour of new measures to limit armaments.

In the 1970s a change was enforced in the development of international relations from the Cold War to peaceful coexistence between states with different social systems: the dominating trend was détente. The successful conclusion of the European Conference on Security and Co-operation (Helsinki, 1975) and progress so far achieved in the implementation of its Final Act have opened up new horizons for all the peace forces in their drive further to improve the international climate in Europe and throughout the world. These positive changes were a result of the new balance of power in the world, and the co-ordinated foreign policy and many initiatives of the states of the socialist community, alongside the activity of all progressive and peace-loving forces.

The increasing menace of the arms race

The work of these broad public forces in expanding and consolidating détente, along with military détente, gains increased importance. Today these tasks are more urgent than ever. Despite progressive political détente and despite the enormous efforts of the socialist countries to achieve international agreements reducing war preparation, the enemies of détente and disarmament still succeed in building up the arms race. The continuing arms race harbours the danger of a new world war. It threatens already achieved successes in the struggle to strengthen peace and to slow down the process of international détente now in progress. The arms race results in a massive waste of the resources needed to meet vitally important social and economic needs.

This make the struggle to bring war preparations to an end ever more imperative since it proves to be a decisive factor in the effort to eliminate completely the threat of world war, preserve life and safeguard a bright future for mankind. The genuine dialectics of the arms race increasingly contradicts man's vital interests, a fact which extends the objective conditions for involving a growing number of workers, peasants, scientists, artists, young people, women, fighters against colonialism and for national independence, environmentalists and, finally, realistically minded members of the bourgeoisie in anti-militarist activities. It must also be emphasized that these conditions do not come about all by themselves. Of decisive importance is the subjective factor primarily stemming from the ability of democratic movements and organizations to mobilize the broad popular masses for the purpose of curbing the arms race.

The dangerous turn being taken by the arms race today has heightened the urgent need for different peace forces to take common action against the foes of détente and disarmament.

Major problems in the struggle against the arms race and for world disarmament

An important achievement of the present-day anti-imperialist struggle is the fact that numerous peace movements and organizations have worked out a common approach towards a wide range of disarmament issues and adopted a platform of joint or co-ordinated activities in order to solve them, and especially important, taken steps to affirm the agreements by putting them into effect. What, then, are the specific details of this common approach and of the platform of joint action adopted by various peace forces?

In analysing the documents adopted by representative public forums in recent years, the conclusion can be drawn that a large number of non-governmental organizations from various social, political and philosophical systems and with different traditions, status, levels and methods of working have recognized the acute and pressing need for curbing the arms race and attaining disarmament and that general and complete disarmament must be the final objective that public peace forces are working for; furthermore, and very importantly, they came to the realization that the solution to these problems requires united and ever-increasing efforts on the part of public movements and organizations. The concept attaching great importance to partial disarmament or arms-reduction measures as helping to lead to general and complete disarmament also gained acceptance. The documents and activities of peace movements emphasize the interrelation between disarmament and campaigning for a more solid and stable peace, the betterment of both the material and spiritual living standards of the people, the elimination of all centres of colonialism and racism, national independence, mankind's social progress and the solution of the major problems modern civilization is facing today. They point out that disarmament is not an issue concerning only individual countries or the great powers alone. They also note that middle-sized and small countries also spend enormous sums on arms to the detriment of the living conditions enjoyed by their peoples and that the successful struggle against the arms race is of vital interest for all forces working for peace in the world. The documents of the public forums held in recent years do not only name the true advocates of the arms race: the military-industrial complexes operating in imperialist states, racist and other reactionary regimes, political, professional and financial quarters opposing international détente; they also formulate guidelines on how to counteract their power and influence.

Efforts to ban weapons of mass destruction are the centre-point of the unified platform and practical activities of public peace organizations. While making a substantial contribution to the struggle against nuclear and other weapons of mass destruction, public peace organizations view the promotion of the universal and effective application of existing international treaties, agreements and conventions limiting nuclear and chemical warfare, as well as those banning bacteriological weapons, whose object is to eliminate an entire category of the most dangerous means of mass destruction, as one of the most urgent tasks. Special attention is being paid to getting all the militarily important states, and above all the nuclear powers, to adhere to these international instruments.

Public peace organizations are hoping that the Soviet-United States negotiations on strategic arms limitation will quickly bring positive results. Public disarmament forums emphasize the urgency of strategic arms reductions and hail steps taken in this direction. They also call upon other nuclear powers to take part in the process of strategic arms limitation.

The common platform of the different peace forces deals not only with disarmament issues which are global in nature but also with specific issues which affect individual continents, regions and groups of countries. The public campaign to consolidate peace contributes to the struggle of those peoples fighting for freedom and political and economic independence. On its part, the general public of the developing countries takes an active part in this movement and makes a significant contribution to the joint struggle for peace and international security. Special attention is given to strengthening the co-ordination of efforts by peace forces to stop the arms race and to the efforts of the peoples and governments of the developing countries to achieve and consolidate their political and economic independence. Those aspects of disarmament concerning the developing countries are being given more and more importance. These are the possibilities disarmament offers for helping the countries in solving their urgent economic problems, eradicating poverty, and advancing along the road to progress, they deal with the banning of all arms supplies and of the transfer of knowhow to countries at present engaged in colonial wars and to regimes that put the weapons supplied to them to aggressive use or use them to take repressive or other measures against their peoples.

Various peace movements and organizations maintain fruitful co-operation in their efforts to eradicate the vestiges of the cold war still surviving in peoples' minds and to create an atmosphere of trust and mutual understanding between nations and peoples which would make general and complete disarmament more attainable. These joint activities include a broad range of measures intended to shape and mobilize public opinion in favor of disarmament. It includes a well-founded denunciation of the spurious arguments invoked by apologists for the arms race (e.g., that war preparations allegedly boost economic and scientific progress, that disarmament measures are technically unfeasible, that security and national interests are guaranteed by the 'balance of terror', 'deterrent force', and so forth). The activation of the broadest sections of the public in the movement, the strengthening of the unity of all peace-loving forces, the development of vigorous actions to curb the arms race and for the utilization of all favourable possibilities arising in the process of détente to isolate the military circles and to advance towards disarmament and the elimination of the danger of devastating war is gaining in importance.

39

Non-governmental organizations and disarmament

Homer Jack
World Conference on Religion and Peace, New York

Introduction

The lack of progress in disarmament negotiations is in particular attributed to the lack of political volition which, it is widely believed, can be enhanced by world public opinion—especially in the field of disarmament. Public opinion is both stimulated by, and reflected in, non-governmental organizations (NGOs) and the media. Both NGOs and the mass media have been increasingly involved with the United Nations system. NGO involvement, however, is very recent.

The United Nations Charter provided an explicit role for NGOs under Article 71, on which authority the Secreteriat of the Economic and Social Council (ECOSOC) has evolved consultative arrangements with several hundred NGOs over three decades. These arrangements have been confined, however, to economic and social issues, and disarmament has been considered only tangentially.

Outside of Article 71, specialized and other agencies within the United Nations system, notably the United Nations Educational, Scientific and Cultural Organization (Unesco), the Food and Agriculture Organization (FAO), the United Nations Children's Fund (UNICEF), and the United Nations Environment Programme (UNEP), gave official recognition to NGOs.

In addition, there has been a succession of General Assembly resolutions referring to NGOs. These have tended to ask help of NGOs either in obtaining material for United Nations studies or in distributing these studies once made. One of the earliest, in 1965, requested information about studies on the economic and social consequences of disarmament 'undertaken by non-governmental organizations'. 'The value of holding conferences of experts and scientists from various countries on the problems of the arms race and disarmament' had already been affirmed in 1971, and 'universities and academic institutes' urged to establish 'continuing courses and seminars to study problems of the arms race'. In 1976, NGOs were called upon 'to further the goals of the Disarmament Decade'. However, no resolution was adopted which gave NGOs a consultative role in disarmament matters equal to that in the economic and social field.

Shortened version of the chapter 'NGOs and Disarmament' from *SIPRI Yearbook 1979*, Stockholm International Peace Research Institute, 1979.

A Special NGO Committee on Disarmament was created in Geneva in 1969—one of several committees created in Geneva and New York by the Conference of Non-Governmental Organizations in Consultative Status with the United Nations Economic and Social Council (CONGO). In 1973, the NGO Committee on Disarmament was established and set up at United Nations Headquarters. Both committees focused the concerns of dozens of general and specialized NGOs on disarmament issues as they arose in the United Nations system.

Outside of the United Nations system, NGOs have been involved in the First Committee, the Conference of the Committee on Disarmament (CCD), several ad hoc committees (on the Indian Ocean and a World Disarmament Conference), and in the first Non-Proliferation Treaty Review Conference in 1975.

At a conference sponsored by the International Peace Bureau at Bradford, United Kingdom, in August 1974, to support efforts to convene a World Disarmament Conference (WDC), far-reaching proposals were made for NGOs. Thirty NGOs, with full rights of participation other than voting rights, should be invited and receive adequate funds to ensure the preparation and distribution of documentation and to ensure proper representation at the WDC. All NGOs in consultative status with ECOSOC should be given normal observer status at the WDC, and all relevant documentation should be circulated by the United Nations to and from NGOs directly concerned with disarmament. This declaration was subsequently endorsed by many international and national NGOs.

NGOs within the United Nations field of disarmament

A role for NGOs

In 1975, a resolution was adopted to create an Ad Hoc Committee on the Review of the Role of the United Nations in the Field of Disarmament. This was viewed by some states and many NGOs as a possible venue to discuss and establish a future role for NGOs. In June 1976, thirteen international NGOs submitted to the Ad Hoc Committee a joint statement on strengthening the role of international NGOs in the field of disarmament. This proposed that NGOs: (a) be accorded observer status in the First Committee of the General Assembly; (b) be associated with the preparation, proceedings and implementation of any future Special Session on Disarmament or a WDC; (c) be asked to communicate their views and suggestions on disarmament matters to the Secretary-General wherever such views are required of Member States and Specialized Agencies; (d) be accorded official or unofficial hearings by disarmament bodies; (e) be given all United Nations documents on disarmament issues; (f) be urged to participate in the preparation and proceedings of review conferences; and (g) be given some access to disarmament negotiating forums.

Preparations for the Special Session

In 1976, the non-aligned states introduced a resolution convening a Special Session Devoted to Disarmament in mid-1978. NGOs saw the Special Session as an opportunity, not unlike the League of Nations Disarmament Conference, to make a special impact.

In the first session of the Preparatory Committee, in March 1977, it was stated that the Special Session would involve 'world public opinion and the organizations, governmental and non-governmental, that are active in mobilizing this opinion'.

At the opening meeting of the second session of the Preparatory Committee on 9 May, it was reported that the Bureau—the Chairman, the Rapporteur, and Vice-Presidents from eight states—had unanimously approved the following proposals relating to NGOs. The Committee then adopted these by consensus.

1. A well-informed public opinion, be it at national or international levels, can bring significant contributions toward progress in the field of disarmament. The non-governmental organizations, whose dedication and interest in this field is well known and highly appreciated by the members of this Committee, could play a stimulating and constructive role in channeling the public concerns in this matter.

2. The officers of this Committee are pleased to realize the NGOs' interest in closely following the development of its work and hope that this association will be further strengthened by the continued presence of its representatives in the usual places in this room.

3. Notwithstanding the frequent and useful contacts or exchanges that take place between NGOs and individual delegations, and in order to facilitate the knowledge of non-governmental contributions, the Secretariat will provide lists of general circulation of the communications received from the NGOs and institutions known to be conducting research in the field of disarmament. The lists will indicate where the communications and any annexed documentation will be available to delegations.

NGOs were quick to implement the formal roles assigned to them in the Preparatory Committee. Several dozen international and national NGOs—the Committee made no distinction—sent observers to the five sessions of the Committee. These included such international organizations as the Friends World Committee for Consultation, the Women's International League for Peace and Freedom, the World Council of Churches, the World Conference on Religion and Peace, and the Stockholm International Peace Research Institute (SIPRI). National groups sending observers included the Maryknoll Fathers, Project Ploughshares of Canada, and the Stanley Foundation. Such efforts were partly co-ordinated by the NGO Committee on Disarmament whose officers were in constant consultation with the officers of the Preparatory Committee, many delegates, and members of the Secretariat.

NGOs took advantage of the new procedure of submitting statements and other materials. The Secretariat released lists of these submissions as official documents. A very wide range of organizations submitted statements and the Secretariat helped make the NGO literature immediately available to delegates.

Other NGO activity

This NGO activity in United Nations Headquarters during the sessions of the Preparatory Committee was the result of much greater NGO activity at both the international and national levels. A number of NGOs sponsored, individually or collectively, conferences, seminars and other meetings to learn about the issues of the Special Session, to formulate their own policies, and in some cases to start dialogues with diplomats and governments.

NGOs working especially with diplomats included the Stanley Foundation, the Quaker United Nations Office (which sponsored a lengthy series of meetings for Third World diplomats), the Carnegie Endowment/Arms Control Association and the International Peace Academy.

The International NGO Conference on Disarmament, held in Geneva in early 1978, was yet another opportunity for a large group of NGOs to discuss the Special Session. Sponsored by the two NGO committees on disarmament in Geneva and New York, 500 individuals representing more than 250 NGOs attended. Recommendations were made and NGO strategy suggested.

A number of international NGOs held special meetings devoted to the Special Session, often bringing together members from several continents. These included the World Council of Churches, the World Assembly of Youth, and the World Peace Council. Out of these various international meetings, a sheaf of NGO literature on the Special Session was published. Quite apart from those arising out of the several NGO conferences involving diplomats, pamphlets were issued by such groups as Operation Turning Point and the World Conference on Religion and Peace (WCRP).

An even greater number of national NGO activities were held in preparation for the Special Session. These involved, in the first instance, educating the leadership of the individual organizations and, secondly, relating this learning to national disarmament policies—NGOs in several countries were successful in urging governments to schedule meetings or hearings on their policies for the Special Session.

The NGO Committee on Disarmament (at United Nations Headquarters) published *SSD News*, a modest newsletter indicating the depth and breadth of NGO activity related to the Special Session in various parts of the world. Also the first issue of the new periodical of the United Nations Centre for Disarmament, *Disarmament*, reflected some of this NGO activity.

During the third session of the Preparatory Committee, the question arose about the role of NGOs at the Special Session itself. The Preparatory Committee recommended to the General Assembly that 'non-governmental organizations concerned with disarmament should be accorded the same facilities at the Special Session as those which they have received at the preparatory committee'.

NGO Day

During the fourth and fifth sessions of the Preparatory Committee, early in 1978, an enlarged role for NGOs during the Special Session emerged. The Preparatory Committee agreed by consensus to invite up to twenty-five NGOs to speak to the Ad Hoc Committee on 12 June. At the opening plenary meeting of the Special Session, the report of the Preparatory Committee was approved by consensus.

Early in 1978, national, regional and international NGOs began to correspond with the United Nations Secretariat concerning attendance at the Special Session. The Secretariat set up an informal Register, accepting any NGOs expressing interest in the Special Session whether or not they had been previously related to the United Nations. A total of 237 organizations and institutions expressed an advance intention to be represented. In addition, a special group of 502 Japanese, representing 200 organizations, attended for one week. The United Nations Centre estimated that, on a rotating basis, a total of approximately 1,300 individuals representing some 430 organizations and institutions were actively involved at one point or another.

A further dimension of NGO activity—a function of Member States and not of the United Nations—was the appointment of NGOs to the official delegations of several Member States. NGOs were appointed at least from Canada, Sweden, the United Kingdom and the United States.

NGO Day was held on 12 June, when speakers were heard from the following organizations: the Afro-Asian Peoples' Solidarity Organization, the Asian Buddhist Conference for Peace, the Commission of the Churches on International Affairs of the World Council of Churches, the Friends World Committee for Consultation, the Gandhi Peace Foundation, the International Association for Religious Freedom, the International Co-operative Alliance, the International Fellowship of Reconciliation, the International Peace Bureau, the International Youth and Student Movement for the United Nations, the Liaison Conference of Japanese National NGOs at the Special Session of the General Assembly Devoted to Disarmament, the Organization of Traditional Religions of Africa, Pugwash Conferences on Science and World Affairs, Socialist International, the Women's International Democratic Federation, the Women's International League for Peace and Freedom, the World Association of World Federalists, the World Conference on Religion and Peace, the World Federation of Democratic Youth, the World Federation of Scientific Workers, the World Federation of United Nations Associations, the World Peace Council, the World Union of Catholic Women's Organizations, the World Veterans Foundation, and the Yugoslav League for Peace, Interdependence and Equality of Peoples.

Six research institutes were heard the next day: the Institute for World Economics and International Relations, Academy of Sciences of the USSR, Moscow; the Center for Defense Information, Washington; the International Institute for Peace, Vienna; the International Peace Research Association; the Stanley Foundation, Iowa; and the Stockholm International Peace Research Institute.

The meeting was opened with the assertion that 'disarmament is not the province of governments alone'. It was hoped that, 'far from arousing political confrontations', NGOs would be 'a positive factor in cementing a climate of confidence and understanding on the basis of which it will be possible only to make real progress to curb the arms race'.

At the concluding session, the association of NGOs with the work of the General Assembly was considered fully justified and likely to mark the beginning of a new stage in the work of the United Nations in the field of disarmament.

Part VIII.   Between peace
and war:
the challenge
of disarmament

40

Peace or oblivion?
An inescapable choice
in the atomic age

Philip Noel-Baker
Nobel Peace Prize Winner 1959

The struggle for disarmament

For nearly sixty years I have watched the struggle between men who want peace—men who believe that world disarmament is the only condition by which lasting peace can be obtained, such as Robert Fishill, Fridtjof Nansen, Arthur Henderson, Aristide Briand, Paul Boncour, Pierre Cot, and many more from France—and those strange alienated militarists who believe that lasting peace is an idle pipe-dream, that wars are sure to come, and who therefore give their lives to armaments and war.

After I came back from my freshman year at an American college in 1907 I began to work on armaments. I helped my father prepare his papers for a deputation at The Hague, a deputation powerful in constitution and in numbers which demanded the ending of the arms race and the compulsory arbitration of all international disputes. Then I did four years at the front in the First World War, and ever since I have lived in the League of Nations and the United Nations.

In those decades I watched the militarists defeat those who wanted lasting peace; they destroyed the Hague conferences.

In 1908, a naval shipbuilder went to Germany and came back with a story for which there was no foundation at all: the tale that Germany was secretly building dreadnoughts. England went mad. The dreadnought race was a major cause of the First World War. And the dreadnought battle of Jutland almost brought Britain to her knees.

I watched the militarists defeat the Hague Disarmament Conference of 1932. I was the assistant to the Conference President, Arthur Henderson, and knew everything that went on. I know how near to success that conference was with a proposal from President Hoover of the United States, and I know that it was the British militarists making delays which allowed the arms manufacturers of Germany—Krupp, Thyssen, Hugenberg, and all the rest—to bring Hitler into power. If the conference had succeeded, as it nearly did, we should have had no Hitler; we should have had no Second World War.

From an address at a Unesco Peace Forum. *The Bulletin of the Atomic Scientists*, September 1977.

And now today, I watch the militarists. I know the men working against the United Nations, working against disarmament. That is why I took part half a century ago, and in 1932, in very serious and very hopeful disarmament negotiations. There have been no serious negotiations since 1964. Because what are called negotiations are carried on by men who do not believe in what they are asked to do.

I am going to submit that there is really only one major problem before mankind, that is, to demilitarize the governments and the societies of the world. We must release the resources wasted on what is now called defence, when there is no defence, to solve our other problems.

When is enough enough?

In the year 1945, after the Second World War ended, there was a bitter and bruising conflict in the United States Congress between those who wanted the Atomic Energy Commission to be under civilian control and those who wanted it to be under military control. Victory in the end went to those who stood for civilian control, and in due course Gordon Dean became the first chairman of the Commission.

Dean pursued his duties for five years with great zeal, great imagination and great success. He built up a large stock of nuclear bombs for the American forces. He developed many uses of atomic energy for peaceful purposes. And when he had been there five years, he made a public speech in which he asked a question: 'When is enough enough? When you can destroy the cities of your enemy, when you can smash his industry and his military power, have you got enough? Should you go on making more?'

Some people didn't like his question, and within a period of months he had ceased to be the chairman of the Commission.

His place was taken by a military man, Admiral Lewis L. Strauss. He won world fame by saying that if he was allowed to go on with nuclear tests, he could produce a 'humane H-bomb': it would destroy London or New York, but would have no fallout—it would be 'humane'.

Gordon Dean did not lose his interest in the subject. When he regained his freedom, he wrote a book and defined his theme as follows:

The atomic age has introduced another factor that must be taken into all calculations. Whereas before the problem was simply one of war or peace, it is now one of oblivion or peace. Yet man, even in the atomic age, has not chosen peace. He has also not chosen war, and he seems to think he can go on forever without deciding upon one or the other. Maybe he can, but the risks are enormous.[1]

Dean went on in his book to propose a plan—a programme to change the psychology of nations. A campaign by every government to make people understand what a nuclear war would mean. With the United States in the lead, the White House, Congress, the Department of State, the governors and legislators

374

of the fifty constituent states of the union should all play their part in educating the nation to understand the issues that were involved. If Dean were alive today, he would be a youthful 71. His would be the most powerful voice in the world on atomic war today.

Our only yardstick

I have a friend who is an authority almost as eminent as Gordon Dean on nuclear weapons—Sir Solly, now Lord, Zuckerman. Sir Solly was on Eisenhower's staff on D-Day. For many years he was chief scientific adviser to the British Ministry of Defence. He is an eminent scientist. Agreeing with Gordon Dean's dogma—'peace or oblivion'—he says: if we want to measure the chances of oblivion, we must judge it by the only yardstick of actual experience that we have—the Hiroshima bomb.

I was moved by this saying of Zuckerman's to visit Hiroshima. I've made the pilgrimage three times. In 1975 I stood, with the citizens of Hiroshima by the Cenotaph, while they recalled the thirtieth anniversary of the day on which the bomb was dropped:

6 August 1945. 8.15 a.m.—The streets are full of people; people going to work, people going to shop, children going to school. It is a lovely summer morning, sunshine and blue sky. A blue sky stands for happiness in Japan.

The air raid siren sounds. No one pays attention. There's only a single enemy aircraft in the sky. The aircraft flies across the city. Above the centre of the town something falls. It is hard to see; the bomb is very small, and appears little larger than a tennis ball in size. It falls for 10 to 15 seconds. Then there is a sudden searing flash of light, brighter and hotter than a thousand suns. Those who are looking directly at it had their eyes burnt in their sockets. They never looked again on men or things.

In the street below there was a businessman in charge of large affairs walking to his work; a lady, as elegant as she was beautiful; a brilliant student, the leader of his class; a little girl laughing as she ran, and in a moment, they were gone. They vanished from the earth. They were utterly consumed by the furnace of the flash. There were not even ashes on the pavement. Nothing but their black shadows on the stones. Scores of thousands more, sheltered by walls or buildings from the flash, were driven mad by intolerable thirst from the heat. They ran in frenzied hordes toward the seven rivers of the delta on which Hiroshima is built. They fought like maniacs to reach the water. If they succeeded, they stooped to drink the poisoned stream. In a month they, too, were dead.

Then came the blast, thousands of miles an hour. Buildings in all directions for miles flattened to the ground. Lorries, cars, milk-carts, human beings, prams, picked up and hurled like lethal projectiles, hundreds of feet through the air. The blast piled its victims in frightful heaps, seven or eight corpses deep. Then the fireball touched the Earth, and scores of conflagrations, fanned by hurricane winds, joined in a firestorm.

And many thousands more trapped by walls of flame, that leaped higher than the highest tower in the town, were burnt to death, swiftly or in longer agony. Then all went black as night. The mushroom cloud rose to 40,000 feet. It blotted out the sun. It dropped its poison dust, its fallout, on everything that still remained non-lethal in Hiroshima. And death by radioactive sickness from the fallout was the fate of those who had survived the flash, the river, the blast, the firestorm.

'On that fatal morning,' wrote the science editor of the London *Times* on 6 August 1975, 'two hundred and forty-thousand people died within an hour. Today, in Hiroshima, many young people, who were only embryos in their mother's womb when the bomb fell, show the fatal seeds of leukemia.' And, he added, 'let's remember that the Hiroshima bomb was a nuclear midget'.

Many of the present weapons are a hundred times as powerful, and some a thousand times. The stockpiles of the world, if they were used, would serve to exterminate mankind three or four times over.

Peace or oblivion?

Powers of darkness

What of the other problems that we have to face? Democracy and freedom? I think they're vital. I'm a Social Democrat, but a British Democrat to the bone. But in country after country, year after year, we have watched militarism and guns destroying democracy and freedom, and they are destroying them still.

Torture? Torture is a horror. Torture is a shame to all mankind, yet today it is practised in sixty to eighty countries. Torture is the logical, perhaps inevitable, result of government by guns, not by law.

Hunger, world hunger? It's a question of resources. We could feed the hungry people within five years. We could double the food production within ten. But we must divert the $300 billion that now go to arms.

Illiteracy? A billion people who cannot read or write; the door to social, cultural, political progress closed to them. And the number is growing. We could end illiteracy for a fraction of the money given to military research.

Population explosion? Contraceptives, family planning—call it what you like. Raising the standard of living is the way to bring the birthrate down.

Inflation? For a century, all economists have called armaments—the product of armament expenditure—'unproductive'. It was Nixon's deficit budgeting for the Viet Nam war that broke the dollar. And the major cause, incomparably more important than all others put together, is armament expenditure. More money, too much money, chasing too few goods. Vast purchasing power and nothing that people want to buy.

And social justice? Decent houses for people to live in, instead of loathsome slums. Hospitals for the sick. Help for the widows and orphans. Education for the people. Education to make them read, really to read, not only to absorb the stuff about sex and sport. Music and the arts, not for the élite only, but for all. What has happened to social justice? What has happened to housing and hospitals, and all the other things? They've been sacrificed on the shrine of Moloch. And it is time that these sacrifices were forever ended, and that we went back to the principles which Unesco was set up to teach.

Two centuries ago, a radical, before the Revolution in France, Tom Paine, said that 'an army of principles will penetrate, where an army of soldiers cannot pass'. If we believe in the principles of Unesco, if we believe that they can defeat the powers of darkness, then most assuredly victory will be ours.

Note

1. Gordon Dean, *Report on the Atom: What You Should Know about the Atomic Energy Program of the United States*, New York, Knopf, 1953.

41

Medical nuclear warning

Medical Working Group
Pugwash Conferences

As doctors of medicine and scientists in health-related fields from many countries present at the thirtieth Pugwash Conference including: Brazil, Chile, Czechoslovakia, Egypt, Finland, France, Kenya, Netherlands, Nigeria, Poland, United Kingdom, United States, USSR and Venezuela, we issue a warning, based on medical and other scientific data, that should become widely known:

That medical disaster-planning for a nuclear war is futile

A nuclear war would result in human death, injury, and disease on a scale that has no precedent in history, dwarfing all previous plagues and wars. There is no possible effective medical response after a nuclear attack—in one major city alone, in addition to the hundreds of thousands of sudden deaths, there would be hundreds of thousands of people with severe burns, trauma, and radiation sickness—all demanding intensive care. Even if all medical resources were intact, the care of these immediate survivors would be next to impossible. In fact, most hospitals would be destroyed, medical personnel among the dead and injured, most transportation, communication and energy systems inoperable, and most medical supplies unavailable. As a result, most of those requiring medical attention would die.

Medical problems that would be minor and curable in normal times —infections and fractures for example—would prove fatal for many. Numerous deaths would also occur from the interaction of multiple, simultaneous injuries which would be trivial if each occurred singly. Large numbers of those who escaped an acute death would suffer mutilating injuries. Furthermore, under the conditions of rampant chaos and terror, the incidence of psychiatric disorders would sharply rise. The risk of long-term effects, such as cancer, would increase during their entire lifetime for many survivors, and possibly for their offspring as well.

Report of the Medical Working Group at the thirtieth Pugwash Conference, Breukelen, Netherlands, August 1980.

That effective civil defence against a nuclear attack is impossible

Bomb shelters in cities under nuclear attack would be useless owing to the blast, heat, and radiation effects. Shelters as far as ten kilometres from the centre of even a one-megaton surface nuclear explosion would become ovens for their occupants—the great surface fires would cook and asphyxiate them. At greater distance, shelters would provide only temporary protection against the high levels of radio-active fallout. In a nuclear war, one would emerge from a shelter into an environment that was a nightmare—water would be undrinkable, food contaminated, and the economic, ecological, and social fabric, on which human life depends, destroyed. For the survivors, the risk of epidemics would be great, as a result of the unburied human and animal corpses everywhere, multiplication of viruses, bacteria, fungi and insects, which are highly resistant to radiation, and the high sensitivity to radiation of the human body's ability to fight infection.

In sum, there are no defences against the lethal effects of nuclear weapons, and there is no effective treatment for those who initially survived a nuclear attack. Under all conditions, medically, nuclear war would be an unparalleled catastrophe.

As doctors of medicine and scientists in health-related fields; we conclude, therefore, that nuclear weapons are so destructive to human health and life that they must never be used. Prevention of nuclear war offers the only possibility for protecting people from its medical consequences. There is no alternative.

42

On the brink of the final abyss

Lord Mountbatten[1]

Do the frightening facts about the arms race, which show that we are rushing headlong towards a precipice, make any of those responsible for this disastrous course pull themselves together and reach for the brakes?

The answer is 'no' and I only wish that I could be the bearer of the glad tidings that there has been a change of attitude and we are beginning to see a steady rate of disarmament. Alas, that is not the case.

I am deeply saddened when I reflect on how little has been achieved in spite of all the talk there has been, particularly about nuclear disarmament. There have been numerous international conferences and negotiations on the subject and we have all nursed dreams of a world at peace but to no avail. Since the end of the Second World War, thirty-four years ago, we have had war after war. There is still armed conflict going on in several parts of the world. We live in an age of extreme peril because every war today carries the danger that it could spread and involve the superpowers.

And here lies the greatest danger of all. A military confrontation between the nuclear powers could entail the horrifying risk of nuclear warfare. The Western powers and the USSR started by producing and stockpiling nuclear weapons as a deterrent to general war. The idea seemed simple enough. Because of the enormous amount of destruction that could be wreaked by a single nuclear explosion, the idea was that both sides in what we still see as an East-West conflict would be deterred from taking any aggressive action which might endanger the vital interests of the other.

It was not long, however, before smaller nuclear weapons of various designs were produced and deployed for use in what was assumed to be a tactical or theatre war. The belief was that were hostilities ever to break out in Western Europe, such weapons could be used in field warfare without triggering an all-out nuclear exchange leading to the final holocaust.

I have never found this idea credible. I have never been able to accept the

Speech on the occasion of the award of the Louise Weiss Foundation Prize to the Stockholm International Peace Research Institute (SIPRI) on 11 May 1979. *Pugwash Newsletter*, Vol. 17, No. 4, April 1980.

reasons for the belief that any class of nuclear weapons can be categorized in terms of their tactical or strategic purposes.

Next month I enter my eightieth year. I am one of the few survivors of the First World War who rose to high command in the Second and I know how impossible it is to pursue military operations in accordance with fixed plans and agreements. In warfare the unexpected is the rule and no one can anticipate what an opponent's reaction will be to the unexpected.

As a sailor I saw enough death and destruction at sea but I also had the opportunity of seeing the absolute destruction of the war zone of the western front in the First World War, where those who fought in the trenches had an average expectation of life of only a few weeks.

Then in 1943 I became Supreme Allied Commander in South-East Asia and saw death and destruction on an even greater scale. But that was all conventional warfare and, horrible as it was, we all felt we had a 'fighting' chance of survival. In the event of a nuclear war there will be no chances, there will be no survivors—all will be obliterated.

I am not asserting this without having deeply thought about the matter. When I was Chief of the British Defence Staff I made my views known. I have heard the arguments against this view but I have never found them convincing. So I repeat, in all sincerity as a military man I can see no use for any nuclear weapons which would not end in escalation, with consequences that no one can conceive.

And nuclear devastation is not science fiction—it is a matter of fact. Thirty-four years ago there was the terrifying experience of the two atomic bombs that effaced the cities of Hiroshima and Nagasaki from the map. In describing the nightmare a Japanese journalist wrote as follows:

Suddenly a glaring whitish, pinkish light appeared in the sky accompanied by an unnatural tremor which was followed almost immediately by a wave of suffocating heat and a wind which swept away everything in its path. Within a few seconds the thousands of people in the streets in the centre of the town were scorched by a wave of searing heat. Many were killed instantly, others lay writhing on the ground screaming in agony from the intolerable pain of their burns. Everything standing upright in the way of the blast—walls, houses, factories and other buildings, was annihilated . . . Hiroshima had ceased to exist.

But that is not the end of the story. We remember the tens and tens of thousands who were killed instantly or, worse still, those who suffered a slow painful death from the effect of the burns; we forget that many are still dying horribly from the delayed effects of radiation. To this knowledge must be added the fact that we now have missiles a thousand times as dreadful; I repeat, a thousand times as terrible.

One or two nuclear strikes on this great city of Strasbourg with what today would be regarded as relatively low-yield weapons would utterly destroy all that we see around us and immediately kill probably half its population. Imagine what the picture would be if larger nuclear strikes were to be levelled against not just Strasbourg but ten other cities in, say, a 200-mile radius. Or even worse, imagine what the picture would be if there was an unrestrained exchange of nuclear weapons—and this is the most appalling risk of all since, as I have already said, I cannot imagine a situation in which nuclear weapons would be used as battlefield weapons without the conflagration spreading.

381

Could we not take steps to make sure that these things never come about? A new world war can hardly fail to involve the all-out use of nuclear weapons. Such a war would not drag on for years. It could all be over in a matter of days.

And when it is all over what will the world be like? Our fine great buildings, our homes will exist no more. The thousands of years it took to develop our civilization will have been in vain. Our works of art will be lost. Radio, television, newspapers will disappear. There will be no means of transport. There will be no hospitals. No help can be expected for the few mutilated survivors in any town to be sent from a neighbouring town—there will no neighbouring towns left, no neighbours, there will be no help, there will be no hope.

How can we stand by and do nothing to prevent the destruction of our world? Einstein, whose centenary we celebrate this year, was asked to prophesy what weapons would be used in the Third World War. I am told he replied to the following effect:

'On the assumption that a Third World War must escalate to nuclear destruction, I can tell you what the Fourth World War will be fought with—bows and arrows.'

The facts about the global nuclear arms race are well known and as I have already said SIPRI has played its part in disseminating authoritative material on world armaments and the need for international efforts to reduce them. But how do we set about achieving practical measures of nuclear arms control and disarmament?

To begin with, we are most likely to preserve the peace if there is a military balance of strength between East and West. The real need is for both sides to replace the attempts to maintain a balance through ever-increasing and ever more costly nuclear armaments by a balance based on mutual restraint. Better still, by reduction of nuclear armaments I believe it should be possible to achieve greater security at a lower level of military confrontation.

I regret enormously the delays which the United States and the USSR have experienced in reaching a SALT II agreement for the limitation of even one major class of nuclear weapons with which it deals. I regret even more the fact that opposition to reaching any agreement which will bring about a restraint in the production and deployment of nuclear weapons is becoming so powerful in the United States. What can their motives be?

As a military man who has given half a century of active service I say in all sincerity that the nuclear arms race has no military purpose. Wars cannot be fought with nuclear weapons. Their existence only adds to our perils because of the illusions which they have generated.

There are powerful voices around the world who still give credence to the old Roman precept—if you desire peace, prepare for war. This is absolute nuclear nonsense and I repeat—it is a disastrous misconception to believe that by increasing the total uncertainty one increases one's own certainty.

This year we have already seen the beginnings of a miracle. Through the courageous determination of Presidents Carter and Sadat and Prime Minister Begin we have seen the first real move towards what we all hope will be a lasting peace between Egypt and Israel. Their journey has only just begun and the path they have chosen will be long and fraught with disappointments and obstacles.

But these bold leaders have realized the alternative and have faced up to their duty in a way which those of us who hunger for the peace of the world applaud.

Is it possible that this initiative will lead to the start of yet another even more vital miracle and someone somewhere will take that first step along the long stony road which will lead us to an effective form of nuclear-arms limitation, including the banning of tactical nuclear weapons?

After all it is true that science offers us almost unlimited opportunities but it is up to us, the people, to make the moral and philosophical choices and since the threat to humanity is the work of human beings, it is up to man to save himself from himself.

The world now stands on the brink of the final abyss. Let us all resolve to take all possible practical steps to ensure that we do not, through our own folly, go over the edge.

Note

1. Earl Louis Mountbatten of Burma was Supreme Allied Commander in South-East Asia during the Second World War. He was the last Viceroy of India and first Governor-General. He was later Admiral of the Fleet, Chief of the British Defence Staff and Chairman of the NATO Military Committee. Lord Mountbatten was killed by a terrorist bomb in August 1979.

43

Unable to visualize nuclear war

Lord Zuckermann
Chief Scientific Adviser
to the British Government (1964–71)

We need education . . .

We all accept that the devastation which would be caused in a nuclear war would be vast and terrible. But I believe that the greatest danger of nuclear weapons being used is that people do not realize, that they are unable to visualize, what this would mean.

Even at this meeting, we began with too depersonalized, too clinical, an account of what would be the result of the explosion of nuclear weapons. We speak of them as though they imply single isolated disasters. We have not tried to visualize the picture of the virtually total destruction, not of one, but of several related cities or, given an 'all-out' nuclear exchange, not just of several cities, but in effect of the effacement of the major cities of Western Europe, of the USSR, and of the United States, beyond all possibility of reconstruction in any realistic period of time.

Writers in the United States, a country which did not suffer damage in any of the wars of this century, talk about 'levels of acceptable damage', of 'assured destruction', of '100 million American citizens being killed in a nuclear exchange'. Words like these carry no meaning. To understand our subject we should have had at our table a survivor of Hiroshima, or of Hamburg or Dresden, or someone who had been on the spot when some vast area of London was flattened. Drawing concentric circles on a map showing the areas where radiation would be lethal, where fire would spread, and where blast would have its effects provides no glimmering of what would be the consequence of the explosion of a single-megaton or a seven-megaton bomb on a city of, say, a million inhabitants. If a single-megaton bomb were ever to burst over a British city like Birmingham, about a third of its population would be immediately killed or crushed under debris. The remaining two-thirds would be extricating themselves from radio-active rubble as they sought help and shelter. There would be floods and fire. There would be nowhere to turn, no possibility of help if at the same time neighbouring cities had been struck. In modern society, when one major focus of destruction interacts with another, there is a multiplying effect.

Remarks at the thirtieth Pugwash Symposium at Toronto, May 1978, *The Dangers of Nuclear War*, University of Toronto Press, 1979.

When the Soviet Union carried out its last series of atmospheric tests, Nikita Khrushchev, referring to a 57-megaton burst, said that it could have been made bigger, but the danger then was that all the windows of Moscow, hundreds of miles away, might have been broken. This was a gruesome joke; but I believe he understood what he was saying! My first point is that one real danger of the possibility of nuclear war is that we have ceased to understand what we are talking about. How can one imagine the reality: the possible elimination, not only of, say, half the population of the northern hemisphere, but also the elimination of the better part of the cultural history of our globe? We need education in these matters. Each new sequence of generals, of admirals, of air marshals who come to positions of power, need to be educated afresh about these things. So, too, do politicians and prime ministers. They come and go but, as someone said earlier at this symposium, they come as freshmen to a university. One generation of freshmen, as it moves on to its second year, does not inoculate the one that follows with its wisdom. And the wisdom becomes thinner as the years pass.

If we go on talking about the use of nuclear weapons as though this was a real option in world politics, then they will be used. That is a danger I see worsening in the years ahead.

Lowering the nuclear threshold

The second and related danger which I see is a technological trend that aims at obliterating the critical difference between nuclear weapons on the one hand and so-called conventional weapons on the other. We persuade ourselves that nuclear weapons can be made small and precise, and not as harmful as an equally precise conventional weapon with more destructive power. In my view this trend undoubtedly lowers the nuclear threshold, at least partly because it encourages people to believe that nuclear weapons (for example, so-called neutron bombs used ostensibly to hold up a massive tank incursion) can be real weapons of choice.

This leads into the third danger I see: the growing belief that nuclear weapons could be used in what is now fashionably called a 'theatre war'. I do not believe that any scenario exists which suggests that nuclear weapons could be used in field warfare between two nuclear states without escalation resulting. I know of several such exercises. They all lead to the opposite conclusion. There is no Marquess of Queensberry who would be holding the ring in a nuclear conflict. I cannot see teams of physicists attached to military staffs who would run to the scene of a nuclear explosion and then back to tell their local commanders that the radiation intensity of a nuclear strike by the other side was such and such, and that therefore the riposte should be only a weapon of equivalent yield. If the zone of lethal or wounding neutron radiation of a so-called neutron bomb would have, say, a radius of half a kilometre, the reply might well be a 'dirty' bomb with the same zone of radiation, but with a much wider area of devastation due to blast and fire.

To the best of my knowledge, no one has yet suggested a mutually agreed mechanism for controlling escalation on a battlefield. Until we are assured that there could be one, we have to see any degree of nuclear destruction as part of a continuous spectrum of devastation. Having some knowledge of the way generals and air marshals discharge their responsibilities in war—having understood why they do as they do—I have no faith that they would behave differently in any future war. What Admiral Miller has told us about the chain of command in the control of the use of nuclear weapons makes it inevitable that, if the concept of tactical nuclear warfare were to have any meaning at all, there would have to be the authority for 'prior-release' as soon as hostilities begin. Another speaker, in his explanation of the concept, has told us that if a division or a brigade feared that it was going to be overwhelmed then, according to NATO doctrine, it would have to resort to the use of nuclear weapons. Were this indeed to happen, we would be talking not of nuclear tactital warfare, but about kamikaze warfare leading to mutual annihilation. Wars are fought on the ground, and by men, and not in accordance with some preordained scenario, and not by moving little flags around on maps on a wall in Moscow or Washington or Paris or London. Wars may start as central planners predict; but history shows that they rarely, if ever, proceed, or indeed end, as predicted.

Nuclear proliferation, deterrence and nuclear superiority

The next, and again related, danger which I see as possibly leading to nuclear warfare is, of course, the proliferation of nuclear-weapon states. Some countries which might 'go nuclear' are undoubtedly encouraged by the belief that nuclear weapons—weapons which we cannot wish away—have a tactical or battlefield value. This promotes a belief in their utility. There is also a false belief that the possession of nuclear weapons implies political power. But the greater the number of nuclear-weapons states, the more difficult the maintenance of the present situation of deterrence between the few existing nuclear powers.

People forget that when nuclear weapons were first developed in the United States, in the United Kingdom, and then in the USSR, it was believed that in effect they were just super-bombs capable of providing, in a phrase now happily forgotten, 'more bang for a buck'. It was only when the risks associated with their possible use became appreciated that the concept of mutual nuclear deterrence emerged. The idea of deterrence then moved inexorably to the idea of equivalence of nuclear power, and then to questions of control. But today, even though knowledgeable men, for example Kissinger, ask what meaning can be attached to the concept of 'nuclear superiority', even when wise men have long known that 'enough is enough', the nuclear arms race continues unabated.

There is, of course, a danger of the control system that maintains the state of deterrence inadvertently breaking down. We have heard at this meeting that, during the Cuba crisis of 1962, some American warships were not fully under command from the top. In times of war, control systems do become precarious. When asked what he thought of the political control of nuclear weapons in Europe, Field Marshal Montgomery said publicly that he would seek permission to fire only after he had fired. The present system could also break down because national sovereignty implies that the much smaller nuclear arsenals of the United Kingdom and France could independently trigger nuclear war. If a British ship in, say, the Indian Ocean were to launch nuclear missiles at Soviet targets, how would the Soviet Union know under which flag they had been fired?

I keep asking myself whether it was wrong to treat Szilard's solution—to have built under Moscow a nuclear fortress manned by American personnel in communication with Washington, with a corresponding fortress manned by Russians under Washington—as a joke.

The momentum of the technological arms race

The next danger which might trigger nuclear war derives from the momentum of the technological arms race itself. We in the West are fearful of the build-up of Warsaw Pact conventional forces in the same way as the Soviet Union is fearful of the possible introduction of cruise missiles and other new types of delivery systems. As we have been told by Admiral Miller, who knows more about strategic targeting than most of us, new nuclear warheads have to be assigned targets as they are produced, whether or not there is a requirement for additional destructive capability. Political fears and reciprocal suspicions have inevitable reactions. The technological arms race cannot but be politically destabilizing.

Finally, I see as another danger which might trigger nuclear war, the continuing competition in the sale of arms—conventional arms, it is true—but none the less a transfer of destructive power which might generate situations in which nuclear weapons could be used.

These are the dangers I see. What then would be my priorities in their reduction? Here I agree completely with Dr Arbatov that the first thing to do is to slow down the arms race, and if possible to reverse it. I am not a dreamer. I do not visualize disarmament as a practical goal; I would be content with arms control.

The first measure which I regard as important is the reduction in the race of proliferation of nuclear weapons. The United Kingdom is committed to the Non-Proliferation Treaty and to such other treaties that have been agreed in order to reduce the dangers which face us. I see as critical to the Non-Proliferation Treaty an unqualified complete test ban. When states began to negotiate for a non-proliferation treaty, they were concerned with the spread of nuclear weapons to non-nuclear countries. Then we started hearing about the 'horizontal proliferation' which the nuclear powers wanted to prevent, and the concept of 'vertical proliferation' which non-nuclear states, for example India, saw as continuing between the nuclear powers. I believe it to be essential that a Comprehensive Test Ban (CTB) is agreed in such a way that potential nuclear powers will not be able to build up their own arsenals, and the nuclear powers will be unable to elaborate what they already have. That, in all logic, comes first.

Next, I believe it is essential for the world that the SALT talks achieve some measure of success, and that they succeed in full public view. There should be no hitches here. It is a fact of history that with every delay in reaching an agreement in the control of nuclear arms—due to a failure to agree to this or that at any given moment—nuclear stocks build up at such a rate that the best that could be achieved later is worse than the worst that might have been concluded a year or two before. With every delay, our mutual peril becomes greater.

44

The mad nuclear scramble

Gene R. La Roque
Center for Defense Information, Washington, D.C.

Role of the military

Nuclear war is an unrelenting and growing threat to hundreds of millions of people. A third world war, with nuclear weapons, can happen and almost certainly will happen unless all governments confront this most uncomfortable reality.

I am a citizen of the United States and a career military officer. I served in the navy of my country for thirty-one years. I have fought in combat and held command posts at sea and on land and participated in strategic and nuclear planning. I have experienced at first hand the impact that nuclear weapons have had on military affairs.

Since retiring from active duty, I have been the director of a non-governmental research organization, the Center for Defense Information, a project of the Fund for Peace. We are a source of independent, objective analysis of military developments. Our centre is particularly active in providing factual information about the nuclear arms race and the consequences of nuclear war.

The traditional role of all the military in all countries, in case of war, is to win. The military profession, to be blunt, has always sought superiority. Military men tend to be uncomfortable with notions of military balance or equilibrium. We military men constantly seek to strengthen the defence of our countries and maintain our advantages. I believe that the military in all countries share this impulse. We are not diplomats; we are soldiers, sailors and airmen. We feel reassured by big military establishments; we believe that the security of our people is enhanced by spending for additional war-fighting and war-winning capabilities.

There may be places in the world where warfare can occur on a limited scale without threatening wider destruction. But those areas are few and shrinking. My experience in the United States military has convinced me that nuclear weapons have changed the traditional rules of warfare. To use an American phrase, 'It's a whole new ball game.'

I am, of course, speaking primarily of the relationship between the United

---

1. Statement at the Special Session of the United Nations General Assembly Devoted to Disarmament, 13 June 1978. (Verbatim record A/S-10/AC. 1/PV.8.)

States and the Soviet Union and their respective military alliances. Despite the constant friction and conflict, that have occurred over many decades, there has never been a war between our two countries. But today, as irrational as it may seem, Soviet and American leaders are planning and arming for nuclear war.

A recent top-level United States Government study concluded that, at a minimum, 140 million people in the United States, and 113 million people in the Soviet Union would be killed in a major nuclear war. Almost three quarters of the economy of each country would be destroyed. In such a conflict, the analysis concluded, 'neither side could conceivably be described as a winner'.

Nor would the rest of the world be safe. Radiation would poison vast stretches of the planet not directly involved in the war. And the threat of ozone damage and ecological disruption leaves us no assurance that the earth would remain habitable for life as we know it.

Preparing for nuclear war

Despite this, the United States and the Soviet Union continue to approach the accumulation of military power in the nuclear age very much as they have in the past. Both countries constantly seek to improve their nuclear and conventional forces.

Many of us are shocked and sobered by the mad nuclear scramble of the superpowers. It seems so obvious that they have diminished their own security in the nuclear competition. We all know that a balance of terror provides a precarious peace.

The Soviet Union and the United States are, in part, victims of modern military technology. Advances in weaponry, particularly better delivery systems, have dramatically compressed time and space. Thus, military leaders believe they must maintain large forces on a close-to-war status. In a nuclear war, each nation could destroy the other in thirty minutes. Nuclear missiles launched from submarines could land within fifteen minutes. There is no defence, regardless of who strikes first.

The prospect of immediate mass destruction seems to compel high states of military readiness, and this situation inspires mutual suspicion and rhetorical harshness.

The continuation of the nuclear arms race is also made possible by widespread apathy about the danger of nuclear war. Many people believe nuclear weapons will never be used. But as someone who has been directly involved in United States nuclear planning, I can tell representatives that my country has plans and forces for actually fighting in a nuclear war.

Our military field manuals detail the use of nuclear weapons. Our troops, airmen and sailors train and practise for nuclear war. Nuclear war is an integral part of American military planning and the United States is prepared to use nuclear weapons anywhere in the world. I believe the Soviet Union is as nuclear-oriented in its military preparations as is the United States. The military in both countries see nuclear weapons as a central instrument of military power. They are prepared to use them now and in many contingencies.

As a citizen of the United States, I do not hesitate to point out that my country has generally taken the lead in the nuclear arms race. The United States is a rich country with vast technological resources. We have been, on the average, five years ahead of the Soviet Union in introducing new nuclear weapons. We were the first to develop the atomic bomb, the hydrogen bomb, the intercontinental bomber, effective intercontinental ballistic missiles, modern nuclear-powered strategic submarines, and multiple warheads (MIRVs) for our missiles.

The United States continues to maintain, as President Carter recently asserted, a significant edge over the Soviet Union in the effectiveness of our strategic weapons as measured by such factors as missile accuracy and numbers of nuclear weapons.

In recent years, the United States has not been sitting on its hands in the nuclear competition. The United States has added more nuclear weapons to its arsenal than has the Soviet Union, going from 4,000 strategic nuclear weapons in 1970 to 9,000 in 1978. During this same period, the Soviet Union increased its strategic nuclear weapons from 1,800 to 4,500. The United States has maintained a two-to-one edge in deliverable nuclear weapons throughout the period 1970 to 1978.

This discrepancy in numbers, however, makes no sense and no difference, as each country can obliterate the entire urban and industrial complex of the other regardless of who strikes first. The United States has thirty-five strategic nuclear weapons for every Soviet city of over 100,000 inhabitants. The Soviet Union has twenty-eight strategic nuclear weapons for every American city of over 100,000 inhabitants.

The United States Secretary of Defense, Harold Brown, asserted in his annual report on the fiscal year 1979 military budget that American nuclear-war plans include 'destruction of a minimum of 200 major Soviet cities'.

The greater danger is that both countries are moving towards a first strike. Improvements in the accuracy of missiles, particularly land-based missiles, stimulate fears about the adequacy of existing nuclear forces in the Soviet Union and the United States.

Enormous destructive potential

If everyone, including military officials, were more conscious of the tremendous destructive potential of nuclear weapons we might stop worrying about questions of 'advantage' in the nuclear arms race. For example, just two United States Poseidon submarines which carry 320 nuclear weapons can destroy all the major Soviet cities, with the destructive potential of 1,000 Hiroshima-size weapons.

Today the United States, with forty-one strategic submarines, has more than twenty-one such submarines at sea constantly. The United States now maintains round the clock some 3,000 strategic nuclear weapons at sea in submarines off the coast of the Soviet Union. The Soviet Union, normally deploying far fewer strategic submarines at sea, keeps a formidable force of approximately 200 sea-based nuclear weapons constantly targeted on the United States.

The United States is now deploying a more powerful warhead, the Mark 12A, on its Minuteman III land-based missiles. Just one of these missiles will contain the destructive power of 80 Hiroshima-size weapons. Individual Soviet missiles contain an even larger destructive potential.

Both the United States and the Soviet Union are now stepping up their nuclear-weapons developments. The Soviet Union, following the path of the United States, is substantially increasing its intercontinental nuclear weapons by putting more than one nuclear weapon on its strategic missiles.

Under the present United States administration, funding for the production of new nuclear warheads has risen 70 per cent to produce warheads for Trident missiles, Minuteman III missiles, air-launched cruise missiles, artillery shells and other nuclear weapons. Military secrecy in the Soviet Union prevents us from knowing the new weapons that may be planned in that country.

The recital of the details of the nuclear competition could go on endlessly. It can take place in the absence of full information about military forces. There is widespread ignorance on the part both of citizens and of government officials about world military activity. I have often been struck by the lack of awareness even on the part of military officers of the enormous size of nuclear arsenals.

This matter of information brings me to the suggestions which I would offer for consideration at this Special Session. What should be done?

I cannot offer a broad-scale programme of action or a magic key to the nuclear maze, but I do have a few thoughts about practical steps that can be taken.

Steps to be taken

First, the role of the United Nations as a repository of information on world military activity should be strengthened. All governments should submit a report each year on their military spending and force levels and the United Nations should publish that information in an annual military yearbook. The United Nations Centre for Disarmament Studies could be an appropriate agency to collect and publish that material.

Article 47 of the United Nations Charter charges the United Nations Military Staff Committee to 'advise and assist the Security Council on all questions relating to . . . the regulation of armaments, and possible disarmament'.

The Military Staff Committee, with a more representative membership, could serve as a source of information and analysis of disarmament efforts. As a beginning, that committee should report to this year's session of the General Assembly on its performance to date in fulfilling the Charter's charge.

Secondly, both the United States and the Soviet Union should adopt measures crucial to the control of the proliferation of nuclear weapons. Preventing the spread of nuclear weapons is essential for the survival of the United States and the Soviet Union. It has been estimated that in twenty years a hundred countries will possess the materials and the knowledge necessary to produce nuclear weapons. By the year 2000, the total amount of plutonium produced as a by-product of global nuclear power will be the equivalent of a million nuclear bombs.

Both countries should pledge themselves never to use nuclear weapons against non-nuclear states—I really wish they would pledge themselves never to use

391

nuclear weapons at all. I can think of no military utility, though, in the use of nuclear weapons by the superpowers against non-nuclear countries.

Stopping production of fissionable materials for weapons has been proposed by previous United States administrations and is more feasible today than ever before. The United States and the Soviet Union have enormous stocks of nuclear weapons and weapons material and have no military need to continue the production of fissionable material. They now have more than they will ever need. The halting of production could be followed by a complete moratorium on all manufacture of nuclear weapons, since both the United States and the Soviet Union now have more weapons than they will ever need.

The ending of all nuclear-weapons testing also is feasible right now. The United States has tested more than 600 nuclear weapons; the Soviet Union has tested more than 350. Both should now have learnt all that is necessary. This Special Session should urge all nations to stop producing fissionable material, stop making nuclear weapons and stop testing nuclear weapons.

Thirdly, without significantly reducing their military capabilities the United States and the Soviet Union could eliminate most, if not all, nuclear weapons from their naval surface ships. With the ships of both navies roaming the far reaches of the world's oceans, the potential for nuclear war arising out of naval incidents increases. Both navies are extensively nuclearized, with several thousand nuclear weapons aboard surface ships of the United States Navy.

Fourthly, a start should be made on the reduction of the huge nuclear arsenals of the United States and the Soviet Union by the dismantling, over a five-year period, of all land-based intercontinental ballistic missiles (ICBMs). The United States has about 1,000 ICBMs and the Soviet Union about 1,400. The scrapping of ICBMs would solve many of the problems that at present preoccupy the military and the press, particularly in the United States. Both the United States and the Soviet Union are becoming increasingly worried about the vulnerability of their ICBMs. I consider the attacks they fear to be unlikely in the extreme, but giving up the traditional attachment to ICBMs would make both countries feel safer.

The elimination of ICBMs would be easier for the United States than for the Soviet Union, since the Soviet Union today has a much smaller proportion of its strategic weapons on bombers and on submarines. However, it is expected that the Soviet Union will shortly begin to put multiple warheads on its many sea-based missiles and become much less reliant on ICBMs. Nuclear deterrence can be accomplished without ICBMs.

Conclusion

In conclusion, this Special Session Devoted to Disarmament, with 149 countries present, demonstrates the realization on the part of all countries that their territory could provide the spark that could ignite nuclear war. Knowledgeable military men are aware that there would be worldwide consequences from a nuclear war. There is no defence, nowhere to hide.

The governments of the United States and the Soviet Union have carelessly let their relations deteriorate to an alarming extent. Political leaders must take control of events and not permit the military, or technology, to control them. The non-nuclear countries can act as the burr under the saddle to push the nuclear powers in the direction of reason. If we are to survive on this planet, the arms race must be slowed, stopped and reversed, and the time to start is now.

Note

1. Rear Admiral United States Navy (Ret.); Director of the Center for Defense Information, Washington, D.C.

45

Détente: the only reasonable policy for the future

Georgi A. Arbatov[1]
Institute of the United States and Canada,
Academy of Sciences of the USSR, Moscow

Assessing the dangers of nuclear war

We are attempting to assess the dangers of nuclear war by the year 2000. In discussing the dangers of war, and ways to avert it, we must pay great attention to the arms race itself, seeking ways to curb it and begin a process of disarmament. There are few who do not acknowledge that bad political relations and an atmosphere charged with mistrust encourage arms-race activity. Today, in addition, we know that such behaviour can flourish under different circumstances. The arms race, as we have recently learned, can go on even in a time of remarkable political improvement and can eventually undermine good relations by fomenting mistrust and suspicion. The conditions are then set for a deterioration in the political atmosphere and in relations between countries.

The arms race, in the opinion of many people—and I share this opinion—has become a major source of danger of nuclear war. Today, the world finds itself on the threshold of a new round of the arms race which is fraught with grave dangers. These dangers are not simply in the possibility of development of some particular weapons but in the pace of development of weapons technology under present political conditions, a trend which can be detrimental to stability and peace.

The continuing military rivalry between major world powers cannot but increase the danger of proliferation of nuclear weapons. Recognition of this truth should not be an excuse for those leaders and governments that may in the years to come opt for nuclear armaments. Under any circumstances such an option will be a bad and dangerous one. It can only greatly impair the security of any country choosing this road and jeopardize international security as a whole. All nuclear powers will continue to bear a special responsibility; if they fail to curb the arms race, the risk of proliferation of nuclear weapons may increase and even become inevitable in certain political situations.

However serious the problem of proliferation of nuclear weapons may be, it is not the only danger in the continuing arms race. The number of stockpiled

Remarks at the thirtieth Pugwash Symposium at Toronto, May 1978. *The Dangers of Nuclear War*, University of Toronto Press, 1979.

weapons of mass destruction, the emergence of new systems, and the new strategic concepts that appear as a result of these, increase the danger of nuclear war. The development of MIRVs, despite all the justifications given by the United States at the time, resulted in a growth in the number of nuclear warheads that far surpassed the needs of 'deterrence'. Military planners immediately began to seek a rationale for the 'redundant' warheads or, in other words, to look for new targets for them. In this way, the idea of 'counterforce' use of strategic weapons was revived at a new and more dangerous level. This led in turn to the development of new programmes designed, among other things, to improve accuracy, terminal guidance, flexibility in retargeting, and miniaturization of warheads.

Destabilizing trends

It is clear that, cumulatively, all of these developments can have far-reaching consequences. In particular, the achievements of military technology have given a fresh impetus to the idea that nuclear war is a possible instrument of foreign policy. In this context the restatement by the United States in 1975 of its policy of possible first use of nuclear weapons seemed particularly alarming. All the more so since it came in the context of new attempts to convince the public that increased accuracy and development of small-yield weapons or neutron weapons would reduce losses in a possible nuclear war to 'acceptable' dimensions. It was argued that these would be used 'only' against military targets and the hostilities would thus not escalate into an all-out nuclear war. All this doubtless contained a good measure of blackmail levelled against political adversaries of the United States. However, it is rightly pointed out both in the Soviet Union and other countries that a by-product of this campaign was to scale down public opposition to nuclear war, to make the idea of such a war a 'thinkable' alternative in the eyes of the public.

Set against the background of possible future breakthroughs in the sphere of anti-submarine warfare, the revival of the 'counterforce' concept and the relevant armament programmes gives a new impulse to fears of a 'first-strike' capability. I do not believe that qualified experts, let alone responsible statesmen, would consider a first strike truly feasible. There would, for example, always remain the possibility of countering this threat by developing mobile launching installations or, as a last resort, relying upon a 'launch on warning' strategy, however dangerous this may be.

One cannot fail to see, however, that these trends in the arms race will destabilize the strategic situation and increase the risk of a dramatic, fatal mistake under conditions of acute international crisis. Moreover, another menace may be discerned: the arms race could take a course (and to a certain extent is beginning to do so) which would make new agreements on limiting and reducing armaments far more difficult, if not altogether impossible, due to the insurmountable obstacles entailed in verification of some new weapons. This is, for instance, one of the negative consequences of the development of the strategic cruise missile or the MX mobile missile.

It must be stressed that the continuing arms race is highly unlikely to produce any immediate, let alone long-term, advantages for either side. But it does create grave threats for both parties as well as for world peace and security. This is so because the arms race increases the danger of nuclear war even though no government may want such a war or plans deliberately to unleash one. In this sense, the decades ahead may differ sharply from the 1960s and 1970s. These developments are already under way. We must act and act quickly to avoid the dangers. One has to agree with Ambassador George Kennan who recently warned that time is running out for all of us.

Mutual interests

I believe that there is increasing need to understand that the Soviet Union and the United States, East and West, face in their relations and their negotiations —including arms-control negotiations—an impersonal adversary that overrides any specific threat one side may see in the other. This adversary is the looming danger of nuclear war, whatever may be its concrete scenario. With all our differences and contradictions we have an overwhelming mutual interest in seeking to avert the threat of war. This interest compels us to be persistent in our efforts to promote détente and to secure arms control and disarmament.

Another mutual interest, one which transcends the borders of each state and which also demands détente and disarmament, is the increasing complexity and urgency of global problems. It seems to me that actions which impede détente not only hinder the strengthening of peace and world security but also ignore the fundamental requirements of social progress all over our planet. I have in mind the emergence of such problems as limited energy resources and shortages of other raw materials, difficulties in providing food for the world's growing population, pollution of the environment and so forth. It is good that in recent years active discussion of these problems has begun. But it is a pity that they are so rarely posed in the context of their interconnection with and dependence on the world situation. Yet such a relationship exists and it is a direct one.

Scientists estimate that by the year 2000 the earth's population will increase by the number of people our planet had at the beginning of this century. A colossal amount of building will be required since in less than a quarter of a century the world will have to build as much as was constructed in several previous centuries. If present trends continue, about 900 million people on the earth will need jobs by the beginning of the next century. Development of the Third World will pose tasks of unprecedented dimensions. Energy and food problems will become increasingly acute.

These are only some of the global challenges we will face in the year 2000. Even allowing for error on the part of scientists, it must be admitted that they are very grave. Yet they can and must be solved.

If problems of this magnitude are on the agenda one may legitimately ask whether the people of the world, especially those in countries with the most advanced economies, science, and technology, can afford to continue to spend an enormous portion of their brain and labour power, of their means and resources, on the arms race and the needs of war. Can these countries afford not to make maximum efforts to concentrate their resources on tackling the global problems mentioned above, on developing the closest and broadest possible co-operation to this end and on establishing an international political atmosphere that is conducive to such co-operation? It is true that détente will not solve all the world's problems by itself. But without it mankind will hardly be able to start coping with them in any sort of fundamental way.

Political realism

We have, then, tremendously important mutual interests which make détente not only desirable but the only reasonable policy for the future. At the same time we have to be aware of the fact that states, like people, have not always acted in keeping with their own best interests—otherwise history would have spared us a great many wars and conflicts. Efforts to curb the arms race lag far behind the pace of military technology. This could lead once more to an unwanted major conflict. Special efforts must be made to avoid this development. Quick and effective measures in the field of arms control are imperative.

The Soviet Union considers arms control and disarmament to be the dominant objective in all its efforts in international policy. The Soviet Union keeps coming up with fresh proposals aimed at curbing and ending the arms race. We are hopeful for the future of détente. As President Brezhnev said to the heads of diplomatic missions in Moscow in July 1977: 'We trust, we firmly trust, that political realism and the will for détente and progress will ultimately overcome, and mankind will be able to step into the twenty-first century in a peace as secure as never before. We will do all we can to make it happen.'

Note

1. Candidate Member, Central Comittee of the Communist Party of the Soviet Union, and Academician and Director, Institute of the United States and Canada, Academy of Sciences of the USSR.

46

Disarmament, development, and a just world order

Rajni Kothari
Centre for the Study of Development Societies, Delhi

The dilemma before humanity

The issues relating to disarmament, and the growing sense of urgency about it at the end of the 1970s, derive from considerations somewhat different from those in earlier decades. This is not just because of the terrifying magnitudes that the stockpiling and continuing refinement of deadly armaments are taking, or because, as in the opinion of many authorities, of the arms race 'getting out of hand'; it is also because this is happening at a time when the world has entered a period of major transformation in several dimensions. It is a transformation that could lead either to a world more peaceful and secure as well as more just and humane, or to a world racked by increasing turbulence, by a greater sense of insecurity among the major centres of power and, hence, to a further tightening of the structures of domination, producing in its wake an intensification of the arms race, a pre-emption of countermoves by encouraging regional conflagration, and an eventual holocaust.

While there is a growing awareness and heightened sensitivity among leading thinkers and intellectuals that the world we live in is undergoing some rapid and perhaps profound transformation, there are varying perceptions of the precise nature of the transformation. These perceptions bring out a number of dimensions: of techno-economics, of demography, of sources of energy, of the availability and distribution of material resources, of military and political power, and of cultural configurations and encounters. A satisfactory interpretation of this transformation must take account of all these dimensions. On the impact of these changes on the international system, however, there are three different, though not necessarily conflicting, perceptions.

Three perceptions

One view is that the age of Western domination is coming to an end, and that a new framework of 'interdependence' is emerging, in which wealth and power will

Shortened version of a working paper prepared for the International Workshop on Disarmament, Delhi (India), March 1978, *Bulletin of Peace Proposals*, Vol. 9, No. 3, 1978.

be more widely distributed among a much larger number of nation-states. The only issue is whether the Western powers and their counterparts in the Soviet sphere of influence will accommodate this change peacefully and in a spirit of co-operation or continue to seek to dominate the world, encouraging in the process turbulence and war, and the institution of repression and brutalization of the social process through the spread of militarization around the globe. There is much merit (and, indeed, a great deal of truth) in this way of looking at the global transformation, limited though it is.

There are others who see the transformation as emanating from a gradual disintegration of the nation-state system. The argument is that the problems of poverty and starvation, energy and ecology, and, above all, prevention of cataclysmic wars and nuclear disaster, have become too massive to be managed within the nation-state framework. Again, there is much in this argument that is not only persuasive but is almost self-evident. However, the idea of disintegration of the nation-state system is negative. Therefore, it is unlikely to cause enough effort to carve out an alternative system of governance at various levels that would give hope to people and engage them in the process of fundamental reconstruction.

There are few who, while recognizing the truth in the above perceptions, see a far more comprehensive and deeper transformation at work which emanates from a fundamental process of erosion of the existing structures and the culture that dominates them. There is a delegitimization of authority structures and processes at various levels arising from a breakdown of the myths and symbols and identities that provided security within the prevailing state system, and from a growing sense of rigidity and ossification of the framework of international relations. There is also a growing sense of futility about the dominant cultural paradigms and techno-economic 'models' that were once held to be universal and hence benign for all, but which have, in fact, produced a schism in the condition of men and societies. This has led to a widespread feeling of vulnerability of the self and the social fabric that gives it anchor and, above all, to a deep and pervasive and a very real sense of injustice at the prevailing order.

The twofold response

The response to this transition from an old order which has lost its utility and credibility, while a new one is yet to take shape, is twofold. On the one hand, the fact that territorial man—based on settled agricultural and industrial units and an organized state—today finds himself adrift is sought to be met with a 'world order' that spans the entire globe; indeed, outer space and the oceans as well. This consists of new corporate structures that transcend territorial boundaries in the wake of new technologies, economic penetration of diverse regions by global enterprises aided by intelligence agencies, and a global structure of power that is supposed to provide 'stability' through military and strategic 'balance' between the two superpowers at the top and a set of subsidiary as well as ancillary balances in the various regions. Both the trilateral approach of world capitalism and its subsidiary partners in parts of the developing world and the Soviet approach of hegemony of the socialist world—despite the Chinese challenge and, to a lesser

399

extent, that of parts of the developing world—are increasingly becoming the co-ordinate parts of this 'world order'. Its basic thrust comes from a comprehensive process of homogenization based on technology transfer, corporate economic management, a co-ordinated framework of governance that is monitored from global and regional power centres, and, above all, a military establishment supposed to ensure security for all.

On the other hand, the newly enfranchised societies—emerging out of a colonial past and struggling to achieve an independence based on national self-determination and economic self-reliance, respect for diversity and opposition to external interventions and hegemonies of all kinds—are engaged in a collective effort that seeks to produce a just and equitable world order by removing sources of inequity and exploitation and, simultaneously, to evolve a structure of peace and harmony by removing the sources of tension and turbulence that are bound to arise in an unequal and divided world. For 'peace', unless it emanates from and is rooted in a social structure widely seen to be just and fair, can be highly stultifying and may prove to be repressive of the forces of change and reconstruction. Those strongly entrenched in a given social and political order have always wanted peace so that the 'order' they preside over would endure and remain unchallenged.

There are different reasons for which different groups desire peace. Those not so entrenched—including both the newly ascendant and the as yet deprived —want peace on the basis of justice and a share in power and decision-making; for, in their view, a structure of inequity and exploitation is the primary source of conflict and violence. These observations apply as much to the international order as to the national and regional ones. It is characteristic of the world we live in that this structure of inequity extends to both socio-economic and politico-strategic dimensions. It is a situation of cumulative inequity in which a fantastic command over instruments of violence and military power reinforces and supports a system of economic and political domination: hence the interest of those outside the dominant structure of power in peace and disarmament. But the essential nature of this interest and striving should be understood. The process of disarmament should start within the citadels of arms race, involving, through their co-operation, the rest of the world. Disarmament should thus be looked upon as an essential component of a global development effort that directs the considerable human and technological resources available towards building a more just and equitable world community.

Pacification of the challenge from the South

There is, of course, a different kind of argument which has gained currency of late, especially since 1973, which signalled the economic ascendancy of the OPEC countries, stimulating a measure of confidence among the Third World élites who tended to close ranks despite wide economic gaps and persisting regional conflicts. Then came the process of defusing the economic power of the Middle East and its induction into the dominant establishment of the world.[1] In this process of pacification of the sources of challenge from the South, the technological and military power of the North has played a very major role.

The economic challenge that 1973 posed has been met by deploying the military and technological power of the highly industrialized countries in the *nouveau riche* societies. And the new sense of power and autonomy that was generated in the wake of the new-found riches has been channelled into the acquisition of new symbols and artefacts of national grandeur that once again have made these countries dependent states. The same processes have been at work in meeting the challenge of the ascendant countries in Latin America, Africa, and South-East Asia. In all these regions, although diplomatic man-oeuvres, economic penetration through multinationals, political subversion of uncomfortable regimes, and hard-headed economic bargaining for maintaining favourable terms of trade for the dominant nations (in the face of increases in oil and commodity prices) have been employed, it is the induction of armaments and the culture of militarization that has ensured the perpetuation of the global status quo. As this kind of penetration spreads wider and becomes systemic to the structure of global management, the dominant role of military power in the design of the states system is likely to increase. And, as the global structure of military power is basically hierarchical and hegemonical (with the two superpowers possessing a disproportionate share in it), the world model that is likely to take shape will also be hierarchical and hegemonical, and essentially bipolar.

Issues facing the developing countries

It is in the light of this analysis, which brings out the fact that the arms race and the global military-industrial culture are an essential component of the whole design of the prevailing world model, that we have to consider two interrelated issues: (a) the serious obstacles in the way of any overall design for disarmament in a manner that reduces, and not accentuates, inequity and injustice in the world, and (b) the prospects before the developing world for restructuring the world economic and political order in the face of what we have earlier described as a situation of cumulative inequity.

The two issues, closely intertwined as they are, need to be faced together as part of a common task. It is a difficult and challenging task, and calls for a widespread movement for change, in the developing countries, in the centres of industrial and military power, in the various world bodies, and in the public opinion forums and communication channels that have an extended international reach. Such a movement for change will have to be in respect of both the basic perception of the human condition in our time and the strategies for redesigning it. It will involve a major educational effort towards reorienting the basic concepts and interpretations of objective reality as well as a simultaneous political effort towards altering the framework of objective reality itself. Such efforts to change the dominant predispositions as well as the structure of dominance are especially needed for dealing with the twin tasks of arresting the arms race and combating the dominance structure in international relationships.

Supremacy in global power relations

This movement will no doubt be resisted by those used to the present world model and the perceptions on which it is based. The situation is further complicated in two respects. First, despite the persistence of important differences and points of discord between the United States and the Soviet Union, on the two crucial issues posed here they seem to converge more than diverge. This means that the earlier leverages that the developing countries had are no longer available. The efforts called for will, therefore, have to be new.

Second, despite the success of the United States and other industrialized countries in containing the economic consequences of the OPEC threat in 1973, concern and anxiety still prevail in the establishment circles in these countries over the growing 'challenge from the South' which, in their perception, might pose a threat to the maintenance and continuous rise in the living standards of their people, upset the balance on which the present system of power relations rests, and ultimately erode the long-established supremacy of the West in world affairs.

Such a perception of threat, and the need to evolve contingency plans against it, are clearly set forth in a recent report by the Rand Corporation to the United States Department of Defense.[2] A careful reading of this document makes it clear that underlying its logic of defending economic supremacy is a deeper motivation: namely, the maintenance of supremacy in global power relations and, hence necessarily, in the global structure of strategic and military balances. Indeed, such a perspective is laid out fairly early in the document:

As a superpower cast by history in a role of world leadership, the United States would be expected to use its military force to prevent the total collapse of the world order or, at least, to protect specific interests of American citizens in the absence of an international rule of law.

Such contingencies might generate military requirements without precedent in the experience of American military planners, who may not yet fully comprehend the significance of events that are already happening, such as the intersection between the old East-West conflict, the new North-South conflict, and the accelerating consequences of planetary mismanagement.

More attention may have to be devoted to the development of doctrine, plans, weapons and force structures in anticipation of possible uses of military force in some novel crisis situations. The American people may demand that its national interests be protected by all available means if global turbulence prevails in the 1980s. . . .

The military posture implications of such a situation are not self-evident. If a harsh international environment were to develop in the 1980s, additional military capabilities might be required besides the forces directly dedicated to Soviet and other well-understood contingencies.

The depth of the crisis

If such is their perception of the emergence of the developing countries after a long period of suppression and tutelage, and if such is their calculated response to it—namely, of halting the rise of the developing countries, if need be by use of force—one can see the depth of the crisis facing humanity. Add to this the prevailing doctrine of the necessity of stockpiling of a wide range of nuclear and conventional armaments by the superpowers, presumably as a means of deterring a world war between them; add to it also the attempt to weave a net of military dependence through spreading the military virus to various regions of the world, and you have the full spectre of the accelerating arms race and its crucial role in maintaining the present pattern of domination and the overall culture of power politics.

This culture militates not only against the values of peace and human dignity that should inform the creation of a just world order, but also against the great need to concentrate all efforts and resources for the tasks of development—of providing human beings everywhere with basic necessities, of discovering new sources of energy and new forms of technology, and of preserving the environment, the sea-bed, and outer space from being destroyed in the race for state power and technological prowess on which nations seem to put a very high premium. If, indeed, they do not turn back from the scramble for power based on the prevailing military-industrial-academic complex, the high technology that it breeds and the corrosive arms race that it has engendered, the prospects of development seem to be dim. Nor will the consequences of this be limited to the economic prospects of the developing world. The search for a place in the techno-military world must lead to the rise of a technocratic élite everywhere, to the erosion of political institutions and cultural autonomy, and, before long, to the end of civil government and democratic rights everywhere, including in liberal democratic societies.

Movement for a new world order

It is essential that these trends be arrested and the nations of the world be made to engage in the movement for change discussed above. In this task, the non-aligned and the developing countries must play a leading role. Instead of merely responding to an agenda set by the big powers, they must take initiatives themselves for both halting the arms race and changing the present structure of inequity and domination in global power relations. Such initiatives will also have predictable responses from the 'developed' world. For it is also caught in the dilemma of an unending arms race that fails to provide security, transforms its own world into a battle camp and threatens it with ecological erosion, and political breakdown of both the liberal-capitalist and the state-socialist systems. There is also a growing sense of futility and anomie in these countries, especially among the junior allies and the relatively independent and neutral countries, among the younger generation, and, gradually, among the masses as well. There is, here, a vast human constituency that the developing countries can depend on. It is nothing short of a movement for a new world order in which the intellectuals of the world, starting with political initiatives of the non-aligned and the developing world, have to engage.

Notes

1. For an analysis of the implications thereof for the North-South relations, see Rajni Kothari, *Sources of Conflict in the 1980s.* (Adelphi Papers, No. 134.)
2. Guy J. Pauker, *Military Implications of a Possible World Order Crisis in the 1980s: A Project AIR FORCE Report Prepared for the United States Air Force,* Santa Monica, The Rand Corporation, 1977.

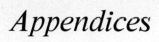

Appendices

Appendix I. Glossary of terms, acronyms and abbreviations frequently used in writings dealing with military policy and in arms control and disarmament negotiations*

ABM. See *Antiballistic missiles.*

Active penetration aid. A weapon that helps a nuclear delivery system breach enemy defences. Air-to-air and air-to-surface missiles are examples. See also *Passive penetration aid.*

Active sonar. Sound navigation and ranging equipment that transmits pulses, then records reflections to detect and locate hostile submarines. See also *Passive sonar.*

Aerospace defence. An inclusive term encompassing all measures to intercept and destroy hostile aircraft, missiles, and space vehicles, or otherwise neutralize them. See also *Air defence; Antiballistic missiles.*

Aggregate. The SALT II agreement provides for several 'aggregate' numerical limits on various categories of strategic offensive arms. The term 'aggregate' refers principally to the overall aggregate of ICBM launchers, SLBM launchers, heavy bombers, and ASBMs.

Airborne alert. A state of readiness designed to reduce reaction time and increase survivability by maintaining combat-equipped aircraft aloft on a continuing basis or during times of tension. See also *Ground alert.*

Airborne warning and control system (AWACS). An air-based defence system carrying radar and navigation and communications equipment designed to detect, track and intercept attacking aircraft.

Airbreather. Any delivery system that operates entirely within the earth's atmosphere. Manned aircraft and cruise missiles are examples.

Air defence. All measures to intercept and destroy hostile aircraft and cruise missiles, or otherwise neutralize them. Equipment includes interceptor aircraft, surface-to-air missiles, surveillance devices, and ancillary installations.

*The present glossary has been prepared from the following sources: 'Glossary', *The Annals of the American Academy of Political and Social Sciences*, Vol. 433, 1977, pp. 175–7; 'Selected Glossary of Terms and Weapons', *Arms Uncontrolled*, (prepared by Frank Barnaby and Ronald Huisken), 1975, pp. 219–23; 'SALT II Glossary', *SIPRI Yearbook 1980*, pp. 212–23; 'Glossary of Terms', document prepared for the Committee on International Relations of the U.S. House of Representatives, 1975, pp. 193–8. The selection of terms has been made to facilitate access to technical literature, and the terms are not necessarily those used in the readings reproduced in this publication. This glossary does not imply any approval or disapproval by Unesco of the definitions given.

1. American Christian Church

Air-launched ballistic missiles. Any ballistic missile transported by and launched from land- or sea-based aircraft and/or lighter-than-air conveyances, such as blimps, balloons and dirigibles.

Air-launched cruise missile (ALCM). A cruise missile designed to be launched from an aircraft. See also *Cruise missile (CM)*.

Airmobile missile. Any missile transported by and launched from an aerial platform. See also *Air-launched ballistic missile; Air-launched cruise missile*.

ALBM. See *Air-launched ballistic missile*.

ALCM. See *Air-launched cruise missile*.

Air-to-surface ballistic missile (ASBM). A ballistic missile launched from an aeroplane against a target on the earth's surface.

Air-to-surface ballistic missile (ASBM) carrier. An airborne carrier for launching a ballistic missile capable of a range in excess of 600 km against a target on the earth's surface.

Anti-aircraft defence. See *Air defence*.

2. **Antiballistic missile (ABM).** Any missile used to intercept and destroy hostile ballistic missiles, or otherwise neutralize them. Antiballistic-missile defence equipment includes weapons, target acquisitions, tracking and guidance radar, plus ancillary installations with the same purpose.

Antisubmarine warfare (ASW). All measures to reduce or nullify the effectiveness of hostile submarines.

Area target. A target whose dimensions encompass two or more geographic co-ordinates on operational maps. Cities and military bases are representative.

Arms control. Any measure limiting or reducing forces, regulating armaments, and/or restricting the deployment of troops or weapons which is intended to induce responsive behaviour or which is taken pursuant to an understanding with another state or states. See also *Arms limitation; Disarmament*.

Arms limitation. An agreement to restrict quantitative holdings of or qualitative improvements in specific armaments or weapons systems. See also *Arms control; Disarmament*.

Arms race. The competitive or cumulative improvement of weapons stocks (qualitatively or quantitatively) or the build-up of armed forces based on the conviction of two or more states that only by trying to stay ahead in military power can they avoid falling behind.

ASBM. See *Air-to-surface ballistic missile*.

Assured destruction. A highly reliable ability to inflict unacceptable damage on any aggressor or combination of aggressors at any time during the course of a nuclear exchange, even after absorbing a surprise first strike.

ASW. See *Antisubmarine warfare*.

Atomic bomb. A weapon based on the rapid fissioning of combinations of selected materials, thereby inducing an explosion (along with the emission of radiation).

Atomic effects. Blast and shock, thermal radiation, initial nuclear radiation, and residual radiation generated by the detonation of fission or fusion weapons.

Attack aircraft. Tactical aircraft used primarily for interdiction and close-air-support purposes.

AWACS. See *Airborne warning and control system*.

B-1. A new American strategic bomber with a 34,000 kilogram payload capable of flying intercontinental missions without refuelling.

B-52. All-jet heavy bomber used in the United States Strategic Air Command since 1955.

Backfire. The NATO designation of a modern Soviet two engine, swing-wing bomber.

Ballistic missile. A pilotless projectile propelled into space by one or more rocket boosters. Thrust is terminated at some early stage, after which re-rentry vehicles follow trajectories that are governed mainly by gravity and aerodynamic drag. Mid-course corrections and terminal guidance permit only minor modifications to the flight path.

Bomb. A weapon dropped from a manned aircraft of any sort. Gravity is the primary force, but 'smart' bombs can be guided electronically.

Breeder reactors. Reactors in which the process of fission enhances the concentrations of fissionable materials in the fuel or in a 'jacket' covering the reactor, thereby producing more fuel than is used.

Captor. An American antisubmarine weapon system consisting of a homing torpedo inserted into a mine casing and a sonar device. If a submarine passes within about 3 kilometres of the mine it releases the torpedo which then seeks out the target. This weapon can be deployed at great depths (around 800 metres).

Carrier. Any vehicle designed to deliver weapons to a target or to stand-off release points. Aircraft, aircraft carriers, and submarines are examples. See also *Stand-off (missile and carrier)*.

CEP. See *Circular error probable*.

Circular error probable (CEP). A measure of the delivery accurate of a weapon system. It is the radius of a circle around a target of such size that a weapon aimed at the target has a 50 per cent probability of falling within the circle.

Civil defence. Passive measures designed to minimize the effects of enemy action on all aspects of civil life, particularly to protect the population and production base. Includes emergency steps to repair or restore vital utilities and facilities.

Coercion. The attempt to induce a change in behaviour through actual punishment, supposedly applicable when compellance fails. See also *Compellance*.

CM. See *Cruise missile*.

CMC. See *Cruise-missile carrier*.

Cold launch. A 'pop-up' technique that ejects ballistic missiles from silos or submarines using power-plants that are separate from the delivery vehicles. Primary ignition is delayed until projectiles are safely removed from containers/carriers.

Collateral casualties and damage. Physical harm done to persons and property co-located with or adjacent to targets. Collateral effects may be welcome or unwanted, depending on circumstances.

Combat radius. The distance an aircraft loaded as required can fly from base to target and return employing axes, speeds and altitudes most likely to guarantee success against armed opposition.

Command/control. An arrangement of facilities, equipment, personnel, and procedures used to acquire, process and disseminate information needed by decision-makers in planning, directing and controlling operations.

Compellance. The attempt to induce a change in behaviour through threatening undesirable consequences in the event of refusal. See also *Coercion*.

Conflict spectrum. A continuum of hostilities that ranges from subcrisis manoeuvring in cold-war situations to the most violent form of general war. See also *General war*.

Conventional (forces, war, weapons). Military organizations, hostilities, and hardware that exclude nuclear, chemical and biological capabilities.

Counterforce strategy. A strategy of using nuclear weapons to destroy the opponent's nuclear and general military forces. The main consequences of adopting such a strategy is the need for large numbers of extremely accurate nuclear weapons.

Counter-insurgency. Any military effort undertaken by an established government to overcome armed resistance by insurgent or anti-government forces.

Countervalue strategy. A strategy of targeting nuclear weapons on the opponent's cities and industrial areas. When compared with a counterforce strategy, this strategy requires fewer and less accurate nuclear weapons.

Cruise missile (CM). A guided missile which uses aerodynamic lift to offset gravity and propulsion to counteract drag. A cruise missile's flight path remains within the earth's atmosphere.

Cruise-missile carrier (CMC).   An aircraft equipped for launching a cruise missile.

Damage limitation.   A term used in nuclear-strategy debates to indicate a situation in which one side, feeling that an attack is imminent, launches a pre-emptive strike with the objective of reducing the opponent's nuclear forces and therefore the severity of the expected attack.

Defence in depth.   Protective measures in successive positions along axes of enemy advance, as opposed to a single line of resistance. Designed to absorb and progressively weaken enemy penetrations.

Delivery system.   See *Nuclear delivery system.*

'Delousing'.   Procedures used by American submarines to ascertain whether hostile ASW forces have picked up their trail as they leave port. Affirmative answers result in evasive action or other responses, depending on the circumstances.

Deterrence.   The prevention from action by fear of the consequences. Deterrence is a state of mind brought about by the existence of a credible threat of unacceptable counteraction. See also *Nuclear deterrence.*

Direct support.   Logistic and administrative assistance dedicated to a specific combat unit by elements that respond directly to requests. Supply, maintenance and service forces organic to aircraft and missile squadrons are representative. See also *General support.*

Disarmament.   The reduction of a military establishment to some level set by international agreement. See also *General and complete disarmament.*

Dispersal base.   An operating base used by strategic bombers only during periods of increased alert caused by mounting international tensions or crimes. See also *Main operating base; Satellite base.*

Dual-purpose forces.   Military forces that can be used effectively to perform two or more unrelated missions or functions. Strategic and conventional operations constitute typical dual-purpose applications. Strategic bombing coupled with post-strike surveillance constitutes another.

ECM.   See *Electronic countermeasures.*

Electronic countermeasures.   A form of electronic warfare that prevents or degrades effective enemy uses of the electromagnetic spectrum. Jamming is a typical tactic. See also *Electronic counter-countermeasures.*

Electronic counter-countermeasures.   A form of electronic warfare taken to ensure effective use of the electromagnetic spectrum despite enemy ECM efforts.

Encryption.   Encoding communications for the purpose of concealing information.

Escalation.   An increase (deliberate or unpremeditated) in the scope or intensity of a conflict.

F-14 (Tomcat).   A highly sophisticated variable-sweep wing all-weather interceptor, first deployed operationally in 1973 on an American aircraft carrier. It is armed with a machine-gun and short-, medium- and long-range air-to-air missiles. The fire-control system for the long-range Phoenix missile is capable of simultaneously tracking and engaging six targets.

Fighter aircraft.   Tactical aircraft used primarily to gain and maintain air superiority.

Fighter-bomber.   See *Attack aircraft.*

First-strike capability.   The ability to destroy all, or very nearly all, of the enemies' strategic nuclear forces in a pre-emptive nuclear attack. See also *Pre-emptive strike ; Second strike capability.*

First-strike strategy.   A strategy adopted perforce by a country which possesses nuclear weapons that are vulnerable to an attack and must therefore be used before such an attack is made.

Fissile material (or Fissionable material).   Isotopes (variants) of certain elements, such as plutonium, thorium and uranium, which emit neutrons in such large numbers that a

410

sufficient concentration will be self-sustaining, that is, will continue to produce increasing numbers of neutrons until it is damped down, explodes, or the material is exhausted.

Flexibility.   Capabilities that afford countries and weapons systems a range of options, and facilitate smooth adjustment when situations change.

Flight-test.   For the purposes of SALT II, a flight-test of a missile is an actual launch of the missile (as distinct from a static test) conducted for any purpose, including for development of the missile, for demonstration of its capabilities, and for training of crews.

FOBS.   See *Fractional orbital bombardment system.*

Fractional orbital bombardment system (FOBS).   A missile that achieves an orbital trajectory but fires a set of retrorockets before the completion of one revolution in order to slow down, re-enter the atmosphere and release the warhead it carries into a ballistic trajectory toward its target.

Fractionation.   The division of the payload of a missile into several warheads. The use of a MIRV payload is an example of fractionation.

Fratricide.   The destruction or neutralization of one nuclear weapon by another belonging to the same country of coalition. Blast, heat and radiation all may contribute.

FRODs.   See *Functionally related observable differences.*

Functionally related observable differences (FRODs).   The means by which SALT II provides for distinguishing between those aircraft capable of performing certain SALT-limited functions and those that are not. FRODs are differences in the observable features of aeroplanes which specifically determine whether or not they can perform the mission of a heavy bomber, whether or not they can perform the mission of a bomber equipped for cruise missiles capable of a range in excess of 600 kilometres, or whether or not they can perform the mission of a bomber equipped for ASBMs.

Fusion.   A process whereby the atoms of light, non-fissionable elements such as lithium are transformed under pressure, yielding helium and energy in the form of radiation.

GEM.   See *Ground-effects machine.*

General and complete disarmament.   The goal established by the United Nations General Assembly in the field of disarmament which involves disbanding armed forces, dismantling military establishments, eliminating stockpiles of nuclear, chemical, bacteriological and other weapons of mass destruction, and discontinuance of military expenditure according to an agreed sequence of balanced measures under strict and effective international control with the ultimate outcome that states will have at their disposal only those non-nuclear armaments, forces, facilities and establishments as are agreed to be necessary to maintain internal order and protect the personal security of citizens.

General war.   Armed conflict between major powers in which the total resources of the belligerents are employed, and the national survival of a major belligerent is in jeopardy. Commonly reserved for a showdown between the United States and the USSR, featuring nuclear weapons.

General-purpose forces.   All combat forces not designed primarily to accomplish strategic offensive or defensive missions. Tactical aircraft are an example. See also *Strategic forces.*

General support.   Logistic and administrative assistance provided to several combat units by elements that operate independently. Supply, maintenance and service forces at depot level are representative. See also *Direct support.*

GLCM.   See *Ground-launched cruise missile.*

Ground alert.   A state of readiness designed to reduce reaction time and increase survivability by maintaining combat-equipped aircraft and crews ready to take off quickly. It may be a routine procedure or be practised only during times of tension. See also *Airborne alert.*

Ground-effects machine. An air-cushion vehicle that 'floats' over terrain when in motion. Considered as a potential off-the-road carrier for land-mobile missiles.

Ground-launched cruise missile (GLCM). A cruise missile launched from ground installations or vehicles. See also *Cruise missile (CM)*.

Hard target. A target protected against the blast, heat and radiation produced by nuclear explosions. There are many degrees of hardening.

Heavy ballistic missile. For the purposes of SALT II, ballistic missiles are divided into two categories according to their throw-weight and launch-weight, light and heavy. Heavy missiles (ICBMs, SLBMs and ASBMs) are those missiles that have a launch-weight greater or a throw-weight greater than the launch-weight or throw-weight of the Soviet SS-19 ICBM.

Heavy bomber. The term used in SALT II to describe those aircraft included in the aggregate limitations of the agreement. See also *Strategic bomber*.

Horizontal proliferation. The spread of nuclear capabilities across states and/or non-governmental entities.

Hueycobra (AH-IG). An American high-speed anti-tank helicopter armed with a machine gun, a grenade launcher, and eight TOW anti-tank missiles. Advanced weapon-aiming equipment is installed, including a laser range-finder.

IAEA. See *International Atomic Energy Agency*.

ICBM. See *Intercontinental ballistic missile*.

Inertial guidance. A system that measures acceleration and relates it to distances travelled in certain directions. Designed to steer ballistic missiles over predetermined courses, using data generated solely by devices in the missiles.

Infra-red signature. The image produced by sensing electro-magnetic radiations emitted or reflected from a given target surface in the infra-red spectrum (approximately 0.72 to 1,000 microns).

Instability. See *Strategic stability*.

Interceptor. An air-defence aircraft designed to identify and/or destroy hostile air-breathing weapons systems such as bombers and cruise missiles.

Intercontinental ballistic missile (ICBM). A land-based fixed or mobile rocket-propelled vehicle capable of delivering a warhead to intercontinental ranges. Once they are outside the atmosphere, ICBMs fly to a target on an elliptical trajectory. An ICBM consists of a booster, one or more re-entry vehicles, possibly penetration aids, and, in the case of a MIRVed missile, a post-boost vehicle. For the purposes of SALT II, an ICBM is considered to be a land-based ballistic missile capable of a range in excess of 5,500 kilometres (about 3,000 nautical miles).

Intercontinental ballistic missile (ICBM) silo launcher. An ICBM silo launcher, a 'hard' fixed ICBM launcher, is an underground installation, usually of steel and concrete, housing an intercontinental ballistic missile and the equipment for launching it.

Intermediate-range ballistic missile (IRBM). A ballistic missile with a range of 1,500 to 3,000 nautical miles (2,800–5,500 km). See also *Ballistic missile*.

Intermediate-range cruise missile (IRCM). An air-breathing missile with a range of 1,500 to 3,000 nautical miles (2,800–5,500 km). See also *Cruise missile*.

International Atomic Energy Agency (IAEA). The international organization belonging to the United Nations system charged, among other things, with monitoring the production and use of special fissionable materials.

IRBM. See *Intermediate-range ballistic missile*.

IRCM. See *Intermediate-range cruise missile*.

Kiloton. One thousand tons (of TNT equivalent).

Launcher. That equipment which launches a missile. ICBM launchers are land-based launchers which can be either fixed or mobile. SLBM launchers are the missiles tubes on a ballistic missile submarine. An ASBM launcher is the carrier aircraft with associated equipment. Launchers for cruise missiles can be installed on aircraft, ships, or land-based vehicles or installations.

Launch-on-warning. Retaliatory strikes triggered upon notification that an enemy attack is in progress, but before hostile forces or ordnance violate friendly soil.

Launch-weight. The weight of the fully loaded missile itself at the time of launch. This would include the aggregate weight of all booster stages, the post-boost vehicle (PBV), and the payload.

Loiter time. The length of time an aircraft can remain aloft in any given location, pending receipt of further orders. Depends primarily on fuel capacity, consumption rates, refuelling capabilities, and pilot fatigue. Loiter capabilities for missiles are a future possibility.

M-20. A French nuclear missile first deployed in 1977 with a maximum range of 5,000 kilometres.

MAD. See *Magnetic anomaly detection.*

Magnetic anomaly detection (MAD). ASW equipment designed to pinpoint the location of hostile submarines by detecting disturbances in normal magnetic fields of force.

Main operating base. The primary airfield used by strategic bombers. Includes the headquarters and diversified support elements. See also *Dispersal base; Satellite base.*

Manoeuvrable re-rentry vehicle (MaRV). A ballistic missile warhead or decoy whose accuracy can be improved by terminal guidance mechanisms.

Manned penetrator. Strategic bombers and tactical aircraft whose performance depends on pilots and/or crews.

MaRV. See *Manoeuvrable re-entry vehicle.*

MBFR. Mutual and Balanced Force Reductions or Mutual Balanced Force Reduction. See *Mutual force reduction.*

Medium bomber. A multi-engined aircraft that lacks intercontinental range without in-flight refuelling, but is suitable for strategic bombing under special circumstances. See also *Strategic bomber.*

Medium-range ballistic missile (MRBM). A ballistic missile with a range of 600 to 1,500 nautical miles (1,100–2,800 km). See also *Ballistic missile.*

Medium-range cruise missile (MRCM). An air-breathing missile with a range of 600 to 1,500 nautical miles (1,100–2,800 km). See also *Cruise missile.*

MFR. See *Mutual force reduction.*

Mid-course correction. An in-flight amendment to the trajectory of ballistic or cruise missile, by any means whatsoever, for the purposes of improving accuracy. See also *Terminal guidance.*

Minuteman III. An American light ICBM, introduced in 1970. Range 7,000 nautical miles (13,000 km) and a payload consisting of three 165-kiloton independently targetable warheads, i.e. 3×165 KT (MIRV).

MIRV. See *Multiple independently targetable re-rentry vehicle.*

Mobile missile. Any ballistic or cruise missile that depends partly or entirely on mobility to ensure pre-launch survivability. Carriers may be aircraft, ships or motor vehicles.

Mobile target. Any target in motion at the time it is attacked.

MRBM. See *Medium-range ballistic missile.*

MRCM. See *Medium-range cruise missile.*

MRV. See *Multiple re-entry vehicle.*

Multiple independently targeted re-entry vehicle (MIRV). A missile payload comprising two or more warheads that can engage separate targets. See also *Multiple re-entry vehicle; Re-entry vehicle.*

Multiple re-entry vehicle (MRV). A missile payload comprising two or more warheads that engage the same target. See also *Multiple independently targeted re-entry vehicle; Re-entry vehicle.*

Mutual and balanced force reductions (MBFR). See *Mutual force reduction.*

Mutual force reduction (MFR). Negotiations between nineteen NATO and Warsaw Pact countries begun in Vienna in 1973 to discuss the mutual reduction of forces and armaments in Central Europe.

Mya-4 Bison (NATO code). Soviet four-jet long-range strategic bomber. First deployment 1956. It has an estimated payload of 10,000 kilograms, a maximum speed of 900 kilometres per hour, and a typical range of 6,000 nautical miles (11,200 km).

National command authority (NCA). The top national security decision-makers of a country.

National technical means of verification (NTM). Assets that are under national control for monitoring compliance with the provisions of an agreement. NTM include photographic reconnaissance satellites, aircraft-based systems (such as radar and optical systems), as well as sea- and ground-based systems (such as radar and antennae for collecting telemetry).

NCA. See *National command authority.*

Non-Proliferation Treaty (NPT). The multi-lateral agreement officially known as the Treaty on the Non-Proliferation of Nuclear Weapons, signed in London, Moscow and Washington on 1 July 1968, and entered into force on 5 March 1970, which prohibits: (a) the transfer by nuclear-weapon states to any recipient whatsoever of nuclear weapons or other nuclear explosive devices or of control over them; (b) the assistance, encouragement or inducement of any non-nuclear-weapon state to manufacture or otherwise acquire such weapons or devices; and (c) the receipt, manufacture or other acquisition by non-nuclear-weapon states of nuclear weapons or other nuclear explosive devices.

NPT. See *Non-Proliferation Treaty.*

NTM. See *National technical means of verification.*

Nuclear delivery system. A nuclear weapon, together with its means of propulsion and associated installations. Includes carriers such as aircraft, ships and motor vehicles. See also *Nuclear weapon.*

Nuclear deterrence. A strategic doctrine based on the assumption that a potential aggressor can be dissuaded from provocative action or war by the threat of 'unacceptable damage' and 'assured destruction' through the use of or retaliation with nuclear weapons.

Nuclear device. A nuclear explosive which may (a) be intended for non-military uses such as construction, hence peaceful nuclear explosive, or (b) be too heavy and/or too cumbersome for delivery on military targets and hence useful only for test purposes.

Nuclear effects. See *Atomic effects.*

Nuclear-free zone. A region or group of states from which all nuclear weapons are banned.

Nuclear material. See *Fissile material.*

Nuclear parity. Rough equivalence between the nuclear forces of opposing countries. Equivalence can be defined in a number of ways: number of launchers; number of individually deliverable warheads; total deliverable explosive power, so-called 'throw-weight'.

Nuclear proliferation. The process by which one state after another comes into possession of some form of nuclear weaponry, and with it the potential of launching a nuclear attack on other states.

Nuclear reactor. A mechanism fuelled by fissionable materials which give off neutrons, thereby inducing heat. Reactors are of three general types: (a) power reactors, in which the heat generated is transformed into power in the form of electricity; (b) production reactors, which are designed primarily to increase concentration of certain fissionable materials, such as plutonium, Pu-239; (c) research reactors, which are designed primarily to produce isotopes (variants) for some materials and/or to induce radioactivity in others, for applications in genetics, medicine and so forth.

Nuclear reprocessing. The separation of radioactive waste (spent fuel) from a nuclear-powered plant into its fissile constituent materials. One such material is plutonium, which can then be used in the production of atomic bombs.

Nuclear safeguards. Any number of ways to protect nuclear power or production reactors from accidental spillage of nuclear waste, from theft of nuclear materials, or from the diversion to these to unauthorized purposes, such as weapons production.

Nuclear terrorism. Terrorism is the systematic use of terror as a means of coercion. Nuclear terrorism involves the use (or threatened use) of nuclear weapons or radioactive materials by an actor, either state or non-government.

Nuclear weapon. A bomb, missile, warhead or other deliverable ordnance item (as opposed to an experimental device) that explodes as a result of energy released by atomic nuclei by fission, fusion or both.

Nuclear (weapons) state. One possessing nuclear weapons, whether fission, fusion or both.

Observable differences (ODs). Externally observable design features used to distinguish between those heavy bombers of current types capable of performing a particular SALT-limited function and those that are not. These differences need not be functionally related but must be an externally observable design feature.

ODs. See *Observable differences*.

Operations and maintenance. All activities of armed forces, in peace and in war, to carry out strategic, tactical, training, logistic and administrative missions.

Overkill. A destructive capacity in excess of that required to achieve stated objectives.

PAL. See *Permissive action links*.

Passive penetration aid. A harmless device that helps a nuclear delivery system breach enemy defences. Chaff and electronic countermeasures are examples. See also *Active penetration aid*.

Passive sonar. Sound navigation and ranging equipment that listens for sounds radiated by hostile submarines. See also *Active sonar*.

Payload. The ordnance delivered by any system, expressed in numbers of bombs, stand-off weapons, and missiles warheads, and/or in terms of yield (kilotons, megatons).

PBV. See *Post-boost vehicle*.

Penetration aids (Penaids). Devices employed by offensive weapon systems, such as ballistic missiles and bombers, to increase the probability of penetrating enemy defences. They are frequently designed to simulate or to mask an aircraft or ballistic missile warhead in order to mislead enemy radar and/or divert defensive anti-aircraft or anti-missile fire. See also *Active penetration aid; Passive penetration aid*.

Permissive action links (PAL). Electronic systems for the control of nuclear warheads whereby these can be armed only if positive action to this end is taken by a duly constituted authority, such as the President of the United States or the Supreme Allied Commander, Europe.

Pershing IA. An American missile first deployed in 1962 with a maximum range of approximately 750 kilometres.

Pershing II. An American nuclear missile scheduled for deployment in 1983 with a maximum range of approximately 1,600 kilometres.

Plutonium recycling. A process whereby plutonium in the spent-fuel of reactors is separated from other fissile materials and reused either as reactor fuel (see *Breeder reactors*) or for atomic weapons.

Point target. A target located by a single set of geographic co-ordinates on operational maps. Missile silos are representative.

Polaris. An American submarine-launched ballistic missile in three versions: A1, first deployed in 1960 with a range of 2,200 kilometres and a 1-megaton nuclear warhead, no longer operational; A2, first deployed in 1962 with a range of 1,500 nautical miles (2,750 km) and an 800-kilton nuclear warhead, no longer operational; A3, first deployed in 1964 with a range of 2,500 nautical miles (4,600 km) and three 200-kiloton warheads (not independently targetable), operational on fourteen strategic submarines.

Poseidon C-3. An American SLBM first deployed in 1971. Range 2,500 nautical miles (4,600 km) and a payload consisting of ten to fourteen 50-kiloton independently targetable warheads.

Positive control. Standard procedures prohibit the accidental launch of ballistic missiles. Aircraft launched on warning return to base unless they receive coded voice instructions that can be authenticated.

Post-boost vehicle (PBV). Often referred to as a 'bus', the PBV is that part of a missile's payload carrying the re-entry vehicles, a guidance package, fuel and thrust devices for altering the ballistic flight path so that the re-entry vehicles can be dispensed sequentially toward different targets. Ballistics missiles with single RVs also might use a PBV to increase the accuracy of the RV by placing it more precisely into the desired trajectory.

Post-launch survivability. The ability of any given delivery system to breach enemy defences and attack designated targets. See also *Pre-launch survivability*.

Post-strike assessment. The acquisition and evaluation of data that indicates the success of a nuclear attack and thereby assists subsequent decision-making.

Pre-emptive strike. An attack launched in the expectation that an attack by an adversary is imminent and designed to forestall that attack or to lessen its impact. Usually refers to a strike on an adversary's delivery vehicles, weapons stocks, and other components of nuclear forces.

Pre-launch survivability. The ability of any given delivery system to weather a surprise first-strike successfully and retaliate. See also *Post-launch survivability*.

Quick-reaction alert. Readiness procedures designed to reduce reaction times and increase the survivability of tactical aircraft, mainly in the NATO area. See also *Ground alert*.

Radar cross-section. The picture produced by recording radar waves reflected from a given target surface. The size of the image is not determined entirely by the size of objects. Structural shape, the refractory characteristics of materials, and locations with regard to receivers are all important.

Radioactive materials. Those giving off Beta rays, Gamma rays or other forms of radiation. Radioactive materials may or may not be fissionable.

Rapid reload capability. The ability of a delivery system to conduct multiple strikes. This characteristic is at present confined to aircraft, but land-mobile missiles and hard-site ICBMs have the potential. Submarines conceivably could be replenished at sea, but a significantly greater time-lag would occur.

Recall capability. The ability to retrieve weapons and/or carriers after launch on warning. Recall may be directed by communications or occur spontaneously in the absence of authenticated orders to attack targets.

Re-entry vehicle (RV). That portion of a ballistic missile which carries the nuclear warhead. It is called a re-entry vehicle because it re-enters the earth's atmosphere in the terminal portion of the missile trajectory.

Release point. The spot from which stand-off weapons are launched from carriers.

RV. See *Re-entry vehicle*.

SAM-D. An American anti-aircraft missile. The fire-control system for the missile includes a phased-array radar that searches for, acquires, tracks and engages the target. The missile is supersonic with either a nuclear or high-explosive warhead.

SALT. See *Strategic arms limitation talks*.

Satellite base. An operating base used routinely by strategic bombers to reduce congestion at main bases, and thus reduce vulnerabilities to nuclear attack. See also *Dispersal base; Main operating base*.

416

Saturation attack. The use of weapons *en masse* to overload enemy defences and/or blanket areas that contain known or suspected targets.

Second-strike capability. The ability to mount a nuclear attack after a first strike by the opponent. For a strategy of deterrence the object is to convince the enemy that no matter what he does (in a first strike), you will retain the capability to deliver an unacceptable severe second strike. See also *First-strike capability; First-strike strategy.*

Shelter. A revetment or other protective construction above ground, designed as a pre-launch shield for a nuclear delivery system and/or crew. Effective in varying degrees against atomic effects, depending on weapon yields and distances from ground zero. See also *Silo.*

Short-range attack missile (SRAM). An air-to-ground missile with a nuclear warhead deployed on American strategic bombers (FB-111 and B-52) since 1972. Its main purpose is to attack enemy aircraft defences (for example, anti-aircraft missile sites) to enable the bombers to penetrate to their primary targets. Maximum range 160 kilometres. See also *Cruise missile.*

Short-range ballistic missile (SRBM). A ballistic missile with a range of less than 1,000 kilometres. See also *Ballistic missile.*

Short-range cruise missile (SRCM). See *Short-range attack missile.*

Show of force. The purposeful exhibition of armed might before an enemy or potential enemy, usually in a crisis situation, to reinforce deterrent demands.

Silo. Underground facilities for a hard-site ballistic missile and/or crew, designed to provide pre-launch protection against atomic effects. High-yield, precision weapons are needed to destroy the most durable construction. See also *Shelter.*

Single integrated operational plan (SIOP). The United States' plan for nuclear retaliation. If deterrence fails, it affords the President many options, regardless of circumstances.

SIOP. See *Single integrated operational plan.*

SLBM. See *Submarine-launched ballistic missile.*

SLCM. See *Submarine-launched cruise missile.*

Soft target. A target not protected against the blast, heat and radiation produced by nuclear explosions. There are many degrees of softness. Some missiles and aircraft, for example, are built in ways that ward off certain effects but they are 'soft' in comparison with shelters and silos. See also *Hard target.*

Sonar. See *Active sonar; Passive sonar.*

Sortie. One operational flight by one aircraft.

Spent fuel. Fuel which has been in use in a reactor for some time and which in conse-quence has changed composition and diminished in its ability to give off neutrons.

SRAM. See *Short-range attack missile.*

SRBM. See *Short-range ballistic missile.*

SRCM. See *Short-range cruise missile.*

S-2. A French nuclear missile first deployed in 1971 with a maximum range of 3,000 kilometres.

SS-4. American designation for a Soviet nuclear missile first deployed in 1959 having a maximum range of 2,000 km.

SS-5. American designation for a Soviet nuclear missile first deployed in 1961 having a maximum range of 2,200 nautical miles (4,100 km).

SS-11 Mod. 1. American designation for the most numerous Soviet ICBM. Introduced in 1965. This missile has a range of 5,700 nautical miles (10,500 km) and a single 1- to 2-megaton warhead.

SS-11 Mod. 3. A development of the SS-11 mod. 1 introduced in 1973 with a payload consisting of three 100 to 300 kiloton warheads (not independently targetable).

SS-12. American designation for a Soviet nuclear missile first deployed in 1969 having a maximum range of approximately 800 km.

417

SS-17. American designation for a Soviet light ICBM first deployed in 1975, with a range of 5,400 nautical miles (10,00 km), that has been flight tested with a single RV and with MIRVs. Mod. 1: 4 × 900 kilotons (MIRV); Mod. 2: 1 × 5 megatons operational.

SS-18. American designation of the heaviest of the heavy Soviet ICBMs in terms of launch-weight and throw-weight. First deployed in 1975 with a range of 5,700 nautical miles (10,500 km). It has been flight tested with a single RV and with MIRVs. Mod. 1 has a warhead of 18 to 25 megatons; Mod. 2: 8 × 2 megatons (MIRV); Mod. 4 has a warhead of 10 to 50 megatons.

SS-19. American designation of the heaviest of the light Soviet ICBMs in terms of launch-weight and throw weight. First deployment in 1975, with a maximum range of 6,000 nautical miles (11,000 km). It has been flight tested with a single RV and with MIRVs. Mod. 1: 6 × 500 kilotons (MIRV); Mod. 2: 1 × 5 megatons (tested).

SS-20. American designation for a Soviet ICBM first deployed in 1977 with a maximum range of 4,000 nautical miles (7,400 km). Mod. 1 has a warhead of 1.5 megatons; Mod. 2: 3 × 150 kilotons (MIRV); Mod. 3: 1 × 50 kilotons.

SS-N-5. American designation for a Soviet SLBM first deployed in 1964 with a maximum range of approximately 600 nautical miles (1,120 km), and a warhead of 1 to 2 megatons.

SS-N-6. American designation for Soviet SLBM first deployed in 1969. Range (Mod. 3) 1,600 nautical miles (3,000 km) and believed to have multiple but not independently targetable warheads. Currently deployed on thirty-three strategic submarines. Mod. 1 and 2 each have a warhead of 1 to 2 megatons (tested) and Mod. 3: 2 × 3 kilotons range (MRV).

SS-N-8. American designation for Soviet SLBM introduced in 1972. Range 4,300 nautical miles (8,000 km). Has a warhead of 1 to 2 megatons.

SS-N-18. American designation for a Soviet SLBM that has been flight tested with a single RV and with MIRVs. First deployed in 1978. Range 4,500 nautical miles (8,000 km). Its MIRV warheads are of 1 to 2 megatons each.

SST. See *Supersonic transport.*

Stability. See *Strategic stability.*

Stand-off (missile and carrier). Any system in which a conveyance of any sort delivers any missile to a designated launch point. The missile then proceeds to the target under its own power, while the transport returns to base.

Strategic arms limitation talks (SALT). The discussions between the United States and the USSR on the limitation of strategic armaments which have been under way since 1970.

Strategic bomber. A multi-engine aircraft with intercontinental range, designed specifically to engage targets whose destruction would reduce an enemy's capacity and/or will to wage war. See also *Medium bomber.*

Strategic forces. Commonly refers to American nuclear weapons able to engage targets in the Soviet Union and China, and to Soviet/Chinese weapons able to engage targets in the United States. Also includes aerospace defensive elements. See also *General-purpose forces.*

Strategic nuclear operations. The use of nuclear weapons against an enemy's homeland so as to reduce his capacity and/or will to wage war. Also includes actions to defend friendly assets from similar forays by foes.

Strategic stability. A state of equilibrium that encourages prudence by opponents facing the possibility of general war. Tendencies toward an arms race are restrained, since manoeuvring for marginal advantage is meaningless.

Strip alert. See *Ground alert.*

Submarine-launched ballistic missile (SLBM). Any ballistic missile transported by and

418

launched from a submarine. May be short-, medium-, intermediate-, or long-range. See also *Ballistic missile.*

Submarine-launched cruise missile (SLCM). Any air-breathing missile transported by and launched from a submarine. May be short-, medium-, intermediate-, or long-range. See also *Cruise missile.*

Supersonic transport (SST). A general term for civilian aircraft capable of flying faster than the speed of sound.

Surgical strike. An American term used to indicate a selective attack with nuclear weapons in contrast to an all-out first strike or retaliatory second strike. The desirability of being able to carry out a surgical strike is being used to justify the development and procurement of nuclear weapons with counterforce capabilities.

Suppliers' club. A name used in reference to those countries that have the ability to make nuclear reactors and other essential equipment and that have banded together to discuss policies for the sale of nuclear plants to other countries.

Survivability. See *Pre-launch survivability; Post-launch survivability.*

System. See *Nuclear delivery system.*

Tactical aircraft. Land- and carrier-based aircraft designed primarily as general-purpose forces. Selected American elements are routinely assigned strategic nuclear missions. See also *General-purpose forces; Strategic nuclear operations.*

Tactical forces. See *General-purpose forces.*

Target of opportunity. An unanticipated target that is identified in combat.

Targeting doctrine. Principle governing the selection of targets to be attacked in the event of war, the allocation of weapons to those targets, and the order in which they will be (or can be) attacked.

Technical reliability. The mechanical dependability of any delivery system without regard for its survivability or the proficiency of its crew before or after launch.

Telemetry. This refers to data, transmitted by radio to the personnel conducting a weapon test, that monitor the functions and performance during the course of the test.

Tercom. See *Terrain contour matching.*

Terminal guidance. In flight corrections to the trajectory of a ballistic or cruise missile during its final approach to the target, for the purpose of improving accuracy. See also *Mid-course correction.*

Terrain contour matching. A system that correlates contour-map data with terrain being overflown by ballistic or cruise missiles. The results provide position fixes at intervals. These can be used to correct inertial guidance errors, and thereby improve accuracy. See also *Inertial guidance; Mid-course correction.*

Throw-weight. Ballistic missile throw-weight is the useful weight placed on a trajectory towards the target by the boost stages of the missile. For the purposes of SALT II, throw-weight is defined as the sum of the weight of: (a) the RV or RVs; (b) any PBV or similar device for releasing or targeting one or more RVs; and (c) any anti-ballistic missile penetration aids, including their release devices.

Time-sensitive target. Any target that can move to avoid being struck. Includes weapons that can be launched or redeployed before hostile aircraft or missiles arrive.

Trident C-4. An American SLBM with a range of 4,000 nautical miles and multiple-independently targetable warheads.

Verification. Inspection and/or surveillance measures to determine compliance with arms-control agreements. See also *Arms control; Arms limitation.*

Vertical proliferation. The development and enlargement of a state's nuclear capacity in terms of further refinement, accumulation and deployment of nuclear weapons.

Vulnerability. The susceptibility of a weapons system to any action by any means through which its combat effectiveness may be diminished.

War-fighting. Combat actions, as opposed to deterrence (which is designed to prevent rather than prosecute wars).

Warhead. That part of a missile, projectile, torpedo, rocket or other munition which contains either the nuclear or thermonuclear system, the high-explosive system, the chemical or biological agents, or the inert materials intended to inflict damage.

Yield. The energy released in an explosion. The energy released in the detonation of a nuclear weapon is generally measured in terms of the kilotons or megatons of TNT required to produce the same energy release (1 kiloton = 1,000 tons of TNT; 1 megaton = 1 million tons of TNT).

Appendix II. Tables of world military expenditure, arms importers and exporters

Exporting country	Total value	Percentage of Third World total
United States of America	27 727	45
USSR	16 914	27.5
France	5 894	10
United Kingdom	3 044	5
Italy	1 868	3
Third World exporters	1 805	3
Federal Republic of Germany	1 444	2.3
China	787	1.3
Netherlands	515	0.8
Australia	421	0.7
Canada	323	0.5
Sweden	196	0.3
Czechoslovakia	154	0.2
Spain	110	0.2
Ireland	87	0.1
Poland	80	0.1
Switzerland	55	—
Yugoslavia	47	—
New Zealand	13	—
Belgium	5	—
Japan	3	—
TOTAL	≃ 61 000	100.0

1. Figures are SIPRI trend-indicator values, as expressed in constant $ millions, at constant 1975 prices.
Source : SIPRI Yearbook, 1980.

TABLE 2. Rank order of major Third World arms importers. 1975–79

Importing region	SIPRI total indicator value of arms imports (1975 $m)	Percentage of Third World total	Largest recipient countries	SIPRI total indicator value of country's arms imports (1975 $m)	Percentage of region's total	Largest supplier to each country	Percentage of country's total	Four largest suppliers per region	Percentage of region's total
Middle East	20 141	48	Iran	6 229	31	United States	81	United States	61
			Saudi Arabia	2 806	14	United States	79	USSR	15
			Jordan	2 615	13	United States	98	France	7
			Iraq	2 418	12	USSR	93	United Kingdom	5
			Israel	2 008	10	United States	95		
			Syria	1 170	6	USSR	84		
Far East	6 679	16	Rep. of Korea	2 515	38	United States	98	United States	49
			Viet Nam	1 094	16	USSR	91	USSR	21
			Taiwan	845	13	United States	95	France	2
			Malaysia	325	5	United States	54	China	1
			Philippines	307	5	United States	61		
			Indonesia	306	5	United States	36		
North Africa	4 848	11	Libya	3 151	65	USSR	79	USSR	62
			Morocco	863	20	France	81	France	19
			Algeria	660	14	USSR	79	United States	3
			Tunisia	72	1	Italy	38	United Kingdom	1
Sub-Saharan Africa	4 021	10	South Africa	969	24	France	53	USSR	31
			Ethiopia	533	13	USSR	95	France	21
			Angola	350	9	USSR	99	United States	7
			Mozambique	315	9	USSR	100	United Kingdom	5
			Sudan	232	6	France	64		
			Nigeria	188	5	United Kingdom	22		
South America	3 963	9	Brazil	965	24	United States	34	United States	21
			Peru	806	20	USSR	41	United Kingdom	18
			Argentina	692	17	United Kingdom	26	France	11
			Chile	543	14	France	22	Italy	11
			Venezuela	511	13	Italy	51		
			Ecuador	304	8	France	45		
South Asia	2 031	5	India	1 055	52	USSR	57	USSR	42
			Pakistan	564	28	France	53	France	18
			Afghanistan	253	13	USSR	100	United Kingdom	14
			Bangladesh	59	3	China	78	China	7
			Nepal	7	0.3	France	57		
			Sri Lanka	4	0.2	France	50		
Central America	624	1.5	Cuba	279	45	USSR	100	USSR	45
			Mexico	172	28	United Kingdom	74	United Kingdom	21
			Bahamas	37	6	United States	100	United States	8
			Honduras	34	5	United States	50	France	3
			El Salvador	30	5	Israel	83		
			Guatemala	23	4	Israel	39		
Oceania	8	0.02	Papua New Guinea	5	63	Australia	100	Australia	63
			Fiji	3	37	United States	100	United States	37
THIRD WORLD TOTAL	42 315	100.5							

Source : SIPRI Yearbook, 1980. SIPRI's trade registers cover primarily the four categories of 'major weapons': i.e. aircraft, missiles, ships and armoured vehicles. As a result of the exclusion of small arms, ammunition and artillery, the coverage of arms imports by Third World countries is estimated to reflect only about half the total procurement of military equipment in this region.

TABLE 3. World military expenditure summary, in constant price figures (figures are in $ millions at 1978 prices and exchange-rates)

	1950	1955	1960	1965	1970	1975	1976	1977	1978	1979
United States	39 475	98 252	100 001	107 192	130 872	110 229	104 261	108 540	108 357	110 145
Other NATO	27 885	44 328	50 386	60 891	63 094	74 699	76 669	78 183	80 438	81 728
Total NATO	67 360	142 580	150 387	168 083	193 966	184 928	180 930	186 723	188 795	191 873
USSR	[37 700]	[51 200]	[48 000]	[65 900]	[92 500]	[99 800]	[102 700]	[104 200]	[105 700]	
Other WTO	...	...	3 388	5 423	8 263	10 530	11 138	11 756	12 006	12 256
Total WTO	[40 700]	[54 200]	[51 388]	[71 323]	[100 763]	[110 330]	[112 438]	[114 456]	[116 206]	[117 956]
Other Europe	(2 800)	(5 140)	(5 867)	7 552	8 595	10 579	11 111	11 052	11 139	11 544
Middle East	[800]	[1 400]	[2 400]	[4 500]	(10 500)	33 879	36 271	35 366	(34 636)	[33 103]
South Asia	[1 240]	[1 415]	[1 555]	3 376	3 424	4 037	4 558	4 541	(4 648)	[4 747]
Far East (excl. China)	[4 400]	[5 200]	[6 100]	8 000	11 990	15 771	16 880	[18 780]	[20 275]	[21 580]
China	[12 900]	[11 800]	[13 100]	[25 300]	[37 900]	[40 300]	[40 400]	[41 700]	[42 900]	[44 200]
Oceania	987	1 583	1 485	2 279	3 068	3 232	3 194	3 206	3 204	3 175
Africa (excl. Egypt)	[125]	[400]	[900]	2 898	5 330	9 134	(9 720)	(9 950)	[10 130]	[10 250]
Central America	[400]	[420]	[575]	742	987	1 266	1 500	1 825	[2 070]	[2 275]
South America	[2 000]	[2 250]	(2 485)	(3 312)	3 981	5 489	5 858	6 120	[5 950]	[5 455]
WORLD TOTAL	133 710	226 390	236 245	297 265	380 510	418 945	422 860	433 719	439 953	446 158

Source : SIPRI Yearbook 1980

423

TABLE 4. World military expenditure, NATO, WTO and other Europe in constant-price figures (figures are in $ millions, at 1978 prices and exchange-rates)

	1950	1955	1960	1965	1970	1975	1976	1977	1978	1979
NATO										
North America:										
Canada	1 271	4 134	3 422	3 167	3 256	3 468	3 702	3 939	4 087	3 877
United States	39 475	98 252	100 001	107 192	130 872	110 229	104 261	108 540	108 357	110 145
Europe :										
Belgium	783	1 459	1 582	1 839	2 174	2 758	2 902	2 978	3 175	3 327
Denmark	329	691	741	1 026	1 038	1 277	1 260	1 266	1 315	1 322
France	6 320	9 520	12 603	13 867	14 458	16 169	16 934	17 687	18 623	18 993
Federal Republic of Germany	4 959	7 799	11 685	16 760	16 872	20 847	20 657	20 522	21 417	21 636
Greece	297	353	437	990	1 714	(1 814)	(2 044)	(2 117)	[2 281]	
Italy	2 154	2 749	3 231	4 344	4 831	5 607	5 580	5 990	6 246	6 283
Luxembourg	14.1	46.0	18.5	30.1	22.7	32.2	34.4	33.8	36.7	37.6
Netherlands	1 535	2 433	2 168	2 896	3 349	4 036	4 002	4 454	4 307	4 434
Norway	316	622	603	885	1 018	1 171	1 200	1 223	1 307	1 346
Portugal	204	299	367	712	983	774	605	570	623	687
Turkey	609	775	892	1 318	1 448	(2 351)	(3 208)	(3 320)	(2 557)	(1 968)
United Kingdom	9 094	13 448	12 636	13 552	12 654	14 495	14 771	14 156	14 627	15 536
TOTAL NATO Europe	26 614	40 194	46 964	57 724	59 838	71 231	72 967	74 244	76 351	77 851
TOTAL NATO	67 360	142 580	150 387	168 083	193 966	184 928	180 930	186 723	188 795	191 873
WTO										
Bulgaria			208	267	365	611	664	(597)	(624)	(666)
Czechoslovakia	1 116	1 217	1 025	1 181	1 645	2 008	2 115	(2 148)	(2 105)	[2 160]
German Dem. Rep.			456	1 414	2 605	3 364	3 580	(3 968)	(4 170)	(4 380)
Hungary			235	437	703	766	721	750	819	791
Poland	283	963	1 140	1 672	2 290	2 907	3 107	(3 316)	(3 218)	(3 195)
Romania			324	452	655	874	951	977	1 070	(1 064)
USSR	[37 700]	[51 200]	[48 000]	[65 900]	[92 500]	[99 800]	[101 300]	[102 700]	[104 200]	[105 700]
TOTAL WTO	[40 700]	[54 200]	[51 388]	[71 323]	[100 763]	[110 330]	[112 438]	[114 456]	[116 206]	[117 956]
TOTAL WTO (excl. USSR)			3 388	5 423	8 263	10 530	11 138	11 756	12 006	12 256
Other Europe										
Albania	104	34			116	155	191	196	201	204
Austria	151	214	309	399	490	642	657	679	741	762
Finland			254	329	350	490	499	461	463	473
Ireland	58.2	75.8	75.6	93.4	110	186	197	178	196	(170)
Spain	339	851	966	1 189	1 662	2 308	2 472	2 478	2 461	2 662
Sweden	1 169	1 763	1 888	2 530	2 696	2 924	2 919	2 933	2 980	3 066
Switzerland	681	931	1 080	1 584	1 697	1 638	1 856	1 758	1 762	1 791
Yugoslavia	274	1 224	1 240	1 358	1 474	2 236	2 320	(2 369)	(2 335)	(2 416)
TOTAL other Europe	(2 800)	(5 140)	(5 867)	7 552	8 595	10 579	11 111	11 052	11 139	11 544

Source: *SIPRI Yearbook 1980*

TABLE 5. World military expenditure, Middle East in constant price figures (figures are in $ millions, at 1978 prices and exchange-rates)

	1950	1955	1960	1965	1970	1975	1976	1977	1978	1979
Bahrain	..	..	..	..	..	21.4	29.9	41.1	[44.7]	[47.8]
Cyprus				16.8	13.9	23.2	22.7	30.1	[23.2]	[17.4]
Egypt	206	489	513	974	2 271	5 756	5 004	5 239	[3 325]	[2 840]
Iran	212	291	577	862	1 906	10 168	11 031	8 902	9 506	(4 943)
Iraq	58	140	313	563	841	2 049	2 010	2 100	1 988	..
Israel	57	49	189	385	2 016	3 160	3 158	2 726	2 377	(3 063)
Jordan	56	109	181	191	279	246	232	275	307	387
Kuwait		..	53	97	393	860	1 073	1 189	1 091	..
Lebanon	13	27	38	68	94	165	137	85	..	..
Oman					36	698	785	686	767	[695]
Saudi Arabia	..	..	..	1 035	2 094	(9 430)	[11 375]	[11 900]	(12 700)	(14 640)
Syria	58	68	170	242	429	1 088	1 086	1 097	1 151	(1 937)
United Arab Emirates	..	..	..			74	(153)	(904)	(1 066)	(1 195)
Yemen Arab Republic	..	..	..	12	58	(102)	(122)	(134)	(132)	..
Yemen, Democratic	..	..	..	..	45.8	38.2	52.1	57.9	74.6	..
TOTAL MIDDLE EAST	[800]	[1 400]	[2 400]	[4 500]	(10 506)	33 879	36 271	35 366	(34 636)	[33 103]

Source: SIPRI Yearbook, 1980.

TABLE 6. World military expenditure, in constant price figures: Africa (figures are in $ millions, at 1978 prices and exchange-rates).

	1950	1955	1960	1965	1970	1975	1976	1977	1978	1979
Algeria				252	226	373	426	473	465	[500]
Benin			(2.1)	4.4	5.3	5.7	7.8	(11.9)	(19.9)	
Burundi				4.0	5.7	12.1	11.2	13.3		
Cameroon			31.5	44.5	55.7	63.0	66.2	63.6	60.7	61.3
Central African Empire			3.5	5.9	12.8	10.8	10.5	9.3		
Chad			0.1	9.7	36.5	26.0	37.4	(34.7)	(41.3)	
Congo			6.0	12.2	(20.1)	44.8	46.2	44.1	38.1	
Equatorial Guinea					3	4				
Ethiopia			53	117	87	216	173	[146]	[159]	[308]
Gabon		78	3.7	9.4	14.2	24.3	26.9	34.9	(53.9)	(60.1)
Ghana			268	267	375	350	253	135		
Guinea			5.1	14.0	[22.7]	(22.4)		(33.1)		
Ivory Coast			13.4	42.2	50.3	70.3	66.7		87.8	78.6
Kenya		14.9	7.1	25.0	39.8	77.0	111	230	251	
Liberia				7.0	7.7	5.4	6.1	7.2		
Libya			13	60	(331)	(1 048)	(1 602)	(1 579)		
Madagascar			4.7	23.7	26.9	33.1	41.4	50.7	52.2	
Malawi				1.7	2.6	10.3	10.9	15.7	19.4	
Mali			[17.1]	17.9	24.6	(32.5)	38.6	37.6	(30.9)	
Mauritania			[6.9]	5.9	6.2	35	(51)	(66)		
Mauritius			0.7	0.7	7.0	11.5				
Morocco		74	119	149	201	539	755	867	825	1.086
Mozambique						14	(41)	44	(85)	87
Niger			4.5	19.1	11.0	9.1	10.0			
Nigeria		28.2	101	203	1 643	2 925	2 545	2 637	(2 040)	[1 471]
Rwanda				7.0	9.0	12.4	14.2	(118.7)		
Senegal			8.9	38.2	38.6	39.6	44.4	50.5	49.4	60.8
Sierra Leone			4.5	4.4	6.3	7.9	7.2	[7.9]		
Somalia			10.4	12.9	26.0	32.5	32.4	35.5		(86)
South Africa	96	151	141	523	628	1 430	1 769	2 000	2 180	2 187
Sudan	27	32	67	136	255	152	194	220	(213)	[290]
Tanzania				82	101	182	186	195	(301)	(283)
Togo			(0.7)	7.2	8.0	11.9	17.2	18.3	21.2	
Tunisia		7.6	36.0	31.5	43.6	65.4	73.5	80.1	84.3	91.2
Uganda		20	11.0	83	168	(1217)	170	136		
Upper Volta			4.2	9.1	11.2	(23.6)	(33.1)	(31.2)		
Zaire				585	658	(471)	(297)	(267)		
Zambia			21	47	67	[353]	[291]	[259]	[240]	[248]
Zimbabwe				36	[88]	173	215	(318)	(385)	(487)
TOTAL AFRICA	[125]	[400]	[900]	2 898	5 330	9 134	(9 720)	(9 950)	[10 130]	[10 250]

Sources: SIPRI Yearbook 1980

TABLE 7. World military expenditure, in constant price figures: Central and South America (figures are in $ millions, at 1978 prices and exchange-rates)

	1950	1955	1960	1965	1970	1975	1976	1977	1978	1979
Central America										
Costa Rica	...	(9.8)	10.5	10.7	7.6	13.7	17.7	19.5	22.1	...
Cuba	...	...	222	270	367	(413)	...	...	992	1 065
Dominican Republic	...	...	85.6	78.7	66.1	72.0	73.7	78.6	[87]	[151]
El Salvador	11.6	14.6	13.4	20.4	20.4	37.8	48.0	56.8	59.0	(62)
Guatemala	12.2	17.4	20.6	31.1	58.0	57.7	60.3	84.0	[59]	[64]
Haiti	...	13.5	18.1	16.6	14.8	11.3	11.6	11.9	13.5	...
Honduras	6.5	6.3	8.4	10.7	14.1	25.8	27.2	(26.8)	(31.4)	...
Jamaica	...	...	...	10.1	10.5	(21.2)	27.3	[28.2]	...	...
Mexico	125	125	180	266	385	557	610	(719)	(699)	[740]
Nicaragua	...	...	15.2	17.0	22.4	32.5	43.5	[43.1]	...	...
Panama	...	...	...	[5.6]	12.7	16.7	(16.7)	...	...	...
Trinidad and Tobago	...	...	...	5.5	7.9	7.4	8.2	8.9	...	...
TOTAL CENTRAL AMERICA	[400]	[420]	[575]	742	987	1 266	[1 500]	[1 825]	[2 070]	[2 275]
South America										
Argentina	1 012	824	1 004	974	1 122	1 515	1 721	[1 771]	[1 492]	...
Bolivia	...	10.6	13.3	37.7	31.3	72.1	79.0	78.0	91	[81]
Brazil	673	823	820	1 268	1 596	1 756	2 023	[2 069]	1 951	[1 842]
Chile	62	100	83	86	177	420	431	[484]	[714]	[665]
Colombia	49.1	133	99	213	204	193	198	182	167	[188]
Ecuador	15.3	46.8	54.0	56.7	80.6	141	129	215	[170]	...
Guyana	...	...	...	...	13.9	42.0	55.3	...	...	...
Paraguay	...	...	[15.1]	[18.0]	26.3	31.9	29.3	34.1	28.6	...
Peru	69.2	75.7	110	176	297	(488)	(615)	(498)	[592]	[401]
Uruguay	...	...	45.3	72.9	92.7	123	95	100	...	...
Venezuela	92	160	227	307	340	707	482	631	590	587
TOTAL SOUTH AMERICA	[2 000]	[2 250]	(2 485)	(3 212)	3 981	5 489	5 858	(6 120)	[5 950]	[5 455]

Source: SIPRI Yearbook 1980

TABLE 8. World military expenditure, in constant price figures: South Asia, Far East and Oceania (figures are in $ millions, at 1978 prices and exchange-rates)

	1950	1955	1960	1965	1970	1975	1976	1977	1978	1979
South Asia										
Afghanistan	..	..	..	63	43.0	47.1	56.9	58.8	..	..
Bangladesh	..	..	..	..	..	68.3	109	133	125	121
India	858	995	1 112	2 595	2 538	2 980	3 447	3 383	3 444	3 523
Nepal	..	..	[5]	[5.2]	8.1	13.5	15.1	15.9	(16.0)	..
Pakistan	333	358	369	705	823	914	917	934	989	1 001
Sri Lanka	0.8	4.0	10.1	8.0	11.9	14.1	13.0	16.1	14.0	24.0
TOTAL SOUTH ASIA	[1 240]	[1 415]	(1 555)	3 376	3 424	4 037	4 558	4 541	(4 648)	[4 747]
Far East										
Brunei				12.8	22.3	48.1	73.1	133	130	163
Burma	57	180	213	228	220	148	149	(169)		
Hong Kong				19.3	26.8	(31)	(70)	(73)	(83)	
Indonesia	634	486	898	338	811	1 324	1 178	1 411	1 545	1 705
Japan	2 656	2 856	2 860	3 927	5 725	7 899	7 983	8 232	8 875	(9 516)
Kampuchea, Democratic			[80]	80	210	[105]	[38]			
Korea, North			[276]	[429]	(878)	922	1 004	1 022	1 194	
Korea, South		207	313	311	617	1 359	1 855	2 362	2 560	2 723
Laos	7.5			40	37	[26]				
Malaysia		124	99	224	353	(451)	370	440	506	[465]
Mongolia			[20]	[20]	[50]	124	136	135	141	160
Philippines	71	102	112	110	174	443	583	744	651	[667]
Singapore					239	347	444	520	500	(513)
Taiwan		371	511	833	1 073	1 199	1 390	1 655	(1 810)	(1 882)
Thailand	53	109	159	206	419	496	596	716	839	
Viet Nam, North	..	..	..	[620]	[585]	[605]	..	..	..	..
Viet Nam, South	..	..	226	602	550	[244]	..	..	..	..
Viet Nam, Socialist Rep. of	..	..	..	..	..	..	..	..	..	..
TOTAL FAR EAST, EXCL. KAMPUCHEA, LAOS AND VIET NAM	[4 000]	[4 700]	(5 487)	6 658	10 608	14 791	15 831	17 612	(19 016)	(20 240)
TOTAL FAR EAST	[4 400]	[5 200]	[6 100]	8 000	11 990	15 771	[16 880]	[18 780]	[20 275]	[21 580]
Oceania										
Australia	873	1 380	1 280	2 025	2 804	2 939	2 912	2 921	2 902	2 893
Fiji	..	..	..	..	1.0	1.6	2.5	2.9	..	..
New Zealand	114	203	205	254	263	291	279	282	299	(278)
TOTAL OCEANIA	987	1 583	1 485	2 279	3 068	3 232	3 194	3 206	3 204	3 175

Source: SIPRI Yearbook 1980

Select bibliography

This bibliography is highly selective in that it is limited to basic readings in the English language on the subject of this book. For publications in other languages, consult the United Nations and Unesco bibliographies listed under 'Bibliographical resources'.

Bibliographical resources

ALBRECHT, U.; EIDE, A.; KALDOR, M.; LEITENBERG, M.; ROBINSON, J. P. *A Short Research Guide on Arms and Armed Forces.* London, Croom Helm, 1978.

BOULDING, E.; PASSMORE, J. R.; GASSLER, S. R. *Bibliography on World Conflict and Peace,* 2nd ed., Boulder, Colo., Westview Press, 1979.

BURNS, R. D. *Arms Control and Disarmament, A Bibliography* (incl. index). Santa Barbara, Calif., American Bibliographical Center/Clio Press, 1977.

JACK, H. A. *A Bibliography on Disarmament: A Classified Listing of 271 Volumes.* New York, World Conference of Religion and Peace, 1972.

UNESCO. *Review of Research Trends and an Annotated Bibliography: Social and Economic Consequences of the Arms Race and of Disarmament.* Paris, Unesco, 1978.

UNITED NATIONS. DAG HAMMARSKJÖLD LIBRARY. *Disarmament: A Select Bibliography, 1962–67.* New York, United Nations, 1968.

——. *Disarmament: A Select Bibliography, 1967–1972.* New York, United Nations, 1973.

——. *Disarmament: A Select Bibliography, 1973–1977.* New York, United Nations, 1978.

Yearbooks and reference books

INTERNATIONAL INSTITUTE FOR STRATEGIC STUDIES, LONDON. *The Military Balance.* (A survey of military forces around the world, issued annually since 1959.)

——. *Strategic Survey.* (Annual review of security related events and trends.)

SIVARD, R. L. *World Military and Social Expenditures* (editions of 1974, 1976, 1977, 1978, 1979). Leesburg, Va., WMSE Publications.

STOCKHOLM INTERNATIONAL PEACE RESEARCH INSTITUTE (SIPRI). *World Armaments and Disarmament, SIPRI Yearbook* (annual editions starting from 1968/69, 1969/70, 1972, 1973 . . . 1981.

———. *SIPRI Yearbooks 1968–1979, Cumulative Index.* Stockholm, 1980.

———. *Armaments and Disarmament in the Nuclear Age, A Handbook.* Ed. by M. Thee. Stockholm, 1976 (available in English, French, German, Japanese, Serbo-Croatian, Finnish and Norwegian).

United Nations Centre for Disarmament. *The United Nations Disarmament Yearbook* Vol. I : 1976. Vol. II : 1977. Vol. III : 1977. New York, United Nations, (1977–79).

United States Arms Control and Disarmament Agency. *Documents on Disarmament* (issued annually since 1960; the first two volumes contained documentation for 1945–56 and 1957–59).

———. *World Military Expenditures and Arms Trade, 1963–73.*

———. *World Military Expenditures and Arms Transfers, 1967–76.*

———. *World Military Expenditures and Arms Transfers, 1968–77.*

———. *Arms Control and Disarmament Agreements, Texts and History of Negotiations.* Washington, D.C., ACDA, 1980.

Studies from the Stockholm International Peace Research Institute

The Arms Trade with the Third World, 1971.

The Problem of Chemical and Biological Warfare, 6 volumes, 1971–75.

Chemical Disarmament: Some Problems of Verification, 1973.

Force Reductions in Europe, 1974.

Nuclear Proliferation Problems, 1974.

Oil and Security, 1974.

Tactical and Strategic Antisubmarine Warfare, 1974.

Arms Trade Registers: The Arms Trade with the Third World, 1975.

The Nuclear Age, 1975.

Safeguards Against Nuclear Proliferation, 1975.

Chemical Disarmament: New Weapons for Old, 1975.

Delayed Toxic Effects of Chemical Warfare Agents, 1975.

Incendiary Weapons, 1975.

Medical Protection against Chemical-Warfare Agents, 1976.

The Law of War and Dubious Weapons, 1976.

Southern Africa, The Escalation of a Conflict, 1976.

Ecological Consequences of the Second Indo-China War, 1976.

Strategic Disarmament, Verification and National Security, 1977.

Weapons of Mass Destruction and the Environment, 1977.

Anti-personnel Weapons, 1978.

Tactical Nuclear Weapons: European Perspectives, 1978.

Outer Space—Battlefield of the Future?, 1978.

Arms Control, A Survey and Apprisal of Multilateral Agreements, 1978.

Postures for Non-Proliferation, Arms Limitation and Security Policies to Minimize Nuclear Proliferation, 1979.

Nuclear Energy and Nuclear Weapon Proliferation, 1979.

Warfare in a Fragile World, Military Impact on the Human Environment, 1980.
Chemical Weapons: Destruction and Conversion, 1980.
Internationalization to Prevent the Spread of Nuclear Weapons, 1980.
The NPT, The Main Political Barrier to Nuclear Weapon Proliferation, 1980.

Other books and studies

ALEXANDER, A. S. et al. *The Control of Chemical and Biological Weapons*. New York, Carnegie Endowment for International Peace, 1971.

ALFORD, J. *The Future of Arms Control: Confidence-Building Measures*, London, IISS, 1979 (Adelphi Papers, No. 149).

ALLISON, G. T. *Questions about the Arms Race: Who's Racing Whom? A Bureaucratic Perspective*. Cambridge, Mass., Harvard University, Public Policy Program, 1974.

ANDREN, N.; BIRNBAUM, K. (eds.) *Beyond Detente: Prospects for East-West Cooperation in Europe*. Leiden, A. W. Stijhoff, 1976.

ARON, R. *Peace and War*. New York, Praeger, 1967.

BAILEY, S. D. *Prohibitions and Restraints in War*. London, Oxford University Press, 1972.

BARNABY, C. F.; HUISKEN, R. (eds). *Arms Uncontrolled*. Cambridge, Mass., Harvard University Press, 1975.

BARNET, R. J. *The Giants. Russia and America*. New York, Simon & Schuster, 1977.

BARTON, J. H.; WEILER, L. D. (eds.). *International Arms Control, Issues and Agreements*, Stanford, Calif., Stanford University Press, 1976.

BENOIT, E.; BOULDING, K. (eds.). *Disarmament and the Economy*. New York, Harper & Row, 1963.

BENOIT, E. (ed.). *Disarmament and World Economic Interdependence*. Oslo, Universitetsforlaget, 1967.

BENOIT, E. *Defense and Economic Growth in Developing Countries*. Lexington, Mass., Lexington Books, 1973.

BERTRAM, C. (ed.). *The Diffusion of Power. I: Proliferation of Force*. London, IISS, 1977. (Adelphi Papers, No. 133.)

——. *The Diffusion of Power. II: Conflict and Its Control*. London, IISS, 1977. (Adelphi Papers, No. 134.)

——. *The Future of Arms Control. I: Beyond SALT II*. London, IISS, 1978. (Adelphi Papers, No. 141.)

——. *The Future of Arms Control. II: Arms Control and Technological Change: Elements of a New Approach*. London, IISS, 1978. (Adelphi Papers, No. 146.)

——. *New Conventional Weapons and East-West Security*. London, Macmillan, 1979.

BIRNBAUM, K. E. (ed) *The Politics of East-West Communication in Europe*. Westmead, Saxon House, 1979.

——. *Arms Control in Europe: Problems and Prospects*. Laxenburg: Austrian Institute for International Affairs, 1980.

BLECHMAN, B. M.; KAPLAN, S. S. (eds.). *Force Without War: United States Armed Forces as a Political Instrument*. Washington, D. C., The Brookings Institution, 1978.

BOSERUP, A.; MACK, A. *War Without Weapons*. New York, Schoken Books, 1974.

BOULDING, K. E. *Conflict and Defense: A General Theory*. New York, Harper & Row, 1962.

——. (ed.). *Peace and the War Industry*. New York, Trans-action Books, 1970.

——. *Stable Peace*. Austin, University of Texas Press, 1978.

BREDOW, W. (ed.). *Economic and Social Aspectes of Disarmament*. Oslo, BBP Publications, 1975.

BRENNAN, D. G. (ed.). *Arms Control, Disarmament and National Security*. New York, George Brazillier, 1961.

BRODIE, B. *Strategy in the Missile Age*. Princeton, Princeton University Press, 1959.

BROWN, F. J. *Chemical Warfare: A Study in Restraints*. Princeton, Princeton University Press, 1968.

BUCHAN, A. *Power and Equilibrium in the 1970s*. New York, Praeger, 1973.

BULL, H. *Control of the Arms Race*. London, Weidenfeld & Nicolson, 1961.

BURT, R. *New Weapon Technologies: Debate and Directions*, London, IISS, 1976. (Adelphi Papers, No. 126.)

BURTON, J. *Peace Theory*. New York, Knopf, 1962.

CARLTON, D.; SCHARF, C. (eds.). *The Dynamics of the Arms Race*. London, Croom Helm, 1975.

——. *Arms Control and Technological Innovation*. London, Croom Helm, 1978.

CLARK, G.; SOHN, L. B. *World Peace Through World Law*. Cambridge, Mass., Harvard University Press, 1960.

CLARKE, R. H. *The Science of War and Peace*. London, Jonathan Cape, 1971.

COFFEY, J. I. *Arms Control and European Security: A Guide to East-West Negotiations*. London, Macmillan, 1979.

COX, A. M. *The Dynamics of Detente: How to End the Arms Race*. New York, W. W. Norton, 1976.

DEUTSCH, K. W. *Arms Control and the Atlantic Alliance*. New York, Wiley, 1967.

DIGBY, J. F. *Precision-Guided Weapons*, London, IISS, 1975. (Adelphi Papers, No. 118.)

DOUGHERTY, J. E. *How to Think About Arms Control and Disarmament*. New York, Crane, Russak, 1973.

DRIVER, C. P. *The Disarmaments: A Study in Protest*. London, Hodder, 1964.

EDWARDS, D. V. *Arms Control in International Politics*. New York, Holt, Rinehart & Winston, 1969.

EIDE, A.; THEE, M. (eds.). *Problems of Contemporary Militarism*. London, Croom Helm, 1980.

ENTHOVEN, A.; SMITH, W. *How Much is Enough? Shaping the Defense Program*. New York, Harper Row, 1971.

EPSTEIN, W. *The Last Chance: Nuclear Proliferation and Arms Control*. New York, The Free Press, 1976.

FALK, R. A.; KIM, S. S. (eds.). *The War System: An Interdisciplinary Approach*. Boulder, Colo., Westview Press, 1980.

FARRAR, L. L. (ed.). *War. A Historical, Political and Social Study*. Oxford University Press, 1978.

FELD, B. T.; GREENWOOD, T.; RATHJENS, G. W.; WEINBERG, S. (eds.). *Impact of New Technologies on the Arms Race*. Cambridge, Mass.: MIT Press, 1971.

FRANK, L. A. *The Arms Trade in International Relations*. New York, Praeger, 1969.

GAILBRAITH, J. K. *How to Control the Military*. New York, Doubleday, 1969.

GALTUNG, J. *Essays in Peace Research. I: Peace Research, Education, Action. II: Peace, War and Defence*. Copenhagen, Christian Ejlers, 1975/76.

GARDINER, R. W. *The Cool Arm of Destruction: Modern Weapons and Moral Insensivity*. Philadelphia, Westminster Press, 1974.

GLAGOLEV, I. *Why We Need Disarmament.* Moscow, Novosti Press, 1973.

GRIFFITH, F.; POLANYI, J. C. (eds.). *The Dangers of Nuclear War.* Toronto, University of Toronto Press, 1979.

HABERMANN, F. W. (ed.). *Nobel Lectures: Peace.* Vol. I: 1901–25, Vol. II: 1926–50, Vol. III: 1951–70, Amsterdam, Elsvier, 1972.

HAMILTON, M. P. *To Avoid Catastrophe: A Study in Future Nuclear Weapon Policy.* Grand Rapids, Mich., William B. Erdmans, 1977.

HARKAVY, R. E. *The Arms Trade and International Systems.* Cambridge, Ballinger, 1975.

HOLST, J. J.; NERLICH, U. (eds.). *Beyond Nuclear Deterrence: New Aims, New Arms.* New York, Crane, Russel, 1977.

IKLE, F. C. *How Nations Negotiate.* New York, Praeger, 1964.

JACK, H. A. *The United Nations Special Session and Beyond.* New York, World Conference on Religion and Peace, 1978.

JOHANSEN, R. C. *The National Interest and Human Interest. An Analysis of United States Foreign Policy.* Princeton, Princeton University Press, 1980.

JOYCE, J. A. *The War Machine. The Case against the Arms Race.* London, Quartet Books, 1980.

KALDOR, M.; EIDE, A. (eds.). *The World Military Order: The Impact of Military Technology on the Third World.* London, Macmillan, 1979.

KALYADIN, A. *Nuclear Energy and International Security.* Moscow, Novosti Press, 1970.

KALYADIN, A.; KADE, G. (eds.). *Détente and Disarmament: Problems and Perspectives.* Vienna, Gazzetta Publishing House, 1976.

KING-HALL, S. *Defence in the Nuclear Age.* London, Gollancz, 1958.

KINKADE, W. H.; PORRO, J. D. (eds.). *Negotiating Security, An Arms Control Reader.* Washington, D.C., The Carnegie Endowment for International Peace, 1979.

KISSINGER, H. A. *Nuclear Weapons and Foreign Policy.* New York, Doubleday, 1958.

KISTIAKOWSKY, G. *A Scientist in the White House. The Private Diary of President Eisenhower's Special Assistant for Science and Technology.* London, Harvard University Press, 1976.

LAPP, R. E. *Kill and Overkill· The Strategy of Annihilation.* London, Weidenfeld & Nicolson, 1963.

LEFEVER, E. W. *Nuclear Arms in the Third World.* Washington, D.C., The Brookings Institution, 1979.

LEITENBERG, M. NATO and WTO Long Range Theater Nuclear Forces. In: K. E. Birnbaum (ed.). *Arms Control in Europe: Problems and Perspectives.* Laxenburg, Austrian Institute for International Affairs, 1980.

LIDER, J. *On the Nature of War.* Farnborough, Saxon House, 1977.

LIDER, J. *The Political and Military Laws of War. An Analysis of Marxist-Leninist Concepts.* Farnborough, Saxon House, 1979.

LOKSHIN, G. (ed.). *Socio-Economic Problems of Disarmament.* Vienna, International Institute for Peace, 1978.

LONG, F. A.; RATHJENS, G. W. (eds.). *Arms, Defense Policy and Arms Control.* New York, Norton, 1976.

LUTTWAK, E. N. *Strategic Power: Military Capabilities and Political Utility.* London, Sage Publications, 1976.

MADARIAGE, S. DE, *Disarmament.* New York, Coward McCann, 1929.

MARKS, A. W. (ed.). *NPT: Paradoxes and Problems.* Washington, D.C., Carnegie Endowment for International Peace, 1975.

MARKS, S. et al. Disarmament Education. Special issue of the *Bulletin of Peace Proposals*, Vol. 11, No. 3, 1980.

MARTIN, L. W. *The Sea in Modern Strategy*. London, Chatto & Windus, 1967.

MELMAN, S. *The Permanent War Economy: American Capitalism in Decline*. New York, Simon & Schuster, 1974.

MEYERS William (ed.). *Conversion from War to Peace: Social, Economic and Political Problems*. New York, 1972.

MYRDAL, Alva. *The Game of Disarmament. How the United States and Russia Run the Arms Race*. New York, Pantheon Books, 1976.

NOEL-BAKER, P. *The Arms Race: A Programme for World Disarmament*. London, Calder, 1958.

PRANGER, R. J. (ed.). *Détente and Defence, A Reader*. Washington, D.C., American Enterprise Institute for Public Policy Research, 1976.

PRIMAKOV, E. et al. *International Detente and Disarmament, Contributions by Finnish and Soviet Scolars*. Tampere (Finland), Tampere Peace Research Institute, 1977.

RANGER, R. *Arms and Politics 1958–78. Arms Control in a Changing Political Context*. Toronto, Macmillan of Canada, 1978.

RAPOPORT, A. *Strategy and Conscience*. New York, Harper & Row, 1964.

RASKIN, M. G. *The Politics of National Security*. New Brunswick, Transaction Books, 1979.

RICHARDSON, L. F. *Statistics of Deadly Quarrels*. Chicago, Quadrangle Press, 1961.

ROBERTS, A. *The Strategy of Civilian Defence*. London, Faber & Faber, 1967.

——. (ed.). *Civilian Resistance as a National Defense: Nonviolent Action Against Aggression*. Harrisburg, Pa., Stackpole Books, 1968.

——. *Total Defence and Civil Resistance*. Stockholm, The Research Institute of Swedish National Defence, 1972.

——. *Nations in Arms: Theory and Practice of Territorial Defence*. London, Chatto & Windus, 1976.

ROSENCRANCE, R. *Strategic Deterrence Reconsidered*, London, IISS, 1975. (Adelphi Papers, No. 116.)

RUSSET, B. M. (ed.). *Peace, War, and Numbers*. London, Sage Publications, 1972.

SAMPSON, A. *The Arms Bazaar*. London, Hodder and Stoughton, 1977.

SARKESIAN, S. (ed.). *The Military-Industrial Complex: A Reassessment*. London/Beverly Hills, 1972.

SCHELLING, T. C. *Strategy of Conflict*. Cambridge, Mass., Harvard University Press, 1960.

SCHELLING, T. C.; HALPERIN, M. H. *Strategy and Arms Control*. New York, Twentieth Century, 1961.

SCOVILLE, H.; OSBORN, R. *Missile Madness*. Boston, Houghton Mifflin, 1970.

SHARP, G. *The Politics of Nonviolent Action*. Boston, Porter Sargent, 1973.

SHARP, J. M. O. *Opportunities for Disarmament*. New York, Carnegie Endowment for International Peace, 1978.

SIMS, N. A. *Approaches to Disarmament*. London, Quaker Peace and Service, 1979.

SINGER, J. D. *Deterrence, Arms Control and Disarmament*. Columbus, Ohio State University Press, 1962.

——. *Disarmament. International Encyclopedia of the Social Sciences*, Vol. II. New York, Macmillan, 1968.

——. (ed.). *The Correlates of War*, 2 vols. New York, The Free Press, 1979–80.

SMITH, D. *The Defence of the Realm in the 1980s.* London, Croom Helm, 1980.

SOKOLOVSKY, M. V. D. *Military Strategy: Soviet Doctrine and Concepts.* New York, Praeger, 1963.

STANTON, J.; PEARTON, M. *The International Trade in Arms.* London, Chatto & Windus, 1972.

THAYER, G. *The War Business: The International Trade in Armaments.* New York, Simon & Schuster, 1969.

THEE, M. (ed.). European Security and the Arms Race, Special issue of the *Bulletin of Peace Proposals.* Vol. 10, No. 1, 1979.

THOMPSON, E. P.; SMITH, D. (eds.). *Protest and Survive.* Harmondsworth, Penguin Books, 1980.

TSIPIS, K.; FELD, B. T. (eds.). *The Future of the Sea-Bed Deterrent.* Cambridge, Mass., MIT Press, 1973.

UDIS, B. (ed.). *The Economic Consequences of Reduced Military Spendings.* Lexington, Mass., D. C. Heath & Co., 1974.

UNITED NATIONS, *Basic Problems of Disarmament.* Reports of the Secretary-General, New York, United Nations, 1970.

——. *The United Nations and Disarmament, 1945–70.* New York, United Nations, 1970.

——. *The United Nations and Disarmament, 1970–75.* New York, United Nations, 1976.

——. SECRETARIAT, *An Analytic Summary of the United Nations Studies describing the Effects of the Possible Use of Nuclear Weapons, Chemical Weapons, Bacteriological (Biological) Weapons and Napalm and Other Incendiary Weapons, as well as Those Dealing with the Reduction of Military Budgets, with the Economic and Social Consequences of the Arms Race and Disarmament, and with the Relationship between Development and Disarmament.* Working paper 1977. (UN Doc. A/Ac 187/72.)

UNITED STATES ARMS CONTROL AND DISARMAMENT AGENCY, *Economic Impact of Military Base Closings.* 2 vols. Washington, D.C., ACDA, 1970.

——. *The Economic Impact of Reductions of Defense Spendings.* Washington, D.C., ACDA, 1972.

UNITED STATES LIBRARY OF CONGRESS. CONGRESSIONAL RESEARCH SERVICE, *United States Policy on the Use of Nuclear Weapons, 1945–75* (by H. Y. Schader). Washington, D.C., 1975.

——. *Nuclear Proliferation Factbook.* Washington, D.C., United States Government Printing Office, 1977.

VIERA GALLO, J. A. (ed.). *The Security Trap: Arms Race, Militarism and Disarmament, A Concern for Christians.* Rome, IDOC International, 1979.

WALLENSTEEN, P. (ed.). *Experiences in Disarmament: On Conversion of Military Industry and Closing of Military Bases.* Uppsala (Sweden), Uppsala University, 1978.

WESTON, B. H. (ed.). Peace Education, Special issue of the *Bulletin of Peace Proposals.* Vol. 10, No. 4, 1979.

WATSON, P. *War on the Mind. The Military Use of Psychology.* London, Hutchinson, 1978.

WEIDENBAUM, M. L. *The Economics of Peacetime Defense.* New York, Praeger, 1974.

WOLFE, T. W. *Soviet Power and Europe, 1945–70.* Baltimore, The Johns Hopkins Press, 1970.

World Health Organization, *Health Aspects of Chemical and Biological Weapons.* Geneva, WHO, 1970.

WRIGHT, Q. *A Study of War,* Chicago, Chicago University Press, 1971.

WULF, C. (ed.). *Handbook on Peace Education.* Frankfurt, International Peace Research Association, 1974.

YARMOLINSKY, A. *The Military Establishment.* New York, Harper & Row, 1971.

YORK, H. F. (ed.). *Arms Control. Readings from* The Scientific American. San Francisco, W. H. Freeman, 1973.

YORK, H. F. *Race to Oblivion: A Participants View of the Arms Race.* New York, Simon & Schuster, 1970.

YORK, H. F. *The Advisers: Oppenheimer, Teller and the Super-Bomb.* San Francisco, W. H. Freeman, 1976.

YOUNG, E. A., *A Farewell to Arms Control?* Harmondsworth, Penguin, 1973.

Index

Prepared by A. Varela and J. Finklestein